FEMINIST
LOCAL AND GLOBAL
THEORY
PERSPECTIVES
READER

CAROLE R. McCANN AND SEUNG–KYUNG KIM

ROUTLEDGE

NEW YORK AND LONDON

Published in 2003 by
Routledge
29 West 35th Street
New York, NY 10001
www.routledge-ny.com

Published in Great Britain by
Routledge
11 New Fetter Lane
London EC4P 4EE
www.routledge.co.uk

Routledge is an imprint of the Taylor & Francis Group.
Printed in the United States of America on acid-free paper.

10 9 8 7 6 5 4

Library of Congress Cataloging-in-Publication Data

Feminist theory reader : local and global perspectives /
[edited] By
Carole R. McCann and Seung-kyung Kim.
        p. cm.
        ISBN 0-415-93152-5 — ISBN 0-415-93153-3
1. Feminist theory. I. McCann, Carole R. (Carole Ruth), 1955–
II.
Kim, Seung-Kyung, 1934–
        HQ1190 .F46346 2002
        305.42' 01—dc21

                                                                    2002005200

FEMINIST
THEORY
READER

CONTENTS

SECTION II
THEORIZING INTERSECTING IDENTITIES

SECTION III
THEORIZING FEMINIST AGENCY AND POLITICS

ACKNOWLEDGMENTS

We started to work on this project two years ago, however, the idea of working together on compiling a feminist theory anthology goes back to 1995 when we first met at the Ford Foundation's Summer Institute on Women and Gender in an Era of Global Change, a faculty development seminar offered by the Curriculum Transformation Project at the University of Maryland, College Park. Since we began to collaborate on transforming the syllabus of "Feminist Theories" into the one that embraced more global perspectives, we discussed the possibility of doing an anthology that would mainstream writings of women of color in the United States and contextualized them in a global setting. We have tried out several versions of syllabi in order to see whether certain articles worked in our classrooms or not; in so doing, we coauthored an article, "Internationalizing Theories of Feminism" (1998). The experience of collaboration for the past seven years has been truly rewarding for both of us: We not only became close personal friends (talking about children and aging parents) but also sounding boards for each other's individual research interests. We can proudly claim that this collaboration is a feminist methodology: We learned from each other's strength and we turned our learning into something quite new, an innovative approach. Although the past two years have been most demanding of us, we are very proud of our anthology: It has gone through several metamorphoses since we conceptualized it, and we hope the changes made it better.

There are many individuals who have helped us along the way. First and foremost, we would like to thank our students in the "Theories in Feminism" upper-level class on both campuses. They have gone through one of the most demanding classes in the women's studies curriculum, sometimes complaining and sometimes enjoying the endless readings we required them to do. Their insights, critiques, and suggestions have been invaluable for us in making this anthology accessible.

We would like to thank Debby Rosenfelt, Director of Curriculum Transformation Project and Summer Institute at the University of Maryland, College Park, who provided an opportunity for us to meet and work together. Debby has been supportive of our project throughout the past seven years and included our first collaborative article in *Women's Studies Quarterly*. Her continuous words of encouragement have meant a lot for us. We would also like to thank Claire Moses, chair of the Women's Studies Department, University of Maryland, College Park, and the editor of *Feminist Studies*. We have included a number of articles previously published in Feminist Studies, and Claire made it affordable for us. We have learned a lot from many discussions on feminist theories with her. We would also like to express our gratitude to our colleagues in the Department of Women's Studies and Women's Studies Program: Elsa Barkley Brown, Evi Beck, Lynn Bolles, Bonnie Dill, Katie King, Jason Louiglio, Pat McDermott, Erin Senack, and Ruth Zambrana.

We would like to thank the various reviewers for this anthology. We would specifically like to thank Sally Kitch, Kathy Ferguson, and Noël Sturgeon for their invaluable comments. We have benefited tremendously from their insightful suggestions and incorporated many of them into this anthology.

We have been very lucky to have various graduate assistants in Women's Studies to help us. We would like to thank Heather Rellihan, Ayu Saraswati, and Sarah Tillery for their work on securing copyright permissions, scanning the articles, and proofreading them. Their work has made this process much easier.

We would like to thank Ilene Kalish, our editor, for recognizing the value of this anthology and her continuing support throughout the long process of publication.

Lastly, we would like to thank our family: Carole thanks Rustin, Marj, and Carole; and Seung-kyung thanks John, Anna, and Ellen.

FEMINIST THEORY: LOCAL AND GLOBAL PERSPECTIVES

The term "feminism" usually refers in its most general sense to political activism by women on behalf of women. Widely used in the "second wave"[1] of the U.S. women's movement beginning in the 1970s, it seems to have originated in France in the 1880s. It combines the French word for woman, "femme," with the suffix meaning political position, "ism," and was used in that time and place to refer to those who defended the cause of women (Cott 1986; Moses 1998). Second wave feminists may have become familiar with the term through the French philosopher Simone De Beauvoir's use of it in *The Second Sex*, one of the few books on women's situation that was readily available to women activists in the early 1970s (Mitchell and Oakley 1986). However, beyond the general description of defending the cause of women, the meaning of feminism has never been historically stable or fixed (Delmar 1986; Moses 1998). Meanings of feminism have shifted across time and space and have often been the subject of intense debate, both by those who have used the term proudly and by those who question its usefulness. With all its ambiguity and limitations, the term nonetheless signals an emancipatory politics on behalf of women. Feminism involves the implicit claim that the prevailing conditions under which women live are unjust and must be changed. Such a claim assumes that change is indeed possible. It also assumes that a group of historical agents, in this case, women, can recognize the injustices they confront and will to change their conditions.

Feminist theories, like other political philosophies, provide intellectual tools by which historical agents can examine the injustices they confront, and can build arguments to support their particular demands for change. Feminist theorists apply their tools to building knowledge of women's oppression[2] and, based on that knowledge, to developing strategies for resisting subordination and improving women's lives. Feminist theories respond to questions such as: How are women subordinated as women? How can we understand the ways in which specific events might be part of social oppression based on sex, rather than unique individual misfortunes? How can we be sure that we have clear understandings of oppressive situations? How can women resist subordination? How should we work for changes that will improve women's lives? In what arenas of life should we focus efforts for change? What kinds of changes are needed? How is women's subordina-

tion as women connected to related oppressions based on race, ethnicity, nationality, class, and sexuality? Answers to these questions make assumptions about who
"we" are, how and why things got to be the way they are, and what changes may be
needed. In other words, answers to these questions rest on some notion of ontology (theories of being and reality), epistemology (theories of how knowledge is
produced), and politics (relations and practices of power). The last term is perhaps
the most important purpose of theory: to inform effective politics. Feminist theory
should be accountable to politics. It should make sense of women's situations; it
should account for women's experiences; and it should point to effective strategies
for change. How well this relationship between theory and political practice has
developed is itself an issue of debate. Nonetheless, feminist theories endeavor to
answer the above questions through descriptions and analyses of women's lives.

This anthology assembles readings that present key aspects of the conversations and debates[3] within multiracial U.S. feminisms and places those local conversations and debates within a global perspective. The idea for this anthology
emerged in 1995 at the Ford Foundation's Summer Institute on Women and
Gender in an Era of Global Change, a faculty development seminar offered by the
Curriculum Transformation Project at the University of Maryland, College Park,
where we first met. Both of us have taught theories of feminism courses over the
past ten years. In many ways our trajectories as feminist scholars, teachers, and as
editors of this volume have paralleled that of U.S. Women's Studies.[4] We belong to
the generation who lived through the women's movements in Korea and the
United States in the 1970s, and who received graduate training in Women's Studies
in the U.S. in the 1980s. Through our training and subsequent teaching experiences in the 1990s, we became convinced that "women's studies core curricula that
remain exclusively oriented to U.S. content and Western feminist perspectives no
longer meet the standards of scholarly rigor and political relevance that define our
field" (McDermott 1998: 88).[5] We each decided to participate in the faculty development seminar as a way to begin to incorporate into our courses "the experiences,
voices, and strategies for change of women around the world" (Rosenfelt 1998: 4).
Discovering our common goal, we began to work together.

While revising our courses, we often complained to each other about the difficulty we had in locating a suitable reader for upper-level feminist theory courses.
We were forced to develop our own selection of course readings, and our feminist
theory courses became the experimental sites where we tried, revised, and retried
various collections of articles to find out how they worked in the classroom. In
addition, the process of our collaborative work shaped the final form of this
anthology in a very fundamental way. Over the several years of reading and teaching we engaged in an extended dialogue that we found incredibly valuable.
Through our own efforts to construct a coherent textbook of feminist theory without losing the particularity of different locations and opportunities for creating
feminist theory, we constructed a strong personal friendship and a professional
association that has greatly enriched our other scholarship and our teaching. Our
collaborative process embodied the kind of dialogue that is often recommended as

a productive way, in an era of ever-increasing globalization, to build effective feminist knowledge and alliances between women of the North and South (Taylor 1993).[6] We end the anthology with readings that present models of negotiation across differences and of coalitions among women's groups who reside in diverse social positions because these models incorporate insights that we found particularly useful.

As Amrita Basu observes in the essay included here, the term "global" "may connote the breadth and universality that is often associated with Western feminism." On the other hand, as she notes, the term "local" often "can connote the supposed particularism, provincialism and primordialism of the Third World." Instead she offers a more specific definition, which we follow. Thus we use the term "local" to refer to "indigenous and regional" feminist theories and movements, in whatever region they arise. And we use the term "global" to refer to theories and movements that emerge within "transnational" locations and discourses. In juxtaposing feminist voices from the United States, Europe, Latin America, Asia, Africa, and Australia we hope to highlight the complex relationship of local and global feminist theories to transnational women's movements. Transnational refers to the literal movement of people, ideas, and resources across national boundaries. Notice that most of the authors from the South included here are transnational in both their personal and professional identities. The global feminisms Basu identifies are emerging from the linkages, networks, and alliances between "a diverse array of organizations," movements, and "issue-based campaigns" that have developed within "global civil society"(Basu 2000: 71). In the context of the four conferences on women convened by the United Nations since 1975, international political leaders and nongovernmental women's groups from around the world have articulated international law relating to women's rights, struggled over the terms of international women's activism, and developed enduring linkages and alliances. Transnational feminist organizations, movements, and campaigns are firmly grounded in the rights articulated in the 1979 Convention on the Elimination of All Forms of Discrimination Against Women.[7] But the new space of feminist agency and transnational women's movements created within global civil society is not one in which all women are suddenly equal nor one in which all women have the same concerns. Global civil society reverberates with historical power relations of race, colonialism, class, and sex. These shifting sites of power continue to shape the possibilities and limits for feminist politics even as new forms of domination emerge with new forms of globalization.

Throughout this anthology, we tried to capture some of the insights that emerged from conversations and debates about how to understand and resist the systematic oppression of women that has occurred in a variety of social-historical locations across the world throughout the twentieth century. However, given that women live in so many different social, economic, cultural, and political circumstances, there can be no single theory of women's subordination or a best strategy for change. Nor has the development of feminist theory been linear or unidirectional. Thus the articles brought together here do not present a singular homogeneous picture. We do not claim that this collection of essays speaks "for everybody, to everybody, nor about everything"(Young 1990: 13). There are interruptions, overlaps, disagreements, disjunctures, and contradictions among the essays. The feminist identities articulated within this anthology also shift and change with these interruptions, overlaps, disjunctures, and contradictions. As Judith Butler has noted elsewhere, "gender identities emerge...shift and vary so that different 'identifications' come into play depending upon the availability of legitimating cultural norms and opportunities"(Butler 1990: 331). Yet much useful knowledge is generated through ongoing debates about what feminism is and can be; about how to do feminist theory; about which theories adequately explain women's status in different social groups and historical locations; and about which theories offer the best strategies for change. We believe that, taken together, the essays effectively represent the multivocal feminist theory of this historical moment as well as the multiple and shifting sites of feminist identities. We hope the resonance and discord among the multiple voices and perspectives in this collection of essays will push readers to examine their own assumptions, the explanatory power and limits of the theories, and the relationships between feminist theories and practices.

Assembling this anthology posed a great challenge because our objectives have frequently been at cross-purposes. We wanted to provide a framework for the anthology that would make the theoretical foundations of U.S. Women's Studies intelligible to contemporary students in the field, so we have tried to maintain a balance of old and new material that represented pivotal moments of theoretical insight. By balancing the writings of women of color—representing numerous ethnic identities and postcolonial locations—with those of Western women and white women, we hope to reframe discussion of feminist theory. We particularly shift away from a narrow focus on gender to emphasize some of the ways in which race, ethnicity, class, nationality, and sexuality intersect with gender to shape women's situations and women's identities. Yet, because even the word "feminism" is not used throughout the world, our framing of the conversations threatened to reimpose Western categories and chronology on transnational women's movements and gender politics. Realizing that the framework for understanding the debates could easily slip into a U.S.-centric view of the world, we have tried to expose the limits of the framework even as it is set in place. We did not simply add a section about global feminism. Nor did we provide readings that either exoticize Third World women or portray them as homogeneous victims of global capitalism and local patriarchal culture. Instead, we incorporated global perspectives throughout the anthology in order to continually challenge Western hegemonic concepts and categories. Also, we did not merely incorporate the challenges made by women of color and women of the South to themes and agendas defined by white and Northern feminists. We have included conversations among women of color about issues of gender, race, colonialism, and sexuality and conversations within local U.S. feminism informed by insights generated by women of color and women of the South as well. Thus we have tried to "...incorporate ideas that have been developed by emergent and postcolonial feminists in a way that centralizes their theoretical perspectives in U.S. classrooms, rather than just using their experience to illustrate predefined Western feminist theories" (McDermott 1998: 90). Throughout the anthology we hope to challenge readers, as we challenged ourselves in conceptualizing the anthology, "to rethink the meanings of 'difference' in contexts outside of... Western feminism" (Rosenfelt 1998: 6). In so doing, we hope to move closer to "a curriculum that illuminates the multiple levels of colonization at work in globalization and tracks the power of its political logic as it crosses international boundaries" (Mohanty 1996, cited in McDermott 1998: 95).

The question of how to place the voices of women of color and postcolonial feminists was not the only one with which we were concerned. We also struggled with how to locate the voices of feminists that rely on white, Northern, middleclass, and heterosexual women's experiences as *the* experience of women. This was especially pressing because so many articles, especially early ones, construct and recapitulate this normative women's experience, which we hope to destabilize. We decided the best strategy was to include some articles that rely on the normative subject of feminist theory and juxtapose them with counter voices that trouble the privileges and exclusions within those texts. We felt it is better to retain these historical artifacts and encourage readers to examine closely how easily white, middle-class, heterosexual, U.S. feminist theories assume that that local experience of sexism is generalizable to all women. We also included readings that examine how this error hinges on the following faulty logic: If one is not a member of a subordinate group, then one is unaffected by the processes of domination which define that group; and, further, since they are unmarked by race, class, colonial, and neocolonial processes of domination, the experience of white, middle-class, heterosexual women of the North offers the purest case of sexism (Spelman 1988). This logic ignores the privileges such processes of dominations confer on those defined as the superior group. We have attempted to disrupt the normative feminist subject by situating her within conversations that include many voices inside and outside the United States, and that analyze gender in the context of race, nationality, class, and sexuality (Sandoval 1990). Thus we located theories based upon white, middle-class, heterosexual Northern women as another variety of local feminist theory and practice, which has dominated feminist discourse. In so doing, we have taken "the task of unmasking privilege seriously by trying to locate the places it finds a home, rather than simply noting that it must be at work" (Spelman 1998: 77; Taylor 1993).[8]

The conversations and debates we present here are anchored by four theoretical concepts—gender, women's experiences, the personal is political, and difference—which have been integral to late-twentieth-century feminisms.[9] These concepts, defined in greater depth in the Section I Introduction, recur in feminist theories in a variety of times and locations. They are foundational concepts upon which feminists have built analyses of women's subordination and proposed various strategies for change. These concepts are found in U.S. feminist theory that instituted a normative feminist subject. And they are concepts that women of color, feminists from the South, and lesbians have used and contested in challenging the normative feminist subject of white, Western feminism. But these concepts do not represent the only thread of conversation between the articles gathered here; the essays included here speak to more than just these four concepts. Various themes, like home, identity, autonomy, and otherness also resonate across the readings. While there are other ways to frame feminist theory, we found that tracing these four concepts and the tensions between them played out in debates within local U.S. and global feminist theories provides a very effective way of learning feminist theory in twenty-first-century globalized society. However, we hope that the plethora of themes and issues within the readings will generate wide-ranging discussion in the classroom.

The book has three sections. Section introductions set up the framework that brings the readings together; they locate the historical context of the readings, and, where appropriate, they point to critical additional readings not included here. Section I provides a survey of feminist themes and movements in broad sweeps. Section II looks at debates about differences and includes a variety of theoretical perspectives. Section III reverses this and looks at standpoint theories and post-structuralist theories and includes a variety of issues of difference.

Section I: Definitions and Movements introduces early articulations of four key feminist concepts: gender, women's experiences, the personal is political, and difference. Gender is the concept that feminists have most often used to define women as a social group. The readings offer readers early explanations of how the sex/gender system produces girls who "act like women" and boys who "act like men." In their elaborations of the concept of gender as a socially constructed identity, feminist theoretical debates have both used and contested women's experience as a source of knowledge about women's lives and social status. Challenges raised by feminists of color about which women's experiences are embodied in feminist theory begin to highlight the limits of using experience to build knowledge of a diverse social group. The phrase, "the personal is political," is an early political slogan that has evolved into a theoretical claim that power relationships structure women's personal lives, and thus feminist politics must confront those personal issues in public through political activism. Difference, which initially referred primarily to sex differences between men and women, is a concept most fully articulated by women of color. Through this concept, feminist theorists have argued that the analysis of differences in women's experiences shaped by related oppressions is crucial to any adequate theory of gender subordination. In these debates, theorists have also examined some of the ways in which difference disrupts the very notion of a stable identity, arguing instead that identity positions are multiple, fragmented, and mobile. The readings in the "Movements" subsection address issues of women's human rights, frameworks for feminist politics across national boundaries, reproductive rights, sexual violence, social and economic issues, and ecofeminism. The readings highlight how feminist theories serve as a resource for feminist movements.

Section II: Theorizing Intersecting Identities deals with questions of differences among women and the intersecting identities and dominations that shape women's lives. These readings further illuminate the exclusions created by the initial definitions of feminist theory's early core concepts. They point to the false universalism and essentialism of those concepts and examine lived differences among women, focusing on international structures of class, the social construction of race, ethnicity, nationality, and sexuality. Each group of readings presents efforts to elaborate the intersections of gender with these dimensions of oppression. Although they continue to rely on the key feminist concepts of gender, women's experience, difference, and the politics of personal life, they point out that one's location within the intersecting systems of oppression shapes knowledge and experience, and they criticize feminist theories for ignoring this fact. The subsections are not meant to suggest that the various axes of domination that intersect with gender in women's and men's lives are neatly separated into categories. Instead, like a kaleidoscope in which a jumble of objects are refracted through a prism in constantly shifting patterns, the organizational scheme is offered as a shifting prism of difference through which to examine the mobile and multiple configurations of domination in women's lives. The organization of section II moves through each subsection, foregrounding one specific category as if each were discrete. The readings on race present analyses by women of color about how gender and race are intertwined, elaborating the vital concepts of "difference" among women and the "matrix of domination." The readings also examine how gender has served as a token in colonial and postcolonial discourse, and discussions of racial and ethnic difference. The readings about class focus on the intersections of class and gender, particularly on the interconnections of capitalism, patriarchy, and globalization. The readings on sexuality address the question of the relationship between anatomical sex, gender, and sexuality. The institution of heterosexuality is discussed, as is the relationship between sexism and homophobia, and racial, ethnic, and national identity. However the readings address multiple issues and continually disrupt the boundaries of the categories. They unsettle the notion that race, nation, class, sexuality, or gender can be treated as independent categories. In particular, colonialism is not presented as a separate category.[10] This organization is designed to interrupt and unsettle U.S.-focused theories of difference captured under the race, class, and sexuality rubric. Through these essays, readers will gain an understanding of the multiple identities that women negotiate, although not all the negotiations carry the same risks and privileges. All of the essays encourage readers to reflect on the multiple identities they negotiate in their own lives. They also demonstrate how these debates can lead, and have led, to fragmentation of feminist politics/organizations.

After confronting many intertwined issues of difference and identity, **Section III: Theorizing Feminist Perspectives** presents two central solutions offered by feminist theorists for constructing grounds for feminist politics: feminist standpoint theories, and poststructuralist analyses of gendered discourse, power, and performativity. This section highlights efforts to answer the questions posed and insights generated by the multiplicity of voices present in section II. With such a multiplicity of women's social locations and experiences, how can a feminist subject be constructed? What is the basis upon which a feminist constituency can act? With the variety of political claims based upon this multiplicity, how can one negotiate differences and build effective politics? Throughout these debates feminist theorists have struggled over how best to build a political constituency aimed at challenging sexism. And they have asked whether it is possible to find or construct the basis for political common ground among women in the face of their considerable heterogeneity. With respect to standpoint theories, discussions have focused on how to build coalitions among women instead of a movement grounded on some mythic sense of unity. Standpoint theories argue that women's social location is a resource for the construction of a uniquely feminist perspective on social reality, which, in turn, can ground feminist political struggles for change. Taken together, the selections lead readers to consider that there might be a multiplicity of feminist standpoints. With respect to poststructuralism, discussions have concerned how power operates in any/every articulation of a feminist subject, suggesting that any assertion of a stable gender identity or stable unity among women involves an exclusion of some kind. The basic concepts of poststructuralist theory, including the relationship of language and subjectivity, and of discourse and power, are presented along with selections that raise questions about the essentialism of the concepts, "woman" and "experience." Through the essays, readers will begin to see the normative functions of discourse and a feminist critique of identity politics. The readings particularly argue that the homogenization of differences among women privileges white/heterosexual western feminist identities.

The last group of readings highlights the issue of location in feminist perspectives and politics in a series of essays that model how women in diverse social positions might locate themselves in feminist politics and build coalitions with women of different backgrounds. Thus, this section also offers readers from diverse backgrounds models for how to negotiate the conflicts and contests that comprise feminist activism in an era of globalization. What is key about the readings is the sense of hopefulness they offer that such negotiation, while a struggle, can accomplish something: more effective political coalitions, strategies, and better knowledge of women's conditions. The readings may not offer easy answers based on an illusory sense of unity, or commonality; or even offer a clear resolution of tensions between gender, women's experience, and difference. But, we hope they offer useful guidance on how to think about and enact feminist strategies for change in one's local situation within a transnational world.

Notes

1. The first usage of this term was apparently in the preface of Kate Millett's book *Sexual Politics*, which is one of the earliest feminist critiques published by the mainstream U.S. press.
2. For definitions of oppression, see Marilyn Frye 1983, chapter 1, where she defines oppression as constraints and limitations of life options because of one's identity as a member of a subordinated group. See also Iris Marion Young 1990, chapter 2, where she identifies five forms of oppression: exploitation, marginalization, powerlessness, cultural imperialism, and violence.
3. The sense of conversations we intend here is informed by definitions in Katie King 1994. She distinguishes between conversations and debates: The former involves "political contours," the latter "theoretical contents." She also describes conversations not as a single thing in which we all share, but as ongoing, overlapping, and shifting. See pp. xi, 56, 87.

4. Although we have argued elsewhere (Kim and McCann 1998: 117–19) that a common feminist taxonomy (liberal, radical, Marxist, poststructural) provides a useful heuristic device by which students can grasp the historical and intellectual development of feminist theory, we have abandoned it as the organizing principle for this book. We found we could not effectively mainstream the writings of women of color and put U.S. multiracial feminism in global perspectives without abandoning that taxonomy.

5. Patrice McDermott was a fellow participant in the Summer Institute, and the publication cited above discusses our mutual projects.

6. Appropriate labels for regions of the postcolonial world are always imprecise. Although this geographic terminology does not adequately convey the political configuration of the world, we use it as the best approximation available today.

7. Work on international women's rights laws by the UN Committee on the Status of Women began almost immediately after the 1946 Declaration of Human Rights was passed by the United Nations. This culminated in the 1979 Convention. More than one hundred nations have signed the Convention, but the United States is not one of them.

8. In her cogent analysis of who the *we* is in Simone de Beauvoir's *The Second Sex*, Elizabeth Spelman argues that "we honor her work by asking how such privilege functions in her own thinking." (1988: 77)

9. The first three concepts are drawn from our reading of Judith Grant 1993, to which we add the fourth, difference.

10. In the Introduction to her 2001 anthology on race and feminism, Kum Kum Bhavnani argues that "three strands—identity, difference, and colonialism—represent the strength" and "diversity"of writings on "'race' and feminism" (2001: 3).

SECTION I
DEFINITIONS AND MOVEMENTS

INTRODUCTION

Throughout the world, activism around women's issues seemed to explode in the 1960s and 1970s. This activism was part of ongoing historical struggles over the situation of women. Earlier in the twentieth-century United States and across the world, women's movements often allied with anticolonial liberation movements and labor activism, and promoted a good deal of change in women's social status and their political rights. In many nations, women's activism focused on notions of public justice for women, including citizenship, education, and marriage rights. The first reading, by Inji Aflatun, who contests conventional arguments for denying women full political rights as they were made in Egypt in 1949, provides one example of this activism. But efforts to end male domination have also ebbed and flowed, a fact which is exemplified by the eagerness with which women take up or eschew the label of feminist (Moses 1998). In the 1970s, feminists came together around the UN Decade of Women to further the women's rights agenda internationally. At the same time, some feminists raised claims about social influences on women's identity and about power in private relationships between women and men. In this section, we try to present key threads of historical and contemporary theoretical debates, as well as key issues around which women's activism coalesced in the last decades of the twentieth century.

Feminist challenges to women's subordinate status rest both on activist struggles and on intellectual efforts to change the dominant conventions about sex differences. Differential treatment based on sex dominated the social practices, law, and religion in the nineteenth century and much of the twentieth century in both the liberal capitalist nation states of the North and their colonial regimes across the South.[1] There have been many explanations for the need for differential treatment. At numerous times and in numerous locations, the belief that women's bodies, souls, character, intelligence, or skills differed from men's was used to justify their different social positions, spiritual authority, political rights, and economic opportunities. Frequently, these explanations derived from cultural meanings given to women's reproductive capacities. The biological fact that women have the potential to give birth has grounded many scientific, spiritual, political, and social explanations for their differential rights, roles, and obligations. Feminist intellectual challenges to conventional ideas about women in the 1970s were built on several central concepts: gender, women's experience, the personal is political, and difference. These concepts were initially articulated within political struggles involving issues of equal rights, social conventions of femininity and sexuality, reproductive self-determination, violence, poverty, and environmentalism, among others.

Prior to the 1970s, gender was a concept that had no social meaning in English; it was merely a grammatical feature of some European languages. But in the 1970s, feminist theorists began to use the concept to ground their arguments that biology (sex) is not destiny, and to assert, instead, that meanings attributed to sex differences (gender) are defined in historically specific ways through culture and politics and, as "man-made" interpretations, secure male dominance over women. While some, such as Simone de Beauvoir, had presented such ideas earlier in the century, the concept of gender ignited an explosion of feminist scholarship in the 1970s that continues today. The concept and analyses using it in interdisciplinary perspectives provide the foundation of the field of Women's Studies internationally.

British sociologist, Ann Oakley's *Sex, Gender, and Society* (1972) is an example of the initial articulation of the concept of gender. Published in both Britain and the United States, Oakley's book is a painstaking review of empirical data on sex differences, including biological differences (e.g., height, hormones, illnesses), psychological differences (intelligence and personality), behavioral differences (childhood play and adult work), and sexual differences (sex drive, practices, and satisfaction). Through this review, Oakley makes two arguments commonly made by feminist theorists at that time, which influenced the direction of much of subsequent theorizing.[2] First, she repeatedly notes that data demonstrate the substantial similarities between the sexes. Height is a classic example. On average, men are taller than women, but the overlap between men and women is extensive and the range of difference within each group is greater than the differences between the groups. The social stereotype that men are taller than women thus obscures the similarity in height between the sexes by exaggerating the actual differences. The comparison by average height also obscures the range of differences within each group. Oakley uses the fact of exaggerated differences to support her claim that modern society's continued emphasis on sex differences betrays its ongoing patriarchal bias. She also notes the patriarchal bias reflected in the fact that it is always women who must explain their difference from men; men are not required to explain themselves in terms of women (Oakley 1972: 208). Second, she repeatedly notes the wide variations in the activities and personality characteristics associated with men and women across cultures. The variance in how societies define the differences between the sexes suggests that sex differences are socially, not biologically, determined.

In opposition to the discredited evidence of extensive natural sex differences, she delineates the concept of gender. She defines gender as the end product of the social process of learning and internalizing appropriate behaviors, roles, and personality traits for one's sex, and she asserts that the genders that result from the process are completely separate and distinct from biological sex, and yet, overstate sex differences. She concludes that observed sex differences are largely social, not natural; and further, biological differences are minimal, have been made irrelevant by modern technology and contraception, and are completely obscured by social institutions, practices, and prejudices (Oakley 1972: 11–15, 187).

The concept of gender within Oakley's work is, however, ambiguous. Sometimes she uses the concept to describe a sense of identity, and sometimes the concept refers to the processes by which the politics of sex difference get thought out, struggled over, enacted in cultural practices, and inscribed in social institutions. Oakley's dual sense of gender is typical of much feminist theorizing in the North at the time. Sometimes gender refers to characteristics of individuals, the meanings of sex differences ingrained on bodies, minds, and identities. Sometimes it refers to the processes by which the socially constructed meanings of gender are deployed by social institutions (schools, courts, hospitals, the media) and incorporated into cultural practices (ceremonies, customs, traditions). In any case, a key claim of feminist theory is that power relations are implicit in the struggles by which sexual differences are defined, constituted, identified with, and reproduced. The focus of feminist theories of gender have been to gain greater understanding of these processes and of operations of power within them.

Throughout the United States in the 1970s a great deal of research in fields such as psychology and sociology linked observed sex differences in personality and achievement behaviors to sex-based differences in the context of socialization.[3] At the same time, anthropologists produced an enormous amount of research cataloging the various meanings given to sex differences in cultures worldwide. This research concentrated on differential meanings of masculinity and femininity in different cultures, and especially differences in the sex-based division of labor (appropriate work activities as defined by the sex of the worker).[4] Most anthropological theories identified the family and kinship systems[5] as key institutions for producing and reproducing gender relations. Gayle Rubin's 1975 essay "The Traffic in Women: Notes on the Political Economy of Sex" provided a systematic theory of the processes whereby gender and sexuality are produced as features of cultures, bodies, and identities. This sex/gender system, she argues, takes the raw material of human babies/bodies and produces gendered beings whose skills and personalities complement each other to such an extent that the social and sexual bonding between them in marriage produces the basic social unit of human groups. Rubin argues that women are positioned as subordinate within such kinship systems inasmuch as they are exchanged between men. As tokens exchanged between men, women cannot also be self-possessed parties to the exchange (Rubin 1975: 172–75). The influence of Rubin's sex/gender system can be seen in section II, where Heidi Hartmann uses it to articulate a Marxist-feminist theory of gender and class structures, and in section III, where it underlies Nancy Hartsock's standpoint theory and Judith Butler's theories of sexed and gendered bodies.

Rubin treated the distinction between sex and gender as a settled matter, sharing Oakley's conclusion that biological sex differences are minor, and that our knowledge of those differences are hopelessly obscured by social practices. Typical of feminist theories of its time and place, Rubin theorizes biological sex as the raw material that cultures mold into genders and sexualities. Rubin's argument is remarkable for at least one other feature. Throughout her explication of the sex/gender system, she peppers her discussion with examples of "exotic"[6] gender and sexual practices drawn from studies of cultures in the South produced by anthropologists from the North. This is one early example of the rhetorical practice among feminist theorists in the North of appropriating examples of different cultural practices in the South to bolster their arguments for social change.[7] In this way, feminists of the North universalize their own local struggles to the struggles of all women. The examples Rubin cites work simultaneously to provide evidence of the diversity of the content of sex/gender categories and as evidence of the ubiquity of the sex/gender system. Thus, even though the details may differ, all women are subjected to the same underlying sex/gender system. This rhetorical practice treats all women as subject to the same patriarchal power relations, and thereby conflates differences of history, culture, and location even as it also positions women of the South as resources for the political struggles and theorizing of women in the North (hooks 1984).

In the 1990s, postmodernism, queer theory, transgendered politics, and activism by intersexed persons have theorized a far more complex and contingent relationship between bodies, sexes, sexualities, and genders than earlier feminist theories accounted for. Thus, interestingly enough, recent feminist scholarship has returned to the relationship between biology and culture to consider how much of what we call anatomical sex difference is shaped by culture and to critique the binary opposition of sexes, sexualities, and genders that prevails in most social, including feminist, theory.[8] Also in the 1990s, the emergence of poststructural challenges to any notion of settled or stable identity has shifted the focus of feminist theorizing to questions of the construction and performance of gendered bodies and identities in cultural discourse and practices. Debates about whether anatomical sex, sexuality, and/or gender are stable, and whether they are coherent facts of individuals' lives throughout their lives, will continue to shape feminist theories in the future. The shifting understandings of sex and gender in contemporary feminist theory and their limitations are well summarized in the Christine Delphy reading.

As outlined in the discussion of the concept of difference below, some feminist theorists, initially mostly women of color and lesbians in the North and South, immediately challenged this universalized view of gender.[9] Universal claims of gender oppression that define the characteristics of the gender group women in terms of their differences from the gender group men, they argued, wrongly glossed over differences among women. They particularly objected to the nearly exclusive focus on sex and gender in feminist theories and agendas articulated by white and Western women. This focus deems other dimensions of social life to be less important in understanding women's experience as women. Within such theories, even if differences among women are acknowledged, those differences are not seen as shaping women's experience as women. Looking back at Ann Oakley's work, it is clear that the focus of her discussion of difference is that between women and men. Likewise, Simone de Beauvoir specifically notes that it is difference from men that marks women as subordinate. Such a focus obscures the difference in women's experiences as women that are shaped by the interconnections of race, ethnicity, nation, and class with gender (Spelman 1988: 66–71). Thus, this fundamental feminist concept—gender—does not have an uncontested definition, even if it is central to feminist theory and political agency.

In displacing the notion that natural sex differences made male domination inevitable, the concept of gender created another problem. Without the female body/soul/nature as the thing that makes women *women*, what would be the basis of women's common identity? On what grounds would women come together as a group to demand change? In other words, what would be the basis of women's political agency as women? Experience is the principal concept feminist theorists have used to replace female nature as the common element defining women as women. Many feminist theorists have asserted that women's identity as a distinct and specific social group begins with their lived experiences as women—beings whose lives, rights, opportunities, pleasures, and responsibilities are often dictated by the value their cultures give to the sex of their bodies as distinct from that of men. Thus a shared experience of oppression is what women have in common. This shared experience defines them as a social group who can act in concert to resist gender oppression and improve their lives. Moreover, critical examination of those experiences provides the grounds for building a feminist political agenda. In 1970s feminist activism, consciousness-raising held a privileged place as a source of critical knowledge that could inform resistance to oppression.[10] Consciousness-raising involved sharing experiences with other women in groups. From these conversations, feminist activists believed, women would come to identify with each other. In turn, the conversations would help identify the common elements in women's individual experiences and thus clarify the systematic nature of women's subordination and the institutional mechanisms of their oppression as women. Such analyses would reveal the most pressing issues for women, would explicate how power works to dominate women, and would point to liberatory strategies. The Gwendolyn Mikell article provides an example of this process. Mikell examines the issues and processes through which women's groups in several African nations coalesced around gender issues during the 1990s. She argues that although the women do not all embrace the label "feminist," an African feminism was emerging from those events. The Corcoran-Nantes article, on the other hand, raises questions about the relationship between women's political activism and feminism. Through an examination of women's activism in popular movements in Brazil, she endeavors to distinguish instances when women mobilized as women around gender issues from instances in which women mobilized around other aspects of identity such as class.

The concept of women's experience also provides the grounds for challenging conventional cultural wisdom about "women's nature." Feminist scholars have observed that much of what passes for knowledge of women's (or men's) nature has historically been constructed from the point of view of the social group men, who benefit most from women's continued subordination. Suspicious of arguments that derive their power from nature, feminist theorists have argued that the value and meaning of women's lives must be defined in social context. Moreover, as de Beauvoir points out, men define themselves as the exemplary case of humanity, and they define women as dependent on men. Given this, it is not surprising that much of what is "known" about women's "nature" justifies their subordination. In that case, feminist theorists have argued, "knowledge" that justifies male domination is untrustworthy precisely because of the interest men have in continuing that dominance. Thus, such theorists conclude, the value and meaning of women's lives must be defined from women's point of view, from the inside of their experiences rather from some outside view.

As you will see in the Kreps essay, it was argued that because women have a "common experience" as women that is distinct from that of men, women are in the best position to define how social structures and cultural beliefs shape women's subordination. In this way, women's gender-based differences from men constitute grounds upon which feminist claims of women's political agency rest. Those differences, feminists such as de Beauvoir have argued, mean that men cannot adequately represent women's interests, and thus women must address for ourselves "how the fact of being women will affect our lives. What opportunities precisely have been given us and what withheld? What fate awaits our younger sisters, and what directions should they take?"

Yet the claim that women share a common experience has been challenged since it was articulated. Some feminist theorists, mostly women of color and lesbians in the North and South, have continually contended that the differences between women's social positions and cultural contexts are so extensive that women may not have a "common experience" at all. However, even while women of color in the North and South challenged the notion of a "common women's experience" and have opposed the dominance of white and Western women's issues in feminist theory and politics, they have often pursued theoretical strategies that embrace the core concept of experience. They often offer alternative narratives that give voice to women's experiences and women's personal lives, as exemplified in section II.[11] Thus, the relationship between one's sense of identity as a woman and one's knowledge of oppression continues to be crucially important for a variety of feminisms. This linkage formed the base for the identity politics that dominated feminist activism in the 1980s and early 1990s. Identity politics are based on the premise that those who experience specific configurations of oppression are best suited to articulate an adequate theory of that oppression and an adequate strategy for change. Thus, as with gender, the concept of experience is central to feminist theorizing but its meaning and usefulness have been continually contested.

So if women's experiences are to be the basis of knowledge in feminist theory, which women's experiences should be the focus of consciousness-raising and critical analysis? The concept of the personal is political succinctly expresses the experiences privileged in second wave feminism in the North. It started out as a political slogan used by self-named radical feminists[12] in the United States and conveys several related notions. It encapsulates the relationship of theory to politics noted above. This concept incorporates the notion underlying the practice of consciousness-raising, that experience is the best grounds for building feminist knowledge and is the best way to define effective feminist politics. At the same time, it expresses the claim that the system of male domination is deeply entrenched in intimate relationships between women and men (Grant 1993: 37). Many of the most pressing issues for feminists in the North have involved women's most personal and intimate experiences—inequality in marriage, male-centered sexuality, reproductive self-determination, and male sexual violence.[13] Examination of those experiences through consciousness-raising, it was argued, would reveal the system of male domination, often called patriarchy in early feminist theory,[14] and would expose the underlying power relations that bound those personal experiences together.

This slogan also challenges the conventional view of politics as limited to formal processes of governments and market relationships in the public sphere, which tend to treat issues of marriage, sexuality, reproduction, and sexual violence as nonpolitical because they are part of private life. Instead, radical feminists defined politics as relations of power that operate within all human relationships in which "one group rules another" (Millet 1970: 111, as cited in Grant 1993: 34). This view of politics was articulated against criticisms from the U.S. left and liberals that the issues U.S. women sought to address related to personal problems, not political issues (Grant 1993: 33–34).

An example of U.S. radical feminism, Bonnie Kreps lays out four key principles. The first two are political and economic rights for all women.[15] But she adds two that are central concerns of the second wave of feminism in the North: women's right to bodily integrity and a critique of femininity. Kreps delineates the idea that women are entitled to bodily integrity, that women's bodies are their property and should not be interfered with by individual men or by governments. This concept, elaborated in depth in the Correa and Petchesky essay, underlies feminist claims for reproductive self-determination as well as activism against rape and domestic violence. In her critique of femininity, Kreps articulates a central concern of U.S. second wave feminism: women's authentic nature. If socialization to femininity through educational institutions and mass media requires women to adapt to oppression, what might they be like if not so coerced?[16] Kreps asks: What might women aspire to if their talents and creativity had free reign? The reading "No More Miss America" asks a related question: What might women look like if not coerced by male-dominant culture to conform to conventional definitions of feminine appearance? This historical document is the leaflet calling for the first protest at a Miss America pageant in 1968. This is the event that produced the caricature by the mainstream media of women's liberationists as bra burners. In criticizing the pageant, however, the document articulates a far more nuanced analysis of the politics of appearance. It argues that standards of conventional feminine beauty and the male-dominated beauty industry require women to conform and contort their bodies for the (white capitalist) male gaze.

The notion of the personal is political was not limited to changes in private relationships, however. It also informs claims upon governments to recognize and change laws and institutional practices that constrained women within private relationships. The concept of autonomy as self-possession, implied in the notion of women's bodily integrity, extends liberal rights of the public sphere into the private sphere. The Correa and Petchesky essay on reproductive rights, and the Margaret Stetz essay on sexual violation of comfort women, each discuss issues at this intersection of the personal and conventionally political. Stetz's account of activism by former "comfort women" highlights strategies of feminist movements to reform rape and domestic violence laws, such as public articulations of women's personal experiences of rape, violence, and institutional disregard for those experiences. The Stetz article also raises the critical question of state-sanctioned sexual violence against women. In her review of local and global feminist politics, Amrita Basu identifies these issues of reproductive and sexual health and safety as those for which there is the strongest global coalitions.

However, at the same time, women of the South question the extent to which feminist theory in the North privileges personal experiences in private life. For instance, Gwen Mikell finds this sentiment within emergent African feminism, in which it is believed feminists in the North have overemphasized individual sexual issues. Basu expresses a similar sentiment in noting that questions of poverty and basic needs are still more likely to be raised by feminists of the South. Thus, as with gender and experience, the concept that the personal is political has been contested as well. Therefore, even the experiences feminist theories focus on in order to understand women's oppression as women are not fixed, but must be defined in specific historical times and places, as Basu recommends.

The need to continually specify time and location in all feminist theorizing is one key insight that has resulted from feminist theorizing about differences. bell hooks makes this point brilliantly by noting that feminists often argue that women want equal rights to men. But she asks which men do women want to be equal to? The abstract individual who possesses full human rights in national and international law is in practice not just male, but is white, middle-class, resides in the North, and is heterosexual as well. She asserts that an adequate feminist theory and practice cannot lay claim to rights of women in general to equality with men in general. As history has shown, hooks notes, feminist activism based on such generalized notions of women and women's experiences often finds it expedient to sacrifice the rights of some groups of women in the interests of securing rights for other groups of women. Such a situation is unacceptable to hooks. For her, freedom for all women is the bedrock of feminist advocacy, and requires the elimination of all forms of domination. In order to begin to pursue this goal of freedom, feminist theories must take account of differences among women.[17]

Conversations and debates about the importance and composition of differences between women became a generative engine for feminist theory in the 1980s.[18] Through this concept, feminist theorists have grappled with questions of how race, nationality, class, and sexuality shape women's lives. Theorizing difference has generated invaluable insights into gender power relations and how those power relations interact with dominations of race, nationality, class, and sexuality, which are the focus of section II.

Questions raised by efforts to articulate the intersections of dominations within women's lives have also led to a critical reassessment of the concept of identity itself. In debating whether and how it might be (im)possible to ever separate the gender aspects of experience from other aspects of experience, such as race, nationality, class, and sexuality, the basic attributes of experience have themselves been cast into doubt. The poststructural notion of difference and power disturb the notion of a stable identity. Poststructural feminist theories ask how differences within a person shape her sense of experience, her sense of identity, her sense of self, her agency. They question if experience is ever a constant or singular thing, even within an individual. Poststructuralist theories suggest that identities are the consequences of shifting relations of power. Therefore, poststructuralist theories understand identity as mobile sites of difference and extol the possibilities of those flexible and changing identities. Women's movements have necessarily shifted along with the fluid complexities of women's identities. Focusing on the issue of environmentalism, the Sturgeon essay speaks to a specific feminist movement and historical moment when questions on how identity categories might inform feminist politics played out in the global civil society. She looks at the flexibility of the concept that women, especially native women, are closer to nature as it was taken up in ecofeminist and Third World environmentalist movements. She argues that the concept, while problematic because it both essentializes women and appropriates the experiences of native women, nonetheless provided the basis for "useful interventions" in discourses and politics of women and development. Therefore, she concludes, in rightly criticizing the universalizing tendencies within Western feminism, we should not overlook the uses Third World women have made of those concepts in their global activism.

Difference is also the primary concept through which those who have been excluded from the dominant feminist theories have challenged the falsely universal claims embedded in those theories and have laid bare the key mechanisms of domination within feminist theoretical practices. bell hooks and Elizabeth Martinez reflect the anger and disillusionment on the part of women of color, while Charlotte Bunch's essay expresses anger among lesbians at the exclusion of lesbian experience from the category of women's experiences. hooks and Martinez object to the way in which the exclusive focus on sex and gender in fact assumes a white, middle-class version of women's experience. Recall the example of height given earlier where gender, defined in terms of differences between women and men, elides differences among women. As with height, in which a statistical average becomes a social norm for appropriate height, the focus on differences between men and women allowed a dominant group to formulate their particular experience as the normative experience of all women. Experiences of white, middle-class, apparently heterosexual women residing in the North became the experiences that typify women's experiences. Intertwining race, class, heterosexual, and imperialist privilege gave (and continue to give) those women greater access to publishing and related means to disseminate their perspectives on their experiences as women's experiences. Silencing all other experiences, this culturally and economically dominant group's experiences as women became the normative women's experience against which other women had to compare themselves.

The effects of this dominance can be clearly seen by hooks, Mikell, and Martinez, who each cast their arguments against a normative feminist subject who is white, middle-class, and of the dominant (imperialist) culture. Bunch's essay, in a similar manner, must counter the heterosexism by which lesbians' concerns are defined as outside of the women's movement, suggesting that they are not really women. White, middle-class, and heterosexual women in the North are rarely called upon to cast their arguments in terms of their differences from other women. Instead, women of color, women of the South, and lesbians/bisexual/ transgendered persons are called upon to locate themselves within "women's experience as women" or to name their "differences" from that "experience." The requirement for such an explanation is framed as if the differences in their experiences are attributable to something other than gender, and as if middle-class, Northern, heterosexual, white women's experience of gender is not shaped by privileges of race, class, nation, and sexuality. Thus, critiques offered by women of color and lesbians reveal that feminist core concepts—gender, women's experience, the personal is political—have recapitulated racial, class, colonial, and heterosexual dominations even as they have sought to articulate a liberatory gender politics (Spellman: 1988).

hooks's view of feminist advocacy directed at the elimination of all forms of domination offers an expansive vision of feminist politics. "The Combahee River Collective" reading in section II, which represents an early articulation of identity politics, signals what would become a central feature of feminist politics in the 1980s: a social movement fragmented into organizations based on identity categories.[19] Fragmentation of feminist politics in the 1980s reflected the challenges involved in women's situation. If articulations of women's experience in feminist theory hinged on excluding some women and some women's experiences (racism, orientalism, homophobia) and privileging others (white, Western, heterosexual), then feminist political agendas based on those theories would not succeed in liberating *all* women, as they have claimed to do. With a variety of experiences shaped along axes of domination that intertwine with gender, then, as Elizabeth Spelman has so eloquently noted, "the paradox at the heart of feminism" is how to weigh the things women have in common with the differences among us (Spelman 1988: 3). A continuing challenge of feminist theory is finding the grounds to argue effectively for the end of oppression of all women. Basu, whose assessment of local and global feminist politics occurs at a moment after many of the initial conflicts between women of color and women of the South with white Northern feminisms, suggests that common goals should be the focus of the answer to this paradox. With all the differences among us, what women can have in common are political goals, defined in specific historical times and places.

Notes

1. Sorting out the relationship between gender-based differential treatment imposed through colonial regimes and any that may have existed before colonial occupation is complex and has been a central concern of feminist theorists, especially those concerned with women's issues in the South. See especially, Mani and Helie-Lucas in this volume. Equal treatment of the sexes was not recognized by the U.S. Supreme Court until the 1970s, and then only partially. In international law, equal treatment of the sexes is implied in the 1946 Declaration of Human Rights. However, sex equality only became an explicit doctrine with the Convention on the Elimination of All Forms of Discrimination of Women in 1979.

2. We are not suggesting that Oakley's work singlehandedly shaped subsequent theory. Instead, we offer it as an exemplar of the kind of conversations/debates of the moment that shaped subsequent theorizing.

3. The most widely cited example of behavioral differences were aggressiveness and passivity, in which the social context encourages aggressiveness in boys and passivity in girls through differential rewards and sanctions for those behaviors. This research is summarized in a 1979 episode of the PBS science series, NOVA, entitled "The Pinks and the Blues." Differential academic achievement has also been shown to be related to the kind and amount of attention girls and boys get from teachers. American Association of University Women and the Wellesley College Center for Research on Women, "How Schools Shortchange Girls: The AAUW Report" (New York: Marlowe and Company, 1992).

4. Two early collections are Michelle Rosaldo and Louise Lamphere, eds., *Woman, Culture, and Society.* (Palo Alto, CA: Stanford University Press, 1974) and Rayna Reiter, ed., *Toward an Anthropology of Women* (New York : Monthly Review Press, 1975).

5. This term is from anthropology and captures not only a Euro-American sense of family, but also a sense of social organization based on familial ties, which the field specifically identifies with "traditional cultures." The term carries both a complex view of the institution of the family and pejorative colonial assessments of primitive cultures. At the same time, feminist critiques of kinship systems as oppressive for women, and criticisms of socialization practices in nuclear families account for why 1970s–U.S. feminists are often caricatured as antifamily.

6. As it was first used in 1599, exotic simply meant "alien, introduced from abroad, not indigenous." By the end of the nineteenth century, however, the term had come to connote something exciting, stimulating, and slightly dangerous with which to spice up the more mundane domestic world (Ashcroft et. al 1998: 94).

7. See for example Rubin 1975: 166, 168, 172, 174–75, 181. We do not intend to single Rubin out; she is not unique in this regard. See also Mary Daly 1978; Audre Lorde 1981 critiquing Daly; and Chandra Talpade Mohanty 1991 critiquing the Zed Press book list. We intended to include the Rubin article here, but the author declined permission to reprint it.

8. For instance, Suzanne Kessler (2000) examines the practice of surgical alteration of the ambiguous genitalia of intersexed persons to fit medical categories of sexually dimorphic bodies. Although feminist theorists, including Kessler, argued for socially constructed genders, they nonetheless easily fell into step with the medical logic of two distinct sexes and two distinct genders, both marked by distinct body types. See also Ann Fausto-Sterling (2000), which examines how biological knowledge of sex, gender, and sexuality shapes—and is shaped by—politics and culture, and how both are literally embodied in our physiology.

9. See for example Chela Sandoval (1991: 1); and Patrice McDermott (1994), who provides an invaluable analysis of the impact of the "difference debate" on feminist academic journals.

10. The notion of consciousness-raising owes much to the theories of the consciousness of oppression developed by W. E. B. DuBois (1969) and Paulo Friere (1970).

11. The continuing importance of experience narratives for women of the South and women of color can be seen in Shari Stone-Mediatore (2000) and the recent superb collection by The Latina Feminist Group (2001). See also Grant 1993: 27.

12. Radical feminists took the name *radical* from the new left politics of the moment that positioned itself against both liberalism and the old left of the 1950s. See also Grant 1993: 18–19.

13. Published guidelines for consciousness-raising groups helped set up this process of defining the most pressing issues by providing lists of suggested topics. See "Consciousness Raising," 1970. This piece defines the appropriate composition and process for consciousness-raising groups and lists the topics of family, childhood and adolescence, men, marital status, motherhood, sex, women, behavior, ambitions, and movement activity.

14. See Hartmann in this volume, Gayle Rubin, 1975; Zillah Eienstein, 1978; and Maria Mies, 1986.

15. Since liberalism seemed to provide a theoretical understanding of political rights—which women's groups were working to secure—and Marxism explained workplace issues, feminists could concentrate on explicating the gendered power relations within personal life, as neither liberals or the left were inclined to do. See Grant 1993: 33–34. Norma Chincilla (1997) argues that the relationship of Marxism to feminism in Latin America produced a far different formulation of feminist theory and politics. This is reflected in the Molyneux and Corcoran-Nantes pieces.

16. This question reverberates with those asked in earlier centuries, for instance by Mary Wollstonecraft 1975; John Stuart Mill 1883; and Harriet Taylor 1983, who in the eighteenth and nineteenth centuries asked what women's character might be like if they were not educated to be pleasing to men.

17. Barbara Smith makes a similar claim two years earlier in 1982, when she argues that "racism is a feminist issue" because "feminism is the political theory and practice that struggles to free *all* women.... anything less than this vision of total freedom is not feminism, but merely female self-aggrandizement" (Hull et al. 1982: 49).

18. There is a vast literature on the significance of differences between women and men produced in the 1980s, including debates about gender differences in moral reasoning (Carol Gilligan 1982), in knowledge production (Mary Belenky et al. 1986, and Hester Eisenstein and Alice Jardine, 1980), in relationality (Nancy Chodorow 1978, and Sara Ruddick 1989), in sexuality (Catharine MacKinnon 1987). Outside of standpoint theories, (which some would include in this literature on gender difference), this branch of feminist theory is not well represented in this anthology. Our inclination to give greater emphasis to differences among women and space limitations account for this gap.

19. The problematic implications of this process of identification at the base of identity politics is key to later feminist theories of subjectivity and agency developed in section III.

DEFINITIONS

1.
WE EGYPTIAN WOMEN
Inji Aflatun

To the women of Egypt
To the ten million women who constitute one half of this people
The Egyptian woman peasant, worker, civil servant, young girl, wife and mother
To our liberal writers: Qasim Amin, Abd al-Rahman al Rafiq, Taha Husain, Salama Musa,
*   Khalid Mohammad Khalid, Ismail Mazhar, whose writings reflect their free conscience and*
*   not dissent and prejudices*
To the young feminist movement
To the true militants of the Egyptian feminist cause, not the amateurs and sycophants giving
*   themselves airs and looking for personal profit, or those crawling far behind*
To the Egyptian woman, her supporters, men and women
I dedicate this book ...

In Egypt today there is a fierce debate about women's rights, between those who uphold equality between men and women and those who oppose it. We are surrounded by the clamour of both groups.

Newspapers and reviews are full of articles expressing conflicting ideas. Although their abundance does not dry up, they are far from clearly presenting the true situation of women in modern Egyptian society. They all revolve around issues which are not supported by facts or based on tangible evidence. I do not suggest that it is the duty of the press to undertake this scientific analysis, supported by facts and based on material evidence. This is the duty of writers rather than newsmen. However, let us recognize here the real need of Egyptian literature for a true scientific study of the status of the Egyptian woman, her problems and her demands. It would be helpful to keep this bitter debate about women's rights a true and matter-of-fact discussion. The present book offered today to the reader is only a quick attempt and a modest contribution. It does not ignore the tumult over the woman issue, but rather explains more clearly and realistically the condition and status of the woman in Egyptian society.

There is no doubt that this book will not be viewed with favour by the enemies of woman, whom Qasim Amin rightly said are the enemies of progress and democracy. It is also certain that it will not be appreciated by certain feminists who pretend to defend the rights of the Egyptian woman but who are actually following in the footsteps of the enemies of woman, crawling behind them and looking only for honours and advantages befitting their elegant personages. The avowed enemies of women are those who proclaim 'Woman's liberation!' This originates in the play of words in which our opponents excel. The slogan 'woman at home' actually means the disruption of this home and the displacement of women and children, and husbands along with them. This means that there will be no contact between the woman working within the house and the society in which she lives. She will know nothing about it, she will not participate in any way in its administration and the solution of its problems. This means the subjection of women to the dominion of men which will result in the obliteration of their personality, dignity, and humanity. Society will be deprived of the endeavours of half its members. This means depriving the home of an articulate mistress, conscious of her rights and duties towards her family and society, able to make her family the good and happy centre of a good and happy society.

But these arguments will not suffice to silence the enemies of women. The best way to counter their craft is to confront them with some concrete proofs and plain figures. This is what current Egyptian literature needs and this is the purpose of the book. Because it is their custom to hide behind the ramparts of tradition and religious custom and to use vague terms intended to sow doubt and confusion in people's minds, we invite our opponents to participate in an honest and open discussion.

A final word is needed to defend this book. Today the Egyptian people, on the eve of general elections, are about to be betrayed by its deputies and representatives, a betrayal of the democratic system. Indeed, the right of the Egyptian women to vote and to be elected should be requested at the start of a new age. The recognition of their oppressed rights would be an implementation of the principles of democracy of a representative regime.

I hope this book will fulfil its purpose and will help convince the public of the justice of women's demands and help free them from the fetters which have bound them in their private and public life. It would enable Egypt to join the countries which have granted women their rights and equality with men and enable the country to enter modern civilisation.

Women and Political Rights

The Egyptian woman is deprived of political rights. She is denied the right to vote or to run for parliament. This deprivation is the worst of the prejudices which a woman has to endure in the Egyptian society. This deprivation conflicts with the most basic principles of democracy. Democracy recognises the political rights of every member of society, without distinction between rich and poor, influential or otherwise, and advocates the participation of the people in the power structure through the mediation of representatives elected by them through universal suffrage. If we deprive half the members of the nation of the right to enjoy political rights, if we deprive half of the Egyptian people of the right to elect its representatives to parliamentary organisation through universal suffrage, we are going against the fundamental principles of a democratic regime, and will thus find ourselves faced with a demi-democracy instead of a total one. It is our duty to oppose this glaring violation of the principles of a representative regime, and to fill in the lacuna by granting the right to enjoy the privileges of democracy to the second half of society as well. Woman's participation in the political life of society constitutes an important element in a healthy democratic regime and a prime factor in the evolution and development of this society. Women in modern societies are not inactive members living on the fringe of life (as their enemies would like them to be) with no right to participate in politics or power. No, rather they constitute half of the people and have the same importance as the first half in the continued existence and development of society. We have proved that they can participate in every field of labour, culture and science on the same footing as man, and are able to be as productive as man while performing the best services.

It is not true that women constitute an isolated part of society, one which cannot feel its sufferings, its needs, or formulate and give directives, thus rendering their participation in political life and power unnecessary. Quite the contrary, women are citizens who are particularly aware of economic, social, and national problems. They understand the needs of their country and people, in internal and external matters. Every day they are confronted with the main problems of society, clothing, food, children, housing, health care, education, et cetera.

To deprive woman of her civil rights constitutes not only an injustice towards her, but also a harmful obstacle in the path of the development and evolution of the people, a lacuna in the country's democratic process.

Now let us listen to the wailings of the enemies of woman who deceive the public with their lies. From their ivory tower, these gentlemen claim that woman should not enjoy the same political rights as man, because this would lead to her degeneration, would make her neglect her duty to the home and children. Woman at home, woman always at home; that is their slogan. For the nth time let us tell these gentlemen that woman, whether they like it or not, has participated effectively in political life in most countries of the world. There is no way to prevent her from participating in various fields of activities, whether they like it or not.

Woman has obtained political rights in India, China, and other countries with oriental traditions. Even so, no fanatic would have pretended that families over there were broken or ruined, or that the home in China has no proper structure any longer.

It would be absurd to pretend that woman's participation in universal suffrage once every five years would keep her away from her home, her family, and her children. This would lead us to suggest that man's participation in this suffrage distracts him from the task entrusted him as well, whether he be a physician, engineer or civil servant. This would imply that universal suffrage constitutes an alienation for the totality of the population.

Let us follow these gentlemen through their wily reasoning. They pretend that what they mean is a female candidate for parliament and other high functions, such as minister, ambassador, et cetera. But we will always expose such impudent falsehoods. The fact that woman offers her candidacy to parliament or various diplomatic jobs constitutes only a job that woman accomplishes in society similar to the work of a teacher, physician or peasant. We have already shown the importance of woman's work. We have shown that the combination of running a home and a job is not an illusion. Our efforts to help woman in her work, by supplying her means to accomplish her double duty, will effectively render her 'a woman for society.'

On the other hand, it is frankly ridiculous to assert that the participation of women in parliament or other political offices would lead her to neglect her home and allow her children to go astray. After all, such arguments misinterpreted in this fashion force us to the conclusion that man's participation in parliament or ministries, be he a physician, professor, lawyer, or worker, goes against the interest of medicine, teaching, law and industry. We would have to consider universal suffrage as a delaying factor in society's productivity. The theories of these gentlemen would thus lead us to disavow democracy, to destroy the principles of a parliamentary and representative government lest they prevent the whole people, male and female, from attending to their chores.

This is the clear proof that the enemies of woman are the fiercest enemies of democracy.

But these gentlemen return to the fray, stating that men who quit their jobs for politics leave their duties to others, and that thus productivity is not impaired. These arguments completely destroy their claims, since women fulfilling political functions can also entrust the tasks which they cannot accomplish at home and in their family to others.

Thus, this sterile discussion is closed. Is there anything more ridiculous than to ask an educated woman to devote herself to washing dishes, sweeping floors, and cooking for the family? If she does not do it, people start whining. They claim that the home has been destroyed and that children have been thrown into the street. With no arguments left, the enemies of woman beat a retreat and look for excuses to justify their unrealistic opinions. Thus, it is not surprising to see these gentlemen raise another factor: Egyptian women are ignorant, illiteracy is twice as high among them as among men. It is easy to reject these faulty pretexts. People should not wait to enjoy democracy in order to learn. On the contrary, obscurantism will only be eradicated and education will only spread under a democratic regime. The Egyptian people realised this fact as a result of their painful experiences. British imperialism dominated Egypt for nearly forty years, during which time illiteracy increased among the people. When the victories of the national movement led to the signing of the 1923 constitution, the illiteracy rate among the Egyptian people exceeded by far the current rate among Egyptian women.

If these gentlemen mean that we have to deprive the people of its democratic rights and of a parliamentary government as well, all this on the pretext that it has a high rate of illiteracy, their theory is tantamount to a disavowal of democracy as well as the ruin of parliamentarism and popular expression.

This is additional proof, even more blatant, that the enemies of woman are also the enemies of democracy.

Today all our intellectual and political leaders are convinced that the political rights of women will inevitably have to be recognised. But the enemies of democracy are fighting to invalidate women's rights. They are fighting to have voting rights granted only to the educated members of the Egyptian nation, both men and women. We are sorry to note that one of the leaders of the Egyptian feminist movement shares the dangerous opinion of these gentlemen and their destructive doctrines. In one of her calls, she has declared: "How can you allow ignorant and illiterate men to take part in Egyptian political life, while depriving educated women of this same participation? Grant the educated woman her political rights; she deserves them more that illiterate men."

We must draw attention to the dangers hidden in such views. The opinions held by these gentlemen mean the limitation of political rights to an educated minority of the members of the nation, men and women. This would bring about the destruction of our democratic government rather than its fulfillment. The majority of men in Egypt would be deprived of political rights in exchange for the granting of these same rights to a small minority of women.

Have we not said that the enemies of women—even if they pose as supporters of educated women—are always the enemies of democracy. The struggle of Egyptian women for their political rights is part of the struggle for the strengthening of democracy in Egypt. The use of this struggle against the democratic regime itself cannot be allowed. Those men and women who are in favour of granting political rights to educated women exclusively, the same people who deny these same rights to ignorant women and illiterate men, should devote their efforts to the immediate eradication of illiteracy and the spreading of education, then the people, men as well as women, will be able to use political rights instead of depriving the overwhelming majority of this people of their natural right to free choice of its representatives and governors.

The solution to the problem is therefore not to deprive illiterate people of their political rights, but to educate them so that they can make good use of these rights. Democracy is not the exclusive prerogative of men, nor of educated men or women only; it is the power of the whole people, men and women together.

The problem of the political rights of women has taken on an international magnitude since the end of the Second World War and the birth of the United Nations. In its preamble, the UN charter states the necessity of equality between men and women. Likewise, the Declaration of Human Rights adopted by the UN General Assembly on 10 December 1948, upholds this equality. Furthermore, on 19 November 1946, the UN General Assembly adopted a resolution recommending that its members implement the equality of rights between men and women in cases where this equality has not yet been established. The UN Economic and Social Council has established a special commission to investigate the woman question and asked it to study the rights and conditions of women in various countries. The deprivation of the Egyptian woman of her political rights is a blatant violation of the United Nations Charter, of the Declaration of Human Rights, as well as of the recommendations of the UN General Assembly of which Egypt is a member. This unlawful attitude adopted by Egypt as a civilised nation doubtless contributes to the decline of her prestige and is detrimental to her reputation in the international arena.

We have recently seen the Syrian government hurriedly recognising political rights for the Syrian woman, but this was limited to educated women. Nonetheless, it is certain that the Syrian woman deserves to be congratulated for having won her cause up to a point. She is the first woman in the Arab East to gain recognition—however partial and limited—of her rights. This step will be followed by others.

Translated from the Arabic
by Michelle Raccagni

2.
THE SECOND SEX: INTRODUCTION
Simone de Beauvoir

For a long time I have hesitated to write a book on woman. The subject is irritating, especially to women; and it is not new. Enough ink has been spilled in the quarreling over feminism, now practically over, and perhaps we should say no more about it. It is still talked about, however, for the voluminous nonsense uttered during the last century seems to have done little to illuminate the problem. After all, is there a problem? And if so, what is it? Are there women, really? Most assuredly the theory of the eternal feminine still has its adherents who will whisper in your ear: "Even in Russia women still are *women*"; and other erudite persons—sometimes the very same—say with a sigh: "Woman is losing her way, woman is lost." One wonders if women still exist, if they will always exist, whether or not it is desirable that they should, what place they occupy in this world, what their place should be. "What has become of women?" was asked recently in an ephemeral magazine.[1]

But first we must ask: what is a woman? "*Total mulier in utero*," says one, "woman is a womb." But in speaking of certain women, connoisseurs declare that they are not women, although they are equipped with a uterus like the rest. All agree in recognizing the fact that females exist in the human species; today as always they make up about one half of humanity. And yet we are told that femininity is in danger; we are exhorted to be women, remain women, become women. It would appear, then, that every female human being is not necessarily a woman; to be so considered she must share in that mysterious and threatened realm known as femininity. Is this attribute something secreted by the ovaries? Or is it a Platonic essence, a product of the philosophic imagination? Is a rustling petticoat enough to bring it down to earth? Although some women try zealously to incarnate this essence, it is hardly patentable. It is frequently described in vague and dazzling terms that seem to have been borrowed from the vocabulary of the seers, and indeed in the times of St. Thomas it was considered an essence as certainly defined as the somniferous virtue of the poppy....

If her functioning as a female is not enough to define woman, if we decline also to explain her through "the eternal feminine," and if nevertheless we admit, provisionally, that women do exist, then we must face the question: what is a woman?

To state the question is, to me, to suggest, at once, a preliminary answer. The fact that I ask it is in itself significant. A man would never get the notion of writing a book on the peculiar situation of the human male.[2] But if I wish to define myself, I must first of all say: "I am a woman"; on this truth must be based all further discussion. A man never begins by presenting himself as an individual of a certain sex; it goes without saying that he is a man. The terms *masculine* and *feminine* are used symmetrically only as a matter of form, as on legal papers. In actuality the relation of the two sexes is not quite like that of two electrical poles, for man represents both the positive and the neutral, as is indicated by the common use of *man* to designate human beings in general; whereas woman represents only the negative, defined by limiting criteria, without reciprocity. In the midst of an abstract discussion it is vexing to hear a man say: "You think thus and so because you are a woman"; but I know that my only defense is to reply: "I think thus and so because it is true," thereby removing my subjective self from the argument. It would be out of the question to reply: "And you think the contrary because you are a man," for it is understood that the fact of being a man is no peculiarity. A man is in the right in being a man; it is the woman who is in the wrong. It amounts to this: just as for the ancients there was an absolute vertical with reference to which the oblique was defined, so there is an absolute human type, the masculine. Woman has ovaries, a uterus; these peculiarities imprison her in her subjectivity, circumscribe her within the limits of her own nature. It is often said that she thinks with her glands. Man superbly ignores the fact that his anatomy also includes glands, such as the testicles, and that they secrete hormones. He thinks of his body as a direct and normal connection with the world, which he believes he apprehends objectively, whereas he regards the body of woman as a hindrance, a prison, weighed down by everything peculiar to it. "The female is a female by virtue of a certain *lack* of qualities," said Aristotle; "we should regard the female nature as afflicted with a natural defectiveness." And St. Thomas for his part pronounced woman to be an "imperfect man," an "incidental" being. This is symbolized in Genesis where Eve is depicted as made from what Bossuet called "a supernumerary bone" of Adam.

Thus humanity is male and man defines woman not in herself but as relative to him; she is not regarded as an autonomous being. Michelet writes: "Woman, the relative being...." And Benda is most positive in his *Rapport d' Uriel*: "The body of man makes sense in itself quite apart from that of woman, whereas the latter seems wanting in significance by itself.... Man can think of himself without woman. She cannot think of herself without man." And she is simply what man decrees; thus she is called "the sex," by which is meant that she appears essentially to the male as a sexual being. For him she is sex—absolute sex, no less. She is defined and differentiated with reference to man and not he with reference to her; she is the incidental, the inessential as opposed to the essential. He is the Subject, he is the Absolute—she is the Other.[3] ...

Thus it is that no group ever sets itself up as the One without at once setting up the Other against itself. If three travelers chance to occupy the same compartment, that is enough to make vaguely hostile "others" out of all the rest of the passengers on the train. In small-town eyes all persons not belonging to the village are "strangers" and suspect; to the native of a country all who inhabit other countries are "foreigners"; Jews are "different" for the anti-Semite, Negroes are "inferior" for

American Racists, aborigines are "natives" for colonists, proletarians are the "lower class" for the privileged....

The parallel drawn by Bebel between women and the proletariat is valid in that neither ever formed a minority or a separate collective unit of mankind. And instead of a single historical event it is in both cases a historical development that explains their status as a class and accounts for the membership of *particular individuals* in that class. But proletarians have not always existed, whereas there have always been women. They are women in virtue of their anatomy and physiology. Throughout history they have always been subordinated to men, and hence their dependency is not the result of a historical event or a social change—it was not something that *occurred*. The reason why otherness in this case seems to be an absolute is in part that it lacks the contingent or incidental nature of historical facts. A condition brought about at a certain time can be abolished at some other time, as the Negroes of Haiti and others have proved; but it might seem that a natural condition is beyond the possibility of change. In truth, however, the nature of things is no more immutably given, once for all, than is historical reality. If woman seems to be the inessential which never becomes the essential, it is because she herself fails to bring about this change. Proletarians say "We"; Negroes also. Regarding themselves as subjects, they transform the bourgeois, the whites, into "others." But women do not say "We," except at some congress of feminists or similar formal demonstration; men say "women," and women use the same word in referring to themselves. They do not authentically assume a subjective attitude. The proletarians have accomplished the revolution in Russia, the Negroes in Haiti, the Indo-Chinese are battling for it in Indo-China; but the women's effort has never been anything more than a symbolic agitation. They have gained only what men have been willing to grant; they have taken nothing, they have only received.[4]

The reason for this is that women lack concrete means for organizing themselves into a unit which can stand face to face with the correlative unit. They have no past, no history, no religion of their own; and they have no such solidarity of work and interest as that of the proletariat. They are not even promiscuously herded together in the way that creates community feeling among the American Negroes, the ghetto Jews, the workers of Saint-Denis, or the factory hands of Renault. They live dispersed among the males, attached through residence, housework, economic condition, and social standing to certain men—fathers or husbands—more firmly than they are to other women. If they belong to the bourgeoisie, they feel solidarity with men of that class, not with proletarian women; if they are white, their allegiance is to white men, not to Negro women. The proletariat can propose to massacre the ruling class, and a sufficiently fanatical Jew or Negro might dream of getting sole possession of the atomic bomb and making humanity wholly Jewish or black; but woman cannot even dream of exterminating the males. The bond that unites her to her oppressors is not comparable to any other. The division of the sexes is a biological fact, not an event in human history. Male and female stand opposed within a biological fact, not an event in human history. Male and female stand opposed within a primordial *Mitsein*, and woman has not broken it. The couple is a fundamental unity with its two halves riveted together, and the cleavage of society along the line of sex is impossible. Here is to be found the basic trait of woman: she is the Other in a totality of which the two components are necessary to one another. . . .

Master and slave, also, are united by a reciprocal need, in this case economic, which does not liberate the slave. In the relation of master to slave the master does not make a point of the need that he has for the other; he has in his grasp the power of satisfying their need through his won action; whereas the slave, in his dependent condition, his hope and fear, is quite conscious of the need he has for his master. Even if the need is at bottom equally urgent for both, it always works in favor of the oppressor and against the oppressed. That is why the liberation for the working class, for example, has been slow.

Now, woman has always been man's dependent, if not his slave; the two sexes have never shared the world in equality. And even today woman is heavily handicapped, though her situation is beginning to change. Almost nowhere is her legal status the same as man's, and frequently it is much to her disadvantage. Even when her rights are legally recognized in the abstract, long-standing custom prevents their full expression in the mores. In the economic sphere men and women can almost be said to make up two castes; other things being equal, the former hold the better jobs, get higher wages, and have more opportunity for success than their new competitors. In industry and politics men have a great many more positions and they monopolize the most important posts. In addition to all this, they enjoy a traditional prestige that the education of children tends in every way to support, for the present enshrines the past and in the past all history has been made by men. At the present time, when women are beginning to take part in the affairs of the world, it is still a world that belongs to men—they have no doubt of it at all and women have scarcely any. To decline to be the Other, to refuse to be a party to the deal—this would be for women to renounce all the advantages conferred upon them by their alliance with the superior caste. Man-the-sovereign will provide woman-the-liege with material protection and will undertake the moral justification of her existence; thus she can evade at once both economic risk and the metaphysical risk of a liberty in which ends and aims must be contrived without assistance. Indeed, along with the ethical urge of each individual to affirm his subjective existence, there is also the temptation to forgo liberty and become a thing. This is an inauspicious road, for he who takes it—passive, lost, ruined—becomes henceforth the creature of another's will, frustrated in his transcendence and deprived of every value: But it is an easy road; on it one avoids the strain involved in undertaking an authentic existence. When man makes of woman the *Other*, he may, then, expect her to manifest deep-seated tendencies toward complicity. Thus, woman may fail to lay claim to the status of subject because she lacks definite resources, because she feels the necessary bond that ties her to man regardless of reciprocity, and because she is often very well pleased with her role as the *Other*.

But it will be asked at once: how did all of this begin? It is easy to see that the duality of the sexes, like any duality, gives rise to conflict. And doubtless the winner will assume the status of absolute. But why should man have won from the start? It seems possible that women could have won the victory; or that the outcome of the conflict might never have been decided. How is it that this world has always belonged to the men and that things have begun to change only recently? Is this change a good thing? Will it bring about an equal sharing of the world between men and women?...

It was only later, in the eighteenth century, that genuinely democratic men began to view the matter objectively. Diderot, among others, strove to show that woman is, like man, a human being. Later John Stuart Mill came fervently to her defense. But these philosophers displayed unusual impartiality. In the nineteenth century the feminist quarrel became again a quarrel of partisans. One of the consequences of the industrial revolution was the entrance of women into productive labor, and it was just here that the claims of the feminist emerged from the realm of theory and acquired an economic basis, while their opponents became the more aggressive. Although landed property lost power to some extent, the bourgeoisie clung to the old morality that found the guarantee of private property in the solidity of the family. Woman was ordered back into the home all the more harshly as her emancipation became a real menace. Even within the working class, the men endeavored to restrain woman's liberation, because they began to see the women as dangerous competitors—even more so because they were accustomed to working for lower wages.[5]

In proving woman's inferiority, the antifeminists then began to draw not only upon religion, philosophy, and theology, as before, but also upon science—biology, experimental psychology, et cetera. At most they were willing to grant "equality in difference" to the *other* sex. That profitable formula is most significant; it is precisely like the "equal but separate" formula of the Jim Crow laws aimed at the North American Negroes. As is well known, this so-called equalitarian segregation has resulted only in the most extreme discrimination. The similarity just noted is in no way due to chance, for whether it is a race, a caste, a class, or a sex that is reduced to a position of inferiority, the methods of justification are the same. "The eternal feminine" corresponds to "the black soul" and to "the Jewish character." True, the Jewish problem is on the whole very different from the other two—to the anti-Semite the Jew is not so much an inferior as he is an enemy for whom there is to be granted no place on earth, for whom annihilation is the fate desired. But there are deep similarities between the situation of woman and that of the Negro. Both are being emancipated today from a like paternalism, and the former master class wishes to "keep them in their place"—that is, the place chosen for them. In both cases the former masters lavish more or less sincere eulogies, either on the virtues of "the good Negro" with his dormant, childish, merry soul—the submissive Negro—or on the merits of the woman who is "truly feminine"—that is, frivolous, infantile, irresponsible—the submissive woman. In both cases the dominant class bases its argument on a state of affairs that it has itself created. As George Bernard Shaw puts it, in substance, "the American white relegates the black to the rank of shoeshine boy; and he concludes from this that the black is good for nothing but shining shoes." This vicious circle is met within all analogous circumstances; when an individual (or a group of individuals) is kept in a situation of inferiority, the fact is that he *is* inferior. But the significance of the verb *to be* must be rightly understood here; it is in bad faith to give it a static value when it really has the dynamic Hegelian sense of "to have become." Yes, women on the whole *are* today inferior to men; that is, their situation affords them fewer possibilities. The question is: should that state of affairs continue?. . .

. . . But men profit in many more subtle ways from the otherness, the alterity of woman. Here is miraculous balm for those afflicted with an inferiority complex, and indeed no one is more arrogant toward women, more aggressive or scornful, than the man who is anxious about his virility. Those who are not fear-ridden in the presence of their fellow men are much more disposed to recognize a fellow creature in woman; but even to these the myth of woman, the Other, is precious for many reasons.[6] They cannot be blamed for not cheerfully relinquishing all the benefits they derive from the myth, for they realize what they would lose in relinquishing woman as they fancy her to be, while they fail to realize what they have to gain from the woman of tomorrow. Refusal to pose oneself as the Subject, unique and absolute, requires great self-denial. Furthermore, the vast majority of men make no such claim explicitly. They do not *postulate* woman as inferior, for today they are too thoroughly imbued with the ideal of democracy not to recognize all human beings as equals.

In the bosom of the family, woman seems in the eyes of childhood and youth to be clothed in the same social dignity as the adult males. Later on, the young man, desiring and loving, experiences the resistance, the independence of the woman desired and loved; in marriage, he respects woman as wife and mother, and in the concrete events of conjugal life she stands there before him as a free being. He can therefore feel that social subordination as between the sexes no longer exists and that on the whole, in spite of differences, woman is an equal. As, however, he observes some points of inferiority—the most important being unfitness for the professions—he attributes these to natural causes. When he is in a cooperative and benevolent relation with woman, his theme is the principle of abstract equality, and he does not base his attitude upon such inequality as may exist. But when he is in conflict with her, the situation is reversed: his theme will be the existing inequality, and he will even take it as justification for denying abstract equality.[7]

So it is that many men will affirm as if in good faith that women *are* the equals of man and that they have nothing to clamor for, while *at the same time* they will say that women can never be the equals of man and that their demands are in vain. It is, in point of fact, a difficult matter for man to realize the extreme importance of social discriminations which seem outwardly insignificant but which produce in woman moral and intellectual effects so profound that they appear to spring from her original nature.[8] The most sympathetic of men never fully comprehend woman's concrete situation. And there is no reason to put much trust in the men when they rush to the defense of privileges whose full extent they can hardly measure. We shall not, then, permit ourselves to be intimidated by the number and violence of the attacks launched against women, nor to be entrapped by the self-seeking eulogies bestowed on the "true woman," nor to profit by the enthusiasm for woman's destiny manifested by men who would not for the world have any part of it.

We should consider the arguments of the feminists with no less suspicion, however, for very often their controversial aim deprives them of all real value. If the "woman question" seems trivial, it is because masculine arrogance has made of it a "quarrel"; and when quarreling, one no longer reasons well. People have tirelessly sought to prove that woman is superior, inferior, or equal to man. Some say that, having been created after Adam, she is evidently a secondary being; others say on the contrary that Adam was only a rough draft and that God succeeded in producing the human being in perfection when He created Eve. Woman's brain is smaller; yes, but it is relatively larger. Christ was made a man; yes, but perhaps for his greater humility. Each argument at once suggests its opposite, and both are often fallacious. If we are to gain understanding we must get out of these ruts; we must discard the vague notions of superiority, inferiority, equality which have hitherto corrupted every discussion of the subject and start afresh.

Very well, but just how shall we pose the question? And, to begin with, who are we to propound it at all? Man is at once judge and party to the case; but so is woman. What we need is an angel—neither man nor woman—but where shall we find one? Still, the angel would be poorly qualified to speak, for an angel is ignorant of all the basic facts involved in the problem. With a hermaphrodite we should be no better off, for here the situation is most peculiar; the hermaphrodite is not really the combination of a whole man and a whole woman, but consists of parts of each and thus is neither. It looks to me as if there are, after all, certain women who are best qualified to elucidate the situation of woman. Let us not be misled by the sophism that because Epimenides was a Cretan he was necessarily a liar; it is not a mysterious essence that compels men and women to act in good or in bad faith, it is their situation that inclines them more or less toward the search for truth. Many of today's women, fortunate in the restoration of all the privileges pertaining to the estate of the human being, can afford the luxury of impartiality—we even recognize its necessity. We are no longer like our partisan elders; by and large we have won the game. In recent debates on the status of women the United Nations has persistently maintained that the equality of the sexes is now becoming a reality, and already some of us have never had to sense in our femininity an inconvenience or an obstacle. Many problems appear to us to be more pressing than those which concern us in particular, and this detachment even allows us to hope that our attitude will be objective. Still, we know the feminine world more intimately than do the men because we have our roots in it, we grasp more immediately than do men what it means to a human being to be feminine; and we are more concerned with such knowledge. I have said that there are more pressing problems, but this does not prevent us from seeing some importance in asking how the fact of being women will affect our lives. What opportunities precisely have been given us and what withheld? What fate awaits our younger sisters, and what directions should they take? It is significant that books by women on women are in general animated in our day less by a wish to demand our rights than by an effort toward clarity and understanding. As we emerge from an era of excessive controversy, this book is offered as one attempt among others to confirm that statement.

But it is doubtless impossible to approach any human problem with a mind free from bias. The way in which questions are put, the points of view assumed, presuppose a relativity of interest; all characteristics imply values, and every so-called objective description implies an ethical background. Rather than attempt to conceal principles more or less definitely implied, it is better to state them openly at the beginning. This will make it unnecessary to specify on every page in just what sense one uses such words as *superior, inferior, better, worse, progress, reaction,* and the like. If we survey some of the works on woman, we note that one of the points of view most frequently adopted is that of the public good, the general interest; and one always means by this the benefit of society as one wishes it to be maintained or established. For our part, we hold that the only public good is that which assures the private good of the citizens; we shall pass judgment on institutions according to their effectiveness in giving concrete opportunities to individuals. But we do not confuse the idea of private interest with that of happiness, although that is another common point of view. Are not women of the harem more happy than women voters? Is not the housekeeper happier than the working-woman? It is not too clear just what the word *happy* really means and still less what true values it may mask. There is no possibility of measuring the happiness of others, and it is always easy to describe as happy the situation in which one wishes to place them.

In particular, those who are condemned to stagnation are often pronounced happy on the pretext that happiness consists in being at rest. This notion we reject, for our perspective is that of existentialist ethics. Every subject plays his part as such specifically through exploits or projects that serve as a mode of transcendence; he achieves liberty only through a continual reaching out toward other liberties. There is no justification for present existence other than its expansion into an indefinitely open future. Every time transcendence falls back into immanence, stagnation, there is a degradation of existence into the "*en-soi*"—the brutish life of subjection to given conditions—and of liberty into constraint and contingence. This downfall represents a moral fault if the subject consents to it; if it is inflicted upon him, it spells frustration and oppression. In both cases it is an absolute evil. Every individual concerned to justify his existence feels that his existence involves an undefined need to transcend himself, to engage in freely chosen projects.

Now, what peculiarly signalizes the situation of woman is that she—a free and autonomous being like all human creatures—nevertheless finds herself living in a world where men compel her to assume the status of the Other. They propose to stabilize her as object and to doom her to immanence since her transcendence is to be overshadowed and forever transcended by another ego (*conscience*) which is essential and sovereign. The drama of woman lies in this conflict between the fundamental aspirations of every subject (ego)—who always regards the self as the essential—and the compulsions of a situation in which she is the inessential. How can a human being in woman's situation attain fulfillment? What roads are open to her? Which are blocked? How can independence be recovered in a state of dependency? What circumstances limit woman's liberty and how can they be overcome? These are the fundamental questions on which I would fain throw some light. This means that I am interested in the fortunes of the individual as defined not in terms of happiness but in terms of liberty.

Quite evidently this problem would be without significance if we were to believe that woman's destiny is inevitably determined by physiological, psychological, or economic forces. Hence I shall discuss first of all the light in which woman is viewed by biology, psychoanalysis, and historical materialism. Next I shall try to show exactly how the concept of the "truly feminine" has been fashioned—why woman has been defined as the Other—and what have been the consequences from man's point of view. Then from woman's point of view I shall describe the world in which women must live; and thus we shall be able to envisage the difficulties in their way as, endeavoring to make their escape from the sphere hitherto assigned them, they aspire to full membership in the human race.[9]

Notes

1. *Franchise*, dead today.
2. The Kinsey Report [Alfred C. Kinsey and others: *Sexual Behavior in the Human Male* (W. B. Saunders Co., 1948)] is no exception, for it is limited to describing the sexual characteristics of American men, which is quite a different matter.
3. E. Lévinas expresses this idea most explicitly in his essay *Temps et l'Autre*. "Is there not a case in which otherness, alterity [*altérité*], unquestionably marks the nature of a being, as its essence, an instance of otherness not consisting purely and simply in the opposition of two species of the same genus? I think that the feminine represents the contrary in its absolute sense, this contrariness being in no wise affected by any relation between it and its correlative and thus remaining absolutely other. Sex is not a certain specific difference . . . no more is the sexual difference a mere contradiction. . . . Nor does this difference lie in the duality of two complementary terms, for two complementary terms imply a pre-existing whole. . . . Otherness reaches its full flowering in the feminine, a term of the same rank as consciousness but of opposite meaning."

   I suppose that Lévinas does not forget that woman, too, is aware of her own consciousness, or ego. But it is striking that he deliberately takes a man's point of view, disregarding the reciprocity of subject and object. When he writes that woman is mystery, he implies that she is mystery for man. Thus his description, which is intended to be objective, is in fact an assertion of masculine privilege.
4. See Part II, ch. viii.
5. See Part II, pp. 129–31.
6. A significant article on this theme by Michel Carrouges appeared in No. 292 of the *Cahiers du Sud*. He writes indignantly: "Would that there were no woman-myth at all but only a cohort of cooks, matrons, prostitutes, and bluestockings serving functions of pleasure or usefulness!" That is to say, in his view woman has no existence in and for herself; she thinks only of her *function* in the male world. Her reason for existence lies in man. But then, in fact, her poetic "function" as a myth might be more valued than any other. The real problem is precisely to find out why woman should be defined with relation to man.
7. For example, a man will say that he considers his wife in no way degraded because she has no gainful occupation. The profession of housewife is just as lofty, and so on. But when the first quarrel comes he will exclaim: "Why, you couldn't make your living without me!"
8. The specific purpose of Book II of this study is to describe this process.
9. Final paragraph refers to original publication.

3.
LA CHICANA
Elizabeth Martinez

The history and problems of La Chicana are similar to those of Latin-American women. Although the native Indian women of the Americas was, before the Spanish conquest, far from being completely free, she often participated more fully in the life of the society than did her sister under Spanish rule. The coming of the European, with his Catholic Church and feudal social system, was a turning point. Our roots lie in the act of rape: the rape of women, the rape of an entire continent and its people.

Inside the borders of the United States, the women of La Raza lived first under Spanish rule, then Mexican rule, and beginning in 1848 under U.S. imperialist rule. That year, the process of rape was resumed. The Chicana was raped by the invading gringo both in the literal, physical sense as well as in the sense of those forms of oppression imposed on all our people, both men and women.

Today we can say that the Chicana suffers from a triple oppression. She is oppressed by the forces of racism, imperialism, and sexism. This can be said of all non-white women in the United States. Her oppression by the forces of racism and imperialism is similar to that endured by our men. Oppression by sexism, however, is hers alone. (By sexism, we mean oppression based on sex just as racism is oppression based on race. Sexism includes both social structures and attitudes of male superiority that are rooted in those structures.)

The Chicana of working class origin, like her Third World sisters in the United States, is born into a life pattern that we see again and again. If she finishes her secondary education, she is lucky. The Chicana who does agricultural work is almost never able to accomplish this; she must go to work in the fields at an early age, along with other members of the family, and move with them around the country as they search for work. Eventually, the Chicana will marry and become pregnant—or simply become pregnant. After one, two, or three children, it is likely that her husband will leave the home. This will not necessarily happen because he does not love the woman and children but more often because of economic pressures. He simply cannot find work to support the family. Even if he doesn't leave the home, the situation is very hard and psychological tension grows between the couple.

This tension is increased when the woman is able to find work while the man cannot. This often happens because certain kinds of jobs, such as domestic service or working in the garment industry, are available to uneducated women. One of the ugliest forms of these economic pressures arises from the U.S. welfare system. Under that system, a woman with children cannot receive financial aid if there is a man in the house (her husband or any other). But she can receive it if there is no man. Some couples deliberately separate so that the woman and children can qualify for welfare aid. This was the case of Reies Lopez Tijerina, leader of the land struggle in New Mexico, and his first wife Maria Escobar. Despite the hard life faced by the working class Chicana—and we have barely suggested it here—she is expected to live according to attitudes and prejudices imposed by sexism. These include ideas about virginity, false definitions of femininity, and the double standard (one standard of sexual behavior for women, a different standard for men). The Chicana may be working 16 hours a day to support and care for her children, but she will still be viewed as a sexual object rather than as a human being. Unless she is over the age of 35 or 40, she will be seen more as a face and body than as a fellow worker and fellow victim of oppression.

All this holds true not only for the working class Chicana—who forms the great majority of our women—but also for the Chicana of middle-class origin. Often the spiritual growth of this Chicana is even more stunted. From birth, her life is a predestined pattern based on passing from her parents control to that of her husband. She goes through high school acquiring a strong sense of competition with other Chicanas for the attention of the boys. This is the dominant feature of her high school years. Although she is expected to become a wife and mother, the whole subject of sexual functions and physiology is treated like a dark secret. Femininity is turned into capitalist consumerism. Her womanhood is channeled into buying clothes and makeup and driving her husband to worry about making more money so that he can buy more material possessions that will give the family "status."

In the last 10 or 20 years, there has been a growing number of Chicanas from middle-class backgrounds who go on from high school to university study and sometimes become professional workers. This group also falls prey to the values of consumerism, but some members do develop a stronger political awareness. This group has added a new element to the picture of the Chicana today.

Today—with literally thousands of Chicano women drawn into activity—there is a wide variety of positions held by Chicanas concerning their role. They might be drawn out as follows:

- The position that women should seek no change in their roles and should never challenge the status quo. This position is found among Chicanas of all classes and ages.
- The position that women are very capable, and can make important contributions as women without raising a fuss about it—in other words, without challenging the present, general situation. This position is generally held by older, working-class Chicanas who often have strong individual personalities.
- The position that women must fight sexism constantly, but as an isolated phenomenon. This position is generally held by younger Chicanas, often university students.

- The position that women should and can be revolutionaries at every level of the struggle. They should struggle against sexism without fear, but within the context of our whole struggle as a people.

We will not win our liberation struggle unless the women move together with the men rather than against them. We must work to convince the men that our struggle will become stronger if women are not limited to a few, special roles. We also have the right to expect that our most enlightened men will join in the fight against sexism; it should not be our battle alone.

We have only begun to grapple with the question of La Chicana and we have much to learn.

What has been the reaction of the men to all this? In some cases, the men have seen how they themselves are oppressed by the sexist attitudes that we call "machismo." They perceive how Chicanos waste time, energy, and even their lives in so-called fights over women. They perceive how our oppressor uses "machismo" against us—for example, by appealing to a Chicano's sense of supposed manhood in order to get him to kill Vietnamese. Sexism is a useful tool to the colonizer; the men are oppressed but they can beat and mistreat women, who thus serve as targets for a frustration that might otherwise become revolutionary. Some men understand very well that the full participation of women is needed if our people are to win the liberation struggle.

The truth is that we need to reexamine and redefine our culture. Some of us do not believe that in our culture, femininity has always meant: weak, passive, delicate looking...in other words, qualities that inflate the male ego. The woman of La Raza is traditionally a fighter and revolutionary. In the history of Mexico the nation closest to us, we find a long line of heroines—from the war of independence against Spain through the 1910 revolution and including the rebellions of the Yaqui Indians. The same holds true for other nations.

The woman of La Raza is also, by tradition, a worker. These are the traditions, this is the culture, that the revolutionary Chicana wants to revive. These are the traditions that a revolutionary nationalism will revive.

The revolutionary Chicana does not identify with the so-called women's liberation movement in the United States because up to now that movement has been dominated by white women of middle-class background. Some of the demands of that movement have real meaning for the Chicana—such as free daycare centers for children and reform of the welfare system. But more often our demands and concerns do not meet with theirs. For example, the women's liberation movement has rejected traditional family. For us, the family has been a source of unity and our major defense against the oppressor.

Up to now, the U.S. women's liberation movement has been mainly concerned with sexism and ignored or denied the importance of racism. For the Chicana, the three types of oppression cannot be separated. They are all a part of the same system, they are three faces of the same enemy. They must all be fought with all our courage and strength. As we said earlier, the rape of our continent, our people, is historically linked. To undo the wrong, we Chicanas must understand that link, and struggle as a united force with our men and our allies.

Notes

1. From *Ideal*, September 5–20, 1972: pp. 1–2.

4.
RADICAL FEMINISM 1[1]
Bonnie Kreps[2]

Put very bluntly, the traditional view of woman can be summed up in the words of Aristotle:

> The female is a female by virtue of a certain *lack* of qualities; we should regard the female nature as afflicted with a natural defectiveness.

This may be a rather crass over-statement of the male chauvinist attitude, but the philosophical assumption exhibited here lies at the crux of the problem at hand: that is, man has consistently defined woman not in terms of herself but in relation to him. She is not regarded as an autonomous being; rather, he is the Subject, he is Absolute—she is the Other. Simone de Beauvoir has argued convincingly that, throughout history, one group has never set itself up as the One without at once setting up in opposition the Other, which then tends to become an object. Otherness, she argues, is a fundamental category of human thought. Thus, good-evil, right-wrong, nationalism, racism, anti-Semitism, and male chauvinism.

In accepting the traditional view of herself as secondary and inferior, woman has provided justification for the charge of inferiority. We are all familiar with the contention that women are different *in their nature* from men. Biological differences which no one can deny are used with great enthusiasm by those who wish to justify the status quo vis-à-vis women, by those to whom freedom for women seems a profound threat to something deep in themselves.

Whatever biology may determine for us all—and the question is debatable—I think it is an obvious truth that one is not born, but rather becomes, a woman or a man. One is born a female or male child with certain given characteristics and certain potentials which are hereditarily and environmentally determined and must, therefore, be viewed developmentally. To understand woman's so-called "nature," we must, therefore, examine her situation: her history, the myths about her, her social environment, her education, and so forth. A look at history and mythology, for instance, will show that women have been written out of history and represented from a male point of view in mythology. The great figures of history and mythology are always male; as de Beauvoir says:

> Representation of the world, like the world itself, is the work of men; they describe it from their own point of view, which they confuse with absolute truth.

Woman's immediate social environment puts enormous pressure on her to submit to male dominance. She is exhorted to play out the role of Cinderella, expecting fortune and happiness from some Prince Charming rather than to venture out by herself. Be pretty, be pleasant, use mouthwash and deodorant, never have an intellectual thought, and Prince Charming will sweep you off to his castle, where you will live happily ever after. Such is the carrot, and behind it is the stick: "Men don't make passes at girls who wear glasses," "wall flower," "spinster," "old maid," "loose woman,"… the list goes on, and its message is: to have caught a man is proof of a woman's desirability as a human being; to be without a man is a social and moral disgrace.

The economic discrimination against the working woman is highly conducive to her seeing marriage as a liberation from ill-paid drudgery. She usually faces the prospect of being an underpaid worker in society's lowest echelons. She faces a discrimination based on sex which racial groups no longer tolerate. So it is little wonder that her desire to find a husband is reinforced.

Society's most potent tool for making female human beings into dependent adults is a socialization process. We have a society which is based on arbitrary and strictly enforced sex roles. We may see a loosening of this condition with the next generation, but it is still unhappily true that a certain role is now ascribed purely on the basis of sex. And what does this mean for the female sex? It means that the essential characteristic of the so-called "feminine" character is passivity. Through her upbringing and education, from girlhood up, a girl's sense of self is progressively crushed. Whereas boys get experimental, control-oriented toys, girls get role-playing toys. Boys get tractors, rockets, microscopes, et cetera.; girls get dolls and vacuum cleaners. Whereas boys are dressed practically and are expected to get dirty, little girls are all too often dressed to be "ladylike"—in other words, they are dressed to be pretty objects, like dolls. Whereas boys are encouraged to be rough, tough and aggressive, girls are trained to become timid and docile (put euphemistically: good listeners, feminine, real helpmates, et cetera). Whereas boys prepare themselves to become creators of their own future, girls are trained to relate through others and taught that to please they must *try* to please and therefore renounce their autonomy.

To please is to abdicate. That is the lesson the young girl learns. It is the lesson which finds its apotheosis in a recent best-seller by the American movie star, Arlene Dahl—its commercial success is redoubtable, its title totally indicative of its message: *Always Ask a Man.*

As long as marriage and motherhood are conceived of as a woman's entire destiny and the fulfillment of her "nature," her lot will involve the acceptance of a situation imposed from the outside rather than a free choice according to her individuality. As long as woman accepts this situation, she will endanger her individuality and possibility for growth as a human being. She will, in short, be abdicating the potential of her nature by giving in to the demands of her situation.

We all know about the alcohol and pill consumption of women, the large influx of female psychiatric patients with unspecified ailments, and the myriad symptoms which suggest that something is troubling a great many women. When we add to that the enormous success of feminist books like *The Second Sex* and *The Feminine Mystique*, and the rising waves of new feminists in Europe and America, I think it becomes apparent to all but the most pig-headed that the picture of the happy housewife, the fulfilled woman who has bought all the garbage of the Feminine Mystique, that this picture is a gross distortion. The true picture spells out in large letters: FRUSTRATION.

For those many women who have acknowledged their sense of emptiness, their frustration, there has often followed a feeling of guilt. They feel that there must be something peculiarly wrong with them and that they should be able somehow to cope with their frustration. (Note here the rising success of the tension-reducing pill named COPE). We are still the beneficiaries of Freud's claim that neurosis is a sign of sickness.

There has emerged recently, however, a new school of psychology with a new definition of sickness and health. Called, loosely, "The Third Force," it contrasts sharply with Freud and the behaviorists. Some of its major tenets are these: Each of us has an essential core, a potential and personality, which tends strongly to persist. One might liken it to the body's drive for health. If this psychological drive for health is frustrated or stunted, sickness results. No psychological health is possible unless this essential core of the person is fundamentally accepted, loved, and respected by others and by himself. And, they add, "adjustment is, very definitely, *not* necessarily synonymous with psychological health."

On this basis, it would seem that woman's present situation is not consonant with her optimal growth; further, that the frustrations engendered by attempting to force these disparities into consonance—these frustrations are a sign, not of mental sickness, but of mental health.

The most reasonable conclusion reached from the above arguments is therefore, I would think, that the traditional view of women and its attendant Feminine Mystique are a fraud. While they are to men's advantage in many (though ultimately not all) respects, they mean loss of growth, of full-humanness, to the woman who submits to their edicts. Such a woman will risk a loss of identity, she will risk becoming a thing.

Modern woman is in the grip of a vicious circle and in urgent need of liberation. The more she resigns herself to the demands of her situation, the more she will stunt her human growth, and the more she will thus be unable to escape from her situation. The ultimate success of the slave system was, after all, that it ultimately convinced the slaves themselves that they were fit for nothing else but being slaves and that being a slave wasn't all that bad. We women can learn a lot from the emergence of black people who are fighting for black dignity. The question for women is, what are the mechanics of our particular kind of oppression and how do we best fight it?

First of all, we must recognize that the liberation of women must be collective, it must be aimed at freedom for all women. Our goal must be that any and all women who want to escape from the sex role foisted upon them will have the freedom to do so. Therefore, no "token integration," no relieving of symptoms without getting at the causes. Second, we must get full economic rights for women, because only economic liberty can guarantee women that their theoretic civil liberties will provide them with liberty in practice. We must do away with the woman-as-economic-parasite notion. Third, women must be freed from their present partial or complete slavery to the species. They must have the right to decide over their own bodies. Fourth, and most generally, girls and women must be encouraged to seek self-fulfillment as human beings rather than merely as females.

The statement that girls should seek fulfilment as human beings rather than as females has enormous implications. It is the starting point for the very large philosophical and political area known as radical feminism.

To explain somewhat further: The Women's Liberation Movement is a generic term covering a large spectrum of positions. Broadly speaking, the movement can be divided into three areas: (1) The largely economically oriented (usually Marxist) segment which sees liberation for women as part of a socialist revolution; (2) liberal groups like the National Organization for Women. This segment is analogous to the NAACP in the black struggle; it is working for some kind of integration of women into the main fabric of society; and (3) radical feminism, which chooses to concentrate exclusively on the oppression of women *as women* (and not as workers, students, etc.). This segment therefore concentrates its analysis on institutions like love, marriage, sex, masculinity and femininity. It would be opposed specifically and centrally to sexism, rather than capitalism (thus differing from the Marxists), and would not he particularly concerned with "equal rights," "equal pay for equal work," and other major concerns of the NOW segment.

The point I would like to make is that all three broad segments have their own validity, all three are important. One belongs in one segment rather than another because of personal affinity with the aims being striven for. Personally, I find radical feminism most congenial, because it seems to me to get at the fundamentals of the sexual oppression which is so prevalent in today's society. Most of the really important books which recently have come out on the subject are written by radical feminists: Kate Millett's *Sexual Politics*, for example, and the very important *Notes From the Second Year* and *Notes From the Third Year*.

In short, radical feminism is concerned with the analysis of the oppression of women *as women*. Its basic aim could fairly be stated as "There shall be no characteristics, behaviour, or roles ascribed to any human being on the basis of sex." In other words, we must fight the myth of the so-called "female" character (men should fight the myth of the "male"); we must fight the corrupt notion we now call "love," which is based on control of another rather than on love for the growth of another; we must fight the institutionalization of the oppression of women— especially the institution of marriage.

Radical feminism is called "radical" because it is struggling to bring about really fundamental changes in our society. We, in this segment of the movement, do not believe that the oppression of women will be ended by giving them a bigger piece of the pie, as Betty Friedan would have it. We believe that the pie itself is rotten. We do not believe that women should be integrated into the male world so that they can be "just as good as men." We believe that the male world as it now exists is based on the corrupt notion of "maleness vs. femaleness," that the oppression of women is based on this very notion and its attendant institutions. "Separate but equal" will get us nowhere; we must eradicate the sexual division on which our society is based. Only then do men and women have a hope of living together as human beings.

Notes

1. Copyright 1972 by Bonnie Kreps. This is an updated version of an article originally printed in *Notes From the Second Year*, and here reprinted with the permission of the author.
2. Bonnie Kreps is a founder of the radical feminist movement in Canada. This article is based on a brief presented to the Royal Commission on the Status of Women in Canada in June, 1968. It was the basis for a speech used widely during the formation of the Toronto New Feminists, Canada's first radical feminist group. Bonnie Kreps is a feminist filmmaker whose films include "After the Vote: A Report from Down Under" and "Portrait of My Mother."

5.
FEMINISM: A MOVEMENT TO END SEXIST OPPRESSION
bell hooks

A central problem within feminist discourse has been our inability to either arrive at a consensus of opinion about what feminism is or accept definition(s) that could serve as points of unification. Without agreed upon definition(s), we lack a sound foundation on which to construct theory or engage in overall meaningful praxis. Expressing her frustrations with the absence of clear definitions in a recent essay, "Towards A Revolutionary Ethics," Carmen Vasquez comments:

> We can't even agree on what a "Feminist" is, never mind what she would believe in and how she defines the principles that constitute honor among us. In key with the American capitalist obsession for individualism and anything goes so long as it gets you what you want. Feminism in American has come to mean anything you like, honey. There are as many definitions of Feminism as there are feminists, some of my sisters say, with a chuckle. I don't think it's funny. (Vasquez 1983: 11)

It is not funny. It indicates a growing disinterest in feminism as a radical political movement. It is a despairing gesture expressive of the belief that solidarity between women is not possible. It is a sign that the political naïveté which has traditionally characterized woman's lot in male-dominated culture abounds.

Most people in the United States think of feminism or the more commonly used term "women's lib" as a movement that aims to make women the social equals of men. This broad definition popularized by the media and mainstream segments of the movement, raises problematic questions. Since men are not equals in white supremacist, capitalist, patriarchal class structure, which men do women want to be equal to? Do women share a common vision of what equality means? Implicit in this simplistic definition of women's liberation is a dismissal of race and class as factors that, in conjunction with sexism determine the extent to which an individual will be discriminated against, exploited, or oppressed. Bourgeois white women interested in women's rights issues have been satisfied with simple definitions for obvious reasons. Rhetorically placing themselves in the same social category as oppressed women, they were not anxious to call attention to race and class privilege.

Women in lower class and poor groups, particularly those who are non-white, would not have defined women's liberation as women gaining social equality with men since they are continually reminded in their everyday lives that all women do not share a common social status. Concurrently, they know that many males in their social groups are exploited and oppressed. Knowing that men in their groups do not have social, political, and economic power, they would not deem it liberatory to share their social status. While they are aware that sexism enables men in their respective groups to have privileges denied them, they are more likely to see exaggerated expressions of male chauvinism among their peers as stemming from the male's sense of himself as powerless and ineffectual in relation to ruling male groups, rather than an expression of an overall privileged social status. From the very onset of the women's liberation movement, these women were suspicious of feminism precisely because they recognized the limitations inherent in its definition. They recognized the possibility that feminism defined as social equality with men might easily become a movement that would primarily affect the social standing of white women in middle- and upper-class groups while affecting only in a very marginal way the social status of working-class and poor women.

Not all the women who were at the forefront of organized women's movement shaping definitions were content with making women's liberation synonymous with women gaining social equality with men. On the opening pages of *Woman Power: The Movement for Women's Liberation*, Cellestine Ware, a black woman active in the movement, wrote under the heading "Goals":

Radical feminism is working for the eradication of domination and elitism in all human relationships. This would make self-determination the ultimate good and require the downfall of society as we know it today. (Ware 1970: 3)

... Many feminist radicals now know that neither a feminism that focuses on woman as an autonomous human being worthy of personal freedom nor one that focuses on the attainment of equality of opportunity with men can rid society of sexism and male domination. Feminism is a struggle to end sexist oppression. Therefore, it is necessarily a struggle to eradicate the ideology of domination that permeates Western culture on various levels as well as a commitment to reorganizing society so that the self-development of people can take precedence over imperialism, economic expansion, and material desires. Defined in this way, it is unlikely that women would join feminist movement simply because we are biologically the same. A commitment to feminism so defined would demand that each individual participant acquire a critical political consciousness based on ideas and beliefs.

All too often the slogan "the personal is political" (which was first used to stress that woman's everyday reality is informed and shaped by politics and is necessarily political) became a means of encouraging women to think that the experience of discrimination, exploitation, or oppression automatically corresponded with an understanding of the ideological and institutional apparatus shaping one's social status. As a consequence, many women who had not fully examined their situation never developed a sophisticated understanding of their political reality and its relationship to that of women as a collective group. They were encouraged to focus on

:ng voice to personal experience. Like revolutionaries working to change the lot of colonized people globally, it is necessary for feminist activists to stress that the ability to see and describe one's own reality is a significant step in the long process of self-recovery; but it is only a beginning. When women internalized the idea that describing their own woe was synonymous with developing a critical political consciousness, the progress of feminist movement was stalled. Starting from such incomplete perspectives, it is not surprising that theories and strategies were developed that were collectively inadequate and misguided. To correct this inadequacy in past analysis, we must now encourage women to develop a keen, comprehensive understanding of women's political reality. Broader perspectives can only emerge as we examine both the personal that is political, the politics of society as a whole, and global revolutionary politics.

Feminism defined in political terms that stress collective as well as individual experience challenges women to enter a new domain—to leave behind the apolitical stance sexism decrees is our lot and develop political consciousness. Women know from our everyday lives that many of us rarely discuss politics. Even when women talked about sexist politics in the heyday of contemporary feminism, rather than allow this engagement with serious political matters to lead to complex, in-depth analysis of women's social status, we insisted that men were "the enemy," the cause of all our problems. As a consequence, we examined almost exclusively women's relationship to male supremacy and the ideology of sexism. The focus on "man as enemy" created, as Marlene Dixon emphasizes in her essay, "The Rise and Demise of Women's Liberation: A Class Analysis," a "politics of psychological oppression" which evoked world views which "pit individual against individual and mystify the social basis of exploitation." By repudiating the popular notion that the focus of feminist movement should be social equality of the sexes and emphasizing eradicating the cultural basis of group oppression, our own analysis would require an exploration of all aspects of women's political reality. This would mean that race and class oppression would be recognized as feminist issues with as much relevance as sexism.

When feminism is defined in such a way that it calls attention to the diversity of women's social and political reality, it centralizes the experiences of all women, especially the women whose social conditions have been least written about, studied, or changed by political movements. When we cease to focus on the simplistic stance "men are the enemy," we are compelled to examine systems of domination and our role in their maintenance and perpetuation. Lack of adequate definition made it easy for bourgeois women, whether liberal or radical in perspective, to maintain their dominance over the leadership of the movement and its direction. This hegemony continues to exist in most feminist organizations. Exploited and oppressed groups of women are usually encouraged by those in power to feel that their situation is hopeless, that they can do nothing to break the pattern of domination. Given such socialization, these women have often felt that our only response to white, bourgeois, hegemonic dominance of feminist movement is to trash, reject, or dismiss feminism. This reaction is in no way threatening to the women who wish to maintain control over the direction of feminist theory and praxis. They prefer us to be silent, passively accepting their ideas. They prefer us speaking against "them" rather than developing our own ideas about feminist movement.

Feminism is the struggle to end sexist oppression. Its aim is not to benefit solely any specific group of women, any particular race or class of women. It does not privilege women over men. It has the power to transform in a meaningful way all our lives. Most importantly, feminism is neither a lifestyle nor a ready-made identity or role one can step into. Diverting energy from feminist movement that aims to change society, many women concentrate on the development of a counter-culture, a woman-centered world wherein participants have little contact with men. Such attempts do not indicate a respect or concern for the vast majority of women who are unable to integrate their cultural expressions with the visions offered by alternative woman-centered communities. In *Beyond God the Father*, Mary Daly urged women to give up "the securities offered by the patriarchal system" and create new space that would be woman-centered. Responding to Daly, Jeanne Gross pointed to the contradictions that arise when the focus of feminist movement is on the construction of new space:

> Creating a "counterworld" places an incredible amount of pressure on the women who attempt to embark on such a project. The pressure comes from the belief that the only true resources for such an endeavor are ourselves. The past which is totally patriarchal is viewed as irredeemable...If we go about creating an alternative culture without remaining in dialogue with others (and the historical circumstances that give rise to their identity) we have no reality check for our goals. We run the very real risk that the dominant ideology of the culture is re-duplicated in the feminist movement through cultural imperialism. (Gross 1977: 54)

Equating feminist struggle with living in a counter-cultural, woman-centered world erected barriers that closed the movement off from most women. Despite sexist discrimination, exploitation, or oppression, many women feel their lives as they live them are important and valuable. Naturally the suggestion that these lives could be simply left or abandoned for an alternative "feminist" lifestyle met with resistance. Feeling their life experiences devalued, deemed solely negative and worthless, many women responded by vehemently attacking feminism. By rejecting the notion of an alternative feminist "lifestyle" that can emerge only when women create a subculture (whether it is living space or even space like women's studies that at many campuses has become exclusive) and insisting that feminist struggle can begin wherever an individual woman is, we create a movement that focuses on our collective experience, a movement that is continually mass-based.

Over the past six years, many separatist-oriented communities have been formed by women so that the focus has shifted from the development of woman-centered space towards an emphasis on identity. Once woman-centered space exists, it can be maintained only if women remain convinced that it is the only place where they can be self-realized and free. After assuming a "feminist" identity, women often seek to live the "feminist" lifestyle. These women do not see that it undermines feminist movement to project the assumption that "feminist" is but another pre-packaged role women can now select as they search for identity. The willingness to see feminism as a lifestyle choice rather than a political commitment reflects the class nature of the movement. It is not surprising that the vast majority of women who equate feminism with alternative lifestyle are from middle-class backgrounds, unmarried, college-educated, often students who are without many of the social and economic responsibilities that working-class and poor women who are laborers, parents, homemakers, and wives confront daily. Sometimes lesbians have sought to equate feminism with lifestyle but for significantly different reasons. Given the prejudice and discrimination against lesbian women in our society, alternative communities that are woman-centered are one means of creating positive, affirming environments. Despite positive reasons for developing woman centered space, (which does not need to be equated with a "feminist" lifestyle) like pleasure, support, and resource-sharing, emphasis on creating a counter-culture has alienated women from feminist movement, for such space can be in churches, kitchens, et cetera.

Longing for community, connection, a sense of shared purpose, many women found support networks in feminist organizations. Satisfied in a personal way by new relationships generated in what was called a "safe," "supportive" context wherein discussion focused on feminist ideology, they did not question whether masses of women shared the same need for community. Certainly many black women as well as women from other ethnic groups do not feel an absence of community among women in their lives despite exploitation and oppression. The focus on feminism as a way to develop shared identity and community has little appeal to women who experience community, who seek ways to end exploitation and oppression in the context of their lives. While they may develop an interest in a feminist politic that works to eradicate sexist oppression, they will probably never feel as intense a need for a "feminist" identity and lifestyle.

Often emphasis on identity and lifestyle is appealing because it creates a false sense that one is engaged in praxis. However, praxis within any political movement that aims to have a radical transformative impact on society cannot be solely focused on creating spaces wherein would-be-radicals experience safety and support. Feminist movement to end sexist oppression actively engages participants in revolutionary struggle. Struggle is rarely safe or pleasurable.

Focusing on feminism as political commitment, we resist the emphasis on individual identity and lifestyle. (This should not be confused with the very real need to unite theory and practice.) Such resistance engages us in revolutionary praxis. The ethics of Western society informed by imperialism and capitalism are personal rather than social. They teach us that the individual good is more important than the collective good and consequently that individual change is of greater significance than collective change. This particular form of cultural imperialism has been reproduced in feminist movement in the form of individual women equating the fact that their lives have been changed in a meaningful way by feminism "as is" with a policy of no change need occur in the theory and praxis even if it has little or no impact on society as a whole, or on masses of women.

To emphasize that engagement with feminist struggle as political commitment we could avoid using the phrase "I am a feminist" (a linguistic structure designed to refer to some personal aspect of identity and self-definition) and could state "I advocate feminism." Because there has been undue emphasis placed on feminism as an identity or lifestyle, people usually resort to stereotyped perspectives on feminism. Deflecting attention away from stereotypes is necessary if we are to revise our strategy and direction. I have found that saying "I am a feminist" usually means I am plugged into preconceived notions of identity, role, or behavior. When I say "I advocate feminism" the response is usually "what is feminism?" A phrase like "I advocate" does not imply the kind of absolutism that is suggested by "I am." It does not engage us in the either/or dualistic thinking that is the central ideological component of all systems of domination in Western society. It implies that a choice has been made, that commitment to feminism is an act of will. It does not suggest that by committing oneself to feminism, the possibility of supporting other political movements is negated.

As a black woman interested in feminist movement, I am often asked whether being black is more important than being a woman; whether feminist struggle to end sexist oppression is more important than the struggle to end racism and vice-versa. All such questions are rooted in competitive either/or thinking, the belief that the self is formed in opposition to an other. Therefore one is a feminist because you are not something else. Most people are socialized to think in terms of opposition rather than compatibility. Rather than see anti-racist work as totally compatible with working to end sexist oppression, they are often seen as two movements competing for first place. When asked "Are you a feminist?" it appears that an affirmative answer is translated to mean that one is concerned with no political issues other than feminism. When one is black, an affirmative response is likely to be heard as a devaluation of struggle to end racism. Given the fear of being misunderstood, it has been difficult for black women and women in exploited and oppressed ethnic groups to give expression to their interest in feminist concerns. They have been wary of saying "I am a feminist." The shift in expression from "I am a feminist" to "I advocate feminism" could serve as a useful strategy for eliminating the focus on identity and lifestyle. It could serve as a way women who are concerned about feminism as well as other political movements could express their support while avoiding linguistic structures that give primacy to one particular group. It would also encourage greater exploration in feminist theory.

The shift in definition away from notions of social equality towards an emphasis on ending sexist oppression leads to a shift in attitudes in regard to the development of theory. Given the class nature of feminist movement so far, as well as racial hierarchies, developing theory (the guiding set of beliefs and principles that become the basis for action) has been a task particularly subject to the hegemonic dominance of white academic women. This has led many women outside the privileged race/class group to see the focus on developing theory, even the very use of the term, as a concern that functions only to reinforce the power of the elite group. Such reactions reinforce the sexist/racist/classist notion that developing theory is the domain of the white intellectual. Privileged white women active in feminist movement, whether liberal or radical in perspective, encourage black women to contribute "experiential" work, personal life stories. Personal experiences are important to feminist movement but they cannot take the place of theory. Charlotte Bunch explains the special significance of theory in her essay, "Feminism and Education: Not By Degrees":

> Theory enables us to see immediate needs in terms of long-range goals and an overall perspective on the world. It thus gives us a framework for evaluating various strategies in both the long and the short run and for seeing the types of changes that they are likely to produce. Theory is not just a body of facts or a set of personal opinions. It involves explanations and hypotheses that are based on available knowledge and experience. It is also dependent on conjecture and insight about how to interpret those facts and experiences and their significance. (Bunch 1979: 7–8)

Since bourgeois white women had defined feminism in such a way as to make it appear that it had no real significance for black women, they could then conclude that black women need not contribute to developing theory. We were to provide the colorful life stories to document and validate the prevailing set of theoretical assumptions.[1] Focus on social equality with men as a definition of feminism led to an emphasis on discrimination, male attitudes, and legalistic reforms. Feminism as a movement to end sexist oppression directs our attention to systems of domination and the inter-relatedness of sex, race, and class oppression. Therefore, it compels us to centralize the experiences and the social predicaments of women who bear the brunt of sexist oppression as a way to understand the collective social status of women in the United States. Defining feminism as a movement to end sexist oppression is crucial for the development of theory because it is a starting point indicating the direction of exploration and analysis.

The foundation of future feminist struggle must be solidly based on a recognition of the need to eradicate the underlying cultural basis and causes of sexism and other forms of group oppression. Without challenging and changing these philosophical structures, no feminist reforms will have a long-range impact. Consequently, it is now necessary for advocates of feminism to collectively acknowledge that our struggle cannot be defined as a movement to gain social equality with men; that terms like "liberal feminist" and "bourgeois feminist" represent contradictions that must be resolved so that feminism will not be continually co-opted to serve the opportunistic ends of special interest groups.

Note

1. An Interesting discussion of black women's responses to feminist movement may be found in the essay "Challenging Imperial Feminism" by Valerie Amos and Pratibha Parmar in the Autumn 1984 issue of *Feminist Review*.

6.
RETHINKING SEX AND GENDER[1]
Christine Delphy[2]

Until now, most work on gender, including most feminist work on gender, has been based on an unexamined presupposition: that sex precedes gender. However, although this presupposition is historically explicable, it is theoretically unjustifiable, and its continued existence is holding back our thinking on gender. It is preventing us from rethinking gender in an open and unbiased way. Further, this lack of intellectual clarity is inextricably bound up with the political contradictions produced by our desire as women to escape domination on the one hand, and our fear that we might lose what seem to be fundamental social categories on the other.

What is common to these intellectual impasses and political contradictions is an inability (or a refusal) to think rigorously about the relationship between *division* and *hierarchy*, since the question of the relationship between sex and gender not only parallels this question, but is, in fact, the self-same issue.

What I want to do here is argue that in order to understand reality, and hence eventually to have the power to change it, we must be prepared to abandon our certainties and to accept the (temporary) pain of an increased uncertainty about the world. Having the courage to confront the unknown is a precondition for imagination, and the capacity to imagine another world is an essential element in scientific progress. It is certainly indispensable to my analysis.

From Sex Roles to Gender

The notion of gender developed from that of sex roles, and, rightly or wrongly, the person who is credited with being the founding mother of this line of thought is Margaret Mead. Put very briefly, it is her thesis (Mead, 1935) that most societies divide the universe of human characteristics into two, and attribute one half to men and the other to women. For Mead, this division is quite arbitrary, but she does not condemn it unreservedly. She sees it as having disadvantages, for example, it leads to some 'maladjustments,' in particular to homosexuality. But overall she sees it as having many advantages for society, culture, and civilisation.

Mead herself does not deal with either the sexual division of labour or differences in the status of men and women. As far as she is concerned, the division of labour is natural, and the few comments she does make about it show that she attributes it to the different reproductive roles of males and females and to differences in physical strength between the sexes. These are, of course, the 'classic' rea-

sons within anthropological, as within 'commonsense' (including feminist) thinking. Mead also does not question the hierarchy between the sexes. She either
ignores it or considers it legitimate. Nor does she discuss the prescribed differences
between the sexes except within the very limited domain of 'temperament' (under
which heading she groups abilities, aptitudes, and emotional personality).

For a long time, Mead's analysis of prescribed differences was the major theme
in the critique of sex roles—a critique which arose from a concern to defend the
rights of individuals to express their individualities freely. In the process, it was
implied that 'masculine' and 'feminine' traits together constitute and exhaust the
whole of human possibilities.

Although the term is frequently accredited to her, Mead herself rarely uses the
term 'sex roles' because she was not in fact concerned about these roles, still less
with critiquing them. Her concern was rather the analysis and critique of feminine
and masculine 'temperaments.' In fact, the idea of sex roles was critically developed
from the 1940s to the 1960s, that is, the decades commonly considered to be a
period when feminism was 'latent'—through the work of Mira Komarovsky
(1950), Viola Klein and Alva Myrdal (Myrdal & Klein, 1956), and Andrée Michel
(1959, 1960). All these authors worked within a Parsonian sociological perspective
and saw a *role* as the active aspect of a *status*. Broadly speaking, 'status' was the
equivalent of the level of prestige within society, and each status had roles which
the individuals who held that status had to fulfill. This perspective is clearly sociological in the true sense of the word: People's situations and activities are held to
derive from the social structure, rather than from either nature or their particular
capacities.

Thus, when these authors spoke of the 'roles' of women and men they were
already taking a large step towards denaturalising the respective occupations and
situations of the sexes. Their approach was not actually opposed to Mead's anthropological approach, but rather developed it in two ways:

1. They confirmed the arbitrary aspect of the division of qualities between the
sexes, this time by an epistemological diktat, that is, by their postulate that everyone plays roles.

2. More importantly, they considered a social 'role' to be not simply the 'psychological' characteristics Mead had spoken about, but also (and principally) the
work associated with a rung on the social ladder (a status), and, hence, a position
in the division of labour.

The division of labour and the hierarchy between men and women, therefore,
began to be accorded a cultural character, whereas Mead had considered them to
be natural, and since they were cultural rather than natural, the authors stressed
they were arbitrary. In addition, since the concept of sex roles also emerged within
the framework of a feminist critique (even when the term feminist was not explicitly used), these authors all stressed that as the position of women was socially
determined, it was changeable. Even though the concepts they used were Parsonian
in origin, they questioned Parson's theory and its premise of harmony between the
sexes, and Andrée Michel in particular strongly criticized the containment of

women within traditional roles, and also Parson's idea that this was good for women and for society.

The term 'sex roles' then remained in use for a long time, until the concept of gender, which derived directly from it, appeared in the early 1970s.

If we take one of the first works directly on 'gender,' Ann Oakley's *Sex, Gender and Society*, published in 1972, we find the following definition:

> 'Sex' is a word that refers to the biological differences between male and female: the visible difference in genitalia, the related difference in procreative function. 'Gender' however is a matter of culture: it refers to the social classification into 'masculine' and 'feminine'. (Oakley, 1985, p. 16)

This book is devoted partly to a critical account of recent research on the differential psychology of the sexes: to innate and acquired elements of aptitude ('talents,' in Mead's terminology) and attitude ('temperamental') differences between women and men, and partly to an account of what anthropological research can teach us about the division of labour between the sexes. According to Oakley, psychological differences between the sexes are due to social conditioning, and there is no research which allows us to infer any biological determinism whatever. She also says that while a division of labour by sex is universal, the content of the tasks considered to be feminine or masculine varies considerably according to the society.

Oakley's use of the concept of gender thus covers *all the established differences between men and women*, whether they are individual differences (studied by psychologists), or social roles or cultural representations (studied by sociologists and anthropologists). In addition, in her work the concept of gender covers everything that is variable and socially determined—variability being the proof that it is social in origin. She says "The constancy of sex must be admitted, but so too must the variability of gender." (1985, p. 16)

But one thing which is missing from Oakley's definition, although it was already present in the work on sex roles, and which has become central to the feminist positions which have been developed subsequently, is the fundamental *asymmetry* (Hurtig & Pichevin, 1986) and *hierarchy* (Delphy, 1981; Varikas, 1987) between the two groups, or roles, or sexes, or genders.

Sex and Gender

With the arrival of the concept of gender, three things became possible (which does not mean they have happened):

1. All the differences between the sexes which appeared to be social and arbitrary, whether they actually varied from one society to another or were merely held to be susceptible to change, were gathered together in one concept.

2. The use of the singular ('gender' as opposed to 'genders') allowed the accent to be moved from the two divided parts to the principle of partition itself.

3. The idea of hierarchy was firmly anchored in the concept. This should, at least in theory, have allowed the relationship between the divided parts to be considered from another angle.

As studies have accumulated showing the arbitrariness of sex roles and the lack of foundation for stereotypes in one area after another, the idea that gender is independent of sex has progressed. Or rather, since it is a question of the content, the idea that both genders are independent of both sexes has progressed, and the aspects of 'sex roles' and sexual situations which are recognised to be socially constructed rather than biologically determined has grown. Everyone working in the field has certainly not drawn the dividing line between what is social and cultural and what is natural in the same place, but then it would have been astonishing if they had. It is right that the question should remain open.

What is problematic, however, is that the ongoing discussion around this question has presumed epistemological and methodological paradigms which should actually have been questioned. We have continued to think of gender in terms of sex: to see it as a social dichotomy determined by a natural dichotomy. We now see gender as the *content* with sex as the *container*. The content may vary, and some consider it *must* vary, but the container is considered to be invariable because it is part of nature, and nature, 'does not change.' Moreover, part of the nature of sex itself is seen to be its *tendency to have a social content*/to vary culturally.

What should have happened, however, is that recognising the independence of the genders from the sexes should have led us to question whether gender is in fact independent of sex. But this question has not been asked. For most authors, the issue of the relationship between sex and gender is simply 'what sort of social classification does sex give rise to? Is it strong or weak, equal or unequal?' What they never ask is why sex should give rise to any sort of social classification. Even the neutral question 'we have here two variables, two distributions, which coincide totally. How can we explain this covarience?' does not get considered.

The response is always: sex comes first, chronologically and hence logically—although it is never explained why this should be so. Actually, whether or not the precedence gets explained does not make much difference. The very fact of suggesting or admitting the precedence of sex, even implicitly, leads to one being located, objectively, in a theory where sex causes, or explains, gender. And the theory that sex causes gender, even if it does not determine the exact forms gender divisions take, can derive from only two logical lines of argument.

1. In the first line of argument, biological sex, and particularly the different functions in procreation between males and females which it provokes, necessarily gives rise to a minimal division of labour.

I would include in this line of argument, with its naturalist premises, most contemporary anthropological accounts, feminist as well as patriarchal, from George Murdock (1949) to Martha Moia (1981) by way of Gayle Rubin (1975) [with just a few notable exceptions, such as Mathieu (1991) and Tabet (1982)]. It fails to explain satisfactorily: (a) the nature and the natural reason for this first division of labour; and (b) the reasons it is extended into all fields of activity, that is, why it is not limited to the domain of procreation. It therefore fails to explain gender other than by suppositions which reintroduce upstream one or more of the elements it is supposed to explain downstream.

2. The second line of argument sees biological sex as a physical trait which is not only suitable, but destined by its intrinsic 'salience' (in psycho-cognitive terms) to be a receptacle for classifications.

Here it is postulated that human beings have a universal need to establish classifications, independently of and prior to any social organisation; and that they also need to establish these classifications on the basis of physical traits, independently of any social practice.[3] But, these two human needs are neither justified nor proven. They are simply asserted. We are not shown *why* sex is more prominent than other physical traits, which are equally distinguishable, but which do not give birth to classifications which are (i) dichotomous and (ii) imply social roles which are not just distinct but hierarchical.

I call this latter line of argument 'cognitivist,' not because it is particularly held by the 'Cognitivists,' but because it presumes certain 'prerequisites' of human cognition. The best-known academic version of such theories is that of Lévi-Strauss who, while not a psychologist, bases all his analyses of kinship and (by extension) human societies on an irrepressible and presocial (hence psychological) need of human beings to divide everything in two (and then in multiples of two). Lévi-Strauss (1969) was very much influenced by linguistics, in particular by Saussure's phonology (1959), and he devised by analogous construction what the social sciences call 'structuralism.'

A rather more recent version of this thesis has been presented by Derrida (1976) and his followers, who say that things can only be distinguished by opposition to other things. However, while Saussure is concerned purely with linguistic structures, Derrida and his clones want to draw philosophical conclusions about the importance of 'différance.' These conclusions themselves incorporate presuppositions on the conditions for the possibility of human knowledge, hence on the human spirit, which are very similar to those of Lévi-Strauss. Saussure's theory had no such ambitions and its validity in its own field of reference—linguistics—should not be taken as a guarantee of its applicability elsewhere. We may agree things are only known by distinction and hence by differentiation, but these differentiations can be, and often are, multiple. Alongside cabbages and carrots, which are not 'opposites' of each other, there are courgettes, melons, and potatoes. Moreover, distinctions are not necessarily hierarchical: vegetables are not placed on a scale of value. Indeed they are often used as a warning against any attempt to hierarchisation: We are told not to compare (or to try to add) cabbages and carrots. They are incommensurable. They do not have a common measure. Therefore, they cannot be evaluated in terms of being more or less, or better or worse than one another.

Those who adhere to Derrida's thesis thus fail to distinguish between the differences on which language is based and differences in social structures. The characteristics of cognition, in so far as they can be reduced to the characteristics of language, cannot account for social hierarchy. This is external to them. They therefore cannot account for gender—or they can do so only at the expense of dropping hierarchy as a constitutive element of gender.

Hence, neither of the two lines of argument which might justify a causal link from sex to gender is satisfactory. The presupposition that there *is* such a causal link remains, therefore, just that: a presupposition.

But if we are to think about gender, or to think about anything at all, we must leave the domain of presuppositions. To think about gender we must rethink the question of its relationship to sex, and to think about this we must first actually ask the question. We must abandon the notion that we already know the answer. We must not only admit, but also explore, two other hypotheses:

1. That the statistical coincidence between sex and gender is just that, a coincidence. The correlation is due to chance.

This hypothesis is, however, untenable, because the distribution is such that the coincidence between so-called biological sex and gender *is* 'statistically significant.' It is stronger than any correlation could be, which is due to chance.

2. That *gender* precedes sex: that sex itself simply marks a social division; that it serves to allow social recognition and identification of those who are dominants and those who are dominated. That is, that sex is a sign, but that since it does not distinguish just any old thing from anything else, and does not distinguish equivalent things but rather important and unequal things it has historically acquired a symbolic value.

The symbolic value of sex has certainly not escaped the theoreticians of psychoanalysis. But what has entirely escaped them is that this should be one of the final *conclusions* of a long progression: the point of arrival and not of departure. Unfortunately this blind spot is one which many feminists share with psychoanalysts.

Since society locates the sign which marks out the dominants from the dominated within the zone of physical traits, two further remarks need to be made:

1. The marker is not found in a pure state, all ready for use.

As Hurtig and Pichevin (1986) have shown, biologists see sex as made up of several indicators which are more or less correlated one with another, and the majority are continuous variables (occurring in varying degrees). So in order for sex to be used as a dichotomous classification, the indicators have to be reduced to just one. And as Hurtig and Pichevin (1985) also say, this reduction 'is a social act.'

2. The presence or absence of a penis[4] is a strong predictor of gender (by definition one might say). However, having or not having a penis correlates only weakly with procreational functional differences between individuals. It does not distinguish tidily between people who can bear children and those who cannot. It distinguishes, in fact, just some of those who cannot. Lots of those who do not have penises also cannot bear children, either because of constitutional sterility or due to age.

It is worth pausing here, because the 'cognitivists' think sex is a 'prominent trait' because they think physical sex is strongly correlated with functional differences, and because they assume that the rest of humanity shares this 'knowledge.' But they only think biological sex is a 'spontaneous perception' of humanity because they themselves are convinced that it is a natural trait that no one could ignore. To them, it is self-evident that there are two, and only two, sexes, and that this dichotomy exactly cross-checks with the division between potential bearers and non-bearers of children.

To try to question these 'facts' is indeed to try to crack one of the toughest nuts in our perception of the world.

We must therefore add to the hypothesis that gender precedes sex the following question: When we connect gender and sex, are we comparing something social with something natural, or are we comparing something social with something which is *also* social (in this case, the way a given society represents 'biology' to itself)?

One would think that this would logically have been one of the first questions to be asked, and it is doubtless the reason why some feminists in France (e.g., Guillaumin, 1982, 1985; Mathieu 1980; and Wittig, 1992) are opposed to using the term 'gender.' They believe it reinforces the idea that 'sex' itself is purely natural. However, not using the concept of gender does not mean one thereby directly questions the natural character of sex. So economising on the concept of gender does not seem to me the best way to progress.

'Sex' denotes and connotes something natural. It is therefore not possible to question 'sex' head on, all at once, since to do so involves a contradiction in terms. ('Naturalness' is an integral part of the definition of the term.) We must first demonstrate that 'sex' is applied to divisions and distinctions which are social. Then we must not only *separate* the social from the original term, which remains defined by naturalness, but make the social *emerge*. This is what the notions of first 'sex roles' and then 'gender' did. Only when the 'social part' is clearly established *as* social, when it has a *name* of its own (whether it be 'sex roles' or 'gender'), then and only then can we come back to the idea we started with. We must first define and lay claim to a territory for the social, having a different conceptual location from that of sex but tied to the traditional sense of the word 'sex,' in order to be able, from this strategic location, to challenge the traditional meaning of 'sex.'

To end this section, I would say that we can only make advances in our knowledge if we initially increase the unknown: if we extend the areas which are cloudy and indeterminate. To advance, we must first renounce some truths. These 'truths' make us feel comfortable, as do all certainties, but they stop us asking questions—and asking questions is the surest, if not the only way of getting answers.

Divisions, Differences, and Classifications

The debate on gender and its relationship to sex covers much the same ground as the debate on the priority of the two elements—division and hierarchy—which constitute gender. These are empirically indissolubly united, but they need to be distinguished analytically. If it is accepted that there is a line of demarcation between 'natural' and socially constructed differences, and that at least some differences are socially constructed, then there is a framework for conceptualizing gender. This means, or should mean, recognising that hierarchy forms the foundation for differences—for all differences, not just gender.

However, even when this is accepted as an explanation, it is not accepted as a politics nor as a vision of the future, by feminists. It is not their Utopia. All feminists reject the sex/gender hierarchy, but very few are ready to admit that the logical consequence of this rejection is a refusal of sex roles, and the disappearance of gender. Feminists seem to want to abolish hierarchy and even sex roles, but not difference itself. They want to abolish the contents but not the container. They all want to keep some elements of gender. Some want to keep more, others less, but at the very least they want to maintain the classification. Very few indeed are happy to contemplate there being simple anatomical sexual differences which are not given any social significance or symbolic value. Suddenly the categories they use for analysis, which elsewhere clearly distinguish those who think difference comes *first* and hierarchy *afterwards* from those who think the *contents* of the divided groups are the product of the hierarchical division become muzzy, and the divergence between the two schools fades away.

This is especially clear in the debate on values. Feminist (and many other!) theorists generally accept that values are socially constructed and historically acquired, but they seem to think they must nonetheless be preserved. There are two typical variants on this position: One says, we must distribute masculine and feminine values through the whole of humanity; the other says that masculine and feminine values must each be maintained in their original group. The latter view is currently especially common among women who do not want to share feminine values with men. I am not sure whether this is because they believe men are unworthy or incapable of sustaining these values, or because they know men do not want them anyway. But we might well ask how women who are 'nurturant' and proud of it are going to become the equals of unchanged men-who are going to continue to drain these women's time? This is not a minor contradiction. It shows, rather, that if intellectual confusion produces political confusion, it is also possible to wonder, in a mood of despair, if there is not a deep and unacknowledged desire *not* to change anything at work behind the intellectual haze.

In any case, both variants of the debate show an implicit interpretation of the present situation which contradicts the problematic of gender:

1. On the one hand, there is a desire to retain a system of classification, even though (it is said) it has outlived its function of *establishing* a hierarchy between individuals—which would seem to indicate that people do not *really* think that gender is a social classification.

2. On the other, there is a vision of values which is very similar to Margaret Mead's, which can be summarised as: All human potentialities are already actually represented, but they are divided up between men and women. 'Masculine' plus 'feminine' subcultures, in fact culture itself, is not the product of a hierarchical society. It is independent of the social structure. The latter is simply superimposed upon it.

Hierarchy as Necessarily Prior to Division

This last view is contrary to everything we know about the relationship between social structure and culture. In the marxist tradition, and more generally in contemporary sociology whether marxist or not, it is held that the social structure is primary. This implies, as far as values are concerned, that they are, and cannot but be, appropriate to the structure of the society in question. Our society is hierarchical, and consequently its values are also hierarchically arranged. But this is not the only consequence, since Mead's model also allows for this.

Rather, if we accept that values are appropriate to social structures, then we must accept that values are *hierarchical* in general, and that those of the dominated are no less hierarchical than those of the dominants. According to this hypothesis, we must also accept that masculinity and femininity are not just, or rather not at all, what they were in Mead's model—a division of the traits which are (i) present in a potential form in both sexes, or (ii) present in all forms of possible and imaginable societies. According to the 'appropriateness' paradigm (i.e., the social construction of values), masculinity and femininity are the cultural creations of a society based on a gender hierarchy (as well, of course, as on other hierarchies). This means not only that they are linked to one another in a relationship of complementarity and opposition, but also that this structure determines the *content of each of these categories* and not just their relationship. It may be that together they cover the totality of human traits *which exist today*, but we cannot presume that even together they cover the whole spectrum of human potentialities. If we follow the 'appropriateness' paradigm, changing the respective statuses of the groups would lead to neither an alignment of all individuals on a single model, nor a happy hybrid of the two models.

Both the other sorts of conjecture presuppose, however, that these 'models' (i.e., the 'feminine' and the 'masculine') exist *sui generis*, and both imply a projection into a changed future of traits and values which exist now, prior to the change in the social structure.

To entrust oneself to this sort of guesswork, which moreover is totally implicit, requires a quite untenable, static view of culture. Even if it was progressive when Margaret Mead was writing just to admit that cultures varied and that values were arbitrarily divided between groups, this view is no longer tenable because it assumes the invariability of a universal human subject, and this has been invalidated by historians' studies of 'mentalities,' and by the social constructionist approaches inspired (even if generally unwittingly) by the marxist principles discussed above.

This vision of culture as static is, however, fundamental to all the variants of the notion of positive complementarity between men and women (even if those who hold such views do not recognise it).[5] They all presuppose that values precede their hierarchical organisation (as in Mead's model) and this stasis can only lead us back to 'nature,' in this case, human nature.

Such a point of view, and only such a point of view, can explain why Mead was afraid that everyone would become the same, which was counter to nature. The fear that a generalised sameness, or absence of differentiation, would be provoked by the disappearance of what is apparently the only kind of difference that we know (for this view point ignores all other sorts of variance)[6] is, of course, not new; though currently the fear that the world will align on a single model often takes the more specific form that the single model will be the current masculine model. This (it is said) will be the price we shall have to pay for equality; and (it is said) it is (perhaps) too high a price. However this fear is groundless since it is based on a static, hence essentialist, vision of women and men, which is a corollary to the belief that hierarchy was in some way added on to an essential dichotomy.

Within a gender framework such fears are simply incomprehensible. If women were the equals of men, men would no longer equal themselves. Why then should women resemble what men would have ceased to be? If we define men within a gender framework, they are first and foremost dominants with characteristics which enable them to remain dominants. To be like them would be also to be dominants, but this is a contradiction in terms. If in a collective couple—constituted of dominants and dominated—either of the categories is suppressed, then the domination is *ipso facto* suppressed. Hence the other category of the couple is also suppressed. Or to put it another way, to be dominant one must have someone to dominate. One can no more conceive of a society where everyone is 'dominant' than of one where everyone is 'richer.'

It is also not possible to imagine the values of a future egalitarian society as being the sum, or a combination, of existing masculine and feminine values, for these values were created in and by hierarchy. So how could they survive the end of hierarchy?

This vision of a society where values existed as 'entities,' prior to their being organised into a hierarchy is, as I have said, static and ultimately naturalist. But it is also not an isolated idea. It is part of a whole ensemble of ideas which includes:

1. commonsense and academic theories of sexuality which involve a double confusion: a confusion of anatomical sex with sexuality, and sexuality with procreation; and

2. a deep cultural theme to which these theories themselves refer back: vis-á-vis that each individual is essentially incomplete in so far as he or she is sexed. Emotional resistance and intellectual obstacles to thinking about gender both originate from this: from the individual and collective consciousness.

This is what I earlier called 'a set of confused representations turning around a belief in the necessity of close and permanent relations between most males and most females' (Delphy, 1981). I wanted to call this *set* (of representations) 'heterosexuality,' but it has been suggested it would be better called 'complementarity.' Its emblem is the image of heterosexual intercourse, and this gives it a social meaning and an emotional charge which is explicable only by its symbolic value. It could therefore equally be called a set of representations of 'fitting together.'

It would be interesting to develop this reflection further in relation to two main sets of questions:

1. how this whole set of ideas forms a view of the world as a whole which is more than the sum of its parts, which possesses a mystical and nonrational character (a cosmogony); and

2. how this cosmogony informs and determines the explicit and implicit premises of much scientific research—including feminist research and lesbian research.

Imagination and Knowledge

We do not know what the values, individual personality traits, and culture of a nonhierarchical society would be like, and we have great difficulty in imagining it. But to imagine it we must think that it is possible. And it *is* possible. Practices produce values; other practices produce other values.

Perhaps it is our difficulty in getting beyond the present, tied to our fear of the unknown, which curbs us in our utopian flights, as also in our progress at the level of knowledge—since the two are necessary to one another. To construct another future we obviously need an analysis of the present, but what is less recognised is that having a utopian vision is one of the indispensable staging-posts in the scientific process—in *all* scientific work. We can only analyse what *does* exist by imagining what does *not* exist, because to understand what is, we must ask how it came about. And asking how it came to exist must involve two operations. The first I described earlier when I said that we must admit we do not know the answers even when we think that we do (Descartes's famous 'suspension of judgement'). The second operation is admitting, even if it is contrary to the evidence of our senses, that something which exists, need not exist.

In conclusion, I would say that perhaps we shall only really be able to think about gender on the day when we can imagine nongender. But if Newton could do it for falling apples, we should be able to do it for ourselves as women.

Notes

1. An earlier version of this paper, "Penser le genre: Quels problemes?" appeared in Marie-Claude Hurtig, Michele Kail, & Helene Rouch (eds.): *Sexe et genre: De la hierarchie entre les sexes*, Editions du Centre National de la Recherche Scientifique, Paris, 1991.
2. Translated by Diana Leonard Centre for Research on Education and Gender, Institute of Education, University of London.
3. See, for example, Archer and Lloyd (1985), who say gender will continue because it is a 'practical way of classifying people.'
4. This is 'the final arbiter' of the dichotomous sex classification for the state, according to Money and Ehrhardt (1972, quoted by Hurtig & Pichevin, 1985).
5. There is, however, no single meaning to complementarity. The paradigm of hierarchy as the basis of division *also* implies complementarity, although in a negative sense.
6. This would mean that I would only talk to a male baker since I would no longer be able to distinguish a female baker from myself.

7.
GLOBALIZATION OF THE LOCAL/LOCALIZATION OF THE GLOBAL: MAPPING TRANSNATIONAL WOMEN'S MOVEMENTS
Amrita Basu

It may be time to replace the bumper sticker that exhorts, "Think Globally, Act Locally," with one that reads, "Think Locally, Act Globally". Or perhaps it's time simply to retire the bumper sticker, for with the growth of transnational social movements, we need to rethink entirely relations between the local and the global.

I am interested in exploring the implications for women's movements in the South of the growth of the transnational networks, organizations, and ideas. In the essay that follows I want to ask how North-South tensions around the meaning of feminism and the nature of women's movements have changed. What new opportunities have emerged and what new tensions have surfaced? What is the relationship between the transnationalism of the '90s and the feminism of the '60s and '70s, when Robin Morgan aptly and controversially claimed, "Sisterhood Is Global"?

My point of departure is an anthology of writings I edited in preparation for the 1995 Beijing women's conference entitled *The Challenge of Local Feminisms: Women's Movements in Global Perspective*. I found myself attempting to navigate twin dangers: resisting, on the one hand, the tendency narrowly to equate women's movements with autonomous urban, middle-class feminist groups, and, on the other hand, of defining women's movements so broadly that the term includes virtually all forms of women's activism. I highlighted the local origins and character of women's movements crossnationally and argued that women's movements must be situated within the particular political economics, state policies, and cultural politics of the regions in which they are active.

The question I now propose to ask is whether we need to rethink once again the relationship between local and global feminisms. Is it possible that the 1995 Beijing conference, which my book was designed to commemorate, in fact marked the coming of age of transnational feminism and the eclipse of locally based women's movements? This question is prompted by the appearance of more transnational women's movement activity than we ever have seen.

Before proceeding, a word about my terms: I am aware that *local* can connote the supposed particularism, provincialism, and primordialism, of the Third World while *global* may connote the breadth and universality that is often associated with Western feminism. By contrast, I use the term *local* to refer to indigenous and regional, and *global* to refer to the transnational. I employ these terms because they correspond to the levels at which a great deal of women's activism is organized, namely at the grass roots and transnational levels. As I will discuss, it is also important to inject into that dynamic attention to the national level.

There is considerable controversy about the significance of transnational movements, NGOs, networks, and advocacy groups. While some scholars speak of the emergence of a global civil society, others are more skeptical.[1] How to evaluate the transnationalization of women's movements is no less complicated. From one perspective it represents a signal achievement—particularly for women in the South. For example, Valentine Moghadam (1996) argues that transnational networks are organizing women around the most pressing questions of the day: reproductive rights, the growth of religious fundamentalism, and the adverse effects of structural adjustment policies. Moghadam also comments favorably on the recent emergence of networks, which she believes have a broader and more far reaching impact than local movements.[2] From another perspective as women's movements have become more transnational, their commitment to grass roots mobilization and cultural change has diminished. Sonia Alvarez (1997, 1998, 2000) argues that women's movements are becoming increasingly bureaucratized as they have come to work more closely with NGOs, political parties, state institutions, and multilateral agencies.[3] What explains the differences in these two perspectives? Which is correct?

I emphasize the indeterminate character of transnational activism in the late 1990s and early 2000s. It is inaccurate to depict local women's movements as simply being subsumed by global ones or as engaging in sustained overt resistance to global influences. Rather what prevails is a more complex and varied situation in which local and transnational movements often exist independently of one another and experience similar challenges and dilemmas. Furthermore, while transnational ideas, resources, and organizations have been extremely successful around certain issues in some regions, their success with these issues is more circumscribed elsewhere. After discussing these questions within the global context, I will turn to the Indian women's movement to illuminate my broader argument.

Women's Movements in Global Perspective

The international women's conferences that occurred in Mexico City (1975), Copenhagen (1980) Nairobi (1985) and Beijing (1995) provide a fruitful opportunity to explore changing relationships among women's organizations transnationally. The two-tier system of conferences, namely the United Nations–convened official conferences of heads of states, and the non-governmental conferences convened by women's groups and movements, provide insights into the workings of the international state system and of what some describe as a burgeoning global civil society.

International feminism might be periodized as comprising two broad phases. The first phase, between 1975 and 1985, was marked by bitter contestation over the meaning of feminism and over the relationship between the local and the global. The second decade-long phase, which begin with the Nairobi conference in 1985 and culminated in the Beijing conference in 1995, was marked by a growth of networks linking women's activism at the local and global levels.

Fierce struggles over the meaning and significance of feminism took place at international women's conferences of activists and policy makers from 1975 to 1985. Some of these debates identified the South with the local and the North with the global. A typical scenario would be one in which women from the South would argue that women's major priorities were both local and material, for instance, the needs for potable drinking water, firewood for fuel, and more employment opportunities. Meanwhile, women from the North typically would focus on women's broad transnational identities and interests.

It would be inaccurate to imply that tensions along North-South lines had disappeared entirely by the 1995 Beijing women's conference. Even today the organizations that sponsor campaigns to extend women's civil and political rights are Northern-based while Southern-based groups are more apt to address poverty, inequality, and basic needs. Esther Ngan-ling Chow (1996) notes, "Even when they agree on the importance of all issues such as human rights, women from various world regions frame it differently. While Western women traditionally have based their human rights struggles on issues of equality, non-discrimination and civil and political rights, African, Asian, and Latin American women have focused their struggles on economic, social and cultural rights."[4]

These differences, however, were less striking at the Beijing conference than significant areas of agreement that were established across North-South lines. Charlotte Bunch and Susan Fried (1996) argue that the entire Platform of Action was an affirmation of the human rights of women: "The incorporation of women's human rights language and concepts by governments and organizations from all parts of the world and in all manner of ways indicates more than a rhetorical gesture. It represents a shift in analysis that moves beyond single-issue politics or identity-based organizing and enhances women's capacity to build global alliances based on collective political goals and a common agenda."[5]

One important explanation for the diminution of tension between women's movements in the North and South is the increasingly important influence of women of color in shaping debates about feminism in the United States. Recall that some of the earliest and most important critiques of feminist universalism came from African American and Latina women in the United States. Years later, in preparation for the 1995 Beijing women's conference, American women of color formed a coalition with women from the South and drafted language for the platform document about women who face multiple forms of discrimination.[6]

At the same time, women from the South increasingly have worked to correct nationalism's exclusions by proposing non-discriminatory policies in newly formed states. Thanks to the influence of its women's movement, Namibia's constitution forbids sex discrimination, authorizes affirmative action for women, and recognizes only those forms of customary law which do not violate the constitution. The South African constitution similarly provides equal rights for women and prohibits discrimination on grounds of sexual orientation. Palestinian women have drafted a bill of rights and sought legislation protecting women from family violence.

Furthermore, with the end of the Cold War, the character of international gatherings changed quite significantly. Early meetings, like the Mexico City conference in 1975, were dominated by national political leaders who sought to use these forums to pursue their own agendas. Whereas many of the delegates attending the 1975 Mexico City conference were the wives, daughters, and widows of male politicians, by the 1985 Nairobi conference, the representatives included many women who were powerful in their own right. Even more important was the growth of women's movements globally and their increasingly important roles relative to those of states.

As nongovernmental organizations and movements have grown, they have become more diverse, and divisions that cross-cut the North-South and East-West divide have become more salient. Both transnational networks of feminists and of conservative activists have grown. For example, a coalition of conservative Islamic groups and Christian anti-abortion activists sought to shape the agenda of the Cairo conference on population and development in 1994 and to influence the World Plan of Action at the Beijing conference in 1995.[7] The coalition included some powerful nongovernmental organizations, such as the International Right to Life Committee and Human Life International; religious bodies, like the Vatican; and some states, preeminently the Islamic Republic of Iran. Like women's organizations, this coalition functions at local, national, and transnational levels.

The growth of transnational networks of the religious Right has reduced North-South polarization. Some of the staunchest opponents of feminism are North American or European, and among its staunchest supporters are Asians, Africans, and Latin Americans. The ability of Muslim, Protestant, and Catholic groups to transcend national differences and arrive at common positions on motherhood, pornography, abortion, homosexuality, and premarital sexuality has encouraged feminist groups similarly to seek out areas of agreement.

Charting the Terrain

It is tempting to treat international conferences as synonymous with transnational women's movements, since they have grown simultaneously. However to conflate the two is to underestimate the extent to which new forms of transnationalism emerge from civil society and include a diverse array of organizations, including NGOs, social movements, issue and identity networks, project coalitions, and issue-based campaigns.

The growth of transnational women's movements entails the spread and growing density of groups and linkages among groups within transnational civil society.

It also refers to a flow of resources, generally from the North to the South, to support women's organizations. Southern-based NGOs have come to rely heavily on financial support from Northern affiliates, foundations, and academic institutions. But it is not just individuals, groups, and currencies that cross borders with greater ease and frequency than in the past. Certain discourses—and this is a second dimension—have acquired greater importance among women in both the North and the South. One of the most important is that the violation of women's rights is a human rights abuse. Thus women's movements can be said to have become increasingly transnational when they appeal to universal principles of human rights and seek redress in global arenas.

The past few years have witnessed the growth of all these dimensions of transnational activism. There also has been a vast expansion in the number of NGOs which engage in international networking, from the one hundred fourteen that attended the NGO forum in Mexico City in 1975 to the three thousand that participated in the Beijing NGO forum in 1995. Today, tens of thousands of NGOs participate in international conferences and gatherings. Many of these are organized at the regional level by women activists from the South, independent of both the United Nations and national governments.

In keeping with the multifaceted character of globalization, transnational women's movements are themselves extremely diverse. A minority among them seek to challenge the feminization of poverty and class inequality that globalization entails. One important example is Development Alternatives with Women for a New Era (DAWN), which researchers and activists formed in 1984 to promote alternative approaches to state sponsored macroeconomic policies. DAWN includes membership from the Caribbean, Latin America, Africa, South and South-East Asia, and the Middle East. It earlier was based in Bangalore and now is based in Rio.

A much larger group of women's organizations has sought to extend women's civic and political rights, particularly to address violence against women and the denial of women's rights by religious nationalists. An important example is the coalition of one hundred thirty women's and human rights groups—including the National Organization for Women, the Feminist Majority, Human Rights Watch, the National Political Congress of Black Women, and the Women's Alliance for Peace and Human Rights—which organized a campaign protesting the repressive measures that the Taleban has exercised against Afghan women since assuming power in September 1996 and urging the international community to deny investments and recognition to the Taleban. It has organized a website documenting the Taleban's abuses, a petition campaign and demonstrations protesting them, and various fundraising activities. Among its victories has been to dissuade Unocal, an American oil company, from building a pipeline through Afghanistan.

The amount of international funding available for women's organizations, women's studies programs, and women's movements has grown dramatically over the past decade. Grants by major U.S. foundations to groups working on women's rights and violence against women increased from $241,000 in 1988 to $3,247,000 in 1993 (Keck and Sikkink 1998). The Ford Foundation underwrote almost half of this amount. In India alone, for example, the large majority of women's NGOs receive foreign funding.

As far as transnational discourses are concerned, neither conventions on international human rights nor the campaign for women's human rights is new. What is relatively new is the extent to which coalitions of transnational women's organizations have lobbied to demand recognition for women's rights as human rights. The year 1993 marked a turning point for the women's human rights movement, for during that year the Vienna Human Rights Declaration and Program of Action and the UN Declaration on the Elimination of Violence Against Women recognized violence against women as a human rights abuse and defined gender violence to include violence against women in the public and the private sphere. Women's human rights activists consolidated their gains at the Beijing conference and since have increasingly employed human rights appeals. With the collapse of communism and the decline of the organized Left, democratic movements have taken the place formerly occupied by socialism, and liberal principles of human rights have become hegemonic.

What are the implications of the transnationalization of women's movements for women in the South? Does the diminution of overt North-South tensions at the Beijing conference and other international forums reflect the increasingly important leadership and agenda-setting roles of women from the South? Or, conversely, are Southern-based organizations less able to oppose Northern domination because of their greater dependence on Northern funding sources? There is no one simple response to this question.

It would be inaccurate to see transnational networks and movements simply as vehicles for Northern domination. Networks like DAWN and WLUML (Women Living under Muslim Law) were organized by and for women from the South. Although these networks accept external funding, they formulate their objectives independently of donor organizations. Furthermore, certain problems may be more effectively addressed at the transnational than at the local level. A good example concerns some of the problems women face as a result of the growth of religious fundamentalism. Afghan women's groups are subject to such extreme repression that they could not organize effectively without outside support. Furthermore, transnational networks of women have been a vital counterweight to transnational networks of the religious Right.

The campaign against the Taleban also illuminates the possibilities of combining global and local appeals. While the campaign has made extensive use of the website and of e-mail petition campaigns, it also has organized demonstrations locally, including one in Amherst, Massachusetts, where women marched through the town commons with banners in their hands and pieces of mesh fabric pinned to their lapels to evoke the *burqua* (veil). Terming the campaign an attempt to stop "gender apartheid" in Afghanistan, the coalition identified the crimes against Afghan women

with the evils of apartheid in South Africa. This simple, indeed simplistic characterization, provided an effective means of generating support for the campaign.

Another tool that the campaign against the Taleban and other campaigns
against religious fundamentalism have employed is to record the stories of women
who are stoned, beaten, or publically humiliated for having worked, married,
divorced, or done nothing at all. These individual narratives not only permit a personal identification with the victims but also invite activism against those who per-
petrate abuse. The coalition against sexual apartheid in Afghanistan distributes a
video entitled "A Shroud of Silence" which recounts these stories in a particularly
graphic form.

The very conditions for the success of global campaigns like the one against
the Taleban in Afghanistan suggest some of the limitations of the strategy. Global
campaigns are much more likely to succeed when women's civil and political rights
rather than their economic rights (food, shelter, housing) have been violated. They
are more effective in challenging physical violence than structural violence against
women. Although this organizing problem exists locally, it is much more significant at the transnational level.

Struggles opposing violence against women are nested within the context of
women's class and sometimes ethnic struggles more often at the local than at the
transnational level. In India struggles against marital abuse often have emerged
amidst social movements of the urban and rural poor. Women who protest the
complicity of the state with illicit liquor producers in Andhra Pradesh, for example, readily appreciate the connections between violence against women and
unemployment, state corruption, and a range of other issues. By contrast, when
women come together in global forums as victims of gender violence, their identities as Bosnian, African American, or poor women may be muted.

Women's groups most enthusiastically have supported transnational campaigns against sexual violence in countries where the state is repressive or indifferent and women's movements are weak. Conversely, transnationalism has provoked
more distrust in places where women's movements have emerged, grown, and
defined themselves independently of Western feminism. Indeed, one explanation
for the differences between the positions of Valentine Moghadam (1996) and Sonia
Alvarez (1998) is that they examine such different contexts. Moghadam's optimism
about the role of transnational networks may be born of the pessimism she feels
about the potential for women's movements in face of the growth of Islamic fundamentalism in the Middle East. By contrast, Alvarez expresses concern about
cooptation because historically women's movements in Latin America have been
strong and closely tied to left-wing parties and human rights movements.

It is precisely in situations where women's movements are grappling with how
to organize more inclusively to overcome social hierarchies that transnational linkages may pose the greatest challenge. In such situations, transnationalism may
deepen divisions between globalized elites, who belong to transnational networks,
and the large majority of women, who do not. The result may be a deradicalization
of women's movements. Or, there may be growing rifts between those who have

access to international funding and those who do not. In this event, some activists become more mobile, while others remain stuck at the local level. The dependence of transnational activists on the internet, which requires specialized skills and technology, further accentuates class divisions among activists. . . .

How should we evaluate the growing exchanges among women's movements transnationally? To what extent are transnational forms of activism overcoming the tensions that until recently bedeviled women's movements across North-South lines? Are new networks, coalitions, and alliances addressing the key issues that women face transnationally? These questions are of more than academic relevance. The major funding organizations are committed to strengthening civil society both locally and cross-nationally and have identified women's movements as key to this endeavor. For women's movement activists in the South, the question of what kind of transnational alliances to forge and resources to accept is a key concern.

Transnational networks, campaigns, and discourses seem to be most effective where support for a particular demand exists locally, but its expression is constrained where the state is either indifferent or repressive towards women; and where the violation involves physical violence and redress can be found by asserting women's civil rights. Examples of such situations include the mass rape of Bosnian women, the Taleban's violence against Afghan women, and the recalled plight of East Asian comfort women during the Second World War. By contrast, transnational networks, campaigns, and discourses have been less effective in strengthening women's movements where strong local movements already exist. Furthermore, activists derive less benefit from transnational connections when the state concedes, however partially, to their demands.

Although transnational women's networks have grown considerably, there is a danger of both crediting and blaming them too much. In India, as in many other places, the principal location of the women's movements is the national rather than the transnational level. Its priority is to influence the state. Women's groups have formed vital roles in nation-building in Namibia, South Africa, and Nicaragua; in conflict resolution in war-torn Ireland, Israel, and Bosnia-Herzegovia; and in the democratization of authoritarian states in central Europe and Latin America.[8]

In all contexts, transnational linkages are likely to be most effective when redress can be sought by asserting women's civil and political rights, rather than their economic well-being, and when transnational linkages are not primarily designed to provide resources. The extent to which women's organizations in the South have come to depend on Northern funding as impeded the open-ended, two-way flow of ideas that has been so critical to the development of feminism. Economic reliance on Western foundations fosters the ever-present possibility of dependence and resentment. These problems are quite independent of the intentions of Northern-based funding organizations, many of which have become quite sensitive to the issues.

Meanwhile, women's economic situation remains perilous. Women constitute 70 percent of the 1.3 billion people living in absolute poverty and two-thirds of the world's illiterate population. Accordingly, the Beijing platform for action called on non-governmental women's organizations to strengthen antipoverty programs and improve women's health, education, and social services. It called on NGOs to take responsibility for ensuring women's full and equal access to economic resources, including the right to inheritance, ownership of land, and natural resources. Interestingly, the only recommendation that NGOs have seriously embraced is to provide women with greater access to savings and credit mechanisms and institutions. Important as microcredit schemes are in allowing women a larger share of the pie, they do not contribute to rethinking the implications of macroeconomic policies for women.[9]

Transnational networks and activists seem to be most effective when the basis for mobilization is sexual victimization. Moreover, the victims who generate the most sympathy generally are women from the South who experience genital mutilation, stoning, or public humiliation. Important as campaigns like the coalition against gender apartheid in Afghanistan may be, they draw sympathy partly because of pervasive anti-Arab sentiment in the U.S., which is gendered. Muslim women often are considered victims of the Islamic faith and of the misogyny of men of their community. The dissemination of pieces of mesh fabric to signify the *burqua* by the coalition against the Taleban certainly implies that the *purdah* is inevitably associated with the degradation of women, thereby inadvertently exacerbating anti-Muslim sentiment.

That there is an alternative to the choice between a religious politics which undermines women's rights and universalist, liberal feminism, which undermines women's religious and nationalist loyalties, is illustrated by the network Women Living under Muslim Law (WLUML). Established in 1985, it provides information, solidarity, and support both to women in Muslim countries and to Muslim women living elsewhere. The network was formed in response to the rise of religious "fundamentalist" movements and the attempt by certain states to institute family codes that would deny women full citizenship rights. By making Muslim women both its objects of concern and its leaders, and by showing how Islam provides both sympathetic and adverse characterizations of women's rights, the WLUML avoids disparaging characterizations of Muslim women. What the WLUML campaign suggests is that global visions need to be further infused with local realities, while appreciating that the local is not merely local, but infused with global influences.

Notes

1. For a sampling of the debates on global civil society, see Ronnie Lipschutz, "Reconstructing World Politics: The Emergence of Global Civil Society," *Millennium* 21: 3 (1992): 389–420; Paul Wapner, "Politics Beyond the State: Environmental Activism and World Civic Politics," *World Politics* 47 (April 1995): 311–40; and Margaret E. Keck and Kathryn Sikkink, *Activists Beyond Borders: Advocacy Networks in International Politics* (Ithaca: Cornell University Press, 1998).

2. Valentine M. Moghadam, "Feminist Networks North and South: DAWN, WIDE and WLUML," *Journal of International Communication* 3:1 (1996): 111–25.

3. Sonia E. Alvarez, "Latin American Feminisms 'Go Global': Trends of the 1990s and Challenges for the New Millennium," in *Cultures of Politics/Politics of Cultures: Revisioning Latin American Social Movements*, edited by Sonia E. Alvarez, Evelina Dagnino, and Arturo Escobar (Boulder, Colo.: Westview, 1998), and "Even Fidel Can't Change That": Trans/national Feminist Advocacy Strategies and Cultural Politics in Latin America" (unpublished paper presented at the Department of Cultural Anthropology, Duke University, October 1997). Also see Sonia Alvarez's contribution to this issue.

4. Esther Ngan-ling Chow, "Making Waves, Moving Mountains: Reflections on Beijing '95 and Beyond," *Signs* 22 (Autumn 1996): 187.

5. Charlotte Bunch and Susana Fried, "Beijing '95: Moving Women's Human Rights From Margin to Center," *Signs* (Autumn 1996): 203.

6. Chow, "Making Waves, Moving Mountains," 189.

7. Valentine E. Moghadam, "The Fourth World Conference on Women: Dissension and Consensus," *Bulletin of Concerned Asian Scholars*, 28 (Jan–March 1996).

8. Cynthia Cockburn, *The Space Between Us: Negotiating Gender and National Identities in Conflict* (London: Zed, 1998).

9. Cecelia Lynch points to the ineffectiveness of social movements in confronting globalization in "Social Movements and the Problem of Globalization," *Alternatives* 23 (1998): 149–73.

MOVEMENTS

8.
NO MORE MISS AMERICA!

On September 7th [1968] in Atlantic City, the Annual Miss America Pageant will again crown "your ideal." But this year, reality will liberate the contest auction-block in the guise of "genyooine" de-plasticized, breathing women. Women's Liberation Groups, black women, high school and college women, women's peace groups, women's welfare and social-work groups, women's job-equality groups, pro-birth control and pro-abortion groups—women of every political persuasion—all are invited to join us in a day-long boardwalk-theater event, starting at 1:00 p.m. on the Boardwalk in front of Atlantic City's Convention Hall. We will protest the image of Miss America, an image that oppresses women in every area in which it purports to represent us. There will be: Picket Lines; Guerrilla Theater; Leafleting; Lobbying Visits to the contestants urging our sisters to reject the Pageant Farce and join us; a huge Freedom Trash Can (into which we will throw bras,[1] girdles, curlers, false eyelashes, wigs, and representative issues of *Cosmopolitan, Ladies' Home Journal, Family Circle*, etc.—bring any such woman-garbage you have around the house); we will also announce a Boycott of all those commercial products related to the Pageant, and the day will end with a Women's Liberation rally at midnight when Miss America is crowned on live television. Lots of other surprises are being planned (come and add your own!) but we do not plan heavy disruptive tactics and so do not expect a bad police scene. It should be a groovy day on the Boardwalk in the sun with our sisters. In case of arrests, however, we plan to reject all male authority and demand to be busted by policewomen only. (In Atlantic City, women cops are not permitted to make arrests—dig that!)

Male chauvinist-reactionaries on this issue had best stay away, nor are male liberals welcome in the demonstrations. But sympathetic men can donate money as well as cars and drivers.

Male reporters will be refused interviews. We reject patronizing reportage. *Only newswomen will be recognized.*

The Ten Points

We Protest:
1. *The Degrading Mindless-Boob-Girlie Symbol.* The Pageant contestants epitomize the roles we are all forced to play as women. The parade down the runway blares the metaphor of the 4-H Club county fair, where the nervous animals are judged

for teeth, fleece, etc., and where the best "specimen" gets the blue ribbon. So are women in our society forced daily to compete for male approval, enslaved by ludicrous "beauty" standards we ourselves are conditioned to take seriously.

2. *Racism with Roses.* Since its inception in 1921, the Pageant has not had one Black finalist, and this has not been for a lack of test-case contestants. There has never been a Puerto Rican, Alaskan, Hawaiian, or Mexican-American winner. Nor has there ever been a *true* Miss America—an American Indian.

3. *Miss America as Military Death Mascot.* The highlight of her reign each year is a cheerleader-tour of American troops abroad—last year she went to Vietnam to pep-talk our husbands, fathers, sons and boyfriends into dying and killing with a better spirit. She personifies the "unstained patriotic American womanhood our boys are fighting for." The Living Bra and the Dead Soldier. We refuse to be used as Mascots for Murder.

4. *The Consumer Can-Game.* Miss America is a walking commercial for the Pageant's sponsors. Wind her and up and she plugs your product on promotion tours and—all in an "honest, objective" endorsement. What a shill.

5. *Competition Rigged and Unrigged.* We deplore the encouragement of an American myth that oppresses men as well as women: the win-or-you're-worthless competitive disease. The "beauty contest" creates only one winner to be "used" and forty-nine losers who are "useless."

6. *The Woman as Pop Culture Obsolescent Theme.* Spindle, mutilate, and then discard tomorrow. What is so ignored as last year's Miss America? This only reflects the gospel of our society, according to Saint Male: women must be young, juicy, malleable—hence age discrimination and the cult of youth. And we women are brainwashed into believing this ourselves!

7. *The Unbeatable Madonna-Whore Combination.* Miss America and Playboy's centerfold are sisters over the skin. To win approval, we must be both sexy and wholesome, delicate but able to cope, demure yet titillatingly bitchy. Deviation of any sort brings, we are told, disaster: "You won't get a man!!"

8. *The Irrelevant Crown on the Throne of Mediocrity.* Miss America represents what women are supposed to be: unoffensive, bland, apolitical. If you are tall, short, over or under what weight The Man prescribes you should be, forget it. Personality, articulateness, intelligence, commitment—unwise. Conformity is the key to the crown—and, by extension, to success in our society.

9. *Miss America as Dream Equivalent To—?* In this reputedly democratic society, where every little boy supposedly can grow up to be President, what can every little girl hope to grow to be? Miss America. That's where it's at. Real power to control our own lives is restricted to men, while women get patronizing pseudo-power, an ermine clock and a bunch of flowers; men are judged by their actions, women by their appearance.

10. *Miss America as Big Sister Watching You.* The pageant exercises Thought Control, attempts to sear the Image onto our minds, to further make women oppressed and men oppressors; to enslave us all the more in high-heeled, low-status roles; to inculcate false values in young girls; to use women as beasts of buying; to seduce us to prostitute ourselves before our own oppression.

NO MORE MISS AMERICA

Note

    1. Bras were never burned. Bra-burning was a whole-cloth invention of the media.—ed. [note in original]

9.
LESBIANS IN REVOLT[1]
Charlotte Bunch

The development of lesbian-feminist politics as the basis for the liberation of women is our top priority; this article outlines our present ideas. In our society, which defines all people and institutions for the benefit of the rich, white male, the lesbian is in revolt. In revolt because she defines herself in terms of women and rejects the male definitions of how she should feel, act, look, and live. To be a lesbian is to love oneself, woman in a culture that denigrates and despises women. The lesbian rejects male sexual/political domination; she defies his world, his social organization, his ideology, and his definition of her as inferior. Lesbianism puts women first while the society declares the male supreme. Lesbianism threatens male supremacy at its core. When politically conscious and organized, it is central to destroying our sexist, racist, capitalist, imperialist system.

Lesbianism is a Political Choice

Male society defines lesbianism as a sexual act, which reflects men's limited view of women: they think of us only in terms of sex. They also say lesbians are not real women, so a real woman is one who gets fucked by men. We say that a lesbian is a woman whose sense of self and energies, including sexual energies, center around women—she is woman-identified. The woman-identified-woman commits herself to other women for political, emotional, physical, and economic support. Women are important to her. She is important to herself. Our society demands that commitment from women be reserved for men.

The lesbian, woman-identified-woman, commits herself to women not only as an alternative to oppressive male/female relationships but primarily because she *loves* women. Whether consciously or not, by her actions, the lesbian has recognized that giving support and love to men over women perpetuates the system that oppresses her. If women do not make a commitment to each other, which includes sexual love, we deny ourselves the love and value traditionally given to men. We accept our second-class status. When women do give primary energies to other women, then it is possible to concentrate fully on building a movement for our liberation.

Woman-identified lesbianism is, then, more than a sexual preference; it is a political choice. It is political because relationships between men and women are essentially political: they involved power and dominance. Since the lesbian actively rejects that relationship and chooses women, she defies the established political system.

Lesbianism, By Itself, Is Not Enough

Of course, not all lesbians are consciously woman-identified, nor are all committed to finding common solutions to the oppression they suffer as women and lesbians. Being a lesbian is part of challenging male supremacy, but not the end. For the lesbian or heterosexual woman, there is no individual solution to oppression.

The lesbian may think that she is free since she escapes the personal oppression of the individual male/female relationship. But to the society she is still a woman, or worse, a visible lesbian. On the street, at the job, in the schools, she is treated as an inferior and is at the mercy of men's power and whims. (I've never heard of a rapist who stopped because his victim was a lesbian.) This society hates women who love women, and so, the lesbian, who escapes male dominance in her private home, receives it doubly at the hands of male society; she is harassed, outcast, and shuttled to the bottom. Lesbians must become feminists and fight against woman oppression, just as feminists must become lesbians if they hope to end male supremacy.

U.S. society encourages individual solutions, apolitical attitudes, and reformism to keep us from political revolt and out of power. Men who rule, and male leftists who seek to rule, try to depoliticize sex and the relations between men and women in order to prevent us from acting to end our oppression and challenging their power. As the question of homosexuality has become public, reformists define it as a private question of whom you sleep with in order to sidetrack our understanding of the politics of sex. For the lesbian-feminist, it is not private; it is a political matter of oppression, domination, and power. Reformists offer solutions that make no basic changes in the system that oppresses us, solutions that keep power in the hands of the oppressor. The only way oppressed people end their oppression is by seizing power: people whose rule depends on the subordination of others do not voluntarily stop oppressing others. Our subordination is the basis of male power.

Sexism is the Root of All Oppression

The first division of labor, in prehistory, was based on sex: men hunted, women built the villages, took care of children, and farmed. Women collectively controlled the land, language, culture, and the communities. Men were able to conquer women with the weapons that they developed for hunting when it became clear that women were leading a more stable, peaceful, and desirable existence. We do not know exactly how this conquest took place, but it is clear that the original imperialism was male over female: the male claiming the female body and her services as his territory (or property).

Having secured the domination of women, men continued this pattern of suppressing people, not on the basis of tribe, race, and class. Although there have been numerous battles over class, race, and nation during the past three thousand years, none has brought the liberation of women. While these other forms of oppression must be ended, there is no reason to believe that our liberation will come with the smashing of capitalism, racism, or imperialism today. Women will be free only when we concentrate on fighting male supremacy.

Our war against male supremacy does, however, involve attacking the latter-day dominations based on class, race, and nation. As lesbians who are outcasts from every group, it would be suicidal to perpetuate these man-made divisions among ourselves. We have no heterosexual privileges, and when we publicly assert our Lesbianism, those of us who had them lose many of our class and race privileges. Most of our privileges as women are granted to us by our relationships to men (fathers, husbands, boyfriends) whom we now reject. This does not mean that there is no racism or class chauvinism within us, but we must destroy these divisive remnants of privileged behavior among ourselves as the first step toward their destruction in the society. Race, class, and national oppressions come from men, serve ruling-class white male interests, and have no place in a woman-identified revolution.

Lesbianism Is the Basic Threat to Male Supremacy

Lesbianism is a threat to the ideological, political, personal, and economic basis of male supremacy. The lesbian threatens the ideology of male supremacy by destroying the lie about female inferiority, weakness, passivity, and by denying women's "innate" need for men. Lesbians literally do not need men, even for procreation.

The lesbian's independence and refusal to support one man undermines the personal power that men exercise over women. Our rejection of heterosexual sex challenges male domination in its most individual and common form. We offer all women something better than submission to personal oppression. We offer the beginning of the end of collective and individual male supremacy. Since men of all races and classes depend on female support and submission for practical tasks and feeling superior, our refusal to submit will force some to examine their sexist behavior, to break down their own destructive privileges over other humans, and to fight against those privileges in other men. They will have to build new selves that do not depend on oppressing women and learn to live in social structures that do not give them power over anyone.

Heterosexuality separates women from each other; it makes women define themselves through men; it forces women to compete against each other for men and the privilege that comes through men and their social standing. Heterosexual society offers women a few privileges as compensation if they give up their freedom: for example, mothers are "honored," wives or lovers are socially accepted and given some economic and emotional security, a woman gets physical protection on the street when she stays with her man, et cetera. The privileges give heterosexual women a personal and political stake in maintaining the status quo.

The lesbian receives none of these heterosexual privileges or compensations since she does not accept the male demands on her. She has little vested interest in maintaining the present political system since all of its institutions—church, state, media, health, schools—work to keep her down. If she understands her oppression, she has nothing to gain by supporting white rich male America and much to gain from fighting to change it. She is less prone to accept reformist solutions to women's oppression.

Economics is a crucial part of woman oppression, but our analysis of the relationship between capitalism and sexism is not complete. We know that Marxist economic theory does not sufficiently consider the role of women or lesbians, and we are presently working on this area.

However, as a beginning, some of the ways that lesbians threaten the economic system are clear: in this country, women work for men in order to survive, on the job and in the home. The lesbian rejects this division of labor at its roots; she refuses to be a man's property, to submit to the unpaid labor system of housework and child care. She rejects the nuclear family as the basic unit of production and consumption in capitalist society.

The lesbian is also a threat on the job because she is not the passive/part-time woman worker that capitalism counts on to do boring work and be part of a surplus labor pool. Her identity and economic support do not come through men, so her job is crucial and she cares about job conditions, wages, promotion, and status. Capitalism cannot absorb large numbers of women demanding stable employment, decent salaries, and refusing to accept their traditional job exploitation. We do not understand yet the total effect that this increased job dissatisfaction will have. It is, however, clear that as women become more intent upon taking control of their lives, they will seek more control over their jobs, thus increasing the strains on capitalism and enhancing the power of women to change the economic system.

Lesbians Must Form Our Own Movement to Fight Male Supremacy

Feminist-lesbianism, as the most basic threat to male supremacy, picks up part of the women's liberation analysis of sexism and gives it force and direction. Women's liberation lacks direction now because it has failed to understand the importance of heterosexuality in maintaining male supremacy, and because it has failed to face class and race as real differences in women's behavior and political needs. As long as straight women see lesbianism as a bedroom issue, they hold back the development of politics and strategies that would put an end to male supremacy and they give men an excuse for not dealing with their sexism.

Being a lesbian means ending identification with, allegiance to, dependence on, and support of heterosexuality. It means ending your personal stake in the male world so that you join women individually and collectively, in the struggle to end your oppression. Lesbianism is the key to liberation and only women who cut their ties to male privilege can be trusted to remain serious in the struggle against male dominance. Those who remain tied to men individually or in political theory, cannot always put women first. It is not that heterosexual women are evil or do not care about women. It is because the very essense, definition, and nature of heterosexuality is men first. Every woman has experienced that desolation when her sister puts her man first; in the final crunch heterosexuality demands that she do so. As long as women still benefit from heterosexuality, receive its privileges and security they will at some point have to betray their sisters, especially lesbian sisters who do not receive those benefits.

Women in women's liberation have understood the importance of having meetings and other events for women only. It has been clear that dealing with men divides us and saps our energies, and that it is not the job of the oppressed to explain our oppression to the oppressor. Women also have seen that collectively, men will not deal with their sexism until they are forced to do so. Yet, many of these same women continue to have primary relationships with men individually and do not understand why lesbians find them oppressive. Lesbians cannot grow politically or personally from the situation which denies the basis of our politics: that lesbianism is political, that heterosexuality is crucial to maintaining male supremacy.

Lesbians must form our own political movement in order to grow. Changes that will have more than token effects in our lives will be led by woman-identified lesbians who understand the nature of our oppression and are therefore in a position to end it.

Note

1. "Lesbians in Revolt," first appeared in *The Furies*, vol. I, no. 1 (January 1972).

10.
REPRODUCTIVE AND SEXUAL RIGHTS: A FEMINIST PERSPECTIVE
Sônia Correa and Rosalind Petchesky

In current debates about the impact of population policies on women, the concept of reproductive and sexual rights is both stronger and more contested than ever before. Those who take issue with this concept include religious fundamentalists, as well as opponents of human rights in general, who associate human rights with individualist traditions deriving from Western capitalism. Some feminists, too, are skeptical about the readiness with which advocates of fertility reduction programs, whose primary concern is neither women's health nor their empowerment, have adopted the language of reproductive rights to serve their own agendas. As a Southern and a Northern feminist who have written about and organized for women's reproductive health for many years, we are conscious of the tensions and multiple perspectives surrounding this conceptual territory. Our purpose in this chapter is not to impose a concept, but to explore a different way of thinking about it in order to advance the debate. We define the terrain of reproductive and sexual rights in terms of power and resources: power to make informed decisions about one's own fertility, childbearing, child rearing, gynecologic health, and sexual activity; and resources to carry out such decisions safely and effectively. This terrain necessarily involves some core notion of "bodily integrity," or "control over one's body." However, it also involves one's relationships to one's children, sexual partners, family members, community, caregivers, and society at large; in other words, the body exists in a socially mediated universe. . . .

Epistemological and Historical Premises

Contrary to many social critics, we are not convinced that reproductive and sexual rights (or human rights) are simply a "Western" concept. As Kamla Bhasin and Nighat Khan (1986) have argued with regard to feminism in South Asia, "an idea cannot be confined within national or geographic boundaries." Postcolonial writers and Southern governments have readily adopted, and adapted, the theories of Marx, Malthus, or Milton Friedman to suit their own purposes. Democracy movements in postcolonial societies easily invoke rights when it comes to voting, or forming political parties or trade unions. Why should concepts like "reproductive rights," "bodily integrity," and women's rights to sexual self-determination be any less adaptable?...

The term "reproductive rights" is of recent—and probably North American[1]—origin, but its roots in ideas of bodily integrity and sexual self-determination have a much older and culturally-broader genealogy. The idea that a woman in particular must be able "to decide whether, when, and how to have children" originated in the feminist–birth control movements that developed at least as early as the 1830s among the Owenite socialists in England and spread to many parts of the world over the course of a century (Chesler 1992; Gordon 1976; Huston 1992; Jayawardena 1993; Ramusack 1989; Weeks 1981). Leaders of these movements in Western countries, like Margaret Sanger in North America and Stella Browne in England, linked "the problem of birth control" not only with women's struggle for social and political emancipation, but also with their need to "own and control" their bodies and to obtain sexual knowledge and satisfaction (Sanger 1920). Their counterparts among women's rights advocates in nineteenth-century Europe and America and among the early–birth control pioneers in twentieth-century Asia, North Africa, and Latin America were more reticent about women's sexuality, emphasizing instead a negative right: that of women (married or single) to refuse unwanted sex or childbearing.

Underlying both the defensive and the affirmative versions of these early feminist prototypes of reproductive rights language were the same basic principles of *equality, personhood, and bodily integrity*. They held a common premise: in order for women to achieve equal status with men in society, they must be respected as full moral agents with projects and ends of their own; hence they alone must determine the uses—sexual, reproductive, or other—to which their bodies (and minds) are put.[2]

In the late 1970s and early 1980s, women's health movements emerged throughout Asia, Latin America, Europe and North America (DAWN 1993; Garcia-Moreno and Claro 1994). These movements aimed at achieving the ability of women, *both* as individuals *and* in their collective organizational forms and community identities, to determine their own reproductive and sexual lives in conditions of optimum health and economic and social well-being. They did not imagine women as atoms completely separate from larger social contexts; rather, they consciously linked the principle of "women's right to decide" about fertility and childbearing to "the social, economic and political conditions that make such decisions possible" (Women's Global Network for Reproductive Rights 1991).

Increasingly, as women of color in Northern societies and women from Southern countries have taken leadership in developing the meanings of sexual and reproductive rights for women, these meanings have expanded. They have come to encompass both a broader range of issues than fertility regulation (including, for example, maternal and infant mortality, infertility, unwanted sterilization, malnutrition of girls and women, female genital mutilation, sexual violence, and sexually transmitted diseases); and a better understanding of the structural conditions that constrain reproductive and sexual decisions (such as reductions in social sector expenditures resulting from structural adjustment programs; lack of transportation, water, sanitation, and child care; illiteracy; and poverty). In other words, the concept of sexual and reproductive *rights* is being enlarged to address the *social needs* that erode reproductive and sexual choice for the majority of the world's women, who are poor (Desai 1994; Petchesky and Weiner 1990).

In the past decade, the integral tie between reproductive rights and women's sexual self- determination, including the right to sexual pleasure, has gained recognition not only in the North, but in Latin America, Africa, and Asia.[3] As the Women's Resource and Research Center (WRRC) in the Philippines states in its Institutional Framework and Strategies on Reproductive Rights (Fabros 1991), "self-determination and pleasure in sexuality is one of the primary meanings of the idea of 'control over one's body' and a principal reason for access to safe abortion and birth control." Anchoring the possibility of women's *individual* right to health, well-being, and "self-determined sexual lives" to the *social* changes necessary to eliminate poverty and empower women, this framework dissolves the boundary between sexuality, human rights, and development. It thus opens a wider lens not only on reproductive and sexual rights, but on rights in general.

Rights Discourse: Rethinking Rights as Individual and Social

The discourse of (human) rights has come under heavy assault in recent years, from, among others, feminist, Marxist, and postmodernist sources (Olsen 1984; Tushnet 1984; Unger 1983)....

While these criticisms are theoretically compelling, they offer no alternative discourse for social movements to make collective political claims. Whatever its theoretical weaknesses, the polemical power of rights language as an expression of aspirations for justice across widely different cultures and political-economic conditions cannot easily be dismissed (Heller 1992). In practice, then, the language of rights remains indispensable but needs radical redefinition. Feminist theorists and activists have figured prominently in efforts to shed the abstract universality, formalism, individualism and antagonism encumbering rights language (Bunch 1990; Crenshaw 1991; Friedman 1992; Nedelsky 1989; Petchesky 1994; Schneider 1991; Williams 1991). Allying themselves with worldwide struggles for democratization among indigenous peoples, ethnic minorities, sexual minorities, immigrant groups, and oppressed majorities—all of whom invoke the language of "human rights"—they seek to recast rights discourse in a more inclusive "referential universe" (Williams 1991). The purpose is to transform the classical liberal rights model in order: (1) to emphasize the *social*, not just individual, nature of rights, thus shifting the major burden of correlative duties from individuals to public agencies; (2) to acknowledge the *communal* (relational) *contexts* in which individuals act to exercise or pursue their rights; (3) to foreground the *substantive* basis of rights in human needs and a redistribution of resources; and (4) to recognize the bearers of rights in their self-defined, multiple identities, including their gender, class, sexual orientation, race, and ethnicty....

Feminist writings and actions in defense of women's human rights build on these critiques to challenge the customary reluctance of states and international agencies to intervene in traditionally defined "family matters." Through vigorous international campaigns leading up to and beyond the United Nations Human Rights Conference in Vienna in 1993, they have called for national and international sanctions against gender-based violations of human rights, and they have shown how such violations occur most frequently in the supposedly private realms of family, reproduction, and sexuality (for example, through endemic violence against women). Inaction by public authorities in response to such violations— whether at the hand of state officials, nongovernmental organizations (NGOs), or spouses—constitutes, they argue, a form of acquiescence (Bunch 1990; Cook 1993b; Copelon 1994; Freedman and Isaacs 1993; Heise 1992).

By prying open the "citadel of privacy," feminist legal and political theory offers a wedge with which to challenge the claims of "tradition" and "local culture" used to defeat domestic application of international human rights norms (see Boland, Rao, and Zeidenstein, 1994). Feminist deconstructions of the public-private division also point to a model of reproductive and sexual behavior that is socially contextualized[.]...

A social model of human behavior does not assume that individuals make decisions in a vacuum or that "choices" are equally "free" for everyone. Group identities that are complex and "intersectional" (across gender, class, ethnicity, religion, age, nationality) pull women's decisions in multiple directions. Moreover, because of existing social inequalities, the resources and range of options women have at their disposal differ greatly, affecting their ability to exercise their rights (Crenshaw 1991; Eisenstein 1994; Williams 1991).

How does this interactive, socially-embedded model of personal decision making apply to the realm of sexual and reproductive rights? Qualitative data across a variety of cultural and historical settings suggest that the extent to which reproductive and sexual decisions are "freely" made eludes easy classification; but "free" or "voluntary," whatever its meaning, is not the same as isolated or individualistic. In each concrete case we must weigh the multiple social, economic, and cultural factors that come to bear on a woman's decision and constitute its local meaning. Women's decisions about whether or not to bring a pregnancy to term are most frequently made in consultation with, under the constraint of, and sometimes in resistance against networks of significant others—mothers, mothers-in-law, sisters, other kin, neighbors; sometimes husbands or male partners, sometimes not (Adams and Castle 1994; Ezeh 1993; Gilligan 1982; Jeffery, Jeffery, and Lyon 1989; Khattab 1992; Petchesky 1990)....

Here we confront the nagging problem, always a dilemma for feminist advocates, of how to critique the kinds and range of choices available to women without denigrating the decisions women do make for themselves, even under severe social and economic constraints.[4] The debate concerning sterilization prevalence rates in Brazil provides a striking illustration. In a context of rapid fertility decline, female sterilization has become a "preferred" method in Brazil, used by 44 percent of current contraceptors. In some regions, the sterilization rate reaches more than 64 percent, as in the case of the Northeast, and the average age of sterilization has rap-

idly declined since the early 1980s (15 percent of sterilized women in the Northeast
are under 25 years of age). A complex mix of factors explains this trend: concerns
about the side effects or effectiveness of reversible contraception, failure of the
public health system to provide adequate information about and access to other
methods, severe economic conditions, women's employment patterns, and cultural
and religious norms making sterilization less "sinful" than abortion (Correa 1993;
Lopez 1993; Petchesky 1979).

In their analysis of the sterilization trends, Brazilian feminists are caught
between the urgent need to denounce the inequities in sterilization rates—particularly among black women—and the evidence of research findings that many
women have consciously chosen and paid for the procedure and are satisfied with
their decision. On the one hand, this is a clear example of the "constrained choices"
that result from circumstances of gender, poverty, and racism; the very notion that
women in such conditions are exercising their "reproductive rights" strains the
meaning of the term (Lopez 1993). On the other hand, the call for criminal sanctions against sterilization by some groups in Brazil seems a denial of women's
moral agency in their search for reproductive self-determination.

We need to develop analytical frameworks that respect the integrity of women's
reproductive and sexual decisions, however constrained, while also condemning
social, economic, and cultural conditions that may force women to "choose" one
course over another. Such conditions prevail in a range of situations, curtailing
reproductive choices and creating dilemmas for women's health activists. Women
desperate for employment may knowingly expose themselves to reproductively
hazardous chemicals or other toxins in the workplace. Women hedged in by economic dependence and the cultural preference for sons may "choose" abortion as a
means of sex selection. Where female genital mutilation is a traditional practice,
women must "choose" for their young daughters between severe health risk and
sexual loss on the one hand, and unmarriageable pariah status on the other.

For reproductive decisions to be in any real sense "free," rather than compelled
by circumstance or desperation, requires the presence of certain *enabling conditions.* These conditions constitute the foundation of reproductive and sexual rights
and are what feminists mean when they speak of women's "empowerment." They
include material and infrastructural factors, such as reliable transportation, child
care, financial subsidies, or income supports, as well as comprehensive health services that are accessible, humane, and well staffed. The absence of adequate transportation alone can be a significant contributor to higher maternal mortality and
failure to use contraceptives (see Asian and Pacific Women's Resource Collection
Network 1990; and McCarthy and Maine 1992). They also include cultural and
political factors, such as access to education, earnings, self-esteem, and the channels of decisionmaking. Where women have no education, training, or status outside that which comes from bearing sons, childbearing may remain their best
option (Morsy 1994; Pearce 1994; Ravindran 1993).

Such enabling conditions, or social rights, are integral to reproductive and sexual rights and directly entail the responsibility of states and mediating institutions

(for example, population and development agencies) for their implementation. Rights involve not only *personal liberties* (domains where governments should leave people alone), but also *social entitlements* (domains where affirmative public action is required to ensure that rights are attainable by everyone). They thus necessarily imply public responsibilities and a renewed emphasis on the linkages between personal well-being and social good, including the good of public support for gender equality in all domains of life.

This is not meant to suggest a mystical "harmony of interests" between individual women and public authorities, nor to deny that conflicts between "private" and "public" interests will continue to exist.... These realities prompt us to rethink the relationship between the state and civil society, and to map out an ethical framework for reproductive and sexual rights in the space where the social and the individual intersect.

The Ethical Content of Reproductive and Sexual Rights

We propose that the grounds of reproductive and sexual rights for women consist of four ethical principles: *bodily integrity, personhood, equality,* and *diversity*. Each of these principles can be violated through acts of invasion or abuse—by government officials, clinicians and other providers, male partners, family members, and so on or through acts of omission, neglect, or discrimination by public (national or international) authorities. Each also raises dilemmas and contradictions that can be resolved only under radically different social arrangements from those now prevailing in most of the world.

Bodily Integrity

Perhaps more than the other three principles, the principle of bodily integrity, or the right to security in and control over one's body, lies at the core of reproductive and sexual freedom. As suggested in our introduction, this principle is embedded in the historical development of ideas of the self and citizenship in Western political culture. Yet it also transcends any one culture or region, insofar as some version of it informs all opposition to slavery and other involuntary servitude, torture, rape, and every form of illegitimate assault and violence. As the Declaration of the International Women's Year Conference in Mexico City put it in 1975, "the human body, whether that of women or men, is inviolable and respect for it is a fundamental element of human dignity and freedom" (quoted in Freedman and Isaacs 1993).

To affirm the right of women to "control over" or "ownership of" their bodies does not mean that women's bodies are mere things, separate from themselves or isolated from social networks and communities. Rather, it connotes the body as an integral part of one's self, whose health and wellness (including sexual pleasure) are a necessary basis for active participation in social life. Bodily integrity, then, is not just an individual but a social right, since without it women cannot function as responsible community members (Freedman and Isaacs 1993; Petchesky 1990, 1994). Yet in its specific applications, the bodily integrity principle reminds us that while reproductive and sexual rights are necessarily social, they are also irreducibly *personal.* While they can never be realized without attention to economic development, political empowerment, and cultural diversity, ultimately their site is individual women's bodies (DAWN 1993; Petchesky 1990).

Bodily integrity includes both "a woman's right *not to be alienated from her sexual and reproductive capacity* (e.g., through coerced sex or marriage,... [genital mutilation], denial of access to birth control, sterilization without informed consent, prohibitions on homosexuality) and...her right to the *integrity of her physical person* (e.g., freedom from sexual violence, from false imprisonment in the home, from unsafe contraceptive methods, from unwanted pregnancies or coerced childbearing, from unwanted medical interventions)" (Dixon-Mueller 1993)....

But bodily integrity also implies *affirmative* rights to enjoy the full potential of one's body—for health, procreation, and sexuality. Each of these raises a host of complex questions we can only touch upon here. In regard to health, the very term "integrity" connotes *wholeness*—treating the body and its present needs as a unity, not as piecemeal mechanical functions or fragments....

The question of whether there is a "fundamental right to procreate" based in one's biological reproductive capacity is clearly more complicated than whether one has a right, as a matter of bodily integrity, to prevent or terminate a pregnancy. Yet we can recognize that childbearing has consequences for others besides an individual woman, man, or lineage without subscribing to the claim that women have a duty to society (or the planet!) to abstain from reproducing. Such a duty could begin to exist only when all women are provided sufficient resources for their well-being, viable work alternatives, and a cultural climate of affirmation outside of childbearing so that they no longer depend on children for survival and dignity (Berer 1990; Freedman and Isaacs 1993). And even then, antinatalist policies that depend on coercion or discriminate against or target particular groups would be unacceptable.

Our hesitancy about a "right to procreate" is not based on any simple correlation between population growth, environmental degradation, and women's fertility,...rather, it comes from apprehensions about how patriarchal kinship systems throughout history have used such claims to confine and subordinate women, who alone have bodies that can be impregnated. Procreative rights are, however, an important part of reproductive and sexual rights. They include the right to participate in the basic human practice of raising and nurturing children; the right to bring wanted pregnancies to term in conditions of safety, decency, and good health, and to raise one's children in such conditions; and the right of gay and lesbian families to bear, foster, or adopt children in the same dignity as other families. They also include a transformation in the prevailing gender division of labor so that men are assigned as much responsibility for children's care as women.

Finally, what shall we say of the body's capacity for sexual pleasure and the right to express it in diverse and nonstigmatized ways? If the bodily integrity principle implies such a right, as we believe, its expression surely becomes more complicated and fraught with dangers for women and men in the context of rising prevalence of HIV and STD infection (Berer 1993a; DAWN 1993). In addition to these immediate dangers—compounded by the now well-documented fact that many STDs increase women's susceptibility to HIV—there is the "vicious cycle" in which "women suffering the consequences of sexually transmitted disease find themselves in a social circumstance that further increases their risk of exposure to sexually transmitted infections and their complications" (Elias 1991). This cycle currently affects Sub-Saharan African women most drastically, but is rapidly becoming a worldwide phenomenon. It includes women's lack of sexual self-determination; the high risk they incur of infertility and ectopic pregnancy from STD infection; their dependence on men and in-laws for survival; the threat of ostracism or rejection by the family or male partner following infection or infertility; then the threat of unemployment, impoverishment, and prostitution, followed by still greater exposure to STD and HIV infection (Elias 1991; Wasserheit 1993).

The global crisis of HIV and AIDS complicates but does not diminish the right of all people to responsible sexual pleasure in a supportive social and cultural environment. For women and men of diverse sexual orientations to be able to express their sexuality without fear or risk of exclusion, illness, or death requires sex education and male and female resocialization on a hitherto unprecedented scale. This is why bodily integrity has a necessary social rights dimension that, now more than ever, is a matter of life and death.

Personhood

Listening to women is the key to honoring their moral and legal personhood—that is, their right to self-determination. This means treating them as principal actors and decisionmakers in matters of reproduction and sexuality—as subjects, not merely objects, and as ends, not only means, of population and family planning policies. As should be clear from our earlier discussion emphasizing a relational-interactive model of women's reproductive decisions, our concept of decisionmaking autonomy implies respect for how women make decisions, the values they bring to bear, and the networks of others they choose to consult; it does not imply a notion of solitude or isolation in "individual choices." Nor does it preclude full counseling about risks and options regarding contraception, prenatal care, childbearing, STDs and HIV, and other aspects of gynecologic health.

At the clinical level, for providers to respect women's personhood requires that they trust and take seriously women's desires and experiences, for example, concerning contraceptive side effects. When clinicians trivialize women's complaints about such symptoms as headaches, weight gain, or menstrual irregularity, they violate this principle. Qualitative studies of clinical practices regarding the use of Norplant® in the Dominican Republic, Egypt, Indonesia, and Thailand found that women's concerns about irregular bleeding were often dismissed, and their requests for removal of the implant not honored (Zimmerman et al. 1990).

Respect for personhood also requires that clients be offered a complete range of safe options, fully explained, without major discrepancies in cost or government subsidization. When some contraceptive methods are *de facto* singled out for promotion (for instance, long-acting implants or sterilization), or clinical practices manifest strong pronatalist or antinatalist biases (as in programs governed by demographic targets), or safe legal abortion is denied, respect for women's personhood is systematically abused. "Quality of care" guidelines, which originated in women's health activism and were codified by Judith Bruce, reflect not only good medical practice but an ethic of respect for personhood (Bruce 1990; DAWN 1993; Jain, Bruce, and Mensch 1992; Mintzes 1992).

At the level of national and international policies and programs, treating women as persons in sexual and reproductive decisionmaking means assuring that women's organizations are represented and heard in the processes where population and health policies are made and that effective mechanisms of public accountability, in which women participate, are established to guard against abuses. It also means abandoning demographic targets in the service of economic growth, cost containment, or ethnic or nationalist rivalries and replacing them with reproductive health and women's empowerment goals (see Jain and Bruce 1994). Demographic targeting policies that encourage the use of material incentives or disincentives often work to manipulate or coerce women, particularly those who are poor, into accepting fertility-control methods they might otherwise reject, thus violating their decisionmaking autonomy.

The question of "incentives" is clearly a complicated one, since in some circumstances they may expand women's options and freedom (Dixon-Mueller 1993). Feminists and human rights activists have justly criticized programs that promote particular fertility control methods or antinatalist campaigns through monetary inducements or clothing to "acceptors," fines or denials of child care or health benefits to "offenders," or quotas reinforced with "bonuses" for village officials or clinic personnel (Freedman and Isaacs 1993; Ravindran 1993). What would be our reaction, however, to a system of women-managed comprehensive care clinics that provided child care or free transportation to facilitate clinic visits? A distinct difference exists between these two cases, since the former deploys the targeting and promotional strategies that undermine women's personhood, whereas the latter incorporates the kinds of enabling conditions we earlier found necessary for equalizing women's ability to exercise their reproductive rights. To distinguish *supportive* or *empowering* conditions from *coercive* incentives or disincentives, we need to assure that they respect all four ethical principles of reproductive rights (bodily integrity, personhood, equality, and diversity). When poor or incarcerated women are expected to purchase other rights "for the price of their womb" (for example, a job for sterilization or release from prison for Norplant®), "incentives" become corrupted into bribes (Williams 1991). Women's social location determines whether they are able to make sexual and reproductive decisions with dignity.

Equality

The principle of equality applies to sexual and reproductive rights in two main areas: relations between men and women (gender divisions), and relations among women (conditions such as class, age, nationality, or ethnicity that divide women as a group). With respect to the former, the impetus behind the idea of reproductive rights as it emerged historically was to remedy the social bias against women inherent in their lack of control over their fertility and their assignment to primarily reproductive roles in the gender division of labor. "Reproductive rights" (or "birth control") was one strategy within a much larger agenda for making women's position in society equal to men's. At the same time, this notion contains the seeds of a contradiction, since women alone are the ones who get pregnant, and in that sense, their situation—and degree of risk—can never be reducible to men's.

This tension, which feminists have conceptualized in the debate over equality versus "difference," becomes problematic in the gender-neutral language of most United Nations documents pertaining to reproductive rights and health. For example, article 16(e) of the Convention on the Elimination of All Forms of Discrimination against Women (CEDAW) gives men and women "*the same rights* to decide freely and responsibly on the number and spacing of their children and to have access to the information, education and means to enable them to exercise these rights [emphasis added]." Might this article be used to mandate husbands' consent to abortion or contraception? Why should men and women have "the same" rights with regard to reproduction when, as not only child-bearers but those who in most societies have responsibility for children's care, women have so much greater stake in the matter—when, indeed, growing numbers of women raise children without benefit of male partners? (The language of "couples" in family planning literature raises the same kinds of questions.)

If we take the issue of contraception as an illustration, the principle of equality would seem to require that, where contraceptive methods carry risks or provide benefits, those risks and benefits must be distributed on a fair basis between women and men, as well as among women. This would suggest a population policy that puts greater emphasis on encouraging male responsibility for fertility control and scientific research into effective "male" contraceptives. In fact, many women express a sense of unfairness that they are expected to bear nearly all the medical risks and social responsibility for avoiding unwanted pregnancies (Pies n.d.). But such a policy might also conflict with the basic right of women to control their own fertility and the need many women feel to preserve that control, sometimes in conditions of secrecy and without "equal sharing" of risks.

On the surface, this dilemma seems to be a contradiction within feminist goals, between the opposing principles of equality and personhood. The feminist agenda that privileges women's control in reproductive rights would seem to reinforce a gender division of labor that confines women to the domain of reproduction. Yet exploring the problem more deeply reveals that women's distrust of men's taking responsibility for fertility control and reluctance to relinquish methods women control are rooted in other kinds of gendered power imbalances that work against a "gender equality" approach to reproductive health policies. These include social systems that provide no educational or economic incentives toward men's involvement in child care and cultural norms that stigmatize women's sexuality outside the bounds of heterosexual monogamy. Thus, while a reproductive health policy that encourages the development and use of "male methods" of contraception may increase the total range of "choices," in the long run it will not help to realize women's social rights nor gender equality until these larger issues are also addressed.

Applying the equality principle in the implementation of sexual and reproductive rights also requires attention to potential inequalities *among* women. This means, at the least, that risks and benefits must be distributed on a fair basis and that providers and policy makers must respect women's decision-making authority without regard to differences of class, race, ethnic origin, age, marital status, sexual orientation, nationality, or region (North-South). Returning to our example of contraception, there is certainly ample evidence that access to safe methods of fertility control can play a major role in improving women's health, but some contraceptive methods can have negative consequences for some women's health (National Research Council 1989). Issues of equal treatment may arise when certain methods—particularly those that carry medical risks or whose long-term effects are not well known—are tested, targeted, or promoted primarily among poor women in Southern or Northern countries. Indeed, when clinical trials are conducted among poor urban women, who tend to move frequently or lack transportation, the necessary conditions for adequate medical follow-up may not exist, and thus the trials themselves may be in violation of the equality principle. Meanwhile, issues of discrimination arise when safe, beneficial methods such as condoms or diaphragms, low-dose hormonal pills, or hygienic abortion facilities are available only to women with the financial resources to pay for them.

For governments and international organizations to promote sexual and reproductive rights in ways that respect equality among women requires addressing at least the most blatant differences in power and resources that divide women within countries and internationally. In the case of safe, effective methods of contraception, laws that guarantee the "freedom" of all women to use whatever methods they "choose" are gratuitous without geographic access, high-quality services and supplies, and financing for all women who need them. We are saying that the economic and political changes necessary to create such conditions are a matter not just of development, but of (social) *rights*; indeed, they are a good example of why development *is* a human right and why women's reproductive rights are inseparable from this equation (Sen 1992).

Diversity
While the equality principle requires the mitigation of inequities among women in their access to services or their treatment by health providers and policy makers, the diversity principle requires respect for differences among women—in values, culture, religion, sexual orientation, family or medical condition, and so on. The universalizing language of international human rights instruments, reflecting a Western liberal tradition, needs to be reshaped to encompass such differences (see

Freedman and Isaacs 1993; Cook 1993a, 1993b). While defending the universal applicability of sexual and reproductive rights, we must also acknowledge that such rights often have different meanings, or different points of priority, in different social and cultural contexts.

Differences in cultural or religious values, for example, affect attitudes toward children and childbearing, influencing how diverse groups of women think about their entitlements in reproduction. In her study of market women in Ile-Ife, Nigeria, anthropologist Tola Olu Pearce (1994) found that the high value placed on women's fertility and the subordination of individual desires to group welfare in Yoruba tradition made the notion of a woman's individual right to choose alien. Yet Yoruba women in Ile-Ife have also used methods of fertility control to space their children and "avoid embarrassment" for untold generations and no doubt consider it part of their collective "right" as women to do so. A similar communal ethic governing women's reproductive decisions emerges in a study of Latina single mothers in East Harlem (New York City), who consider their "reproductive rights" to include the right to receive public assistance in order to stay home and care for their children (Benmayor, Torruellas, and Juarbe 1992).

Local religious and cultural values may also shape women's attitudes toward medical technologies or their effects, such as irregular menstrual bleeding. Clinic personnel involved in disseminating Norplant® have not always understood the meanings menstrual blood may have in local cultures and the extent to which frequent bleeding—a common side effect of Norplant®—may result in the exclusion of women from sex, rituals, or community life (Zimmerman et al. 1990). Imposing standards of what is "normal" or "routine" bleeding (for example, to justify refusal to remove the implant upon request) could constitute a violation of the diversity principle, as well as the bodily integrity and personhood principles.[5]

It is important to distinguish between the feminist principle of respect for difference and the tendency of male-dominated governments and fundamentalist religious groups of all kinds to use "diversity" and "autonomy of local cultures" as reasons to deny the universal validity of women's human rights.[6] In all the cases cited above, women's assertion of their particular needs and values, rather than denying the universal application of rights, clarifies what those rights mean in specific settings. Women's multiple identities—whether as members of cultural, ethnic, and kinship groups, or as people with particular religious and sexual orientations, and so forth—challenge human rights discourse to develop a language and methodology that are pluralistic yet faithful to the core principles of equality, personhood, and bodily integrity. This means that the diversity principle is never absolute, but always conditioned upon a conception of human rights that promotes women's development and respects their self-determination. Traditional patriarchal practices that subordinate women—however local or time-worn, or enacted by women themselves (for example, genital mutilation)—can never supersede the social responsibility of governments and intergovernmental organizations to enforce women's equality, personhood, and bodily integrity, through means that respect the needs and desires of the women most directly involved.

Bringing a Feminist Social Rights Approach to Population and Development Policies

The above analysis has attempted to show that the individual (liberty) and the social (justice) dimensions of rights can never be separated, as long as resources and power remain unequally distributed in most societies. Thus the affirmative obligations of states and international organizations become paramount, since the ability of individuals to exercise reproductive and sexual rights depends on a range of conditions not yet available to many people and impossible to access without public support. In this respect, the language of "entitlement" seems to us overly narrow, insofar as it implies claims made by individuals on the state without expressing the idea of a mutual *public* interest in developing empowered, educated, and politically responsible citizens, including all women. Likewise, the language of "choosing freely and responsibly" still contained in most international instruments that address family planning and reproductive rights is at best ambiguous and at worst evasive (see Boland, Rao, and Zeidenstein 1994). What does it mean to choose "responsibly"? Who, in fact, is responsible, and what are the necessary conditions—social, economic, cultural—for individuals to act in socially responsible ways? The correlative duties associated with sexual and reproductive rights belong not only to the bearers of those rights, but to the governmental and intergovernmental agencies charged with their enforcement....

Documents developed in preparation for the 1994 International Conference on Population and Development (ICPD), in Cairo, have begun to reflect the vision of reproductive and sexual rights as social rights that we have presented here. This is true not only of documents produced by women's NGOs, but also of official conference preparatory meetings and summaries, where for the first time in international population discourse, issues of gender equality and women's empowerment overshadow demographic targets and economic growth and are recognized as part of "sustainable development."...

... Years of organizing and advocacy by women's health groups throughout the world have clearly had an important effect *at the level of official rhetoric* on intergovernmental forums concerned with "population" issues. To what extent are we likely to see governments, UN agencies, and international population organizations move from awareness to action to translate this rhetoric into concrete policies and programs that truly benefit women?

Many women's health groups, in both the South and the North, are concerned that feminist-sounding rhetoric is being used by international population agencies to legitimate and gloss over what remain instrumentalist and narrowly quantitative ends. Perceiving the history of population control policies and programs as all too frequently oblivious to women's needs and the ethical principles outlined above, they fear the language of reproductive rights and health may simply be co-opted by the Cairo process to support business as usual.

Our position is slightly more optimistic but nonetheless cautious. Feminists are putting pressure on population- and family-planning agencies to acknowledge women's self-defined needs and our conceptions of reproductive and sexual rights. This should move us closer to social and policy changes that empower women, but whether it does will depend on even more concerted action by women's NGOs, including alliances with many other groups concerned with health, development, and human rights. One such action should be to insist on full participation by women's rights and health groups in all relevant decisionmaking bodies and accountability mechanisms. In the long run, however, it is not enough that we call population agencies to account. To bridge the gap between rhetoric about reproductive and sexual rights and the harsh realities most women face demands a much larger vision. We must integrate, but not subordinate, those rights with health and development agendas that will radically transform the distribution of resources, power, and wellness within and among all the countries of the world (DAWN 1993; Sen 1992). These are the enabling conditions to transform rights into lived capacities. For women, Cairo is just a stop along the way.

Notes

1. The term seems to have originated with the founding of the Reproductive Rights National Network (R2N2) in the United States in 1979. R2N2 activists brought it to the European-based International Campaign for Abortion Rights in the early 1980s; at the International Women and Health Meeting in Amsterdam in 1984, the Campaign officially changed its name to the Women's Global Network for Reproductive Rights (Beret 1993b). Thereafter, the concept rapidly spread throughout women's movements in the South (for example, in 1985, under the influence of feminist members who had attended the Amsterdam meeting, the Brazilian Health Ministry established the Commission on the Rights of Human Reproduction). See also Garcia-Moreno and Claro 1994.

2. In fact, the principle of "ownership of one's body and person" has much deeper roots in the history of radical libertarian and democratic thought in Western Europe. Historian Natalie Zemon Davis traced this idea to sixteenth-century Geneva, when a young Lyonnaise girl, brought before the Protestant elders for sleeping with her fiancé before marriage, invoked what may have been a popular slogan: "*Paris est au roi, et mon corps est à moi.*" (Paris is the king's, and my body is mine). The radical Levellers in seventeenth-century England developed the notion of a "property in one's person," which they used to defend their members against arbitrary arrest and imprisonment (Petchesky 1994). But the principle is not only of European derivation. Gandhi's concept of *Brahmacharya*, or "control over the body," was rooted in Hindu ascetic traditions and the Vedas' admonition to preserve the body's vital fluids. Like that of nineteenth-century feminists and the Catholic church, Gandhi's concept was theoretically gender-neutral, requiring both men and women to engage in sexual restraint except for purposes of procreation (Fischer 1962; O'Flaherty 1980). Islamic law goes further toward a sexually-affirmative concept of self-ownership. Quranic provisions not only entitle women to sexual satisfaction in marriage, as well as condoning abortion and contraception; they also allow that, upon divorce—which wives as well as husbands may initiate—a woman regains her body (Ahmed 1992; Musallam 1983; Ruthven 1984).

3. In Latin America, a new resolution of the Colombian Ministry of Public Health "orders all health institutions to ensure women the right to decide on all issues that affect their health, their life, and their sexuality, and guarantees rights 'to information and orientation to allow the exercise of free, gratifying, responsible sexuality which cannot be tied to maternity' " (quoted in Cook 1993a). In North Africa, Dr. Hind Khattab's field research among rural Egyptian women

has revealed strong sentiments of their sexual entitlement to pleasure and gratification from husbands (Khattab 1993).

4. Feminist theory and practice have witnessed a long history of division over this question. Whether with regard to protective labor legislation, prostitution, pornography, or providing contraceptive implants to teenagers or poor women, conflicts between "liberals" (advocates of "freedom to choose") and "radicals" (advocates of social protection or legal prohibition) have been bitter and protracted.

5. Not only clinicians but feminist activists maybe guilty of imposing their own values and failing to respect diversity. Feminist groups that condemn all reproductive technologies (for examples, technologies that artificially assist fertility) as instruments of medical control over women against "nature" ignore the ways that such technologies may expand the rights of particular women (for example, lesbians seeking pregnancy through artificial insemination or in vitro fertilization).

6. It seems crucial to us to recognize that religious fundamentalist movements are on the upswing in all the world's regions and major religions—Catholicism, Protestantism, Judaism, and Hinduism as well as Islam. Despite vast cultural and theological differences, these fundamentalisms share a view of women as reproductive vessels that is antipathetic to any notion of women's reproductive rights. In an otherwise excellent discussion of the clash between religious and customary law and human rights, Lynn Freedman and Stephen Isaacs (1993) place undue emphasis on Muslim countries and Islamic law.

11.
AFRICAN FEMINISM: TOWARD A NEW POLITICS OF REPRESENTATION
Gwendolyn Mikell

I am convinced that I am observing the birth of feminism on the African continent—a feminism that is political, pragmatic, reflexive, and group oriented.[1] These observations have grown out of my work in various parts of West Africa, in the 1970s and 1980s, and in South Africa, in 1992; out of my dialogues with women from Kenya and other parts of the continent; and most recently out of workshops on women and legal change that I conducted in Liberia, Sierra Leone, and Nigeria during May 1994. My research and involvement with Africa goes back to the early 1970s, when the charismatic energy of nationalist leaders like Kwame Nkrumah and Julius Nyerere had faded, the disillusionment with modernization and the capitalist economy was strong, and a rash of military coups marked the emergence of a new crisis orientation. In the nationalist phase, women had played crucial roles, but their importance in politics had waned by 1971 when I began research on cocoa farmers in Ghana and visited many West African countries. I have watched the episodic rise of women's movements during the United Nations Decade of Women (1975–1985) and during the difficult economic crises and structural adjustment program experiments of the 1980s, but I see the peaking of a new feminism now as African states reinvent themselves in the 1990s.

This recognition of an emerging African feminism has been met with unanticipated enthusiasm by some of my Japanese, female, African studies colleagues who pursue autonomy within their own unique cultural environment, with ambivalence by some colleagues who work in Africa, and with amused tolerance on the part of many Western feminists who saw it as a moot point which I had (fortunately) resolved in the affirmative. There were relatively few African women who used the term "feminism" prior to the 1990s, and those who do so now are explicit in acknowledging the breadth that appears within it. For me, the recognition of a new African feminism represents a gargantuan change, because previously I was unwilling, for several reasons, to apply the feminist label to the African women's movement.

First, there was the recurring issue of hegemony. To a large extent I responded to the anger many African women have felt toward what they perceived as attempts by Western academics and activists to co-opt them into a movement defined by extreme individualism, by militant opposition to patriarchy, and, ultimately, by hostility to males. This has been reflected most cogently in the reaction of African women writers, such as Buchi Emecheta, to the persistent question from Western audiences about why they refused to call themselves feminist. Certainly, the writings of sociologist/novelist Buchi Emecheta (such as *The Bride Price*) portray both traditional and modern African women searching for fulfillment while attempting to overcome oppression by familial and patriarchal elements within their own cultures. In Emecheta's book *Head Above Water*, we see that her own life also reflects such struggles. However, when asked about the feminist label in 1994, Emecheta's heated response was: "I have never called myself a feminist. Now if you choose to call me a feminist, that is your business; but I don't subscribe to the feminist idea that all men are brutal and repressive and we must reject them. Some of these men are my brothers and fathers and sons. Am I to reject them too?"[2]

Second, I was exercising caution born of my knowledge that what we called the African women's "movement" actually consisted of a broad continuum. The Nigerian researcher and writer Nina Mba, in her *Nigerian Women Mobilized* (1982), has shown that separate-gender, "dual-sex" organizing has generated the emergence of a broad spectrum of women's associations. This continuum includes women's associations with largely traditional frames of reference, the organization and activities of educated women who were often engaged in overtly political or advocacy work, as well as the activities of urban women whose realities straddle these cultural worlds. Neither end of the African continuum aligns with the Western feminist continuum, but it does reflect African realities, as Florence Abena Dolphyne, the Ghanaian linguist and women's development organizer, points out in her 1991 book, *The Emancipation of Women: An African Perspective.*[3]

Third, I was resisting the projection of a dichotomy on to this continuum, with educated and elite women seen as ideologically far more advanced (and therefore feminist) and rural/ordinary African women seen as parochial and prefeminist. Class differences do exist in the positions that African women have taken, as well as in their degrees of radicalism and types of activism, but collaboration between classes still occurs. It has been my position that an ideological dichotomy is largely negated by African cultural traditions which legitimate female organizations and collective actions by women in the interest of women,[4] an awareness shared by women at all points along the continuum. This continuum appears to be grounded in African communal, historical, symbolic, an experiential constructs, rather than in cultural constructs based on Western individualism and competition.

The strategic consensus that I see emerging among African women in many parts of the continent is an impressive one. The consensus, which many label "feminist" given the new meanings with which they are endowing the term, is reflected in Filomina Steady's description of African feminism as "dealing with multiple oppressions" and as dealing with woman first and foremost as human, rather than sexual beings.[5] However, I point out that as new subtleties in African women's realities surface, politics is becoming the central point around which a new feminist consensus is emerging. I believe that the pragmatics of women's political representation in the 1990s are shaping the emerging African women's movement.

In the early part of this century, women's declining political status was directly related to the oppressive control of the colonial regime. African women took strength from the fact that their participation was essential if their countries were to end the colonial experience and achieve independence. However, after independence, male suppression of African women's political autonomy increased, despite the contributions women had made to nationalist politics and despite state claims to equitable approaches in education, policies, and laws. Given this, much scholarly discussion has been focused on understanding why African women eschewed an explicitly woman-oriented politics, while being victimized by military regimes and oppressed by males in both public and private life.

The results of such questioning have been greater insights into state and gender interactions, but we have little information on women's ideological and practical configurations.[6] I have for some time observed women's groups in West Africa (Ghana, Cote d'Ivoire, Nigeria), where women's organizations and associations have a long history, and I have followed the interactions of African women with the courts, constitutional issues, and new family laws.[7] I have been disturbed by the obstacles that formerly prevented the construction of national woman-oriented social agendas under whatever label. Now women are striving to overcome these obstacles. The growth of active women in development legal programs, of assertive women's movements in a number of countries, especially in Kenya prior to the 1992 elections, and of the African National Congress (ANC) Women's League's demands for greater female political representation in South Africa are positive signs of this feminist emergence.

I suspect that the greater willingness of African women to embrace feminist politics and gender representation in the 1990s is traceable to the current national crises and political transitions[8] which have been occurring throughout the continent over the past fifteen decades.... [I]t is at these crisis/transition points that the disjuncture between the existing sociocultural compacts and modern political realities becomes most visible, and the audible discourse about gender roles alerts us to the subterranean conflicts that are occurring within the society. The heightening of contradictions and gender discourse may actually open up space for the emergence of a new configuration in the various African women's movements.

The 1990s post–cold war environment provides the first chance that most Africans—in particular, women of different ethnic and religious communities—have had to participate in a serious way in deciding the legal and constitutional rights of people in their own countries and the desired forms of government. During the past two decades, the crisis-initiated space expanded, but African women were sometimes hesitant to move into it because they did not want self-interests to take precedence over state interests, they recognized the existence of increasingly complicated "identity politics" (to use Valentine M. Moghadam's term) occurring around them,[9] and they were primarily concerned with resisting what many saw as Western hegemony in the guise of international feminist support. In addition, those market women's groups or elite women's groups, which were the first to attempt to move into this political space, were in many cases ruthlessly crushed by the government or military forces.[10]

But the harsh pressures exerted by contemporary national economic crises and political failures have removed some of women's fears and much of their reluctance to seek public office. African women's psychic involvement with these national and local processes is more clearly visible, as is their desire for equitable change. They appear strengthened in their beliefs that women's performance can be no worse than those of earlier male politicians, and is likely to be considerably better. Many women are saying that more assertive female actions are necessary to ensure gender-balanced approaches in the aftermath of the 1980s' economic collapses, military coups, civil wars, refugee crises, feminization of poverty, and structural adjustment programs.

Women appear aware that the present climate of political experimentation and "democratization," whether resulting from Western pressures or internal shifts within cultural/religious communities, offers them unique political opportunities to alter their sociopolitical positions. Even in the Muslim communities of Nigeria and Sudan,[11] some women are making use of the new political spaces that national crises and elections have created in order to mobilize women to achieve increased status in many areas of life. They, like women in many other areas, are analyzing the ways in which the lack of legal and policy supports may have affected their ability to play roles in development and politics.[12] In addition, it has not escaped their attention that in 1995, the year of the long-anticipated UN Fourth World Conference on Women (the Beijing Conference), women may have a unique opportunity to formulate a feminist agenda which will be seriously discussed....

Now, almost two decades after the beginning of the United Nations Decade of Women, the discourse of African women's activism displays considerable maturation because it contains more explicit gender-political critiques. It is more woman-action and national/global issue oriented. Still, it has retained some of the earlier focus on rectifying inequities in conjugality and domestic relations, particularly in defining women's rights within marriage.[13] There have always been a few self-proclaimed feminists like the Ghanaian writer Ama Ata Aidoo,[14] who assigns some of the responsibility for women's plight to Western hegemony and an embattled African political economy. However, most women activists still hesitate to use the term "feminism," although they are more willing to seek legal change, promote gender equity, and to label their persistent grievances as "human rights" ones. It has become clear that today, even more than in the 1980s, African women are searching for a new deal,[15] and are more willing to work for the eradication of discrimination against women in customary norms, modern law, and social conventions.[16]...

In May 1994 my workshops on sociolegal change in Monrovia (Liberia), Freetown (Sierra Leone), and in various parts of Nigeria offered me an opportunity to have a dialogue with women from a wide variety of groups—craftswomen, churchwomen, teachers, clerks, nongovernmental (NGO) representatives, professors, businesswomen, lawyers, judges, ministers, and first ladies.[17]...

... Perhaps not surprisingly, the African women I met were intrinsically prona-
tal, operating from shared assumptions that African women value marriage and
motherhood. The major areas that women articulated as problematic were domestic relations (problems of marriage and spousal relationships given polygyny and
lineage systems, as well as the monitoring of male responsibilities in the mainte-
nance/custody of children),[18] women's rights of access to property and other
resources,[19] and that controversial category called "privacy" rights (which includes
many sexual and reproductive issues, as well as violence against women).[20]...

... [W]omen were anxious to discuss the heightening of the above problems in
direct correlation to the economic collapse, structural adjustment, constitu-
tional/democratic stalemates, and war which had engulfed the African state. And
they stressed that they would never be able to address them directly unless they
stepped up to the challenge of direct self-representation and involvement in the
political realm.

The word "feminism" was scarcely used, although some men jokingly called us
feminists and other men angrily pinned the label on these workshops; in addition,
the newspapers occasionally referred to the "feminist talks" taking place. However,
the content of the women's discourse made it clear that they wanted change and
were searching for ideas and strategies through which they could achieve it. The
manner in which they discussed women's problems indicated their awareness
of the decreased capacity of traditional systems to respond to their complaints and
the absolute necessity for women's assertive actions in support of specific legal initiatives. In some cases, they reminded each other that modern laws which address
their situation were on the books, although the social environment did not encourage use of legal remedies; and they discussed how such contradictions could be
eliminated.

In Liberia, the ongoing civil war in the countryside and the trauma of displacement, torture, and starvation appeared to have defused many earlier distinctions and inequities among women[21] and radicalized and mobilized women.
Although we think in terms of ethnic/religious differences (Americo-Liberians
versus indigenous peoples) and class differences as separating Liberians, women
sought to coalesce in ways that bypassed the ethnic rivalries implicit in the civil
war. During 1994, Monrovia, the capital city, was protected by the military operations group of the Economic Community of West African States, as well as by the
United Nations Interim Military forces in Liberia. So, it had been possible for
women to set up shelters and job-training programs for women, such as My Sister's
Place, as well as crafts and agricultural training projects, all of which tended to
lessen the socioeconomic class distinctions between women who were involved....

As Liberian women talked about rape of women by troops of all sides, and
about the climate in which male violence against women was tolerated, they voiced
something I was to hear repeated in each place: "Until the government makes an
explicit commitment to the enforcement of basic human rights for women, our
existing legal rights are irrelevant because men know that they do not need to

respect them." Thus, women intended that one of the anticipated fruits of peace was also to be mechanisms that would protect them as they brought charges against assaulters, regardless of whether they were soldiers or husbands.

The challenges of competitions *within* the women's movement were visible in Freetown, Sierra Leone.... Here, feminism was struggling to coalesce but could not do so easily because of divided class and ethnic interests. Educated women were concerned about the political fragmentation and rebel actions which existed throughout the country, a reality which dominated even their organizational meetings and contributed to a sense of helplessness.[22] Rural women, on the other hand, were concerned about violence and the absence of economic stability, both of which were decimating community life....

...It was clear to me that in the face of an emerging feminism, smart state and military leaders may attempt to co-opt or redirect women's movements, perhaps avoiding confrontations on legal, political, and economic issues where leaders anticipate a divide between gender rights, human rights, and national power....

Some of my most fruitful experiences took place in Nigeria, a formerly oil-rich country, the largest in West Africa, which has had a succession of military coups interspersed with short-lived electoral politics in the years since independence. Increasingly, political instability accompanied by economic restructuring and continued conflict with the United States over corruption and drugs has made Nigerians cynical about achieving democracy within African state structures. Within Nigeria, my most exciting discussions occurred in a workshop at the Lakoja State House, in an area bordering Kaduna, where more than fifty women (rural and urban, educated and illiterate, Muslim and Christian) discussed specific problems of concern. Nigeria has a tradition of diverse public and private roles for women,[23] a history of women's activism in the south, and a growing involvement of women in public organizations in Muslim areas of the north, as Ayesha Imam indicates.[24] However, the sheer multicultural nature of the group forced greater clarity in how women defined and thought about the problems faced by different groups of Nigerian women, and it reinforced the important role of culture in advancing or retarding women's progress. Large numbers of Muslim women attended the workshop, and some confided that they were unwilling to speak in public because of their lack of fluency in English or because their support for "feminist causes" might be reported to husbands. But they vigorously nodded their heads in agreement with certain interpretations of women's problems, leaving no confusion about where they stood. A fascinating discussion ensued about how women's activism need not constitute a rejection of religion or culture (although women wanted to see gender equity introduced into particular aspects of community life and national life) and about how material or legal rights for women could influence the culture in more equitable ways.

Nigerian women repeated the comments I had heard voiced in Monrovia about the priority of explicit state recognition of human rights for women. They wanted to see Nigeria publicize its acceptance of the International Convention on Human Rights, its support for women's rights within the 1979 Lagos Plan of

Action, and a national recognition of women's rights under law and constitution, which they think will reinforce other rights within the domestic, economic, and privacy categories outlined above. . . . For northern Nigerian women, more than for any other group of women I encountered, gender liberation was symbolized in a woman's right to operate in public space—to determine for herself whether she would enter the work force or run for public office. They clearly stated that the economic decline had crystallized for them the fact that work outside the home could be a route out of poverty and that male refusal to allow wives to work was an attempt to oppress women. . . .

The emerging African feminism is intensely prodemocratic and supportive of some sort of rapprochement between the pure market economics and "justice economics." They, like their menfolk, believe that there is a link (implicit or explicit) between structural adjustment[25] and stalemated democratization and that recent verbalization of gender-equity goals might be another tool for internal control. . . . Many Liberian, Nigerian, and Sierra Leonean women are beginning to believe that now may be the time to utilize the expanding political space to correct legal inequities related to the control of resources, which made then the paramount victims of the economic crises of the 1980s. Most African women are concerned that their governments see the link between support for women's rights and economic stability for women and the family. . . .

. . . . To a large extent, much of the emerging feminist consciousness and the current movement toward feminist agendas in each country remains hidden—hidden first because the chaotic economic and political conditions there causes primary emphasis to be placed on survival issues. But they also remain hidden because governments allow political and economic events to monopolize national public media space and foreign attention, thus downplaying the cultural and gender developments which they sometimes find troublesome.

Overt and public feminism has its price, but women now seem willing to pay it. When African women's movements seize the space and command attention, they face ostracism and often severe reprisals. Kenyan women proved the most outstanding examples. Wangari Mathai's Green Belt movement began with issues of urban ecology and gradually taught women that they could become shapers of their own agroeconomic destinies. Led by Mathai, this was a grassroots movement among women to reclaim their environment, restore "green spaces" in which they could produce food, and revive women's agrarian strategies which had been of benefit to them and their communities. The movement helped to produce a large woman-oriented constituency for later politicians, but Mathai herself faced imprisonment, harassment, and victimization even as the movement grew. Other issues, such as the privileging of traditional law over modern law as a regulator of women's rights, have emerged in Kenya with the Wambui Otieno case.[26] However, with President Arap Moi's announcement of elections for December 29, 1992, the National Committee on the Status of Women (NCSW) became the beneficiary of Mathai's consciousness raising among women and helped women elect forty-five female civic leaders and six parliamentarians.[27] Despite the fact that women who stood for election faced ostracism and in some cases were raped as punishment, the successful NCSW is involved in planning systematic women's agendas for education, local government, and legal reform.

My point is that the emergence of African feminism has been in accordance with its own internal clock, evolving in dialogue with the cultural contexts from which it has sprung and only cautiously acknowledging individualism. After many years of observing, it is gratifying to see that an internally driven and aggressively democratic politics appears to be characteristic of the African feminism which is emerging across the continent....

In the search for gender equity, this African feminism has the ability to subject indigenous cultural norms, received legal notions, and new state laws to new scrutiny as it assesses whether they are in women's interest. Such behavior has led me to believe that in charting an African course, this will not be a feminism which will fixate on the female "body," champion woman's autonomy from man the "victimizer," or question the value of marriage and motherhood. Admittedly, the implications for female-male relationships remain to be seen. But feminism is to be judged by women's actions, so there seems little doubt that the emerging African feminism will generate positive changes in African political structures and contribute to greater gender equality before the law on the African continent.

Notes

1. Here, feminism is defined as approaches to addressing the unequal status of women relative to men, with the goal of mediating gender differences and providing women access to the repertoire of valued roles and statuses within society....
2. Buchi Emecheta, giving a lecture at Georgetown University in Washington, D.C., on 8 Feb. 1994.
3. See Florence Abena Dolphyne, *The Emancipation of Women: An African Perspective* (Accra: Ghana University Press, 1991). Dolphyne reports that at the 1980 UN conference in Denmark, African women resisted the Western feminist insistence on abolishing female circumcision, and they also refused to abandon their position of criticizing apartheid in South Africa (x–xi).
4. I have written elsewhere about the existence of several traditional cultural models which structured the polity and gender relations and which contained coherent statements about what constitutes political identity, authority, and legitimacy.... See Gwendolyn Mikell, "Introduction," in "African Women: State of Crisis" (Philadelphia: University of Pennsylvania Press, forthcoming 1996).
5. Filomina Chioma Steady, "African Feminism: A Worldwide Perspective," in *Women in Africa and the African Diaspora*, ed. Rosalyn Terborg-Penn, Sharon Harley, and Andrea Benton Rushing (Washington, D.C.: Howard University Press, 1987), 4.
6. Iris Berger and Claire Robertson, *Women and Class in Africa* (New York: Africana Publishing, 1986).
7. Gwendolyn Mikell, "Pleas for Domestic Relief: Akan Women and Family Courts in Ghana," in *Poverty in the 1990s: The Situation of Urban Women*, ed. Fatima Meer (Geneva: UNESCO, 1994), 65–86.
8. Pearl Robinson's notion of the culture of politics (i.e., "political practice that is culturally legitimated and societally validated by local knowledge") meshes nicely with my notions of gender behavior which grows out of preexisting cultural models as they have been elaborated over time. See Pearl Robinson, "Approaches to the Study of Democratization: Scripts in Search of Reality" (paper presented at the African Studies Association meeting in Boston, 5 Dec. 1993).

9. Valentine M. Moghadam, "Preface" in *Identity Politics and Women: Cultural Reassertions and Feminism in International Perspective*, ed. Valentine M. Moghadam (Boulder: Westview Press, 1993).

10. Ann Fraker and Barbara Harrell-Bond, "Rawlings and the 1979 Revolution" (American Field Service Committee Report, no. 4, 1980).

11. Ayesha Imam and Sonya Hale point out the changing configurations of gender within various Islamic cultural/religious constructs and how these respond to altered local circumstances and power relationships, as well as to national politics. Imam emphasizes the plurality of responses from women, with some Muslim women attempting to move toward a more secularist interpretation of women's roles, while others retain more orthodox interpretations of gender roles. Hale argues that different political ideologies have sought to strategically manipulate the image of woman, often conflating it to the essentialist "ideal woman as mother" stereotype in an attempt to further control women's actions. See Ayesha Imam, "Politics, Islam, and Women in Kano, Northern Nigeria" (123–44); and Sonya Hale, "Gender, Religious Identity, and Political Mobilization in Sudan," both in *Identity Politics and Women*.

12. "Women, Legal Reform, and Development in Sub-Saharan Africa," *Findings*, no. 20 (Africa Technical Department, World Bank, July 1994), 1.

13. See Dorothy Dee Vallenga, "Who Is a Wife? Expressions of Heterosexual Conflict in Ghana," in *Female and Male in West Africa*, ed. Christine Oppong (London: Allen & Unwin, 1983), 144–55. See also the case studies on Ghana and Kenya in *Law and the Status of Women: An International Symposium* (New York: Columbia University School of Law, 1977).

14. See Ama Ata Aidoo, "The African Woman Today," *Dissent*, summer 1992, pp. 319–25; and Ama Ata Aidoo, interview by Mary Mackay, in *belles letters*, fall 1993, pp. 33–35.

15. Filomina Chioma Steady, "African Women at the End of the Decade," in *Africa Report* (March-April 1985): 4–8.

16. Although earlier our focus was on the contradictions involved in using received laws or "imposed law," whether derived from colonialism or global influences, the focus is shifting. African women recognize that global interaction is moving local realities in directions which sometimes cannot be adequately addressed by traditional legal norms and may require resorting to several legal levels or systems. Some important questions concern the nature of the syncretism or blending of legal ideas. See Leopold Pospisil, *Anthropology of Law: A Comparative Theory* (New York: Harper & Row, 1970), 97–126; and Richard Abel, "Western Courts in Non-Western Settings: Patterns of Court Use in Colonial and Neo-Colonial Africa," in *The Imposition of Law: Studies in Law and Social Control*, ed. Sandra Burman and Barbara Harrell-Bond (New York: Academic Press, 1979), 167–200.

17. These activities were sponsored by the AMPART lecture program of the United States Information Agency. USIA has helped to support other women and development activities and workshops, particularly in Nigeria.

18. As one example, in terms of domestic rights, the rights of African women as wives and mothers vary depending upon the type of lineage, ethnic, and legal systems they participate in, that is, whether they are Christian, Muslim, or traditionalists, and the degrees of control that husbands acquire over wives and their activities. Of major concern to women were, first, the registration and equalization of marriages, whether they are under ordinance or statute, whether they are Mohammedan, or whether under customary law. Many women felt that one national law would uniformly entitle a wife to specified rights, including the right to make decisions about the conjugal family and residence, and the right to own conjugal or private property. Second, women are concerned about the equality of women in obtaining divorce and equality after divorce. Here, they voice their needs for some guarantees of male contributions to the maintenance and custody of children should the marriage not endure. They do not want men being given the privilege of ownership of the children but not having the legal responsibility to support the children if women are awarded custody.

19. In addition to clear economic rights to produce and own things of value, to inherit and work, women want other social changes which support these economic rights. For example, equality of

spouses, so that no husband "owns" his wife, despite payment of any brideprice; and no husband matters more before the law than the wife. In Nigeria, this concern is a strong one given that under traditional culture, brideprice provides a major incentive for families to give women in arranged marriage, often at a very young age, or to disrupt a girl's education so that she can marry. Many Nigerian women say equality of women will allow them to be equal as spouses. In addition, Nigerian women say they want recognition of the married couple as economic unit, which takes into consideration contributions the wife may have made to existing property that may be owned in the husband's name. They are concerned about situations in which husbands die, and the paternal families take everything including the domicile and its contents, leaving nothing for the wife and children.

20. Noteworthy is that the women did not even raise the issues of women's right to birth control. Although national women's groups often work on family planning and demographic issues, these issues were not even a part of the conversation of the cross-section of women attending these workshops. See Christine Oppong, *Marriage, Parenthood, and Fertility in West Africa* (Canberra: Australian National University Press, 1978). On the other hand, the issue of forced female circumcision and women's objections to it surfaced in Nigeria as a problem that even educated women and their children faced. Interestingly enough, women argued for private diplomatic interventions and the need to educate men about the hazards of clitoridectomy, so that their wives or daughters would face fewer communal pressures, rather than for legal suppression of female circumcision.

21. Jeanette Carter and Joyce Mends-Coles, *Liberian Women: Their Roles in Food Production and Their Educational and Legal Status* (Monrovia: University of Liberia, USAID, 1982). Also see Mary Moran, *Civilized Women: Gender and Prestige in Southeast Liberia* (Ithaca: Cornell University Press, 1990).

22. There have long been women's groups in Sierra Leone, but they were mostly urban Krio organizations of Christian teachers, churchwomen, lawyers, and so forth, who were quite distinct from the African women leaders and chiefs of ethnic and Muslim communities in the interior. See Adelaide M. Cromwell, *An African Victorian Feminist: The Life and Times of Adelaide Smith Casely-Hayford, 1868–1960* (Washington, D.C.: Howard University Press, 1992), 1–17.

23. Bolanle Awe, *Nigerian Women in Historical Perspective* (Lagos: Sankori/Bookcraft, 1992).

24. Imam, 123–44.

25. In the 1980s, in response to plummeting rural production, declining prices for African exports, and rising external debts, the International Monetary Fund and the World Bank devised a generic program of economic adjustment for African countries. Structural adjustment is designed to achieve sectorial balance within the economy by (1) devaluing currency to destroy parallel markets, moderate imports, and encourage diversified exports; (2) privatizing the economy by cutting subsidies for food, social services, such as education and health, and inputs for farming; (3) creating a legal and economic climate encouraging private investment; (4) liberalizing trade by removing import or producer taxes, thus allowing market principles to operate in setting agricultural and other prices; and (5) trimming government bureaucracy, selling many state-owned enterprises, cutting wages, and retrenching government workers. Women were among the most adversely affected by these changes, particularly in the food, health, and education arenas. This was evident in the feminization of poverty during early phases of structural adjustment programs. But the question is whether many foreign assistance projects which incorporate "women and development" components truly aim to assist women economically or aim to gain greater control over domestic political and economic agendas.

26. In Kenya, the 1989 Wambui Otieno case created considerable concern because the widow was prevented from determining the disposition and burial of her husband's body by the claimed rights of the lineage and ethnic community. See Patricia Stamp, "Burying Otieno: Politics of Gender and Ethnicity in Kenya, " *Signs* 16 (summer 1991): 808–45.

27. The National Committee on the Status of Women, headed by Maria Nzomo, held a national conference which drew Kenyan women from all walks of life and helped organize women's workshops and political training exercises all across the country. See Maria Nzomo, ed., *Empowering Kenyan Women: Report of a Seminar on Post Election Women's Agenda-Forward Looking Strategies to 1997 and Beyond* (Nairobi: NCSW, 1993).

12.
ECOFEMINIST APPROPRIATIONS
AND TRANSNATIONAL ENVIRONMENTALISMS
Noël Sturgeon

The image of women as natural environmentalists has gained ascendancy in popular literature and has been deployed effectively in internationalist political contexts. At the same time, the strong postmodernist turn in contemporary cultural, anthropological, and feminist theory has created an almost automatic rejection of this kind of ecofeminist rhetoric. As I've worked on a study of contemporary U.S. ecofeminist and its interaction with international feminist movements, I've found that ecofeminists who portray women as in their essence closer to nature have been rigorously criticized (Brinda Rao 1991; Bina Agarwal 1992; Cecile Jackson 1993; and Melissa Leach 1994).

In this paper, I will quickly sketch the critique of certain essentialist constructions of Third-World[1] and Native-American women that predominated among U.S. ecofeminists in the late 1980s and early 1990s, essentialisms that I elsewhere call "ecofeminist natures" (Sturgeon 1997). Not satisfied simply to critique these essentialisms, I will then speculate on their function within a particular hegemonic context in post–Cold War international politics that I call "globalizing environmentalisms." During the Cold War, "universal" discourses about freedom, democracy, and human rights were often used to justify Western exploitation of Third World countries in the name of containing Communism. In a post-Communist world, environmentalist discourse is sometimes used as a new justification for the imbalanced relationship between the West and the Third World. Western countries are presented as locations of sane, world-saving scientific and political practices, while Third-World countries are backwards, polluting, and dangerous locations in need of international environmental policing.

We must carefully judge environmentalist discourses and practices, including ecofeminist ones, in the context of this post–Cold War political arena. We cannot judge them simply in terms of abstract scholarly critiques. My argument here is that we should pay attention to the difference between academic and activist arenas. In academic arenas, essentialist rhetorics are problematic because they produce bad scholarship, ignoring important differences within groups of women. In activist arenas, essentialist discourses become problematic when they set up exclusionary categories. At the same time, making claims, even essentialist ones, about the existence of such collectivities as "women" has contributed to the creation of political movements oriented toward protecting the environment, as well as other movements. These movements intervene effectively in on-going contests over power, influence, resource exploitation, and labor processes.

Therefore, though I am theoretically and politically sympathetic to anti-essentialist critiques, I believe that sometimes they can have damaging political consequences, dividing progressive academic intellectuals and feminist environmental activists. Anti-essentialist critiques of social movements undercut the rhetorical claims of these movements and expose their strategies to the powers they oppose. These critiques hamper our ability to understand social movements within their political contexts. Here, ecofeminism can serve as a case study to help us address this question.

The deployment of essentialist visions of women within ecofeminist rhetorics can be a Western appropriation of romanticized "indigenous" peoples, but it can also be an attempt by disempowered Third World women to intervene in the policies and plans of international political elites. It is a tactic that can create "two-way streets" between Western feminists and Third World feminists.[2] That is to say, even though essentialisms may be a part of the dominant and oppressive ideology, they can facilitate communication among subordinate groups and provide new tools for resistance to power (Tsing 1997). Ecofeminism is one political location, though not the only one, in which international feminist coalitions can be formed, despite, and sometimes through, academically problematic essentialist claims about women's stake in environmentalism. To see these possibilities, we have to think through the difference between academic arenas and activist arenas.

"Indigenous Women" as the "Ultimate Ecofeminists"

In the latter half of the 1980s U.S. ecofeminists produced a common set of discourses about difference that idealized "indigenous" women as symbolic representatives of the movement. Often the essentialism was not explicitly stated by ecofeminists but was an outcome of the reliance of white U.S. ecofeminists on activism by Native American and Third World women as examples of ecofeminist practice. Essentialism is the practice of making generalized claims about a group based on notions of an essential, inherent similarity. Such generalized claims assume common characteristics within a group, making it impossible to identify and evaluate important differences among the group's members. An essentialist approach creates exclusionary barriers between groups that display particular characteristics and those that don't. For example, arguments that assume all women are nurturant mothers excludes women who are not mothers. The quality of being a nurturing mother is posited as a natural fact rather than a historically constructed social characteristic, one that has been used to limit women's activity to the domestic sphere. Further, essentialist discourses problematically portray social differences as a result of inherent qualities instead of the result of inequalities of power. As Laura Pulido points out, "Instead of examining how or why various constellations of wealth and power result in different environmental practices, cultural essentialism tends to view variations in environmental practices as originating in 'natural' ethnic or cultural differences" (Pulido 1998: 294).

Third World women are used as symbols for environmental sustainability by white ecofeminists, without respect to the particularity of these women's lives and choices. For example, Irene Diamond, a white U.S. ecofeminist, writes about the slogan, "Green Earth, Women's Power, Human Liberation," belonging to Stri Mukti Sangarsh Calval, the Women's Liberation Struggle Movement in Maharashta: "When I first heard this plea...I was thrilled. It seemed that in the United States, where identities are fractured and thinking compartmentalized we no longer had access to such a humanistic vision...It is not accidental that we find this grounded, Earth-based, hope for freedom and change in a cultural and economic setting where ecological wisdom derives from the practices of daily living in rural communities" (Diamond 1994: 140–41).

To illustrate the strand of ecofeminist theory, prominent in the late 1980s and early 1990s, that privileges "indigenous women" as the "ultimate ecofeminists," I examine two important ecofeminist anthologies, the first published in 1989 (Plant, *Healing the Wounds: The Promise of Ecofeminism*) and the second in 1990 (Diamond and Orenstein, *Reweaving the Web: The Emergence of Ecofeminism*). The "discourse of indigeneity" is prominent in these texts. Native American women are frequently held up as exemplars for white ecofeminists. The covers of both books reference Native American women. In addition to the inclusion of Native American women as authors (even when, as in the case of Marie Wilson, they specifically do not identify as ecofeminists, let alone feminists),[3] white authors present themselves as privy to Native American cultures in ways that allow them to hold them up as ecological resources for white ecofeminists. We are presented, for example, with a white woman who goes on a Native American "vision quest" (Hamilton 1989), or with Dolores La Chapelle, who writes about Native American cultures as "ecosystem cultures" (La Chapelle 1989).

In addition to frequent references to Native American women, these texts tend to reduce Third World women to peasant or tribal Asian Indian women. But why do Indian women serve as the primary example of Third World women? Because India has developed both feminist and environmentalist movements, Indian women have emerged as significant global spokespersons, and they have publicized women's actions to defend the environment. Thus, both *Healing* and *Reweaving* contain several articles by Asian Indian authors dealing specifically with women's environmental struggles, as well as other examples of women's activism, including struggles around the Bhopal toxic-release catastrophe, industrialized fishing in Southern India (Philipose 1989), and women's protection of village forests in numerous locations (Bhatt 1989). Furthermore, *Healing* popularizes the argument of Indian author Corrine Kumar D'Souza's that the metaphor of the "the South" is a way of breaking up the dualistic, linear models of "the East" and "the West" (D'Souza 1989). D'Souza's article does not examine specific activist examples, but rather offers broad claims in an attempt to paint a broad canvas of Third World activism as sources of inspiration for ecofeminism.

But it is the Chipko movement, the protest of village women against the commercial logging of forests in the Gharwal Hills, rather than other possible examples of Indian women's activism, that captures the imagination of the authors in both texts. It is not that other kinds of activism are not examined; the two books, especially *Reweaving*, are rich with various kinds of "ecofeminist" activism. However, references to Chipko, which quickly attained talismanic status in ecofeminist writings of this period, are threaded throughout these texts. The other most common Third World example is Wangari Maathai's Green Belt Movement in Kenya, in which rural women are involved in a program of tree-planting to resist desertification and malnutrition (Wallace 1993). But the story of the Green Belt movement is not elaborated in these anthologies in the way Chipko is, and the image of women planting trees is not made to carry the same symbolic force as the image of women "hugging" trees. Chipko, on the other hand, reappears in a consistent way, often as the only "Third World" example. . . .

To explain this frequent use of Chipko in ecofeminist writings of this time period, we need to look at the writings of Vandana Shiva. In 1988, a year before the publication of *Healing*, Vandana Shiva, an Indian theoretical physicist turned environmentalist researcher, published her book, *Staying Alive: Women, Ecology, and Survival in India*. This book analyzed the failure of the Green Revolution in the Third World, and cited in particular its negative effects on rural women, as a symptom of the patriarchal capitalist project of development, which she calls "maldevelopment." Shiva's analysis was extremely influential among U.S. ecofeminists. She combined environmentalist and feminist analyses of Westernized development policies persuasively and passionately. She also connected her analyses with elements of feminist spirituality and with the valorization of "indigeneity." For Shiva, the "death of the feminine principle," was a necessary part of the project of "maldevelopment." The "feminine principle" was seen as keeping Indian culture in balance with nature, and Shiva meant by it not some notion of matriarchy, or Goddess worship, but the idea of gender complementarity in sexual divisions of labor. The resulting social and political equality-in-difference, she argues, existed in precolonial Indian subsistence cultures, which she claims were more ecological than that of Western patriarchal capitalism. "[Maldevelopment] ruptures the cooperative unity of the masculine and feminine, and puts men, deprived of the feminine principle, above and thus separated from nature and women" (Shiva 1990: 193).

In crucial ways, Shiva's argument parallels those of ecofeminists and feminist theologians who look to a prehistoric European past or Native American tribal cultures for the existence of "ultimate ecofeminists.". . .

Shiva offers the story of the Chipko movement as an example of women reclaiming the "feminine principle" in resistance to patriarchal capitalist development. In doing so, she authorizes the use of this movement as an exemplar for U.S. ecofeminists eager to add Shiva's theory of the relationship of Western colonialism to their parallel analyses of environmental degradation and sexism in the Third World. Thus, for white U.S. ecofeminists, the Chipko become a symbolic center of a discourse about Third World women. These women are portrayed as "natural environmentalists," or "ultimate ecofeminists," reducing them to idealized peasant women who are integrated into "nature" through their daily, lived activities of food gathering and preparation, child-rearing, and the support of village communities.

Ecofeminism and Critiques of Essentialist Discourse

U.S. ecofeminism is a political position based on an analysis of the consequences of Western, patriarchal society's devaluation of nature and of women. An ecofeminist discourse that privileges "indigeneity" is perhaps a stage of U.S. ecofeminist discourse in the late 1980s and early 1990s.[4] Though ecofeminist thinkers include a diversity of viewpoints, and there is much debate over a number of core concepts within ecofeminism, there is basic agreement that the patriarchal Western conceptualization of nature as a feminized, exploitable resource has had negative environmental consequences. In addition, environmental degradation has produced special burdens for women as they carry out their gendered social roles as food producers, caretakers, and health providers. Ecofeminists argue that Western, patriarchal thinkers have seen women, animals, and nature as lesser than men and culture, and this dualistic and hierarchical way of thinking has justified and promoted the exploitation of both women and nature.

While ecofeminism is an incredibly diverse and internally contested set of discourses, and the essentialist tendencies I am criticizing do not characterize *all* ecofeminist writings, these viewpoints are prominent. Western ecofeminists have been critiqued, by myself among others, for two common and problematic tendencies in their political discourse, both characterized by essentialist arguments (Sturgeon 1997; Brinda Rao 1991; Bina Agarwal 1992; Cecile Jackson 1993; and Melissa Leach 1994). One essentialist tendency in U.S. ecofeminism is a gender essentialism, arising from arguments that seem to claim that women are closer to and have special sympathy with nature, and thus are natural environmentalists. The other tendency is a racial essentialism, that claims that nonwhite, non-Western women are even more likely to be natural environmentalists because of "Third World" women's material, lived, grounded, cultural and social integration into and care of "nature." Ironically, by deploying examples of Third World women to combat the gender essentialism of claims that all women are biologically in sympathy with nature, white U.S. ecofeminists have generated a form of racial essentialism. These claims are not found in all ecofeminist arguments, and they are rarely made in uncomplicated, explicit ways. Yet the frequent use of Third World and Native American women's environmental activism as examples of "ecofeminist" practice in writing by U.S. white ecofeminists gives an overall impression that women, and especially nonwhite, non-Western women, are essentially closer to nature and inherently environmentalists.

The use of such "indigenous" women as "ultimate ecofeminists" has been criticized on three grounds. First, such characterizations of these activists as ecofeminists often ignore the material basis upon which grassroots and indigenous women act, attributing to them a set of theories about the connections between patriarchy and environmental degradation that some of these women may specifically, or implicitly, reject. Second, when some forms of ecofeminism simply revalue and see as positive a sexist equivalency between "women" and "nature," they legitimize dominant assumptions in development strategies that posit women as potential "natural resources" for sustainable development programs, discourses that may not have the women's long-term interests at heart. For example, if women are all natural environmentalists, then development planners may see women as the ideal workers in conservation programs without evaluating the needs and commitments of the women themselves. Third, seeing indigenous women as the "ultimate ecofeminists" locates solutions for environmental problems only with so-called "indigenous" or peasant peoples or practices. Doing so conceptually prevents an environmentalist imaginary that could focus on urban problems, account for class differences within regions, generate information about appropriate technologies, or emphasize the environmental responsibilities and possibilities of Western industrialized nations.

By putting "indigenous" in quotes here, I am pointing to the conflation of three ecofeminist discourses on racial difference that partake of the same form and function: that of creating an image of indigenous, grassroots, or peasant women as "the ultimate ecofeminists." In other words, this discourse assumes that certain groups of women are closer to nature, naturally environmentalists, and best suited to manage natural resources simply because they are indigenous peasant farmers or hunters and gatherers. These three discourses of racial difference, located in "indigeneity," concern Native American women, Third World women (in which, as stated, rural Asian Indian women subsistence farmers tend to stand in as generalized "Third World women"), and pre–Christian European pagan women. I have argued elsewhere that the conflation of these three categories into a symbolic "indigeneity" is ironically a form of anti-racist discourse that ends up, despite good intentions, reconstituting white privilege (Sturgeon 1997). All difference between and within the categories "Native American" and "Third World" are erased and the women portrayed as indigenous are constituted as racialized Others to a white Self that is Western, modern, and industrialized....

The ecofeminist critique of the hierarchical dualism of nature/culture at the heart of patriarchal, Western, Enlightenment science and ideology privileges those cultural and economic arrangements that are seen not to divide culture from nature and that do not think of culture as superior to a degraded, inferior nature. This pervasive, and in many respects persuasive, critique of Western, Enlightenment rationalism directs Western ecofeminists to non-Western cultures for examples of ecofeminist politics, culture, and economy....

Ecofeminism in Development Practices

Having presented a sketch of the kind of the theoretical analysis and academic critique that ecofeminist discourses of "indigeneity" have generated, I want to take up the question of the effect of ecofeminist discourses within an international political arena and explore the possibility of their strategic nature in the context of globalizing environmentalisms. In doing so, I am interested in the relation between the local and transnational effects of such discourses.... This is what theorists like Anna Tsing are doing in their recent work (Tsing 1994, 1997), giving us methods of tracing the complex dance of influence and reception among groups of people differentiated by history, culture, language, gender, class, and political location, imbedded within historical and political processes in flux, and occurring within such different action spheres as academic conferences, international UN meetings, or local political actions....

...I do not want to ignore or dispute the dangers of essentialist notions of women, indigenous peoples, cultures, or nature. Rather, I wish to point to the positive potential, though ambiguous and uneven, of ecofeminism as a strategic discourse within a particular historical moment in international politics. As an *international political discourse* rather than a *theoretical tool*, the "discourse of indigeneity" (that is, seeing Third World peasants or Native Americans as "naturally" environmentalist), coupled with the sometimes essentialist claims about women's stake in environmentalism, opens up some possibilities. First, it identifies Third World women as experts, though it may limit that expertise to stereotypical "indigenous" qualities. Second, the feminist and anti-racist intentions of most ecofeminists exists in tension with their desire to idealize nature, women, and indigenous peoples. This contradiction produces opportunities, not just to concur with, but to debate those essentialist notions of women and nature that are already circulating within development discourse. Finally, ecofeminism inserts feminist demands and analyses within a hegemonic discourse of globalizing environmentalisms at an important historical moment.... Leach, though not focused on this level, does note that "when policy-oriented discussions incorporate ecofeminist ideas, they often mix [essentialist and anti-essentialist variants] uncritically" (Leach 1994: 30). However, she does not identify that mix as an opportunity for a strategic notion of "women-as-environmentalists" that can be inserted into dominant political discourses and that contains the seeds of destabilization of its own (and the dominant discourse's) essentialism.

A less reductive story is told of the interweaving of ecofeminism and development discourse approaches by several books on women and development (Braidotti *et al.* 1994; Dankelman and Davidson 1988; Mies and Shiva 1993; Shiva 1994; Van den Homburgh 1993). Ecofeminist discourse has resulted in important benefits for women within a development strategy labeled Women in Development (WID). Women in Development is the name for a shift in development studies and policies in the early 1970s. Women who were previously invisible to development strategists, or who appeared only as housewives and mothers, relegated to a privatized notion of reproduction, became a focus of policy. They were finally understood to be producers and economic actors, especially in the area of agriculture. However, the resulting programs did not often stress the need for gender equity. Rather, women were subjects for research that was aimed at creating more "efficient" and "effective" development policies, and their work was seen as an important resource for the success of development projects, even when those policies benefitted men far more than women (Schroeder 1993). Indeed, as Leach points out, essentialist notions of nature and women, especially poor and rural Third World women, were common in WID discourse before "ecofeminism" became a player within development politics (Leach 1994: 25). Nevertheless, WID was an important location for an internal contest between feminist notions of equality and empowerment and the desire of First World development agencies to craft policies that would successfully export Western products and practices to Third World countries. In practice, WID policies often provided poor women in the Third World with substantial opportunities compared to the previous male-oriented development paradigm.

Indeed, the WID paradigm was intimately intertwined with the growth of an international feminist movement, thus bringing international feminism into close contest and negotiation with Western multinational and state powers. The WID approach became initially institutionalized in the "development bureaucracy" in the West (Braidotti et al. 1994: 80). In 1975, the first UN conference on "Women and Development" was held in Mexico City. Though the growing legitimacy of WID was not the only impetus behind the organization of this conference, it certainly was an important factor in convincing international policymakers engaged in the UN that a conference on women was needed. Their new assumptions were reflected in the title of the conference, connecting women and development.

During the Decade for Women, which was initiated by the 1975 Mexico City conference, both Western and Third World feminists seriously engaged the process of constructing an international feminist movement. In this process of debate and forming of alliances, development policies—especially the exploitation of the Third World by the West in which such policies were embedded—were points of contention among Third World feminists, who accused Western feminists of ethnocentrism and of being tools of Western neo-colonialism. In the 1980s, during a period of worsening conditions for women worldwide caused by the "debt crisis" (Van den Hombergh 1993: 58–60), Third World feminists were organizing to influence the international political processes surrounding the UN apparatus, which had grown up around women as political and economic subjects. In 1984, an organization called "Development with Women for a New Era," or DAWN, was created. DAWN critiqued the WID approach for its acceptance of the "Western development model" and its failure to focus on the empowerment of women as a primary goal (Braidotti et al. 1994: 81). In Nairobi in 1985, during the Second UN Conference on Women, which capped the Decade for Women, the parallel Non-Governmental Organization (NGO) Forum involved numerous lively discussions of the need for approaches such as DAWN's. But throughout the decade of the 1980s, these various feminist positions had also to contend with the growing influence of environmentalisms within the international political arena.

Concurrent with the rise of WID, an increasing concern about environmental questions as part of development studies during the 1980s also began to include a focus on women, in part because of the new stress on women's management of natural resources through their productive roles, and in part because of an early link made between environmental problems and population growth. As a result, as Western consciousness of environmental questions such as resource use, energy production, desertification, and pollution increased during the 1970s, Third World rural women became a major focus of development planning. As Häusler comments: "A powerful image emerged of poor people in the South, with too many children, using too much fuel; the poor were seen to have no choice but to destroy the environment" (Häusler, in Braidotti et al. 1994: 84). The responsibility for population growth and environmental problems was thus placed on poor Third World women rather than on the Western, industrialized nations, which consume most of the world's resources. These assumptions about Third World women's responsibility for dangerous levels of population growth and misguided environmental resource use, widespread in influential reports such as *Limits to Growth*, have been a major focus of challenges both by Western and Third World feminists.

Several events served to embed the relation among environment, women, and development both within development politics and with international feminism, as they interacted during the late 1970s and early 1990s. Within this complicated, rapidly changing political context, the feminist agenda became not only to make women's stake in these issues visible, but to promote women's economic and political empowerment as environmental experts. For example, at the first major international conference on the environment, in 1972 at Stockholm, during the parallel NGO meeting, Sunderlal Bahuguna, a male Indian activist who had played a major role in promoting the Chipko movement, presented Chipko women as exemplars of community-based, sustainable environmental practitioners. Because, as Häusler writes, "women had emerged as the main actors in this movement, it was concluded that rural women understood that it was in their own interests to protect the environment" (Häusler, in Braidotti et al. 1994: 85). The Chipko movement is inserted into the international political context at a moment when the environment becomes a major agenda item, and in Bahuguna's version, Chipko represents a challenge to the notion that Third World women are problematic environmentally; instead, he presents them as natural environmentalists. It is this opening which is later seized by Third World ecofeminists such as Shiva, who offer the Chipko as representing not just women as natural environmentalists, but women as active, political agents with expert knowledge about the environment. Thus, "ecofeminism," through Shiva's intervention in the late 1980s, enters into an international context as a way of attaching earlier feminist efforts to transform WID to a newer environmentalist paradigm that has been called Women, Environment, and Development or WED. In this light, Shiva's arguments about women's greater environmental knowledge became an important political intervention despite the problematic essentialism of some of her discourse. In this context, "ecofeminism" *means* this feminist intervention into environmentalism, more than it represents a set of new, independent theoretical arguments or a coherent social movement. In a political arena in which environmentalist questions are beginning to be seen as vitally important, it was crucial to produce arguments that linked feminist and environmentalist concerns. That this was sometimes done through problematic claims about women, especially Third-World women, as "naturally environmentalist," does not vitiate the need for a politics of connection between feminism and environmentalism.

While this "ecofeminist" position, or WED, thus incorporated political relevance and effectiveness within a political context at a particular time, it also ran the risk of dovetailing with older WID assumptions about women as "natural resources." Many progressive development scholars began to worry about trends in which ecofeminist arguments (such as Shiva's) about women as environmental managers and environmental activists were retranslated in development policies as requiring women to be the primary laborers in conservation schemes that might or might not benefit them directly. These scholars critiqued such arguments as essentialist, though such essentialism had existed as well in older WID discourse (Schroeder 1993). Rather than seeing the reoccurrence of essentialist moments in development discourses on women as being as part of an ongoing process of political struggle stimulated by feminist interventions and aimed at creating collective subjects (such as "women"), these scholars critique "ecofeminism" instead.

Nevertheless, it is clear that the insertion of feminist demands into development policy in the period when it becomes concerned with the environment (in other words, the "ecofeminist" moment), provided particular political and working links between Western feminists and Third-World feminists in a context of "globalizing environmentalisms." I will provide some illustrations of these links below. But first, I want to explain what I mean by "globalizing environmentalisms," in order to underline the importance of feminist interventions into internationalist environmentalist discourses.

By the term "globalizing environmentalisms," I want to point to a convergence of particular concerns (environmentalism, the New World Order, global markets) that illuminate the contours of a specific conjuncture within a post–Cold War hegemonic struggle for dominance. I posit a shift from a Cold War discourse, about "democracy" versus "communism," to a new hegemonic discourse, about "environmentalism" versus "chaos or catastrophe." Within this discursive field, the fact that environmental problems are "global," in that they cross national boundaries, can be either the source of progressive hopes for a new global cooperation tied to a radical environmentalist analysis of the need for "sustainability," or it can serve multinational corporate and technocratic elite interests in order to impose unjust conditions on the poor and the colonized, perceived as an "environmental" threat....

...And we could enumerate the political struggles engaged in this conjuncture and identify them in multiple ways: between the West and the Third World, between class formations, between racial/ethnic groups, between genders, and so forth. Often obscuring this multiplicity, these struggles are presently taking place within internationalized versions of "environmentalism." What strikes me...is ...the relation of the "ending" of the Cold War in the final years of the 1980s to the appearance of global environmentalisms as a discursive tool within these political struggles. Like the discourse of democracy as a world-wide good, environmentalism turns out to be a two-edged sword. For example, the popularity of Robert Kaplan's construction of a connection between environmental disasters and the threatening "chaos" within African nations in his widely-read article, "The Coming Anarchy" (1994), displays the way in which older forms of U.S. racist and Western colonialist fears about the "barbarity" of the Third World are transformed into a concern with environmental disaster, which unleashes new forms of "savagery."

In this political context, "the environment" has served feminists (now often "ecofeminists") as a medium for the connection of critiques of militarism, sexism, capitalism, and neo-colonialism, similar to the way "militarism" functioned in the 1970s and 1980s. The argument that women have a stake in environmentalist politics becomes an especially important strategic position within an international context of "globalizing environmentalism." Positioning women as environmental activists is one moment in a dialectical process of negotiation between dominant interests in development policies and feminist efforts to insert women's concerns into an international arena. While it is important to critique the limits of such ecofeminist interventions, it is equally important to see the way in which these analytic linkages can operate as "two-way streets" between Third World and Western feminist activists. This is particularly the case when ecofeminist arguments contain a tension between essentialist and anti-essentialist analyses, giving an opening for debates around operative definitions of "women" and "nature" that allow the possibility of more nuanced analyses. For example, note the slippage between essentialist and materialist analyses in this quote from Maria Mies: "But not only women in the industrialized countries realized the interconnectedness of all life forms in their struggle against environmental destruction. This was even more clearly expressed by Third World women, particularly those who were/are engaged in a struggle for survival, dignity, and the preservation of their independent subsistence base, like the women in the Chipko movement in India... Therefore their struggle against this type of development is at the same time a struggle for the preservation of nature and a struggle for survival. They cannot separate the two" (Mies 1992:64–5).

The complexity produced by activist discourses connecting women's struggles and environmentalist struggles is not adequately portrayed when an analysis simply focuses on what is said rather than the context in which the discourse is deployed. For example, at Miami, Florida, U.S., in 1991, a recognizably ecofeminist discourse employing versions of essentialist maternalism was used by a new organization, Women, Environment, and Development Organization (WEDO) to bring together 1,500 women from 83 countries to a World Women's Conference for a Healthy Planet. WEDO, arguing "Now It's Time to Mother Earth," successfully gathered support for the need to organize a women's agenda for environmentalism.[5] At this conference, which included many Third World feminist activists and researchers, as well as grassroots activists from around the world, an active debate and discussion between actors with disparate access to international political power generated an intertwined feminist and environmentalist analysis with a number of radical positions on women's health, development policies, and Western economic exploitation of the Third World. And WEDO moved on from this event, mobilizing a diverse constituency of women on the basis of a maternalist version of ecofeminism that also employed an essentialist discourse of "indigeneity," to generate repeated interventions into UN political arenas that promoted a feminist, anticolonialist analysis of environmental problems, despite sometimes essentialist rhetoric.[6] The limits of WEDO's intervention are clear, given the limits of UN politics themselves; nevertheless WEDO's presence opened up a space for Third World women to have access to powerful arenas of action.

In his essay on the "globalization of grassroots politics," Michael Peter Smith points out that in social theory, the local is usually equated with "stasis" and "personal identity," while the global is characterized as the "site of dynamic change, the decentering of meaning, and the fragmentation and homogenization of culture—that is, the *space* of global capitalism" (1994: 15). In contrast, he argues that a transnational grassroots politics has appeared, which confuses these older notions of separate local and global spaces, and which operates within particular transnational arenas. These activities create new transnational political subjects (brought together as "women" or as members of other politically-constructed subjectivities) and create opportunities for dialogue and coalitions.

These political collectivities very well may be constructed by essentialist discourses, but it is also possible that some may be oppositional collectivities built on hard-won unity across great differences. And they may serve the less powerful groups as well as the powerful groups within the new collectivity. For instance, "ecofeminist" discourses about women's nurturing relation to nature may effectively intervene within hegemonic processes in a context of globalizing environmentalisms, and, contingent upon organizational structures that emphasize equal participation among very differently-located political actors, they may serve to destabilize the essentialism of the rhetoric and produce valuable political effects.

Just the construction of these arenas may create new opportunities for the less powerful to gain political leverage. Jane Jacob, in an essay critiquing essentialist Western notions about Aboriginal women's relation to environmental activism, makes a similar point: "In particular, there are specific problems arising from the essentialized notions of Aboriginality and woman that underpin radical environmentalisms and feminisms. Yet to read these alliances only in terms of the reiteration of a politics of Western, masculinist supremacy neglects the positive engagement indigenous women may make with such 'sympathizers' in their efforts to verify and amplify their struggles for land rights" (Jacobs 1994: 169). The ecofeminist intervention into international political arenas, in uneven and unsatisfactory ways, perhaps, can create a network, a space for debate, a mechanism not just for the intervention of feminism, environmentalism, and anticolonial scholarship into policy-making, but also for strategic coalitions to take place among disempowered people and between privileged and underprivileged people in one political collectivity. I think it is useful to keep in mind that, as in the contribution of the international feminist antimilitarist movement to the end of the Cold War, we may need to tolerate, at least initially, "essentialist" rhetoric, which calls women from different locations to act together against power.

But other issues remain, which I hope to raise here for further discussion rather than resolve. If we agree that essentialist claims are often strategic, on what basis do we support women who use essentialist rhetoric in activist efforts? How and when do we support the common assertions of tribal, peasant, or rural women that they see themselves as closer to nature than Westernized peoples (whether as members of the Third World or as Western elites)? How do we judge the material effects of strategic political discourse in global arenas for women in localized struggles? For instance, if an internationalist ecofeminist group holds up the example of a poor rural woman whose practice of sustainable subsistence farming is seen as ideally ecological, are this woman's life chances materially supported or inhibited in any way? Are more sustainable methods of growing food and using natural resources linked firmly to poverty, and how do we bring the necessity of structural economic change into environmentalist discourse? And finally, when and where do we support globalized claims for environmentalism in the context of the increasing dominance of transnational capitalism, which equates exploitative labor and market practices with democracy, civil society, human rights, and environmentalism? These are the kinds of questions I think academics who analyze the discourses and practices of social movements should keep in the forefront of our efforts to understand and support radical activism.

Notes

1. Throughout this paper I use the terms "Third World" and "Western" to indicate what has also been called "Southern" and "Northern," or "over-developed" and "less-developed," or "industrialized" and "developing" peoples and nations. None of these terms is completely satisfactory but it is necessary to use some commonly understood terms to indicate the generalized differentials of power, wealth, and global influence between these two broadly-indicated entities.
2. The notion of theories operation as "two-way" streets for communication between subordinate groups or as new tools for resistance to power, even when those theories may be part of a dominating force, is complexly argued by Anna Tsing (1997).
3. Marie Wilson, a Gitskan woman, is interviewed by Judith Plant in *Healing*, and comments, "When I read about ecofeminism I find that the attitudes towards women and the feelings inside myself are quite different. It's difficult to explain, but it's as if women are separate" (Plant 1989: 212).
4. I have developed the points made in this paragraph more fully in my book (Sturgeon 1997).
5. The phrase "Now It's Time to Mother Earth!" was used on an organizing poster produced by WEDO.
6. I examine WEDO in detail and analyze the production of a feminist, anti-colonialist analysis that promoted the interests of poor Third-World women in "Ecofeminist Natures and Transnational Environmental Politics," Chapter Five (Sturgeon 1997).

13.
FEMALE CONSCIOUSNESS OR FEMINIST CONSCIOUSNESS?: WOMEN'S CONSCIOUSNESS RAISING IN COMMUNITY-BASED STRUGGLES IN BRAZIL[1]

Yvonne Corcoran-Nantes

...My own research in Brazil, from which the empirical data in this chapter originates, was designed specifically to look at aspects of women's political participation in popular urban social movements in order to provide explanations for women's high profile in non-institutional politics. It was clear that by the 1980s women participated in and led popular protest around a wide variety of issues related to urbanization, employment and the provision of basic services, which suggests that this political arena represents something of fundamental importance to women (see Safa 1990; Corcoran-Nantes 1990; Moser 1987). Moreover, the issues that interest women represent the major social and economic problems in developing countries and are also becoming key issues in the advanced industrial nations.

Women of the working poor in Brazil have, over the past two decades, strengthened their presence in non-institutional politics by protesting about the lack of basic services, health provision, transport, housing and unemployment. The methods of organization and political practice of popular urban social movements demonstrate the influence of women in them and similar practices can be found in many developing countries both in grassroots protest politics and women's organizations (see, for example, Mies 1988; Mattelart 1980; Cutrufelli 1983). I have argued elsewhere that these movements were not specifically created *for* women. It is women who form the majority within a social group whose socio-economic experience in Brazilian society is neither reflected nor represented in other forms of political organization (see Corcoran-Nantes 1990). Consequently, women have played a major role in the formation and development of popular movements. Through their participation they have discovered a new public identity in a political sphere which, in many ways, they have made their own. Many women, through their political development in non-institutional politics, have gone on to extend their participation to political parties and trade unions as well as strategic gender protests along with women's organizations and feminist groups around issues such as birth control, rape, and domestic violence.

What seems to have developed is a bifurcated political sphere: male/institutional politics and female/non-institutional politics, which are identifiable by the nature of political/gender organization and action. The political practice in either sphere bears little resemblance to the other as in one the majority of political actors are male and in the other female. What I wish to consider here is the gender specificity of political practices in non-institutional politics and their implications for the relationship between politically reproduced gender spheres.

This chapter will look at the development of political consciousness and solidarity among women of the popular urban movements in São Paulo. It is through these practices and women's influence on them that we can analyse the motivation behind their participation in this political sphere, how women view their role in society and what this represents for them. By looking at the various processes involved in conscientization and politicization such as forms of consciousness raising, self-help groups, oral history, and the struggle for literacy, I will argue that the development of women's political consciousness is far more complex than present analyses demonstrate. In Brazil, as in many other Latin American countries, women have created a political role for themselves based on their social status as wives and mothers but through which they have struggled for recognition of their roles and rights as workers, residents, and citizens.

Gender: The Missing Link in Analyses of Popular Social Movements

Despite evidence to show the predominance of women in non-institutional politics, those who have attempted to analyse popular social movements have tended to ignore the question of gender. Those who have acknowledged or tried to give some explanation for women's participation and political consciousness tend to fall into two different camps. First, there are those like Jaquette (1989) who subsume female participation under the auspices of feminism or women's movements, thereby removing the question of gender from their analysis of popular protest in Latin America. Second, there are those like Chaney (1979) who prefer to confine themselves to a matrifocal analysis where the traditional role of women as wives and mothers and their relation to the reproduction of the labour force becomes the universal explanation, the *sine qua non*, for women's political practice and participation. The role of women in Latin American society is far too multifaceted for us to be satisfied with unitary explanations of their participation in the political sphere.

Political division of labour exists in political parties and trade unions in Latin America and many other parts of the world. Within institutional politics women's groups and women's departments are formed to present programmes and drafts of new laws or to develop a strategy to place women's issues on the political agenda. What this actually does is to take strategic gender issues and other issues that are of importance to women out of the mainstream politics within these organizations. In short, it removes them from the political agenda. Tying women's political participation exclusively to the question of feminism and women's movements is a wholly inaccurate picture of the extent of women's political participation and the motives and interests behind it. The majority of women who participate in the popular social movements are not motivated by a feminist consciousness; feminism for them has very little to do with the reality of their lives. In Latin American society, the marked inequality in the distribution of wealth and resources has further reinforced the idea, among the women of the urban poor, that feminism is a middle-class ideology for women who have all the social and economic advantages. Moreover, the institutionalization of domestic service on the continent has sustained the antagonism between classes whereby 'fortunate' women exploit 'less fortunate' women. The patron/client relationship which has evolved is a major barrier to any longstanding political association between them, and there have been occasions when this relationship has been politically exploited (Corcoran-Nantes 1988; Filet Abreu de Souza 1980; Chuchryk 1989). Consequently, there are considerable class differences in relation to how and in what forms of political organizations women participate.

Writers who do analyse women's participation in popular social movements tend to consider only one aspect (that of the sexual division of labour) as an explanation for their participation, either relating this exclusively to women's domestic role, or this, together with women's relationship to collective consumption (see Cardoso 1984; Safa 1990; Moser 1987; Evers et al. 1982). I have argued elsewhere that women's participation in social movements is also linked to their role in production and that most of the issues around which these movements are organized also affect men (Corcoran-Nantes 1990). Without doubt, women do legitimate their entry into the political spheres as wives and mothers but there are tangible reasons why women do so. In Latin American society *marianismo*, or the cult of Mary, still exists whereby women's status comes from their reproductive role, and this has often been a source of power for women (Stevens 1973). By utilizing this image, women can strengthen and legitimate their political involvement in the eyes of the state. Conversely, the state has also exploited the cultural identity of women, *os supermadres*, to secure their political support (Chuchryk 1989). The *supermadre* approach to politics is legitimated by women, men, and the state. Up to the present time no one has considered, for example, how far men take their role in the family into the political sphere.

Maxine Molyneux in her own work on women in post-revolutionary societies, has presented an excellent working hypothesis for considering the motivations and achievements of women's participation in political struggles. She divides gender interests into two broad categories. One is strategic gender interests which are directly related to women's subordination in a given society and the demands around which women's struggles are based on a strategy to overcome all forms of gender inequality. The other is practical gender interests which derive from women's ascribed role in the sexual division of labour, a response to their immediate practical needs and formulated by women themselves. These are shaped by class and ethnicity and are not necessarily part of a long-term strategy to achieve gender equality. She goes on to argue that in the formulation of strategic gender interests, practical gender interests have to be taken into account and it is 'the politicisation of these practical interests and their transformation into strategic interests which constitutes a central aspect of feminist practice' (Molyneux 1985: 236–7).

It is practical gender interests which are the basis of women's political participation in popular social movements. The transformation of practical gender interests into strategic gender interests requires not only women's recognition of their power to represent their own interests but also that space exists within the prevailing political system to pressure the state into recognizing those interests. This is part of a complex political development process whereby women not only recognize gender interests but do so in relation to and in conjunction with other women, across class and ethnic boundaries.

Political Practice—The Development of Political Consciousness and Solidarity

… It is on the urban periphery of São Paulo that the fieldwork on which this chapter is based was carried out and concentrated on three popular movements: O Movimento de Favela (the Favela Movement—founded in 1976 to secure land title and to improve services and infrastructure in the settlements), O Movimento de Saude (the Health Movement—formed originally in 1973 with the aim of improving medical services at both the local and regional level), and O Movimento dos Desempregados (the Unemployed Movement—formed in 1983 to solve the immediate problems of unemployment through demands for unemployment benefit, funding to set up worker cooperatives and so on).[2] These popular movements are representative of the wide range of movements which existed, and continue to exist, in the urban periphery of São Paulo. One common feature is that participants in these movements are either exclusively or predominantly women.

Health, housing, and unemployment are typical of the kind of social questions that have attracted the interest of low-income women, and movements formed around these issues developed characteristics which reflect their involvement in them. The key factor to take into account here is that while the sexual division of labour tends in general terms to confine women for a large amount of their time to their homes and immediate neighbourhoods, low-income women are often involved in a wide range of activities which span the rather arbitrary divide between production and reproduction, with many having various modes of generating income (see Brydon and Chant 1989: 10–12) Women thus tend to be more responsive than men to issues that relate to socio-economic activities in both the public *and* private sphere. The political participation of women arises from the social bonds which are created via these activities in the community, through which they organize themselves and from which the political contexts of urban social movements are developed.

Moreover, the social, economic and even moral issues which have formed the basis of this type of political protest are directly associated with the nature of dependent capitalist development. They are issues which cannot be solved in the short term and are precisely those which have remained on the periphery of 'mainstream' politics or have been given little or no priority in the programmes of parties and successive governments. It is hardly surprising, therefore, that some social movements have been in existence for over two decades and have only gradually gained improvements in the conditions of life for the urban poor. Various forms of consciousness raising were used by the popular movements, and the ways in which they were implemented differed from one movement to another. First, there was instruction in socialist theories to explain the socio-economic conditions of the urban poor and the importance of the popular movements to the struggle for political change in Brazilian society. This almost always involved the help of supporters of the movements such as the Church or political parties who had political material designed for the conscientization of the urban poor. Second, there was a form of consciousness raising which was a means of self-education and collective counselling, and dealt with issues and problems arising from, and related to, their struggles. This was a method of consciousness raising which women preferred to use in which self-help and the dissemination of information was a part of the process of political participation. The question of self-help also led to the formation of cooperative schemes in low-income neighbourhoods to provide practical solutions to the immediate needs of the local community. Third was the use of oral history, which was probably the most important and effective way of creating political consciousness and solidarity. All the popular movements had some means of recording and registering their political history but it was only in those movements in which women had organizational control that a strong emphasis was placed on the use of oral history as a means of conscientization.

Class Consciousness vis-à-vis Female Consciousness

Consciousness raising based on the propagation of socialist theory was undertaken in various ways. In many cases it was an integral part of the political meetings of the movement itself during which an individual or group, usually with experience in political parties or left-wing Church groups, discussed current political issues relating to the problems of the urban poor. Sometimes it was little more than speech making, but on other occasions simple visual aids such as diagrams or cartoon pictures were used to show the participants how and why they suffered in Brazilian society. Women were quick to point out that in much of this material they were underrepresented and *their* experience in Brazilian society was rarely discussed at all. More sophisticated material was sometimes used, such as films or slides borrowed from the Catholic Church which has produced entire courses for the politicization of the popular classes.

These forms of consciousness raising stimulated interest and discussion both inside and outside the meetings but this was difficult to sustain over a long period of time. Women, in particular, lost interest fairly quickly because their political concerns centred on practical difficulties rather than theorizing struggles. It was, however, a successful way of selecting potential political activists. Experienced activists from political parties or left-wing ecclesiastical groups who participated in the popular movements would often utilize this form of consciousness raising to 'recruit' new activists by inviting those people who demonstrated some 'political aptitude' to attend their meetings. A significant number of women entered local party politics in this way. . . .

In the Unemployed Movement the formation of women's groups spread swiftly from one region to another and the numbers of women committee members rose to 70 percent. In some regions, women's groups were formed as a result of initiatives by women themselves. In others, however, their formation was encouraged by men, who had organizational control of the Unemployed Movement, as a means of removing 'women's issues' out of the general political demands of the movement. Wherever they emerged, they became a forum for the discussion of a wide range of issues such as women's political participation, male domestic violence, and women's role in society. Through the exchange of experiences, particularly those related to their own participation in the popular movements, many women were better able to face the problems arising from their political activities with the support of these groups which served to reinforce their commitment to the movement.[3]

Many women enjoyed the opportunity of talking about themselves and their lives, as well as finding out more about themselves and other women. These groups often developed into a mutual support collective wherein *companheiras* in the struggle became true friends who gave each other help in their personal, working and political lives. Some of these groups were little more than small women's meetings but others went on to join up with other women's groups and organize talks to which feminist speakers were invited to discuss topics such as 'The history of women's political participation in Brazil' and 'Female sexuality: my body, my choice'. Many of these groups joined with women's organizations and feminist groups on demonstrations and political protests about issues such as abortion, violence against women, and family planning. Consequently, these groups, although initially formed as a means of politicizing women within the popular movements through consciousness raising undertaken by women for women, sometimes became a vehicle for contacts with other women's groups or other women in a wide range of political organizations. Irrespective of how these groups developed, they gave women greater confidence in themselves, and many of the women who organized or participated in these groups went on to be elected local and regional coordinators of Committees of the Unemployed.

The Health Movement actually evolved from issues concerning women's health and that of their children. The use of self-education as a form of consciousness raising about these issues was a natural progression from the movement's initial aims and objectives. Their struggle to improve an inadequate and underfunded health service made women conscious of the need to take action themselves in the area of preventive medicine in an attempt to reduce the risk of health problems for themselves and their children. Women of the movement were principally interested in two main topics: first, ways in which they could prevent or reduce the risk of their children suffering from some of the more common child-hood diseases in Brazil; second, access to information on contraception so that women could make an informed choice as to what methods were available and most suitable for them to use. In both cases, women turned to local doctors and nurses to help them produce booklets which they could use in their self-education groups....

The leaflets produced by the Health Movement on family planning were also an invaluable source of information for women. In Brazil there were no official family planning schemes or health advice services for women and the public health service offered little orientation for women who wished to use contraceptives, apart from advice on 'natural' methods of birth control supported by the Catholic Church. In practice, while there was no official line taken by the government on the question of family planning, women of the working poor were often pressured into using sterilization as a permanent solution to their 'problems' without being advised on alternative forms of contraception available to them.[4] The self-educa-tion groups and pamphlets were a means of informing women about the different methods of contraception available in Brazil, showing the advantages and disad-vantages of each one to help women make an informed choice on what method was best for them. Women who did not participate in the Health Movement attended these informal groups on family planning and some of them went on to participate in the movement itself.

Meetings held by the Health Movement about the issues of family health and family planning were invariably held in people's houses, often as 'street meetings' to which women from the movement would invite their friends and neighbours. Working from the pamphlets, women would discuss the questions raised and any practical difficulties which arose. No professional people participated in the groups: they were run by ordinary women who sought practical solutions to health problems which were not resolved within the public health service. The existence of the groups demonstrated the importance of the Health Movement in the strug-gle for a better health service and they reinforced or developed women's commit-ment to the movement.

This type of consciousness raising developed for women by women raised female consciousness in relation to strategic gender interests. It stimulated and developed a complex matrix of inter- and intra-class alliances between women around gender-specific issues. As women acquired a greater sense of themselves and gender inequality through their political practices in popular struggles, women's organizations in the low-income neigbourhoods emerged and grew in strength. By developing a political identity as women of the working poor, they were able to define their relationships clearly with other organizations, both inside and outside institutional politics. Consequently, when they entered political protests in association with political parties and trade unions on the one hand, or feminist groups and women's organizations on the other, in general or gender-specific political struggles, such as the Campaign for Direct Elections or Women against Violence Campaign, they were able to defend this identity and their practical gender interests from a position of greater political strength.

The Demand for Literacy and Politicization

Adult literacy courses based on the methods of Paulo Freire, which use short literacy courses as a means of politicization, were also a popular and constructive form of conscientization.[5] Many of the urban poor who participate in the popular movements are illiterate. Women in particular have had few chances to educate themselves, and when they begin to undertake organizational roles in the movement there is tremendous pressure on them to obtain basic literacy skills. Dealing with members of the government, participating in negotiations and the need to take notes at meetings present difficulties to those who are unable to read or write.

Women often bypass these difficulties by using tape-recorders or by taking their children along to the regional or state meetings to take notes, so that they are able to recall the main points of discussion or proposals to report back to members of their group or the movement. However, the high rate of illiteracy amongst those who participate in the popular movements often gives a privileged position to people who can read or write. There are women with valuable political skills who have been elected as representatives or coordinators in the movements who hide the fact that they are illiterate. Whether it is from a feeling of inadequacy or as a result of internal or external pressure, it is invariably the leaders or representatives of the movements who instigate literacy courses as a means of educating both themselves and others in the popular movements.

Literacy courses are always undertaken with the help of activists from either the Church or the political parties who have experience in this field. These activists are invited by the movements initially to teach the literacy course, but eventually one or two members of the movement are shown how to deliver the course and this eliminates the need for outside help. The courses are nearly always oversubscribed and it is frequently women who are the most interested in becoming literate. This interest derives, primarily, from the desire to enhance and expand their new-found political skills; to be able to make notes, to vote in government elections, to read political material, or even to write their own placards were all skills that these women wanted to acquire. Thus, it was these factors which made this type of literacy course based on politicization ideal for the popular movements.

Community Action as Political Action

Cooperative work and mutualist schemes were two other activities which developed and strengthened the solidarity between those who participated in the popular movements. Amongst the urban poor they were a means of resolving immediate and socio-economic problems and could be of a short- or long-term nature. Cooperative work schemes usually entailed the sale of goods or commodities and only benefited those who participated in them. Mutualist schemes, on the other hand, involved the provision of services and frequently benefited those who did not participate in them as well as those who did. Irrespective of the schemes' beneficiaries, they arose from the political practice of the popular movements. These schemes became an integral part of their political organization and extended the members' political commitment to the idea of collectivism into the local community.

It was the Unemployed Movement that used cooperative work schemes as an immediate solution to the subsistence problems of its members and in the period 1983–85 they became popular amongst the unemployed throughout Brazil. Some state governments financed projects submitted by the unemployed, but in São Paulo the majority of financing came from the Paulista Association of Solidarity in Unemployment (APSD) and was only given to groups registered with the Association.[6] Once again it was women who were most interested in the schemes which covered a wide range of petty commodity production such as bread making, confectionary, tailoring, and craft production.[7] These schemes were 'tailor-made' for women: they were located near the home, they used flexible work rota systems and initially there were few expectations that the financial remuneration would do more than help to sustain the family unit during periods of unemployment. However, some of these cooperatives became extremely successful and the share of the profits was comparable to women's wages in the formal sector. Some cooperatives were more successful than others, in financial terms, but most of them managed to provide subsistence wages for the unemployed who participated in them. Furthermore, some of the cooperatives gave a small percentage of their profits to the funds of the Unemployed Movement to help finance political action....

Oral History: The Story Told and Retold

The use of oral history as a form of politicization was fundamental to the creation of a political identity for the movements themselves and for those who participated in them. Many of the popular movements do write down the history of their organization and struggles and use this material for the conscientization of new members. But the use of oral history is a rich and personalized tribute to past events and the contribution of each of the participants to the movement's "success." An oral history is developed from individual and collective experiences of those who participate in the movements. It is a vivid, living testimony of their political defeats and victories which are recalled at any and every opportunity to demonstrate the courage, tenacity, and commitment of those who participate in them. Women, without a doubt, are the most avid subscribers to this form of politicization. They take great pride in their ability to recall events and even conversations in the minutest detail, often dramatizing the conflicts and confrontations with government or the police during their struggles. It is the way in which they reaffirm the importance of their participation in this form of political organization and the viability of the popular movements as an instrument for political change and social change.

In the meetings held after a political protest has been carried out, those who participated recall their personal experiences of the struggle and how they felt about it. Not everyone who participates in the popular movements can or will participate in their protests and demonstrations. The practice of using individual accounts of events informs those who were not present, but it is also a means of encouraging far more people to participate. Everyone is given a chance to speak or ask questions; the emphasis is on the individual contribution to the collective; the relaxed, enthusiastic atmosphere of these meetings alleviates the inevitable anticlimax which follows the intense period of political activity leading up to collective action. For those who participate in the popular movement, *every* struggle is a success which is counted not only by the concrete victories obtained through the struggle in relation to the demands of the movement but also by its impact on both the government *and* the participants....

The oral history of the popular movements catalogues both the triumphs and tribulations of their political practice, and those who participate in the movements are the ones who make and develop this history. The past successes of a movement are often what sustains its organization and the political commitment of those who participate in the movements in some of the more difficult and less successful periods of its political action. Women in particular are eager to record their political experiences, to create for themselves and reaffirm a specific political identity, one in which women are not inconsequential but successful political actors. In this way, oral history is not merely an adjunct to the political action of the popular movements but one of the key elements of their political practice.

The Transformation of Gender Interests

The many forms of political action employed by the popular urban social movements, as we can see here, have many different functions. The need for conscientization or the creation of solidarity within the movements themselves was not always the initial purpose of these practices but often became the reason for continuing or developing them. Some practices arose from a simple need or idea expressed by those who participate in the movements whilst others were a direct attempt to conscientize the popular classes. Irrespective of the impetus for or the development of such forms of political practice used by the popular movements, in most cases they reflected the desires and needs of the women who dominated this form of political organization. In doing so, it gave many women the chance to 'improve' themselves and develop both socially and politically by utilizing a wide range of skills to enhance and expand their new-found political ones.

The political mobilization of low-income women arose from their practical gender interests as well as structural class differences in Brazilian society. Their daily battles for economic survival prioritized political action around issues related to the access of the popular classes to the benefits of economic development. The provision of urban infrastructure, adequate healthcare and transport not only affect women's activities in the reproductive sphere but also have limiting effects on their access to employment and income-generating activities. Nevertheless, as opposed to gender "neutral" analyses (Slater 1985), it would be wrong to describe urban social movements as women's social movements (Safa 1990); this would fail to acknowledge not only the participation of men in these movements but also the affects of gender relations within and between these movements and institutional politics.

In the popular movements men can account for up to 40 percent of the participants. Gender relations in this context are different to those in institutional politics. Women acquire political experience in association with men, but in a sphere where they predominate it is frequently on their own terms. As we have seen here, the political practices of the movements are strongly influenced by women and as such their political development is directly related to their gender subordination in society. They are able to strengthen and legitimate their political role and become experienced political actors. Those who go on to enter institutional politics are able to do so from a much stronger position and with greater confidence in their political abilities (Corcoran-Nantes 1988; Moser 1987).

Through their struggles around practical gender interests, women who have a similar socio-economic experience in Brazilian society develop greater solidarity and awareness in relation to strategic gender interests. Opposition to women's political participation at a personal political level reinforces their experience of gender inequality in other spheres. Through their contact with political parties and trade unions they develop cross-class links with other women from feminist groups and women's organizations. These links have been strengthened by their association in struggles around strategic gender interests. By developing a political practice which emphasizes not only class inequality but also gender inequality, these women began to construct a gender identity around strategic interests based on their socio-economic experience. Consequently, low-income women were able to articulate their priorities and interests in relation to other class-based feminist groups and organizations and to pursue strategic gender interests through their political action.

Nevertheless, for low-income women practical gender interests take priority in their political struggles and it is here that they have built the necessary basis for unity and solidarity. Class oppression, to which their gender subordination is directly related, has forced women to organize around issues related to their very survival and that of their families. These issues comprise the major social and economic problems in developing countries, and in this context, strategic gender issues take a secondary role or may not be considered at all. In Brazil, however, amongst women of the urban poor, female consciousness has developed around strategic gender interests, and whether they choose to describe these as feminist or not is irrelevant. What is important for women of the popular classes is that their concerns are firmly on the political agenda.

Notes

1. This chapter is dedicated to Elisabeth Souza-Lobo.
2. The material on which this chapter is based arises out of a wider research project conducted on the role of women in the organization and formation of popular urban social movements in Brazil during the period 1983–85. The research was funded by a postgraduate award from the Economic and Social Research Council. Fieldwork was carried out in nine low-income neighbourhoods from three different regions of the Greater São Paulo metropolitan area: Embu and Sta Emilia in the Southern Zone; Vila Rica, Vila Antonieta, Vila Sezamo, and São Matheus in the Eastern Zone; and Diadema, São Caetano do Sul and Maua in the "ABC" region to the far east of the metropolitan area. Interviews were held with over 200 women who were active participants in popular movements. All material and quotations used in this chapter are from the author's primary data, unless otherwise stated.
3. Many women faced strong opposition to their political involvement from their partners. In many regions, women's self-help groups gave practical help and support to those who were victims of domestic violence or who wished to separate from their partners.
4. The Health Movement in conjunction with feminist groups and women's organizations had strongly opposed all family planning proposals by the government for being far too authoritarian. For example, in 1985 the Head of the Armed Forces insisted that the question of family planning should come under their jurisdiction because it was a matter of National Security!
5. Paulo Freire created a literacy course which utilized political material as subject matter to teach adults, in the space of forty lessons, the basic skills of reading and writing while at the same time developing a political consciousness in the student. In recent years the Brazilian Catholic Church has adapted this method for the conscientization of the popular classes, and many political militants attend weekend courses, held by the Church, to learn how to deliver this course.
6. The APSD was one of the successful outcomes of political action by the Unemployed Movement. This Association was sponsored by various ecumenical bodies and Churches in São Paulo to give financial support to cooperatives and employment schemes initiated by the unemployed themselves.
7. In all the Brazilian states where help was offered by the government, the majority of projects were either submitted by women or were to be carried out by them.

14.
WARTIME SEXUAL VIOLENCE AGAINST WOMEN: A FEMINIST RESPONSE
Margaret D. Stetz

There has always been sexual violence directed against women during war. Sometimes the acts of aggression and domination have been individual, and sometimes collective. Sometimes they have been spontaneous, but other times, they have been organized and officially sanctioned, especially when dealing with the procurement of women for sexual use by combatants.

To acknowledge this historical record will take us through many cultures and settings. It will lead us back to what George Hicks has identified as a prototype for the "comfort system" in the Roman Empire, when "Slavery ensured a regular supply of captive females for the military brothels which were attached to every Roman garrison or campaigning army."[1] With many examples along the way, especially from the British Empire's nineteenth-century expansion,[2] it will carry us to the turn of the twentieth century, to Elizabeth Salas's research on the Mexican Revolution; in that conflict, revolutionary forces and federal soldiers alike kidnaped and raped women, called them prostitutes, and compelled them to perform both sexual service and housekeeping at the front lines.[3] It will bring us to the early 1970s and to Susan Brownmiller's investigations into the abduction and gang rapes of women, both in Bangladesh, by Pakistani soldiers, and in Vietnam, by American soldiers.[4] It will, of course, send us to the testimony of the former inmates of the Bosnian rape camps collected by Alexandra Stiglmayer.[5] And it will force us to read the headlines of so late a date as 23 September 1996, when the *New York Times* surveyed the plight of thousands of women who, during the Rwandan civil war, were "raped by individuals, gang-raped, raped with sharpened stakes and gun barrels and held in sexual slavery, sometimes alone and sometimes in groups."[6] It will even lead us to the very threshold of the twenty-first century with the abductions and rapes by Serbian soldiers and police of ethnic Albanian women fleeing Kosovo in the spring of 1999.

The chronological record of wartime rape is long. So, too, is the history of how systematic sexual violence by invading or occupying military forces has been disguised as "prostitution," to mitigate atrocities by dismissing them as ordinary commerce. But only recently have there been feminist movements, activists, or scholars to expose these abuses and address these concerns. In the context of the subject of Asian "comfort women"—the question of some two hundred thousand women, roughly 80 percent of whom were Korean, forced to provide sexual service to the

Japanese military before and during World War II—I want to ask, what difference has the presence of feminist analysis made, especially in Asia and the West, over the past twenty-five years? What stories have become visible because of it, and what changes in thought and action may now result? If, as many feminists have argued, rape is a "weapon" of war,[7] in what ways does feminism itself serve as a counter weapon?

I would like to propose that shared Asian and Western feminist perspectives not only have made it possible to confront the subject of wartime rape in new ways, but also to confront it at all. Through the concerted efforts of feminist academics and activists, rape has become a subject that can be spoken about, and the victims of rape themselves have become speaking subjects on the international stage. Because of feminist-initiated research, not only does the world know more about the so-called "comfort system" of World War II, but it also recognizes that this system has appeared in many forms, whenever and wherever military imperialism has combined with masculine privilege. Most recently, feminist pressure worldwide has resulted in a changed legal concept of rape as a war crime—a development that, for the first time ever, holds out hope for the prosecution and punishment by international tribunals of those who commit sexual violence, or who order it to occur.

When I speak of the work of feminists, of course, I am not referring to women alone, but to both female and male thinkers who put the critical examination of gender and its relationship to power at the center of their analyses. And by gender, I mean the dynamic through which human beings are constructed as masculine or feminine subjects within a given cultural and historical framework, then made to occupy unequal social roles.

Perhaps the chief service that feminist analysis has performed is in distinguishing what is customary and familiar from that which is biologically ordained and thus inevitable. In other words, feminism has made it possible to say that, although there has always been sexual violence against women during war, there is nothing normal or justifiable about it. As Ruth Seifert writes, "The most popular and effective myth is that rape has to do with an uncontrollable male drive that, insofar as it is not restrained by culture, has to run its course in a manner that is unfortunate, to be sure, but also unavoidable."[8] To counter such a myth, academic feminists have produced research demonstrating that "rape is not an aggressive manifestation of sexuality, but rather a sexual manifestation of aggression" and that such assaults, whether spontaneous or systematic, "are acts of extreme violence implemented by sexual means."[9]

When sexual violence against women is part of warfare, moreover, feminists have urged the world to look beyond individual perpetrators, to the culture, laws, military systems, and governments that license and encourage it. In the view, for instance, of Larry May and Robert Strikwerda,

> [rape] is something that men, as a group, are collectively responsible for, in a way which parallels the collective responsibility of a society for crimes against humanity

perpetrated by some members of their society. Rape is indeed a crime against humanity, not merely a crime against a particular woman.... [And] men receive strong
encouragement to rape from the way they are socialized as men.[10]

To understand that rape is not an inevitable "release" for male sexuality and
that governments themselves acknowledge this, we have an interesting example
before us. For a period of six months in 1996, two nations put male and female
personnel together into a prolonged situation of unimaginable physical danger,
stress, fear, loneliness, and absolute isolation—that is, aboard the space station *Mir*.
Yet neither Russia nor the United States expected astronaut Shannon Lucid to be
raped, nor was she. She was not raped because it had been made clear that rape was
not being anticipated, permitted, or condoned, regardless of the extreme conditions and absence of other outlets, and that rape would have gone against the two
nations's political interests. Therefore, when governments argue that men "need"
sex with women, and that if women are not provided, rape is the unavoidable
result, feminist analysis enables us to see that the argument conceals another
agenda—that the government in question must, in fact, view a situation in which
women are being violated, dominated, humiliated, and treated as chattel as serving
its political interests. When it is not in the political interests of a government or of
its military arm, then rape stops.

But feminists have not only provided new methods of looking at these questions; they have also demanded new sorts of listening. Around the globe, they have
focused on the silencing of women, emphasized the importance of attending to
women's speech, and uncovered its political implications. Through great struggle,
they have created a climate in which it has been possible for surviving former
"comfort women" to break their silence and politically impossible for governments
to pretend not to hear them. In 1985, when Joan Ringelheim interviewed Jewish
female concentration camp survivors who described being raped both by the SS
and by male prisoners, such women still feared that their abuse represented a trivial, or merely personal misfortune. One survivor told Ringelheim "that it 'was not
important...except to me.' She meant that it had no significance within the larger
picture of the Holocaust."[11] Today, thanks to Asian and Western feminist agitation,
no historian, government, or international tribunal can afford to treat the story of
any individual "comfort woman" as lacking "significance within the larger picture."

In defiance of cultural norms, feminists have heeded and acted on the oral testimony of rape victims, a group often discredited by antifeminists. This has been a
crucial development in making the plight of the "comfort women" known. As
George Hicks noted in 1994, "The central evidence that coercion and deception were
used by the Japanese military to recruit women for the comfort system comes, as this
book has shown, from the women themselves. At the time of writing, there are no
official documents to back up such evidence."[12] Feminists have asserted, too, that a
woman's past sexual history does not invalidate a charge of rape—an important
point for the testimony of some women (including some Japanese women) who

worked in the sex trade, before being used in the "comfort system." Even prostitutes are raped, and when they are, the crimes against them, too, must be prosecuted.

Recently, prosecutions have become more likely, thanks to feminists such as Rhonda Copelon, who repeatedly criticized the old definitions of the Geneva Conventions, under which wartime rapes were "categorized as crimes against honor, not as crimes of violence comparable to murder, mutilation, cruel and inhuman treatment and torture," and thus not deserving separate legal redress.[13] After a long struggle, feminist activism has succeeded in altering this way of thinking. The *New York Times* and other newspapers reported on 28 June 1996 that the UN's International Criminal Tribunal of the Hague broke precedent and, for the first time in any such court, indicted eight Bosnian Serb military and police officials for rape, treating it separately as a war crime in and of itself. On 9 March 1998, this development brought concrete results; Dragoljub Kunarac pleaded guilty to the charge of rape as a crime against humanity (although he later reversed his plea)—the very first such conviction by an international court, but surely the first of many in the future. More recently, in August 1999, a paramilitary leader named Radomir Kovac, a Bosnian Serb, was indicted by the International Criminal Tribunal for the Former Yugoslavia on charges of having run a military "brothel" in Foca, where Muslim women were imprisoned and repeatedly raped by Serbian soldiers, much as women were in Asian "comfort stations" during World War II. The interviewing of ethnic Albanian women by human rights workers in the Balkans, immediately following the war in Kosovo in the spring of 1999, will doubtless soon lead to the indictments of Serbian officials for that round of wartime rapes, too.

Feminist attention to the testimony of rape victims has also produced a new understanding of the physical and mental effects of rape—of why it must be seen as a weapon of destruction and suffering, both in wartime and in what we may choose to call peacetime. (And, of course, feminists have remarked upon the likeness between peace and war, if we consider the role that sexual violence or its imminence plays in women's daily lives around the world.) Moreover, feminist psychologists such as Laura S. Brown and Patricia A. Resick have been responsible for implementing new forms of therapy to treat the trauma of women recovering from war atrocities.[14]

Through feminist efforts, the stories of women raped during war are being broadcast globally, and are becoming the stuff of international legal action and of historical narratives, forcing the rewriting of war to highlight crimes based on gender. Susan Brownmiller warns of what happens when such feminist pressure is not exerted: "The plight of raped women as casualties of war is given credence only at the emotional moment when the side in danger of annihilation cries out for world attention. When the military histories are written...the stories are glossed over, discounted as exaggerations, deemed not serious enough for inclusion in scholarly works."[15]

But new sorts of histories are appearing, and Japanese feminists, in particular, deserve credit for bringing the gendered crimes of militarism, along with the plight of Asian "comfort women" of World War II, into the official Japanese story. I would single out, from among many, Tomiyama Taeko, the artist who has used both visual and verbal means to record the horrors of an imperialist past, and also Takazato Suzuyo, city councillor in Okinawa, who in the 1990s led investigations not only into the use of "comfort women" on Okinawa by Japanese soldiers, but also by American forces, after the island's invasion and capture. Matsui Yayori, a retired journalist who now heads a major Asian feminist organization, has been instrumental, as well, in leading protests against the censorship of Japanese war crimes in textbooks and in recording and disseminating interviews with the surviving former sex slaves of the Japanese military. Japanese feminists' determined resistance to further efforts at silencing has been unceasing, as has been their readiness to work together with Asian and Western women alike in networks of support. During December 2000, for instance, in her role as chairperson of the Violence against Women in War Network—Japan, Matsui Yayori helped to organize and to host the Women's International War Crimes Tribunal on Japan's Military Sexual Slavery, which was intended to bring representatives from women's groups from around the globe to Tokyo with the express purpose of documenting fully the crimes of the past, identifying the perpetrators, seeking their punishment, and making the Japanese government at last accept its legal responsibility toward the former "comfort women." In raising both domestic and international awareness, Miki Mutsuko—widow of Japan's former prime minister, Miki Takeo—has also been an important ally. Her championing of the cause of the survivors of military sex slavery has led her to denounce (perhaps most publicly at "The 'Comfort Women' of World War II: Legacy and Lessons," the conference on "comfort women" held at Georgetown University from 30 September to 4 October 1996) the Japanese government's efforts to avoid paying reparations by creating a so-called private fund for compensation.

Throughout Asia, academic and nonacademic feminists alike have united both within and across national boundaries to build coalitions around these issues. No clearer example of successful action and coalition-formation exists than in the Philippines. The Task Force on Filipino Comfort Women began in 1992 largely thanks to the initiatives of Filipina feminist leaders such as Nelia Sancho and Indai Sajor. Soliciting the stories and participation of victims of the "comfort system," Sancho and Sajor brought to the fore "comfort women" such as Maria Rosa Henson (1928–1996), a remarkable woman who had survived not only a year of sexual slavery by the Japanese imperial forces, but postwar Philippine revolutionary struggles and government crackdowns that had resulted in the murder of members of her family. Until Henson's death, Filipina feminists worked with her in a variety of capacities, including the filing of a lawsuit in a Tokyo district court for financial redress from the Japanese government. Along with other members of the task force, moreover, Sancho and Sajor helped to record, preserve, and circulate Henson's important testimonial, which has recently been issued in English as *Comfort Woman: A Filipina's Story of Prostitution and Slavery under the Japanese*

Military and which has given to the history of this subject a personal voice and a new immediacy for readers everywhere.[16]

Feminists have been linking internationally over the issue of sexual victimization. But even now, there are conservative movements in the United States that wish to frighten American feminists out of such alliances by demonizing the examination of oppression—demonizing even the use of that word—and by deriding the term "victim," along with any correlative analysis of what victimhood means or of the forces that produce this status.

Contrary to what their detractors have said, feminists know quite well that "woman" and "victim" are not identical and interchangeable terms. Victimhood is not the defining status of women, either as a class or as individuals. But ignoring the concept of victimization and failing to embrace the cause of those who have been victimized would be moral cowardice. American feminists must stand up to the new effort at silencing by certain antifeminist, right-wing forces and stand with their Asian counterparts. They must stand with the feminist scholars who have awakened the world to the plight of victims of wartime sexual violence, and they must stand with the survivors themselves.

The world has learned the stories of "comfort women" through the pioneering work of feminist academics such as Professor Yun Chung Ok of South Korea. She, in turn, has inspired a further generation of activist professors in South Korea, such as Professor Shin Heisoo of Hanil Presbyterian University, a prominent member of the organization called the Korean Council for the Women Drafted for Military Sexual Slavery by Japan, as well as faculty at institutions of higher education in the Philippines, Australia, and elsewhere throughout the Pacific region. In Japan, the government has had to confront the subject of past war crimes, due to pressure not only from opposition politicians and journalists (and from important public figures such as Miki Mutsuko, who has used her access to political inner circles and to the media alike to great effect), but also from academics such as Professor Emerita Tsurumi Kazuko, who spoke out on NHK-TV on the fiftieth anniversary of the end of World War II, about the need to uncover all the buried history and to take responsibility for it. These examples should encourage Western feminist academics to involve themselves in the world outside the academy—to appreciate the deep and essential connections between the history we unearth as scholars and the situation of women today, which our research can influence and change.

Yet there are growing numbers of organizations in the United States that are trying to sever this connection between scholarship and women's lives around the globe, insisting that universities must confine themselves to the study of classical texts, the works of Western thinkers, and the histories of great men. Using threats to cut off funding, these rightwing groups hope to discourage American academics from engaging in research or teaching that could be read as "political" and to send us back to the ivory tower. I would remind everyone that a tower made of ivory grows sinister, if we consider what ivory is, where it comes from, and how it is procured. It is all white; it is constructed out of the takings of imperial conquest and despoilation; it represents the valuing of the dead object over the living subject.

At the moment, former "comfort women" are still living subjects. For almost twenty years, they have been telling their stories again and again, and governments have begun to respond. Progress continues to occur in the quest for official apologies and reparations, although it will not come fast enough to benefit many of the survivors, who are now both old and ill. When the last witnesses are gone, historians must repeat their stories everywhere, and a new generation must listen. But it has been and will be the special responsibility of feminist scholars, both in Asia and the West, not merely to attend to these stories, but to study and teach them. For it is up to us, using the methods and philosophy developed through our scholarship, to elucidate and transmit the lessons of this legacy—a legacy that has also begun to inform the worlds of the visual arts, literature, theater, film, and video on both sides of the Pacific.

In her book *Rape Warfare*, Beverly Allen, a professor of women's studies, calls on her readers: "[Our] task . . . is to aid the survivors, judge the perpetrators, and do anything else that will guard against such atrocity in the future. Thus shall we move toward new formulations of community and justice and peace."[17] But only if we move together can such a possibility be realized. Let that be our commitment, as feminists and as academics, and let that be our goal.

Notes

1. George Hicks, *The Comfort Women: Japan's Brutal Regime of Enforced Prostitution in the Second World War* (London and New York: W. W. Norton, 1994), p. 29.
2. Luise White, *The Comforts of Home: Prostitution in Colonial Nairobi* (Chicago: University of Chicago Press, 1990), p. 3.
3. Elizabeth Salas, *Soldaderas in the Mexican Military: Myth and History* (Austin: University of Texas Press, 1990), pp. 39–40.
4. Susan Brownmiller, "Making Female Bodies the Battlefield," in *Mass Rape: The War against Women in Bosnia-Herzegovina*, ed. Alexander Stiglmayer (Lincoln: University of Nebraska Press, 1994), pp. 180–182.
5. Alexandra Stiglmayer, "The Rapes in Bosnia-Herzegovina," in *Mass Rape: The War against Women in Bosnia-Herzegovina*, ed. Alexandra Stiglmayer (Lincoln: University of Nebraska Press, 1994), pp. 82–169.
6. James C. McKinley Jr., "Legacy of Rwanda Violence: The Thousands Born of Rape," *New York Times*, 23 Sept. 1996, sec. A, p. 3.
7. Melinda Lorenson, "No Woman Was Spared," *Ms.* (May/June 1996): 25.
8. Ruth Seifert, "War and Rape: A Preliminary Analysis," in *Mass Rape: The War against Women in Bosnia-Herzegovina*, ed. Alexandra Stiglmayer (Lincoln: University of Nebraska Press, 1994), p. 55.
9. Ibid.
10. Larry May and Robert Strikwerda, "Men in Groups: Collective Responsibility for Rape," in *Special Issue: Feminism and Peace*, ed. Karen J. Warren and Duane L. Cady, *Hypatia* 9 (spring 1994): 135–137.
11. Joan Ringelheim, "Women and the Holocaust: A Reconsideration of Research," in *SIGNS: Journal of Women in Culture and Society* 10 (summer 1985): 745.
12. Hicks, *Comfort Women*, p. 270.

13. Rhonda Copelon, "Gendered War Crimes: Reconceptualizing Rape in Time of War," in *Women's Rights, Human Rights: International Feminist Perspectives*, ed. Julie Peters and Andrea Wolper (New York: Routledge, 1995), p. 200.

14. See Laura S. Brown, "From Alienation to Connection: Feminist Therapy with Post-Traumatic Stress Disorder, pp. 13–26, and Patricia A. Resick, "PostTraumatic Stress Disorder in a Vietnam Nurse: Behavioral Analysis of a Case Study," pp. 55–65, in *Another Silenced Trauma: Twelve Feminist Therapists and Activists Respond to One Woman's Recovery from War*, ed. Esther D. Rothblum and Ellen Cole (New York: Harrington Park Press, 1986).

15. Brownmiller, "Making Female Bodies the Battlefield," p. 182.

16. See Maria Rosa Henson, *Comfort Woman: A Filipina's Story of Prostitution and Slavery under the Japanese Military* (Lanham, MD: Rowman & Littlefield, 1999).

17. Beverly Allen, *Rape Warfare: The Hidden Genocide in Bosnia-Herzegovina and Croatia* (Minneapolis: University of Minnesota Press, 1996), p. 144.

SECTION II
THEORIZING INTERSECTING
IDENTITIES

INTRODUCTION

From the early days of the second wave women's movement in the United States, "difference" among women has been thinly camouflaged under a hegemonic "gender difference" that was supposed to unite all women. However, as early as the 1970s, "difference" was articulated not only as "gender difference that united women as distinct from men" but also "as an index of incommensurability among women of different races, classes, ethnicities, and sexualities" (Schmitz et al. 1995: 710). Moreover, "women of color" were already challenging the way "women's experiences" were constructed as an exclusionary practice by white, middle class, heterosexual women: "Frances Beal's 1971 essay in *Sisterhood Is Powerful* warned that women's liberation was fast becoming a 'white women's movement' because it insisted on organizing along the gender demarcation male/female alone..." (Sandoval 1991, cited in King 1994: 25). Despite their constant challenges, these voices were often kept at the periphery of U.S. feminist theorizing.

As bell hook's book title *From Margin to Center*[1] signifies, the ideas and experiences of women of color were relegated to the margins of feminist theorizing. At best they were appropriated to provide experiential evidence for white feminist theory. However, the 1980s saw a full-blown critique of feminist theoretical frameworks based solely on the concept of gender that was launched by many women of color, Third World women, socialist feminists, and lesbian feminists. While this critique began as a challenge to exclusion from feminist theory, it also opened up the space to examine the significance of differences among women and to discuss the ways that women's lives are shaped by race, nationality, class, and sexuality as well as by gender. As with theorizing, which fragmented around identity categories, the U.S. feminist movement also fragmented around identity categories. In global context, the tensions between North and South erupted at each of the UN conferences during the Decade on Women, 1975–1985. The document from the 1995 Beijing Conference reflects the long struggle to develop alliances among women that are built on respect for racial, sexual, class, religious, and locational differences.[2]

The essays in this section reflect the struggles to build feminist theories of differences among women. The readings are gathered together under the categories of race and nation, class, and sexuality. Through these essays, readers will gain an understanding of the multiple identities that women must negotiate and are encouraged to reflect on the multiple identities they must negotiate in their own lives.

We recognize the problems involved in approaching women's differences based on such discrete categories. As we have already seen with the category "women," where there is not a common identity, there are dangers in treating race, nationality, class, and sexuality as if each category captures some perfectly shared common experience or identity. The discussion of differences can also be oversimplified by treating the experiences captured within these categories as if they are each analytically discrete and separate from the others. Furthermore, in treating one factor as the principle focus of analysis, important interactions with simultaneously present other factors can easily be obscured or misconstrued. Thus, with a narrow focus on gender, it is impossible to see how gender is raced. Likewise, with a narrow focus on race, one can not see the specificity of nationality within racial groups; one cannot see the specificity of class or sexualities within nationalities and racial groups; and so on. Further, there are also hazards in delineating differences among women as if all the important differences are containable within the three categories of race, class, and sexuality. As Grewal and Kaplan have urged, we must be aware of emerging new orthodoxies, for example, how "race, class, and gender are fast becoming the holy trinity that every feminist feels compelled to address even as this trinity delimits the range of discussion around women's lives. What is often left out of these U.S.-focused debates are other complex categories of identity and affiliation that apply to non-U.S. cultures and situations" (Grewal and Kaplan 1994: 19).

Although the categories may not be discrete in history or social experience, they do represent recurrent tensions within feminist conversations and debates around which theorizing has often fractured. Intellectual efforts to understand these phenomena have been located in separate although sometimes overlapping intellectual communities. Thus, in these multiple–identity based sites of theorizing, feminists, North and South, struggled to understand the specific connections and disconnections between gender domination with race, nationality, class, and sexuality. Sometimes this theorizing considered the intersections of several systems of domination simultaneously, sometimes not. The framework used in this section, "Theorizing Intersecting Identities," was constructed with these problems and tensions in mind. Like a kaleidoscope in which a jumble of objects are refracted through a prism in constantly shifting patterns, the organizational scheme is offered as a shifting prism of difference through which to examine the mobile and multiple configurations of domination in women's lives. The organization of section II moves through each subsection, foregrounding one specific category, as if it were discrete. But the readings within each subsection continually disrupt the boundaries of the category they are grouped under. They unsettle the notion that race, nation, class, sexuality, or gender can be treated as independent categories. In particular, colonialism is not presented as a separate category.[3] Instead, each subsection includes readings that specifically address issues of locational identity and experiences within non-U.S. contexts. This organization is designed to interrupt and unsettle U.S.-focused theories of difference captured under the race, class, and sexuality rubric. This organizational scheme thus encourages readers to see differences as relational rather than discrete; and to see that the meanings of difference are produced through those relations and are not an inherent quality of each category. We also hope the repeated transgressions of the categorical boundaries will encourage discussion of intersectionality of complex and conflicting aspects of identity in women's lives. We hope it will encourage readers to reflect on the shifting identities they must negotiate, although the readings also demonstrate that not all negotiations carry the same risks and privileges.

The readings in "Race and Nation" trace the turbulent shifts in feminist theories of oppression. In the early 1980s, when feminist scholars debated how racial and national differences might be connected, there was a great deal of talk about how gender, race, and nation fit together. Did the combination of race and gender oppression produce a kind of "double-jeopardy," in which the injuries of sexism and racism added up to a double dose of oppression? (Beal 1970). And what would happen if one was also subject of class-based domination, colonialism, or heterosexual domination? Did that constitute a situation of multiple jeopardy, in which dominations were added together, creating ever greater misery? (King 1988). Or did each additional element of domination produce greater suffering and the possibility of greater insight? There was also talk of a hierarchy of oppression, in which some forms of domination were judged to be more politically important than others. Questions of whether any one dimension of domination was primary or was historically prior to all others stirred ongoing and often contentious debates among theorists and activists.[4] Some argued that class, or gender, or race, or sexuality were *the* first oppression, *the* model of all other oppressions. Marxist movements traditionally argued that the class system is the basic division of society and that racism, imperialism, and sexism derive from it. Socialist feminists and black feminists, like the Combahee River Collective included here, contend instead that sexism and racism derive from separate systems.[5] Radical feminist theorists also have argued that the oppression of women by men is the original oppression, which serves as the model for all others (Burris 1973; Rich 1979). Throughout such discussions, recurrent claims have been made about who is most oppressed, and therefore who has the clearest insight, the greatest claim to articulate political strategies, and who would be the subject of revolutionary change. Such discussions shaped the context out of which the standpoint theories presented in section III emerged.

Through this struggle to understand the intersecting identities and dominations women experience, the analytic framework of an additive model of oppression gave way to the recognition of the simultaneity, not a hierarchy, of oppression (Spelman 1988) and a theoretical framework of intersectionality, or a "matrix of domination" (Hill Collins 1990). Audre Lorde, herself an older, disabled, working-class, African-Carribean lesbian argued against privileging a hierarchy of oppression (Lorde 1984).[6] Likewise, the women of the Combahee River Collective, in the essay included here, argue that the conditions of our lives result from the synthesis of simultaneous and "interlocking systems of domination." The interlocking systems they note include, race, sexual, heterosexual, and class oppression. However, the analysis of simultaneous oppression that they offer still depends on a hierarchy of oppression, in which black women are positioned "at the bottom." This essay also provides an early definition of identity politics. They argue that black feminism is formed in its troubled connections to the "Second Wave of the American women's movement" and "the movement for black liberation," both of which failed to address the unique political struggles of black women adequately. Therefore, they conclude "the most profound and potentially the most radical politics come directly out of our own identity, as opposed to working to end somebody else's oppression." Black feminism, they argue, emerges from "the political realization that comes from the seemingly personal experiences of individual black women's lives."

In this process of understanding the significance of racial and national differences among women, theorists also confronted the questions of who are "we" who were left out of the white women's movement and feminist theory. By what name should "we" be known? The term "women of color" was an organizing category at the 1981 National Women's Studies Association's conference at Storrs, Connecticut, which became a watershed event in U.S. Women's Studies. The topic of the conference was "Women Respond to Racism," and included consciousness-raising sessions structured according to identity categories. While categories for white women were divided by class, sexuality, and immigrant status, women who were not white found their differences were collapsed into a single category, "women of color." This category was offered by feminists of color involved in organizing the conference and the label was in response to criticism that the discussions of racism among U.S. feminists often dichotomized race into black and white. The Combahee River Collective's essay provides an example of the erasure of racial differences beneath the hegemony of black/white definitions of race in U.S. feminisms. They argue that black feminism is the political movement to combat the oppressions all women of color face. This essay constructs the normative woman of color as an African American woman. The term, "women of color" was intended to be more inclusive of women's racial identities and experiences of racism. However, conference participants intensely deliberated whether or not this was an appropriate term. Chela Sandoval, in her essay recounting the conference events, describes the fragility of the term "women of color" even as it was accepted. The group of women who were involved were aware that the differences this term "threatened to hide include, for example, culture, ethnicity, national associations, religion, skin color, race, language, class, and sexual differences" (cited in King 1994: 64).

Other possible terms included "Third World women," a term that was already widely used. The term "Third World" originates in the context of Cold War–era development politics. The First World was a label designating the first nations to go through industrialization, the liberal-capitalist nation states of Western Europe and the United States. The Second World referred to the socialist nations that industrialized in the context of communist revolutions. The Third World referred to those nations that were not aligned with either in Cold War political contests after World War II.[7] While the label "women of color" highlights race as the grounds of common oppression and political solidarity, "Third World women" highlights imperialism as the grounds of oppression and solidarity. The debate itself points to the historical nexus of race, colonialism, and nation,

Race is the term for the classification of humans into physically recognizable groups who possess distinct genetic constitutions. Racial classifications emerged with the European expansion that began four hundred years ago and coincides with European colonialism, but their fullest articulation came in European and American racial sciences of the late-nineteenth century (Omi and Winant 1994). Race has never been just about skin color or content of character, it is part of the "construction and naturalization of unequal form of intercultural relations" (Ashcroft et al. 1998: 46). The concept has been central to the organization of the global inequality that accompanied colonial expansion and accomplished European cultural and economic imperialism.

Colonialism refers to that form of empire-building imperialism, in which regions outside of Europe were claimed by European countries and settled. This occupation of territory was justified through a racialized colonial discourse about the necessity of civilizing the world.[8] One reason for racial classifications is to provide a natural basis for the rigid hierarchy of difference between the colonizer and the colonized. Another reason is to provide a natural basis for the rigid hierarchy between slaves and slave owners. Both provide an assumption of natural superiority that legitimates European acquisition and domination of territory across the globe (Ashcroft et al. 1998: 46, 201).

Like the classification of humans by race, the idea of the nation, "natural and immutable formations based on shared collective values," is a product of European expansion (Ashcroft et al., 1998: 151). The idea of the nation emerged through confrontation with the colonized. As an "imagined community" it became the entity for which the colony was claimed. Its welfare and prosperity justified the subordination of other people and places (Anderson 1983).

European colonialism certainly involved the dispersal of Europeans across the world, a "Europeanization of the globe" (Ashcroft et al. 1998: 123). However, it also involved additional movements of peoples from their homelands to other regions. For instance, the slave trade involved the involuntary movement of millions of Africans to North and South America and the Carribean. In addition, after slavery was outlawed in Europe in the nineteenth century, systems of indentured labour resulted in world-wide colonial diasporas.[9] "... [L]arge populations of poor agricultural labourers from population rich areas, such as India and China, [were transported] to areas where they were needed to service plantations." Descendants of these groups have developed their own cultures, which "preserve and often extend and develop their originary cultures." Today, the major diasporic movements involve the movement of "colonized peoples back to the metropolitan centres" (Ashcroft et al. 1998: 69–70).

In Europe and in colonies where large numbers of Europeans settled, the boundaries between the nation (us) and the colonized (them), were set up by erasing differences within the nation through a homogenized myth of national tradition (Ashcroft et al. 1998: 150–51).[10] However, the nation is always unstable, because the homogenizing effects of those national myths are always disrupted by reemergent differences. Most recently, the "counter-publics" generated by diasporic cultures contest the national myths of colonial discourses in Europe and the United States (Fraser 1992). At the same time, the nation has also extended into the colonized world as liberation movements directed at ending colonialism established new nations, which likewise depend on the erasure of internal difference. These erasures are not enacted only in national myths, but as the twentieth-century histories of genocide demonstrate, they are often violently enacted on national landscapes.[11]

Another aspect of the nexus of race, colonialism, and nation is the way it is gendered. The status of women within a culture has often been used as a marker in constructing a hierarchy of nations. While building their empire, the British used to say, one could judge how civilized a culture was by the way they treated their women. Of course, the British treatment of women represented the pinnacle, even though they had few political, economic, or social rights (Said 1978: 14). Thus, judgment about the level of civilization a culture had attained depended on how closely it matched European gender conventions and constraints. Moreover, colonial rule often justified cultural intervention in the name of improving the status of women. Such practices make women's situation a political token within the hierarchical relationships of colonialism. When the status of women is used in this way, it becomes really challenging for feminists in or from postcolonial cultures to criticize the gender politics of our culture. To do so could result in our complaints being used as evidence that the men of our culture are not as civilized as Western men, and thus, our complaints may be seen as traitorous by our culture.[12] Helie-Lucas's essay examines the way in which local gender politics can be shaped by these broader politics of colonialism. She argues that within a variety of Islamic fundamentalisms, women's status has become a central element of resistance to Western hegemony in the 1990s. In the process of articulating a defense of Islam against colonialism, imperialism, and debased Western ideologies, the private sphere has been identified as the core of an embattled Muslim identity. To protect the private sphere from encroachment, fundamentalists have focused on the place of women within it. In many Muslim nations, fundamentalist movements endeavored to pass "Personal Laws that they believed enforced the authentic Islamic tradition that existed before colonial occupation." Helie-Lucas examines the ways in which the discourses and practices of fundamentalist resistence to the cultural hegemony of the West have limited the strategies for feminist resistance to regressive political measures embodied in fundamentalist "Personal Laws."

In the United States in the 1980s and 1990s, "women of color" became one concept that designated the multifaceted nexus of race, colonialism, and nation. On the other hand, "Third World women" continued to be used to denote non-U.S. locations and identities (Mohanty et al. 1991). As the readings make clear, both can imply the notion of a diasporic identity. Recently, the term transnational has been used to refer to women from Third World nations/ethnicities who resided in First World countries. Many scholars who contributed to the feminist theorizing about gender difference in postcolonial contexts fit within this category. The location of such individuals within the political struggles of their originary cultures can be quite complicated. As Aiwha Ong asks, "do Third World feminists who now write in the anglophone world enjoy a privileged positionality in representing the 'authentic experiences' of women from our ancestral cultures or not?" As Lydia Liu notes, it is not clear, "exactly how the post-colonial theorist relates to the 'Third World' except that s/he travels in and out of it and points out its difference from that of the 'First World.'" The term "transnational" tries to capture the notion that such scholars are, as Ong notes, "multiply inscribed subjects," who engage complicated cultural power relations in crossing national boundaries (quoted in Kim and McCann 1998: 117).

Despite the unstable nature of the terms "women of color," "Third World women," and "transnational women," they can denote a strategic temporary unity from which "oppositional consciousness" and significant theoretical insights can emerge (Spivak 1990). The years after the Storrs conference saw the explosion of writings by women of color, Third World, and transnational feminist scholars. These writings embody vibrant debates about the significance of intersections of race, colonialism, nation, and gender for understanding women's complex situations. Sandoval also cautions that the unity constructed by these terms is necessarily temporary, noting: "The meaning of our sisterhood will change. If society's powers are ever mobile and in flux, as they are, then our oppositional moves must not be ideologically limited to one, single, frozen, 'correct' response" (Sandoval 1990: 66).

One of the most important writings during this period was *This Bridge Called My Back* in 1981. It was one of the first anthologies by self-defined women of color in the United States. It is the anthology in which that very phrase "women of color," gets constructed as a community of nonwhite women defined not in terms of the negation of whiteness, but as an acclamation of a positive identity. In the preface, the editors Cherri Moraga and Gloria Anzaldúa claim the anthology as an intervention in and a critique of the "hegemonic feminist theory." The writings included theoretical pieces, poems, and prose, which often relied on the feminist concepts of gender, experience, personal is political, and difference.[13]

Donna Rushin's poem expresses the frustration of a woman of color who has continuously been used as a bridge to connect people in different locations. She has had enough of doing work for others so that they can realize the limits and potentials of their positions. The bridge in the poem, and in the anthology title, thus signifies how women of color have been walked over, literally and figuratively, as others find themselves and their freedom. She tells the reader to either "stretch or drown," because she is no longer going to be there to fill the gap. Instead she is going to focus her energies on building a bridge "to her own power" to her "true self." The anthology editor, Gloria Anzaldua, declares "there are no more bridges, one builds them as one walks" (Moraga and Anzaldúa 1981).

Drawing on her personal experience as a Nisei Japanese American, Mitsuye Yamada depicts Asian American women as "the visible minority that is invisible." Yamada reflects on the process by which her colleagues translated her protests over gender discrimination as a "front for those feminists." Because her colleagues saw her stereotypically as a quiet, respectful Asian woman, she was seen as too nice to be engaged in such agitation. Yamada concludes that when she did not actively engage in resisting the stereotypes of Asian American women, she was being complicit in the construction and reconstruction of those stereotypes. Thus, as well, her resistance was misread and therefore it was rendered invisible. She urges us to refuse to be relegated to an invisible group, noting that "we need to raise our voices a little more, even as they say to us 'This is so uncharacteristic of you.'"

In using these concepts, theorists also reconfigured them in important ways. As Mohanty says, "the point is not just 'to record' one's history of struggle, or consciousness, but how they are recorded; the way we read, receive and disseminate such imaginative records is immensely significant" (1991a: 34). In *This Bridge Called My Back*, various authors use their marginalized experience "...to remember and to renarrate everyday experiences of domination and resistance, and to situate these experiences in relation to broader historical phenomena..." (Stone-Mediatore 2000: 117). Hence, these marginalized experiences were not simply told or uncovered. They worked as an expression of "oppositional consciousness" to intervene into the flow of "hegemonic feminist theory," and the value of the book lies in this intervention and the affirmation of the theorizing ability of "women of color."[14] One very important contribution of the book was to provide analyses of the differences in experiences of racism. Essays demonstrated that the racial experiences and identities of women of color are constructed in historically-specific intersections of race, colonialism, and nationalism.

An exemplar of the generative insights of reconfiguring experience can be seen in Gloria Anzaldúa's essay herein. Using her experience as a Mexican American lesbian, Anzaldúa traces her shifting identity through her shifting locations. These experiences of shifting identity, she argues, are the grounds for a new consciousness of the multiple logics of power. Anzaldúa constructs a "new higher consciousness," which she calls a new mestiza consciousness. The mestiza is usually understood as mixed race, connoting negative sterility of the hybrid (McCann 1994). To the contrary, Anzaldúa asserts, "this mixture of races, rather than resulting in an inferior being, provides hybrid progeny, a mutable, more malleable species with a rich gene pool." The mestiza, in juggling cultures and contexts each time she crosses the borders, has a plural personality. While the experiences of multiple, shifting identities is painful, she not only "sustains contradictions, she turns the ambivalence into something else." That "something else" is a perspective that "includes rather than excludes.... Nothing is thrust out, the good, the bad, and the ugly, nothing is rejected, nothing abandoned." Going through the experience of border crossing, one can emerge with a new understanding of contradictions and ambiguities that emerge in the experience of multiple cultures and locations. In the borderlands, the new mestiza learns to shift identities between contexts, to bridge cultures, and thus, to come up with new strategies (Mohanty 1991a).

Fifteen years after the publication of *This Bridge*, questions of how linkages and alliance among women of color might be forged remain. In a review of the 1995 UN Conference on Women in Beijing, Mallika Dutt considers the issues of organizing among women of color in global contexts. She is particularly concerned with how U.S. women of color can locate themselves with respect to issues of gender and race in global civil society. What kinds of coalitions are possible? What are the points of tensions and struggle? She particularly highlights the network of indigenous peoples worldwide as a model that can inform effective global alliances among women of color.

The readings about class focus most sharply on the relationship between feminism and Marxism. Heidi Hartmann's essay summarizes much of the debate that occurred in the United States in the 1970s about the relationship of gender and class, explaining why this relationship is so important. In a variety of anticapitalist political communities, the debate about whether socialism would end women's oppression, as communists claimed earlier in the century, was renewed in the 1960s and 1970s.[15] Hartmann's essay, which circulated in mimeographed form for many years before it was formally published, offers an example of such a critique and elaborates on one socialist-feminist solution: dual systems theory.[16] For Hartmann, the class system, represented in the current historical moment by capitalism, did not underlie sexism, and thus socialism would not eliminate sexism. Instead, an independent system, patriarchy, shaped the social relations of gender, and these would have to be changed to end women's oppression.

Hartmann begins with Marx's notion of historical materialism. Marx argued that "as individuals express their lives, so they are." By this he meant that the ways people organize the activities of making the things they need to live—food, clothing, shelter, tools—and of making human beings themselves are the key factors that shape history (Marx 1977: 161, 162; Engels 1972: 71–72). Thus historical materialism, as a method for understanding society and history, focuses on this material reality, the forces and relations of production and reproduction. In practice as Hartmann notes, Marx and Marxists ignored the relations and forces of reproduction, and with it the system of patriarchy that she argues accounts for sexism. She defines patriarchy as the "set of social relations between men, ... though hierarchical ... that enable them to dominate women." She argues that, like the class system, the patriarchy has a material base: men's control of women's sexuality and their access to resources. Where Marx mistakenly saw the sexual division of labor as natural, Hartmann theorizes it as social. Following Rubin, Hartmann calls the system that underlies patriarchy "the sex/gender system." After detailing mechanisms by which the sex/gender system secures male domination of women, she examines the partnership that has developed between capitalism and patriarchy. Thus, she concludes that any adequate theory of class must take account of the sex/gender system. Also, while she does note that race, like gender, serves as a system of domination, she does not elaborate a theory of the intersections of gender, class, and race.

Linda Lim complicates the question of the relationship of class and gender by situating the experience of Third World women in capitalist, patriarchal, and imperialist relations of production. She argues that "the interplay of capitalist, imperialist, and patriarchal relations of production" produce "simultaneously exploitative and liberating consequences.... [The] complexities involved in an analysis of female employment in multinational export factories in developing countries [point up the] inadequacy of simplistic anti-capitalist, anti-imperialist, and anti-patriarchal... strategies to relieve exploitation." In a similar vein, Molyneux's essay addresses the relationship between "socialist revolution and women's emancipation." She provides a case study of this relationship in an analysis of the circumstances in which women became engaged in the movement to oust the authoritarian Somoza government from Nicaragua in 1979.[17] Arguing that women's political activism emerges from their distinctive position within the sexual division of labor and the class structure, she delineates a theory of women's complex strategic and practical gender interests. Yet, she concludes, feminists cannot assume that women will always recognize their gender interests, nor that women will be unified on gender issues. History shows that gender unity "tends to collapse under the pressure of acute class conflict." While she notes that racial, ethnic, and national conflicts also can undercut womens unity, these categories do not figure in her basic analysis. The clearest cases of this collapse of gender unity, she argues, can be seen in the midst of socialist revolutions. This, she argues, may account for the fact that such revolutions seem not to address women's issues adequately. However, the case of Nicaragua also provides some evidence that it is not inevitable that socialist governments will ignore gender interests.

In section I, Charlotte Bunch delineated the lines of tension in conversations about women's sexuality in the U.S.-based women's movement and feminist theorizing. The discussion of sexuality in this section begins with a classic piece by Anne Koedt, which raises many issues that have become the topic of tension and extensive theorizing. She starts with the observation that what we know about women's sexuality has been constructed from the point of view of male pleasure. Thus female sexuality has been socially constructed to fit with the requirements of male heterosexual pleasure. This observation suggests that heterosexuality might be compulsory for women, and not dictated by the nature of women's desire or pleasure. Following the form of analysis common to U.S.–radical feminist theorizing, she asks, what would women's sexuality be if not constructed to fit male-dominated conventions of heterosexuality? Koedt raises the question of whether men are even necessary to women's sexual pleasure. In so doing, she poses but leaves unanswered the question of the relationship between sexism, heterosexism, and homophobia.

An early postmodernist perspective on the position of lesbians in the women's movement is represented by Monique Wittig's piece. Within her essay she raises the question of the relation between women and the myth of woman, that dominant cultural representation that marks actual women. Arguing that women are made in culture and not born in nature, she poses this as a political question—How can we distinguish strategies for the liberation of women and strategies for securing the dominion of the myth of woman? The myth of woman is that representation of natural woman to which actual women are made to conform. How can we distinguish when women are speaking for the myth of woman and when they are resisting it? The answers to these questions hinge on developing the insights of lesbian feminists, who because of their exclusion from it, have a unique vantage point from which to analyze the myth of woman.

In 1980, Adrienne Rich published "Compulsory Heterosexuality and Lesbian Existence," in which she made a sustained case for the notion that heterosexuality was not natural but was imposed on women. This argument extended feminist theoretical insights about the social construction of gender to sexuality. Likewise, Rich argued, compulsory heterosexuality is the essence of male domination. That is, heterosexuality is the institutional structure at the base of women's oppression as women. While the social construction of sexuality was noted earlier, such as by Rubin, and lesbian feminist theorists had argued that heterosexuality was the mainstay of patriarchy (Bunch 1975; Radicalesbians 1973), Rich elaborated the argument more fully and grounded it in key principles of Western feminist thinking. Rich's argument was grounded on feminist psychoanalytic theories of gender, in which mother love was the primary emotional connection for all humans and the ground of women's unique gender-based skills/qualities. This primacy of mother love indicated that woman-centered emotional and erotic attachments were central for all women. Through this argument Rich makes the case that homophobia and repression of lesbians is an issue central to the women's movement, because it is one example on the continuum of repression of female solidarity, desire, and creative energies.[18] She also makes the case for a politics of separatism, the withdrawal of women's support from men and male-dominated institutions.

However, just as with the category of women and women's experiences, the category of lesbian and lesbian experiences constructed in feminist theory has often imposed a binary opposition between heterosexuality and homosexuality and often excluded lesbians of color and lesbians of the South and sexual practices and identities that do not abide by the rigid distinction. The strategy of separatism, which was a primary strategy of white Western lesbian-feminist theory and practice in the late 1970s and 1980s, has been criticized by lesbians of color as one more example of the exclusive focus on gender politics. As Barbara Smith notes, in several places, lesbians of color have good reasons for solidarity with men of color (Smith and Smith 1881; Smith 1983). Audre Lorde, as well, continuously raised cautions about the interconnectedness of gender, race, and sexual identity that made separatism an unworkable strategy for lesbians of color (Lorde 1984). Yet while separatism is unworkable, she sees that organizing around difference is very challenging as well. In the piece included here, Lorde addressed the exclusions within their racial/ethnic/cultural communities that lesbians of color have had to confront. Audre Lorde notes the complexity of heterosexism and homophobia by which her identity as a lesbian is subsumed under her identity as a black woman in race-based identity politics, forcing her to hide to gain inclusion. She notes that "heterosexism and homophobia are two grave barriers to organizing among Black women." Challenging black women to see how they have clung to heterosexual privilege as one of the few privileges afforded African American women, Lorde recounts her antiracist activism as a lesbian and asserts, "I want to be recognized. I am a black lesbian, and I am your sister." She argues that black women must find ways to organize around "genuine" difference without either "denying them" or "blowing them out of proportion." Lorde delineates the challenges of organizing around difference in specific relationship to homophobia within the U.S. black community. However, the observations she makes can be extended to a variety of contexts within the intersections of oppressions.

Gestures of colonialism have been frequent within the feminist conversations about women's sexuality in the United States and in Europe. Rich's essay provides a vivid example. Following her observation of the primacy of women-centered attachments, she provides a catalog of violent acts of male power. This time the list of atrocities is marshaled to prove that same-sex erotic attachment is the thing men most fear and repress through their dominance over women. In the list, the sexuality of women of color and women in the South are used as examples of the pervasiveness and violence of male power. The first example given is "clitoridectomy and infibulation," early 1980s terms for female genital surgeries. Feminist theorists of the South, such as Chandra Talpade Mohanty, have criticized such listings because they cast the sexuality of women of the South entirely as experiences of victimization (Mohanty 1991b).[19] The construction of the sexuality of women of the South within colonial discourse as either exotic or victimized, raises particular dilemmas for organizing around sexuality within transnational communities of color.

Karin Aguilar-San Juan and Gayatri Gopinath both raise issues of sexuality in transnational communities of color. Both consider the challenges of organizing around issues of sexual identity in diaspora. Gopinath raises the issue of gender in articulations of community and ethnic identity in diaspora. Reacting to the pejorative representations within colonial discourses, she argues that disaporic communities tend to replicate conventional ideologies of gender and sexuality, in which "certain bodies" are "rendered invisible" or are "marked as other." In addressing the questions of how those "outside a normative space of monogamous heterosexuality forge diasporic networks for our own particular purposes," she provides an analysis of the uses of Hindi film songs in queer South Asian spaces. These uses, she argues, can inform a theory of South Asian queerness that does not "replicate existing power structures between the west and the rest." Instead "such forms of transnational popular practice mean radically different things in different contexts." For Gopinath, this requires, like Anzaldua's mestiza consciousness, a flexible, mobile subject. It also requires a model of organizing, like Anzaldua's bridge-building metaphor, "where queerness and ethnicity are being contested and made anew every step of the way."

Aguilar-San Juan focuses on the "problem of authenticity" that confronts communities that organize around "some aspect of identity." Although she notes that "acknowledging our experience in terms of our sexuality is a central part of our community building process," she cautions that "appealing to an authentic experience can make a misleading claim to truth." Following the criticism of feminist theorizing from experience offered by feminist historian Joan Scott, Aguilar

San-Juan points out that in seeking to give voice to a silenced category of people by speaking from experience, we may fail to reveal the reasons for that silencing in the first place. For Aguilar-San Juan, the repeated marginalization of queer Asian Americans within sexual discourses and practices on one hand, and within ethnic/postcolonial discourses on the other, is the central problem involved in giving voice to Asian American lesbian experiences. She argues that "including my voice inadvertently reveals that all perspectives are not given equal footing."[20] Thus, she asserts, when speaking from the margins, attention must be given to the social processes by which some categories are "assumed to be central" while others are "naturally on the margins." She also locates the problem of authenticity in the way that the notion of home has been evoked in queer Asian American conversations. How can one be at home in Asian American communities that require one to deny one's sexual orientation, and yet how can one be at home in a gay and lesbian community that requires one to deny one's cultural heritage? The shifting contexts and meanings of home and identity are complicated by transnational identities, which, if one is not cautious, can replicate colonial dominations in the pursuit of sexual freedom. As an example she examines the talk among U.S.-based Filipina lesbians in their efforts to support lesbians in the Philippines in their struggles against homophobia.

After examining the categories of difference grouped herein, readers will confront again the central dilemma of feminist theory: how to weigh differences both in terms of individual identities and in terms of political configurations of feminist activism. This is a recurrent and insoluble issue. Moreover, the readings demonstrate that the boundaries of difference within and among women must also continually be defined, redefined, and always negotiated. As Patricia Williams has explained,

> while being black has been the most powerful social attribution in my life, it is only one of a number of governing narratives or presiding fictions by which I am constantly reconfiguring myself in the world. Gender is another, along with ecology, pacifism, my peculiar brand of colloquial English, and Roxbury, Massachusetts. The complexity of role identification, the politics of sexuality, the inflections of professionalized discourse—all describe and impose boundary in my life, even as they confound one another in unfolding spirals of confrontation, deflection, and dream. (Patricia Williams 1991: 256)

As Williams eloquently describes, gender—along with others (race/ethnicity, class, and sexuality)—is one axis of the matrix of domination that imposes boundaries on any woman. Furthermore, a woman's identity can never be collapsed to a uni-dimension because identity is not only always relational, ever changing, and fluid, but also inherently contradictory, layered, and conflicting. Because of these multilayered differences, including the inherent differences "within" us, feminist scholars have argued that it is difficult to render identity as a secure anchor for politics (see Trinh Minh-Ha 1989; Judith Butler 1990; Joan Scott 1992; and Wendy Brown 1995). Likewise, feminist scholars have critiqued experience-based knowledge/politics. "The evidence of experience … becomes evidence for the fact of difference, rather than a way of exploring how difference is established, how it operates, how and in what ways it constitutes subjects who see and act in the world" (Scott 1992: 25). Thus "appeals to experience risk naturalizing ideologically conditioned categories that structure our experiences of self and world" (Stone-Mediatore 2001: 110). Despite the questioning, according to Elizabeth Weed, some feminists have employed experience "not to pin down the truth of the individual subject but as a critical effort to open up ideological contradictions" (cited in Stone-Mediatore 2001: 113). Even with the limitations of "women's experience," as Mohanty argues "stories of experiences have been vital to Third World feminist praxis" (Stone-Mediatore 2001: 116). So how do feminist theorists proceed? How can we weigh differences? How can we assess the shifting identities and alliances produced by the intersecting boundaries within the matrix of domination? And, can our experiences usefully inform our knowledge? Section III delineates two important currents of feminist theorizing in a transnational world that offer thoughtful responses to these questions.

Notes

1. The essay by hooks in section I is taken from this 1984 book.
2. For criticism of the narrow focus of feminism in global contexts, see, for instance, Barriosde Chungara 1977; Rao 1991; and *Feminist Studies* 22(3) 1996, Special Issue after Beijing.
3. In the introduction to her 2001 anthology on race and feminism, Kum Kum Bhavnani argues that "three strands—identity, difference, and colonialism … represent the strength [and] diversity [of writings on] race and feminism" (p. 3).
4. We have also seen this is in our feminist theory classrooms, as students engage in conversations about the complexity of gender and difference.
5. See also Omi and Winant 1994, whose concept of racial formation articulates a system of racial relations that is related to but independent of capitalism and imperialism. Similarly, postcolonial theorists argue that colonialism has generated relations of power that are related to capitalism but also are independent. See Bhabha 1990 and 1994.
6. The repeated need to speak against the ranking of oppressions indicates the resilience of this theme in feminist organizations and Women's Studies classrooms.
7. Microsoft Encarta attributes the first use of the term to Frantz Fanon, the renowned anticolonialist theorist. Ashcroft, et al. which defines key concepts of Post Colonial Studies, attributes the term to French demographer, Alfred Sauvy, and notes the rapid development of pejorative and racialized connotations of the term in Western usage. The term was widely used by U.S. feminists. See Burris, 1971; Anzaldúa herein; and Sandoval, 1990.
8. Following Edward Said, colonial discourse is the discourse constructed by colonial regimes, as well as ordinary travelers and explorers about areas/cultures colonized by Europe. This discourse defines the colonized region in an imaginative geography that characterizes the colonized, often in racialized terms, as inferior to the colonizer. Colonial discourse sets up the binary opposition of primitive and civilized, in which Europe is always the civilized member of the pair.
9. Diaspora, first used to describe the situation of Jews in the Middle Ages, has come to refer to "the voluntary and involuntary movement of peoples from their homelands to other regions" (Ashcroft et al. 1998: 68).
10. The idea of the nation also conceals the power and practices of the nation-state. Thus the nation is an "extremely contentious site, on which ideas of self-determination and freedom, of identity, and unity collide with suppression and force, of domination and exclusion" (Ashcroft et al. 1998: 151).

11. See Powers 2002 for a history of twentieth-century genocides and U.S. knowledge of and complicity in those events.
12. This judgment also rebounds on European and First World women, in that our complaints of mistreatment are dismissed with the argument that we have it great in comparison with other countries where other women are treated really badly, and therefore, we should be grateful.
13. See also Combahee River Collective; Mohanty 1991a; and Bhavnani 2001.
14. Although *This Bridge Called My Back* brought attention to differences, as Alarcon argues in section III, the anthology did not break down the hegemony of white feminist theorizing. That struggle is ongoing.
15. See, for example, Combahee River Collective; Humphries 1977; Eisenstein 1978; and Sen 1980.
16. The label "dual systems theory" was coined by Iris Young. See Young 1980 and 1981.
17. For an update discussion of her work that responds to and clarifies some misinterpretations of the 1985 article, see Molyneux 2000.
18. We intended to include the Rich article, but the author declined to allow it to be reprinted here.
19. The 1980 UN conference erupted over this issue. It was resolved at the 1985 conference in Nairobi, when African women declared that they would define the terms of political resistance to female genital surgeries for themselves. See Rao 1991.
20. Yet Aguilar-San Juan and others also suggest that by speaking from the margins one is already complicit in the discourse that constructs that margin and center. Therefore speaking from the margins is not enough, one must also theorize the historical and discursive processes by which both the center and margin are constructed (Kaplan, Alarcon, Moallem 1999: 8).

RACE AND NATION

15.
A BLACK FEMINIST STATEMENT
The Combahee River Collective[1]

We are a collective of black feminists who have been meeting together since 1974.[2] During that time we have been involved in the process of defining and clarifying our politics, while at the same time doing political work within our own group and in coalition with other progressive organizations and movements. The most general statement of our politics at the present time would be that we are actively committed to struggling against racial, sexual, heterosexual, and class oppression and see as our particular task the development of integrated analysis and practice based upon the fact that the major systems of oppression are interlocking. The synthesis of these oppressions creates the conditions of our lives. As black women we see black feminism as the logical political movement to combat the manifold and simultaneous oppressions that all women of color face.

We will discuss four major topics in the paper that follows: (1) The genesis of contemporary black feminism; (2) what we believe, i.e., the specific province of our politics; (3) the problems in organizing black feminists, including a brief herstory of our collective; and (4) black feminist issues and practice.

1. The Genesis of Contemporary Black Feminism

Before looking at the recent development of black feminism we would like to affirm that we find our origins in the historical reality of Afro-American women's continuous life-and-death struggle for survival and liberation. Black women's extremely negative relationship to the American political system (a system of white male rule) has always been determined by our membership in two oppressed racial and sexual castes. As Angela Davis points out in "Reflections on the Black Woman's Role in the Community of Slaves," black women have always embodied, if only in their physical manifestation, an adversarial stance to white male rule and have actively resisted its inroads upon them and their communities in both dramatic and subtle ways. There have always been black women activists—some known, like Sojourner Truth, Harriet Tubman, Frances E. W. Harper, Ida B. Wells Barnett, and Mary Church Terrell, and thousands upon thousands unknown—who had a shared awareness of how their sexual identity combined with their racial identity to make their whole life situation and the focus of their political struggles unique.

Contemporary black feminism is the outgrowth of countless generations of personal sacrifice, militancy, and work by our mothers and sisters.

A black feminist presence has evolved most obviously in connection with the second wave of the American women's movement beginning in the late 1960s. Black, other Third World, and working women have been involved in the feminist movement from its start, but both outside reactionary forces and racism and elitism within the movement itself have served to obscure our participation. In 1973 black feminists, primarily located in New York, felt the necessity of forming a separate black feminist group. This became the National Black Feminist Organization (NBFO).

Black feminist politics also have an obvious connection to movements for black liberation, particularly those of the 1960s and 1970s. Many of us were active in those movements (civil rights, black nationalism, the Black Panthers), and all of our lives were greatly affected and changed by their ideology, their goals, and the tactics used to achieve their goals. It was our experience and disillusionment within these liberation movements, as well as experience on the periphery of the white male left, that led to the need to develop a politics that was antiracist, unlike those of white women, and antisexist, unlike those of black and white men.

There is also undeniably a personal genesis for black feminism, that is, the political realization that comes from the seemingly personal experiences of individual black women's lives. Black feminists and many more black women who do not define themselves as feminists have all experienced sexual oppression as a constant factor in our day-to-day existence.

Black feminists often talk about their feelings of craziness before becoming conscious of the concepts of sexual politics, patriarchal rule, and, most importantly, feminism, the political analysis and practice that we women use to struggle against our oppression. The fact that racial politics and indeed racism are pervasive factors in our lives did not allow us, and still does not allow most black women, to look more deeply into our own experiences and define those things that make our lives what they are and our oppression specific to us. In the process of consciousness-raising, actually life-sharing, we began to recognize the commonality of our experiences and, from that sharing and growing consciousness, to build a politics that will change our lives and inevitably end our oppression.

Our development also must be tied to the contemporary economic and political position of black people. The post–World War II generation of black youth was the first to be able to minimally partake of certain educational and employment options, previously closed completely to black people. Although our economic position is still at the very bottom of the American capitalist economy, a handful of us have been able to gain certain tools as a result of tokenism in education and employment which potentially enable us to more effectively fight our oppression.

A combined antiracist and antisexist position drew us together initially, and as we developed politically we addressed ourselves to heterosexism and economic oppression capitalism.

2. What We Believe

Above all else, our politics initially sprang from the shared belief that black women are inherently valuable, that our liberation is a necessity not as an adjunct to somebody else's but because of our need as human persons for autonomy. This may seem so obvious as to sound simplistic, but it is apparent that no other ostensibly progressive movement has ever considered our specific oppression a priority or worked seriously for the ending of that oppression. Merely naming the pejorative stereotypes attributed to black women (e.g., mammy, matriarch, Sapphire, whore, bulldagger), let alone cataloguing the cruel, often murderous, treatment we receive, indicates how little value has been placed upon our lives during four centuries of bondage in the Western hemisphere. We realize that the only people who care enough about us to work consistently for our liberation is us. Our politics evolve from a healthy love for ourselves, our sisters, and our community which allows us to continue our struggle and work.

This focusing upon our own oppression is embodied in the concept of identity politics. We believe that the most profound and potentially the most radical politics come directly out of our own identity, as opposed to working to end somebody else's oppression. In the case of black women this is a particularly repugnant, dangerous, threatening, and therefore revolutionary concept because it is obvious from looking at all the political movements that have preceded us that anyone is more worthy of liberation than ourselves. We reject pedestals, queenhood, and walking ten paces behind. To be recognized as human, levelly human, is enough.

We believe that sexual politics under patriarchy is as pervasive in black women's lives as are the politics of class and race. We also often find it difficult to separate race from class from sex oppression because in our lives they are most often experienced simultaneously. We know that there is such a thing as racial-sexual oppression which is neither solely racial nor solely sexual, e.g., the history of rape of black women by white men as a weapon of political repression.

Although we are feminists and lesbians, we feel solidarity with progressive black men and do not advocate the fractionalization that white women who are separatists demand. Our situation as black people necessitates that we have solidarity around the fact of race, which white women of course do not need to have with white men, unless it is their negative solidarity as racial oppressors. We struggle together with black men against racism, while we also struggle with black men about sexism.

We realize that the liberation of all oppressed peoples necessitates the destruction of the political-economic systems of capitalism and imperialism as well as patriarchy. We are socialists because we believe the work must be organized for the collective benefit of those who do the work and create the products and not for the profit of the bosses. Material resources must be equally distributed among those who create these resources. We are not convinced, however, that a socialist revolution that is not also a feminist and antiracist revolution will guarantee our liberation. We have arrived at the necessity for developing an understanding of class relationships that takes into account the specific class position of black women who are generally marginal in the labor force, while at this particular time some of us are temporarily viewed as doubly desirable tokens at white-collar and professional levels. We need to articulate the real class situation of persons who are not merely raceless, sexless workers, but for whom racial and sexual oppression are significant determinants in their working/economic lives. Although we are in essential agreement with Marx's theory as it applied to the very specific economic relationships he analyzed, we know that this analysis must be extended further in order for us to understand our specific economic situation as black women.

A political contribution which we feel we have already made is the expansion of the feminist principle that the personal is political. In our consciousness-raising sessions, for example, we have in many ways gone beyond white women's revelations because we are dealing with the implications of race and class as well as sex. Even our black women's style of talking/testifying in black language about what we have experienced has a resonance that is both cultural and political. We have spent a great deal of energy delving into the cultural and experiential nature of our oppression out of necessity because none of these matters have ever been looked at before. No one before has ever mentioned the multilayered texture of black women's lives.

As we have already stated, we reject the stance of lesbian separatism because it is not a viable political analysis or strategy for us. It leaves out far too much and far too many people, particularly black men, women, and children. We have a great deal of criticism and loathing for what men have been socialized to be in this society: what they support, how they act, and how they oppress. But we do not have the misguided notion that it is their maleness, per se—i.e., their biological maleness—that makes them what they are. As black women we find any type of biological determinism a particularly dangerous and reactionary basis upon which to build a politic. We must also question whether lesbian separatism is an adequate and progressive political analysis and strategy, even for those who practice it, since it so completely denies any but the sexual sources of women's oppression, negating the facts of class and race.

3. Problems in Organizing Black Feminists

During our years together as a black feminist collective we have experienced success and defeat, joy and pain, victory and failure. We have found that it is very difficult to organize around black feminist issues, difficult even to announce in certain contexts that we *are* black feminists. We have tried to think about the reasons for our difficulties, particularly since the white women's movement continues to be strong and to grow in many directions. In this section we will discuss some of the general reasons for the organizing problems we face and so talk specifically about the stages in organizing our own collective.

The major source of difficulty in our political work is that we are not just trying to fight oppression on one front or even two, but instead to address a whole range of oppressions. We do not have racial, sexual, heterosexual, or class privilege to rely upon nor do we have even the minimal access to resources and power that groups who possess any one of these types of privilege have.

The psychological toll of being a black woman and the difficulties this presents in reaching political consciousness and doing political work can never be underestimated. There is a very low value placed upon black women's psyches in this society, which is both racist and sexist. As an early group member once said, "We are all damaged people merely by virtue of being black women." We are dispossessed psychologically and on every other level, and yet we feel the necessity to struggle to change our condition and the condition of all black women. In "A Black Feminist's Search for Sisterhood," Michele Wallace arrives at this conclusion:

> We exist as women who are black who are feminists, each stranded for the moment, working independently because there is not yet an environment in this society remotely congenial to our struggle—because, being on the bottom, we would have to do what no one else has done: we would have to fight the world.[3]

Wallace is not pessimistic but realistic in her assessment of black feminists' position, particularly in her allusion to the nearly classic isolation most of us face. We might use our position at the bottom, however, to make a clear leap into revolutionary action. If black women were free, it would mean that everyone else would have to be free since our freedom would necessitate the destruction of all the systems of oppression.

Feminism is, nevertheless, very threatening to the majority of black people because it calls into question some of the most basic assumptions about our existence, i.e., that gender should be a determinant of power relationships. Here is the way male and female roles were defined in a black nationalist pamphlet from the early 1970s.

> We understand that it is and has been traditional that the man is the head of the house. He is the leader of the house/nation because his knowledge of the world is broader, his awareness is greater, his understanding is fuller and his application of this information is wiser.... After all, it is only reasonable that the man be the head of the house because he is able to defend and protect the development of his home.... Women cannot do the same things as men—they are made by nature to function differently. Equality of men and women is something that cannot happen even in the abstract world. Men are not equal to other men, i.e., ability, experience, or even understanding. The value of men and women can be seen as in the value of gold and silver—they are not equal but both have great value. We must realize that men and women are a complement to each other because there is no house/family without a man and his wife. Both are essential to the development of any life.[4]

The material conditions of most black women would hardly lead them to upset both the economic and sexual arrangements that seem to represent some stability in their lives. Many black women have a good understanding of both sexism and racism, but because of the everyday constrictions of their lives cannot risk struggling against them both.

The reaction of black men to feminism has been notoriously negative. They are, of course, even more threatened than black women by the possibility that black feminists might organize around our own needs. They realize that they might not only loose valuable and hard-working allies in their struggles but that they might also be forced to change their habitually sexist ways of interacting with and oppressing black women. Accusations that black feminism divides the black struggle are powerful deterrents to the growth of an autonomous black women's movement.

Still hundreds of women have been active at different times during the three-year existence of our group. And every black woman who came, came out of a strongly felt need for some level of possibility that did not previously exist in her life.

When we first started meeting early in 1974 after the NBFO first eastern regional conference, we did not have a strategy for organizing, or even a focus. We just wanted to see what we had. After a period of months of not meeting, we began to meet again late in the year and started doing an intense variety of consciousness-raising. The overwhelming feeling that we had is that after years and years we had finally found each other. Although we were not doing political work as a group, individuals continued their involvement in lesbian politics, sterilization abuse and abortion rights work, Third World Women's International Women's Day activities, and support activity for the trials of Dr. Kenneth Edelin, Joan Little, and Inez Garcia. During our first summer, when membership had dropped off considerably, those of us remaining devoted serious discussion to the possibility of opening a refuge for battered women in a black community. (There was no refuge in Boston at that time.) We also decided around that time to become an independent collective since we had serious disagreements with NBFOs bourgeois-feminist stance and their lack of a clear political focus.

We also were contacted at that time by socialist feminists, with whom we had worked on abortion rights activities, who wanted to encourage us to attend the National Socialist Feminist Conference in Yellow Springs. One of our members did attend and despite the narrowness of the ideology that was promoted at that particular conference, we became more aware of the need for us to understand our own economic situation and to make our own economic analysis.

In the fall, when some members returned, we experienced several months of comparative inactivity and internal disagreements which were first conceptualized as a lesbian-straight split but which were also the result of class and political differences. During the summer those of us who were still meeting had determined the need to do political work and to move beyond consciousness-raising and serving exclusively as an emotional support group. At the beginning of 1976, when some of the women who had not wanted to do political work and who also had voiced disagreements stopped attending of their own accord, we again looked for a focus. We decided at that time, with the addition of new members, to become a study group. We had always shared our reading with each other, and some of us had written papers on black feminism for group discussion a few months before this decision was made. We began functioning as a study group and also began discussing the possibility of starting a black feminist publication. We had a retreat in the late spring which provided a time for both political discussion and working out interpersonal issues. Currently we are planning to gather together a collection of black feminist writing. We feel that it is absolutely essential to demonstrate the reality of our politics to other black women and believe that we can do this through writing and distributing our work. The fact that individual black feminists are living in isolation all over the country, that our own numbers are small, and that we have some skills in writing, printing, and publishing makes us want to carry out these kinds of projects as a means of organizing black feminists as we continue to do political work in coalition with other groups.

4. Black Feminist Issues and Practice

During our time together we have identified and worked on many issues of particular relevance to black women. The inclusiveness of our politics makes us concerned with any situation that impinges upon the lives of women, Third World, and working people. We are of course particularly committed to working on those struggles in which race, sex, and class are simultaneous factors in oppression. We might, for example, become involved in workplace organizing at a factory that employs Third World women or picket a hospital that is cutting back on already inadequate health care to a Third World community, or set up a rape crisis center in a black neighborhood. Organizing around welfare or daycare concerns might also be a focus. The work to be done and the countless issues that this work represents merely reflect the pervasiveness of our oppression.

Issues and projects that collective members have actually worked on are sterilization abuse, abortion rights, battered women, rape, and health care. We have also done many workshops and educationals on black feminism on college campuses, at women's conferences, and most recently for high school women.

One issue that is of major concern to us and that we have begun to publicly address is racism in the white women's movement. As black feminists we are made constantly and painfully aware of how little effort white women have made to understand and combat their racism, which requires among other things that they have a more than superficial comprehension of race, color, and black history and culture. Eliminating racism in the white women's movement is by definition work for white women to do, but we will continue to speak to and demand accountability on this issue.

In the practice of our politics we do not believe that the end always justifies the means. Many reactionary and destructive acts have been done in the name of achieving "correct" political goals. As feminists we do not want to mess over people in the name of politics. We believe in collective process and a nonhierarchical distribution of power within our own group and in our vision of a revolutionary society. We are committed to a continual examination of our politics as they develop through criticism and self-criticism as an essential aspect of our practice. As black feminists and lesbians we know that we have a very definite revolutionary task to perform and we are ready for the lifetime of work and struggle before us.

Notes

1. The Combahee River Collective is a black feminist group in Boston whose name comes from the guerrilla action conceptualized and led by Harriet Tubman on June 2, 1863, in the Port Royal region of South Carolina. This action freed more than 750 slaves and is the only military campaign in American history planned and led by a woman.
2. This statement is dated April 1977.
3. Michele Wallace, "A Black Feminist's Search for Sisterhood," *The Village Voice*, 28 July 1975, pp. 6–7.
4. Mumininas of Committee for Unified Newark, *Mwanamke Mwananchi* (*The Nationalist Woman*), Newark, N.J., c. 1971, pp. 4–5.

16.
THE BRIDGE POEM

Donna Kate Rushin

I've had enough
I'm sick of seeing and touching
Both sides of things
Sick of being the damn bridge for everybody

Nobody
Can talk to anybody
Without me
Right?

I explain my mother to my father my father to my little sister
My little sister to my brother my brother to the white feminists
The white feminists to the Black church folks the Black church folks
To the ex-hippies the ex-hippies to the Black separatists the
Black separatists to the artists the artists to my friends' parents...

Then
I've got to explain myself
To everybody

I do more translating
Than the Gawdamn U.N.

Forget it
I'm sick of it

I'm sick of filling in your gaps

Sick of being your insurance against
The isolation of your self-imposed limitations
Sick of being the crazy at your holiday dinners
Sick of being the odd one at your Sunday Brunches
Sick of being the sole Black friend to 34 individual white people

Find another connection to the rest of the world
Find someone else to make you legitimate
Find some other way to be political and hip

I will not be the bridge to your womanhood
Your manhood
Your human-ness

I'm sick of reminding you not to
Close off too tight for too long

I'm sick of mediating with your worst self
On behalf of your better selves

I am sick
Of having to remind you
To breathe
Before you suffocate
Your own fool self

Forget it
Stretch or drown
Evolve or die

The bridge I must be
Is the bridge to my own power
I must translate
My own fears
Mediate
My own weaknesses

I must be the bridge to nowhere
But my true self
And then
I will be useful

17.
INVISIBILITY IS AN UNNATURAL DISASTER: REFLECTIONS OF AN ASIAN AMERICAN WOMAN
Mitsuye Yamada

Last year for the Asian segment of the Ethnic American Literature course I was teaching, I selected a new anthology entitled *Aiiieeeee!* compiled by a group of outspoken Asian American writers. During the discussion of the long but thought-provoking introduction to this anthology, one of my students blurted out that she was offended by its militant tone and that as a white person she was tired of always being blamed for the oppression of all the minorities. I noticed several of her classmates' eyes nodding in tacit agreement. A discussion of the "militant" voices in some of the other writings we had read in the course ensued. Surely, I pointed out, some of these other writings have been just as, if not more, militant as the words in this introduction? Had they been offended by those also but failed to express their feelings about them? To my surprise, they said they were not offended by any of the Black American, Chicano or American Indian writings, but were hard-pressed to explain why when I asked for an explanation. A little further discussion revealed that they "understood" the anger expressed by the Black and Chicanos and they "empathized" with the frustrations and sorrow expressed by the American Indian. But the Asian Americans??

Then finally, one student said it for all of them: "It made me angry. *Their* anger made *me* angry, because I didn't even know the Asian Americans felt oppressed. I didn't expect their anger."

At this time I was involved in an academic due process procedure begun as a result of a grievance I had filed the previous semester against the administrators at my college. I had filed a grievance for violation of my rights as a teacher who had worked in the district for almost eleven years. My student's remark "Their anger made me angry...I didn't expect their anger," explained for me the reactions of some of my own colleagues as well as the reactions of the administrators during those previous months. The grievance procedure was a time-consuming and emotionally draining process, but the basic principle was too important for me to ignore. That basic principle was that I, an individual teacher, do have certain rights which are given and my superiors cannot, should not, violate them with impunity. When this was pointed out to them, however, they responded with shocked surprise that I, of all people, would take them to task for violation of what was clearly written policy in our college district. They all seemed to exclaim, "We don't understand this; this is so uncharacteristic of her; she seemed such a nice person, so polite, so obedient, so non-trouble-making." What was even more surprising was once they were forced to acknowledge that I was determined to start the due process action, they assumed I was not doing it on my own. One of the administrators suggested someone must have pushed me into this, undoubtedly some of "those feminists" on our campus, he said wryly.

In this age when women are clearly making themselves visible on all fronts, I, an Asian American woman, am still functioning as a "front for those feminists" and therefore invisible. The realization of this sinks in slowly. Asian Americans as a whole are finally coming to claim their own, demanding that they be included in the multicultural history of our country. I like to think, in spite of my administrator's myopia, that the most stereotyped minority of them all, the Asian American woman, is just now emerging to become part of that group. It took forever. Perhaps it is important to ask ourselves why it took so long. We should ask ourselves this question just when we think we are emerging as a viable minority in the fabric of our society. I should add to my student's words, "because I didn't even know they felt oppressed," that it took this long because we Asian American women have not admitted to ourselves that we were oppressed. We, the visible minority that is invisible.

I say this because until a few years ago I have been an Asian American woman working among non-Asians in an educational institution where most of the decision-makers were men;[1] an Asian American woman thriving under the smug illusion that I was *not* the stereotypic image of the Asian woman because I had a career teaching English in a community college. I did not think anything assertive was necessary to make my point. People who know me, I reasoned, the ones who count, know who I am and what I think. Thus, even when what I considered a veiled racist remark was made in a casual social setting, I would "let it go" because it was pointless to argue with people who didn't even know their remark was racist. I had supposed that I was practicing passive resistance while being stereotyped, but it was so passive no one noticed I was resisting; it was so much my expected role that it ultimately rendered me invisible.

My experience leads me to believe that contrary to what I thought, I had actually been contributing to my own stereotyping. Like the hero in Ralph Ellison's novel *The Invisible Man*, I had become invisible to white Americans, and it clung to me like a bad habit. Like most bad habits, this one crept up on me because I took it in minute doses like Mithradates' poison and my mind and body adapted so well to it I hardly noticed it was there.

For the past eleven years I have busied myself with the usual chores of an English teacher, a wife of a research chemist, and a mother of four rapidly growing children. I hadn't even done much to shatter this particular stereotype: the middle-class woman happy to be bringing home the extra income and quietly fitting into the man's world of work. When the Asian American woman is lulled into believing that people perceive her as being different from other Asian women (the submissive, subservient, ready-to-please, easy-to-get-along-with Asian woman), she is kept comfortably content with the state of things. She becomes ineffectual in the milieu in which she moves. The seemingly apolitical middle-class woman and the apolitical Asian woman constituted a double invisibility.

I had created an underground culture of survival for myself and had become in the eyes of others the person I was trying not to be. Because I was permitted to go to college, permitted to take a stab at a career or two along the way, given "free choice" to marry and have a family, given a "choice" to eventually do both, I had assumed I was more or less free, not realizing that those who are free make and take choices; they do not choose from options proffered by "those out there."

I, personally, had not "emerged" until I was almost fifty years old. Apparently through a long conditioning process, I had learned how *not* to be seen for what I am. A long history of ineffectual activities had been, I realize now, initiation rites toward my eventual invisibility. The training begins in childhood; and for women and minorities, whatever is started in childhood is continued throughout their adult lives. I first recognized just how invisible I was in my first real confrontation with my parents a few years after the outbreak of World War II.

During the early years of the war, my older brother, Mike, and I left the concentration camp in Idaho to work and study at the University of Cincinnati. My parents came to Cincinnati soon after my father's release from Internment Camp (these were POW camps to which many of the Issei[2] men, leaders in their communities, were sent by the FBI), and worked as domestics in the suburbs. I did not see them too often because by this time I had met and was much influenced by a pacifist who was out on a "furlough" from a conscientious objectors' camp in Trenton, North Dakota. When my parents learned about my "boy friend" they were appalled and frightened. After all, this was the period when everyone in the country was expected to be one-hundred percent behind the war effort, and the Nisei[3] boys who had volunteered for the Armed Forces were out there fighting and dying to prove how American we really were. However, during interminable arguments with my father and overheard arguments between my parents, I was devastated to learn they were not so much concerned about my having become a pacifist, but they were more concerned about the possibility of my marrying one. They were understandably frightened (my father's prison years of course were still fresh on his mind) about repercussions on the rest of the family. In an attempt to make my father understand me, I argued that even if I didn't marry him, I'd still be a pacifist; but my father reassured me that it was "all right" for me to be a pacifist because as a Japanese national and a "girl" *it didn't make any difference to anyone.* In frustration, I remember shouting, "But can't you see, *I'm* philosophically committed to the pacifist cause," but he dismissed this with "In my college days we used to call philosophy, foolosophy," and that was the end of that. When they were finally convinced I was not going to marry "my pacifist," the subject was dropped and we never discussed it again.

As if to confirm my father's assessment of the harmlessness of my opinions, my brother Mike, an American citizen, was suddenly expelled from the University of Cincinnati while I, "an enemy alien", was permitted to stay. We assumed that his stand as a pacifist, although he was classified a 4-F because of his health, contributed to his expulsion. We were told the Air Force was conducting sensitive wartime research on campus and requested his removal, but they apparently felt my presence on campus was not as threatening.

I left Cincinnati in 1945, hoping to leave behind this and other unpleasant memories gathered there during the war years, and plunged right into the politically active atmosphere at New York University where students, many of them returning veterans, were continuously promoting one cause or other by making speeches in Washington Square, passing out petitions, or staging demonstrations. On one occasion, I tagged along with a group of students who took a train to Albany to demonstrate on the steps of the State Capitol. I think I was the only Asian in this group of predominantly Jewish students from NYU. People who passed us were amused and shouted "Go home and grow up." I suppose Governor Dewey, who refused to see us, assumed we were a group of adolescents without a cause as most college students were considered to be during those days. It appears they weren't expecting any results from our demonstration. There were no newspersons, no security persons, no police. No one tried to stop us from doing what we were doing. We simply did "our thing" and went back to our studies until next time, and my father's words were again confirmed: it made no difference to anyone, being a young student demonstrator in peacetime, 1947.

Not only the young, but those who feel powerless over their own lives know what it is like not to make a difference on anyone or anything. The poor know it only too well, and we women have known it since we were little girls. The most insidious part of this conditioning process, I realize now, was that we have been trained not to expect a response in ways that mattered. We may be listened to and responded to with placating words and gestures, but our psychological mind set has already told us time and again that we were born into a readymade world into which we must fit ourselves and that many of us do it very well.

This mind set is the result of not believing that the political and social forces affecting our lives are determined by some person, or a group of persons, probably sitting behind a desk or around a conference table.

Just recently I read an article about "the remarkable track record of success" of the Nisei in the United States. One Nisei was quoted as saying he attributed our stamina and endurance to our ancestors whose characters had been shaped, he said, by their living in a country which has been constantly besieged by all manner of natural disasters, such as earthquakes and hurricanes. He said the Nisei has inherited a steely will, a will to endure and hence, to survive.

This evolutionary explanation disturbs me, because it equates the "act of God" (i.e., natural disasters) to the "act of man" (i.e., the war, the evacuation). The former is not within our power to alter, but the latter, I should think, is. By putting the "acts of God" on par with the acts of man, we shrug off personal responsibilities.

I have for too long a period of time accepted the opinion of others (even though they were directly affecting my life) as if they were objective events totally out of my control. Because I separated such opinions from the persons who were making them, I accepted them the way I accepted natural disasters; and I endured them as inevitable. I have tried to cope with people whose points of view alarmed me in the same way that I had adjusted to natural phenomena, such as hurricanes, which plowed into my life from time to time. I would readjust my dismantled feelings in the same way that we repaired the broken shutters after the storm. The Japanese have an all-purpose expression in their language for this attitude of resigned acceptance: "Shikataganai." "It can't be helped." "There's nothing I can do about it." It is said with the shrug of the shoulders and tone of finality, perhaps not unlike the "those-were-my-orders" tone that was used at the Nuremberg trials. With all the sociological studies that have been made about the causes of the evacuations of the Japanese Americans during World War II, we should know by now that "they" knew that the West Coast Japanese Americans would go without too much protest, and of course, "they" were right, for most of us (with the exception of those notable few), resigned to our fate, albeit bewildered and not willingly. We were not perceived by our government as responsive Americans; we were objects that happened to be standing in the path of the storm.

Perhaps this kind of acceptance is a way of coping with the "real" world. One stands against the wind for a time, and then succumbs eventually because there is no point to being stubborn against all odds. The wind will not respond to entreaties anyway, one reasons; one should have sense enough to know that. I'm not ready to accept this evolutionary reasoning. It is too rigid for me; I would like to think that my new awareness is going to make me more visible than ever, and to allow me to make some changes in the "man made disaster" I live in at the present time. Part of being visible is refusing to separate the actors from their actions, and demanding that they be responsible for them.

By now, riding along with the minorities' and women's movements, I think we are making a wedge into the main body of American life, but people are still looking right through and around us, assuming we are simply tagging along. Asian American women still remain in the background and we are heard but not really listened to. Like Muzak, they think we are piped into the airwaves by someone else. We must remember that one of the most insidious ways of keeping women and minorities powerless is to let them only talk about harmless and inconsequential subjects or let them speak freely and not listen to them with serious intent.

We need to raise our voices a little more, even as they say to us "This is so uncharacteristic of you." To finally recognize our own invisibility is to finally be on the path toward visibility. Invisibility is not a natural state for anyone.

Notes

1. It is hoped this will change now that a black woman is Chancellor of our college district.
2. Issei—Immigrant Japanese, living in the U.S.
3. Nisei—Second generation Japanese, born in the U.S.

18.
LA CONCIENCIA DE LA MESTIZA: TOWARDS A NEW CONSCIOUSNESS
Gloria Anzaldúa

Por la mujer de mi raza
hablará el espíritu[1]

Jose Vasconcelos, Mexican philosopher, envisaged *una raza mestiza, una mezcla de razas afines, una raza de color—la primera raza síntesis del globo.* He called it a cosmic race, *la raza cosmica,* a fifth race embracing the four major races of the world.[2] Opposite to the theory of the pure Aryan, and to the policy of racial purity that white America practices, his theory is one of inclusivity. At the confluence of two or more genetic streams, with chromosomes constantly "crossing over," this mixture of races, rather than resulting in an inferior being, provides hybrid progeny, a mutable, more malleable species with a rich gene pool. From this racial, ideological, cultural, and biological cross-pollinization, an "alien" consciousness is presently in the making—a new *mestiza* consciousness, *una conciencia de mujer.* It is a consciousness of the Borderlands.

Una lucha de fronteras/A Struggle of Borders

Because I, a *mestiza,*
continually walk out of one culture
and into another,
because I am in all cultures at the same time,
alma entre dos mundos, tres, cuatro,
me zumba la cabeza con lo contradictorio.
Estoy norteada por todas las voces que me hablan
simultáneamente.

The ambivalence from the clash of voices results in mental and emotional states of perplexity. Internal strife results in insecurity and indecisiveness. The mestiza's dual or multiple personality is plagued by psychic restlessness.

In a constant state of mental nepantilism, an Aztec word meaning torn between ways, *la mestiza* is a product of the transfer of the cultural and spiritual values of one group to another. Being tricultural, monolingual, bilingual, or multilingual, speaking a patois, and in a state of perpetual transition, the *mestiza* faces the dilemma of the mixed breed: which collectivity does the daughter of a dark-skinned mother listen to?

El choque de un alma atrapado entre el mundo del espíritu y el mundo de la técnica a veces la deja entullada. Cradled in one culture, sandwiched between two cultures, straddling all three cultures and their value systems, *la mestiza* undergoes a struggle of flesh, a struggle of borders, an inner war. Like all people, we perceive the version of reality that our culture communicates. Like others having or living in more than one culture, we get multiple, often opposing messages. The coming together of two self-consistent but habitually incompatible frames of reference[3] causes *un choque*, a cultural collision.

Within us and within *la cultura chicana*, commonly held beliefs of the white culture attack commonly held beliefs of the Mexican culture, and both attack commonly held beliefs of the indigenous culture. Subconsciously, we see an attack on ourselves and our beliefs as a threat and we attempt to block with a counterstance.

But it is not enough to stand on the opposite river bank, shouting questions, challenging patriarchal, white conventions. A counterstance locks one into a duel of oppressor and oppressed; locked in mortal combat, like the cop and the criminal, both are reduced to a common denominator of violence. The counterstance refutes the dominant culture's views and beliefs, and, for this, it is proudly defiant. All reaction is limited by, and dependent on, what it is reacting against. Because the counterstance stems from a problem with authority—outer as well as inner—it's a step towards liberation from cultural domination. But it is not a way of life. At some point, on our way to a new consciousness, we will have to leave the opposite bank, the split between the two mortal combatants somehow healed so that we are on both shores at once and, at once, see through serpent and eagle eyes. Or perhaps we will decide to disengage from the dominant culture, write it off altogether as a lost cause, and cross the border into a wholly new and separate territory. Or we might go another route. The possibilities are numerous once we decide to act and not react.

A Tolerance for Ambiguity

These numerous possibilities leave *la mestiza* floundering in uncharted seas. In perceiving conflicting information and points of view, she is subjected to a swamping of her psychological borders. She has discovered that she can't hold concepts or ideas in rigid boundaries. The borders and walls that are supposed to keep the undesirable ideas out are entrenched habits and patterns of behavior; these habits and patterns are the enemy within. Rigidity means death. Only by remaining flexible is she able to stretch the psyche horizontally and vertically. *La mestiza* constantly has to shift out of habitual formations; from convergent thinking, analytical reasoning that tends to use rationality to move toward a single goal (a Western mode), to divergent thinking,[4] characterized by movement away from set patterns and goals and toward a more whole perspective, one that includes rather than excludes.

The new *mestiza* copes by developing a tolerance for contradictions, a tolerance for ambiguity. She learns to be an Indian in Mexican culture, to be Mexican from an Anglo point of view. She learns to juggle cultures. She has a plural personality, she operates in a pluralistic mode—nothing is thrust out, the good the bad and the ugly, nothing rejected, nothing abandoned. Not only does she sustain contradictions, she turns the ambivalence into something else.

She can be jarred out of ambivalence by an intense, and often painful, emotional event which inverts or resolves the ambivalence. I'm not sure exactly how. The work takes place underground—subconsciously. It is work that the soul performs. That focal point or fulcrum, that juncture where the mestiza stands, is where phenomena tend to collide. It is where the possibility of uniting all that is separate occurs. This assembly is not one where severed or separated pieces merely come together. Nor is it a balancing of opposing powers. In attempting to work out a synthesis, the self has added a third element which is greater than the sum of its severed parts. That third element is a new consciousness—a mestiza consciousness—and though it is a source of intense pain, its energy comes from continual creative motion that keeps breaking down the unitary aspect of each new paradigm.

En unas pocas centurias, the future will belong to the mestiza. Because the future depends on the breaking down of paradigms, it depends on the straddling of two or more cultures. By creating a new mythos—that is, a change in the way we perceive reality, the way we see ourselves, and the ways we behave—*la mestiza* creates a new consciousness.

The work of *mestiza* consciousness is to break down the subject-object duality that keeps her a prisoner and to show in the flesh and through the images in her work how duality is transcended. The answer to the problem between the white race and the colored, between males and females, lies in healing the split that originates in the very foundation of our lives, our culture, our languages, our thoughts. A massive uprooting of dualistic thinking in the individual and collective consciousness is the beginning of a long struggle, but one that could, in our best hopes, bring us to the end of rape, of violence, of war.

La excrucijada/The Crossroads

> A chicken is being sacrificed
>   at a crossroads, a simple mound of earth
> a mud shrine for *Eshu*,
>   *Yoruba* god of indeterminacy,
> who blesses her choice of path.
>   She begins her journey.

Su cuerpo es una bocacalle. La mestiza has gone from being the sacrificial goat to becoming the officiating priestess at the crossroads.

As a *mestiza* I have no country, my homeland cast me out; yet all countries are mine because I am every woman's sister or potential lover. (As a lesbian I have no race, my own people disclaim me; but I am all races because there is the queer of me in all races.) I am cultureless because, as a feminist, I challenge the collective cultural/religious male-derived beliefs of Indo-Hispanics and Anglos; yet I am cultured because I am participating in the creation of yet another culture, a new story to explain the world and our participation in it, a new value system with images and symbols that connect us to each other and to the planet. *Soy un amasamiento*, I am an act of kneading, of uniting, and joining that not only has produced both a creature of darkness and a creature of light, but also a creature that questions the definitions of light and dark and gives them new meanings.

We are the people who leap in the dark, we are the people on the knees of the gods. In our very flesh, (r)evolution works out the clash of cultures. It makes us crazy constantly, but if the center holds, we've made some kind of evolutionary step forward. *Nuestra alma el trabajo*, the opus, the great alchemical work; spiritual *mestizaje*, a "morphogenesis,"[5] an inevitable unfolding. We have become the quickening serpent movement.

Indigenous like corn, like corn, the *mestiza* is a product of crossbreeding, designed for preservation under a variety of conditions. Like an ear of corn— a female seed-bearing organ—the *mestiza* is tenacious, tightly wrapped in the husks of her culture. Like kernels she clings to the cob; with thick stalks and strong brace roots, she holds tight to the earth—she will survive the crossroads.

Lavando y remojando el maíz en agua de cal, despojando el pellejo. Moliendo, mixteando, amasando, haciendo tortillas de masa.[6] She steeps the corn in lime, it swells, softens. With stone roller on *metate*, she grinds the corn, then grinds again. She kneads and moulds the dough, pats the round balls into *tortillas*.

> We are the porous rock in the stone *metate*
> squatting on the ground.
> We are the rolling pin, *el maíz y agua*,
> *la masa harina. Somos el amasijo.*
> *Somos lo molido en el metate.*
> We are the *comal* sizzling hot,
> the hot *tortilla*, the hungry mouth.
> We are the coarse rock.
> We are the grinding motion,
> the mixed potion, *somos el molcajete.*
> We are the pestle, the *comino, ajo, pimienta*,
> We are the *chile colorado*,
> the green shoot that cracks the rock.
> We will abide.

El camino de la mestiza/The Mestiza Way

...Her first step is to take inventory. *Despojando, desgranando, quitando paja.* Just what did she inherit from her ancestors? This weight on her back—which is the baggage from the Indian mother, which the baggage from the Spanish father, which the baggage from the Anglo?

Pero es difícil differentiating between *lo heredado, lo adquirido, lo impuesto.* She puts history through a sieve, winnows out the lies, looks at the forces that we as a race, as women, have been a part of. *Luego bota lo que no vale, los desmientos, los desencuentros, el embrutecimiento. Aguarda el juicio, hondo y enraízado, de la gente antigua.* This step is a conscious rupture with all oppressive traditions of all cultures and religions. She communicates that rupture, documents the struggle. She reinterprets history and, using new symbols, she shapes new myths. She adopts new perspectives toward the darkskinned, women and queers. She strengthens her tolerance (and intolerance) for ambiguity. She is willing to share, to make herself vulnerable to foreign ways of seeing and thinking. She surrenders all notions of safety, of the familiar. Deconstruct, construct. She becomes a *nahual*, able to transform herself into a tree, a coyote, into another person. She learns to transform the small "I" into the total Self. *Se hace moldeadora de su alma. Según la concepcíon que tiene de si misma, así será.*

Que no se nos olvide los hombres

> *"Tú no sirves pa' nada—*
> you're good for nothing.
> *Eres pura vieja"*

"You're nothing but a woman" means you are defective. Its opposite is to be *un macho*. The modern meaning of the word "machismo," as well as the concept, is actually an Anglo invention. For men like my father, being "macho" meant being strong enough to protect and support my mother and us, yet being able to show love. Today's macho has doubts about his ability to feed and protect his family. His "machismo" is an adaptation to oppression and poverty and low self-esteem. It is the result of hierarchical male dominance. The Anglo, feeling inadequate and inferior and powerless, displaces or transfers these feelings to the Chicano by shaming him. In the Gringo world, the Chicano suffers from excessive humility and self-effacement, shame of self and self-deprecation. Around Latinos he suffers from a sense of language inadequacy and its accompanying discomfort; with Native Americans he suffers from a racial amnesia which ignores our common blood, and from guilt because the Spanish part of him took their land and oppressed them. He has an excessive compensatory hubris when around Mexicans from the other side. It overlays a deep sense of racial shame.

The loss of a sense of dignity and respect in the macho breeds a false machismo which leads him to put down women and even to brutalize them.

Coexisting with his sexist behavior is a love for the mother which takes precedence over that of all others. Devoted son, macho pig. To wash down the shame of his acts, of his very being, and to handle the brute in the mirror, he takes to the bottle, the snort, the needle, and the fist.

Though we "understand" the root causes of male hatred and fear, and the subsequent wounding of women, we do not excuse, we do not condone, and we will no longer put up with it. From the men of our race, we demand the admission/acknowledgment/disclosure/testimony that they wound us, violate us, are afraid of us and of our power. We need them to say they will begin to eliminate their hurtful put-down ways. But more than the words, we demand acts. We say to them: We will develop equal power with you and those who have shamed us. It is imperative that mestizas support each other in changing the sexist elements in the Mexican-Indian culture. As long as woman is put down, the Indian and the Black in all of us is put down. The struggle of the mestiza is above all a feminist one. As long as *los hombres* think they have to *chingar mujeres* and each other to be men, as long as men are taught that they are superior and therefore culturally favored over *la mujer*, as long as to be a *vieja* is a thing of derision, there can be no real healing of our psyches. We're halfway there—we have such love of the Mother, the good mother. The first step is to unlearn the *puta/virgen* dichotomy and to see *Coatlapopeuh-Coatlicue* in the Mother, *Guadalupe*.

Tenderness, a sign of vulnerability, is so feared that it is showered on women with verbal abuse and blows. Men, even more than women, are fettered to gender roles. Women at least have had the guts to break out of bondage. Only gay men have had the courage to expose themselves to the woman inside them and to challenge the current masculinity. I've encountered a few scattered and isolated gentle straight men, the beginnings of a new breed, but they are confused, and entangled with sexist behaviors that they have not been able to eradicate. We need a new masculinity and the new man needs a movement.

Lumping the males who deviate from the general norm with man, the oppressor, is a gross injustice. *Asombra pensar que nos hemos quedado en ese pozo oscuro donde el mundo encierra a las lesbianas. Asombra pensar que hemos, como feministas y lesbianas, cerrado nuestros corazónes a los hombres, a nuestros hermanos los jotos, desheredados y marginales como nosotros.* Being the supreme crossers of cultures, homosexuals have strong bonds with the queer white, Black, Asian, Native American, Latino, and with the queer in Italy, Australia, and the rest of the planet. We come from all colors, all classes, all races, all time periods. Our role is to link people with each other—the Blacks with Jews with Indians with Asians with whites with extraterrestrials. It is to transfer ideas and information from one culture to another. Colored homosexuals have more knowledge of other cultures; have always been at the forefront (although sometimes in the closet) of all liberation struggles in this country; have suffered more injustices and have survived them despite all odds. Chicanos need to acknowledge the political and artistic contributions of their queer. People, listen to what your *jotería* is saying.

The mestizo and the queer exist at this time and point on the evolutionary continuum for a purpose. We are a blending that proves that all blood is intricately woven together, and that we are spawned out of similar souls.

Somos una gente

> *Hay tantísimas fronteras*
> *que dividen a la gente,*
> *pero por cada frontera*
> *existe también un puente.*
> —Gina Valdés[7]

Divided Loyalties. Many women and men of color do not want to have any dealings with white people. It takes too much time and energy to explain to the downwardly mobile, white middle-class women that it's okay for us to want to own "possessions," never having had any nice furniture on our dirt floors or "luxuries" like washing machines. Many feel that whites should help their own people rid themselves of race hatred and fear first. I, for one, choose to use some of my energy to serve as mediator. I think we need to allow whites to be our allies. Through our literature, art, *corridos*, and folktales we must share our history with them so when they set up committees to help Big Mountain Navajos or the Chicano farmworkers or *los Nicaragüenses* they won't turn people away because of their racial fears and ignorances. They will come to see that they are not helping us but following our lead.

Individually, but also as a racial entity, we need to voice our needs. We need to say to white society: We need you to accept the fact that Chicanos are different, to acknowledge your rejection and negation of us. We need you to own the fact that you looked upon us as less than human, that you stole our lands, our personhood, our self-respect. We need you to make public restitution: to say that, to compensate for your own sense of defectiveness, you strive for power over us, you erase our history and our experience because it makes you feel guilty—you'd rather forget your brutish acts. To say you've split yourself from minority groups, that you disown us, that your dual consciousness splits off parts of yourself, transferring the "negative" parts onto us. (Where there is persecution of minorities, there is shadow projection. Where there is violence and war, there is repression of shadow.) To say that you are afraid of us, that to put distance between us, you wear the mask of contempt. Admit that Mexico is your double, that she exists in the shadow of this country, that we are irrevocably tied to her. Gringo, accept the doppelganger in your psyche. By taking back your collective shadow the intracultural split will heal. And finally, tell us what you need from us.

By Your True Faces We Will Know You

I am visible—see this Indian face—yet I am invisible. I both blind them with my beak nose and am their blind spot. But I exist, we exist. They'd like to think I have melted in the pot. But I haven't, we haven't.

The dominant white culture is killing us slowly with its ignorance. By taking away our self-determination, it has made us weak and empty. As a people we have resisted and we have taken expedient positions, but we have never been allowed to develop unencumbered—we have never been allowed to be fully ourselves. The whites in power want us people of color to barricade ourselves behind our separate tribal walls so they can pick us off one at a time with their hidden weapons; so they can whitewash and distort history. Ignorance splits people, creates prejudices. A misinformed people is a subjugated people.

Before the Chicano and the undocumented worker and the Mexican from the other side can come together, before the Chicano can have unity with Native Americans and other groups, we need to know the history of their struggle and they need to know ours. Our mothers, our sisters and brothers, the guys who hang out on street corners, the children in the playgrounds, each of us must know our Indian lineage, our afro-*mestisaje*, our history of resistance.

To the immigrant *mexicano* and the recent arrivals we must teach our history. The 80 million *mexicanos* and the Latinos from Central and South America must know of our struggles. Each one of us must know basic facts about Nicaragua, Chile and the rest of Latin America. The Latinoist movement (Chicanos, Puerto Ricans, Cubans, and other Spanish-speaking people working together to combat racial discrimination in the marketplace) is good but it is not enough. Other than a common culture we will have nothing to hold us together. We need to meet on a broader communal ground.

The struggle is inner: Chicano, *indio*, American Indian, *mojado, mexicano*, immigrant Latino, Anglo in power, working-class Anglo, Black, Asian—our psyches resemble the bordertowns and are populated by the same people. The struggle has always been inner, and is played out in the outer terrains. Awareness of our situation must come before inner changes, which in turn come before changes in society. Nothing happens in the "real" world unless it first happens in the images in our heads.

El dia de la Chicana

> I will not be shamed again
> Nor will I shame myself.

I am possessed by a vision: that we Chicanas and Chicanos have taken back or uncovered our true faces, our dignity and self-respect. It's a validation vision.

Seeing the Chicana anew in light of her history. I seek an exoneration, a seeing through the fictions of white supremacy, a seeing of ourselves in our true guises and not as the false racial personality that has been given to us and that we have given to ourselves. I seek our woman's face, our true features, the positive and the negative seen clearly, free of the tainted biases of male dominance. I seek new images of identity, new beliefs about ourselves, our humanity and worth no longer in question.

Estamos viviendo en la noche de la Raza, un tiempo cuando el trabajo se hace a lo quieto, en el oscuro. El día cuando aceptamos tal y como somos y para en donde vamos y porque—ese día será el dia de la Raza. Yo tengo el compromiso de expresar mi visíon, mi sensibilidad, mi percepción de la revalidación de la gente mexicana, su mérito, estimación, honra, aprecio y validez.

On December 2nd, when my sun goes into my first house, I celebrate *el día de la Chicana y el Chicano.* On that day I clean my altars, light my *Coatlalopeuh* candle, burn sage and copal, take *el baño para espantar basura,* sweep my house. On that day I bare my soul, make myself vulnerable to friends and family by expressing my feelings. On that day I affirm who we are.

On that day I look inside our conflicts and our basic introverted racial temperament. I identify our needs, voice them. I acknowledge that the self and the race have been wounded. I recognize the need to take care of our personhood, of our racial self. On that day I gather the splintered and disowned parts of *la gente mexicana* and hold them in my arms. *Todas las partes de nosotros valen.*

On that day I say, "Yes, all you people wound us when you reject us. Rejection strips us of self-worth; our vulnerability exposes us to shame. It is our innate identity you find wanting. We are ashamed that we need your good opinion, that we need your acceptance. We can no longer camouflage our needs, can no longer let defenses and fences sprout around us. We can no longer withdraw. To rage and look upon you with contempt is to rage and be contemptuous of ourselves. We can no longer blame you, nor disown the white parts, the male parts, the pathological parts, the queer parts, the vulnerable parts. Here we are weaponless with open arms, with only our magic. Let's try it our way, the mestiza way, the Chicana way, the woman way.

On that day, I search for our essential dignity as a people, a people with a sense of purpose—to belong and contribute to something greater than our *pueblo.* On that day I seek to recover and reshape my spiritual identity. *¡Animate! Raza, a celebrar el día de la Chicana. . . .*

Notes

1. This is my own "take off" on Jose Vasconcelos' idea. Jose Vasconcelos, *La Raza Cósmica: Misión de la Raza Ibero-Americana* (Mexico: Aguilar S.A. de Ediciones, 1961).
2. Ibid.
3. Arthur Koestler termed this "bisociation." Albert Rothenberg, *The Creative Process in Art, Science and Other Fields* (Chicago, IL: University of Chicago Press, 1979), 12.
4. In part, I derive my definitions for "convergent" and "divergent" thinking from Rothenberg, 12–13.
5. To borrow chemist Ilya Prigogine's theory of "dissipative structures." Prigogine discovered that substances interact not in predictable ways as it was taught in science, but in different and fluctuating ways to produce new and more complex structures, a kind of birth he called "morphogenesis," which created unpredictable innovations. Harold Gilliam, "Searching for a New World View," *This World* (January, 1981), 23.
6. *Tortillas de masa harina:* corn tortillas are of two types, the smooth uniform ones made in a tortilla press and usually bought at a tortilla factory or supermarket, and *gorditas,* made by mixing *masa* with lard or shortening or butter (my mother sometimes puts in bits of bacon or *chicharrones*).
7. Gina Valdés, *Puentes y Fronteras: Coplas Chicanas,* trans. Cary F. Baynes (Princeton, NJ: Princeton University Press, 1950), 98.

19.
THE PREFERENTIAL SYMBOL FOR ISLAMIC IDENTITY: WOMEN IN MUSLIM PERSONAL LAWS

Marie-Aimée Hélie-Lucas

Introduction: Fundamental Movements and Muslim Identity

Fundamentalist movements in the Muslim world emerged under diverse political and economic circumstances. Although they are present everywhere and display some similarities, it would be erroneous to analyze them as a single and homogeneous movement.[1] An ahistorical image of fundamentalism can only confound the opportunity to confront politically its various forms. There is not one uniform fundamentalist "monster," but rather several fundamentalisms. This being stated, one should add that what fundamentalisms do have in common pertains to identity politics and affects women directly....

A Question of Definition: Islam and Muslims

Fundamentalists speak in the name of Islam, and unfortunately there is a common tendency to conflate Islam and Muslims. We feel that the adjective Muslim should be used to describe the social reality of the Muslim world as it is—people, countries, states, laws, and customs—without assuming that what Muslims do is Islamic. The term Islam should be used for religion as such, theological reflections and interpretations of the Quran. In other words, we do not believe that Islamic states exist, but that there are Muslim states.

Debates often take place among Muslims about what Islam is or should be. Rather than speculating about a true and authentic Islam, we would simply use the term Muslim to describe what those who claim to believe in Islam and those who claim to live according to rules edicted by their God and those who claim to build nations which abide by those, do in the real world. In other words, Islam as it should be, Muslims as they are.

Women as Pillars and Weak Points in the Construction of Identity

In spite of their diversity, although Muslim fundamentalist groups represent a variety of interests and classes, and fulfill different psychological and political needs, their discourse centers around identity in three senses: identity as threatened; identity as a process of "going back"; and, identity confined to the private sphere. And although the threat is generally external, monolithic and all-evil, educated elites and women are the weak points in the defence system as well as the potential allies of the external enemy. This in turn justifies the closing of identity upon itself, like a fortress, and the closing of women within the fortress.

The practical consequences of this ideological stand shape women's lives as well as their responses to fundamentalists. At a political level, they fear being accused of betrayal, since challenging any aspect of identity is betraying the whole; at a cultural level, traditions are defined as immutable; at a religious level, the end of interpretation of the Quran confines women into a model of society, way of life, dress and behavior as close as possible to the historical model born in the Middle East 14 centuries ago; and finally, at a legal level, the emphasis is on Personal Laws as the means to defend identity.

Fundamentalists do not merely share a common discourse on identity and women; they also achieve common immediate goals: They have successfully put pressure on governments to adjust Personal Laws to their definition of Islamic identity. Personal Laws directly affect women: they pertain to questions of marriage, divorce, child custody, and inheritance. Therefore they also determine what a Muslim woman's behavior should be and link her to the defense of the threatened identity.

To be the guardians of identity and culture is an honor in the fundamentalist discourse. Women are honored for as long as they keep culture and religion in the way they are told to do; breeders and raisers of good Muslims, women should behave as a model for the sons, who are warriors of Islam. Recently published studies on women in Nazi Germany provide elements of comparison with women living under or participating in Muslim fundamentalism.[2] What is common to both is the ideal of Mothers and of Family keepers tied up with the notion of reproducing the best possible group (race or religion) in the context of an economic crisis and expansionist views over other nations. Being the guardian is so central to the threatened identity that it is also identified as the weakest point, the most vulnerable to be protected from alien influences. Being the guardian is being a potential traitor who should therefore be closely watched. Laws should be codified which clearly fix the private sphere as central to protection of the threatened identity, bind women to their role of guardians and prevent them from any possibility to fulfill the dark part of their natural mission, to show the other profile of their Janus face, prevent them from betrayal and the destruction of the community—national, religious, or communal.

Women Living under Muslim Laws

About 450 million women live in Muslim countries and communities, throughout five continents. The majority of them live under "Muslim laws," that is, Muslim Personal Laws, also known as Family Codes. These laws are presented as "Islamic" and consequently as the unique and untouchable transcription of the word of God. They have many commonalities but also significant differences from one

country to the other. This is due to two reasons: the incorporation of local traditions and the political use of religion.

Islam is a religion which constantly expands—probably the only one to do so
nowadays. In the process it invariably incorporates ways of life and customs from
different cultures. Muslim laws as they exist in the real world today result from the
combination of interpretations of the Quran entwined with local traditions. It is
important to fully realize that although they are not "Islamic," traditions are
enforced upon women in the name of Islam. Belonging to a specific Muslim community is equated with accepting all the religio-cultural aspects which make for
this society. The Semitic tradition of veiling and/or secluding women in the Middle
East and North Africa; female genital mutilation in Egypt, Sudan, and other countries of West Africa; or the Hindu tradition of caste and dowry in India and Sri
Lanka are all specific to the regions where they prevail.[3] Nevertheless, Muslim peoples and certainly women are made to believe that their local traditions are part
and parcel of being a Muslim and—in the final analysis—are Islamic.

Muslim states also interpret Islam in ways which suit their local policies, even
on very crucial ideological issues. An example of the fact that Muslim states do not
have a common policy inspired by Islam can be found in the diversity of stands
taken on the question of contraception and abortion. Both are legal in Tunisia;
both are enforced on women in Bangladesh together with sterilization for both
sexes; contraception is allowed but abortion forbidden in Pakistan. Algeria has forbidden both for a long time (from 1962 till 1974) in spite of a *fatwa* issued a year
after independence by the High Islamic council in Algiers; it finally allowed contraception when our annual population growth rate had reached 3.5, threatening the
wealth and privileges of the ex-socialist bureaucrats who by then had turned into a
classical bourgeoisie owning the means of production.[4] All these countries claim
that they defined their population policy according to the spirit of Islam. In each
country, people, and certainly women, are made to believe that the rules enforced
locally or nationally reflect the spirit of Islam and are injunctions of God that
Muslim states apply in their legislation. Moreover, the official discourse implies or
eventually states that these laws are Islamic.

The mere confrontation of women from various Muslim backgrounds is in
itself enlightening insofar as it permits challenging the notion of one homogeneous Muslim world and the existence of a Muslim law which would genuinely be
Islamic.[5] On the contrary, it draws attention to the fact that Muslim Laws are
grounded in history and culture, *hic et nunc*, as well as to the fact that they are used
for political purposes.

Fundamentalists and the State

In July 1984, the first Action Committee of Women Living Under Muslim Laws
defined themselves as "Women whose lives are shaped, conditioned and governed
by laws, both written and unwritten, drawn from interpretations of the Quran tied
up with local traditions." The Action Committee later stated that "generally speak-

ing, men and the State use these [laws] against women, and have done so under various political regimes."[6]

During the past two decades and more especially during the last one, Muslim Personal Laws have been at the center of Muslim identities; new Muslim Personal Laws have been passed, reinforced, or modified in ways which are highly unfavorable to women. This phenomenon could be interpreted as the expression of the power of fundamentalists, and as the collusion of states with fundamentalist movements.[7] No matter whether fundamentalists are in power or in the position of a powerful main opposition party, or whether they are just growing, in most cases, their claim to an "Islamic" private sphere through the adoption of personal laws is very generally heard by those in power.[8] This happens whatever their general political stands would otherwise be.[9] Is it that the woman question is so sensitive, as they pretend, that their authority and their position could be challenged on this issue? Or is it rather that women's subordination is thrown to the crowd to amuse itself with, like crumbs are thrown to the poor, while serious political matters remain in their hands? Are we the *monnaie d'échange* they use to remain in power? Could it also be that the control of women prepares for a brutalization of the society which suits the needs of the powers-that-be to control people? Although states may resist on other points, the rise of fundamentalists, family affairs, and women's subordination are generally, with rare exceptions, the reflection of the fundamentalist definition of identity, and laws are passed or modified in order to meet their demands. The past decade has seen increasingly the collusion of states with fundamentalists in these matters. It is interesting to note that this happens even in countries where fundamentalists are otherwise fought, banned, and imprisoned for their challenge to the state....

Women's Internalization of Identity Politics

Women's responses to this state of affairs show the impact that fundamentalist ideologies have, not only on governments and subsequent legal decisions affecting women, but also on the women's movement itself. Women's organizations range from participating in the fundamentalist movement, to working for reform within the framework of Islam, and to fighting for a secular state and secular laws. In spite of this wide range of tendencies and strategies, all of them have internalized some of the concepts developed and used by fundamentalists. In particular they have internalized the notion of an external monolithic enemy, and the fear of betraying their identity—defined as group identity, rather than their gender identity in the group. To a large extent, they also accept tradition, not as a living history which informs their present and future, but as a dead body to be revived and maintained in its former (imagined) shape. And finally, they acknowledge their central role in identity politics.

In the same way that those who lived for a long time in a state of lack of democracy have difficulties in reinventing democratic practices (even if they fought for reaching such a stage), it is not easy today to step out of ideological constructions of the fundamentalist women-centered discourse on identity. One should not underestimate the impact of this discourse on women's minds. Its consequences are clearly visible in the efforts that women have to make in order to question not only fundamentalist discriminatory practices against women but also the premises which inform these practices.

Internalization by women of fundamentalists' philosophy, concepts, and biased hypotheses has many consequences at the level of their strategies. Internalizing the notion that Islam is in danger—therefore that the community is in danger—implies that in their practices, women must abide by an established set of priorities. Thus they become an easy prey for political manipulation: Since facing an external threat requires total unity of the group, then wars, communal tensions, any suitable political event will be used against women to compel them to join the nation's unity and postpone their demands. We could provide many examples.[10] The Algerian case is a landmark insofar as women not only postponed their demands but were later forced to renounce them until very recently. For decades, they were fully cheated.[11] Even in recent history, in Palestine for instance, where women are trying to build an autonomous movement, priority is still given to the liberation struggle, and women's struggles will still come as their second or third priority.

As the Left before them, women who try to defend their rights in Muslim contexts are generally accused of importing a foreign ideology whenever they ask for more social justice. But while the Left's response was to point at universal values of social justice, women accept the fundamentalist premises that in matters concerning the private sphere, universal is equated to being West-dominated. Consequently, defending universal values of social justice becomes unacceptable when it comes to the woman question. This is why, instead of going straight to the point, women first try to demonstrate that they are truly and genuinely rooted in their own culture, that they are not alienated in nonindigenous ideologies, that they do not side with external enemies. Trying in vain to legitimize themselves and their struggle according to the criteria for legitimacy set by fundamentalists, they expend considerable time and energy trying to distinguish themselves from "Western feminists" as "Third World feminists"—as if these categories too were homogeneous aggregates of interchangeable individuals, without ideological differences, without classes and conflicting interests, a very mechanistic model indeed. To a certain extent, one could say that women thus also abide by the notion of the superiority of Muslims over other religious groups, a xenophobia which theologians denounce as contrary to the spirit of tolerance in Islam, but which is also present in the policies of some contemporary Muslim states.

It sometimes takes very long before individuals dare transgress the "betrayal complex," and try and identify their allies both inside and outside their community. It is only after experiencing again and again that the time for women's demands is never now, but always later (reasons given for it may unfortunately be very convincing, as for instance when Palestine is under brutal attack by Israel, or in Pakistan under Benazir Bhutto,[12] or during the Gulf war) that women dare make a breakthrough out of the fortress of communal, national and religious identity.

Women's Responses and Strategies

...Many women's groups in Muslim countries and communities devote time to research their feminist ancestors, not only in an effort to recover their own history as women, but also in the vain hope of stopping accusations of Westernization by rightists, and in quest for their legitimacy. They may also try and excavate traditions in an attempt to show that traditions were not necessarily unfavorable to women if placed in their historical context.[13] This again refers to a definition of traditions as a thing from the past, to be opposed to "modernity," while modernity should be understood as the present stage of traditions, the normal evolution of tradition and culture evolving from the past to adjust to the present context. However, it is very clear that many traditions which were indeed favorable to women are at present being eradicated,[14] while our rulers introduce new "traditions" directly inspired by Western colonization, without ever being accused of betrayal and collusion with the West, not even by women's groups themselves. In this general context, one can identify three main strategies in the women's movement in Muslim countries and communities:

1. Women joining fundamentalist groups—a strategy which I tend to see as a sort of entryism. On the one hand this strategy avoids challenging Muslim identity, and it frees from the fear of betrayal; on the other hand, because fundamentalist groups have both the will and the funds to do so, they offer various gratifications and advantages to their members, such as grants to study, free medical care, and loans without interest. Women followers also benefit from social and parental recognition, the right and encouragement to study (although they may not freely choose their subject, as there are areas of knowledge which are forbidden to women), a chance to choose their husband within the group instead of going through an arranged marriage, and so on.[15] An increasing number of women join fundamentalist groups throughout the world. We cannot dismiss this important social and political phenomenon by stigmatizing these women and their ideological alienation. Neither can we simply say that there are material benefits which no other group ever offered them. We believe that a serious reason for their choice is that no alternative—at the religious and therefore at the identity level—ever existed until recently.[16] Fundamentalists are the first ones to consider and use women and their needs to try and reach out to them, and to acknowledge them as a political force which can be maneuvered and is worth trying to gain to the cause. The new strategy, described in the following paragraphs, will hopefully provide for the philosophical needs of those who at present see no way out of the religious frame hijacked by fundamentalists.

2. Women working from within the frame of Islam, both at the level of religion and at the level of culture. Although they are not yet very visible, there are feminist theologians and historians within the Muslim world. They represent a very important ideological current and offer a real alternative to the previous strategy. Women theologians in search of a "true" Islam are currently trying to promote a liberation theology in Islam by reviving the tradition of reinterpretation of the Quran.

Several men in recent history have devoted their time and paid with their lives for their progressive interpretations of the Quran[17] and if there were women interpreters of the Quran in modern history, we have lost track of them. But there are now women who have attained a high level in theology and who feel that progressive male interpreters of the Quran have not fully explored it from the point of view of women. They go back to the original Arabic text and will propose, in the spirit of what they believe is true Islam, their own interpretation of the verses on which fundamentalists base their oppression of women.[18] They also point to the historical context of the text which may lead to more enlightened interpretations. Similarly, women historians attempt to track and recapture women's history, to show the historical role of leading women in the transformation of customs and traditions. They stress that this role was seen neither as threatening to the group's identity nor as cutting them off from their cultural or religious roots. Both theologians and historians have worked in isolation for a long time. They now have opportunities to come together and reinforce each other as well as opportunities to reach out to their real audience, to women activists who are craving for such knowledge. Even though such approaches are indeed seen as betrayals by fundamentalists, women feel secure that these strategies do not cut them off from the masses, and challenge the accusation of betrayal by closing themselves within an Islamic frame of thought. We nevertheless believe that if such women theologians and historians would gain audience of women in masses, they will, as their male counterparts did, pay with their lives for the social change that their religious and philosophical work aims at.

3. Women fighting for secularism and for laws which would reflect the present understanding of what human rights are and should be in the world today. Those are under the fiercest attacks. These women are left unprotected because they step out of both religious and cultural frames. Although they state that they did not renounce their religious, cultural, and national identities, they are perceived as having lost them all, and are regarded as outcasts. Not only are they accused and rejected but each of them as a single individual is treated as if their sole betrayal would endanger both their society and the whole of the Muslim world.[19] They advocate that religion is a private affair for individuals to choose and plead for the separation of religion from the state.[20] They believe in values which are neither the property of Muslims nor of the West and tend to turn to internationalism as the only way for them to build up their legitimacy, as well as a strategy for information, support and solidarity amongst themselves across national, religious, and cultural boundaries. But it is interesting to note that internationalism in their view does not transcend and erase their belonging to a cultural-religious compound in which they still want to grow their roots; nor does it come into conflict with forms of nationalism drawn from the full consciousness of imperialism and memories of the time of colonization. Although they are in a minority, they seem to me the only alternative to identity politics as defined and shaped by fundamentalists, the only hope for the recognition of concomitant non-antagonistic, multiple identities in each individual.

Notes

1. One witness's various attempts to globally qualify fundamentalism in political, religious or cultural terms, for instance as totalitarianism, revivalism, traditionalism, etc. We believe these generalizations to be both inadequate and dangerous. See Olivier Roy, "Fundamentalism, Traditionalism and Islam," *Telos* 65 (1985): 122–127; also see Hassan Hanafi, "The Origins of Violence in Contemporary Islam," *Development* 1 (1987), Special issue on Culture and Ethnicity, pp. 56–61; and also Tibi Bassam, "Neo-Islamic Fundamentalism," in *ibid.*, pp. 62–66.

2. Claudia Koonz, *Mothers in the Fatherland, Women in the Family and Nazi Politics* (New York: St Martin's Press, 1986) Cf. *Cahiers du Feminisme*, November 1990, on Women and Nazism.

3. Cf. Dossiers *Women Living Under Muslim Laws*, nos. 1–6 (1986–1989), edited by Marie-Aimée Hélie-Lucas.

4. Marie-Aimée Hélie-Lucas, "La politique de formation en Algérie, comme indicateur d'une situation de classe," *Temps Moderne*, no. special "Du Maghreb," Paris 1974. See also Marie-Aimée Hélie-Lucas, "Women in the Algerian Liberation Struggle and After," presented at a conference at the Transnational Institute, Amsterdam, 1984.

5. See Documents *Women Living Under Muslim Laws Exchange Programme* (1988), and *Aramon Plan of Action* (1986).

6. In 1988 the Women Living Under Muslim Laws network organized an Exchange Programme by which women from 18 different Muslim countries were sent to each others' countries; they were hosted by women's groups and introduced to the diversity of cultures and practices all believed to be inspired by religion. This exercise enabled them to distinguish in their own set up what pertains to religion, what pertains to culture, and what is the political use of both, or, as Salma Sobhan once described it: "It helps us analyze how all these have been woven together to form a particular garment that women have to wear willingly or unwillingly."

7. The debate on the Woman Question and the nature of the State is very important among feminists from Muslim countries. See essays in Deniz Kandiyoti (ed.), *Women, the State and Islam* (London: Macmillan, 1991).

8. In France and in Britain, the debate on "respect of the other's culture" has been raging over the past few years. The traditional Left caught into its white colonial guilt is so afraid to be labeled racist that they have lost all shame and are prepared to cover crimes against women in the name of respect of culture, while feminists try to link up with indigenous women's demands. The most fruitful alliance of this kind is the London-based group "Women Against Fundamentalism," which takes up issues against Christian fundamentalism in Ireland, Muslim fundamentalism in Britain, and racism in the U.K. Britain has accepted that separate schools for Muslim girls be set up, where the curriculum is drastically different from both the curriculum of British children in British schools and of Muslim boys in Muslim schools. Women in France (both French and migrants working together) who take to court parents who practice female genital mutilation on their baby daughters are fiercely attacked both by fundamentalists of all sorts and by the liberal Left who support "the right to be different."

9. On March 15, 1990, the Iraqi Revolutionary Command Council declared it legal for Iraqi men to kill their mothers, wives, daughters and their paternal nieces and cousins accused of *zina* (fornication and adultery); the decree specified that they could "not be brought to justice" for acting as prosecutors and executioners of the suspected women, who then had no chance to even try and prove their innocence. Until recently, the Iraqi Baath government was the main exemplar of a secular Arab state which did not draw on Quranic interpretations for its laws and policies. The fact that it did take inspiration from other Muslim states on the issue of zina in drafting this decree (and made it worse, to the horror of believers who protested) did not attract attention, except from women activists inside and outside the Muslim world.

10. On the Sheenaaz Sheikh case, see *Women Living Under Muslim Laws Dossier* 1 and 2 (1986).

11. Hélie-Lucas, "Bound and Gagged by the Family Code," reproduced in *Women Living Under Muslim Laws Dossier* 5/6 (1989).

12. Under Benazir Bhutto, Pakistani women reproduced the experience of Algerian women under "specific socialism": for fear of giving reasons for fundamentalists to attack the legal govern-

ment, they did not make any demands which could have aggravated the situation, thus losing precious time.

13. Most progressive theologians and interpreters of the Quran introduce a historical factor in their analysis of the improvement that Mohammad brought to women in his time; for instance, they would quote his opposition to female infanticide. Others would research on rights for women to end their marriage or own property, looking at it both from the point of view of religious rights and customary rights.

14. For example, in the Arab and Middle East tradition women would keep their father's name throughout their lives and would be known as X, daughter of Y (or would also be referred to as X, mother of Z). Now bureaucrats are imposing the Western tradition of the husband's name. Considering the number of divorces and repudiations, women will now have to be called by 4 or 5 different names in their life. Their sense of self-identity will certainly be shattered. Bureaucrats do not seem troubled with this introduction of such an alien tradition.

15. Though women who join fundamentalist groups claim that they get all these benefits, it clearly appears as self-justificatory. Nevertheless, one has to admit that neither the Left nor governments have even pretended to cater to the needs of people the way fundamentalists do. As an example, in Algeria in the late 1970s, when there was neither food on the market nor clothing in the shops to buy (regardless of prices), the Muslim Brothers were the ones who distributed semolina (the basis of couscous, a very popular basic dish), as well as "Islamic dress" at the mosques on Fridays. This is how the hijab Iranian style—definitely an untraditional women's dress in Algeria—was introduced in our country. The Muslim Brothers in Algeria and fundamentalist groups in many other countries are the only ones who have both the will and the money to afford to be populists. Their money obviously comes from various state sources, which allow them to generate income and finance their projects. The powerful Arkam, who was visited by a woman activist in Malaysia, has branches in many countries both in Asia and in Africa, as well as in non-Muslim countries (for instance in Australia); they own factories, produce for their own communities who live in autarchy, both in terms of self-subsistence, and for grants, teachings, and religious education.

16. In 1988 the network Women Living Under Muslim Laws planned to explore the possibilities of gathering and circulating information on progressive interpretations of Islam; this project later evolved into identifying feminist interpreters of the Quran, then gathering and circulating their work. In 1988 an international working group on feminist interpretation of the Quran was launched which held its first meeting in July 1990 in Karachi; since then the group meets regularly; the research done is circulated within the network Women Living Under Muslim Laws.

17. Male progressive interpreters of the Quran have often paid with their lives for their decision to undertake *Ijtihad*. In recent years Tahar Haddad was persecuted in Tunisia, Asghar Ali Engineer escaped bombs in India, and the Sudanese Nour Mahmoud Mohamed Tahir was killed in 1984. The latter's books were publicly burnt, his body buried in a hidden place to prevent pilgrimage, and the possession of his books was punishable.

18. See various publications by Women Living Under Muslim Laws network: *Information Kit on Marriage Contracts and the Delegated Right of Divorce Talaq et tafwez* (1989); *Proceedings of the Meeting on Interpretations of the Koran by Women* (1991); *Les Femmes dans le Coran: Kit d'information préparé pour la réunion du Groupe International de Travail sur les Interprétations Coraniques par les Femmes* (Juillet 1990, Karachi: Femmes Sous Lois Musulmanes); *Women in the Qur'an: Information Kit prepared for Women Living Under Muslim Laws* (July 1990); International Working Meeting on Qur'anic Interpretation by Women (Karachi).

19. The claim by fundamentalists that any individual is a threat to the whole of Islam is well illustrated by the Rushdie affair.

20. On the forefront of secularism and the separation of religion from the state are the Algerian women, whose stands are published in *Dossier* no. 7 and 8, *Women Living Under Muslim Laws*.

20.
SOME REFLECTIONS ON U.S. WOMEN OF COLOR AND THE UNITED NATIONS FOURTH WORLD CONFERENCE ON WOMEN AND NGO FORUM IN BEIJING, CHINA

Mallika Dutt

Over a year has passed since 40,000 women gathered at the United Nations Fourth World Conference on Women in Beijing. A watershed event in the history of global women's movements, Beijing had an important impact on women's movements in the United States. Seven thousand U.S. women participated in the conference, and many of them were women of color. This article reflects on the role and participation of women of color in the women's conference and explores the possible implications of the impact of Beijing on political trends in the United States. Conversations with nine women of color organizers and activists (Alice Cardona, Idélisse Malavé, Lori Pourier, Catherine Powell, Beth Richie, Loretta Ross, Peggy Saika, Rinku Sen, and Ingrid Washinawatok) are interwoven into my own analysis of and involvement in the largest United Nations gathering in history. Of the nine women, three are African American, two are Latina, two are Native American, and two are Asian American. Seven of them attended the Beijing conference; the two who did not go were involved in several pre-Beijing activities.

Four main themes emerged from my conversations and observations. The first was the vibrancy and power of the global women's movement and the corresponding lack of unity and strength in U.S. counterparts. The second had to do with the globalization of the world economy and its impact on the United States. The third concerned the tension experienced around the category "women of color," and the fourth led from the profound transformation in consciousness post-Beijing to the struggle to implement that transformation into day-to-day organizing.

Discovering the Power of Global Women's Movements

For most women from the United States, Beijing was an eye-opening, humbling, and transformative experience. U.S. women were startled by the sophisticated analysis and well-organized and powerful voices of women from other parts of the world, particularly those of women from the South. Saddled with years of imperialist history along with its corresponding baggage of U.S. superiority, racism, xenophobia, and insularity, women in the United States seldom connect issues of local organizing to international arenas. Even long-time activists and organizers perceive women in other parts of the world as more oppressed, less organized, less vocal, and certainly not as "feminist" as their U.S. counterparts. Images like female genital mutilation, dowry deaths, and public stoning of women form the dominant perception about the lives of women overseas. The discovery that these "victims" were in fact a far more powerful voice for change in the 1990s than the women's movement in the United States has provided an important starting point in changing the nature of the dialogue between women in the United States and women in other parts of the world.

For women of color, the discovery and connection with strong voices from the South was particularly important. Almost all the women I spoke with described the sense of global solidarity, pride, and affirmation that they experienced in Beijing. This sense of affirmation had greater resonance, because of the sense of siege that pervades the political environment in the United States, with the attacks on women and communities of color, particularly immigrant women, African American women on welfare, and lesbians. Feelings of frustration and impotence that defined women's political activism in the United States were shattered by the atmosphere of collective power that was palpable in Beijing. As Cathy Powell, an attorney with the NAACP Legal Defense Fund, so eloquently stated, "Although I was depressed about the U.S. women's movement, I felt very proud to be part of a global movement which has been a source of great inspiration in my work. I met amazing women in amazing struggles and feel very affirmed by the loose and diverse broader global women's movement."

The global solidarity and breadth of issues that were discussed in Beijing brought into stark relief the constraints of single-issue and single-identity organizing in the United States. For Peggy Saika, an environmental justice activist and executive director of the Asian Pacific Environmental Network, the overarching lesson of Beijing was the interconnectedness of issues and people. Indeed, although activists in the United States see connections when they come together across identity or issue lines, the opportunities to do so are few. In Beijing, Saika felt the connections every day, with 40,000 women from around the world discussing everything from peace to education.

The fragmentation of the U.S. women's movement was visually represented in the dialogues that took place in the regional tents. At the NGO Forum, women from different regions gathered in their geographic tents to share ideas, network, and develop strategies. Idélisse Malavé, a litigator for Puerto Rican civil rights, now vice-president of the Ms Foundation, said the Latin American tent was like a festival where an organizing committee held thematic workshops, meetings, and strategy discussions. Women tried to build a common ideological base through dialogue, a process Malavé found very powerful. In contrast, the North American tent was empty and sterile, used only sporadically as an ad hoc meeting place, while both U.S. women of color and white women from North America and Europe gathered in more active areas.

Understanding the Place of the United States in the Global Arena

Women of color left Beijing with a heightened awareness of the interaction of local and global forces on women in the United States, particularly economic forces. The adverse impact on women of the globalization of the world economy was a central theme at the NGO Forum. Women from the United States discovered that their stories of social service cutbacks, loss of jobs, corporate downsizing, attacks on women on welfare, and an increase in women's poverty were echoed by women from the South who described the impact of structural adjustment programs in their countries. Women from the South, however, had a far more sophisticated analysis of the role of international organizations like the World Bank and the International Monetary Fund (both dominated by the U.S. government), as well as the role of international capital markets and transnational corporations in the economic marginalization and exploitation of women.

Beijing helped Loretta Ross, organizer in the National Black Women's Health Project and executive director of the Center for Human Rights Education, understand that the globalization of the economy had to be an integral part of her organizing in the United States. For her, Beijing meant questioning the "American dream" which assumes the ability to acquire and consume material goods if one works hard enough, an assumption called into question by the world economy, which makes working-class people and people of color dispensable. This meant that the economic assumptions that had guided U.S. social change movements needed to be reevaluated. It became clear to Ross that if U.S. women did not build global movements like an international human rights movement and a global labor movement, they would become part of the global free-fall.

Lori Pourier, who staffs the Indigenous Women's Network, said: "Beijing opened my eyes to the role of international decision makers. My experience of racism was limited to living as an indigenous woman in the border town of Pine Ridge, South Dakota. I had been too focused on the trust responsibilities of the U.S. government and was not looking at the global picture." Meeting indigenous women from other parts of the world who were grappling not only with the impact of dictatorships but also with the impact of institutions like the World Bank, the International Monetary Fund, the World Trade Organization, and transnational corporations, helped Pourier to understand the role of the United States in these organizations as well as the role of global forces within the United States.

Ingrid Washinawatok, a citizen of the Menominee Nation and co-chair of the Indigenous Women's Network, said that Beijing allowed the indigenous women who attended to "step out of their views of their own oppression to go, hear, share, and feel the oppression of other women. This was important because if you stay too localized and only within your own people, it atrophies you, makes you resentful, and leads to inaction."

Searching for Identity and Location in Beijing

For many women of color who sought to create bonds with women from their continents of origin, Beijing was often painful. The difficulties encountered by women of color in connecting with these women were interwoven with the history of their migration to the United States. For African American women, the legacy of slavery meant that few know their specific countries of origin and claiming common ground with African women was more difficult for them than the geographic and cultural connections through which Asian American and Latinas have a ready frame of reference. For indigenous women, whose presence in and claim to the United States precedes all other ethnic and racial communities, ideas of self-determination and sovereignty resonate most closely with indigenous women from other parts of the world. However, despite these differences in location, in Beijing, all women of color had to overcome the suspicion and hostility that came from being perceived as "Americans" by women from the South.

Negatively held perceptions of Americans as interfering, arrogant, ignorant, insensitive, and imperialist were ascribed to women of color as well as to white women from the United States. These attitudes forced women of color constantly to confront the role of the United States as an aggressor and violator of human rights even as they perceived themselves as oppositional forces within the country. Thus, as Rinku Sen, codirector of the Center for Third World Organizing, stated, women of color had continually to make decisions about how they identified themselves in relation to women from the South. Although some expected to make immediate connections with women from their home countries, others were more careful in how they identified themselves—as women from the South living in the North, as women of color from the United States, as immigrant women, or as women from their particular ethnic or racial background. According to Sen, women of color sought self-definitions to avoid rejection by their Southern counterparts.

As many women from both the United States and the South have pointed out, U.S. women have usually been involved with women in other countries in the context of academic research, development aid, or involvement in other women's movements. Thus, hundreds of dissertations have been written about women's lives in the Third World by women from the United States, but rarely do women from the South come to "study" U.S. women or write dissertations on government abuse of women on welfare or the attacks by the religious Right on abortion providers in this country. Similarly, women from other parts of the world have not presumed to define the agenda of U.S. women's movements in the same way that some women from this country have insisted that women's movements in other countries prioritize female genital mutilation, dowry deaths, or religious persecution. This simplistic understanding of women's lives ignores the depth and breadth of women's organizing in other parts of the world. The anger felt by women from other parts of the world at this often racist and culturally biased perception of their work has been exacerbated by the fact that most U.S. women's movements have seldom addressed the role played by their own government in the violations of women's human rights the world over whether through the training of military personnel for dictatorships, the location of military bases, the programs of the World Bank or the International Monetary Fund, or the actions of U.S. corporations overseas.

On Being "Women of Color" and Organizing for Beijing

Women of color today appear to be far more focused on organizing within their own ethnic communities than across color lines. This was particularly apparent among the women I interviewed for this article. The primary self-identification through which women described their experiences around Beijing was as African American or Asian American, Latina, or indigenous women even when their political work was located in a broader context and they had gone to the conference as part of a multiethnic team. The term "women of color" was most easily embraced by African American women, but even they described their experiences primarily through the context of their own racial/ethnic identity. Indigenous women seemed the best organized constituency of women from the United States and articulated their concerns and issues differently from other women of color.

Alice Cardona was dissatisfied with the term "women of color." She said the term came from African American women's attempt to be more inclusive but that it failed to reflect the social context of different communities. Cardona's group, the National Latina Caucus, went to Beijing as Latinas, an identity they used primarily to disassociate from white women who were perceived as imperialist or insensitive. For Cardona, the issue of identity is "a question of community consciousness and not of color."

An interesting phenomenon in Beijing was the contrast between the power of Asian women's movements in the regions compared with the relative marginalization of Asian American women in the United States. Person after person commented on the strength, diversity, and leadership of women's movements in India, the Philippines, Japan, and other parts of Asia. According to Loretta Ross, Asian women were the best organized force in Beijing; she wondered what impact this would have on Asian American women in the United States. Although the visibility of Asian women was affirming for Peggy Saika, it also reinforced the fragility of Asian American women and their inability to be front and center in the U.S. political scene.

Efforts to bring together different communities of women of color for preconference organizing were limited to local and regional initiatives, with the exception of the U.S. indigenous women. Indigenous women in the United States met systematically for nine months and produced an eighty-page document that reflected the feedback, input, and writing of women from around the country. In Beijing, this document became the North American contribution to a global indigenous women's statement of their concerns. Although African American, Latina, and Asian American women also drafted their own statements in Beijing, the statement by indigenous women was the most comprehensive.

Although they were the best organized as a group, indigenous women did not fully identify as "women of color." As Ingrid Washinawatok described it, for indigenous women, solidarity with other women of color in the United States is complicated by the reality that women of color are just as much interlopers on Native people's lands as are white people. Communities of color and immigrant communities are often disrespectful of indigenous peoples; share the same value systems as white people in terms of acquisition of wealth, resources, and power; and can be as insensitive to the needs of indigenous peoples. Thus, the concerns of other women of color conflict with or differ from indigenous women's struggles around self-determination, land, sovereignty, and survival. In Beijing, therefore, the primary focus of U.S. indigenous women was to meet indigenous peoples from around the world and to build an international network. This network will act across common issues of nuclear waste, land rights, and sovereignty issues and to monitor actions at the United Nations which affect indigenous peoples. Alliances with other women of color were useful in certain contexts, but indigenous women did not feel that they always fit into the general agenda of women of color.

Transforming Consciousness into Action

All the women I spoke with described a profound shift in their consciousness post-Beijing. Almost all shared the same vision for future social change organizing, but few have been able to make these ideas concrete. According to Rinku Sen, women have developed a new language describing themselves and their work, but this has not yet changed day-to-day organizing. It has also been difficult for women who were in Beijing to share their experiences adequately with women who did not attend the conference.

Despite the challenges, the common themes articulated by those who went to Beijing provide a shared basis for action. Many women urged increasing the focus on community organizing and base building. Their first priority was organizing within their own ethnic communities. Alice Cardona articulated the need to refocus on one's own community and then connect with other women of color to coalesce around clear goals. Similarly, Peggy Saika described her efforts to build an Asian American and Pacific Islander women's movement that shifted the focus from service-oriented organizations to base-building and advocacy groups. All these women described plans for national post-Beijing meetings of their particular identity groups. They also felt more opportunities to meet across issue and identity lines were crucial, and they called for better international networking and global connections.

Opportunities Lost and Found

Beijing provided women of color with singular opportunities to catapult themselves into leadership within organizations in the United States—opportunities that have not been realized. On the other hand, the energy and excitement of those who went continues to provide hope that new directions will emerge in the organizing of women of color.

Women of color were unable to utilize the pre-Beijing process to build a national movement or network when such a network was critical. Hundreds of meetings and conferences took place prior to Beijing (including ten regional meetings convened by the Women's Bureau of the Department of Labor); yet few attempted to share agendas, goals, ideas, and strategies to develop concerted plans of action. The energy that took women to Beijing did not get transformed into a powerful voice for the human rights of women of color.

Moreover, women of color did not understand the importance of the Beijing Platform for Action as a tool to influence public policy in the United States. The Platform for Action was negotiated by approximately 181 governments, including our own, to reflect the commitments of UN member countries to half the world's population. Although women globally were involved in regional and UN efforts to lobby their governments and establish themselves as players in their own public policy processes, few U.S. women of color even realized that the Beijing conference comprised an official governmental conference as well as an NGO Forum. Because of their lack of preparation, it was difficult for women of color in Beijing to represent their interests adequately or affect the process. Again, the one exception was the indigenous women's caucus. However, their efforts at influencing the Platform would have benefited from a strong and powerful lobby by women of color who had agreed to shared goals.

Despite these missed opportunities, the excitement and energy that Beijing has generated provides the possibility of forging stronger directions, coalitions, agendas, and movements of women of color to address the present political climate. However, some important shifts in consciousness are necessary before such a possibility is realized.

Although women of color must focus on their own ethnic communities in order to build strong bases for political action, it is also critical that they begin to provide much-needed national leadership that crosses ethnic and identity lines. U.S. women's movements today are suffering from an acute crisis in leadership, vision, and direction. Women of color who are local leaders must develop and share their critical lessons, strategies, and analyses with a wider constituency of people. If women of color continue only to define themselves in the context of their communities, they perpetuate the problem of white women being perceived as national leaders while women of color are seen only as speaking for their own particular ethnicity or concern. It is important that leadership be assumed out of a sense of accountability and responsibility, but it is also important that marginalized communities understand their power as well as their victimization.

Women from other parts of the world demonstrated the potential to speak as leaders while articulating a complex analysis of their exploitation and oppression. U.S. women of color returned from Beijing with pride and affirmation, which should provide the basis for moving from margin to center in a way that redefines both. Our ability to build a true democracy that values and protects the human rights of all its constituents hangs in the balance.

CLASS

21.
THE UNHAPPY MARRIAGE OF MARXISM AND FEMINISM: TOWARDS A MORE PROGRESSIVE UNION
Heidi Hartmann

The "marriage" of marxism and feminism has been like the marriage of husband and wife depicted in English common law: marxism and feminism are one, and that one is marxism.[1] Recent attempts to integrate marxism and feminism are unsatisfactory to us as feminists because they subsume the feminist struggle into the "larger" struggle against capital. To continue our simile further, either we need a healthier marriage or we need a divorce.

The inequalities in this marriage, like most social phenomena, are no accident. Many marxists typically argue that feminism is at best less important than class conflict and at worst divisive of the working class. This political stance produces an analysis that absorbs feminism into the class struggle. Moreover, the analytic power of marxism with respect to capital has obscured its limitations with respect to sexism. We will argue here that while marxist analysis provides essential insight into the laws of historical development, and those of capital in particular, the categories of marxism are sex-blind. Only a specifically feminist analysis reveals the systemic character of relations between men and women. Yet feminist analysis by itself is inadequate because it has been blind to history and insufficiently materialist. Both marxist analysis, particularly its historical and materialist method, and feminist analysis, especially the identification of patriarchy as a social and historical structure, must be drawn upon if we are to understand the development of western capitalist societies and the predicament of women within them. In this essay we suggest a new direction for marxist feminist analysis.

... [W]e try to use the strengths of both marxism and feminism to make suggestions both about the development of capitalist societies and about the present situation of women. We attempt to use marxist methodology to analyze feminist objectives, correcting the imbalance in recent socialist feminist work, and suggesting a more complete analysis of our present socioeconomic formation. We argue that a materialist analysis demonstrates that patriarchy is not simply a psychic, but also a social and economic structure. We suggest that our society can best be understood once it is recognized that it is organized both in capitalistic and in patriarchal ways. While pointing out tensions between patriarchal and capitalist interests, we argue that the accumulation of capital both accommodates itself to patriarchal social structure and helps to perpetuate it. We suggest in this context that sexist ideology has assumed a peculiarly capitalist form in the present, illustrating one way that patriarchal relations tend to bolster capitalism. We argue, in short, that a partnership of patriarchy and capitalism has evolved....

I. Marxism and the Woman Question

The woman question has never been the "feminist question." The feminist question is directed at the causes of sexual inequality between women and men, of male dominance over women. Most marxist analyses of women's position take as their question the relationship of women to the economic system, rather than that of women to men, apparently assuming the latter will be explained in their discussion of the former. Marxist analysis of the woman question has taken three main forms. All see women's oppression in our connection (or lack of it) to production. Defining women as part of the working class, these analyses consistently subsume women's relation to men under workers' relation to capital. First, early marxists, including Marx, Engels, Kautsky, and Lenin, saw capitalism drawing all women into the wage labor force, and saw this process destroying the sexual division of labor. Second, contemporary marxists have incorporated women into an analysis of everyday life in capitalism. In this view, all aspects of our lives are seen to reproduce the capitalist system and we are all workers in the system. And third, marxist feminists have focussed on housework and its relation to capital, some arguing that housework produces surplus value and that houseworkers work directly for capitalists....

Engels, in *Origins of the Family, Private Property and the State*, recognized the inferior position of women and attributed it to the institution of private property.[2] In bourgeois families, Engels argued, women had to serve their masters, be monogamous, and produce heirs who would inherit the family's property and continue to increase it. Among proletarians, Engels argued, women were not oppressed, because there was no private property to be passed on. Engels argued further that as the extension of wage labor destroyed the small-holding peasantry, and women and children were incorporated into the wage labor force along with men, the authority of the male head of household was undermined, and patriarchal relations were destroyed.[3]

For Engels, then, women's participation in the labor force was the key to their emancipation. Capitalism would abolish sex differences and treat all workers equally. Women would become economically independent of men and would participate on an equal footing with men in bringing about the proletarian revolution. After the revolution, when all people would be workers and private property abolished, women would be emancipated from capital as well as from men. Marxists were aware of the hardships women's labor force participation meant for women and families, which resulted in women having two jobs: housework and wage work. Nevertheless, their emphasis was less on the continued subordination of women in the home than on the progressive character of capitalism's "erosion" of patriarchal relations. Under socialism housework too would be collectivized and women relieved of their double burden.

The political implications of this first marxist approach are clear. Women's lib- eration requires first, that women become wage workers like men, and second, that they join with men in the revolutionary struggle against capitalism. Capital and private property, the early marxists argued, are the cause of women's particular oppression just as capital is the cause of the exploitation of workers in general.

Though aware of the deplorable situation of women in their time the early marxist failed to focus on the *differences* between men's and women's experiences under capitalism. They did not focus on the feminist questions—how and why women are oppressed as women. They did not, therefore, recognize the vested interest men had in women's continued subordination. As we argue in part III below, men benefited from not having to do housework, from having their wives and daughters serve them, and from having the better places in the labor market. Patriarchal relations far from being atavistic leftover, being rapidly outmoded by capitalism, as the early marxists suggested, have survived and thrived alongside it. And since capital and private property do not cause the oppression of women as *women* their end alone will not result in the end of women's oppression. . . .

Marxist feminists who have looked at housework have also subsumed the fem- inist struggle into the struggle against capital. Mariarosa Dalla Costa's theoretical analysis of housework is essentially an argument about the relation of housework to capital and the place of housework in capitalist society and not about the rela- tions of men and women as exemplified in housework.[4] Nevertheless, Dalla Costa's political position, that women should demand wages for housework, has vastly increased consciousness of the importance of housework among women in the women's movement. The demand was and still is debated in women's groups all over the United States.[5] By making the claim that women at home not only provide essential services for capital by reproducing the labor force, but also create surplus value through that work,[6] Dalla Costa also vastly increased the left's consciousness of the importance of housework, and provoked a long debate on the relation of housework to capital.[7]

Dalla Costa uses the feminist understanding of housework as real work to claim legitimacy for it under capitalism by arguing that it should be waged work. Women should demand wages for housework rather than allow themselves to be forced into the traditional labor force, where, doing a "double day," women would still provide housework services to capital for free as well as wage labor. Dalla Costa suggests that women who receive wages for housework would be able to organize their housework collectively, providing community child care, meal preparation, and the like. Demanding wages and having wages would raise their consciousness of the importance of their work; they would see its *social* significance, as well as its private necessity, a necessary first step toward more comprehensive social change.

Dalla Costa argues that what is socially important about housework is its necessity to capital. In this lies the strategic importance of women. By demanding wages for housework and by refusing to participate in the labor market, women can lead the struggle against capital. Women's community organizations can be subversive to capital and lay the basis not only for resistance to the encroachment of capital but also for the formation of a new society.

Dalla Costa recognizes that men will resist the liberation of women (that will occur as women organize in their communities) and that women will have to struggle against them, but this struggle is an auxiliary one that must be waged to bring about the ultimate goal of socialism. For Dalla Costa, women's struggle are revolutionary not because they are feminist, but because they are anti-capitalist. Dalla Costa finds a place in the revolution for women's struggle by making women producers of surplus value, and as a consequence part of the working class. This legitimates women's political activity.[8]

The women's movement has never doubted the importance of women's struggle because for feminists the *object* is the liberation of women, which can only be brought about by women's struggles. Dalla Costa's contribution to increasing our understanding of the social nature of housework has been an incalculable advance. But like the other marxist approaches reviewed here her approach focuses on capital—not on relations between men and women. The fact that men and women have differences of interest, goals, and strategies is obscured by her analysis of how the capitalist system keeps us all down, and the important and perhaps strategic role of women's work in this system. The rhetoric of feminism is present in Dalla Costa's writing (the oppression of women, struggle with men) but the focus of feminism is not. If it were, Dalla Costa might argue for example, that the importance of housework as a social relation lies in its crucial role in perpetuating male supremacy. That women do housework, performing labor for men, is crucial to the maintenance of patriarchy.

Engels...and Dalla Costa...fail to analyze the labor process within the family sufficiently. Who benefits from women's labor? Surely capitalists, but also surely men, who as husbands and fathers receive personalized services at home. The content and extent of the services may vary by class or ethnic or racial group, but the fact of their receipt does not. Men have a higher standard of living than women in terms of luxury consumption, leisure time, and personalized service.[9] A materialist approach ought not ignore this crucial point.[10] It follows that men have a material interest in women's continued oppression....

...The focus of marxist analysis has been class relations; the object of marxist analysis has been understanding the laws of motion of capitalist society. While we believe marxist methodology can be used to formulate feminist strategy, these marxist feminist approaches discussed above clearly do not do so; their marxism clearly dominates their feminism.

As we have already suggested, this is due in part to the analytical power of marxism itself. Marxism is a theory of the development of class society, of the accumulation process in capitalist societies, of the reproduction of class dominance, and of the development of contradictions and class struggle. Capitalist societies are driven by the demands of the accumulation process, most succinctly summarized by the fact that production is oriented to exchange, not use. In a capitalist system production is important only insofar as it contributes to the making of profits, and the use value of products is only an incidental consideration. Profits derive from the capitalists' ability to exploit labor power, to pay laborers less than the value of what they produce. The accumulation of profits systematically transforms social structure as it transforms the relations of production. The reserve army of labor, the poverty of great numbers of people and the near-poverty of still more, these human reproaches to capital are by-products of the accumulation process itself. From the capitalist's point of view, the reproduction of the working class may "safely be left to itself."[11] At the same time, capital creates an ideology, which grows up along side it, of individualism, competitiveness, domination, and in our time, consumption of a particular kind. Whatever one's theory of the genesis of ideology, one must recognize these as the dominant values of capitalist societies.

Marxism enables us to understand many aspects of capitalist societies: the structure of production, the generation of a particular occupational structure, and the nature of the dominant ideology. Marx's theory of the development of capitalism is a theory of the development of "empty places." Marx predicted, for example, the growth of the proletariat and the demise of the petit bourgeoisie. More precisely and in more detail, Braverman among others has explained the creation of the "places" clerical worker and service worker in advanced capitalist societies.[12] Just as capital creates these places indifferent to the individuals who fill them, the categories of marxist analysis, class, reserve army of labor, wage-laborer, do not explain why particular people fill particular places. They give no clues about why *women* are subordinate to *men* inside and outside the family and why it is not the other way around. *Marxist categories, like capital itself, are sex-blind.* The categories of marxism cannot tell us who will fill the empty places. Marxist analysis of the woman question has suffered from this basic problem....

II. Radical Feminism and Patriarchy

The great thrust of radical feminist writing has been directed to the documentation of the slogan "the personal is political." Women's discontent, radical feminists argued, is not the neurotic lament of the maladjusted, but a response to a social structure in which women are systematically dominated, exploited, and oppressed. Women's inferior position in the labor market, the male-centered emotional structure of middle-class marriage, the use of women in advertising, the so-called understanding of women's psyche as neurotic—popularized by academic and clinical psychology—aspect after aspect of women's lives in advanced capitalist society was researched and analyzed. The radical feminist literature is enormous and defies easy summary. At the same time, its focus on psychology is consistent. The New York Radical Feminists' organizing document was "The Politics of the Ego." "The personal is political" means for radical feminists, that the original and basic class division is between the sexes, and that the motive force of history is the striving of men for power and domination over women, the dialectic of sex.[13]

Accordingly, Firestone rewrote Freud to understand the development of boys and girls into men and women in terms of power.[14] Her characterizations of what are "male" and "female" character traits are typical of radical feminist writing. The male seeks power and domination; he is egocentric and individualistic, competitive and pragmatic; the "technological mode," according to Firestone, is male. The female is nurturant, artistic, and philosophical; the "aesthetic mode" is female.

No doubt, the idea that the aesthetic mode is female would have come as quite a shock to the ancient Greeks. Here lies the error of radical feminist analysis: the dialectic of sex as radical feminist present it project male and female characteristics as they appear in the present back into all of history. The radical feminist analysis has greatest strength in its insights into the present. Its greatest weakness is a focus on the psychological which blinds it to history.

The reason for this lies not only in radical feminist method, but also in the nature of patriarchy itself, for patriarchy is a strikingly resilient form of social organization. Radical feminists use patriarchy to refer to a social system characterized by male domination over women. Kate Millett's definition is classic:

> Our society...is a patriarchy. The fact is evident at once if one recalls that the military, industry, technology, universities, science, political offices, finances—in short, every avenue of power within the society, including the coercive force of the police, is entirely in male hands.[15]

This radical feminist definition of patriarchy applies to most societies we know of and cannot distinguish among them. The use of history by radical feminists is typically limited to providing examples of the existence of patriarchy in all times and places.[16] For both marxist and mainstream social scientists before the women's movement, patriarchy referred to a system of relations between men, which form the political and economic outlines of feudal and some pre-feudal societies, in which hierarchy followed ascribed characteristics. Capitalist societies are understood as meritocratic, bureaucratic, and impersonal by bourgeois social scientists; marxists see capitalist societies as systems of class domination.[17] For both kinds of social scientists neither the historical patriarchal societies nor today's western capitalist societies are understood as systems of relations between men that enable them to dominate women.

Towards a Definition of Patriarchy

We can usefully define patriarchy as a set of social relations between men, which have a material base, and which, though hierarchical, establish or create interdependence and solidarity among men that enable them to dominate women. Though patriarchy is hierarchical and men of different classes, races, or ethnic groups have different places in the patriarchy, they also are united in their shared relationship of dominance over their women; they are dependent on each other to maintain that domination. Hierarchies "work" at least in part because they create vested interests in the status quo. Those at the higher levels can "buy off" those at the lower levels by offering them power over those still lower. In the hierarchy of patriarchy, all men, whatever their rank in the patriarchy, are bought off by being able to control at least some women. There is some evidence to suggest that when patriarchy was first institutionalized in state societies, the ascending rulers literally made men the heads of their families (enforcing their control over their wives and children) in exchange for the men's ceding some of their tribal resources to the new rulers.[18] Men are dependent on one another (despite their hierarchical ordering) to maintain their control over women.

The material base upon which patriarchy rests lies most fundamentally in men's control over women's labor power. Men maintain this control by excluding women from access to some essential productive resources (in capitalist societies, for example, jobs that pay living wages) and by restricting women's sexuality.[19] Monogamous heterosexual marriage is one relatively recent and efficient form that seems to allow men to control both these areas. Controlling women's access to resources and their sexuality, in turn, allows men to control women's labor power, both for the purpose of serving men in many personal and sexual ways and for the purpose of rearing children. The services women render men, and which exonerate men from having to perform many unpleasant tasks (like cleaning toilets) occur outside as well as inside the family setting. Examples outside the family include the harassment of women workers and students by male bosses and professors as well as the common use of secretaries to run personal errands, make coffee, and pro- vide "sexy" surroundings. Rearing children, whether or not the children's labor power is of immediate benefit to their fathers, is nevertheless a crucial task in per- petuating patriarchy as a system. Just as class society must be reproduced by schools, work places, consumption norms, et cetera, so must patriarchal social relations. In our society, children are generally reared by women at home, women socially defined and recognized as inferior to men, while men appear in the domes- tic picture only rarely. Children raised in this way generally learn their places in the gender hierarchy well. Central to this process, however are the areas outside the home where patriarchal behaviors are taught and the inferior position of women enforced and reinforced: churches, schools, sports, clubs, unions, armies, factories, offices, health centers, the media, et cetera.

The material base of patriarchy, then, does not rest solely on childrearing in the family, but on all the social structures that enable men to control women's labor. The aspects of social structures that perpetuate patriarchy are theoretically identi- fiable, hence separable from their other aspects. Gayle Rubin has increased our ability to identify the patriarchal element of these social structures enormously by identifying "sex/gender system":

> a "sex/gender system" is the set of arrangements by which a society transforms, biolog- ical sexuality into products, of human activity, and in which these transformed sexual needs are satisfied.[20]

We are born female and male, biological sexes, but we are created woman and man, socially recognized genders. *How* we are so created is that second aspect of the *mode* of production of which Engels spoke, "the production of human beings themselves, the propagation of the species."

How people propagate the species is socially determined. If, biologically, people are sexually polymorphous, and society were organized in such a way that all forms of sexual expression were equally permissible, reproduction would result only from some sexual encounters, the heterosexual ones. The strict division of labor by sex, social invention common to all known societies, creates two very separate genders and a need for men and women to get together for economic reasons. It thus helps to direct their sexual needs toward heterosexual fulfillment, and helps to ensure biological reproduction. In more imaginative societies, biological reproduction might be ensured by other techniques, but the division of labor by sex appears to be the universal solution to date. Although it is theoretically possible that a sexual division of labor not imply inequality between the sexes, in most known societies, the socially acceptable division of labor by sex is one which accords lower status to women's work. The sexual division of labor is also the underpinning of sexual subcultures in which men and women experience life differently; it is the material base of male power which is exercised (in our society) not just in not doing housework and securing superior employment, but psychologically as well.

How people meet their sexual needs, how they reproduce, how they inculcate social norms, in new generations, how they learn gender, how it feels to be a man or woman—all occur in the realm Rubin labels the sex/gender system. Rubin emphasizes the influence of kinship (which tells you with whom you can satisfy sexual needs) and the development of gender specific personalities via childrearing and the "oedipal machine." In addition, however, we can use the concept of the sex/gender system to examine all other social institutions for the roles they play in defining and reinforcing gender hierarchies. Rubin notes that theoretically a sex/gender system could be female dominant, male dominant, or egalitarian, but declines to label various known sex/gender systems or to periodize history accordingly. We choose to label our present sex/gender system patriarchy, because it appropriately captures the notion of hierarchy and male dominance which we see as central to the present system.

Economic production (what marxists are used to referring to as *the* mode of production) and the production of people in the sex/gender sphere both determine "social organization under which the people of a particular historical epoch and particular country live," according to Engels. The whole of society, then, can be understood by looking at both these types of production and reproduction, people and things.[21] There is no such thing as "pure capitalism," nor does "pure patriarchy" exist, for they must of necessity coexist. What exists is patriarchal capitalism, or patriarchal feudalism, or egalitarian hunting/gathering societies, or matriarchal horticultural societies, or patriarchal horticultural societies, and so on.

There appears to be no necessary connection between *changes* in the one aspect of production and changes in the other. A society could undergo transition from capitalism to socialism, for example, and remain patriarchal.[22] Common sense, history, and our experience tell us, however, that these two aspects of production are so closely intertwined, that change in one ordinarily creates movement, tension, or contradiction in the other.

Racial hierarchies can also be understood in this context. Further elaboration may be possible along the lines of defining color/race systems, arenas of social life that take biological color and turn it into a social category, race. Racial hierarchies, like gender hierarchies, are aspects of our social organization, of how people are produced and reproduced. They are not fundamentally ideological; they constitute that second aspect of our mode of production, the production and reproduction of people. It might be most accurate then to refer to our societies not as, for example, simply capitalist, but as patriarchal capitalist white supremacist.

Capitalist development creates the places for a hierarchy of workers, but traditional marxist categories cannot tell us who will fill which places. Gender and racial hierarchies determine who fills the empty places. *Patriarchy is not simply hierarchical organization*, but hierarchy in which *particular* people fill *particular* places. It is in studying patriarchy that we learn why it is women who are dominated and how. While we believe that most known societies have been patriarchal, we do not view patriarchy as a universal, unchanging phenomenon. Rather patriarchy, the set of interrelations among men that allow men to dominate women, has changed in form and intensity over time. It is crucial that the hierarchy among men, and their differential access to patriarchal benefits, be examined. Surely, class, race, nationality, and even marital status and sexual orientation, as well as the obvious age, come into play here. And women of different class, race, national, marital status, or sexual orientation groups are subjected to different degrees of patriarchal power. Women may themselves exercise class, race, or national power, or even patriarchal power (through their family connections) over men lower in the patriarchal hierarchy than their own male kin.

To recapitulate, we define patriarchy as a set of social relations which has a material base and in which there are hierarchical relations between men and solidarity among them which enable them in turn to dominate women. The material base of patriarchy is men's control over women's labor power. That control is maintained by excluding women from access to necessary economically productive resources and by restricting women's sexuality. Men exercise their control in receiving personal service work from women, in not having to do housework or rear children, in having access to women's bodies for sex, and in feeling powerful and being powerful. The crucial elements of patriarchy as we *currently* experience them are: heterosexual marriage (and consequent homophobia), female childrearing and housework, women's economic dependence on men (enforced by arrangements in the labor market), the state, and numerous institutions based on social relations among men—clubs, sports, unions, professions, universities, churches, corporations, and armies. All of these elements need to be examined if we are to understand patriarchal capitalism.

Both hierarchy and interdependence among men and the subordination of women are *integral* to the functioning of our society; that is, these relationships are *systemic*. We leave aside the question of the creation of these relations and ask, can we recognize patriarchal relations in capitalist societies? Within capitalist societies we must discover those same bonds between men which both bourgeois and marxist social scientists claim no longer exist or are, at the most, unimportant leftovers. Can we understand how these relations among men are perpetuated in capitalist societies? Can we identify ways in which patriarchy has shaped the course of capitalist development?

III. The Partnership of a Patriarchy and Capital

How are we to recognize patriarchal social relations in capitalist societies? It appears as if each woman is oppressed by her own man alone; her oppression seems a private affair. Relationships among men and among families seem equally fragmented. It is hard to recognize relationships among men, and between men and women, as *systematically* patriarchal. We argue, however, that patriarchy as a system of relations between men and women exists in capitalism, and that in capitalist societies a healthy and strong partnership exists between patriarchy and capital. Yet if one begins with the concept of patriarchy and an understanding of the capitalist mode of production, one recognizes immediately that the partnership of patriarchy and capital was not inevitable; men and capitalists often have conflicting interests, particularly over the use of women's labor power. Here is one way in which this conflict might manifest itself: the vast majority of men might want their women at home to personally service them. A smaller number of men, who are capitalists, might want most women (not their own) to work in the wage labor market. In examining the tensions of this conflict over women's labor power historically, we will be able to identify the material base of patriarchal relations in capitalist societies, as well as the basis for the partnership between capital and patriarchy....

The argument that capital destroys the family also overlooks the social forces which make family life appealing. Despite critiques of nuclear families as psychologically destructive, in a competitive society the family still meets real needs for many people. This is true not only of long-term monogamy, but even more so for raising children. Single parents bear both financial and psychic burdens. For working-class women, in particular, these burdens make the "independence" of labor force participation illusory. Single parent families have recently been seen by policy analysts as transitional family formations which become two-parent families upon remarriage.[23]

It could be that the effects of women's increasing labor force participation are found in a declining sexual division of labor within the family, rather than in more

frequent divorce, but evidence for this is also lacking. Statistics on who does housework, even in families with wage-earning wives, show little change in recent years;
women still do most of it.[24] The double day is a reality for wage-working women.
This is hardly surprising since the sexual division of labor outside the family, in the
labor market, keeps women financially dependent on men—even when they earn a
wage themselves. The future of patriarchy does not, however, rest solely on the
future of familial relations. For patriarchy, like capital, can be surprisingly flexible
and adaptable.

Whether or not the patriarchal division of labor, inside the family and elsewhere, is "ultimately" intolerable to capital, it is shaping capitalism now. As we
illustrate below, patriarchy both legitimates capitalist control and delegitimates
certain forms of struggle against capital.

Ideology in the Twentieth Century

Patriarchy, by establishing and legitimating hierarchy among men (by allowing
men of all groups to control at least some women), reinforces capitalist control,
and capitalist values shape the definition of patriarchal good.

The psychological phenomena Shulamith Firestone identifies are particular
examples of what happens in relationships of dependence and domination. They
follow from the realities of men's social power—which women are denied—but
they are shaped by the fact that they happen in the context of a capitalist society.[25]
If we examine the characteristics of men as radical feminists describe them—competitive, rationalistic, dominating—they are much like our description of the dominant values of capitalist society.

This "coincidence" may be explained in two ways. In the first instance, men, as
wage laborers, are absorbed in capitalist social relations at work, driven into the
competition these relations prescribe, and absorb the corresponding values.[26] The
radical feminist description of men was not altogether out of line for capitalist
societies. Secondly, even when men and women do not actually behave in the way
sexual norms prescribe, men *claim for themselves* those characteristics which are
valued in the dominant ideology. So, for example, the authors of *Crestwood Heights*
found that while the men, who were professionals, spent their days manipulating
subordinates (often using techniques that appeal to fundamentally irrational
motives to elicit the preferred behavior), men and women characterized men as
"rational and pragmatic." And while the women devoted great energies to studying
scientific methods of child-rearing and child development, men and women in
Crestwood Heights characterized women as "irrational and emotional."[27]

This helps to account not only for "male" and "female" characteristics in capitalist societies, but for the particular form sexist ideology takes in capitalist societies. Just as women's work serves the dual purpose of perpetuating male domination and capitalist production, so sexist ideology serves the dual purpose of
glorifying male characteristics/capitalist values, and denigrating female character-
istics/social need. If women were degraded or powerless in other societies, the rea-

sons (rationalizations) men had for this were different. Only in a capitalist society does it make sense to look down on women as emotional or irrational. As epithets, they would not have made sense in the renaissance. Only in a capitalist society does it make sense to look down on women as "dependent." "Dependent" as an epithet would not make sense in feudal societies. Since the division of labor ensures that women as wives and mothers in the family are largely concerned with the production of use values, the denigration of these activities obscures capital's inability to meet socially determined need at the same time that it degrades women in the eyes of men, providing a rationale for male dominance. An example of this may be seen in the peculiar ambivalence of television commercials. On one hand, they address themselves to the real obstacles to providing for socially determined needs: detergents that destroy clothes and irritate skin, shoddily made goods of all sorts. On the other hand, concern with these problems must be denigrated; this is accomplished by mocking women, the workers who must deal with these problems.

A parallel argument demonstrating the partnership of patriarchy and capitalism may be made about the sexual division of labor in the work force. The sexual division of labor places women in low-paying jobs, and in tasks thought to be appropriate to women's role. Women are teachers, welfare workers, and the great majority of workers in the health fields. The nurturant roles that women play in these jobs are of low status because capitalism emphasizes personal independence and the ability of private enterprise to meet social needs, emphases contradicted by the need for collectively provided social services. As long as the social importance of nurturant tasks can be denigrated because women perform them, the confrontation of capital's priority on exchange value by a demand for use values can be avoided. In this way, it is not feminism, but sexism that divides and debilitates the working class.

IV. Towards a More Progressive Union

Many problems remain for us to explore. Patriarchy as we have used it here remains more a descriptive term than an analytic one. If we think marxism alone inadequate, and radical feminism itself insufficient, then we need to develop new categories. What makes our task a difficult one is that the same features, such as the division of labor, often reinforce both patriarchy and capitalism, and in a thoroughly patriarchal capitalist society, it is hard to isolate the mechanisms of patriarchy. Nevertheless, this is what we must do. We have pointed to some starting places: looking at who benefits from women's labor power, uncovering the material base of patriarchy, investigating the mechanisms of hierarchy and solidarity among men. The questions we must ask are endless....

The struggle against capital and patriarchy cannot be successful if the study and practice of the issues of feminism is abandoned. A struggle aimed only at capitalist relations of oppression will fail, since their underlying supports in patriarchal relations of oppression will be overlooked. And the analysis of patriarchy is essential to a definition of the kind of socialism useful to women. While men and women share a need to overthrow capitalism they retain interests particular to their gender group. It is not clear—from our sketch, from history, or from male socialists—that the socialism being struggled for is the same for both men and women. For a humane socialism would require not only consensus on what the new society should look like and what a healthy person should look like, but more concretely, it would require that men relinquish their privilege.

As women we must not allow ourselves to be talked out of the urgency and importance of our tasks, as we have so many times in the past. We must fight the attempted coercion, both subtle and not so subtle, to abandon feminist objectives.

This suggests two strategic considerations. First, a struggle to establish socialism must be a struggle in which groups with different interests form an alliance. Women should not trust men to liberate them after the revolution, in part, because there is no reason to think they would know how; in part, because there is no necessity for them to do so. In fact their immediate self-interest lies in our continued oppression. Instead we must have our own organizations and our own power base. Second, we think the sexual division of labor within capitalism has given women a practice in which we have learned to understand what human interdependence and needs are. While men have long struggled *against* capital, women know what to struggle *for*.[28]

As a general rule, men's position in patriarchy and capitalism prevents them from recognizing both human needs for nurturance, sharing, and growth, and the potential for meeting those needs in a nonhierarchical, nonpatriarchal society. But even if we raise their consciousness, men might assess the potential gains against the potential losses and choose the status quo. Men have more to lose than their chains.

As feminist socialists, we must organize a practice which addresses both the struggle against patriarchy and the struggle against capitalism. We must insist that the society we want to create is a society in which recognition of interdependence is liberation rather than shame, nurturance is a universal, not an oppressive practice, and in which women do not continue to support the false as well as the concrete freedoms of men.

Notes

Earlier drafts of this essay appeared in 1975 and 1977 coauthored with Amy B. Bridges. Unfortunately, because of the press of current commitments, Amy was unable to continue with this project, joint from its inception and throughout most of its long and controversial history.

1. Often paraphrased as "the husband and wife are one and that one is the husband," English law held that "by marriage, the husband and wife are one person in law: that is, the very being or legal existence of the women is suspended during the marriage, or at least is incorporated and consolidated into that of the Husband." I. Blackstone, *Commentaries*, 1965, pp. 442–445, cited in Kenneth M. Davidson, Ruth B. Ginsburg, and Herma H. Kay, *Sex Based Discrimination* (St. Paul, Minn.: West Publishing Co., 1974), p. 117.

2. Frederick Engels, *The Origin of the Family, Private Property and the State*, edited, with an introduction by Eleanor Burke Leacock (New York: International Publishers, 1972).

3. Frederick Engels, *The Condition of the Working Class in England* (Stanford, Calif.: Stanford University Press, 1958). See esp. pp. 162–66 and 296.

4. Mariarosa Dalla Costa, "Women and the Subversion of the Community," in *The Power of Women and the Subversion of the Community* by Mariarosa Dalla Costa and Selma James (Bristol, England: Falling Wall Press, 1973; second edition) pamphlet, 78 pages.

5. It is interesting to note that in the original article Dalla Costa suggests that wages for housework would only further institutionalize woman's housewife role (pp. 32, 34) but in a note (n. 16, pp. 52–52 [in original]) she explains the demand's popularity and its use as a consciousness raising tool. Since then she has actively supported the demand. See Dalla Costa, "A General Strike," in *All Work and No Pay: Women, Housework, and the Wages Due*, ed. Wendy Edmond and Suzie Fleming (Bristol, England: Falling Wall Press, 1975).

6. The text of the article reads: "We have to make clear that, within the wage, domestic work produces not merely use values, but is essential to the production of surplus value" (p. 31). Note 12 reads: "What we mean precisely is that housework as work is *productive* in the Marxian sense, that is, producing surplus value" (p. 52, original emphasis). To our knowledge this claim has never been made more rigorously by the wages for housework group. Nevertheless marxists have responded to the claim copiously.

7. The literature of the debate includes Lise Vogel, "The Earthly Family," *Radical America*, Vol. 7, no. 4–5 July–October 1973), pp. 9–50; Ira Gerstein, "Domestic Work and Capitalism," *Radical America*, Vol. 7, no. 4–5 July–October 1973, pp. 101–128; John Harrison, "Political Economy of Housework," *Bulletin of the Conference of Socialist Economists*, Vol. 3, no. 1 (1973); Wally Seccombe, "The Housewife and her Labour under Capitalism," *New Left Review*, no. 83 (January–February 1974), pp. 3–24; Margaret Coulson, Branka Magas, and Hilary Wainwright, "'The Housewife and her Labour under Capitalism,' A Critique," *New Left Review*, no. 89 (January–February 1975), pp. 59–71; Jean Gardiner, "Women's Domestic Labour," *New Left Review*, no. 89 (January–February 1975), pp. 47–58; Ian Cough and John Harrison, "Unproductive Labour and Housework Again," *Bulletin of the Conference of Socialist Economists*, Vol. 4, no. 1 (1975); Jean Gardiner, Susan Himmelweit, and Maureen Mackintosh, "Women's Domestic Labour," *Bulletin of the Conference of Socialist Economists*, Vol. 4, no. 2 (1975); Wally Seccombe, "Domestic Labour: Reply to Critics," *New Left Review*, no. 94 (November–December 1975), pp. 85–96; Terry Fee, "Domestic Labor: An Analysis of Housework and its Relation to the Production Process," *Review of Radical Political Economics*, Vol. 8, no. 1 (Spring 1976), pp. 1–8; Susan Himmelweit and Simon Mohun, "Domestic Labour and Capital," *Cambridge Journal of Economics*, Vol. 1, no. 1 (March 1977), pp. 15–31.

8. In the U.S., the most often heard political criticism of the wages for housework group has been its opportunism.

9. Laura Oren documents this for the working class in "Welfare of Women in Laboring Families: England, 1860–1950," *Feminist Studies*, Vol. 1, no. 3–4 (Winter–Spring 1973), pp. 107–25.

10. The late Stephen Hymer pointed out to us a basic weakness in Engels' analysis in *Origins*, a weakness that occurs because Engels fails to analyze the labor process within the family. Engels argues that men enforced monogamy because they wanted to leave their property to their own children. Hymer argued that far from being a "gift," among the petit bourgeoisie, possible inheritance is used as a club to get children to work for their fathers. One must look at the labor process and who benefits from the labor of which others.

11. This is a paraphrase. Karl Marx wrote: "The maintenance and reproduction of the working class is, and must ever be, a necessary condition to the reproduction of capital. But the capitalist may safely leave its fulfillment to the labourer's instincts of self-preservation and propagation." [*Capital* (New York: International Publishers, 1967), Vol. 1, p. 572.]

12. Harry Braverman, *Labor and Monopoly Capital* (New York: Monthly Review Press, 1975).

13. "Politics of Ego: A Manifesto for New York Radical Feminists," can be found in *Rebirth of Feminism*, ed. Judith Hole and Ellen Levine (New York: Quadrangle Books, 1971), pp. 440–443.

"Radical feminists" are those feminists who argue that the lost fundamental dynamic of history is men's striving to dominate women. "Radical" in this context does *not* mean anti-capitalist, socialist, counter-cultural, etc., but has the specific meaning of this particular set of feminist beliefs or group of feminists. Additional writings of radical feminists, of whom the New York Radical Feminists are probably the most influential, can be found in *Radical Feminism*, ed. Ann Koedt (New York: Quadrangle Press, 1972).

14. Focusing on power was an important step forward in the feminist critique of Freud. Firestone argues, for example, that if little girls "envied " penises it was because they recognized that little boys grew up to be members of a powerful class and little girls grew up to be dominated by them. Powerlessness, not neurosis, was the heart of women's situation. More recently, feminists have criticized Firestone for rejecting the usefulness of the concept of the unconscious. In seeking to explain the strength and continuation of male dominance, recent feminist writing has emphasized the fundamental nature of gender-based personality differences, their origins in the unconscious, and the consequent difficulty of their eradication. See Dorothy Dinnerstein, *The Mermaid and the Minotaur* (New York: Harper Colophon Books, 1977), Nancy Chodorow, *The Reproduction of Mothering* (Berkeley: University of California Press, 1978), and Jane Flax, "The Conflict Between Nurturance and Autonomy in Mother-Daughter Relationships and Within Feminism," *Feminist Studies*, Vol. 4, no. 2 (June 1978), pp. 141–189.

15. Kate Millett, *Sexual Politics* (New York: Avon Books, 1971), p. 25.

16. One example of this type of radical feminist history is Susan Brownmiller's *Against Our Will, Men, Women, and Rape* (New York: Simon & Shuster, 1975).

17. For the bourgeois social science view of patriarchy, see, for example, Weber's distinction between traditional and legal authority, *Max Weber: The Theories of Social and Economic Organization*, ed. Talcott Parson (New York: The Free Press, 1964), pp. 328–357. These views are also discussed in Elizabeth Fee, "The Sexual Politics of Victorian Social Anthropology," *Feminist Studies*, Vol. 1, nos. 3–4 (Winter–Spring 1973), pp. 23–29; and in Robert A. Nisbet, *The Sociological Tradition* (New York: Basic Books, 1966), especially Chapter 3, "Community."

18. See Viana Muller, "The Formation of the State and the Oppression of Women: Some Theoretical Considerations and a Case Study in England and Wales," *Review of Radical Political Economics*, Vol. 9, no. 3 (Fall 1977), pp. 7–21.

19. The particular ways in which men control women's access to important economic resources and restrict their sexuality vary enormously, both from society to society, from subgroup to subgroup, and across time. The examples we use to illustrate patriarchy in this section, however, are drawn primarily from the experience of whites in western capitalist countries. The diversity is shown in *Toward an Anthropology of Women*, ed. Rayna Rapp Reiter (New York: Monthly Review Press, 1975); *Woman, Culture and Society*, ed. Michelle Rosaldo and Louise Lamphere (Stanford, California: Stanford University Press, 1974); and *Females, Males, Families: A Biosocial Approach*, by Liba Leibowitz (North Scituate, Massachusetts: Duxbury Press, 1978). The control of women's sexuality is tightly linked to the place of children. An understanding of the demand (by men and capitalists) for children is crucial to understanding changes in women's subordination.

Where children are needed for their present or future labor power, women's sexuality will tend to be directed toward reproduction and childrearing. When children are seen as superfluous, women's sexuality for other than reproductive purposes is encouraged, but men will attempt to direct it towards satisfying male needs. The Cosmo girl is a good example of a woman "liberated" from childrearing only to find herself turning all her energies toward attracting and satisfying men. Capitalists can also use female sexuality to their own ends, as the success of Cosmo in advertising consumer products shows.

20. Gayle Rubin, "The Traffic in Women," in *Anthropology of Women*, ed. Reiter, p. 159.

21. Himmelweit and Mohun point out that both aspects of production (people and things) are logically necessary to describe a mode of production because by definition a mode of production must be capable of reproducing itself. Either aspect alone is not self-sufficient. To put it simply the production of things requires people, and the production of people requires things. Marx,

though recognizing capitalism's need for people, did not concern himself with how they were produced or what the connections between the two aspects of production were. See Himmelweit and Mohun, "Domestic Labour and Capital" (note 7 above).

22. For an excellent discussion of one such transition to socialism, see Batya Weinbaum, "Women in Transition to Socialism: Perspectives on the Chinese Case," *Review of Radical Political Economics*, Vol. 8, no. 1 (Spring 1976), pp. 34–58.

23. Heather L. Ross and Isabel B. Sawhill, *Time of Transition The Growth of Families Headed by Women* (Washington, D.C.: The Urban Institute, 1975).

24. See Kathryn E. Walker and Margaret E. Woods, *Time Use: A Measure of Household Production of Family Goods and Services* (Washington D.C.: American Home Economics Association, 1976; and Heidi I. Hartmann, "The Family as the Locus of Gender, Class, and Political Struggle: The Example of Housework," *Signs: Journal of Women in Culture and Society*, Vol. 6, no. 3 (Spring 1981).

25. Richard Sennett's and Jonathan Cobb's *The Hidden Injuries of Class* (New York: Random House, 1973) examines similar kinds of psychological phenomena within hierarchical relationships between men at work.

26. This should provide some clues to class differences in sexism, which we cannot explore here.

27, See John R. Seeley et al., *Crestwood Heights* (Toronto: University of Toronto Press, 1956), pp. 382–94. While men's place may be characterized as "in production" this does not mean that women's place is simply "not in production"—her tasks, too, are shaped by capital. Her non-wage work is the resolution, on a day-to-day basis, of production for exchange with socially determined need, the provision of use values in a capitalist society (this is the context of consumption). See Weinbaum and Bridges, "The Other Side of the Paycheck," for a more complete discussion of this argument. The fact that women provide "merely" use values in a society dominated by exchange values can be used to denigrate women.

28. Lise Vogel, "The Earthly Family" (see note 7).

22.
CAPITALISM, IMPERIALISM, AND PATRIARCHY: THE DILEMMA OF THIRD-WORLD WOMEN WORKERS IN MULTINATIONAL FACTORIES
Linda Y. C. Lim

Introduction

Female employment in multinational factories in developing countries has recently become the subject of much academic and political interest. Studies have been done analyzing the growth and spread of such employment and its impact on women in particular countries, and industries.[1] The findings generally point to a central theoretical and political question that as yet remains unanswered: Is the employment of women factory workers by multinational corporations in developing countries primarily an experience of *liberation*, as development economists and governments maintain or one of *exploitation*, as feminists assert, for the women concerned? Does it present a problem or a solution to the task of integrating women into the development of their countries?

This paper examines the theoretical issues raised by the available case study material, in an attempt to resolve this question. It emphasizes economic analysis, and suggests that the interactions between capitalist, imperialist, and patriarchal relations of production are responsible both for the phenomenon of female employment by multinationals and for the dilemma it poses for women workers and for progressive feminist analysis and political action.

Capitalism and the Relocation of Manufacturing Industry to Developing Countries

Capitalism is the economic system prevailing in the parent countries of multinational corporations and in the world market which they dominate. It is a mode of production based on private ownership of capital (the "means of production"), employment of wage labor, and production for exchange on a free market to earn private profit that is accumulated and reinvested for growth and further profit. Whereas the Western nations and Japan are developed economies in a mature or advanced stage of capitalism, many developing countries are embarking on economic programs aimed at further developing the capitalist relations of production first introduced in them by colonialism and world market forces. This colonial heritage, combined with the dominance of the world capitalist system, forces even those new nations that have embraced socialist ideologies of development to tolerate some degree of private enterprise and foreign investment producing for exchange on the world market.

The relocation of manufacturing industry from developed to developing countries by multinational corporations engaged in "offshore sourcing" is part of a new international division of labor and pattern of trade in manufactures.[2] From plants in the Third World, multinational subsidiaries export manufactures to their home countries. From their home countries they import capital and technology in exchange. This is the direct result of two developments in the world capitalist economy which began in the 1960s. First, growth in international trade intensified inter-capitalist competition among the developed nations. In particular, the ascendancy of Japan as a major industrial power and its rapid and highly successful penetration of Western consumer markets led American and European manufacturers to invest in developing countries as a means of reducing costs in competition with the Japanese (Reynis 1976). In the 1970s, the slowing down of growth in Western and world markets further intensified these competitive pressures.

Second, the accelerating development of capitalist relations of production in a number of developing countries resulted in some of their indigenous entrepreneurs manufacturing for export to Western markets, beginning in the 1960s. This placed them in direct competition with Western manufacturers, who were forced to relocate to these same countries in order to be cost competitive in their own home markets. This trend continued through the 1970s on an ever larger and wider scale, particularly in Asian countries like Hong Kong, Taiwan, South Korea, and Singapore, whose larger local firms have themselves become multinationals operating offshore manufacturing plants in other developing countries.

Thus, Western manufacturers in several industries located plants in developing countries in response to the competitive challenge from other mature capitalist countries, especially Japan, and from newly industrializing developing capitalist countries, mainly in Asia. The crucial factor in the competition was and is the cost of production, which differs between mature and developing capitalist economies according to their stage of development. In the 1960s and early 1970s, the mature Western economies experienced tight domestic labor markets—low unemployment rates, high wages, and chronic labor shortages in many industries. Labor-intensive manufacturing industries—those which employ large numbers of workers in generally unskilled or low-skilled jobs—were the most affected, and these countries began to lose their international comparative advantage in industries such as garments, shoes, plastic toys, and electronics assembly. The developing countries, on the other hand, had relatively abundant supplies of labor, reflected in the rural-urban migration of surplus labor off the farms; high urban unemployment rates; and low wages. Cheap labor, combined in many cases with government-subsidized capital costs, including tax holidays and low-interest loans from government banks (Lim 1978), gave these countries a comparative advantage in world trade in labor-intensive products. . . .

Imperialsm, Patriarchy, and Exploitation

Studies of Third World women workers in multinational export factories tend to focus, explicitly or implicitly, on the exploitation of these women by their multinational employers. Absolutely low wages and poor working conditions are often cited as evidence of such exploitation. In an earlier work, I pointed out that the concept of exploitation is an established one in all schools of economics, from the bourgeois to the Marxist, though the particular definition of it may vary. All, however, agree that

> exploitation . . . is a *relative* concept, bearing no direct relation to the *absolute* level of wages paid: so long as the worker does not receive the full value of her product, however defined, she is exploited. A higher wage may also entail a higher rate of exploitation if greater intensity of work, longer working hours, better equipment and organization of production, etc. mean that labor productivity, and hence the value of the worker's output, is proportionally greater in the higher-wage than lower-wage situation. (Lim 1978b)

Thus, focusing on absolute conditions faced by workers does not lend itself to useful theoretical or political analysis.

In the economic sense defined above, all workers employed in capitalist enterprises are exploited to produce profits for their employers. But the degree of exploitation differs among different groups of workers. In addition to being paid less than the value of the output they contribute, Third World women workers in multinational export factories are paid less than women workers in the multinationals' home countries and less than men workers in these countries and in their own countries as well, despite the fact that in relocated, labor-intensive industries their productivity is frequently acknowledged to be higher than that of either of these other groups. Thus, Third World women workers are the most heavily exploited group of workers, both relative to their output contribution and relative to other groups. Although all are subject to capitalist exploitation, Third World women workers are additionally subject to what might be called imperialist exploitation and patriarchal exploitation.

Imperialist exploitation—the differential in wages paid to workers in developed and developing countries for the same work and output—arises from the ability of multinationals to take advantage of different labor market conditions in different parts of the world—a perfectly rational practice in the context of world capitalism. In the developing countries,

> high unemployment, poor bargaining power vis-à-vis the foreign investor, lack of worker organization and representation and even the repression of workers' movements, all combine to depress wage levels, while the lack of industrial experience, igno-

rance and naivete of workers with respect to the labor practices in modern factory employment enable multinational employers to extract higher output from them in certain unskilled operations. (Lim 1978b: 11–12)

Patriarchal exploitation—the differential in wages paid to male and female workers for similar work and output—derives from women's inferior position in the labor market....

Although multinational employers of women factory workers in developing countries do practice all of the above forms of exploitation, they do so only in response to labor market forces, specifically the international and sexual segmentation of labor markets. Differences in the degree of development of capitalist relations of production and natural restrictions on the international mobility of labor are responsible for differential wage rates between countries whereas patriarchal institutions and attitudes limiting the employment opportunities open to women are responsible for the differential wage rates between the sexes. Multinationals may, consciously, attempt to preserve these differentials from which they benefit; but in general they merely take advantage of them since they exist....

Capitalist Development and Liberation from Patriarchy

In developing as in mature industrial economies, the state of development of capitalist relations of production defines the employment opportunities available to wage labor. Patriarchal social structures and cultures divide these opportunities by sex, typically limiting female wage labor to a narrow range of inferior jobs. In this situation the entry of labor-intensive export manufacturing industries and of multinational corporations in particular into sex segregated local labor markets has two somewhat contradictory effects. On the one hand, multinational *and* local employers can take advantage of women's inferior position in the labor market to employ them at lower wages and poorer working conditions than exist for men in the same country and for women in developed countries. This is what I have termed patriarchal and imperialist exploitation. Both local firms and multinationals benefit from the gap between workers' wages in the developing country and final product prices in markets of developed countries.

On the other hand, the expansion of employment opportunities for women in these industries does improve conditions for women in the labor market. In however limited a way, the availability of jobs in multinational and local export factories does allow women to leave the confines of the home, delay marriage and childbearing, increase their incomes and consumption levels, improve mobility, expand individual choice, and exercise personal independence. Working for a local or foreign factory is for many women at least marginally preferable to the alternatives of staying at home, early marriage and childbearing, farm or construction labor, domestic service, prostitution, or unemployment, to which they were previously restricted. Factory work, despite the social, economic, and physical costs it often entails, provides women in developing countries with one of the very few channels they have of at least partial liberation from the confines and dictates of traditional patriarchal social relations.

Given their lack of access to better jobs, women workers usually prefer multinationals as employers over local firms since they offer higher wages and better working conditions and often have more "progressive" labor practices and social relations within the firm (Lim 1978b). Indeed, the more multinationals there are in any one country and the longer they have been established, the stronger the workers' bargaining position becomes. Exclusive employment of female production workers in labor-intensive export industries creates occasional labor shortages, resulting over time in rising wages, greater job security, and improved working conditions for women in indigenous as well as multinational enterprises.[3] Greater competition for female laborers will tend to reduce the degree of exploitation found in women's work.

Whether or not market forces alone will expand women's employment alternatives beyond the traditional "female ghettoes" of low wage, low skill, dead end jobs depends on the state and rate of development of capitalist relations of production in the economy as a whole. In an economy that is rapidly growing, diversifying, and upgrading itself in all sectors, high demand for labor might eventually propel women into skilled industrial and nonindustrial jobs from which they have previously been excluded by custom, education, or employment discrimination. This will improve the wages and working conditions of women who remain in factory employment as production workers, given the reduction in the numbers of women available for work.

So far, such a situation is an exceptional one among the many developing countries that host multinational corporations in female-intensive industries. Even where rapid growth occurs, employers may escape the tightening labor market by importing migrant labor, by automation, and by shifting labor-intensive processes to other countries, as they have done in the home countries of the multinationals and are now doing in rapidly developing countries like Singapore. In this latter country, growth in other industries and sectors has prevented these actions from having a depressing effect on wages, and the government's high wage policy has furthermore forced firms to shed or shift their labor-intensive activities. Also, when women ascend the job hierarchy, it is usually to take jobs vacated by male workers who have since advanced even higher in the hierarchy of skills and incomes. That is to say, although rapid growth may enable women to improve their position in the labor market in absolute terms, relative to men they remain in an inferior position.

Employment of women in modern capitalist industrial enterprises in developing countries does contribute to an expansion of employment opportunities and thus to some economic and social liberation for women in patriarchal societies that customarily restrict them to a domestic role in the family. But such wage employment on its own or combined with generally rapid capitalist development throughout an economy cannot significantly undermine the patriarchal social relations responsible for women's inferior labor market position on which their very employment is predicated. In other words, capitalism cannot wipe out patriarchy, though exploitation in capitalist enterprises can provide some women with an at least temporary escape from traditional patriarchal social relations.

Exploitation and Liberation: A Dilemma for Political Action

The above analysis has identified the relocation of manufacturing industry from mature to developing capitalist countries as the outcome of the expansion of capitalism on a world scale, reflecting differences in the development of capitalist relations of production between nations, particularly of the wage labor market. The relocation is carried out by multinational corporations, whose export manufacturing activities in developing host countries can and do enhance the development of capitalist relations of production. The almost exclusive employment of female labor in many relocated industries is based on women's inferior position in the wage labor market, resulting from patriarchal social relations. Although women workers in these multinational factories are exploited relative to their output, to male workers in the same country, and to female workers in developed countries, their position is often better than in indigenous factories and in traditional forms of employment for women. The limited economic and social liberation that women workers derive from their employment in multinational factories is predicated on their subjection to capitalist, imperialist, and patriarchal exploitation in the labor market and the labor process. This presents a dilemma for feminist policy towards such employment: because exploitation and liberation go hand in hand, it cannot be readily condemned or extolled.

Many of the studies of female employment in multinational export factories in developing countries focus their criticism on the multinational corporation as chief perpetrator of all the forms of exploitation that these women workers are subject to in their employment. But although the multinational does take advantage of national and sexual wage differentials and sometimes reinforces them, it is not responsible for creating them and cannot by its own actions eliminate them. National wage differentials are the result of differences in the development of capitalist relations of production between nations, whereas sex wage differentials originate in indigenous patriarchy.

Removing the multinational—the logical if extreme conclusion of an anti-imperialist political stand—will, in the absence of a credible alternative form of development, drastically reduce employment opportunities for women in developing countries. This will weaken their labor market position and subject them to even greater exploitation by indigenous capitalists and continued subordination to traditional patriarchy. This is clearly undesirable for the economic and social liberation of women. A less radical solution—attempting to reduce imperialist exploitation by imposing reforms on the multinational or local employer—is unlikely to succeed even if host governments were willing, which is doubtful. Export manufacturers operate in highly competitive international markets with generally elastic supply and, in important industries like garments and shoes, inelastic demand. Host governments and workers can neither demand nor enforce better wages and working conditions in profit-oriented multinationals that are mobile between countries. Local firms are often less competitive than multinationals in the world market and, with their lower profits, are unlikely to be able to absorb the costs of such reforms.

Another possibility for reducing imperialist exploitation is through international action to restrict multinationals from exploiting market wage differentials between nations—for example, by standardizing certain terms and conditions of work in particular industries or occupations. This is clearly unrealistic, given the different stages of development of capitalism and different labor market conditions in different countries. Furthermore, workers in developed and developing countries tend to have opposing interests vis-à-vis the relocation of manufacturing industry. National interests inhibit the development of international labor solidarity. For example, protectionist groups of employers and labor unions in the multinationals' home countries have furthered their own self interest by citing exploitation of women workers overseas as a reason why goods made by these workers should be prevented from reaching their destined markets by means of tariffs, quotas, and other restrictive trade practices. This has the effect of pitting workers in mature and developing capitalist countries against each other.

Because patriarchal social relations are at the bottom of women's subjection to imperialist exploitation, it is logical to turn to an attack on traditional patriarchy as a means of improving the position of women. The successful elimination of patriarchal institutions and attitudes, discrimination, differential socialization by sex, and the sexual division of labor within the family would equalize male and female employment opportunities and incomes, ending the sex segregation of the capitalist labor market. This is also difficult to envisage, given the deep cultural and psychological as well as economic and social foundations of patriarchy, which is found in advanced as well as developing capitalist countries and in socialist countries as well. Furthermore, in developing countries, national identity is very much bound up with a traditional, often feudal patriarchal culture. An attack on traditional patriarchy may be construed as an attack on national identity and thus arouse the forces of a reactionary nationalism against the liberation of women. Indeed one of the dangers of multinational exploitation of Third World women workers is that it arouses local antiimperialist sentiment that becomes identified—as in fundamentalist Islamic ideology in Iran—with traditionalism and opposition to wage employment by women.

Even if traditional patriarchy is successfully undermined and equality in the capitalist labor market achieved for women workers, they will remain subject, together with male workers, to capitalist exploitation in a capitalist economy. Capitalist employers themselves are unlikely to be indifferent to the elimination of sex differences in the labor market. Although employers of predominantly female workers may be expected to oppose sex equalization because it would reduce the supply and thus raise the wages of women workers in low skill, labor-intensive, and dead-end jobs, employers in male-intensive industries where labor is scarce may welcome the entry of female labor as a means of increasing the labor supply and reducing wages. The balance between these opposing interests and the attitude of male workers themselves, depends on the state and rate of development of capitalist relations of production. A nation that is rapidly growing and upgrading into high-skill, high-wage industries and occupations and experiences rising demand relative to supply of labor is likely to have greater sex equalization in the labor market than one which is only slowly growing or stagnating, with high employment and a dependence on low-wage, labor-intensive industries. In other words, rapid capitalist development is more conducive to sex equalization in the labor market but by itself cannot be expected to bring about such equalization.

Elimination of worker exploitation altogether can only occur if capitalism itself is eliminated. This presents enormous difficulties for the small developing country in a world dominated by capitalism and imperialism. Domestically, a necessary precondition is the unity of the working class, which is hampered by sex, race, regional, and other differences within the labor force. So long as patriarchal relations of production persist, male and female workers remain divided by occupational segregation and by the tendency for male workers to assume the position of a labor aristocracy. If development is slow and mainly in low-skill industries, male unemployment and low wages will limit this aristocracy to a small segment of the male work force, rather than creating a male elite that opposes female workers. Thus, the elimination of patriarchy would facilitate the elimination of capitalism itself. However, the elimination of capitalist exploitation does not necessarily facilitate the elimination of patriarchal exploitation as the experience of present-day postcapitalist societies indicates. In all the "socialist" countries, including the USSR, China, and eastern Europe, women occupy an inferior position in the labor force and in social and political life relative to men (though the difference may be less than in mature capitalist countries). Indeed, in some cases, the struggle against a capitalism identified with imperialist exploitation can lend itself to a reinforcement of traditional patriarchy and opposition to women's participation in the labor force. Finally, to the extent that socialist societies are likely to be less materially successful than capitalist societies—at least in the short and medium run—the elimination of all forms of exploitation may be achieved at the cost of lower absolute wages and standards of living and working for both men and women.

Conclusion

This paper has sought to spell out the complexities involved in an analysis of female employment in multinational export factories in developing capitalist countries and in any attempt to formulate policy or political action on behalf of these women workers. The interplay of capitalist, imperialist, and patriarchal relations of production and the simultaneously exploitative and liberating consequences of this form of wage employment for women, point out the inadequacy of simplistic anti-capitalist, anti-imperialist, or anti-patriarchal analyses and strategies to relieve exploitation....

Ultimately it is the existing structure of the economy and society that has to be changed if the exploitation of women in the labor force is to be eliminated. Capitalist market forces and employment based on imperialist exploitation cannot liberate women from patriarchal exploitation that is the very condition for their entry into wage labor in multinational factories producing for the world market. In the long run, capitalism and imperialism only perpetuate and may even reinforce patriarchal relations of production, which in turn reinforce capitalist and imperialist relations of production. Although the liberation of women workers as women and as workers can only come about through some combined struggle against capitalist, imperialist, and patriarchal exploitation, the specific strategies to be undertaken depend on the particular historical, social, economic, and political circumstances of each national unit in the context of an international capitalism.

Notes

1. For a few examples of relevant case studies, see Snow 1977, Lim 1978b, Paglaban 1978, Grossman 1979, Fernández Kelly 1980, United Nations Industrial Development Organization (UNIDO) 1980.
2. See, for example, Leontiades 1971, Adam 1975, Moxon 1974, UNIDO 1979, Fröbel, Heinrichs, and Kreye 1980.
3. Indigenous firms have to compete with multinationals in the labor market; multinationals are the leaders in setting wages and working conditions. In Singapore, the improvement of wages and working conditions in the female labor market are illustrated by the following facts: Starting wages have more than doubled in five years (ahead of inflation); fringe benefits have improved (for example, the extension of paid holiday time to two weeks in the year); part-time shifts have been instituted to suit housewives; the desired age of workers has risen from sixteen to twenty-three years to up to fifty years; there has been a dramatic reduction in rotating shifts and microscope work in electronics factories; and a five-day week is typical. Singapore workers have become a "labor aristocracy" in the Southeast Asian region.

23.
MOBILIZATION WITHOUT EMANCIPATION? WOMEN'S INTERESTS, THE STATE, AND REVOLUTION IN NICARAGUA
Maxine Molyneux

The fall of the Nicaraguan dictator, Anastasio Somoza, in July 1979 could not have been achieved without the mass urban insurrections which brought the capital, Managua, and other key cities under the increasing control of the revolutionary forces. This was the culmination of a process of growing popular opposition characterized by the incorporation of a wide cross-section of the population into political activity.

Large numbers of women from all social classes joined the youth and the unwaged poor men who entered the realm of politics in the 1970s, many for the first time. Women's participation in the Nicaraguan revolution was probably greater than in any other recent revolution with the exception of Vietnam. Women made up approximately 30 percent of the FSLN's combat forces, and at its peak in 1979, the women's organization of the FSLN, the Association of Women Confronting the National Problem, or AMPRONAC, had over 8,000 members.[1] Many more women who were not involved in organized politics provided vital logistical and backup support to the revolutionary forces, and still others gave their support silently by refusing to denounce their revolutionary neighbors, or by hiding a fleeing combatant.[2]

The extent of women's participation in the struggle against Somoza has been regarded by many authors as an obvious enough response to the widespread repression and brutality of the regime on the one hand, and the appeal of the FSLN's vision and strategy on the other.[3] The specific ways in which women became political subjects has not been subjected to rigorous analysis, partly because it seems obvious and partly because women's extensive revolutionary activism is seen as the effect of the universalizing character of the opposition to Somoza. In the words of one author, this process dissolved the specificity of political subjects in the generalized struggle against the dictatorship.[4] Put simply, all were united against the dictatorship, and differences of class, age, and gender were transcended. It was this unity that accounted for the strength and ultimate success of the opposition movement.

However, much depends upon what is implied by subjects "losing their specificity" and goals being universalized. For the universalization of the *goals* of revolutionary subjects does not necessarily entail a loss of their specific *identities*, and it is certainly doubtful whether this can be said to have happened in the case of women. As far as women were concerned it would be difficult to argue that a loss of their gender identities occurred, except perhaps to a limited extent among the front line *guerrilleros* where a degree of masculinization and a blurring of gender distinctions took place.[5] Rather, representations of women acquired new connotations, ones that *politicized* the social roles with which women are conventionally associated, but did not dissolve them.

The participation of women in political activity was certainly part of the wider process of popular mobilization, but it was entered into from a distinctive social position to men, one crucially shaped by the sexual division of labor. Moreover, for different classes and groups of women, the meaning of political participation also differed, whether in the case of students, young middle-class women, or the women in the *barrios*.[6] For many poor women, entry into political life began with the earthquake of 1972, when in the aftermath, the neighborhood committees were organized to care for the victims, feed the dispossessed, and tend the wounded. The anger that followed Somoza's misappropriation of the relief funds intensified as the brutal methods used to contain opposition escalated. Many of these women experienced their transition from relief workers to participants in the struggle as a natural extension, albeit in combative form, of their protective role in the family as providers and crucially as mothers. This transition to "combative motherhood" was assisted by the propaganda efforts of the radical clergy, the Sandinistas, and by AMPRONAC, which linked these traditional identities to more general strategic objectives, and celebrated women's role in the creation of a more just and human-itarian social order. The revolutionary appropriation of the symbol of motherhood has since been institutionalized in the FSLN's canonization of the "Mothers of Heroes and Martyrs," a support group which remains an active part of the Sandinistas' political base.[7]

However, if the revolution did not demand the dissolution of women's *identities*, it did require the *subordination* of their *specific interests* to the broader goals of overthrowing Somoza and establishing a new social order. This raises an important question which lies at the heart of debates about the relationship between socialist revolution and women's emancipation. For if women surrender their specific interests in the universal struggle for a different society, at what point are these interests rehabilitated, legitimated, and responded to by the revolutionary forces or by the new socialist state? Some feminist writing implies that they are never ade-quately reestablished and that this is why socialism[8] has failed to fulfill its promise to emancipate women. Such critics point out that not only does gender inequality still persist in these states, but also in some ways women could be considered to be worse off than they were before the revolution. Far from having been "emanci-pated" as the official rhetoric sometimes claims, women's work load has been increased and there has been no substantial redefinition of the relations between the sexes. To the traditional roles of housewife and mother have been added those of full-time wage worker and political activist, while the provision of childcare agencies remains inadequate. As one Soviet woman recently summed it up, "If this is emancipation, then I'm against it."[9]

The negative image of socialist states in this regard is reinforced by their failure to establish anything near sexual parity in the organs of political power, and by the absence of real popular democracy. The conventional explanations of these short-comings—at least in the poorer states—in terms of resource scarcity, international pressure, underdevelopment, or the "weight of tradition," are greeted with increasing skepticism. A feminist writer recently expressed an emerging consensus when she wrote: "if a country can eliminate the tsetse fly, it can get an equal number of men and women on its politburo."[10].

This article focuses on the Nicaraguan revolution and its progress since the seizure of state power by the Sandinistas in July 1979, in order to consider the proposition that women's interests are not served by socialist revolutions....

Women's Interests

The concept of women's interests is central to feminist evaluations of socialist societies and indeed social policies in general. Most feminist critiques of socialist regimes rest on an implicit or explicit assumption that there is a given entity, women's interests, that is ignored or overridden by policymakers. However, the question of these interests is far more complex than is frequently assumed. As the problems of deploying any theory of interest in the analysis of postrevolutionary situations are considerable, the following discussion must be considered an attempt to open up debate rather than to attain closure....

Although it is true that at a certain level of abstraction women can be said to have some interests in common, there is no consensus over what these interests are or how they are to be formulated. This is in part because there is no theoretically adequate and universally applicable causal explanation of women's subordination from which a general account of women's interests can be derived. Women's oppression is recognized as being multicausal in origin and mediated through a variety of different structures, mechanisms, and levels which may vary considerably across space and time. There is therefore continuing debate over the appropriate site of feminist struggle and over whether it is more important to focus attempts at change on objective or subjective elements, "men" or "structures"; laws, institutions, or interpersonal power relations—or all of them simultaneously. Because a general conception of interests (one which has political validity) must be derived from a theory of how the subordination of a determinate social category is secured, it is difficult to see how it would overcome the two most salient and intractable features of women's oppression—its multicausal nature, and the extreme variability of its forms of existence across class and nation. These factors vitiate attempts to speak *without qualification* of a unitary category "women" with a set of already constituted interests common to it. A theory of interests that has an application to the debate about women's capacity to struggle for and benefit from social change must begin by recognizing difference rather than by assuming homogeneity.

It is clear from the extensive feminist literature on women's oppression that a number of different conceptions prevail of what women's interests are, and that these in turn rest implicitly or explicitly, upon different theories of the causes of gender inequality. For the purpose of clarifying the issues discussed here, three conceptions of women's interests, which are frequently conflated, will be delineated. These are women's interests, strategic gender interests, and practical gender interests.

Women's interests. Although present in much political and theoretical discourse, the concept of women's interests is, for the reasons given earlier, a highly contentious one. Because women are positioned within their societies through a variety of different means—among them, class, ethnicity, and gender—the interests they have as a group are similarly shaped in complex and sometimes conflicting ways. It is therefore difficult, if not impossible, to generalize about the interests of women. Instead, we need to specify how the various categories of women might be affected differently, and act differently on account of the particularities of their social positioning and their chosen identities. However, this is not to deny that women may have certain general interests in common. These can be called gender interests to differentiate them from the false homogeneity imposed by the notion of women's interests.

Strategic gender interests. Gender interests are those that women (or men, for that matter) may develop by virtue of their social positioning through gender attributes. Gender interests can be either strategic or practical, each being derived in a different way and each involving differing implications for women's subjectivity. Strategic interests are derived in the first instance deductively, that is, from the analysis of women's subordination and from the formulation of an alternative, more satisfactory set of arrangements to those which exist. These ethical and theoretical criteria assist in the formulation of strategic objectives to overcome women's subordination, such as the abolition of the sexual division of labor, the alleviation of the burden of domestic labor and childcare, the removal of institutionalized forms of discrimination, the attainment of political equality, the establishment of freedom of choice over childbearing, and the adoption of adequate measures against male violence and control over women. These constitute what might be called strategic gender interests, and they are the ones most frequently considered by feminists to be women's "real" interests. The demands that are formulated on this basis are usually termed "feminist" as is the level of consciousness required to struggle effectively for them.[11]

Practical gender interests. Practical gender interests are given inductively and arise from the concrete conditions of women's positioning within the gender division of labor. In contrast to strategic gender interests, these are formulated by the women who are themselves within these positions rather than through external interventions. Practical interests are usually a response to an immediate perceived need, and they do not generally entail a strategic goal such as women's emancipation or gender equality. Analyses of female collective action frequently deploy this conception of interests to explain the dynamic and goals of women's participation in social action. For example, it has been argued that by virtue of their place within the sexual division of labor as those primarily responsible for their household's daily welfare, women have a special interest in domestic provision and public welfare.[12] When governments fail to provide these basic needs, women withdraw their support; when the livelihood of their families—especially their children—is threatened, it is women who form the phalanxes of bread rioters, demonstrators, and petitioners. It is clear, however, from this example that gender and class are closely intertwined; it is, for obvious reasons, usually poor women who are so readily mobilized by economic necessity. Practical interests, therefore, cannot be assumed to be innocent of class effects. Moreover, these practical interests do not in themselves challenge the prevailing forms of gender subordination, even though they arise directly out of them. An understanding of this is vital in understanding the capacity or failure of states or organizations to win the loyalty and support of women.

The pertinence of these ways of conceptualizing interests for an understanding of women's consciousness is a complex matter, but three initial points can be made. First, the relationship between what we have called strategic gender interests and women's recognition of them and desire to realize them cannot be assumed. Even the lowest common denominator of interests which might seem uncontentious and of universal applicability (such as complete equality with men, control over reproduction, and greater personal autonomy and independence from men) are not readily accepted by all women. This is not just because of "false consciousness" as is frequently supposed—although this can be a factor—but because such changes realized in a piecemeal fashion could threaten the short-term practical interests of some women, or entail a cost in the loss of forms of protection which are not then compensated for in some way. Thus the formulation of strategic interests can only be effective as a form of intervention when full account is taken of these practical interests. Indeed, it is the politicization of these practical interests and their transformation into strategic interests that women can identify with and support which constitutes a central aspect of feminist political practice.

Second, the way in which interests are formulated—whether by women or political organizations—will vary considerably across space and time and may be shaped in different ways by prevailing political and discursive influences. This is important to bear in mind when considering the problem of internationalism and the limits and possibilities of cross-cultural solidarity. Finally, because women's interests are significantly broader than gender interests, and are shaped to a considerable degree by class factors, women's unity and cohesion on gender issues cannot be assumed. Although they can form the basis of unity around a common program, such unity has to be constructed—it is never given. Moreover, even when unity exists it is always conditional, and the historical record suggests that it tends to collapse under the pressure of acute class conflict. It is also threatened by differences of race, ethnicity, and nationality. It is therefore difficult to argue, as some feminists have done, that gender issues are primary for women, at all times.[13]

This general problem of the conditionality of women's unity and the fact that gender issues are not necessarily primary is nowhere more clearly illustrated than by the example of revolutionary upheaval. In such situations, gender issues are frequently displaced by class conflict, principally because although women may suffer discrimination on the basis of gender and may be aware that they do, they nonetheless suffer differentially according to their social class. These differences crucially affect attitudes toward revolutionary change, especially if this is in the direction of socialism. This does not mean that, because gender interests are an insufficient basis for unity among women in the context of class polarization, they disappear. Rather, they become more specifically attached to and defined by social class.

An awareness of the complex issues involved serves to guard against any simple treatment of the question of whether a state is or is not acting in the interests of women, that is, whether all or any of these interests are represented within the state. Before any analysis can be attempted it is necessary to specify in what sense the term "interest" is being deployed. A state may gain the support of women by satisfying either their immediate practical demands or certain class interests, or both. It may do this without advancing their strategic objective interests at all. However, the claims of such a state to be supporting women's *emancipation* could not be substantiated merely on the evidence that it maintained women's support on the basis of representing some of their more practical or class interests. . . .

The Nicaraguan Revolution

. . . The Nicaraguan revolution also gave hope to those who supported women's liberation, for here too, the Sandinistas were full of promise. The revolution occurred in the period after the upsurge of the "new feminism" of the late sixties, at a time when Latin American women were mobilizing around feminist demands in countries like Mexico, Peru, and Brazil. The Sandinistas' awareness of the limitations of orthodox Marxism encouraged some to believe that a space would be allowed for the development of new social movements such as feminism. Some members of the leadership seemed aware of the importance of women's liberation and of the need for it in Nicaragua. The early issues of *Somos AMNLAE*, one of two newspapers of the women's organization, contained articles about feminist issues and addressed some of the ongoing debates within Western feminism. Unlike many of its counterparts elsewhere, the FSLN, the revolutionary party, did not denounce feminism as a "counterrevolutionary diversion," and some women officials had even gone on record expressing enthusiasm for its ideals.

In practical terms too, there was promise. The FSLN had shown itself capable of mobilizing many thousands of women in support of its struggle. It had done this partly through AMPRONAC, the women's organization that combined a commitment to overthrow the Somoza regime with that of struggling for women's equality. At its peak in 1979, two years after it was founded, AMPRONAC had attracted over 8,000 members. Feminist observers noted the high level of participation of women in the ranks of the combat forces, epitomized in Dora Maria Tellez's role as Commander Two in the seizure of the Presidential Palace by the guerillas in

1978, and they debated how the Sandinista commitment to women's equality would be realized if they triumphed. . . .

A detailed analysis of the impact of Sandinista social policies is beyond the scope of this paper.[14] Instead, I will briefly summarize some of the relevant conclusions by considering the effects of the reforms in terms of the three categories of interest referred to earlier.

If we disaggregate women's interests and consider how different categories of women fared since 1979, it is clear that the majority of women in Nicaragua were positively affected by the government's redistribution policies. This is so even though fundamental structures of gender inequality were not dismantled. In keeping with the socialist character of the government, policies were targeted in favor of the poorest sections of the population and focused on basic needs provision in the areas of health, housing, education, and food subsidies. In the short span of only five years, the Sandinistas reduced the illiteracy rate from over 50 percent to 13 percent; doubled the number of educational establishments, increased school enrollment, eradicated a number of mortal diseases, provided the population with basic healthcare services, and achieved more in their housing program than Somoza had in his entire period of rule.[15] In addition, the land reform canceled peasants' debts and gave thousands of rural workers their own parcels of land or secured them stable jobs on the state farms and cooperatives.[16] . . .

In terms of *practical* gender interests, these redistributive policies have also had gender as well as class effects. By virtue of their place within the sexual division of labor, women are disproportionately responsible for childcare and family health, and they are particularly concerned with housing and food provision. The policy measures directed at alleviating the situation in these areas has, not surprisingly, elicited a positive response from the women affected by them as borne out by the available research into the popularity of the government. Many of the campaigns mounted by AMNLAE have been directed at resolving some of the practical problems women face, as is exemplified by its mother and child healthcare program, or by its campaign aimed at encouraging women to conserve domestic resources to make the family income stretch further and thus avoid pressure building up over wage demands or shortages.[17] A feature of this kind of campaign is its recognition of women's practical interests, but in accepting the division of labor and women's subordination within it, it may entail a denial of their strategic interests.

With respect to strategic interests, the acid test of whether women's emancipation is on the political agenda or not, the progress which was made is modest but significant. Legal reform, especially in the area of the family, has confronted the issue of relations between the sexes and of male privilege, by attempting to end a situation in which most men are able to evade responsibility for the welfare of their families, and become liable for a contribution paid in cash, in kind, or in the form of services. This also enabled the issue of domestic labor to be politicized in the discussions of the need to share this work equally among all members of the family. . . .

Yet these qualifications are important nonetheless, and have a significance which goes beyond the Sandinista revolution to the wider question of the relationship between socialism and feminism. Three of these issues can be listed here in summary form. The first is that what we have called strategic gender interests—although recognized in the official theory and program of women's emancipation— remains rather narrowly defined, based as they are on the privileging of economic criteria. Feminist theories of sexual oppression, or the critique of the family or of male power have had little impact on official thinking, and indeed are sometimes suppressed as being too radical and too threatening to popular solidarity.[18] There is a need for greater discussion and debate around these questions both among the people and within the organs of political power, so that the issue of women's emancipation remains alive and open, and does not become entombed within official doctrine.

The second issue concerns the relationship established by planners between the goal of women's emancipation and other goals, such as economic development, which have priority. It is not the *linkage* itself that constitutes the problem—principles like social equality and women's emancipation can only be realized within determinate conditions of existence. So linking the program for women's emancipation to these wider goals need not necessarily be a cause for concern because these wider goals may constitute the preconditions for realizing the principles. The question is rather, the nature of the link. Are gender interests *articulated into* a wider strategy of economic development (for example) or are they irretrievably *subordinated to it*? In the first case we would expect gender interests to be recognized as being specific and irreducible, and requiring something more for their realization than is generally provided for in the pursuit of the wider goals. Thus, when it is not possible to pursue a full program for women's emancipation this can be explained and debated. The goal can be left on the agenda, and every effort made to pursue it within the existing constraints. In the latter case, the specificity of gender interests is likely to be denied or its overall importance minimized. The issues are trivialized or buried; the program for women's emancipation remains one conceived in terms of how functional it is for achieving the wider goals of the state. . . .

And this raises the third general issue, which is that of political guarantees. For if gender interests are to be realized only within the context of wider considerations, it is essential that the political institutions charged with representing these interests have the means to prevent their being submerged altogether, and action on them being indefinitely postponed. Women's organizations, the official representatives of women's interests, should not conform to Lenin's conception of mass organizations as mere "transmission belts of the party." Rather, they must enjoy a certain independence and exercise power and influence over party policy, albeit within certain necessary constraints. In other words, the issue of gender interests and their means of representation cannot be resolved in the absence of a discussion of Socialist democracy and the forms of state appropriate to the transition to socialism; it is a question therefore not just of *what* interests are represented in the state, but ultimately and critically of *how* they are represented.

Notes

1. The Association of Women Confronting the National Problem was founded in 1977 to counter Somoza's excesses and promote gender equality. Its general secretary was Lea Guido, now minister of health. See AMNLAE, *Documentos de al Asamblea de AMNLAE*, Managua, 1981, for an account of AMPRONAC's history and its list of aims; and Margaret Randall, *Sandino's Daughters* (London: Zed Press, 1982).

2. For firsthand accounts of these activities see Randall; Jane Deighton, Rossana Horsley, Sarah Stewart, and Cathy Cain, *Sweet Ramparts* (London: War on Want/Nicaragua Solidarity Campaign, 1983); and Susan Ramirez-Horton, "The Role of Women in the Nicaraguan Revolution," in *Nicaragua in Revolution*, ed. Thomas Walker (New York: Praeger, 1982).

3. The women writers have been more interested in this question. See especially Elisabeth Maier, *Nicaragua, La Mujer en la Revolution* (Mexico: Ediciones de Cultura Popular, 1980).

4. José Luis Corraggio, "Posibilidades y limites de la politica en los procesos de transicion: el caso de Nicaragua" (Paper presented at the Amsterdam Latin American Centre [CEDLA] Conference on Nicaragua, 1983). The paper will be published in a forthcoming collection edited by David Slater, CEDLA.

5. Margaret Randall, *Inside the Nicaraguan Revolution* (Vancouver: New Star Books, 1978); and *Sandino's Daughters.*

6. This is usually translated as "poor neighborhoods."

7. This organization is involved in various anti-imperialist and propeace campaigns and gives support to the bereaved and those anxious about daughters or sons in the battle zones.

8. The term "socialist" is used here for the sake of brevity. In relation to most of these states, some qualification is required along the lines suggested by Rudolf Bahro ("actually existing socialism"), for the reasons he advanced in his *The Alternative in Eastern Europe* (London: NLB, 1979). Others have not reached the level of economic socialization that qualifies them for inclusion in this category.

9. See, for example, the attitudes of women to this in Carola Hansson and Karin Liden's book of interviews, *Moscow Women* (New York: Pantheon, 1983)

10. Quoted in Catherine MacKinnon, "Feminism, Marxism, Method, and the State: An Agenda for Theory," *Signs* (Spring 1982). For critical discussions, from differing perspectives, of the record of socialist states, see Maria Markus, "Women and Work: Emancipation at a Dead End," in *The Humanisation of Socialism*, ed. A. Hegedus et al. (London: Alison & Busby, 1976); and Judith Stacey, *Patriarchy and Socialist Revolution in China* (Berkeley: University of California Press, 1983).

11. It is precisely around these issues, which also have an ethical significance, that the theoretical and political debate must focus. The list of strategic gender interest noted here is not exhaustive, but is merely exemplary.

12. See, for example, Temma Kaplan, "Female Consciousness and Collective Action: The Case of Barcelona, 1910–1918," *Signs* 7 (Spring 1982): 546–66; and Olwen Hufton, "Women in Revolution, 1789–1796," *Past and Present*, no. 53 (1971): 90–108.

13. This is the position of some radical feminist groups in Europe.

14. For a fuller account of Sandinista social policies see Thomas Walker, ed., *Nicaragua Five Years On* (New York: Praeger, 1985); and for their policies on women, see my article "Women," chap. 6 in the same volume.

15. See Walker.

16. For a discussion of the agrarian reform and its effects on women, see Carmen Diana Deere, "Cooperative Development and Women's Participation in Nicaragua's Agrarian Reform," *American Journal of Agrarian Economics* (December 1983).

17. MNLAE argued that the implications of women conserving resources under a socialist government were radically different from those under capitalism because in the first case the beneficiaries were the people, and in the second, private interests.

18. This argument was put forward to quash the new Family Law in the council of state. See reports in the national press during November 1982.

SEXUALITY

24.
THE MYTH OF THE VAGINAL ORGASM[1]
Anne Koedt[2]

Whenever female orgasm and frigidity are discussed, a false distinction is made between the vaginal and the clitoral orgasm. Frigidity has generally been defined by men as the failure of women to have vaginal orgasms. Actually the vagina is not a highly sensitive area and is not constructed to achieve orgasm. It is the clitoris which is the center of sexual sensitivity and which is the female equivalent of the penis.

I think this explains a great many things: First of all, the fact that the so-called frigidity rate among women is phenomenally high. Rather than tracing female frigidity to the false assumptions about female anatomy, our "experts" have declared frigidity a psychological problem of women. Those women who complained about it were recommended psychiatrists, so that they might discover their "problem"—diagnosed generally as a failure to adjust to their role as women.

The facts of female anatomy and sexual response tell a different story. Although there are many areas for sexual arousal, there is only one area for sexual climax; that area is the clitoris. All orgasms are extensions of sensation from this area. Since the clitoris is not necessarily stimulated sufficiently in the conventional sexual positions, we are left "frigid."

Aside from physical stimulation, which is the common cause of orgasm for most people, there is also stimulation through primarily mental processes. Some women, for example, may achieve orgasm through sexual fantasies, or through fetishes. However, while the stimulation may be psychological, the orgasm manifests itself physically. Thus, while the cause is psychological, the *effect* is still physical, and the orgasm necessarily takes place in the sexual organ equipped for sexual climax—the clitoris. The orgasm experience may also differ in degree of intensity—some more localized, and some more diffuse and sensitive. But they are all clitoral orgasms.

All this leads to some interesting questions about conventional sex and our role in it. Men have orgasms essentially by friction with the vagina, not the clitoral area, which is external and not able to cause friction the way penetration does. Women have thus been defined sexually in terms of what pleases men; our own biology has not been properly analyzed. Instead, we are fed the myth of the liberated woman and her vaginal orgasm—an orgasm which in fact does not exist.

What we must do is redefine our sexuality. We must discard the "normal" concepts of sex and create new guidelines which take into account mutual sexual enjoyment. While the idea of mutual enjoyment is liberally applauded in marriage manuals, it is not followed to its logical conclusion. We must begin to demand that if certain sexual positions now defined as "standard" are not mutually conducive to orgasm, they no longer be defined as standard. New techniques must be used or devised which transform this particular aspect of our current sexual exploitation.

Freud—Father of the Vaginal Orgasm

Freud contended that the clitoral orgasm was adolescent, and that upon puberty, when women began having intercourse with men, women should transfer the center of orgasm to the vagina. The vagina, it was assumed, was able to produce a parallel, but more mature, orgasm than the clitoris. Much work was done to elaborate on this theory, but little was done to challenge the basic assumptions.

To fully appreciate this incredible invention, perhaps Freud's general attitude about women should first be recalled. Mary Ellman, in *Thinking About Women*, summed it up this way:

> Everything in Freud's patronizing and fearful attitude toward women follows from their lack of a penis, but it is only in his essay *The Psychology of Women* that Freud makes explicit... the deprecation of women which are implicit in his work. He then prescribes for them the abandonment of the life of the mind, which will interfere with their sexual function. When the psychoanalyzed patient is male, the analyst sets himself the task of developing the man's capacities; but with women patients, the job is to resign them to the limits of their sexuality. As Mr. Rieff puts it: For Freud, "Analysis cannot encourage in women new energies for success and acievement, but only teach them the lesson of rational resignation."

It was Freud's feelings about women's secondary and inferior relationship to men that formed the basis for his theories on female sexuality.

Once having laid down the law about the nature of our sexuality, Freud not so strangely discovered a tremendous problem of frigidity in women. His recommended cure for a woman who was frigid was psychiatric care. She was suffering from failure to mentally adjust to her "natural" role as a woman. Frank S. Caprio, a contemporary follower of these ideas, states:

> ... whenever a woman is incapable of achieving an orgasm via coitus, provided the husband is an adequate partner, and prefers clitoral stimulation to any other form of sexual activity, she can be regarded as suffering from frigidity and requires psychiatric assistance. (*The Sexually Adequate Female*, p. 64)

The explanation given was that women were envious of men—"renunciation of womanhood." Thus it was diagnosed as an anti-male phenomenon.

It is important to emphasize that Freud did not base his theory upon a study of woman's autonomy, but rather upon his assumptions of woman as an inferior appendage to man, and her consequent social and psychological role. In their attempts to deal with the ensuing problem of mass frigidity, Freudians created elaborate mental gymnastics. Marie Bonaparte, in *Female Sexuality*, goes so far as to suggest surgery to help women back on their rightful path. Having discovered a strange connection between the non-frigid woman and the location of the clitoris near the vagina,

> it then occurred to me that where, in certain women, this gap was excessive, and cli-toridal fixation obdurate, a clitoridal-vaginal reconciliation might be effected by surgi-cal means, which would then benefit the normal erotic function. Professor Halban, of Vienna, as much a biologist as surgeon, became interested in the problem and worked out a simple operative technique. In this, the suspensory ligament of the clitoris was severed and the clitoris secured to the underlying structures, thus fixing it in a lower position, with eventual reduction of the labia minora. (p. 148)

But the severest damage was not in the area of surgery, where Freudians ran around absurdly trying to change female anatomy to fit their basic assumptions. The worst damage was done to the mental health of women, who either suffered silently with self-blame, or flocked to psychiatrists looking desperately for the hid-den and terrible repression that had kept from them their vaginal destiny.

Lack of Evidence

One may perhaps at first claim that these are unknown and unexplored areas, but upon closer examination this is certainly not true today, nor was it true even in the past. For example, men have known that women suffered from frigidity often dur-ing intercourse. So the problem was there. Also, there is much specific evidence. Men knew that the clitoris was and is the essential organ for masturbation, whether in children or adult women. So obviously women made it clear where *they* thought their sexuality was located. Men also seem suspiciously aware of the clitoral powers during "foreplay," when they want to arouse women and produce the necessary lubrication for penetration. Foreplay is a concept created for male purposes, but works to the disadvantage of many women, since as soon as the woman is aroused the man changes to vaginal stimulation, leaving her both aroused and unsatisfied.

It has also been known that women need no anesthesia inside the vagina during surgery, thus pointing to the fact that the vagina is in fact not a highly sensitive area.

Today, with extensive knowledge of anatomy, with Kelly, Kinsey, and Masters and Johnson, to mention just a few sources, there is no ignorance on the subject. There are, however, social reasons why this knowledge has not been popularized. We are living in a male society which has not sought change in women's role.

Anatomical Evidence

Rather than starting with what women *ought* to feel, it would seem logical to start out with the anatomical facts regarding the clitoris and vagina.

The Clitoris is a small equivalent of the penis, except for the fact that the ure-thra does not go through it as in the man's penis. Its erection is similar to the male erection, and the head of the clitoris has the same type of structure and function as the head of the penis. G. Lombard Kelly, in *Sexual Feeling in Married Men and Women*, says:

> The head of the clitoris is also composed of erectile tissue, and it possesses a very sen-sitive epithelium or surface covering, supplied with special nerve endings called genital corpuscles, which are peculiarly adapted for sensory stimulation that under proper mental conditions terminates in the sexual orgasm. No other part of the female gener-ative tract has such corpuscles. (p. 35)

The clitoris has no other function than that of sexual pleasure.

The Vagina—Its functions are related to the reproductive function. Principally, 1) menstruation, 2) receive penis, 3) hold semen, and 4) birth passage. The interior of the vagina, which according to the defenders of the vaginally caused orgasm is the center and producer of the orgasm, is:

> like nearly all other internal body structures, poorly supplied with end organs of touch. The internal entodermal origin of the lining of the vagina makes it similar in this respect to the rectum and other parts of the digestive tract. (Kinsey, p. 580)

The degree of insensitivity inside the vagina is so high that "Among the women who were tested in our gynecologic sample, less than 14% were at all conscious that they had been touched." (Kinsey, p. 580).

Even the importance of the vagina as an *erotic* center (as opposed to an orgas-mic center) has been found to be minor.

Other Areas—Labia minora and the vestibule of the vagina. These two sensitive areas may trigger off a clitoral orgasm. Because they can be effectively stimulated during "normal" coitus, though infrequently, this kind of stimulation is incorrectly thought to be vaginal orgasm. However, it is important to distinguish between areas which can stimulate the clitoris, incapable of producing the orgasm them-selves, and the clitoris:

> Regardless of what means of excitation is used to bring the individual to the state of sexual climax, the sensation is perceived by the genital corpuscles and is localized where they are situated: in the head of the clitoris or penis. (Kelly, p. 49)

Psychologically Stimulated Orgasm—Aside from the above mentioned direct and indirect stimulations of the clitoris, there is a third way an orgasm may be trig-gered. This is through mental (cortical) stimulation, where the imagination stimu-lates the brain, which in turn stimulates the genital corpuscles of the glans to set off an orgasm.

Women Who Say They Have Vaginal Orgasms

Confusion—Because of the lack of knowledge of their own anatomy, some women accept the idea that an orgasm felt during "normal" intercourse was vaginally caused. This confusion is caused by a combination of two factors. One, failing to locate the center of the orgasm, and two, by a desire to fit her experience to the male-defined idea of sexual normalcy. Considering that women know little about their anatomy, it is easy to be confused.

Deception—The vast majority of women who pretend vaginal orgasm to their men are faking it to "get the job." In a new best-selling Danish book, *I Accuse*, Mette Ejlersen specifically deals with this common problem, which she calls the "sex comedy." This comedy has many causes. First of all, the man brings a great deal of pressure to bear on the woman, because he considers his ability as a lover at stake. So as not to offend his ego, the woman will comply with the prescribed role and go through simulated ecstasy. In some of the other Danish women mentioned, women who were left frigid were turned off to sex, and pretended vaginal orgasm to hurry up the sex act. Others admitted that they had faked vaginal orgasm to catch a man. In one case, the woman pretended vaginal orgasm to get him to leave his first wife, who admitted being vaginally frigid. Later she was forced to continue the deception, since obviously she couldn't tell him to stimulate her clitorally.

Many more women were simply afraid to establish their right to equal enjoyment, seeing the sexual act as being primarily for the man's benefit, and any pleasure that the woman got as an added extra.

Other women, with just enough ego to reject the man's idea that they needed psychiatric care, refused to admit their frigidity. They wouldn't accept self-blame, but they didn't know how to solve the problem, not knowing the physiological facts about themselves. So they were left in a peculiar limbo.

Again, perhaps one of the most infuriating and damaging results of this whole charade has been that women who were perfectly healthy sexually were taught that they were not. So in addition to being sexually deprived, these women were told to blame themselves when they deserved no blame. Looking for a cure to a problem that has none can lead a woman on an endless path of self-hatred and insecurity. For she is told by her analyst that not even in her one role allowed in a male society—the role of a woman—is she successful. She is put on the defensive, with phony data as evidence that she'd better try to be even more feminine, think more feminine, and reject her envy of men. That is, shuffle even harder, baby.

Why Men Maintain the Myth

1. *Sexual Penetration is Preferred*—The best stimulant for the penis is the woman's vagina. It supplies the necessary friction and lubrication. From a strictly technical point of view this position offers the best physical conditions, even though the man may try other positions for variation.

2. *The Invisible Woman*—One of the elements of male chauvinism is the refusal or inability to see women as total, separate human beings. Rather, men have chosen

to define women only in terms of how they benefited men's lives. Sexually, a woman was not seen as an individual wanting to share equally in the sexual act, any more than she was seen as a person with independent desires when she did anything else in society. Thus, it was easy to make up what was convenient about women; for on top of that, society has been a function of male interests and women were not organized to form even a vocal opposition to the male experts.

3. *The Penis as Epitome of Masculinity*—Men define their lives primarily in terms of masculinity. It is a universal form of ego-boosting. That is, in every society, however homogeneous (i.e., with the absence of racial, ethnic, or major economic differences) there is always a group, women, to oppress.

The essence of male chauvinism is in the psychological superiority men exercise over women. This kind of superior-inferior definition of self, rather than positive definition based upon one's own achievements and development, has of course chained victim and oppressor both. But by far the most brutalized of the two is the victim.

An analogy is racism, where the white racist compensates for his feelings of unworthiness by creating an image of the black man (it is primarily a male struggle) as biologically inferior to him. Because of his power in a white male power structure, the white man can socially enforce this mythical division.

To the extent that men try to rationalize and justify male superiority through physical differentiation, masculinity may be symbolized by being the *most* muscular, the most hairy; having the deepest voice, and the biggest penis. Women, on the other hand, are approved of (i.e., called feminine) if they are weak, petite; shave their legs; have high soft voices, and no penis. Since the clitoris is almost identical to the penis, one finds a great deal of evidence of men in various societies trying to either ignore the clitoris and emphasize the vagina (as did Freud), or, as in some places in the Mideast, actually performing clitoridectomy. Freud saw this ancient and still practiced custom as a way of further "feminizing" the female by removing this cardinal vestige of her masculinity. It should be noted also that a big clitoris is considered ugly and masculine. Some cultures engage in the practice of pouring a chemical on the clitoris to make it shrivel up into "proper" size.

It seems clear to me that men in fact fear the clitoris as a threat to masculinity.

4. *Sexually Expendable Male*—Men fear that they will become sexually expendable if the clitoris is substituted for the vagina as the center of pleasure for women. Actually this has a great deal of validity if one considers *only* the anatomy. The position of the penis inside the vagina, while perfect for reproduction, does not necessarily stimulate an orgasm in women because the clitoris is located externally and higher up. Women must rely upon indirect stimulation in the "normal" position.

Lesbian sexuality could make an excellent case, based upon anatomical data, for the extinction of the male organ. Albert Ellis says something to the effect that a man without a penis can make a woman an excellent lover.

Considering that the vagina is very desirable from a man's point of view, purely on physical grounds, one begins to see the dilemma for men. And it forces us as well to discard many "physical" arguments explaining why women go to bed with men. What is left, it seems to me, are primarily psychological reasons why women select men at the exclusion of women as sexual partners.

5. *Control of Women*—One reason given to explain the Mideastern practice of clitoridectomy is that it will keep the women from straying. By removing the sexual organ capable of orgasm, it must be assumed that her sexual drive will diminish. Considering how men look upon their women as property, particularly in very backward nations, we should begin to consider a great deal more why it is not in men's interest to have women totally free sexually. The double standard, as practiced for example in Latin America, is set up to keep the woman as total property of the husband, while he is free to have affairs as he wishes.

6. *Lesbianism and Bisexuality*—Aside from the strictly anatomical reasons why women might equally seek other women as lovers, there is a fear on men's part that women will seek the company of other women on a full, human basis. The establishment of clitoral orgasm as fact would threaten the heterosexual *institution*. For it would indicate that sexual pleasure was obtainable from either men *or* women, thus making heterosexuality not an absolute, but an option. It would thus open up the whole question of *human* sexual relationships beyond the confines of the present male-female role system.

Notes

1. Copyright © by Anne Koedt, 1970, and reprinted with the permission of the author. Section I first appeared in *Notes From the First Year*, June, 1968. The entire article was presented as a paper at the first national women's liberation conference, Thanksgiving weekend 1968, in Chicago and then printed in 1970 in *Notes From the Second Year*.
2. Anne Koedt was a founder of the radical feminist movement in New York (New York Radical Women, The Feminists, and New York Radical Feminists). She has worked with *Notes* from its beginnings as a mimeographed journal (*Notes From the First Year*), and was an editor of *Notes From the Second* and *Third Years*.

25.
ONE IS NOT BORN A WOMAN
Monique Wittig

A materialist feminist[1] approach to women's oppression destroys the idea that women are a "natural group": "a racial group of a special kind, a group perceived *as natural*, a group of men considered as materially specific in their bodies."[2] What the analysis accomplishes on the level of ideas, practice makes actual at the level of facts: by its very existence, lesbian society destroys the artificial (social) fact constituting women as a "natural group." A lesbian society[3] pragmatically reveals that the division from men of which women have been the object is a political one and shows that we have been ideologically rebuilt into a "natural group." In the case of women, ideology goes far since our bodies as well as our minds are the product of this manipulation. We have been compelled in our bodies and in our minds to correspond, feature by feature, with the *idea* of nature that has been established for us. Distorted to such an extent that our deformed body is what they call "natural," what is supposed to exist as such before oppression. Distorted to such an extent that in the end oppression seems to be a consequence of this "nature" within ourselves (a nature which is only an *idea*). What a materialist analysis does by reasoning, a lesbian society accomplishes practically: not only is there no natural group "women" (we lesbians are living proof of it), but as individuals as well we question "woman," which for us, as for Simone de Beauvoir, is only a myth. She said: "One is not born, but becomes a woman. No biological, psychological, or economic fate determines the figure that the human female presents in society: it is civilization as a whole that produces this creature, intermediate between male and eunuch, which is described as feminine."[4]

However, most of the feminists and lesbian-feminists in America and elsewhere still believe that the basis of women's oppression is *biological as well as* historical. Some of them even claim to find their sources in Simone de Beauvoir.[5] The belief in mother right and in a "prehistory" when women created civilization (because of a biological predisposition) while the coarse and brutal men hunted (because of a biological predisposition) is symmetrical with the biologizing interpretation of history produced up to now by the class of men. It is still the same method of finding in women and men a biological explanation of their division, outside of social facts. For me this could never constitute a lesbian approach to women's oppression, since it assumes that the basis of society or the beginning of society lies in heterosexuality. Matriarchy is no less heterosexual than patriarchy: it is only the sex of the oppressor that changes. Furthermore, not only is this conception still imprisoned in the categories of sex (woman and man), but it holds onto the idea that the capacity to give birth (biology) is what defines a woman. Although practical facts and ways of living contradict this theory in lesbian society, there are lesbians who affirm that "women and men are different species or races (the words are used interchangeably): men are biologically inferior to women; male violence is a biological inevitability...."[6] By doing this, by admitting that there is a "natural" division between women and men, we naturalize history, we assume that "men" and "women" have always existed and will always exist. Not only do we naturalize history, but also consequently we naturalize the social phenomena which express our oppression, making change impossible....

A materialist feminist approach shows that what we take for the cause or origin of oppression is in fact only the *mark*[7] imposed by the oppressor: the "myth of woman,"[8] plus its material effects and manifestations in the appropriated consciousness and bodies of women. Thus, this mark does not predate oppression: Colette Guillaumin has shown that before the socioeconomic reality of black slavery, the concept of race did not exist, at least not in its modern meaning, since it was applied to the lineage of families. However, now race, exactly like sex, is taken as an "immediate given," a "sensible given," "physical features," belonging to a natural order. But what we believe to be a physical and direct perception is only a sophisticated and mythic construction, an "imaginary formation,"[9] which reinterprets physical features (in themselves as neutral as any others but marked by the social system) through the network of relationships in which they are perceived. (They are seen as *black*, therefore they *are* black; they are seen as *women*, therefore, they *are* women. But before being *seen* that way, they first had to be *made* that way.) Lesbians should always remember and acknowledge how "unnatural," compelling, totally oppressive, and destructive being "woman" was for us in the old days before the women's liberation movement. It was a political constraint, and those who resisted it were accused of not being "real" women. But then we were proud of it, since in the accusation there was already something like a shadow of victory: the avowal by the oppressor that "woman" is not something that goes without saying, since to be one, one has to be a "real" one. We were at the same time accused of wanting to be men. Today this double accusation has been taken up again with enthusiasm in the context of the women's liberation movement by some feminists and also, alas, by some lesbians whose political goal seems somehow to be becoming more and more "feminine." To refuse to be a woman, however, does not mean that one has to become a man. Besides, if we take as an example the perfect "butch," the classic example which provokes the most horror, whom Proust would have called a woman/man, how is her alienation different from that of someone who wants to become a woman? Tweedledum and Tweedledee. At least for a woman, wanting to become a man proves that she has escaped her initial programming. But even if she would like to, with all her strength, she cannot become a man. For becoming a man would demand from a woman not only a man's external appearance but his consciousness as well, that is, the consciousness of one who disposes by right of at least two "natural" slaves during his life span. This is impossible, and one feature of lesbian oppression consists precisely of making women out of reach for us, since women belong to men. Thus a lesbian *has* to be something else, a not-woman, a not-man, a product of society, not a product of nature, for there is no nature in society.

The refusal to become (or to remain) heterosexual always meant to refuse to become a man or a woman, consciously or not. For a lesbian this goes further than the refusal of the *role* "woman." It is the refusal of the economic, ideological, and political power of a man. This, we lesbians, and nonlesbians as well, knew before the beginning of the lesbian and feminist movement. However, as Andrea Dworkin emphasizes, many lesbians recently "have increasingly tried to transform the very ideology that has enslaved us into a dynamic, religious, psychologically compelling celebration of female biological potential."[10] Thus, some avenues of the feminist and lesbian movement lead us back to the myth of woman which was created by men especially for us, and with it we sink back into a natural group. Having stood up to fight for a sexless society,[11] we now find ourselves entrapped in the familiar deadlock of "woman is wonderful." Simone de Beauvoir underlined particularly the false consciousness which consists of selecting among the features of the myth (that women are different from men) those which look good and using them as a definition for women. What the concept "woman is wonderful" accomplishes is that it retains for defining women the best features (best according to whom?) which oppression has granted us, and it does not radically question the categories "man" and "woman," which are political categories and not natural givens. It puts us in a position of fighting within the class "women" not as the other classes do, for the disappearance of our class, but for the defense of "woman" and its reenforcement. It leads us to develop with complacency "new" theories about our specificity: thus, we call our passivity "nonviolence," when the main and emergent point for us is to fight our passivity (our fear, rather, a justified one). The ambiguity of the term "feminist" sums up the whole situation. What does "feminist" mean? Feminist is formed with the word "femme," "woman," and means: someone who fights for women. For many of us it means someone who fights for women as a class and for the disappearance of this class. For many others it means someone who fights for woman and her defense—for the myth, then, and its reenforcement. But why was the word "feminist" chosen if it retains the least ambiguity? We chose to call ourselves "feminists" ten years ago, not in order to support or reenforce the myth of woman, nor to identify ourselves with the oppressor's definition of us, but rather to affirm that our movement had a history and to emphasize the political link with the old feminist movement.

It is, then, this movement that we can put in question for the meaning that it gave to feminism. It so happens that feminism in the last century could never resolve its contradictions on the subject of nature/culture, woman/society. Women started to fight for themselves as a group and rightly considered that they shared common features as a result of oppression. But for them these features were natural and biological rather than social. They went so far as to adopt the Darwinist theory of evolution. They did not believe like Darwin, however, "that women were less evolved than men, but they did believe that male and female natures had diverged in the course of evolutionary development and that society at large reflected this polarization."[12] "The failure of early feminism was that it only attacked the Darwinist charge of female inferiority, while accepting the foundations of this charge—namely, the view of woman as 'unique.'"[13] And finally it was women scholars—and not feminists—who scientifically destroyed this theory. But the early feminists had failed to regard history as a dynamic process which develops from conflicts of interests. Furthermore, they still believed as men do that the cause (origin) of their oppression lay within themselves. And therefore after some astonishing victories the feminists of this first front found themselves at an impasse out of a lack of reasons to fight. They upheld the illogical principle of "equality in difference," an idea now being born again. They fell back into the trap which threatens us once again: the myth of woman.

Thus it is our historical task, and only ours, to define what we call oppression in materialist terms, to make it evident that women are a class, which is to say that the category "woman" as well as the category "man" are political and economic categories not eternal ones. Our fight aims to suppress men as a class, not through a genocidal, but a political struggle. Once the class "men" disappears, "women" as a class will disappear as well, for there are no slaves without masters. Our first task, it seems, is to always thoroughly dissociate "women" (the class within which we fight) and "woman," the myth. For "woman" does not exist for us: it is only an imaginary formation while "women" is the product of a social relationship. We felt this strongly when everywhere we refused to be called a "*woman's* liberation movement." Furthermore, we have to destroy the myth inside and outside ourselves. "Woman" is not each one of us, but the political and ideological formation which negates "women" (the product of a relation of exploitation). "Woman" is there to confuse us, to hide the reality "women." In order to be aware of being a class and to become a class we first have to kill the myth of "woman" including its most seductive aspects (I think about Virginia Woolf when she said the first task of a woman writer is to kill "the angel in the house"). But to become a class we do not have to suppress our individual selves, and since no individual can be reduced to her/his oppression we are also confronted with the historical necessity of constituting ourselves as the individual subjects of our history as well. I believe this is the reason why all these attempts at new definitions of woman are blossoming now. What is at stake (and of course not only for women) is an individual definition as well as a class definition. For once one has acknowledged oppression, one needs to know and experience the fact that one can constitute oneself as a subject (as opposed to an object of oppression), that one can become *someone* in spite of oppression, that one has one's own identity. There is no possible fight for someone deprived of an identity, no internal motivation for fighting, since, although I can fight only with others, first I fight for myself.

The question of the individual subject is historically a difficult one for everybody. Marxism, the last avatar of materialism, the science which has politically formed us, does not want to hear anything about a "subject."…

…Marxist theory does not allow women any more than other classes of oppressed people to constitute themselves as historical subjects, because Marxism does not take into account the fact that a class also consists of individuals one by one. Class consciousness is not enough. We must try to understand philosophically (politically) these concepts of "subject" and "class consciousness" and how they work in relation to our history. When we discover that women are the objects of oppression and appropriation, at the very moment that we become able to perceive this, we become subjects in the sense of cognitive subjects, through an operation of abstraction. Consciousness of oppression is not only a reaction to (fight against) oppression. It is also the whole conceptual reevaluation of the social world, its whole reorganization with new concepts, from the point of view of oppression. It is what I would call the science of oppression created by the oppressed. This operation of understanding reality has to be undertaken by every one of us: call it a subjective, cognitive practice. The movement back and forth between the levels of reality (the conceptual reality and the material reality of oppression, which are both social realities) is accomplished through language.

It is we who historically must undertake the task of defining the individual subject in materialist terms. This certainly seems to be an impossibility since materialism and subjectivity have always been mutually exclusive. Nevertheless, and rather than despairing of ever understanding, we must recognize the *need* to reach subjectivity in the abandonment by many of us to the myth "woman" (the myth of woman being only a snare that holds us up). This real necessity for everyone to exist as an individual, as well as a member of a class, is perhaps the first condition for the accomplishment of a revolution, without which there can be no real fight or transformation. But the opposite is also true; without class and class consciousness there are no real subjects, only alienated individuals. For women to answer the question of the individual subject in materialist terms is first to show, as the lesbians and feminists did, that supposedly "subjective," "individual," "private" problems are in fact social problems, class problems; that sexuality is not for women an individual and subjective expression, but a social institution of violence. But once we have shown that all so-called personal problems are in fact class problems, we will still be left with the question of the subject of each singular woman—not the myth, but each one of us. At this point, let us say that a new personal and subjective definition for all humankind can only be found beyond the categories of sex (woman and man) and that the advent of individual subjects demands first destroying the categories of sex, ending the use of them, and rejecting all sciences which still use these categories as their fundamentals (practically all social sciences).

To destroy "woman" does not mean that we aim, short of physical destruction, to destroy lesbianism simultaneously with the categories of sex, because lesbianism provides for the moment the only social form in which we can live freely. Lesbian is the only concept I know of which is beyond the categories of sex (woman and man), because the designated subject (lesbian) is *not* a woman, either economically, or politically, or ideologically. For what makes a woman is a specific social relation to a man, a relation that we have previously called servitude,[14] a relation which implies personal and physical obligation as well as economic obligation ("forced residence,"[15] domestic corvée, conjugal duties, unlimited production of children, et cetera), a relation which lesbians escape by refusing to become or to stay heterosexual. We are escapees from our class in the same way as the American runaway slaves were when escaping slavery and becoming free. For us this is an absolute necessity; our survival demands that we contribute all our strength to the destruction of the class of women within which men appropriate women. This can be accomplished only by the destruction of heterosexuality as a social system which is based on the oppression of women by men and which produces the doctrine of the difference between the sexes to justify this oppression.

Notes

1. Christine Delphy, "Pour un féminisme matérialiste," *L'Arc* 61 (1975). Translated as "For a Materialist Feminism," *Feminist Issues* 1, no. 2 (Winter 1981).
2. Colette Guillaumin, "Race et Nature: Système des marques, idée de groupe naturel et rapports sociaux," *Pluriel*, no. 11 (1977). Translated as "Race and Nature: The System of Marks, the Idea of a Natural Group and Social Relationships," *Feminist Issues* 8, no. 2 (Fall 1988).
3. I use the word society with an extended anthropological meaning; strictly speaking, it does not refer to societies, in that lesbian societies do not exist completely autonomously from heterosexual social systems.
4. Simone de Beauvoir, *The Second Sex* (New York: Bantam, 1952), p. 249.
5. Redstockings, *Feminist Revolution* (New York: Random House, 1978), p. 18.
6. Andrea Dworkin, "Biological Superiority: The World's Most Dangerous and Deadly Idea," *Heresies* 6: 46.
7. Guillaumin, op. cit.
8. de Beauvoir, op. cit.
9. Guillaumin, op. cit.
10. Dworkin, op. cit.
11. Atkinson, p. 6: "If feminism has any logic at all, it must be working for a sexless society."
12. Rosalind Rosenberg, "In Search of Woman's Nature," *Feminist Studies* 3, no. 1/2 (1975): 144.
13. Ibid., p. 146.
14. In an article published in *L'Idiot International* (May 1970), whose original title was "Pour un movement de libération des femmes" ("For a Women's Liberation Movement").
15. Christiane Rochefort, *Les stances à Sophie* (Paris: Grasset, 1963).

26.
I AM YOUR SISTER: BLACK WOMEN ORGANIZING ACROSS SEXUALITIES[1]
Audre Lorde

Whenever I come to Medgar Evers College I always feel a thrill of anticipation and delight because it feels like coming home, like talking to family, having a chance to speak about things that are very important to me with people who matter the most. And this is particularly true whenever I talk at the Women's Center. But, as with all families, we sometimes find it difficult to deal constructively with the genuine differences between us and to recognize that unity does not require that we be identical to each other. Black women are not one great vat of homogenized chocolate milk. We have many different faces, and we do not have to become each other in order to work together.

It is not easy for me to speak here with you as a Black Lesbian feminist, recognizing that some of the ways in which I identify myself make it difficult for you to hear me. But meeting across difference always requires mutual stretching, and until you *can* hear me as a Black Lesbian feminist, our strengths will not be truly available to each other as Black women.

Because I feel it is urgent that we not waste each other's resources, that we recognize each sister on her own terms so that we may better work together toward our mutual survival, I speak here about heterosexism and homophobia, two grave barriers to organizing among Black women. And so that we have a common language between us, I would like to define some of the terms I use: *Heterosexism*—a belief in the inherent superiority of one form of loving over all others and thereby the right to dominance; *Homophobia*—a terror surrounding feelings of love for members of the same sex and thereby a hatred of those feelings in others.

In the 1960s, when liberal white people decided that they didn't want to appear racist, they wore dashikis, and danced Black, and ate Black and even married Black, but they did not want to feel Black or think Black, so they never even questioned the textures of their daily living (why should flesh-colored bandaids always be pink?) and then they wondered, "Why are those Black folks always taking offense so easily at the least little thing? Some of our best friends are Black...."

Well, it is not necessary for some of your best friends to be Lesbian, although some of them probably are, no doubt. But it is necessary for you to stop oppressing me through false judgement. I do not want you to ignore my identity, nor do I want you to make it an insurmountable barrier between our sharing of strengths.

When I say I am a Black feminist, I mean I recognize that my power as well as my primary oppressions come as a result of my Blackness as well as my womanness, and therefore my struggles on both these fronts are inseparable.

When I say I am a Black Lesbian, I mean I am a woman whose primary focus of loving, physical as well as emotional, is directed to women. It does not mean I hate men. Far from it. The harshest attacks I have ever heard against Black men come from those women who are intimately bound to them and cannot free themselves from a subservient and silent position. I would never presume to speak about Black men the way I have heard some of my straight sisters talk about the men they are attached to. And of course that concerns me, because it reflects a situation of noncommunication in the heterosexual Black community that is far more truly threatening than the existence of Black Lesbians.

What does this have to do with Black women organizing?

I have heard it said—usually behind my back—that Black Lesbians are not normal. But what is normal in this deranged society by which we are all trapped? I remember, and so do many of you, when being Black was considered *not normal* when they talked about us in whispers, tried to paint us, lynch us, bleach us, ignore us, pretend we did not exist. We called that racism.

I have heard it said that Black Lesbians are a threat to the Black family. But when 50 percent of children born to Black women are born out of wedlock, and 30 percent of all Black families are headed by women without husbands, we need to broaden and redefine what we mean by *family*.

I have heard it said that Black Lesbians will mean the death of the race. Yet Black Lesbians bear children in exactly the same way other women bear children, and a Lesbian household is simply another kind of family. Ask my son and daughter.

The terror of Black Lesbians is buried in that deep inner place where we have been taught to fear all difference—to kill it or ignore it. Be assured: loving women is not a communicable disease. You don't catch it like the common cold. Yet the one accusation that seems to render even the most vocal straight Black woman totally silent and ineffective is the suggestion that she might be a Black Lesbian.

If someone says you're Russian and you know you're not, you don't collapse into stunned silence. Even if someone calls you a bigamist, or a childbeater, and you know you're not, you don't crumple into bits. You say it's not true and keep on printing the posters. But let anyone, particularly a Black man, accuse a straight Black woman of being a Black *Lesbian*, and right away that sister becomes immobilized, as if that is the most horrible thing she could be, and must at all costs be proven false. That is homophobia. It is a waste of woman energy, and it puts a terrible weapon into the hands of your enemies to be used against you to silence you, to keep you docile and in line. It also serves to keep us isolated and apart.

I have heard it said that Black Lesbians are not political, that we have not been and are not involved in the struggles of Black people. But when I taught Black and Puerto Rican students writing at City College in the SEEK program in the sixties I was a Black Lesbian. I was a Black Lesbian when I helped organize and fight for the Black Studies Department of John Jay College. And because I was fifteen years younger then and less sure of myself, at one crucial moment I yielded to pressures that said I should step back for a Black man even though I knew him to be a serious error of choice, and I did, and he was. But I was a Black Lesbian then.

When my girlfriends and I went out in the car one July 4th night after fireworks with cans of white spray paint and our kids asleep in the back seat, one of us staying behind to keep the motor running and watch the kids while the other two worked our way down the suburban New Jersey street, spraying white paint over the black jockey statues, and their little red jackets, too, we were Black Lesbians.

When I drove through the Mississippi Delta to Jackson in 1968 with a group of Black students from Tougaloo, another car full of redneck kids trying to bump us off the road all the way back into town, I was a Black Lesbian.

When I weaned my daughter in 1963 to go to Washington in August to work in the coffee tents along with Lena Horne, making coffee for the marshals because that was what most Black women did in the 1963 March on Washington, I was a Black Lesbian.

When I taught a poetry workshop at Tougaloo, a small Black college in Mississippi, where white rowdies shot up the edge of the campus every night, and I felt the joy of seeing young Black poets find their voices and power through words in our mutual growth, I was a Black Lesbian. And there are strong Black poets today who date their growth and awareness from those workshops.

When Yoli and I cooked curried chicken and beans and rice and took our extra blankets and pillows up the hill to the striking students occupying buildings at City College in 1969, demanding open admissions and the right to an education, I was a Black Lesbian. When I walked through the midnight hallways of Lehman College that same year, carrying Midol and Kotex pads for the young Black radical women taking part in the action, and we tried to persuade them that their place in the revolution was not ten paces behind Black men, that spreading their legs to the guys on the tables in the cafeteria was not a revolutionary act no matter what the brothers said, I was a Black Lesbian. When I picketed for Welfare Mothers' Rights, and against the enforced sterilization of young Black girls, when I fought institutionalized racism in the New York City schools, I was a Black Lesbian.

But you did not know it because we did not identify ourselves, so now you can say that Black Lesbians and Gay men have nothing to do with the struggles of the Black Nation.

And I am not alone.

When you read the words of Langston Hughes you are reading the words of a Black Gay man. When you read the words of Alice Dunbar-Nelson and Angelina Weld Grimké, poets of the Harlem Renaissance, you are reading the words of Black Lesbians. When you listen to the life-affirming voices of Bessie Smith and Ma Rainey, you are hearing Black Lesbian women. When you see the plays and read the words of Lorraine Hansberry, you are reading the words of a woman who loved women deeply.

Today, Lesbians and Gay men are some of the most active and engaged members of Art Against Apartheid, a group which is making visible and immediate our cultural responsibilities against the tragedy of South Africa. We have organizations such as the National Coalition of Black Lesbians and Gays, Dykes Against Racism Everywhere, and Men of All Colors together, all of which are committed to and engaged in antiracist activity.

Homophobia and heterosexism mean you allow yourselves to be robbed of the sisterhood and strength of Black Lesbian women because you are afraid of being called a Lesbian yourself. Yet we share so many concerns as Black women, so much work to be done. The urgency of the destruction of our Black children and the theft of young Black minds are joint urgencies. Black children shot down or doped up on the streets of our cities are priorities for all of us. The fact of Black women's blood flowing with grim regularity in the streets and living rooms of Black communities is not a Black Lesbian rumor. It is a sad statistical truth. The fact that there is widening and dangerous lack of communication around our differences between Black women and men is not a Black Lesbian plot. It is a reality that is starkly clarified as we see our young people becoming more and more uncaring of each other. Young Black boys believing that they can define their manhood between a sixth-grade girl's legs, growing up believing that Black women and girls are the fitting target for their justifiable furies rather than the racist structures grinding us all into dust, these are not Black Lesbian myths. These are sad realities of Black communities today and of immediate concern to us all. We cannot afford to waste each other's energies in our common battles.

What does homophobia mean? It means that high-powered Black women are told it is not safe to attend a Conference on the Status of Women in Nairobi simply because we are Lesbians. It means that in a political action, you rob yourselves of the vital insight and energies of political women such as Betty Powell and Barbara Smith and Gwendolyn Rogers and Raymina Mays and Robin Christian and Yvonne Flowers. It means another instance of the divide-and-conquer routine.

How do we organize around our differences, neither denying them nor blowing them up out of proportion?

The first step is an effort of will on your part. Try to remember to keep certain facts in mind. Black Lesbians are not apolitical. We have been a part of every freedom struggle within this country. Black Lesbians are not a threat to the Black family. Many of us have families of our own. We are not white, and we are not a disease. We are women who love women. This does not mean we are going to assault your daughters in an alley on Nostrand Avenue. It does not mean we are about to attack you if we pay you a compliment on your dress. It does not mean we only think about sex, any more than you only think about sex.

Even if you *do* believe any of these stereotypes about Black Lesbians, begin to practice acting like you don't believe them. Just as racist stereotypes are the problem of the white people who believe them, so also are homophobic stereotypes the problem of the heterosexuals who believe them. In other words, those stereotypes are yours to solve, not mine, and they are a terrible and wasteful barrier to our working together. I am not your enemy. We do not have to become each other's unique experiences and insights in order to share what we have learned through our particular battles for survival as Black women.

There was a poster in the 1960s that was very popular: HE'S NOT BLACK, HE'S MY BROTHER! It used to infuriate me because it implied that the two were mutually exclusive—*he* couldn't be both brother and Black. Well, I do not want to be tolerated, nor misnamed. I want to be recognized.

I am a Black Lesbian, and I *am* your sister.

27.
FUNNY BOYS AND GIRLS:[1] NOTES ON A QUEER[2] SOUTH ASIAN PLANET
Gayatri Gopinath

What does it mean to queer the diaspora[3]? The question was at the back of my mind as I walked into a recent panel discussion entitled "Queer Festivals Go Global," organized by the 1994 New York Experimental Lesbian and Gay Film Festival, and but one of a spate of recent events[4] that seem to be positing a notion of a shared alterior sexuality that exists across national boundaries. As I listened to the discussion, it became increasingly obvious to me how complicated it is to think in terms of a queer diaspora: the notions of both "queer" and "diaspora" connote highly contested terrain, where it is difficult if not impossible to avoid falling into murky territory while trying to negotiate a path around existing and competing discourses on sexuality, class, "culture," and language. In fact, I walked away from the event more aware than ever of the ways in which a project of constructing a diasporic queerness—on the part of queer activists, scholars, and cultural producers—is fraught with both pleasures and dangers.

Rather than develop any totalizing or linear narrative around these questions, I would like here to simply begin a dialogue on just what some of these pleasures and dangers might be, by focusing on the workings of a South Asian diaspora in particular. The subjective "I" in this piece functions not so much as a marker of a representative positionality but rather militates against any such reading, insisting upon the radical contingency of queer South Asian subjectivity.[5] While I am not suggesting that transnational performances of South Asian queerness work to create some kind of purely liberatory space, free from the various violences effected by the disciplinary mechanisms of the state and nation, I do want to explore the possibilities—as well as the limits—of conceptualizing a diasporic or transnational South Asian queer sexuality. Clearly, there are no answers that can be arrived at, no conclusions that can easily be drawn; all that is possible is a more rigorous interrogation of the frameworks within which we attempt to speak of queerness transnationally.

Whose Queer State? Whose Queer Nation?

There have been a number of recent attempts by queer scholars to explicitly link together questions of the state, nation, and queerness. Lisa Duggan's essay on "Queering the State,"[6] for instance, calls for the necessity of formulating new strategies "at the boundary of queer and nation"[7] to combat anti-gay rightwing campaigns. It is only through a creative contestation of the politics of the state within the public sphere, she argues, that queers can hope to counter the rhetorical and legislative violence aimed at them. Similarly, Lauren Berlant's and Elizabeth Freeman's essay on "Queer Nationality"[8] analyzes Queer Nation's project of "coordinating a new nationality" through the "[reclamation of] the nation for pleasure."[9] While Berlant and Freeman express some reservations at using nationalism as a counter-hegemonic model for transgression and resistance,[10] they nevertheless hold that Queer Nation's strategies of spectacular counterpublicity redefine the terms of citizenship and nationality.

I would argue that neither Duggan nor Berlant and Freeman fully address the particularly vexed relation of many queers of color to the disciplinary and regulatory mechanisms of the state and nation, thereby inadvertently pointing up the severe limitations of any nationalist project, however transgressive. The authors suggest that the power of queer activism lies in its ability to exploit the disjuncture between queers having access to the state and its juridical privileges, that is, to citizenship, and being simultaneously denied access to the nation, to full national subjectivity.[11] Implicit in their argument, then, is that queers, for the most part, have unproblematic access to the state and to "queer citizenship"[12]; ultimately, the queer (white) U.S. citizen remains in their framework as the singular subject for and through which the public arena can and must be reterritorialized. Clearly, this uninterrogated assumption of queer citizenship as the starting point of their argument renders it inadequate in addressing the realities faced on a daily basis by a substantial number of queers—particularly those of color. As queer South Asians in the diaspora, "citizenship," queer or otherwise, is not something that we can ever take for granted. Rather, we enact a much more complicated navigation of state regulatory practices and *multiple* national spaces—one that is often profoundly mobile, contingent, and evasive, and that demands a more nuanced theorization of the interplay of state and nation. Indeed, as I hope to make clear in what follows, it is at the interstices of these various strategic negotiations that transnational or diasporic queerness is under construction.

Diasporic Pleasure

Before addressing this question of diasporic queerness, however, we must ask what "diaspora" means for South Asians in the first place. We need to keep in mind the limitations involved in situating ourselves as "diasporic" subjects at all, even while acknowledging that the notion of diaspora is a useful and necessary one for those of us who inhabit simultaneous and often contradictory geographic, political and psychic spaces. As one critic writes, "to be cognizant of oneself as a diasporic subject is always to be aware of oneself, no matter where one is, as from elsewhere, in the process of making a not quite legitimate appeal to be considered as if one were from here."[13] It is this liminality of diasporic experience—of being inside/outside—that is so perfectly captured and negotiated by South Asian transnational popular cultural forms such as bhangra. Originally a Punjabi folk music that has been transformed through its amalgam with house, reggae, rap, and other black diasporic musical forms, bhangra is a tremendously celebratory "affirmation of particularity"[14] that testifies to the (often forced) movements of South Asians between South and East Africa, South Asia, the Caribbean, the United States, Canada, and Great Britain. Bhangra has become a general signifier for South Asian-ness from New York to London to Toronto to Bombay, calling into existence a diasporic network of "affiliation and affect"[15] that cuts across national boundaries with remarkable fluidity. In this sense, bhangra enacts a counter-public space of "diasporic intimacy" (Paul Gilroy's phrase) that resists the exclusionary norms of a bourgeois public sphere.[16] Yet, as with many constructions of community and ethnic identity, however oppositional, current articulations of diaspora tend to replicate and indeed rely upon conventional ideologies of gender and sexuality; once again, certain bodies (queer and/or female) are rendered invisible or marked as other. Within the bhangra music industry, for instance, there remain very few women producers or DJs; similarly, many bhangra lyrics and the stage personas of the performers themselves are deeply masculinist and heterosexist, imagining women as reproducers (both literally and metaphorically) of "culture" and community.[17]

So how do those of us who fall outside a normative space of monogamous heterosexuality forge diasporic networks for our own particular purposes? Perhaps the strategic appropriation of bhangra or Hindu film music by queer South Asians in the west—where both have become staples at parties and parades as a way of signifying South Asian-ness to a mainstream (white) gay community, as well as to other queer people of color—offers a glimpse into what a queered South Asian diaspora could look (and sound) like. The recontextualization of Hindi film songs within the space of queer South Asian parties, for instance, where these songs become parodic performances of conventional gender constructions,[18] indicates but one out of the many proliferating sites and strategies upon and through which new articulations of queer pleasure and desire are emerging. Indeed, it becomes clear that the question of pleasure, of constituting ourselves as desiring subjects, is critical to this project of negotiating a space of queer diasporic intimacy.[19] As one activist observes in *Khush*, Pratiblia Parade's documentary on queer South Asian identity, the pleasures of being gay are for him summed up by "two words: sex and solidarity."[20] His comment seems to speak to what Gina Dent, in her discussion of "black pleasure, black joy,"[21] refers to as "the collective basis of our conception of joy": there is a profoundly affective quality to the experience of walking into a roomful of queer brown folks lip-synching along to *Choli Ke Piche* a phenomenally popular Hindi film song that, as one South Asian gay man playfully commented, has done more for the South Asian queer community than any conference or parade ever has. We know what a high it can be to participate in conferences like Desh Pardesh, an annual, Toronto-based festival that draws progressive South Asians together from all over the globe. Many of us are also a part of more informal networks of friends and lovers that traverse various diasporic locations, creating a transnational politics of affect that is proving to be remarkably malleable and resistant[22] to state regulation.[23] The work of British cultural workers like Paul Gilroy and Isaac Julien have taught us to take seriously this kind of politics of affect, to acknowledge its profound influence on the ways in which we imagine ourselves and our relation to each other.

On another, more formalized level, the works of emerging writers like Canadian-based Shani Mootoo[24] and Shyam Selvadurai trace, with a distinct comic sensibility, the exquisite intricacies of simultaneous sexual, racial, and national immigrations. A recent anthology, *A Lotus of Another Color*,[25] maps the lines of exchange and influence between various global South Asian queer organizations, from (among others) Trikone, Shamakami, and SALGA in the U.S., to Khush in Toronto, to Shakti in London, to Sakhi and Bombay Dost in India. Meanwhile, much of the scholarly and experimental work currently being produced by queer South Asians is critically informed by and responds to the work of (U.K. "Black") British artists and cultural theorists[26]—both Asian and Afro-Caribbean—thereby underscoring the need to theorize a queer South Asian diaspora as marked and inflected by multiple, overlapping diasporas. My brief and rather random citations here are not meant to be exhaustive but rather to sketch out the shifting contours of a South Asian diasporic queerness, and to foreground the centrality of questions of pleasure and desire to the processes—both formal and informal—by which it is taking shape.

Whose Queerness?

So what about the dangers involved in framing queer sexuality diasporically? As one critic reminds us, new constructions of sexual subjectivity "[offer] an ambiguous combination of collective power and vulnerability" in its "focusing and ossifying" of identity.[27] What, then, are the implications of privileging sexuality as a primary "identity" throughout the diaspora? What possible alternative narratives of sexuality may we be shutting down in such a move?[28] How do we allow for the fact that same-sex eroticism exists and signifies very differently in different diasporic contexts,[29] while simultaneously recognizing the common forms of violence that we face everyday because of our sexuality? I would like to return here to the film festival panel and the pitfalls that it ran into, which I think are emblematic of the difficulties inherent in recent formal attempts—like festivals and conferences—in articulating a queer diaspora.

The panelists at this particular program spoke about the problems in transporting queer festivals (that were for the most part conceived of in the west) to India, Brazil, Hong Kong, and other parts of the non-western world. There was a lot of talk among various panelists and audience members about the need to avoid yet another form of "cultural imperialism," where this time around the cultural imperialists would be gay people in the west exporting and imposing their particular brand of queer identity upon unsuspecting non-western "sexual minorities." I could certainly understand where this well-intentioned concern with imposing "alien" paradigms and strategies was coming from, given that the weapon most often wielded against any struggle for queer visibility and self-definition is that same-sex sexuality is a western import, something that is not "authentically" Indian, Brazilian, etc. The necessity we feel to work against and grapple with such notions of cultural validity also plays out in the ongoing debate around what to call ourselves, the language we use to signify alterior sexualities in a way that does not excise particular histories.

Yet in struggling against certain dominant discourses, we find ourselves reconsolidating a number of other, equally problematic ones. One curator at the panel, for instance, talked about how troubled she was that a program on body-piercing she had taken from New York to Brazil prompted a body-piercing trend in the Brazilian city where it was shown. Given my lack of access to the Brazilian context that was being referenced, I can only suggest that there may exist other, more enabling readings of such an instance of translated queer style. While I do not deny the power of global structures of imperialism and neocolonialism in shaping the ways in which we as queer people relate across various diasporas, it should not be assumed that consumption, on the part of the non-western "they" that the audience and panelists were referring to, can be read solely as mimicry.[30] Couching this non-western "they" in such terms negates the ways in which consumption—whether of identities or style or modes of organizing—can be a productive, imaginative act, where what is consumed is not simply and passively digested but more often than not reworked and forced to resignify.[31] The evacuation of agency of the non-western "they" engendered in the name of an anti-imperialist position also necessitates a concurrent evacuation of the possible site of pleasure that a practice like bodypiercing opens up. In denying this non-western "they" the power to (re)invent and claim pleasure, "they" were effectively shut out of the potential dialogue that would construct a queer diasporic subject and sensibility. Even more problematically, such an attribution of motivation (or rather the lack of it) to "other" queer subjects reinscribes the conventional anthropological logic that has been so fundamental to the colonial imagination.

Fabled Territories

Such difficulties in speaking of sexuality diasporically are not easily rectified. But perhaps recognizing the uses to which queer South Asians, as I have alluded to above, put film music or bhangra or any other popular cultural form available to us is to force us to theorize queerness and diaspora in a way that at least confounds this easy cultural imperialism argument. It is to realize that such forms of transnational popular practice mean radically different things in different contexts, that it is not about a one-way flow of commodities, identities, or models of being and organizing; rather, it is about multiple and non-hierarchical sites of exchange, where queerness and ethnicity are being contested and made anew every step of the way. And it seems to do so in a way that formal attempts at forging new sexual subjectivities (the film fests and the panels) have yet to catch up to. This is not to romanticize popular culture, or to deny the dialogic relationship between theory and practice, but I do get the sense that what is going on through informal popular cultural practices exceeds the theoretical models that we have been working with so far. Paying closer attention to these varied performances of a queer South Asian counter-public demands that we theorize queer diaspora in a particular way: not in terms of an immutable, generalized queer subject that inhabits this diasporic space, nor in terms of a notion of both queerness and diaspora that replicates existing power structures between the west and the rest. Instead, the new paradigm of queerness gestured to by queer South Asian diasporic cultural practices is one that interpellates a translated geography of pleasure, what poet and activist Ian Rashid calls a "fabled territory"[32] where new sites of deterritorialized desire are continuously being produced. Yet, even within this translated geography, it remains to be seen if we can fully avoid enacting the various forms of conceptual violences that I have sought to foreground here.

Notes

1. The title contains a reference to Sri Lankan/Canadian writer Shyam Selvadurai's novel, *Funny Boy* (London: Jonathan Cape, 1994).
2. I use the word "queer" in this article as shorthand for indicating an oppositional space outside hetero-normativity. I recognize the term as emerging out of a long and complicated history within a U.S. context (as historian George Chauncey's most recent work attests to), and that it is not one used for self-identification by many South Asians throughout the diaspora. I nevertheless find "queer" useful in that it is (or has the potential to be) gender-neutral, and connotes an entire range of alternative sexual practices and sensibilities in a way that "lesbian," "bisexual," or "gay" do not.
3. Clearly, there is no such thing as "diaspora" as such; it is hardly a given entity or a transparent term but one with an extremely problematic genealogy inflected by class, gender, and heterosexuality. However, I continue to use the term in this essay, even while recognizing its limits, to refer to the global networks of affiliation constantly being produced and reproduced along the lines of race, ethnicity, and/or sexuality.
4. To cite just two examples, the theme of New York City's 1994 Pride Parade was one of "international human rights" for "sexual minorities"; on a much smaller scale, Trikone, a queer South Asian group in San Francisco and the International Gay and Lesbian Human Rights Committee, attempted to organize an international queer film festival and conference in India for December 1994.
5. Concurrently, when I speak of or from a collectivity, an "us" or a "we," it is with the recognition that this collectivity is continuously under construction both within and outside academic discourse, and that it is one that, as I hope this essay will make clear, simultaneously inhabits and transcends identity politics.
6. See Lisa Duggan, "Queering the State," *Social Text* 39 (Summer 1994): 1–14.
7. Ibid., 3.
8. Lauren Berlant and Elizabeth Freeman, "Queer Nationality," *Boundary* 2 (Spring 1992): 149–80.
9. Ibid., 151.
10. Ibid., 154.
11. I am grateful to Qadri Ismail for bringing this point to my attention.
12. For instance, Berlant and Freeman state that "disidentification with U.S. nationality is not, at this moment, even a theoretical option for queer citizens"(154), disregarding the fact that identification with either nationality or citizenship is not an option for many queers (particularly queers of color) in the U.S.

13. Kenneth Warren, "Appeals of (Mis) Recognition: Theorizing the Diaspora." In *The Cultures of United States Imperialism*, ed. Amy Kaplan and Donald E. Pease (Durham: Duke University Press, 1993): 400–401.

14. The phrase is Paul Gilroy's, which he uses to discuss Black diasporic cultural production. See *The Black Atlantic: Modernity and Double Consciousness*, 16.

15. Ibid.

16. I am indebted to José Muñoz's recent lecture on "Latino Bodies, Queer Spaces," given at Columbia University, for this particular formulation of the counter-public.

17. One of the more transparent instances of this includes the hit song "Arranged Marriage" by the British Asian musician Apache Indian.

18. The scope of this essay precludes an adequate discussion of the subject, but it must be noted that such performances cannot be contained within the discourse of camp that is so prevalent in queer theory, but rather demand their own specific theorization. The possibilities opened up by these performances for lesbian spectatorship and desire is also a subject that remains to be further explored.

19. It is necessary to add here that pleasure, so intrinsic to a project of queer subject formation, is always available to recuperation in the service of heternormativity; that pleasure—its policing and denial—can also function as the most powerful weapon in the effacement and foreclosure of such a project.

20. *Khush* Dir. Pratiblia Parmar. Women Make Movies, 1991. 16 mm, 24 min.

21. Gina Dent, "Black Pleasure, Black Joy: An Introduction." In *Black Popular Culture*, ed. Gina Dent (Seattle: Bay Press, 1992): 10.

22. See Lisa Duggan, 12, for a discussion of "malleability and resistance" in conceptualizing an alternative model of queerness.

23. If there is a utopian strain that runs through these various articulations of diasporic queerness, it is one that perhaps gestures to what Greg Tate calls "a certain kind of romance" that even "self-defined antiessentialists" have with inhabiting particular identities (see Greg Tate, quoted in Gina Dent, "Black Pleasure, Black Joy: An Introduction": 13).

24. See Shani Mootoo, *Out on Main Street and Other Stories* (Vancouver: Press Gang Publishers, 1993).

25. Rakesh Ratti, ed., *A Lotus of Another Color: An Unfolding of the South Asian Lesbian and Gay Experience* (Boston: Alyson Publications, 1993).

26. Some of the work I have in mind includes: Paul Gilroy, *The Black Atlantic: Modernity and Double Consciousness* (Cambridge: Harvard University Press, 1993), and *There Ain't No Black in the Union Jack: The Cultural Politics of Race and Nation* (Chicago: University of Chicago, 1987); Kobena Mercer, *Welcome to the Jungle: New Positions in Black Cultural Studies* (New York: Routledge, 1994); *Looking for Langston*, Dir. Isaac Julien. Sankofa, 1989; Hanif Kureishi, *My Beautiful Laundrette and the Rainbow Sign* (Boston: Faber and Faber, 1986), and *The Buddha of Suburbia* (New York: Viking Penguin, 1990); *I'm British, But...* Dir. Gurinder Chadha. Unibi Films, 1988; and *Bhaji on the Beach*, Dir. Gurinder Chadha, 1994.

27. Rosalind Morris, "Three Sexes and Four Sexualities: Redressing the Discourses of Gender and Sexuality in Contemporary Thailand," *Positions* 2 no. 2 (Spring 1994): 29

28. I thank Hiram Peréz for asking this question.

29. We would do well to heed Morris' warning against the "homogenization of differences that emerges when...[particular] forms of alterior sexual identity are considered in fetishism's vacuum, dependent of the culturally specific sex/gender systems from which they emerge": 16.

30. I use "mimicry" here to signify a kind of parodic repetition, in Judith Butler's terms, that fails to displace its conventions.

31. This argument, of course, is not a new one, as work like Dick Hebdige's classic, *Subculture: The Meaning of Style* (London: Methuen, 1979), attests to; yet it bears repeating within the new context of a transnational queer politics.

32. Ian lqbal Rashid, *Black Markets, White Boyfriends and Other Acts of Elision* (Toronto: TSAR, 1991): 11.

28.
GOING HOME: ENACTING JUSTICE IN QUEER ASIAN AMERICA
Karin Aguilar–San Juan

We will, in short, create fictions, not actual cities
or villages, but invisible ones, imaginary homelands, Indias of the
mind.
—*Salmon Rushdie,* Imaginary Homelands.

The Problem of Authenticity

It is a funny thing to be writing an essay about going home when, at the moment, there is really no place I call "home." I was born in Boston but eventually left for Providence. I recently moved to southern California, which has always fascinated me. To go westward is, for an Asian American, to go home, in the sense that many Asian Americans have family in California, in Washington state, or farther west in Hawai'i. But my immediate family is currently scattered around the Midwest.[1]

For many years, I have been concerned with the way we, as Asian American lesbians and gay men, think about going home.[2] Many of us simply cannot do so, at least not openly, because of the intolerance of parents, relatives, or friends who bristle at our "lifestyles." For too many of my friends, going home involves entering a closet of furtive whispers and private pain. Once I went with several AMALGM[3] members to a Boston suburb, where we had been invited by a friend to enjoy a sumptuous Filipino feast with her family. But since our host had not come out to her mother, we disguised ourselves by sitting around the living room in purposeful order: boy, girl, boy, girl. This superficially heterosexual arrangement made home a safe place for our friend, her mother, and ultimately for us. Without feeling threatened, we could continue our meal.

I am wary, here and in general, of portraying Asian American queers as being less able than other people to "go home." Home seems to bring forth intense and mixed feelings for everyone. It is not my intention to reinforce the idea that Asian Americans are somehow more squeamish about homosexuality, or sex, than is any other group. As far as I know, no one has systematically or by any standard measure compared homophobia in various racial and ethnic groups. But it is probably true that we feel that homophobia is most intense at home, wherever we construe that to be, because home matters the most. It seems that for many Asian Americans, home is a place where "Asianness" originates, a place made more compelling by the negation of an Asian American presence elsewhere. Often, we look to the future with anticipation, hoping that the next time we go home, we can be out.

But I do not want to feed into the notion that as *Asian* Americans, we are somehow always foreigners in America, longing for home in another faraway continent. That stereotype conjures up images of exotic aromas and spicy foods and languages that we do not speak (but that somehow we understand through some feat of intergenerational and international memory). Indeed, because of the popular belief that Asian Americans are never really "at home" in America, I find the concept of "going home" so much more interesting to explore.

This essay is a commentary on the difficulties that arise whenever we evoke the notion of "home," "experience," or "community" as a claim to truth,[4] originary places, authenticating devices, or the activism or cultural grounding of metaphors in social movement representation. My shorthand for this issue is the "problem of authenticity," which has been addressed in other ways by other writers, some of whom I cite throughout this chapter. Authenticity is a problem because it suggests that our actions or our representations are true, universal, or just, without explicit criteria by which these actions or representations may be assessed. As I see it, the problem of authenticity particularly confronts communities organized around some aspect of identity. But it is not a problem that is the sole territory of identity politics. Claims to truth are the basis of any social movement; ultimately, the claim to justice is what drives movements for social change. My intention here is to provide some illustrations of the problem of authenticity as I see it, to offer some explanations for why it persists, and to suggest a possible solution. Throughout my discussion, "queer Asian America" is much more than a simple designation of a population group; I use the phrase to refer to the process of building a sense of collectivity which, in its most utopian moment, strives toward community.

Home

In the winter of 1994, a group of Filipino American lesbian activists in the San Francisco Bay Area established The Beth and Vangie Legal Defense Fund (I refer to this group as the Fund). Beth and Vangie were fired from their jobs in a human rights agency in Manila when they became lovers. They filed a complaint with the Philippine National Labor Relations Commission and sought legal counsel from an organization called the Women's Legal Bureau. A network composed of thirteen lesbian and women's groups in the Philippines formed Advocates for Lesbian Rights (ALERT) to support Beth and Vangie's case against their former employer. The Fund, established in San Francisco, opened chapters in other cities in order to garner U.S. support for Beth and Vangie in the form of money, petitions, letters of protest, and publicity. By June 1995, the Fund had produced a newsletter, *Breakout*, published an article featuring a Fund activist in a local lesbian newspaper, and collected a sizable sum of money. The Fund appealed to a collective sense of outrage and indignation at the unfair treatment of our two "sisters" in the Philippines.

Beth and Vangie's new relationship had become known among their twelve coworkers through a breach of confidence. Intra-office gossip eventually cost them their jobs and their privacy. Their employer, the Balay Rehabilitation Center, made the following accusations, citing them as reasons for the firing: (1) for Vangie this was an extramarital affair, (2) Beth and Vangie had "flaunted" the affair in the office, and (3) Beth and Vangie had lobbied for support. Balay also dismissed the four board members who had abstained from the decision to fire the two women.

I was fortunate to attend a benefit party for the Fund on one evening that summer.... At several points during the house party, I became concerned with the way the Fund was positioning itself vis-à-vis Beth and Vangie and, by extension, vis-à-vis lesbian rights in the Philippines (let alone the rest of Asia).[5]

The primary purpose of the party was to collect money. People were invited to donate anywhere from $6 to $50 at the door. Food was free, but soda, beer, and wine were sold at a makeshift bar at the back of the patio. The atmosphere was congenial, and I think most of us were happy to be contributing to a worthy cause. When the night finally turned cold, we congregated inside the house, and the Fund members presented the story of Beth and Vangie. The story was punctuated by quotations from a letter written by Balay's director, Flora Arellano, to a San Francisco human rights commissioner named Jeannette Lazam. The letter seemed full of half-baked excuses for institutionalized homophobia....

... The way we had jumped scale from the relatively small personal interactions among the Balay staff to the international correspondence between Arellano and Lazam to the organizational efforts of the Fund to protect "lesbian rights in Asia" made me nervous. I felt that we (as supporters of the Fund, San Francisco's Filipino dyke community, and possibly even all queer-friendly Americans) had endowed ourselves with all the powers of self-actualization and enlightenment that traditionally have been associated with modernity and Western civilization.

Worsening my fears about the missionary zeal I thought I glimpsed that evening, a friend paraphrased for me a comment that she had overheard during the party: "If worse comes to worst, we'll just bring Beth and Vangie here." I'm not sure whether "here" meant the apartment, the city, or the country. But, in any case, the words encapsulated in my mind the fantasy of "home" as a safe haven for lesbians. It was a loaded statement, full of misleading implications. It was as if we could build our community simply by kidnaping and bringing "home" oppressed queers from all over the world.

The idea of bringing Beth and Vangie here might have been only a silly fantasy in the heart of one overly zealous activist. The fantasy is interesting, though, because of what I see as its colonial impulse: the desire to extend to Beth and Vangie all the freedoms and the luxuries we are thought to enjoy as lesbians in the United States.[6] I wondered to myself, with some sarcasm, *Could we be assuming that every lesbian in the Philippines wants a chance to be out in the Mission[7] and to be free to eat hippie-style tofu, fly a rainbow flag, wear freedom rings, and march under an "international" banner every year at the Gay Parade?*

Lost in the zealousness is a sense of community participation and struggle. What makes living in the Mission and marching at the Gay Parade so thrilling is not (I hope) the opportunity to buy more queer paraphernalia. I suspect that what makes it possible, even for a moment, to fantasize about queer life in the United States is that there are debates and discussions among lesbians and gay men that allow us to build a sense of shared purpose. When it is good (for example, when our daily lives are unencumbered by stereotypes and hostility), it can be really good. When it is bad (for example, when someone gets fired or loses custody of his or her kids), it can be made better by the efforts of people who come together to fight for recognition. For me, what makes "home" a desirable metaphor is the utopian prospect of building a community. Such interaction always involved a bit of insecurity and uncertainty. That, to me, is the joy of queer social life.

Truly, I do not know where in the world Beth and Vangie would be the happiest. Perhaps no place would be absolutely wonderful—or absolutely bad. But I would have been happier at the Fund benefit if we had engaged in a more thoughtful group discussion about home, family, homophobia, and colonialism. That night, I was concerned about the implication that our sense of lesbian freedom is universal. I do not want to be implicated in what seems a condescending gesture of showing lesbians in the Philippines the "true" path to freedom. This is a gesture I have associated with those U.S. feminists who reinscribe colonialist relations by subordinating the experience of Filipina feminists to the rubric of Third World feminism, thereby preserving the evidently neutral territory of feminism for themselves.

In some respects, the effort to support Beth and Vangie meshes curiously with the political trajectory of the Filipino colonial subject. In this trajectory, the Philippines is our first home, our starting point—but America is our final destination. The margin and the center are in this way clearly demarcated. By viewing Asia as the site of a denial of lesbian rights and America as the site of their defense and assertion, the Fund organizers verged dangerously close to reproducing a colonial myth. Coming out as coming home to the United States would be a sapphic twist on that myth.

Experience

> *growing up / for a long time / lost childhood*
> *we began writing in secret*
> *when confession, communion, confirmation,*
> *confession*
> *taught us to lie*
> > —*Elsa Rediva E'Der, "La Puente"*

Just the other day, a young Filipino American man invited me to contribute to an anthology on Filipino American politics. He explained that he and his colleagues have become frustrated with the lack of Filipino American voices in public life and public discourse, an omission that seems particularly egregious given the relative size of the Filipino population in the United States (in 1990 we were the second largest Asian American group). He and I chatted briefly on the phone about the kinds of issues he would like to see covered in the book. Then he said (and I paraphrase), "And, if I'm not mistaken, you're a lesbian, right? Because right now, we don't have anyone writing about that." There was something so final in his designation of me that I was caught off guard. I thought to myself, *He's right, isn't he? What kind of lesbian am I, anyway? Am I the kind of lesbian he means?*

In retrospect, I take no offense at his comment, which I see as an honest invitation to talk about what it means to be a lesbian, a Filipina American lesbian, an activist, and so on. But there is an implication in the question "You *are* a lesbian, right?" that being a lesbian (whatever was meant by that) commands an authenticity of experience—not just any experience, but one that is, from a heterosexual perspective, a marginalized and mysterious experience. By answering, "Yes" to his question, I would be asserting myself, making myself known, validating the life I have so far lived. By answering, "No," I would be disavowing a category called "the lesbian experience." In the end, no matter how I answered the question, something would be deeply wrong.

The appeal to an authentic experience is one way that Asian American lesbians and gay men confer upon ourselves the power of knowledge. Jeffrey Escoffier notes in his essay "Community and Academic Intellectuals: The Contest for Cultural Authority in Identity Politics" that knowledge, whether based in community or in academia, helps to legitimate certain representations and interpretations of political and social life. The knowledge we gain by experiencing queer Asian American community life is devalued in the public sphere, a sphere where Asian Americans are either gangsters or businessmen, hustlers or whores, and none of them is in control of his or her own sexuality. For this reason, acknowledging our experiences in terms of our sexuality is a central part of our community-building processes.

At the same time, however, appealing to an authentic experience can make a misleading claim to truth. Feminist historian Joan W. Scott explores this problem in her essay "The Evidence of Experience." She points out that in seeking to give voice to a silenced category of people, we may fail to reveal the reasons for that silencing in the first place. As she puts it, "The evidence of experience then becomes evidence for the fact of difference, rather than a way of exploring how difference is established, how it operates, how and in what ways it constitutes subjects who see and act in the world" (399–400).

I decided not to contribute to the anthology on Filipino American politics, mostly because I am still thinking through my position with regard to Filipino American studies and, more generally, with regard to the Filipino American community. Still, I worry that my contribution to the book could have served as a "lesbian fact" in a larger collection of "facts" about Filipino American life. In that case, nothing about the points of view of the three editors (who are all Filipino American men) would have needed further interrogation: every perspective would have been construed to have an equally objective basis. The truth is that including my voice (or the voice of any other writer with a claim to the lesbian experience) inadvertently reveals that all perspectives are not given equal footing. But by adding a voice from the margins, what never gets air time is the social process by which certain categories (for example, Filipino American life) are assumed to be "central" while others (for example, Filipino American *lesbian* life) are located "naturally" on the margins.[8]

In using this example to launch my criticism of the appeal to an authentic experience, I should be clear: the broadening of perspective, even one based on the "evidence of experience," is not a worthless endeavor. But I think, along the lines presented by Scott, that incorporating a marginalized perspective in a larger work that does not ask *why certain perspectives are marginalized to begin with* is not sufficient. In my mind, this approach—and I am not assuming that the anthology in my example will inevitably exemplify it—lends itself to cooptation by the status quo.

Ironically, by speaking up, we can marginalize ourselves. The danger of the appeal to authenticity is that even when individuals who feel marginalized shape the agenda, the idea of a center—whether out there or in here—can come alive....

The problem of authenticity arises whenever some dimension of experience is left out despite a concerted effort to include everyone.[9] In the end, no matter how inclusive we try to be—as editors of collections or as activists in social movements—at some point the line we draw must be exclusive of someone, because it is not possible to anticipate the infinite variety of human experiences or the social and historical circumstances that surround us. I see two ways around this problem. The first is simply to acknowledge the lines that we draw. The second calls for deeper transformation, a world without lines. I would bet that in practice we will—and must—draw some lines. But I hope that we can also imagine a more ideal world, where those lines won't matter. That image should remind us that our work—building a sense of collectivity, moving toward justice—is never really done.

Community

> We are gay and straight and bisexual, older and younger, differently able and temporarily able-bodied; and we share an unquenched hope for the survival and sanity of the human community. Believing that no single people can survive being only for itself, we want a base from which to act on our hope.
>
> —Adrienne Rich, "If Not with Others, How?"

How we, as gay men and lesbians who trace our roots to Asia, think about "home" and "experience" matters most when we try to designate the boundaries of our queer Asian American community.[10] Asian American history makes efforts toward queer community—especially those that depend on a notion of home and family—particularly vexing. Asian Americans often have been treated as perpetual foreigners, seen as outsiders no matter how many generations ago the first immigrants arrived. That is why the distinction between Asian and Asian American is often lost on non-Asian Americans. Over the past century, Asian American community building has been shaped by state-regulated labor markets, exclusion acts, antimiscegenation policies, internment, and resettlement.[11] When queer Asian America places home, the family, and community into question, it does so against a historical backdrop that is already littered with such questions.

As if blind to these questions, queer Asian Americans often draw lines in the sand, by referring to "original" places or to "real" feelings in an effort to fix the location, shape, and meaning of community—and our own positions within it. Such references often seem urgent, inescapable, and even desirable; they signal who is "in" (and who is not) and provide guidelines for community building (including the creation of community institutions, the planning and carrying out of community events, outreach to newcomers, and joint activities with other community groups). In my view, the problem of authenticity arises when community-building efforts among Asian American lesbians and gay men treat "home" or "experience" as preordained facts and thus mimic the exclusive and hierarchical frameworks that make efforts toward visibility and recognition necessary in the first place....

The issue of participation in LAAPIS events by transgendered people (TGs) is another example of drawing lines in the sand. Who gets included in community often depends on who is there to advocate for themselves. In O Môi [a Santa Ana–based Vietnamese American organization], TGs participated right from the start, not out of an abstract principle about inclusion but because people were there to fight for themselves. When O Môi members (mostly lesbians and bisexual women) got together to hash out what they had in common besides being Vietnamese, one person suggested, "It's about feeling like a woman." So when another person declared, "But I don't feel like a woman," the problem of authenticity (to use my terminology) reared its ugly head. After all, what on earth does it mean to "feel like" a woman?

The exclusion of TGs from queer Asian America—whether by intent or by oversight—indicates to me that the body is not necessarily the site of home. "Feeling like" a woman or a man is a good way to put it, because the phrase suggests that the appeal to an authentic experience cannot depend on biological categories (understood by most people as "natural" ones) but, instead, more aptly refers to a subjective expression of desire.[12] Bringing TGs into the picture not only problematizes gender and sexuality; it points to ways that gender and sexuality have become naturalized, almost normalized, dimensions of social life, even in queer Asian America.

When I realized how complicated gender and sexual identity are, I wondered for a moment why I bother to call myself a lesbian. Didn't I mean to be more transgressive—perhaps a bit more queer? It seems that lesbian and gay organizing is just the tip of a very huge iceberg. If queer Asian America is interested in challenging the confining categories of gender and sexuality imposed upon us by the status quo, then queer Asian American activists are going to have to do something about the ways that those categories are enforced on us and on other people. I think we must continually reconsider the bases upon which we include some people—but not others—in our community and cultural work.

In the end, O Môi members decided that their commonality lies in "object choice" (that is, a love for women). It's not always a satisfying choice: when butch lesbians face off against female-to-male TGs, who gets called "sir" can be a seriously touchy issue. Unlike O Môi, LAAPIS has come up with a different proviso regarding transgendered people. They want to include only male-to-female TGs, their argument being that the organization is for women or, presumably, people who want to live as women.

Either way, a can of worms has been opened. Evidently, every solution raises ambivalent feelings, even among the TG community. I suspect there is no correct solution, and my intention here is not to offer one. Instead, I want to caution against belittling the issues of inclusion and exclusion—for example, treating transgenderism as a personal predicament only. If queer Asian America has learned nothing else, it has learned that the challenge to sexual normativity is always more than a personal dilemma. The norm of heterosexuality is a social fact that guides hierarchical social practice. Thus, Lorber warns, "Even if some future utopia were not gendered, sexuality is likely to be organized with norms of appropriateness, if not with moral strictures, in the service of community interests.... Whoever has the power in the community will be influential in determining what sexualities will have moral hegemony" (79).

Enacting Justice in Queer Asian America

We who occupy the interstices—whose very lives contain disparate selves—are, of necessity, at home among groups that know little of each other.... We have a deep hunger for a place in which we can be, at one and the same time, whole and part of something larger than ourselves. Our knowledge and desire may at times bring us to action.

—*Yoko Yoshikawa, "The Heat Is On* Miss Saigon *Coalition"*

Community building in queer Asian America requires vigilance regarding the notions of home and experience, especially regarding the ways these concepts may close off further discussion about who's in and who's out of the community and why. (This is not to imply that there is a model leader or organization that can by pass the problem of authenticity to bring all of queer Asian America directly to a copacetic destination called "Justice.") The stories I tell in this essay put forth instances in which that discussion should be encouraged, because—although tireless efforts have produced important results (events held, money raised, networks established, anthologies published)—the truth claims that are inherent in the various references to home and experience may pose stumbling blocks for future community building.

Perhaps there is no way to avoid the problem of authenticity completely as I have laid it out here. Collective action inevitably pushes toward exclusive boundaries and universalizing gestures.[13] The purpose of this essay has been to suggest the ways that those boundaries might be redrawn or those gestures made less universal. I hope to ameliorate the problem, not to circumvent it.

I will not abandon the project of enacting justice. Enacting justice in queer Asian America involves a rearticulation of the utopian possibilities of community building against the disenabling impulses of the dominant social order. Too many scholars have given up on this project, preferring instead to "theorize the subject" by detailing the myriad ways in which we might be thought to exist. Some of those theories are compelling, but some of them seem pointless and detached. Worse, some blur important distinctions between action and negotiation, inclusion and representation, power and powerlessness. Too many activists have given up as well, focusing instead on individual expression and narcissistic explorations of victimization, leaving justice and other lofty ideals to the scholars.

Enacting justice in queer Asian America is a particularly vexing task, because precisely at the moment in which we wish to speak, the problem of authenticity prevents us from doing so. We resist labeling; yet without a label, how can our views and perspectives be given a meaningful context? Ironically, we need to fix ourselves as a stable (read: knowable, nameable, solid) community in order to point a finger at the practices and ideas that deny us that stability from the start.

Like many others who refuse the privileges associated with heterosexuality, queer Asian Americans come out and go home only at the risk of great loss, sometimes terror, even death. Gestures toward home and family seem both necessary and impossible: necessary for a sense of completion, impossible because family requires heteronormativity. Yet, because no closet can be home, there is no choice for queer Asian America but to push toward the other side. Much is at stake in building a queer Asian American community. Precisely because of the high price at which queer Asian America purchases a sense of home, our motivation toward building community and enacting justice must be even stronger.

Notes

1. When my grandmother Ramona Aguilar recently passed away in the Philippines, I decided to dedicate this essay in memory of her. I often wonder what trail I might trace back to her.

2. I direct my discussion of home primarily toward Asian American studies, where the questions of home and family, home and colonialism are already framed in terms of race and nation. If I were to direct the discussion toward queer studies, I would want to anticipate the issue of Asian American specificity, by making reference to home not as the originating point for our "difference" (from a white norm) but as a place from which Asian Americans are always already negated, made invisible, excluded. But that is a topic for another essay.

3. AMALGM stands for the Alliance of Massachusetts Asian Lesbians and Gay Men. The Boston-based group is currently called QAPA, the Queer Asian Pacific Alliance.

4. Professor Bob Lee of Brown University introduced me to this concept, which he used to describe the potential dissonance between historiography and history as it is "actually" lived.

5. I do not intend to diminish the importance of the support for Beth and Vangie or to portray my views of the campaign as superior to or more informed than those held by anyone else. This narrative is intended only to illustrate how the idea of "home" can be evoked in organizing for social change.

6. This is not to deny the observation, made by several Fund members that night, that Asian American lesbians are subject to racism. Still, the fantasy implies that being queer in the racist "Amerika" is still better than being queer in the Philippines.

7. The Mission is a predominantly Latino neighborhood in San Francisco, where quite a few lesbians and gay men of color live.

8. Some activists still talk about the "double" and "triple" oppression of women and lesbians of color. The idea that each label adds another layer of oppression sometimes unintentionally reinforces white heterosexuality as the norm and everything else as marginal. I hope that queer Asian American activists reevaluate the idea of layers of oppression, perhaps starting at "home."

9. In fact, transgendered people (including cross-dressers and transsexuals) are not included, a matter that I address herein.

10. I am grateful to Susette Min for helping me to tie this section into the rest of the chapter.

11. For an in-depth discussion of the legal history behind Asian immigration, see Hing. For insights into labor migration and its effects on community building, see Chan.

12. In her book, *Paradoxes of Gender*, feminist sociologist Judith Lorber points out that the male-female gender dichotomy is so entrenched in our political, legal, and ideological frameworks that we can hardly escape it, even when reality begs to differ. In a chapter provocatively entitled, "How many Opposites? Gendered Sexuality," Lorber explores the multiple statuses we assign to people on the basis of anatomical features and gendered social roles. On the basis of genitalia alone, there are five—not two—sexes: unambiguously male, unambiguously female, hermaphrodite, male-to-female transsexual, and female-to-male transsexual. Lorber sees (at least) three sexual orientations: heterosexual, homosexual, and bisexual. And she sees many more categories of gender displays, emotional bonds, group affiliations, and sexual practices.

13. I thank Joshua Gamson for his comments on this point.

SECTION III
THEORIZING FEMINIST AGENCY
AND POLITICS

INTRODUCTION

Section II discusses social differences in women's lives and experiences, especially those shaped by race, class, nation, and sexual orientation. The variety of experiences and the complexity of intersecting and overlapping forms of oppression it highlights make it difficult to see how feminist theories can proceed in a way that honors the diversity of women's experiences and yet informs an effective feminist politics. Moreover, the strands of conversation in section II insist that feminist theories must come to grips with the ways in which gender identity/oppression intersects, overlaps, imbricates, or otherwise shapes and is shaped by other forms of identity/oppression. In theorizing these interconnections, several questions emerge. What are the appropriate boundaries of feminist theorizing and feminist politics? How should feminist theories expand beyond a narrow focus on gender? Can we turn the insights from the complex and diverse experiences of women into effective knowledge? Can feminists construct a reliable basis for analyzing social systems and for articulating strategies for change that will improve women's lives?

The readings in this section are drawn from two major currents that emerged within feminist theory in the 1980s and 1990s—feminist standpoint theories and poststructural feminist theories—each of which offers answers to the preceding questions. Standpoint theory was developed primarily by social scientists, especially sociologists and political theorists. It extends some of the early insights about consciousness that emerged from Marxist/socialist feminist theories and the wider conversations about identity politics presented in section II. It endeavors to develop a feminist epistemology, or theory of knowledge, that delineates a method for constructing effective knowledge from the insights of women's experiences. Poststructural feminist theory was developed primarily among literary critics and philosophers, as well as by film and cultural studies scholars. It builds on insights about sexual difference and language from psychoanalysis and literary theory, and has been concerned with understanding processes that construct public knowledge and personal identity. It focuses on the ways in which power relationships shape the social construction of the category women, women's experiences, and reality itself (Hesford and Kozol 2001). These two currents of theory have had much to say to each other. To understand fully the conversations between these two schools of thought, it is necessary to take a few steps back and investigate the key principles of each theory. The readings have been selected to illustrate those key principles, to provide examples of application of the theories, as well as to illuminate the debates about the multiplicity of women's perspectives in local U.S. and in global contexts.

In the first reading, Nancy Hartsock defines the elements of a standpoint and delineates the ground for her claim that a feminist standpoint can be constructed from careful analysis of women's experiences. In many ways, Hartsock's essay is a response to Heidi Hartmann's earlier call to apply Marxist methods to feminist ends. The notion of a standpoint derives from Marx's view of human consciousness, which emerges in interactions with nature and other humans as we work to make our lives. These interactions, especially the work we do, shape us and our knowledge. They also set limits on what we can know. Following the insights of Hartmann, among others, Hartsock argues that the sexual division of labor, whereby women are responsible for the activities involved in reproducing children and society, provides the ground for a feminist standpoint: A critical perspective on society from which competent knowledge of women's lives can be developed to inform effective strategies for change. A standpoint is political because, Hartsock argues, differences in perspectives among social groups are shaped by power relations between those groups. Thus the sexual division of labor not only sets up differences between men and women, but also domination of women by men.

Following Marx's theory, Hartsock argues that knowledge produced from the dominant group's perspective distorts reality. As she points out, we can see this in contemporary society in that the accumulation of wealth through the production and exchange of goods and services is the most important activity, if measured by the economic rewards given to those who engage in that activity, if measured by the attention given to the activity within the society, or if measured by the social resources dedicated to the activity by the government. However, the real point of production and exchange is not profit; it is meeting human needs through the use of those goods. The point of making and exchanging things should be to allow us to survive. But in capitalism, the real relationships between people are distorted and inverted so the exchange of commodities is more important than meeting human needs. And human needs get met accidentally, if at all, as a by-product of business activity. Part of the power of dominance is the ability to make your perspective true, to set the rules of the game to your advantage. Thus, even if capitalism distorts human relationships, we all must engage in (or resist) economic activities set up by the rules of capitalist exchange. For instance, our society devalues the work that caregivers, primarily women, do while engaging in raising children, easing the burdens of sickness and old age, and ensuring that workers, usually men, are fed, clothed, and rested so they can return to the business of business each morning. This devaluation is clear in the exclusion of these activities from measures of economic productivity. It does not count as work if you perform it for family members and are not paid a wage. When we do hire people to complete this work, we pay them very low wages in comparison to jobs that manage capital accumulation and exchange.

Given this distorted view of social relationships, subordinated social groups must struggle to see their situation clearly. On the surface, the dominant group's description of the way the world works appears to be sensible and true. It takes concerted effort to get below the surface reality because it requires one to think against the grain of dominant culture. Subordinated group members caught in the contradictions between the rules of the dominant culture and the realities of human need are in a unique position to develop knowledge from the perspective of underlying domination. This insight can become the ground for a critique of dominant culture that points to effective strategies for change. For instance, by living the contradictions involved in doing the crucial work of caregiving in a society that does not value caregiving, Hartsock asserts, women are in a position to see that dominant culture distorts human relationships. The clearest example of this distortion, for Hartsock, is the fact that Western culture valorizes risking death in battle and disparages giving life through birth and caretaking activities. While Hartsock notes that differences among women shape their experiences, she nonetheless argues that the sexual division of labor constructs a singular unique perspective on society from which feminists can effectively challenge male domination.

Patricia Hill Collins also articulates the grounds for a feminist standpoint, in this case a black feminist standpoint, based on the insights of feminism and African American intellectual traditions. As with all standpoint theories, Hill Collins posits that subordinated social groups can have a unique insight into the power relations which subordinate them. For Hill Collins, this position is that of the outsider-within. However, there is an important difference between Hill Collins, Hartsock, and many other theorists in the later twentieth century who argue that the oppressed have a better view on reality (Harding 1986; Smith 1987). A central claim made by standpoint and related theories is that there are certain positions in society from which it is possible, with effort, to see clearly, and others from which clear vision is not possible. This claim to superior vision rests on the fact that subordinated groups not only see the world from their location, which the dominant culture ignores, but they also have to know the dominant culture in order to survive in it. In rejecting either/or thinking on principle, Hill Collins also rejects the claim that any one social group has the best vantage point from which to see the truth about social relations.

Hill Collins sees oppression as a "matrix of domination," consisting of an interlocking web of oppression that works simultaneously in the same social structures. Sometimes they intersect, sometimes they do not. Sometimes they operate in concert and sometimes in conflict. And these interconnections grow, shift, and attenuate over time. Through this concept she posits a very dynamic system of oppressions and with it a vigorous heterogeneity of perspectives. Individual experiences of oppression vary depending on where one falls within the historical web of dominations consisting of, at the least, race, (post)colonialism, class, gender, and sexuality. These dimensions of a woman's life intertwine in ways that affect her life opportunities, her options for resistance, and so on. They are twisted together in ways that are difficult, or impossible, to untangle. Within this matrix of domination, individuals' lives can be constituted of moments of privilege and moments of oppression simultaneously. People can be both privileged and oppressed, at different times, different contexts, and in relation to different people.

Given this complexity, Hill Collins concludes that everybody has a partial view, nobody has the place to stand and see everything clearly. But a partial view of power can still produce valuable, if not complete or perfect, knowledge. For Hill

Collins, some locations make it easier to produce accurate knowledge within these interlocking systems, and from some locations one has to struggle harder to understand it (Smith 1987). So that men have to struggle harder than women to see and understand sexism, white people have to struggle harder than people of color to see and understand racism. And residents of the North have to struggle harder than residents of the South to understand the impact of (post)colonialism. But she recognizes that expressing a collective body of knowledge in a subordinated group's own interests is extremely difficult, precisely because the dominant groups have vested interests in subjugating that knowledge. Thus Hill Collins's black feminist standpoint is constituted in and through the politics of continuous interplay between activism and suppression.

Uma Narayan's essay challenges key components of Western feminist standpoints, arguing that they have built a feminist epistemology that is "noncontextual and nonpragmatic." In so doing, Western feminist epistemologies can "convert important feminist insights...into feminist epistemological dogmas." Using her perspective as a South Asian feminist, she cites several limitations of existing standpoint theories. Her first criticism is that Western feminist standpoints run the risk of romanticizing women's experiences. Western women, living in cultures that devalue qualities associated with women, often suggest that one way to change the status of women is to re-value their contributions to society. This is not necessarily a useful strategy in cultures dominated by a strong "traditional discourse" in which women's contributions are valued, as long as women "stay in their place." She notes in such cases, feminist efforts to revalue women's contributions may be "drowned out by the louder and more powerful voices of traditional discourse" which will reaffirm women's prescribed place. Also there is a tension for feminists in the South between wanting to affirm the value of their culture in the face of Western colonial prejudices and wanting to critique traditions that oppress women. As she notes, liberalism is the politics of colonialism. So from a non-Western perspective, liberalism is not the politics of freedom, it's the politics of oppression. Yet, at the same time, the liberal concept of individual rights is vital for women's resistance to systems of domination. Without a notion of individual rights, it is difficult to argue effectively for women's rights to bodily integrity or autonomy. But it is difficult for non-Western feminists to extract that notion of rights from this history of liberal colonial oppression. For Narayan, the problem is that Western feminist standpoints, because they are noncontextual, gloss over these points of tension. And in so doing, Western feminist standpoints assume a solid basis for coalition among women's groups, where Narayan sees a more fluid and highly charged terrain for global feminist politics (see also Spivak 1988).

Narayan's final challenge is to the tendency of Western–feminist standpoint theorists to valorize the situation of contradiction. Hartsock identifies the contradictory demands in women's lives between the public and the private sphere as providing the possibility of liberatory thought. Likewise, Hill Collins, as noted above, values the position of the outsider-within as empowering resistance. To the contrary Narayan points out, for individuals who must "straddl[e] a multiplicity of contexts," there are many ways that one can cope with contradiction. One can dichotomize one's life and live by the different rules in different contexts. One can alienate oneself from the knowledge of one of the contexts. Or, sometimes, one can simply be overwhelmed by contradictions. In such cases, contradiction does not provide a place for generating liberatory philosophy but instead can be very disempowering.

The Maxine Baca Zinn and Bonnie Thornton Dill essay and that by Cheshire Calhoun provide examples of feminist theorizing from specific perspectives within intersections of the matrix of domination. Building on the work of theorists such as Hill Collins and Chela Sandoval, Maxine Baca Zinn and Bonnie Thornton Dill theorize the intersections of race, ethnic, and gender dominations, laying out principles for effective theory building at those intersections. They articulate several key principles for a multiracial feminism. "Multiracial feminism," they argue, "asserts that gender is constructed by a range of interlocking inequalities." It stresses the "intersectional nature" of all social "hierarchies," as well as the "relational nature of domination and subordination." Multiracial feminism focuses analysis on the "interplay of social structure and women's agency." Together these principles enable multiracial feminism to resolve some of the central problems involved in theorizing difference in women's experiences and identities.

Cheshire Calhoun examines the points of conflict and coincidence within lesbian and feminist theory in the United States since the 1970s. As Heidi Hartmann did with Marxism and feminism, she asks whether the coupling of feminist and lesbian theory has produced an effective basis for, in this case, lesbian politics. Her answer suggests that lesbian theory has been dominated by feminist theory, which has limited our understanding of the institution of heterosexuality. At the same time, articulating the gender-based differences lesbians have from gay men, she argues that queer theory[1] as well has not served lesbian politics effectively. She then proceeds to explore where lesbian, queer, and feminist politics diverge. In pulling apart the sex/gender system into its gender and sexual currents, she provides a thoughtful history of key moments in U.S. lesbian-feminist theory building.

Poststructural feminisms approach the dilemmas of feminist theorizing from a different perspective. Poststructuralist feminisms first emerged within intellectual circles in France. Reworking semiotic theories of language and psychoanalytic theories of subjectivity, they have been most concerned with theorizing the ways in which cultural discourses and social practices shape forms of social organization, knowledge, meaning, subjectivity, and identity.[2] While the details of poststructural theories are beyond the scope of this book, some discussion of key elements is crucial for understanding feminist uses of these theories. In poststructural theory, social reality and human subjectivity are constituted in and through language. What we know about the world and ourselves is defined and contested in the language of historically specific discourses. "Discourses...are ways of constituting knowledge, together with, the social practices, forms of subjectivity, and power relations which inhere in such knowledges" (Weedon 1997: 105). We can never make sense of the real world outside of these discursive fields. But we can analyze the processes by which order and coherence are imposed on the world through the discourses and practices that make up knowledge of the real and of the subjective. Poststructural theories provide tools for those analyses.

Poststructural theories of subjectivity are distinctive in viewing subjectivity as an ongoing process. In much of Western thought, humans are represented as possessing some unique essence (human nature, reason, race, sex) that is inherent in the individual, that exists prior to and outside of the individuals' interaction with society. In contrast, poststructural theories assert that one's subjectivity, one's sense of self, is constituted in the same process through which one learns language, and it is reconstituted each time one thinks, speaks, or acts. For many poststructural feminist theories, the workings of the language and the structure of one's subjectivity are constructed through psychoanalytic processes in which the structure of sexual difference as a binary opposition between masculinity and femininity is central. Thus, gender differences are intricately intertwined with the construction of subjectivity, which is one key reason poststructural theories have been of continuing interest to feminist theorists.

The way in which language works to construct identity, however, involves a fundamental misrecognition of oneself as the author of meaning. This misrecognition derives from the belief that language reflects and expresses the meaning inherent in the world. We think of ourselves as generating meaning through our language use, rather than language generating us. Instead, poststructuralists argue, we are using a symbol system, the rules of which we have been learning since we were young, and the meaning of words and gestures are already defined in discourses before we give them voice. When we are speaking, we are speaking the lines from scripts written for subjects of the discourse we enunciate. Discourses are continually competing for individuals to take up their "I" positions, to become the subject agent of those discourses. When we say, for instance, "I am a feminist," there are certain topics, issues, postures that we have to situate ourselves in relation to, such as: feminism/femininity, feelings about men, and sexual orientation. When we say I am a woman of color, there are certain topics, issues, postures that we have to situate ourselves in relationship to: feminism/femininity, race/racism, feelings about men of our culture and feelings about sexism in our culture. When we say we are a Third World woman, we must situate ourselves in relationship to Western feminism/femininity, colonialism, and feelings about sexism in our culture. These issues are invoked by the discursive struggle to set "the rules" about what it means to be a feminist in different locations. Joan Scott details the meanings of some of these rules through an analysis of the competing meanings of equality and difference as they were deployed in U.S. Federal Court in a 1981 sex discrimination case. In the process, she provides definitions of key poststructural concepts, language, discourse, difference, and deconstruction.

As Scott's essay demonstrates, there is not a singular discourse of gender or sexuality. There are multiple and competing discourses. Identity, for poststructuralists, becomes a site of continual contest among discourses for allegiance of its subjects. What it means to be a woman is the site of continual struggle over the meanings of femininity. "Everything we do signifies compliance or resistance to dominant norms of what it is to be a woman,"(Weedon 1997: 83). The construction of the meanings of femininity is not just a language game. It involves a whole array of speaking parts, a whole range of obligatory gestures, a whole set of appropriate practices. Riot grrl, soccer mom, teenage mother, feminist, professional woman, all of these have outfits and activities that go with them. That is what Barbie dolls are all about in dominant culture discourses of femininity: get the female body (white, thin, rich, and blond) in the right outfits for the right activities. Power operates within these discourses to set the limits of what women can be and the playing field is not level. Poststructualists explode our certainty that we control the meaning of what we say and that our meaning is transparent. For poststructuralists one never controls those meanings, at least not for very long. And any temporarily fixed meaning involves "both interests and questions of power," (Weedon 1997: 171). The subject positions created in discourses then are always "implicated in power relations," (Weedon 1997: 174). Power relations, not as simple binary oppositions between those who have it and those who do not, but as complex relational fields "exercised within discourses in the ways in which the constitute and govern individual subjects," (Weedon 1997: 110).

But while discourses attempt to construct subjectivity, most individuals experience that subjectivity as obvious, as their own, not as an effect of discourse.[3] Norma Alarcon, provides compelling evidence of this process in her essay on the classic feminist theory text, *This Bridge Called My Back*. Alarcon examines the process of identification that occurred for readers of the book. Women of color read the book as speaking to them, speaking for them, articulating things they hadn't yet figured out how to say. In the process of reading, as Alarcon explicates, individuals come to identify with a subject position, political category, and group based on seeing themselves in meaningful ways as like the voices in the book. This is an example of how identity politics work. From that sense of sameness, individuals can build a sense of community and build a sense of shared experience around that axis of identity. At the same time, she argues *This Bridge Called My Back* constructs a new discursive formation, "women of color." This is a subject position that does not exist prior to the publication of this book. Alarcon, reiterating criticisms made by many feminist theorists of color, identifies how by privileging gender above all else, Anglo feminism eliminates the possibility of dealing with differential power relations among women. This exclusion provides the ground for the construction of the category of women of color. It constructs a unity of women of different races, ethnicities, cultures, nations, and language groups based on their identity as members of races, cultures, and language groups subordinated by Anglo culture.

Because they insist that no category—women, experience, the personal—can be taken for granted, poststructural theories have been useful for feminist theorists, both North and South. In particular, the tools of these theories have helped to crack open the normative Western feminist subject on one hand and Orientalist view of women in the South on the other.[4] Lata Mani's analysis of the different ways that her study of the *sati* (ritual widow death in Indian culture) has been received in Britain, the United States, and in India demonstrates the complexity of gender politics in the South. Her analysis examines one specific historical case of a colonial discourse where the status of women became a marker of the level of civilization. This discourse constructed multiple knowledges about women and gender that have persisted through time in different locations. Mani takes up the topic of *sati* in part because of the ethnocentric gestures by which the topic has been addressed in the North. Colonial discourses constructed the practice of *sati* for Westerners. In other words, Northern feminists only know about *sati*, and other cultural practices that they have called gender atrocities, because debates about these practices help to legitimate colonial rule. At the same time, in India, Mani confronts arguments about the practice of sati that raise complex gender politics as well. Such arguments seem to hinge on problematic assumptions about women's agency, as if the matter can be settled by knowing the widow's intention. Mani argues that the challenge for Third World feminist scholars is to "straddle different temporalities of struggle." Narayan speaks to this tension when she talks about the desire both to delineate the suffering of women and yet to shield Indian culture from the nearly automatic (post)colonialist criticisms.

Carolyn Sorisio, a third wave feminist theorist, investigates the representation of feminism in the U.S. media in the 1990s. In order to illuminate the discursive construction of feminists as ideologues of women's victimization, she offers close readings of books by Katie Rophie, Naomi Wolf, and Camille Paglia. She also examines the reception of their work in the mainstream U.S. media, which quickly took up the charge of that feminism in the 1980s became a kind of "victim feminism." This label referred to the prominence of antisexual violence and antipornography activism in women's movements. Sorisio locates feminist theoretical debates about pornography, male sexual violence, and female sexuality within the social-historical context of the United States in the 1980s. In this analysis, she wields the tools of poststructualist feminist literary theory to interrogate the discursive maneuvers of both feminist theory and its popular critics. She concludes that the charge that victim feminism is harmful may be right, but not for the reasons the critics give. Instead, she suggests, the problem with the antimale violence movements is that they employed a rhetoric of sisterhood that absorbed other women's experiences into a universal category that did not fit those experiences.

Returning to de Beauvoir's observation that "one is not born, but becomes a woman," Judith Butler's piece offers a theory of gender construction through performative acts. That is, she argues, we are the gender we act as: We become the gender whose normative qualities we perform in and through our actions in daily life. "Social agents *constitute* social reality through language, gesture, and all manner of symbolic social sign[s]," (emphasis in original). But, Butler says, gender isn't a performance that an individual chooses to engage in. One's subjectivity, indeed one's body, is gendered through these performances, which are "compelled by social sanction and taboo." It is a fiction of liberal humanism that what one, an agent who exists prior to the performance, freely chooses to act in certain ways. "[G]ender is in no way a stable identity o[r] locus of agency from which various acts proceed; rather, it is an identity tenuously constituted in time—an identity instituted through a *stylized repetition of acts*," (emphasis in original). But gender also constitutes "an illusion" that we, audience and actor, believe to be real. Gender's construction is concealed by the fiction of its naturalness. Moreover, Butler asserts that gender is a function of the heterosexual social contract. Thus, gender is performed in the service "of the cultivation of bodies into discrete sexes with 'natural' appearances and 'natural' heterosexual dispositions." Gender performances produce and reproduce the fiction of two distinct and opposite sexes that "naturally" fit together to form the basic unit of society.

Butler wants to understand how this gendering process works at the level of the body in order to change gender performances and thus genders, sexes, and sexualities. "If the ground of gender identity is the stylized repetition of acts through time,...then the possibilities of gender transformation are to be found in the...possibility of a different sort of repeating, in the breaking or subversive repetition of that style." Drawing on the rich gay cultural tradition of camp, she particularly privileges those subversive performances that parody heterosexual normativity. Drag exposes the underlying contingency of the conventional gender norms enacted in the performance. Rather than expressing a natural essence, drag demonstrates that gender is constituted through those normative acts themselves.

The contentions between standpoint feminisms and poststructural feminisms revolve around the questions of power and agency. Poststructural feminisms critique the feminist epistemology constructed by standpoint theorists. In particular, poststructural feminisms question the transparency of women's experiences upon which standpoint theories seem to rely. From the point of view of poststructural theories, standpoint theories rest on the same reflective/expressive model of language that underlies liberal humanism, which feminists heavily criticize for excluding women. Standpoint theories, like liberal humanism, attempt to fix the truth of their insights with the guarantee that experience is a reliable source of knowledge about reality. They assume that an individual, with an already formed sense of identity, has the experience of oppression and, in reflecting on experience through talking with others, sees it clearly. However, as poststructural theory suggests, historically specific discourses within the cultural context, in which individuals narrate their experience, constitute what can be said. Thus, women's articulations of their experience are already implicated in conventional power relations embedded in the rules of narration. Poststructural feminist theorists argue that standpoint theorists have thus only revalued the discursive content of the category women, but they have not altered the power relations that continue to confine women to that category. Effective oppositional strategies must destabilize the operations of power, not just construct a new subject position from which those power relations can be exercised. Given the power relations that inhere in those narratives of experience, poststructural feminists wonder how those narratives can point to liberation (Stone-Mediatore 2000).

On the other hand, standpoint theorists, notably Nancy Hartsock, respond with their own critique of poststructural feminist theories, suggesting that they provide a poor basis for political resistance. They criticize poststructural theorists for proposing so contingent and contradictory a sense of subjectivity that they remove the ground for feminist agency. If individuals are merely the sites of power struggles among competing discourses, what agency is left to them to think of or engage in resistance? Thus they suggest that a poststructural theory that defines one's identity primarily as an artifact of dominant power relations exercised in discursive fields disempowers effective political struggle against dominant culture. Also, without some way to guarantee of the accuracy of knowledge, standpoint theorists wonder how we can distinguish between the merits of competing discourses about women. If subjects are the effects of discourse, is feminism just as good a discourse about women as any other discourse about women? Experience may well be contradictory, and changing, but standpoint theorists argue, it may be the best strategic basis upon which feminists can ground demands for autonomy and freedom for women. Also, standpoint theorists note, it is at exactly the moment in history when those silenced in much of Western thought give voice to their experiences that Western thought declares that experience is an unreliable source of knowledge. It is at the moment when subordinated social groups are demanding recognition of their self-articulated perspectives that doubt is cast on the status of the subject. Perhaps, then poststructuralist feminism also reproduces dominant operations of power (Hartsock 1990: 163–64).

Donna Haraway connects the strengths of standpoint theory with the insights of poststructural feminisms in her discussion of situated knowledge. She argues against the extremes of some social constructionists for whom "facts are part of the powerful art of rhetoric." She also argues against any superior vantage point from which to see everything clearly. Instead, reminding readers that vision is an embodied sense, she argues for an embodied, situated, and partial feminist knowledge. She posits "the joining of partial views and halting voices into a collective subject position that promises a vision . . . of living within limits and contradictions—views from somewhere." These views from somewhere, would trust the vantage points of the subjugated, but these vantage points must also be reexamined, decoded, and deconstructed. In an example of the analysis she theorizes, she calls into question the distinction of sex and gender that prevailed in much feminist theory until recently.

Haraway's argument reiterates a theme that reverberates across many of the readings in this section: Any adequate feminist theory must locate the specific social-historical context of its underlying assumptions. The last group of readings takes up the questions of how to locate one's analysis, how to negotiate differences within specific locations, and how feminist political activism, expanded beyond a narrow focus on gender, might be pursued. We end the anthology with readings that present models of negotiation across differences and of coalitions between women's groups that reside in diverse social positions because, in an era of ever-increasing globalization, they incorporate insights into productive ways to build effective feminist knowledge and alliances between women of the North and South (Taylor 1993). The insights in these readings provide guidance for the kind of global feminist activism Basu recommends in her essay in section I.

A vision of twenty-first century feminist politics based on coalitions was articulated by Bernice Johnson-Reagon in "Coalition Politics: Turning the Century," in 1983.[5] Speaking at a moment in the U.S. women's movement when fragmentation around identity categories dislocated the notion that there was a single unified women's movement, Johnson-Reagon challenged the notion that the movement must be based on unity. She argued instead for a vision of the women's movement as consisting of principled coalitions among identity-based groups. She insisted that effective politics emerge from coalitions based on shared issues and mutual respect for differences, rather than the creation of safe spaces based on common identity. Certainly, she argued we all need safety sometimes—to recuperate from the struggle, to heal from the wounds of oppression. And identity-based groups can provide such a safety zone. However, political struggle is never comfortable or safe. Women's groups must recognize this and purposefully decide when safety and when struggle are most needed, and build alliances accordingly. Chandra Talpade Mohanty contrasts Johnson-Reagon's vision of coalition with the vision of global sisterhood based on common identity as women offered by Robin Morgan, in her book, *Sisterhood Is Global.* Mohanty's reading of the text draws out the discursive practices by which Morgan constructs a common identity of women, based on the essential female experience of victimization by men. The global sisterhood Morgan constructs decontextualizes women's specific cultural historical experiences, and, Mohanty argues, in so doing it reaffirms the dominance of the normative feminist subject of women's movements in the North. In drawing out the limitations of the kind of unity Morgan premises for global sisterhood, Mohanty demonstrates how Johnson-Reagon's vision of coalition is a more effective metaphor and method for negotiating differences within any women's movement, local or global.

In recounting the shifting alliances that are possible among the different sites of power she encounters in traveling to and from the Bahamas, June Jordan's essay demonstrates the changing basis for common cause. She finds that the bases for common cause are not always the obvious ones. This meditation asks when various intersections of race, class, and gender experiences might facilitate or might hinder both identification with another person and collective action. Adrienne Rich's essay meditates on location and power as she struggles to situate herself in her thinking, her body, and in geography shaped by history and politics. Her efforts to locate herself and her local, specific, and limited experience as a white, Jewish, U.S. lesbian feminists are continually undercut by universalizing gestures in her writing. Even though she continually tries to interrupt them, these discursive gestures of dominance by which white Western women's experiences become the normative experience are almost automatic reflexes.

The last essay, by third-wave feminist, JeeYeun Lee, speaks in the voice of a new generation struggling with shifting identities. She sees the central tension of feminism as "an uneasy balancing act between the imperatives of outreach and inclusion on the one hand, and the risk of tokenism and further marginalization on the other. She speaks of the experience of unease in Women's Studies classrooms and in API[6] activist organizations. In her reflections on these experiences, her concerns about coalitional identities and the insecurity of home resonate with the same chords that Bernice Johnson-Reagon did in 1983. However, she ends with an observation which we find hopeful: The new generation of feminists starts with the realization that "Coming together and working together are by no means natural and easy." These tasks are and always will be complex and conditional, and that suggests possibility.

Notes

1. Queer refers to the space outside hetero-normativity. See footnote 2 in Gopinath herein.
2. The "Special Section on French Feminism," *Signs* 7(Autumn 1981): 5–86, included essays by/about Julia Kristeva, Luce Irigaray, and Helene Cixous. See also Moses 1998b.
3. Teresa de Lauretis argues that "what one 'perceives and comprehends as subjective' is constructed through a continuous process, an ongoing constant renewal based on an interaction with the world, which she defines as experience." Quoted in Alcoff 1988: 423, who summarizes Lauretis's argument nicely in contrast to the humanist subject underlying cultural feminism.
4. Edward Said defines Orientalism as "the Western style of dominating, restructuring, and having authority over the Orient" (1978: 3). It makes that region a resource for Western culture. As an imaginative geography, all that is Oriental is defined in comparison to the West, the Occident. The comparison always reaffirms the superiority of Western culture, thought, law, politics, et cetera.
5. We intended to include the Johnson-Reagon essay here, but the author declined permission to reprint it.
6. API is the acronym for Asian and Pacific Islander.

STANDPOINTS

29.
THE FEMINIST STANDPOINT: TOWARD A SPECIFICALLY FEMINIST HISTORICAL MATERIALISM
Nancy C. M. Hartsock

The different understandings of power put forward by women who have theorized about power implicitly pose the question of the extent to which gender is a world-view-structuring experience. In this chapter I explore some of the epistemological consequences of claiming that women's lives differ systematically and structurally from those of men. In particular, I suggest that, like the lives of proletarians according to Marxian theory, women's lives make available a particular and privileged vantage point on male supremacy, a vantage point that can ground a powerful critique of the phallocratic institutions and ideology that constitute the capitalist form of patriarchy. I argue that on the basis of the structures that define women's activity as contributors to subsistence and as mothers, the sexual division of labor, one could begin, though not complete, the construction of a feminist standpoint on which to ground a specifically feminist historical materialism. I hope to show how just as Marx's understanding of the world from the standpoint of the proletariat enabled him to go beneath bourgeois ideology, so a feminist standpoint can allow us to descend further into materiality to an epistemological level at which we can better understand both why patriarchal institutions and ideologies take such perverse and deadly forms and how both theory and practice can be redirected in more liberatory directions.

The reader will remember that the concept of a standpoint carries several specific contentions. Most important, it posits a series of levels of reality in which the deeper level both includes and explains the surface or appearance. Related to the positing of levels are several claims:

1. Material life (class position in Marxist theory) not only structures but sets limits on the understanding of social relations.
2. If material life is structured in fundamentally opposing ways for two different groups, one can expect that the vision of each will represent an inversion of the other, and in systems of domination the vision available to the rulers will be both partial and perverse.
3. The vision of the ruling class (or gender) structures the material relations in which all parties are forced to participate and therefore cannot be dismissed as simply false.

4. In consequence, the vision available to the oppressed group must be struggled for and represents an achievement that requires both science to see beneath the surface of the social relations in which all are forced to participate and the education that can only grow from struggle to change those relations.

5. As an engaged vision, the understanding of the oppressed, the adoption of a standpoint exposes the real relations among human beings as inhuman, points beyond the present, and carries a historically liberatory role.

Because of its achieved character and its liberatory potential, I use the term "feminist" rather than "women's standpoint." Like the experience of the proletariat, women's experience and activity as a dominated group contains both negative and positive aspects. A feminist standpoint picks out and amplifies the liberatory possibilities contained in that experience.

Women's work in every society differs systematically from men's. I intend to pursue the suggestion that this division of labor is the first, and in some societies the only, division of labor; moreover, it is central to the organization of social labor more generally.[1] On the basis of an account of the sexual division of labor, one should be able to begin to explore the oppositions and differences between women's and men's activity and their consequences for epistemology. While I cannot attempt a complete account, I put forward a schematic and simplified account of the sexual division of labor and its consequences for epistemology. I sketch out a kind of ideal type of the social relations and world view characteristic of men's and women's activity in order to explore the epistemology contained in the institutionalized sexual division of labor. In so doing, I do not mean to attribute this vision to individual women or men (any more than Marx or Lukács meant their theory of class consciousness to apply to any particular worker or group of workers). My focus is instead on institutionalized social practices and on the specific epistemology and ontology manifested by the institutionalized sexual division of labor. Individuals, as individuals, may change their activity in ways that move them outside the outlook embodied in these institutions, but such a move can be significant only when it occurs at the level of society as a whole.

I discuss the "sexual division of labor" rather than "gender division of labor" to stress, first, my desire not to separate the effects of "nature and nurture," or biology and culture, and my belief that the division of labor between women and men cannot be reduced to simply social dimensions. One must distinguish between what Sara Ruddick has termed "invariant and *nearly* unchangeable" features of human life, and those that, despite being "*nearly* universal," are "certainly changeable."[2] Thus the fact that women and not men *bear* children is not (yet) a social choice, but that women and not men rear children in a society structured by compulsory heterosexuality and male dominance is clearly a societal choice. A second reason to use the term "sexual division of labor" is to keep hold of the bodily aspect of existence, perhaps to grasp it overfirmly in an effort to keep it from evaporating altogether. There is some biological, bodily component to human existence. But its size and substantive content will remain unknown until at least the certainly changeable aspects of the sexual division of labor are altered.

On the basis of a schematic account of the sexual division of labor, I begin to fill in the specific content of the feminist standpoint and begin to specify how women's lives structure an understanding of social relations, that is, begin to follow out the epistemological consequences of the sexual division of labor. In addressing the institutionalized sexual division of labor, I propose to lay aside the important differences among women and instead to search for central commonalities across race and class boundaries. I take some justification from the fruitfulness of Marx's similar strategy in constructing a simplified, two-class, two-man model in which everything was exchanged at its value. Marx's schematic account in volume I of *Capital* left out of account such factors as imperialism; the differential wages, work, and working conditions of the Irish; the differences between women, men, and children; and so on. While all these factors are important to the analysis of contemporary capitalism, none changes either Marx's theories of surplus value or alienation, the two most fundamental features of the Marxian analysis of capitalism. My effort here takes a similar form, in an attempt to move toward a theory of the extraction and appropriation of women's activity and women themselves. Still, I adopt this strategy with some reluctance, since it contains the danger of making invisible the experience of lesbians or women of color.[3] At the same time, I recognize that the effort to uncover a feminist standpoint assumes that there are some things common to all women's lives in Western class societies.

The feminist standpoint that emerges through an examination of women's activities is related to the proletarian standpoint, but deepergoing. Women and workers inhabit a world in which the emphasis is on change rather than stasis, a world characterized by interaction with natural substances rather than separation from nature, a world in which quality is more important than quantity, a world in which the unification of mind and body is inherent in the activities performed. Yet there are some important differences, differences marked by the fact that the proletarian (if male) is immersed in this world only during the time his labor power is being used by the capitalist. If, to paraphrase Marx, we follow the worker home from the factory, we can once again perceive a change in the *dramatis personae.* He who before followed behind as the worker, timid and holding back, with nothing to expect but a hiding, now strides in front, while a third person, not specifically present in Marx's account of the transactions between capitalist and worker (both of whom are male) follows timidly behind, carrying groceries, baby, and diapers.

Given what has been said about the life activity of the proletarian, one can see that, because the sexual division of labor means that much of the work involved in reproducing labor power is done by women, and because much of the male worker's contact with nature outside the factory is mediated by women, the vision of reality which grows from the female experience is deeper and more thoroughgoing than that available to the worker.

The Sexual Division of Labor

Women's activity as institutionalized has a double aspect: their contribution to subsistence and their contribution to childrearing. Whether or not all women do both, women as a sex are institutionally responsible for producing both goods and human beings, and all women are forced to become the kinds of persons who can do both. Although the nature of women's contribution to subsistence varies immensely over time and space, my primary focus here is on capitalism, with a secondary focus on the class societies that preceded it.[4] In capitalism, women contribute both production for wages and production of goods in the home, that is, they, like men, sell their labor power and produce both commodities and surplus value, and produce use values in the home. Unlike men, however, women's lives are institutionally defined by their production of use values in the home.[5] Here we begin to encounter the narrowness of Marx's concept of production. Women's production of use values in the home has not been well understood by socialists. It is no surprise to feminists that Engels, for example, simply asks how women can continue to do the work in the home and also work in production outside the home. Marx, too, takes for granted women's responsibility for household labor. He repeats, as if it were his own, the question of a Belgian factory inspector: If a mother works for wages, "how will [the household's] internal economy be cared for; who will look after the young children; who will get ready the meals, do the washing and mending?"[6]

Let us trace both the outlines and the consequences of women's dual contribution to subsistence in capitalism. Women's labor, like that of the male worker, is contact with material necessity. Their contribution to subsistence, like that of the male worker, involves them in a world in which the relation to nature and to concrete human requirement is central, both in the form of interaction with natural substances whose quality, rather than quantity, is important to the production of meals, clothing, and so forth and in the form of close attention in a different way from men's. While repetition for both the wages and even more in household production involves a unification of mind and body for the purpose of transforming natural substances into socially defined goods. This, too, is true of the labor of the male worker.

There are, however, important differences. First, women as a group work more than men. We are all familiar with the phenomenon of the "double day," and with indications that women work many more hours per week than men.[7] Second, a larger proportion of women's labor time is devoted to the production of use values than men's. Only some of the goods women produce are commodities—however much they live in a society structured by commodity production and exchange. Third, women's production is structured by repetition in a different way from men's. While repetition for both the woman and the male worker may take the form of production of the same object, over and over—whether apple pies or brake linings—women's work in housekeeping involves a repetitious cleaning.[8]

Thus the man, in the process of production, is involved in contact with necessity and interchange with nature as well as with other human beings, but the process of production or work does not consume his whole life. The activity of a woman in the home as well as the work she does for wages keeps her continually in contact with a world of qualities and change. *Her* immersion in the world of use—in concrete, many-qualitied, changing material processes—is more complete than his. And if life itself consists of sensuous activity, the vantage point available to women on the basis of their contribution to subsistence represents an intensification and deepening of the materialist world view available to the producers of commodities in capitalism, an intensification of class consciousness. The availability of this outlook to even nonworking-class women has been strikingly formulated by a novelist: "Washing the toilet used by three males, and the floor and walls around it, is, Mira thought, coming face to face with necessity. And that is why women were saner than men, did not come up with the mad, absurd schemes men developed: they were in touch with necessity, they had to wash the toilet bowl and floor."[9]

The focus on women's subsistence activity rather than men's leads to a model in which the capitalist (male) lives a life structured completely by commodity exchange and not at all by production, and at the farthest distance from contact with concrete material life. The male worker marks a way station on the path to the other extreme—the constant contact with material necessity present in women's contribution to subsistence. There are of course important differences along the lines of race and class. For example, working-class men seem to do more domestic labor than men higher up in the class structure—car repairs, carpentry, and the like. And until very recently, the wage work done by most women of color replicated the housework required by their own households. Still, there are commonalities present in the institutionalized sexual division of labor that make women responsible for both housework and wage work.

Women's contribution to subsistence, however, represents only a part of women's labor. Women also produce/reproduce men (and other women) on both a daily and a long-term basis. This aspect of women's "production" exposes the deep inadequacies of the concept of production as a description of women's activity. One does not (cannot) produce another human being in anything like the way one produces an object such as a chair. Much more is involved, activity that cannot easily be dichotomized into play or work. Helping another to develop, the gradual relinquishing of control, the experiencing of the human limits of one's actions—all these are important features of women's activity as mothers. Women, as mothers, even more than as workers, are institutionally involved in processes of change and growth, and more than workers, must understand the importance of avoiding excessive control in order to help others grow.[10] The activity involved is far more complex than instrumentally working with others to transform objects. (Interestingly, much of women's wage work—nursing, social work, and some secretarial jobs in particular—requires and depends on the relational and interpersonal skills women learned by being mothered by someone of the same sex.)

This aspect of women's activity, too, is not without consequences. Indeed, it is in the production of men by women and the appropriation of this labor, and women themselves, by men, that the opposition between feminist and masculinist experience and outlook is rooted, and it is here that features of the proletarian vision are enhanced and modified for the woman and diluted for the man.

Women's experience in reproduction represents a unity with nature that goes beyond the proletarian experience of interchange with nature. As another theorist has put it, "reproductive labor might be said to combine the functions of the architect and the bee: Like the architect, parturitive woman knows what she is doing; like the bee, she cannot help what she is doing." And just as the worker's acting on the external work changes both the world and the worker's nature, so too "a new life changes the world and the consciousness of the woman."[11] In addition, in the process of producing human beings, relations with others may take a variety of forms with deeper significance than simple cooperation with others for common goals—forms that range from a deep unity with another through the many-leveled and changing connections mothers experience with growing children. Finally, women's experience in bearing and rearing children involves a unity of mind and body more profound than is possible in the worker's instrumental activity.

Motherhood in the large sense, that is, motherhood as an institution rather than an experience, including pregnancy and the preparation for motherhood almost all female children receive in being raised by a woman, results in the construction of female existence as centered within a complex relational nexus.[12] One aspect of this relational existence is centered on the experience of living in a woman's rather than a man's body. There are a series of what our culture treats as boundary challenges inherent in female physiology, challenges that make it difficult to maintain rigid separation from the object world. Menstruation, coitus, pregnancy, childbirth, lactation—all represent challenges to bodily boundaries.[13] Adrienne Rich has described the experience of pregnancy as one in which the embryo was both inside and yet "daily more separate, on its way to becoming separate from me and of-itself. In early pregnancy the stirring of the fetus felt like ghostly tremors of my own body, later like the movements of a being imprisoned in me; but both sensations were *my* sensations, contributing to my own sense of physical and psychic space."[14]

In turn, the fact that women but not men are primarily responsible for young children means that the infant first experiences itself as not fully differentiated from the mother and then as an I in relation to an *It* that it later comes to know as female.[15] Nancy Chodorow and Jane Flax have argued that the object-relations school of psychoanalytic theory puts forward a materialist psychology, one that I propose to treat as a kind of empirical hypothesis. If the account of human development provided by object relations is correct, one ought to expect to find consequences—both psychic and social.[16] According to object-relations theory, the process of differentiation from a woman, by both boys and girls, reinforces boundary confusion in women's egos and boundary strengthening in men's. Individuation is far more conflictual for male than for female children, in part because both mother and son experience the other as a definite "other." The experience of oneness on the part of both mother and infant seems to last longer with girls.[17]

The complex relational world inhabited by women has its start in the experience and resolution of the oedipal crisis, cleanly resolved for the boy, whereas the girl is much more likely to retain both parents as love objects. The nature of the crisis itself differs by sex: The boy's love for the mother is an extension of mother-infant unity and thus essentially threatening to his ego and independence. Masculine ego formation necessarily requires repressing this first relation and negating the mother.[18] In contrast, the girl's love for the father is less threatening both because it occurs outside this unity and because it occurs at a later stage of development. For boys, the central issue to be resolved concerns gender identification; for girls, the issue is psychosexual development.[19] Chodorow concludes that girls' gradual emergence from the oedipal period takes place in such a way that empathy is built into their primary definition of self, and they have a variety of capacities for experiencing another's needs or feelings as their own. Put another way, girls, because of female parenting, are less differentiated from others than boys, more continuous with and related to the external object world. They are differently oriented to their inner object world as well.[20]

The more complex female relational world is reinforced by the process of socialization. Girls learn roles from watching their mothers; boys must learn roles from rules that structure the life of an absent male figure. Girls can identify with a concrete example present in daily life; boys must identify with an abstract set of maxims only occasionally concretely present in the form of the father. Thus, not only do girls learn roles with more interpersonal and relational skills, but the process of role learning itself is embodied in the concrete relation with the mother. The male, in contrast, must identify with an abstract, cultural stereotype and learn abstract behaviors not attached to a well-known person. Masculinity is idealized for boys, whereas femininity is concrete for girls.[21]

Women and men, then, grow up with personalities affected by different boundary experiences, differently constructed and experienced inner and outer worlds, and preoccupations with different relational issues. This early experience forms an important ground for the feminine sense of self as connected to the world and the masculine sense of self as separate, distinct, and even disconnected. By retaining the preoedipal attachment to the mother, girls come to define and experience themselves as continuous with others. In sum, girls enter adulthood with a more complex layering of affective ties and a rich, ongoing inner set of object relations. Boys, with a simpler oedipal situation and a clear and early resolution, have repressed ties to another. As a result, women define and experience themselves relationally, and men do not.[22]

Chodorow's argument receives support from Robert Stroller's work on sexual excitement and his search for the roots of adult sexual behavior in infant experience. Attempting to understand why men are more perverse than women (i.e., why men's sexual excitement seems to require more gross hostility than women's) led him to suggest that boys may face more difficulties in individuating than girls.[23] He puts forward a theory of what he terms "primary femininity." Because the male infant is merged with the mother, who is a woman, the boy may experience himself as female. Stoller suggests that it may be that the boy does not start out as heterosexual, as Freud thought, but must separate himself to achieve heterosexuality. The oneness with the mother must be counteracted.[24] Thus, "masculinity in males starts as a movement away from the blissful and dangerous, forever remembered and forever yearned for, mother-infant symbiosis.[25] To become masculine, the boy must separate himself both externally from his mother's body, and within himself, from his own already formed primary identification with femininity.[26] This requires the construction of barriers to femininity directed both inward and outward. The mother may be represented as an evil creature, a witch, to counteract the wish to merge with her. Or the barrier may be constructed and sustained by fantasies of harming the mother.[27] Inwardly, the boy must develop a character structure that forces the feminine part of himself down and out of awareness.[28]. . .

Abstract Masculinity and the Feminist Standpoint

This excursion into psychoanalytic theory has served to point to the differences in men's and women's experience of self resulting from the sexual division of labor in childrearing. These different psychic experiences both structure and are reinforced by the differing patterns of men's and women's activity required by the sexual division of labor, and are thereby replicated as epistemology and ontology. This differential life activity in class society leads on the one hand toward a feminist standpoint and on the other toward an abstract masculinity.

Because the problem for the boy is to distinguish himself from the mother and protect himself against the real threat she poses for his identity, his conflictual and oppositional efforts lead to the formation of rigid ego boundaries. The way Freud takes for granted the rigid distinction between the "me and not-me" makes the point well: "Normally, there is nothing of which we are more certain than the feeling of ourself, of our own ego. This ego appears to us as something autonomous and unitary, marked off distinctly from everything else." At least toward the outside, "the ego seems to maintain clear and sharp lines of demarcation."[29] Thus, the boy's construction of self in opposition to unity with the mother, his construction of identity as differentiation from the mother, sets a hostile and combative dualism at the heart of both the community men construct and the masculinist world view by means of which they understand their lives. . . .

The construction of the self in opposition to another who threatens one's very being reverberates throughout the construction of both class society and the masculinist world view and results in a deep-going and hierarchical dualism. First, the man's experience is characterized by the duality of concrete versus abstract.[30] Material reality as experienced by the boy in the family provides no model, and is unimportant in the attainment of masculinity. Nothing of value to the boy occurs within the family, and masculinity becomes an abstract ideal to be achieved over the opposition of daily life.[31] Masculinity must be attained by means of opposition to the concrete world of daily life, by escaping from contact with the female world of the household into the masculine world of politics or public life. This experience of two worlds, one valuable, if abstract and deeply unattainable, the other useless and demeaning, if concrete and necessary, lies at the heart of a series of dualisms—abstract/concrete, mind/body, culture/nature, ideal/real, stasis/change. And these dualisms are overlaid by gender; only the first of each pair is associated with the male.

Dualism, along with the dominance of one side of the dichotomy over the other, marks phallocentric society and social theory. These dualisms appear in a variety of forms—in philosophy, sexuality, technology, political theory, and the organization of class society itself....

The oedipal roots of these hierarchical dualisms are memorialized in the overlay of masculine and feminine connotations. It is not accidental that women are associated with quasi-human and nonhuman nature, that the woman is associated with the body and material life, that the lives of women are systematically used as examples to characterize the lives of those ruled by their bodies rather than their minds.[32]

Both the fragility and fundamental falseness of the masculinist ideology and the deeply problematic nature of the social relations from which it grows are apparent in its reliance on a series of counterfactual assumptions and contentions. Consider how the following contentions run counter to lived experience: The body is both irrelevant and in opposition to the (real) self, an impediment to be overcome by the mind; the female mind either does not exist (Do women have souls?) or works in such incomprehensible ways as to be unintelligible (the "enigma of woman"); what is real and primary is imperceptible to the senses and impervious to nature and natural change. What is remarkable is not only that these contentions have absorbed a great deal of philosophical energy but, along with a series of other counterfactuals, have structured social relations for centuries.

Interestingly enough, the epistemology and society constructed by men, suffering from the effects of abstract masculinity, have a great deal in common with the society and ideology imposed by commodity exchange. The separation and opposition of social and natural worlds, of abstract and concrete, of permanence and change, the effort to define only the former of each pair as important, the reliance on a series of counterfactual assumptions—all this is shared with the exchange abstraction. Abstract masculinity shares still another of its aspects with the exchange abstraction: It forms the basis for an even more problematic social synthesis. Hegel's analysis makes clear the problematic social relations available to the self that maintains itself by opposition: Each of the two subjects struggling for recognition tries to kill the other. But if the other is killed, the subject is once again alone. In sum, then, masculine experience when replicated as epistemology leads to a world conceived as (and in fact) inhabited by a number of fundamentally hostile others whom one comes to know by means of opposition (even death struggle) and yet with whom one must construct a social relation in order to survive.

Women's construction of self in relation to others leads in an opposite direction—toward opposition to dualisms of any sort; valuation of concrete, everyday life; a sense of a variety of connectednesses and continuities both with other persons and with the natural world. If material life structures consciousness, women's relationally-defined existence, bodily experience of boundary challenges, and activity of transforming both physical objects and human beings must be expected to result in a world view to which dichotomies are foreign. Women experience others and themselves along a continuum whose dimensions are evidenced in Adrienne Rich's argument that the child carried for nine months can be defined "*neither* as me or as not-me," and she argues that inner and outer are not polar opposites but a continuum.[33] What the sexual division of labor defines as women's work turns on issues of change rather than stasis—the changes involved in producing both use values and commodities, but more profoundly in the activity of rearing human beings who change in both more subtle and more autonomous ways than any inanimate object. Not only the qualities of things but also the qualities of people are important in women's work; quantity becomes peripheral. In addition, far more than the instrumental cooperation of the workplace is required; the mother-child relation and the maintenance of the family, while it has instrumental aspects, is not defined by them. Finally, the unity of mental and manual labor and the directly sensuous nature of much of women's work leads to a more profound unity of mental and manual labor, social and natural worlds, than is experienced by the male worker in capitalism. The unity grows from the fact that women's bodies, unlike men's, can be themselves instruments of production: In pregnancy, giving birth, or lactation, arguments about a division of mental from manual labor are fundamentally foreign.

That this is indeed women's experience is documented in both the theory and practice of the contemporary women's movement and needs no further development here.[34] The more important question here is whether women's experience and the world view constructed by women's activity can meet the criteria for a standpoint. If we return to the five claims carried by the concept of a standpoint it seems clear that women's material life activity has important epistemological and ontological consequences for both the understanding and construction of social relations. Women's activity, then, does satisfy the first requirement for a standpoint.

I can now take up the second claim made by a standpoint: that women's experience not only inverts that of men but forms a basis on which to expose abstract masculinity as both partial and fundamentally perverse, as not only occupying only one side of the dualities it has constructed but reversing the proper valuation of human activity. The partiality of the masculinist vision and of the societies that support this understanding is evidenced by its confinement of activity proper to the man to only one side of the dualisms. Its perverseness, however, lies elsewhere. Perhaps the most dramatic (though not the only) reversal of the proper order of things characteristic of masculine experience is the substitution of death for life.

The substitution of death for life results at least in part from the sexual division of labor in childrearing. The self surrounded by rigid ego boundaries, certain of what is inner and what is outer, the self experienced as walled city, is discontinuous with others. Georges Bataille has made brilliantly clear the ways in which death emerges as the only possible solution to this discontinuity and has followed the logic through to argue that reproduction itself must be understood, not as the creation of life, but as death. The core experience to be understood is that of discontinuity and its consequences. As a consequence of this experience of discontinuity and aloneness, penetration of ego boundaries, or fusion with another, is experienced as violent. The pair "lover-assailant" is not accidental. Nor is the connection of reproduction and death.

"Reproduction," Bataille argues, "implies the existence of *discontinuous* beings." This is so because "beings which reproduce themselves are distinct from one another, and those reproduced are likewise distinct from each other, just as they are distinct from their parents. Each being is distinct from all others. His birth, his death, the events of his life may have an interest for others, but he alone is directly concerned in them. He is born alone. He dies alone. Between one being and another, there is a *gulf*, a discontinuity."[35] (Clearly the gulf of which he speaks is better characterized as a chasm). In reproduction, sperm and ovum unite to form a new entity, but they do so from the death and disappearance of two separate beings. Thus, the new entity bears death with itself.

Although death and reproduction are intimately linked, Bataille stresses that "it is only death which is to be identified with [the transition to] continuity"; he holds to this position despite his recognition that reproduction is a form of growth. The growth, however, he dismisses as not "ours," as being only "impersonal."[36] This is not the female experience, in which reproduction is hardly impersonal, nor experienced as death. It is, of course, in a literal sense, the sperm that is cut off from its source and lost. Perhaps we should not wonder, then, at the masculinist preoccupation with death, and the feeling that growth is "impersonal," not of fundamental concern to oneself. Beneath Bataille's theorization of continuity as death lies the conflictual individuation of the boy: Continuity with another, continuity with the mother, carries not just danger but inevitable death as a separate being. But this complete dismissal of the experience of another bespeaks a profound lack of empathy and refusal to recognize the very being of another. It manifests the chasm that separates each man from every other being and from the natural world, the chasm that marks and defines the problem of community.

The preoccupation with death instead of life appears as well in the argument that is the ability to kill (and for centuries, the practice) that sets humans above animals. Even Simone de Beauvoir has accepted that "it is not in giving life but in risking life that man is raised above the animal: that is why superiority has been accorded in humanity not to the sex that brings forth but to that which kills."[37] That superiority has been accorded to the sex which kills is beyond doubt. But what kind of vision can take reproduction, the creation of new life, and the force of life in sexuality, and turn it into death, not just in theory but in the practice of rape and sexual murder? Any why give pride of place to killing? That is not only an inversion of the proper order of things but also a refusal to recognize the real activities in which men as well as women are engaged. The producing of goods and the reproducing of human beings are certainly life-sustaining activities. And even the deaths of the ancient heroes in search of undying fame were pursuits of life and represented the attempt to avoid death by attaining immortality. The search for life, then, represents the deeper reality that lies beneath the glorification of death and destruction.

Yet one cannot dismiss the substitution of death for life as simply false. Men's power to structure social relations in their own image means that women too must participate in social relations that manifest and express abstract masculinity. The most important life activities have consistently been held by the powers that be to be unworthy of those who are fully human, most centrally because of their close connections with necessity and life: motherwork (the rearing of children), housework, and until the rise of capitalism in the West any work necessary to subsistence. In addition, these activities in contemporary capitalism are all constructed in ways that systematically degrade and destroy the minds and bodies of those who perform them.[38] The organization of motherhood as an institution in which a woman is alone with her children, the isolation of women from each other in domestic labor, the female pathology of loss of self in service to others—all mark the transformation of life into death, the distortion of what could have been creative and communal activity into oppressive toil, and the destruction of the possibility of community present in women's relational self-definition. The ruling gender's and class's interest in maintaining social relations such as these is evidenced by the fact that when women set up other structures in which the mother is not alone with her children, isolated from others, as is frequently the case in working-class communities or the communities of people of color, these arrangements are described as pathological deviations.

The real destructiveness of the social relations characteristic of abstract masculinity, however, is now concealed beneath layers of ideology. Marxian theory needed to go beneath the surface to discover the different levels of determination that defined the relation of capitalist and (male) worker. These levels of determination and laws of motion or tendency of phallocratic society must be worked out on the basis of female experience. This brings me to the fourth claim for a standpoint: its character as an achievement of both analysis and political struggle occurring in a particular historical space. The fact that class divisions should have proved so resistant to analysis and required such a prolonged political struggle before Marx was able to formulate the theory of surplus value indicates the difficulty of this accomplishment. And despite the time that has passed since the theory was worked out, rational control of production has yet to be achieved.

Feminists have only begun the process of revaluing the female experience, searching for the common threads that connect the diverse experiences of women, and searching for the structural determinants of these experiences. The difficulty of the problem faced by feminist theory can be illustrated by the fact that it required a struggle even to define household labor, if not done for wages, as work, to argue that what are held to be acts of love instead must be recognized as work.[39] Both the revaluation of women's experience and the use of this experience as a ground for critique are required. That is, the liberatory possibilities present in women's experience must be, in a sense, read out and developed. Thus, a feminist standpoint may be present on the basis of the commonalities within women's experience, but it is neither self-evident nor obvious.

Finally, because it provides a way to reveal the perverseness and inhumanity of human relations, a standpoint forms the basis for moving beyond these relations. Just as the proletarian standpoint emerges out of the contradiction between appearance and essence in capitalism, understood as essentially historical and con- stituted by the relation of capitalist and worker, the feminist standpoint emerges both out of the contradiction between the systematically differing structures of men's and women's life activity in Western cultures. It expresses women's experi- ence at a particular time and place, located within a particular set of social rela- tions. Capitalism, Marx noted, could not develop fully until the notion of human equality achieved the status of universal truth.[40] Despite women's exploitation, both as unpaid reproducers of the labor force and as a sex-segregated labor force available for low wages, then, capitalism poses problems for the continued oppres- sion of women. Just as capitalism enables the proletariat to raise the possibility of a society free from class domination, so too it provides space to raise the possibility of a society free from all forms of domination. The articulation of a feminist stand- point based on women's relational self-definition and activity exposes the world men have constructed and the self-understanding that manifests these social rela- tions as both partial and perverse. More important, by drawing out the potentiality available in the actuality and thereby exposing the inhumanity of human relations, it embodies a distress that requires a solution. The experience of continuity and relation—with others, with the natural world, of mind with body—provide an ontological base for developing a nonproblematic social synthesis, a social synthe- sis that need not operate through the denial of the body, the attack on nature, or the death struggle between the self and other, a social synthesis that does not depend on any of the forms taken by abstract masculinity.

What is necessary is the generalization of the potentiality made available by the activity of women—the defining of society as a whole as propertyless producer both of use values and of human beings. To understand what such a transformation would require, we should consider what is involved in the partial transformation represented by making the whole of society into propertyless producers of use val- ues: socialist revolution. The abolition of the division between mental and manual labor cannot take place simply by means of adopting worker self-management tech- niques, but instead requires the abolition of private property, the seizure of state power, and lengthy post-revolutionary class struggle. Thus I am not suggesting that shared parenting arrangements can abolish the sexual division of labor. Doing away with this division of labor would of course require institutionalizing the participa- tion of both women and men in childrearing. But just as the rational and conscious control of the production of goods and services requires a vast and far-reaching social transformation, so too the rational and conscious organization of reproduc- tion would entail the transformation both of *every* human relation and of human relations to the natural world. The magnitude of the task is apparent if one asks what a society without institutionalized gender differences might look like.

Generalizing the human possibilities present in the life activity of women to the social system as a whole would raise, for the first time in human history, the possibility of a fully human community, a community structured by a variety of connections rather than separation and opposition. One can conclude then that women's life activity does form the basis of a specifically feminist materialism, a materialism that can provide a point from which to both critique and work against phallocratic ideology and institutions.

NOTES

1. This is Iris Young's point. I am indebted to her persuasive arguments for taking what she terms the "gender differentiation of labor" as a central category of analysis. See Young, "Dual Systems Theory," *Socialist Review* 50, 51 (March–June 1980): 185. My use of this category, however, differs to some extent from hers. Young focuses on the societal aspects of the division of labor and chooses to use the term "gender division" to indicate that focus. I want to include the relation to the natural world as well. In addition, Young's analysis of women in capitalism does not seem to include marriage as a part of the division of labor. She is more concerned with the division of labor in capitalism in the productive sector.
2. See Sara Ruddick, "Maternal Thinking," *Feminist Studies* 6, no. 2 (Summer 1980): 364.
3. See, for a discussion of this danger, Adrienne Rich, "Disloyal of Civilization: Feminism, Racism, Gynephobia," in *On Lies, Secrets, and Silence* (New York: Norton, 1979), pp. 275–310; Elly Bulkin, "Racism and Writing: Some Implications for White Lesbian Critics," *Sinister Wisdom*, no. 6 (Spring 1980); bell hooks, *Ain't I a Woman* (Boston: South End Press, 1981), p. 138.
4. Some cross-cultural evidence indicates that the status of women varies with the work they do. To the extent that women and men contribute equally to subsistence, women's status is higher than it would be if their subsistence work differed profoundly from that of men; that is, if they do none or almost all of the work of subsistence, their status remains low. See Peggy Sanday, "Female Status in the Public Domain," in *Woman, Culture and Society*, ed. Michelle Rosaldo and Louise Lamphere (Stanford: Stanford University Press, 1974), p. 199. See also Iris Young's account of the sexual division of labor in capitalism, mentioned in note 1.
5. It is irrelevant to my argument here that women's wage labor takes place under different circumstances than men's—that is, their lower wages, their confinement to only a few occupational categories, et cetera. I am concentrating instead on the formal, structural features of women's work. There has been much effort to argue that women's domestic labor is a source of surplus value, that is, to include it within the scope of Marx's value theory as productive labor, or to argue that since it does not produce surplus value it belongs to an entirely different mode of production, variously characterized as domestic or patriarchal. My strategy here is quite different from this. See, for the British debate, Mariarosa Dalla Costa and Selma James, *The Power of Women and the Subversion of the Community* (Bristol: Falling Wall Press, 1975); Wally Secombe, "The Housewife and Her Labor Under Capitalism," *New Left Review* 83 (January–February 1974); Jean Gardiner, "Women's Domestic Labour," *New Left Review* 89 (March 1975); and Paul Smith, "Domestic Labour and Marx's Theory of Value," in *Feminism and Materialism*, eds. Annette Kuhn and Ann Marie Wolpe (Boston: Routledge and Kegan Paul, 1978). A portion of the American debate can be found in Ira Gerstein, "Domestic Work and Capitalism," and Lisa Vogel, "The Earthly Family," *Radical America* 7, nos. 4/5 (July–October 1973); Ann Ferguson, "Women as a New Revolutionary Class," in *Between Labor and Capital*, ed. Pat Walker (Boston: South End Press, 1979).

6. Frederick Engels, *Origins of the Family, Private Property and the State* (New York: International Publishers, 1942); Karl Marx, *Capital* (New York: International Publishers, 1967) 1: 671. Marx and Engels have also described the sexual division of labor as natural or spontaneous. See Mary O'Brien, "Reproducing Marxist Man," in *The Sexism of Social and Political Thought*, ed. Lorenne Clark and Lynda Lange (Toronto: University of Toronto Press, 1979).

7. For a discussion of women's work, see Elise Boulding, "Familial Constraints of Women's Work Roles," in *Women and the Workplace*, ed. Martha Blaxall and B. Reagan (Chicago: University of Chicago Press, 1976), esp. pp. 111, 113. An interesting historical note is provided by the fact that Nausicaa, the daughter of a Homeric king, did the household laundry. See M. I. Finley, *The World of Odysseus* (Middlesex, England: Penguin, 1979), p. 73. While aristocratic women were less involved in actual labor, the difference was one of degree. And as Aristotle remarked in the *Politics*, supervising slaves is not a particularly uplifting activity. The life of leisure and philosophy, so much the goal for aristocratic Athenian men, then, was almost unthinkable for any woman.

8. Simone de Beauvoir holds that repetition has a deeper significance and that women's biological destiny itself is repetition. See *The Second Sex*, trans. H. M. Parshley (New York: Knopf, 1953), p. 59. But see also her discussion of housework in ibid., pp. 423 ff. There, her treatment of housework is strikingly negative. For her the transcendence of humanity is provided in the historical struggle of self with other and with the natural world. The oppositions she sees are not really stasis vs. change, but rather transcendence, escape from the muddy concreteness of daily life.

9. Marilyn French, *The Women's Room* (New York: Jove, 1978), p. 214.

10. Sara Ruddick, "Maternal Thinking," presents an interesting discussion of these and other aspects of the thought which emerges from the activity of mothering. Although I find it difficult to speak the language of interests and demands she uses, she brings out several valuable points. Her distinction between maternal and scientific thought is very intriguing and potentially useful (see esp. pp. 350–53).

11. Mary O'Brien, "Reproducing Marxist Man," p. 115, n. 11.

12. It should be understood that I am concentrating here on the experience of women in Western culture. There are a number of cross-cultural differences that can be expected to have some effect. See, for example, the differences that emerge from a comparison of childrearing in ancient Greek society with that of the contemporary Mbuti in central Africa. See Philip Slater, *The Glory of Hera* (Boston: Beacon, 1968); and Colin Turnbull, "The Politics of Non-Aggression," in *Learning Non-Aggression*, ed. Ashley Montagu (New York: Oxford University Press, 1978). See also Isaac Balbus, *Marxism and Domination* (Princeton: Princeton University Press, 1982).

13. See Nancy Chodorow, "Family Structure and Female Personality," in Rosaldo and Lamphere, *Women, Culture, and Society*, p. 59.

14. Adrienne Rich, *Of Woman Born* (New York: Norton, 1976), p. 63.

15. I rely on the analyses of Dinnerstein and Chodorow but there are difficulties in that they are attempting to explain why humans, both male and female, fear and hate the female. My purpose here is to invert their arguments and to attempt to put forward a positive account of the epistemological consequences of this situation. What follows is a summary of Nancy Chodorow, *The Reproduction of Mothering* (Berkeley: University of California Press, 1978).

16. See Chodorow, *Reproduction*; and Jane Flax, "The Conflict Between Nurturance and Autonomy in Mother-Daughter Relations and in Feminism," *Feminist Studies* 6, no 2 (June 1978).

17. Chodorow, *Reproduction*, pp. 105–9.

18. This is Jane Flax's point.

19. Chodorow, *Reproduction*, pp. 127–31, 163.

20. Ibid., p. 166.

21. Ibid., pp. 174–78. Chodorow suggests a correlation between father absence and fear of women (p. 213), and one should, treating this as an empirical hypothesis, expect a series of cultural differences based on the degree of father absence. Here the ancient Greeks and the Mbuti provide a fascinating contrast. (See above, note 12.)

22. Ibid., p. 198. The flexible and diffuse female ego boundaries can of course result in the pathology of loss of self in responsibility for and dependence on others (the obverse of the male pathology of experiencing the self as walled city).

23. He never considers that single-sex childrearing may be the problem and also ascribes total responsibility to the mother for especially the male's successful individuation. See Robert Stoller, *Perversion* (New York: Pantheon, 1975), p. 154 and p. 161, for an awesome list of tasks to be accomplished by the mother.

24. Ibid., pp. 137–138.

25. Ibid., p. 154. See also his discussion of these dynamics in Chapter 2 of Robert Stoller, *Sexual Excitement* (New York: Pantheon, 1979).

26. Stoller, *Perversion*, p. 99.

27. Ibid., pp. 150, 121, respectively.

28. Ibid., p. 150.

29. Sigmund Freud, *Civilization and Its Discontents* (New York: Norton, 1961), pp. 12–13.

30. I use the terms abstract and concrete in a sense much influenced by Marx. "Abstraction" refers not only to the practice of searching for universal generalities but also carries derogatory connotations of idealism and partiality. By "concrete," I refer to respect for complexity and multidimensional causality, and mean to suggest as well as a materialism and completeness.

31. Alvin Gouldner has made a similar argument in his contention that the Platonic stress on hierarchy and order resulted from a similarly learned opposition to daily life rooted in the young aristocrat's experience of being taught proper behavior by slaves who could not themselves engage in this behavior. See Gouldner, *Enter Plato* (New York: Basic Books, 1965), pp. 351–55.

32. See Elizabeth Spelman, "Metaphysics and Misogyny: The Soul and Body in Plato's Dialogues" (mimeo). One analyst has argued that its basis lies in the fact that "the early mother, monolithic representative of nature, is a source, like nature, of ultimate distress as well as ultimate joy. Like nature, she is both nourishing and disappointing, both alluring and threatening. . . . The infant loves her . . . and it hates her because, like nature, she does not perfectly protect and provide for it . . . The mother, then—like nature, which sends blizzards and locusts as well as sunshine and strawberries—is perceived as capricious, sometimes actively malevolent." Dorothy Dinnerstein, *The Mermaid and the Minotaur* (New York: Harper & Row, 1976), p. 95.

33. Rich, *Of Woman Born*, pp. 64, 167. For a similar descriptive account, but a dissimilar analysis, see David Bakan, *The Duality of Human Existence* (Boston: Beacon Press, 1966).

34. My arguments are supported with remarkable force by both the theory and practice of the contemporary women's movement. In theory, this appears in different forms in the work of Dorothy Riddle, "New Visions of Spiritual Power," *Quest: a feminist quarterly 1*, no. 3 (Spring 1975); Griffin, *Woman and Nature*, esp. Book IV, "The Separate Rejoined"; Rich, *Of Woman Born*, esp. pp. 62–68; Linda Thurston, "On Male and Female Principle," *The Second Wave 1*, no. 2 (Summer 1971). In feminist political organizing, this vision has been expressed as an opposition of leadership and hierarchy, as an effort to prevent the development of organizations divided into leaders and followers. It has also taken the forms of an insistence on the unity of the personal and the political, a stress on the concrete rather than on abstract principles (an opposition to theory), and a stress on the politics of everyday life. For a fascinating and early example, see Pat Mainardi, "The Politics of Housework," in *Voices of Women's Liberation*, ed. Leslie Tanner (New York: New American Library, 1970).

35. Georges Bataille, *Death and Sensuality* (New York: Arno Press, 1977), p. 12; italics mine.

36. Ibid., pp. 95–96.

37. de Beauvoir, *The Second Sex*, p. 58.

38. Consider, for example, Rich's discussion of pregnancy and childbirth, chaps. 6, 7, and *Of Woman Born*. And see also Charlotte Perkins Gilman's discussion of domestic labor in *The Home* (Urbana, Ill.: University of Illinois Press, 1972).

39. The Marxist-feminist efforts to determine whether housework produces surplus value and the feminist political strategy of demanding wages for housework represent two (mistaken) efforts to recognize women's activity as work.

40. Marx, *Capital*, 1: 60.

30.
THE PROJECT OF FEMINIST EPISTEMOLOGY: PERSPECTIVES FROM A NONWESTERN FEMINIST
Uma Narayan

A fundamental thesis of feminist epistemology is that our location in the world as women makes it possible for us to perceive and understand different aspects of both the world and human activities in ways that challenge the male bias of existing perspectives. Feminist epistemology is a particular manifestation of the general insight that the nature of women's experiences as individuals and as social beings, our contributions to work, culture, knowledge, and our history and political interests have been systematically ignored or misrepresented by mainstream discourses in different areas.

Women have been often excluded from prestigious areas of human activity (for example, politics or science) and this has often made these activities seem clearly "male." In areas where women were not excluded (for example, subsistence work), their contribution has been misrepresented as secondary and inferior to that of men. Feminist epistemology sees mainstream theories about various human enterprises, including mainstream theories about human knowledge, as one-dimensional and deeply flawed because of the exclusion and misrepresentation of women's contributions.

Feminist epistemology suggests that integrating women's contribution into the domain of science and knowledge will not constitute a mere adding of details; it will not merely widen the canvas but result in a shift of perspective enabling us to see a very different picture. The inclusion of women's perspective will not merely amount to women participating in greater numbers in the existing practice of science and knowledge, but it will change the very nature of these activities and their self-understanding.

It would be misleading to suggest that feminist epistemology is a homogenous and cohesive enterprise. Its practitioners differ both philosophically and politically in a number of significant ways (Harding 1986). But an important theme on its agenda has been to undermine the abstract, rationalistic, and universal image of the scientific enterprise by using several different strategies. It has studied, for instance, how contingent historical factors have colored both scientific theories and practices and provided the (often sexist) metaphors in which scientists have conceptualized their activity (Bordo 1986; Keller 1985; Harding and O'Barr 1987).

It has tried to reintegrate values and emotions into our account of our cognitive activities, arguing for both the inevitability of their presence and the importance of the contributions they are capable of making to our knowledge (Gilligan 1982; Jaggar 1989; and Tronto 1989). It has also attacked various sets of dualisms characteristic of western philosophical thinking—reason versus emotion, culture versus nature, universal versus particular—in which the first of each set is identified with science, rationality, and the masculine and the second is relegated to the nonscientific, the nonrational, and the feminine (Harding and Hintikka 1983; Lloyd 1984; Wilshire 1989).

At the most general level, feminist epistemology resembles the efforts of many oppressed groups to reclaim for themselves the value of their own experience. The writing of novels that focused on working-class life in England or the lives of black people in the United States shares a motivation similar to that of feminist epistemology—to depict an experience different from the norm and to assert the value of this difference.

In a similar manner, feminist epistemology also resembles attempts by third-world writers and historians to document the wealth and complexity of local economic and social structures that existed prior to colonialism. These attempts are useful for their ability to restore to colonized peoples a sense of the richness of their own history and culture. These projects also mitigate the tendency of intellectuals in former colonies who are westernized through their education to think that anything western is necessarily better and more "progressive." In some cases, such studies help to preserve the knowledge of many local arts, crafts, lore, and techniques that were part of the former way of life before they are lost not only to practice but even to memory.

These enterprises are analogous to feminist epistemology's project of restoring to women a sense of the richness of their history, to mitigate our tendency to see the stereotypically "masculine" as better or more progressive, and to preserve for posterity the contents of "feminine" areas of knowledge and expertise—medical lore, knowledge associated with the practices of childbirth and child rearing, traditionally feminine crafts, and so on. Feminist epistemology, like these other enterprises, must attempt to balance the assertion of the value of a different culture or experience against the dangers of romanticizing it to the extent that the limitations and oppressions it confers on its subjects are ignored.

My essay will attempt to examine some dangers of approaching feminist theorizing and epistemological values in a noncontextual and nonpragmatic way, which could convert important feminist insights and theses into feminist epistemological dogmas. I will use my perspective as a nonwestern, Indian feminist to examine critically the predominantly Anglo-American project of feminist epistemology and to reflect on what such a project might signify for women in nonwestern cultures in general and for nonwestern feminists in particular. I will suggest that different cultural contexts and political agendas may cast a very different light on both the "idols" and the "enemies" of knowledge as they have characteristically been typed in western feminist epistemology.

In keeping with my respect for contexts, I would like to stress that I do not see nonwestern feminists as a homogenous group and that none of the concerns I express as a nonwestern feminist may be pertinent to or shared by *all* nonwestern feminists, although I do think they will make sense to many....

Nonwestern Feminist Politics and Feminist Epistemology

Some themes of feminist epistemology may be problematic for nonwestern feminists in ways that they are not problematic for western feminists. Feminism has a much narrower base in most nonwestern countries. It is primarily of significance to some urban, educated, middle-class, and hence relatively westernized women, like myself. Although feminist groups in these countries do try to extend the scope of feminist concerns to other groups (for example, by fighting for childcare, women's health issues, and equal wages issues through trade union structures), some major preoccupations of western feminism—its critique of marriage, the family, compulsory heterosexuality—presently engage the attention of mainly small groups of middle-class feminists.

These feminists must think and function within the context of a powerful tradition that, although it systematically oppresses women, also contains within itself a discourse that confers a high value on women's place in the general scheme of things. Not only are the roles of wife and mother highly praised, but women also are seen as the cornerstones of the spiritual well-being of their husbands and children, admired for their supposedly higher moral, religious, and spiritual qualities, and so on. In cultures that have a pervasive religious component, like the Hindu culture with which I am familiar, everything seems assigned a place and value as long as it keeps to its place. Confronted with a powerful traditional discourse that values woman's place as long as she keeps to the place prescribed, it may be politically counterproductive for nonwestern feminists to echo uncritically the themes of western feminist epistemology that seek to restore the value, cognitive and otherwise, of "women's experience."

The danger is that, even if the nonwestern feminist talks about the value of women's experience in terms totally different from those of the traditional discourse, the difference is likely to be drowned out by the louder and more powerful voice of the traditional discourse, which will then claim that "what those feminists say" vindicates its view that the roles and experiences it assigns to women have value and that women should stick to those roles.

I do not intend to suggest that this is not a danger for western feminism or to imply that there is no tension for western feminists between being critical of the experiences that their societies have provided for women and finding things to value in them nevertheless. But I am suggesting that perhaps there is less at risk for western feminists in trying to strike this balance. I am inclined to think that in nonwestern countries feminists must still stress the negative sides of the female experience within that culture and that the time for a more sympathetic evaluation is not quite ripe.

But the issue is not simple and seems even less so when another point is considered. The imperative we experience as feminists to be critical of how our culture and traditions oppress women conflicts with our desire as members of once colonized cultures to affirm the value of the same culture and traditions.

There are seldom any easy resolutions to these sorts of tensions. As an Indian feminist currently living in the United States, I often find myself torn between the desire to communicate with honesty the miseries and oppressions that I think my own culture confers on its women, and the fear that this communication is going to reinforce—however unconsciously—western prejudices about the "superiority" of western culture. I have often felt compelled to interrupt my communication, say on the problems of the Indian system of arranged marriages, to remind my western friends that the experiences of women under their system of "romantic love" seem no more enviable. Perhaps we should all attempt to cultivate the methodological habit of trying to understand the complexities of the oppression involved in different historical and cultural settings while eschewing, at least for now, the temptation to make comparisons across such settings, given the dangers of attempting to compare what may well be incommensurable in any neat terms.

The Nonprimacy of Positivsim as a Problematic Perspective

As a nonwestern feminist, I also have some reservations about the way in which feminist epistemology seems to have picked positivism as its main target of attack. The choice of positivism as the main target is reasonable because it has been a dominant and influential western position and it most clearly embodies some flaws that feminist epistemology seeks to remedy.

But this focus on positivism should not blind us to the facts that it is not our only enemy and that nonpositivist frameworks are not, by virtue of that bare qualification, any more worthy of our tolerance. Most traditional frameworks that nonwestern feminists regard as oppressive to women are not positivist, and it would be wrong to see feminist epistemology's critique of positivism given the same political importance for nonwestern feminists that it has for western feminists. Traditions like my own, where the influence of religion is pervasive, are suffused through and through with values. We must fight not frameworks that assert the separation of fact and value but frameworks that are pervaded by values to which we, as feminists, find ourselves opposed. Positivism in epistemology flourished at the same time as liberalism in western political theory. Positivism's view of values as individual and subjective related to liberalism's political emphasis on individual rights that were supposed to protect an individual's freedom to live according to the values she espoused.

Nonwestern feminists may find themselves in a curious bind when confronting the interrelations between positivism and political liberalism. As colonized people, we are well aware of the facts that many political concepts of liberalism are both suspicious and confused and that the practice of liberalism in the colonies was marked by brutalities unaccounted for by its theory. However, as feminists, we often find some of its concepts, such as individual rights, very useful in our attempts to fight problems rooted in our traditional cultures.

Nonwestern feminists will no doubt be sensitive to the fact that positivism is not our only enemy. Western feminists too must learn not to uncritically claim any nonpositivist framework as an ally; despite commonalities, there are apt to be many differences. A temperate look at positions we espouse as allies is necessary since "the enemy of my enemy is my friend" is a principle likely to be as misleading in epistemology as it is in the domain of Realpolitik....

...[F]eminists should be cautious about assuming that they necessarily have much in common with a framework simply because it is nonpositivist. Nonwestern feminists may be more alert to this error because many problems they confront arise in nonpositivist contexts.

The Political Uses of "Epistemic Privilege"

Important strands in feminist epistemology hold the view that our concrete embodiments as members of a specific class, race, and gender as well as our concrete historical situations necessarily play significant roles in our perspective on the world; moreover, no point of view is "neutral" because no one exists unembedded in the world. Knowledge is seen as gained not by solitary individuals but by socially constituted members of groups that emerge and change through history.

Feminists have also argued that groups living under various forms of oppression are more likely to have a critical perspective on their situation and that this critical view is both generated and partly constituted by critical emotional responses that subjects experience vis-à-vis their life situations. This perspective in feminist epistemology rejects the "Dumb View" of emotions and favors an intentional conception that emphasizes the cognitive aspect of emotions. It is critical of the traditional view of the emotions as wholly and always impediments to knowledge and argues that many emotions often help rather than hinder our understanding of a person or situation (see Jaggar 1989).

Bringing together these views on the role of the emotions in knowledge, the possibility of critical insights being generated by oppression, and the contextual nature of knowledge may suggest some answers to serious and interesting political questions. I will consider what these epistemic positions entail regarding the possibility of understanding and political cooperation between oppressed groups and sympathetic members of a dominant group—say, between white people and people of color over issues of race or between men and women over issues of gender.

These considerations are also relevant to questions of understanding and cooperation between western and nonwestern feminists. Western feminists, despite their critical understanding of their own culture, often tend to be more a part of it than they realize. If they fail to see the contexts of their theories and assume that their perspective has universal validity for all feminists, they tend to participate in the dominance that western culture has exercised over nonwestern cultures.

Our position must explain and justify our dual need to criticize members of a dominant group (say, men or white people or western feminists) for their lack of attention to or concern with problems that affect an oppressed group (say, women or people of color or nonwestern feminists, respectively), as well as for our frequent hostility toward those who express interest, even sympathetic interest, in issues that concern groups of which they are not a part.

Both attitudes are often warranted. On the one hand, one cannot but be angry at those who minimize, ignore, or dismiss the pain and conflict that racism and sexism inflict on their victims. On the other hand, living in a state of siege also necessarily makes us suspicious of expressions of concern and support from those who do not live these oppressions. We are suspicious of the motives of our sympathizers or the extent of their sincerity, and we worry, often with good reason, that they may claim that their interest provides a warrant for them to speak for us, as dominant groups throughout history have spoken for the dominated.

This is all the more threatening to groups aware of how recently they have acquired the power to articulate their own points of view. Nonwestern feminists are especially aware of this because they have a double struggle in trying to find their own voice: they have to learn to articulate their differences, not only from their own traditional contexts but also from western feminism.

Politically, we face interesting questions whose answers hinge on the nature and extent of the communication that we think possible between different groups. Should we try to share our perspectives and insights with those who have not lived our oppressions and accept that they may fully come to share them? Or should we seek only the affirmation of those like ourselves, who share common features of oppression, and rule out the possibility of those who have not lived these oppressions ever acquiring a genuine understanding of them?

I argue that it would be a mistake to move from the thesis that knowledge is constructed by human subjects who are socially constituted to the conclusion that those who are differently located socially can never attain *some* understanding of our experience or *some* sympathy with our cause. In that case, we would be committed to not just a perspectival view of knowledge but a relativistic one. Relativism, as I am using it, implies that a person could have knowledge of only the sorts of things she had experienced personally and that she would be totally unable to communicate any of the contents of her knowledge to someone who did not have the same sorts of experiences. Not only does this seem clearly false and perhaps even absurd, but it is probably a good idea not to have any a priori views that would imply either that all our knowledge is always capable of being communicated to every other person or that would imply that some of our knowledge is necessarily incapable of being communicated to some class of persons.

"Nonanalytic" and "nonrational" forms of discourse, like fiction or poetry, may be better able than other forms to convey the complex life experiences of one group to members of another. One can also hope that being part of one oppressed group may enable an individual to have a more sympathetic understanding of issues relating to another kind of oppression—that, for instance, being a woman may sensitize one to issues of race and class even if one is a woman privileged in those respects.

Again, this should not be reduced to some kind of metaphysical presumption. Historical circumstances have sometimes conspired, say, to making working-class men more chauvinistic in some of their attitudes than other men. Sometimes one sort of suffering may simply harden individuals to other sorts or leave them without energy to take any interest in the problems of other groups. But we can at least try to foster such sensitivity by focusing on parallels, not identities, between different sorts of oppressions.

Our commitment to the contextual nature of knowledge does not require us to claim that those who do not inhabit these contexts can never have any knowledge of them. But this commitment does permit us to argue that it is *easier* and *more likely* for the oppressed to have critical insights into the conditions of their own oppression than it is for those who live outside these structures. Those who actually *live* the oppressions of class, race, or gender have faced the issues that such oppressions generate in a variety of different situations. The insights and emotional responses engendered by these situations are a legacy with which they confront any new issue or situation.

Those who display sympathy as outsiders often fail both to understand fully the emotional complexities of living as a member of an oppressed group and to carry what they have learned and understood about one situation to the way they perceive another. It is a commonplace that even sympathetic men will often fail to perceive subtle instances of sexist behavior or discourse.

Sympathetic individuals who are not members of an oppressed group should keep in mind the possibility of this sort of failure regarding their understanding of issues relating to an oppression they do not share. They should realize that nothing they may do, from participating in demonstrations to changing their lifestyles, can make them one of the oppressed. For instance, men who share household and child-rearing responsibilities with women are mistaken if they think that this act of choice, often buttressed by the gratitude and admiration of others, is anything like the woman's experience of being forcibly socialized into these tasks and of having others perceive this as her natural function in the scheme of things.

The view that we can understand much about the perspectives of those whose oppression we do not share allows us the space to criticize dominant groups for their blindness to the facts of oppression. The view that such an understanding, despite great effort and interest, is likely to be incomplete or limited, provides us with the ground for denying total parity to members of a dominant group in their ability to understand our situation.

Sympathetic members of a dominant group need not necessarily defer to our views on any particular issue because that may reduce itself to another subtle form of condescension, but at least they must keep in mind the very real difficulties and possibility of failure to fully understand our concerns. This and the very important need for dominated groups to control the means of discourse about their own situations are important reasons for taking seriously the claim that oppressed groups have an "epistemic advantage."

The Dark Side of "Double Vision"

I think that one of the most interesting insights of feminist epistemology is the view that oppressed groups, whether women, the poor, or racial minorities, may derive an "epistemic advantage" from having knowledge of the practices of both their own contexts and those of their oppressors. The practices of the dominant groups (for instance, men) govern a society; the dominated group (for instance, women) must acquire some fluency with these practices in order to survive in that society.

There is no similar pressure on members of the dominant group to acquire knowledge of the practices of the dominated groups. For instance, colonized people had to learn the language and culture of their colonizers. The colonizers seldom found it necessary to have more than a sketchy acquaintance with the language and culture of the "natives." Thus, the oppressed are seen as having an "epistemic advantage" because they can operate with two sets of practices and in two different contexts. This advantage is thought to lead to critical insights because each framework provides a critical perspective on the other.

I would like to balance this account with a few comments about the "dark side," the disadvantages, of being able to or of having to inhabit two mutually incompatible frameworks that provide differing perspectives on social reality. I suspect that nonwestern feminists, given the often complex and troublesome inter-relationships between the contexts they must inhabit, are less likely to express unqualified enthusiasm about the benefits of straddling a multiplicity of contexts. Mere access to two different and incompatible contexts is not a guarantee that a critical stance on the part of an individual will result. There are many ways in which she may deal with the situation.

First, the person may be tempted to dichotomize her life and reserve the framework of a different context for each part. The middle class of nonwestern countries supplies numerous examples of people who are very westernized in public life but who return to a very traditional lifestyle in the realm of the family. Women may choose to live their public lives in a "male" mode, displaying characteristics of aggressiveness, competition, and so on, while continuing to play dependent and compliant roles in their private lives. The pressures of jumping between two different lifestyles may be mitigated by justifications of how each pattern of behavior is appropriate to its particular context and of how it enables them to "get the best of both worlds."

Second, the individual may try to reject the practices of her own context and try to be as much as possible like members of the dominant group. Westernized intellectuals in the nonwestern world often may almost lose knowledge of their own cultures and practices and be ashamed of the little that they do still know. Women may try both to acquire stereotypically male characteristics, like aggressiveness, and to expunge stereotypically female characteristics, like emotionality. Or the individual could try to reject entirely the framework of the dominant group and assert the virtues of her own despite the risks of being marginalized from the power structures of the society; consider, for example, women who seek a certain sort of security in traditionally defined roles.

The choice to inhabit two contexts critically is an alternative to these choices and, I would argue, a more useful one. But the presence of alternative contexts does not by itself guarantee that one of the other choices will not be made. Moreover, the decision to inhabit two contexts critically, although it may lead to an "epistemic advantage," is likely to exact a certain price. It may lead to a sense of totally lacking roots or any space where one is at home in a relaxed manner.

This sense of alienation may be minimized if the critical straddling of two contexts is part of an ongoing critical politics, due to the support of others and a deeper understanding of what is going on. When it is not so rooted, it may generate ambivalence, uncertainty, despair, and even madness, rather than more positive critical emotions and attitudes. However such a person determines her locus, there may be a sense of being an outsider in both contexts and a sense of clumsiness or lack of fluency in both sets of practices. Consider this simple linguistic example: most people who learn two different languages that are associated with two very different cultures seldom acquire both with equal fluency; they may find themselves devoid of vocabulary in one language for certain contexts of life or be unable to match real objects with terms they have acquired in their vocabulary. For instance, people from my sort of background would know words in Indian languages for some spices, fruits, and vegetables that they do not know in English. Similarly, they might be unable to discuss "technical" subjects like economics or biology in their own languages because they learned about these subjects and acquired their technical vocabularies only in English.

The relation between the two contexts the individual inhabits may not be simple or straightforward. The individual subject is seldom in a position to carry out a perfect "dialectical synthesis" that preserves all the advantages of both contexts and transcends all their problems. There may be a number of different "syntheses," each of which avoids a different subset of the problems and preserves a different subset of the benefits.

No solution may be perfect or even palatable to the agent confronted with a choice. For example, some Indian feminists may find some western modes of dress (say trousers) either more comfortable or more their "style" than some local modes of dress. However, they may find that wearing the local mode of dress is less socially troublesome, alienates them less from more traditional people they want to work with, and so on. Either choice is bound to leave them partly frustrated in their desires.

Feminist theory must be temperate in the use it makes of this doctrine of "double vision"—the claim that oppressed groups have an epistemic advantage and access to greater critical conceptual space. Certain types and contexts of oppression certainly may bear out the truth of this claim. Others certainly do not seem to do so; and even if they do provide space for critical insights, they may also rule out the possibility of actions subversive of the oppressive state of affairs.

Certain kinds of oppressive contexts, such as the contexts in which women of my grandmother's background lived, rendered their subjects entirely devoid of skills required to function as independent entities in the culture. Girls were married off barely past puberty, trained for nothing beyond household tasks and the rearing of children, and passed from economic dependency on their fathers to economic dependency on their husbands to economic dependency on their sons in old age. Their criticisms of their lot were articulated, if at all, in terms that precluded a desire for any radical change. They saw themselves sometimes as personally unfortunate, but they did not locate the causes of their misery in larger social arrangements.

I conclude by stressing that the important insight incorporated in the doctrine of "double vision" should not be reified into a metaphysics that serves as a substitute for concrete social analysis. Furthermore, the alternative to "buying" into an oppressive social system need not be a celebration of exclusion and the mechanisms of marginalization. The thesis that oppression may bestow an epistemic advantage should not tempt us in the direction of idealizing or romanticizing oppression and blind us to its real material and psychic deprivations.

31.
THE POLITICS OF BLACK FEMINIST THOUGHT
Patricia Hill Collins

In 1831 Maria W. Stewart asked, "How long shall the fair daughters of Africa be compelled to bury their minds and talents beneath a load of iron pots and kettles?" Orphaned at age five, bound out to a clergyman's family as a domestic servant, Stewart struggled to gather isolated fragments of an education when and where she could. As the first American woman to lecture in public on political issues and to leave copies of her texts, this early U.S. Black woman intellectual foreshadowed a variety of themes taken up by her Black feminist successors (Richardson 1987).

Maria Stewart challenged African-American women to reject the negative images of Black womanhood so prominent in her times, pointing out that race, gender, and class oppression were the fundamental causes of Black women's poverty. In an 1833 speech she proclaimed, "Like King Solomon, who put neither nail nor hammer to the temple, yet received the praise; so also have the white Americans gained themselves a name . . . while in reality we have been their principal foundation and support." Stewart objected to the injustice of this situation: "We have pursued the shadow, they have obtained the substance; we have performed the labor, they have received the profits; we have planted the vines, they have eaten the fruits of them" (Richardson 1987, 59).

Maria Stewart was not content to point out the source of Black women's oppression. She urged Black women to forge self-definitions of self-reliance and independence. "It is useless for us any longer to sit with our hands folded, reproaching the whites; for that will never elevate us," she exhorted. "Possess the spirit of independence. . . . Possess the spirit of men, bold and enterprising, fearless and undaunted" (p. 53). To Stewart, the power of self-definition was essential, for Black women's survival was at stake. "Sue for your rights and privileges. Know the reason you cannot attain them. Weary them with your importunities. You can but die if you make the attempt; and we shall certainly die if you do not" (p. 38).

Stewart also challenged Black women to use their special roles as mothers to forge powerful mechanisms of political action. "O, ye mothers, what a responsibility rests on you!" Stewart preached. "You have souls committed to your charge. . . . It is you that must create in the minds of your little girls and boys a thirst for knowledge, the love of virtue . . . . and the cultivation of a pure heart." Stewart recognized the magnitude of the task at hand. "Do not say you cannot make any thing of your children; but say . . . we will try" (p. 35).

Maria Stewart was one of the first U.S. Black feminists to champion the utility of Black women's relationships with one another in providing a community for Black women's activism and self-determination. "Shall it any longer be said of the daughters of Africa, they have no ambition, they have no force?" she questioned. "By no means. Let every female heart become united, and let us raise a fund ourselves; and at the end of one year and a half, we might be able to lay the corner stone for the building of a High School, that the higher branches of knowledge might be enjoyed by us" (p. 37). Stewart saw the potential for Black women's activism as educators. She advised, "Turn your attention to knowledge and improvement; for knowledge is power" (p. 41).

Though she said little in her speeches about the sexual politics of her time, her advice to African-American women suggests that she was painfully aware of the sexual abuse visited upon Black women. She continued to "plead the cause of virtue and the pure principles of morality" (p. 31) for Black women. And to those Whites who thought that Black women were inherently inferior, Stewart offered a biting response: "Our souls are fired with the same love of liberty and independence with which your souls are fired.... [T]oo much of your blood flows in our veins, too much of your color in our skins, for us not to possess your spirits" (p. 40).

Despite Maria Stewart's intellectual prowess, the ideas of this extraordinary woman come to us only in scattered fragments that not only suggest her brilliance but speak tellingly of the fate of countless Black women intellectuals. Many Maria Stewarts exist, African-American women whose minds and talents have been suppressed by the pots and kettles symbolic of Black women's subordination (Guy-Sheftall 1986).[1] Far too many African-American women intellectuals have labored in isolation and obscurity and, like Zora Neale Hurston, lie buried in unmarked graves.

Some have been more fortunate, for they have become known to us, largely through the efforts of contemporary Black women scholars (Hine et al. 1993; Guy-Sheftall 1995b). Like Alice Walker, these scholars sense that "a people do not throw their geniuses away" and that "if they are thrown away, it is our duty as artists, scholars, and witnesses for the future to collect them again for the sake of our children.... if necessary, bone by bone" (Walker 1983, 92).

This painstaking process of collecting the ideas and actions of "thrown away" Black women like Maria Stewart has revealed one important discovery. Black women intellectuals have laid a vital analytical foundation for a distinctive standpoint on self, community, and society and, in doing so, created a multifaceted, African-American women's intellectual tradition. While clear discontinuities in this tradition exist—times when Black women's voices were strong, and others when assuming a more muted tone was essential—one striking dimension of the ideas of Maria W. Stewart and her successors is the thematic consistency of their work.

If such a rich intellectual tradition exists, why has it remained virtually invisible until now. In 1905 Fannie Barrier Williams lamented, "The colored girl...is not known and hence not believed in; she belongs to a race that is best designated by the term 'problem,' and she lives beneath the shadow of that problem which envelops and obscures her" (Williams 1987, 150). Why are African American women and our ideas not known and not believed in?

The shadow obscuring this complex Black women's intellectual tradition is neither accidental nor benign. Suppressing the knowledge produced by any oppressed group makes it easier for dominant groups to rule because the seeming absence of dissent suggests that subordinate groups willingly collaborate in their own victimization (Scott 1985). Maintaining the invisibility of Black women and our ideas not only in the United States, but in Africa, the Caribbean, South America, Europe, and other places where Black women now live, has been critical in maintaining social inequalities. Black women engaged in reclaiming and constructing Black women's knowledges often point to the politics of suppression that affect their projects. For example, several authors in Heidi Mirza's (1997) edited volume on Black British feminism identify their invisibility and silencing in the contemporary United Kingdom. Similarly, South African businesswoman Danisa Baloyi describes her astonishment at the invisibility of African women in U.S. scholarship: "As a student doing research in the United States, I was amazed by the [small] amount of information on Black South African women, and shocked that only a minuscule amount was actually written by Black women themselves" (Baloyi 1995, 41).

Despite this suppression, U.S. Black women have managed to do intellectual work, and to have our ideas matter. Sojourner Truth, Anna Julia Cooper, Ida B. Wells-Barnett, Mary McLeod Bethune, Toni Morrison, Barbara Smith, and countless others have consistently struggled to make themselves heard. African women writers such as Ama Ata Aidoo, Buchi Emecheta, and Ellen Kuzwayo have used their voices to raise important issues that affect Black African women (James 1990). Like the work of Maria W. Stewart and that of Black women transnationally, African-American women's intellectual work has aimed to foster Black women's activism.

This dialectic of oppression and activism, the tension between the suppression of African-American women's ideas and our intellectual activism in the face of that suppression, constitutes the politics of U.S. Black feminist thought. More important, understanding this dialectical relationship is critical in assessing how U.S. Black feminist thought—its core themes, epistemological significance, and connections to domestic and transnational Black feminist practice—is fundamentally embedded in a political context that has challenged its very right to exist.

The Suppression of Black Feminist Thought

The vast majority of African-American women were brought to the United States to work as slaves in a situation of oppression. Oppression describes any unjust situation where, systematically and over a long period of time, one group denies another group access to the resources of society. Race, class, gender, sexuality, nation, age, and ethnicity among others constitute major forms of oppression in the United States. However, the convergence of race, class, and gender oppression characteristic of U.S. slavery shaped all subsequent relationships that women of African descent had within Black American families and communities, with employers, and among one another. It also created the political context for Black women's intellectual work.

African-American women's oppression has encompassed three interdependent dimensions. First, the exploitation of Black women's labor essential to U.S. capitalism—the "iron pots and kettles" symbolizing Black women's long-standing ghettoization in service occupations—represents the economic dimension of oppression (Davis 1981; Marable 1983; Jones 1985; Amott and Matthaei 1991). Survival for most African-American women has been such an all-consuming activity that most have had few opportunities to do intellectual work as it has been traditionally defined. The drudgery of enslaved African-American women's work and the grinding poverty of "free" wage labor in the rural South tellingly illustrate the high costs Black women have paid for survival. The millions of impoverished African-American women ghettoized in Philadelphia, Birmingham, Oakland, Detroit, and other U.S. inner cities demonstrate the continuation of these earlier forms of Black women's economic exploitation (Brewer 1993; Omolade 1994).

Second, the political dimension of oppression has denied African-American women the rights and privileges routinely extended to White male citizens (Burnham 1987; Scales-Trent 1989; Berry 1994). Forbidding Black women to vote, excluding African-Americans and women from public office, and withholding equitable treatment in the criminal justice system all substantiate the political subordination of Black women. Educational institutions have also fostered this pattern of disenfranchisement. Past practices such as denying literacy to slaves and relegating Black women to underfunded, segregated Southern schools worked to ensure that a quality education for Black women remained the exception rather than the rule (Mullings 1997). The large numbers of young Black women in inner cities and impoverished rural areas who continue to leave school before attaining full literacy represent the continued efficacy of the political dimension of Black women's oppression.

Finally, controlling images applied to Black women that originated during the slave era attest to the ideological dimension of U.S. Black women's oppression (King 1973; D. White 1985; Carby 1987; Morton 1991). Ideology refers to the body of ideas reflecting the interests of a group of people. Within U.S. culture, racist and sexist ideologies permeate the social structure to such a degree that they become hegemonic, namely, seen as natural, normal, and inevitable. In this context, certain assumed qualities that are attached to Black women are used to justify oppression. From the mammies, jezebels, and breeder women of slavery to the smiling Aunt Jemimas on pancake mix boxes, ubiquitous Black prostitutes, and ever-present welfare mothers of contemporary popular culture, negative stereotypes applied to African-American women have been fundamental to Black women's oppression.

Taken together, the supposedly seamless web of economy, polity, and ideology function as a highly effective system of social control designed to keep African-American women in an assigned, subordinate place. This larger system of oppression works to suppress the ideas of Black women intellectuals and to protect elite White male interests and worldviews. Denying African-American women the credentials to become literate certainly excluded most African-American women from positions as scholars, teachers, authors, poets, and critics. Moreover, while Black women historians, writers, and social scientists have long existed, until recently these women have not held leadership positions in universities, professional associations, publishing concerns, broadcast media, and other social institutions of knowledge validation. Black women's exclusion from positions of power within mainstream institutions has led to the elevation of elite White male ideas and interests and the corresponding suppression of Black women's ideas and interests in traditional scholarship (Higginbotham 1989; Morton 1991; Collins 1998, 95–123). Moreover, this historical exclusion means that stereotypical images of Black women permeate popular culture and public policy (Wallace 1990; Lubiano 1992; Jewell 1993).

U.S. and European women's studies have challenged the seemingly hegemonic ideas of elite White men. Ironically, Western feminisms have also suppressed Black women's ideas (duCille 1996, 81–119). Even though Black women intellectuals have long expressed a distinctive African-influenced and feminist sensibility about how race and class intersect in structuring gender, historically we have not been full participants in White feminist organizations (Giddings 1984; Zinn et al. 1986; Caraway 1991). As a result, African-American, Latino, Native American, and Asian-American women have criticized Western feminisms for being racist and overly concerned with White, middle-class women's issues (Moraga and Anzaldua 1981; Smith 1982; Dill 1983; Davis 1989).

Traditionally, many U.S. White feminist scholars have resisted having Black women as full colleagues. Moreover, this historical suppression of Black women's ideas has had a pronounced influence on feminist theory. One pattern of suppression is that of omission. Theories advanced as being universally applicable to women as a group upon closer examination appear greatly limited by the White, middle-class, and Western origins of their proponents. For example, Nancy Chodorow's (1978) work on sex role socialization and Carol Gilligan's (1982) study of the moral development of women both rely heavily on White, middle-class samples. While these two classics made key contributions to feminist theory, they simultaneously promoted the notion of a generic woman who is White and middle class. The absence of Black feminist ideas from these and other studies placed them in a much more tenuous position to challenge the hegemony of mainstream scholarship on behalf of all women.

Another pattern of suppression lies in paying lip service to the need for diversity, but changing little about one's own practice. Currently, some U.S. White women who possess great competence in researching a range of issues acknowledge the need for diversity, yet omit women of color from their work. These women claim that they are unqualified to understand or even speak of "Black women's experiences" because they themselves are not Black. Others include a few safe, "hand-picked" Black women's voices to avoid criticisms that they are racist. Both examples reflect a basic unwillingness by many U.S. White feminists to alter the paradigms that guide their work.

A more recent pattern of suppression involves incorporating, changing, and thereby depoliticizing Black feminist ideas. The growing popularity of post modernism in U.S. higher education in the 1990s, especially within literary criticism and cultural studies, fosters a climate where symbolic inclusion often substitutes for bona fide substantive changes. Because interest in Black women's work has reached occult status, suggests Ann duCille (1996), it "increasingly marginalizes both the black women critics and scholars who excavated the fields in question and their black feminist 'daughters' who would further develop those fields" (p. 87). Black feminist critic Barbara Christian (1994), a pioneer in creating Black women's studies in the U.S. academy, queries whether Black feminism can survive the pernicious politics of resegregation. In discussing the politics of a new multiculturalism, Black feminist critic Hazel Carby (1992) expresses dismay at the growing situation of symbolic inclusion, in which the texts of Black women writers are welcome in the multicultural classroom while actual Black women are not.

Not all White Western feminists participate in these diverse patterns of suppression. Some do try to build coalitions across racial and other markers of difference, often with noteworthy results. Works by Elizabeth Spelman (1988), Sandra Harding (1986, 1998), Margaret Andersen (1991), Peggy McIntosh (1988), Mab Segrest (1994), Anne Fausto-Sterling (1995), and other individual U.S. White feminist thinkers reflect sincere efforts to develop a multiracial, diverse feminism. However, despite their efforts, these concerns linger on.

Like feminist scholarship, the diverse strands of African-American social and political thought have also challenged mainstream scholarship. However, Black social and political thought has been limited by both the reformist postures toward change assumed by many U.S. Black intellectuals (Cruse 1967; West 1977–78) and the secondary status afforded the ideas and experiences of African-American women. Adhering to a male-defined ethos that far too often equates racial progress with the acquisition of an ill-defined manhood has left much U.S. Black thought with a prominent masculinist bias.

In this case the patterns of suppressing Black women's ideas have been similar yet different. Though Black women have played little or no part in dominant academic discourse and White feminist arenas, we have long been included in the organizational structures of Black civil society. U.S. Black women's acceptance of subordinate roles in Black organizations does not mean that we wield little authority or that we experience patriarchy in the same way as do White women in White organizations (Evans 1979; Gilkes 1985). But with the exception of Black women's organizations, male-run organizations have historically either not stressed Black women's issues (Beale 1970; Marable 1983), or have done so under duress. For example, Black feminist activist Pauli Murray (1970) found that from its founding in 1916 to 1970, the *Journal of Negro History* published only five articles devoted exclusively to Black women. Evelyn Brooks Higginbotham's (1993) historical monograph on Black women in Black Baptist churches records African-American women's struggles to raise issues that concerned women. Even progressive Black organizations have not been immune from gender discrimination. Civil rights activist Ella Baker's experiences in the Southern Christian Leadership Conference illustrate one form that suppressing Black women's ideas and talents can take. Ms. Baker virtually ran the entire organization, yet had to defer to the decision-making authority of the exclusively male leadership group (Cantarow 1980). Civil rights activist Septima Clark describes similar experiences: "I found all over the South that whatever the man said had to be right. They had the whole say. The woman couldn't say a thing" (C. Brown 1986, 79). Radical African-American women also can find themselves deferring to male authority. In her autobiography, Elaine Brown (1992), a participant and subsequent leader of the 1960s radical organization the Black Panther Party for Self-Defense, discusses the sexism expressed by Panther men. Overall, even though Black women intellectuals have asserted their right to speak both as African-Americans and as women, historically these women have not held top leadership positions in Black organizations and have frequently struggled within them to express Black feminist ideas (Giddings 1984).

Much contemporary U.S. Black feminist thought reflects Black women's increasing willingness to oppose gender inequality within Black civil society. Septima Clark describes this transformation:

> I used to feel that women couldn't speak up, because when district meetings were being held at my home...I didn't feel as if I could tell them what I had in mind...But later on, I found out that women had a lot to say, and what they had to say was really worthwhile....So we started talking, and have been talking quite a bit since that time (C. Brown 1986, 82).

African-American women intellectuals have been "talking quite a bit" since 1970 and have insisted that the masculinist bias in Black social and political thought, the racist bias in feminist theory, and the heterosexist bias in both be corrected (see, e.g., Bambara 1970; Dill 1979; Jordan 1981; Combahee River Collective 1982; Lorde 1984).

Within Black civil society, the increasing visibility of Black women's ideas did not go unopposed. The virulent reaction to earlier Black women's writings by some Black men, such as Robert Staples's (1979) analysis of Ntozake Shange's (1975) choreopoem, *For Colored Girls Who Have Considered Suicide*, and Michele Wallace's (1978) controversial volume, *Black Macho and the Myth of the Superwoman*, illustrates the difficulty of challenging the masculinist bias in Black social and political thought. Alice Walker encountered similarly hostile reactions to her publication of *The Color Purple*. In describing the response of African-American men to the outpouring of publications by Black women writers in the 1970s and 1980s, Calvin Hernton offers an incisive criticism of the seeming tenacity of a masculinist bias:

The telling thing about the hostile attitude of black men toward black women writers is that they interpret the new thrust of the women as being "counter-productive" to the historical goal of the Black struggle. Revealingly, while black men have achieved outstanding recognition throughout the history of black writing, black women have not accused the men of collaborating with the enemy and setting back the progress of the race. (1985, 5)

Not all Black male reaction during this period was hostile. For example, Manning Marable (1983) devotes an entire chapter in *How Capitalism Underdeveloped Black America* to how sexism has been a primary deterrent to Black community development. Following Marable's lead, work by Haki Madhubuti (1990), Cornel West (1993), Michael Awkward (1996), Michael Dyson (1996), and others suggests that some U.S. Black male thinkers have taken Black feminist thought seriously. Despite the diverse ideological perspectives expressed by these writers, each seemingly recognizes the importance of Black women's ideas.

Black Feminist Thought as Critical Social Theory

Even if they appear to be otherwise, situations such as the suppression of Black women's ideas within traditional scholarship and the struggles within the critiques of that established knowledge are inherently unstable. Conditions in the wider political economy simultaneously shape Black women's subordination and foster activism. On some level, people who are oppressed usually know it. For African-American women, the knowledge gained at intersecting oppressions of race, class, and gender provides the stimulus for crafting and passing on the subjugated knowledge[2] of Black women's critical social theory (Collins 1998, 3–10).

As an historically oppressed group, U.S. Black women have produced social thought designed to oppose oppression. Not only does the form assumed by this thought diverge from standard academic theory—it can take the form of poetry, music, essays, and the like—but the *purpose* of Black women's collective thought is distinctly different. Social theories emerging from and/or on behalf of U.S. Black women and other historically oppressed groups aim to find ways to escape from, survive in, and/or oppose prevailing social and economic injustice. In the United States, for example, African-American social and political thought analyzes institutionalized racism, not to help it work more efficiently, but to resist it. Feminism advocates women's emancipation and empowerment, Marxist social thought aims for a more equitable society, while queer theory opposes heterosexism. Beyond U.S. borders, many women from oppressed groups also struggle to understand new forms of injustice. In a transnational, postcolonial context, women within new and often Black-run nation-states in the Caribbean, Africa, and Asia struggle with new meanings attached to ethnicity, citizenship status, and religion. In increasingly multicultural European nation-states, women migrants from former colonies encounter new forms of subjugation (Yuval-Davis 1997). Social theories expressed by women emerging from these diverse groups typically do not arise from the rarefied atmosphere of their imaginations. Instead, social theories reflect women's efforts to come to terms with lived experiences within intersecting oppressions of race, class, gender, sexuality, ethnicity, nation, and religion (see, e.g., Alexander and Mohanty 1997; Mirza 1997).

Black feminist thought, U.S. Black women's critical social theory, reflects similar power relationships. For African-American women, critical social theory encompasses bodies of knowledge and sets of institutional practices that actively grapple with the central questions facing U.S. Black women as a collectivity. The need for such thought arises because African-American women as a *group* remain oppressed within a U.S. context characterized by injustice. This neither means that all African-American women within that group are oppressed in the same way, nor that some U.S. Black women do not suppress others. Black feminist thought's identity as a "critical" social theory lies in its commitment to justice, both for U.S. Black women as a collectivity and for that of other similarly oppressed groups.

Historically, two factors stimulated U.S. Black women's critical social theory. For one, prior to World War II, racial segregation in urban housing became so entrenched that the majority of African-American women lived in self-contained Black neighborhoods where their children attended overwhelmingly Black schools, and where they themselves belonged to all-Black churches and similar community organizations. Despite the fact that ghettoization was designed to foster the political control and economic exploitation of Black Americans (Squires 1994), these all-Black neighborhoods simultaneously provided a separate space where African-American women and men could use African-derived ideas to craft distinctive oppositional knowledges designed to resist racial oppression.

Every social group has a constantly evolving worldview that it uses to order and evaluate its own experiences (Sobel 1979). For African-Americans this worldview originated in the cosmologies of diverse West African ethnic groups (Diop 1974). By retaining and reworking significant elements of these West African cultures, communities of enslaved Africans offered their members explanations for slavery alternative to those advanced by slave owners (Gutman 1976; Webber 1978; Sobel 1979). These African-derived ideas also laid the foundation for the rules of a distinctive Black American civil society. Later on, confining African-Americans to all-Black areas in the rural South and Northern urban ghettos fostered the solidification of a distinctive ethos in Black civil society regarding language (Smitherman 1977), religion (Sobel 1979; Paris 1995), family structure (Sudarkasa 1981b), and community politics (Brown 1994). While essential to the survival of U.S. Blacks as a group and expressed differently by individual African-Americans, these knowledges remained simultaneously hidden from and suppressed by Whites. Black oppositional knowledges existed to resist injustice, but they also remained subjugated.

As mothers, othermothers, teachers, and churchwomen in essentially all-Black rural communities and urban neighborhoods, U.S. Black women participated in constructing and reconstructing these oppositional knowledges. Through the lived experiences gained within their extended families and communities, individual African-American women fashioned their own ideas about the meaning of Black womanhood. When these ideas found collective expression, Black women's self-definitions enabled them to refashion African-influenced conceptions of self and community. These self-definitions of Black womanhood were designed to resist the negative controlling images of Black womanhood advanced by Whites as well as the discriminatory social practices that these controlling images supported. In all, Black women's participation in crafting a constantly changing African-American culture fostered distinctively Black and women-centered worldviews.

Another factor that stimulated U.S. Black women's critical social theory lay in the common experiences they gained from their jobs. Prior to World War II, U.S. Black women worked primarily in two occupations—agriculture and domestic work. Their ghettoization in domestic work sparked an important contradiction. Domestic work fostered U.S. Black women's economic exploitation, yet it simultaneously created the conditions for distinctively Black and female forms of resistance. Domestic work allowed African-American women to see White elites, both actual and aspiring, from perspectives largely obscured from Black men and from these groups themselves. In their White "families," Black women not only performed domestic duties but frequently formed strong ties with the children they nurtured, and with the employers themselves. On one level this insider relationship was satisfying to all concerned. Accounts of Black domestic workers stress the sense of self-affirmation the women experienced at seeing racist ideology demystified. But on another level these Black women knew that they could never belong to their White "families." They were economically exploited workers and thus would remain outsiders. The result was being placed in a curious *outsider-within* social location (Collins 1986), a peculiar marginality that stimulated a distinctive Black women's perspective on a variety of themes (see, e.g., Childress 1986).

Taken together, Black women's participation in constructing African-American culture in all-Black settings and the distinctive perspectives gained from their outsider-within placement in domestic work provide the material backdrop for a unique Black women's standpoint. When armed with cultural beliefs honed in Black civil society, many Black women who found themselves doing domestic work often developed distinct views of the contradictions between the dominant group's actions and ideologies. Moreover, they often shared their ideas with other African-American women. Nancy White, a Black inner-city resident, explores the connection between experience and beliefs:

> Now, I understand all these things from living. But you can't lay up on these flowery beds of ease and think that you are running your life, too. Some women, white women, can run their husband's lives for a while, but most of them have to...see what he tells them there is to see. If he tells them that they ain't seeing what they know they are seeing, then they have to just go on like it wasn't there! (in Gwaltney 1980, 148)

Not only does this passage speak to the power of the dominant group to suppress the knowledge produced by subordinate groups, but it illustrates how being in outsider-within locations can foster new angles of vision on oppression. Ms. White's Blackness makes her a perpetual outsider. She could never be a White middle-class woman lying on a "flowery bed of ease." But her work of caring for White women allowed her an insider's view of some of the contradictions between White women thinking that they are running their lives and the patriarchal power and authority in their households.

Practices such as these, whether experienced oneself or learned by listening to African-American women who have had them, have encouraged many U.S. Black women to question the contradictions between dominant ideologies of American womanhood and U.S. Black women's devalued status. If women are allegedly passive and fragile, then why are Black women treated as "mules" and assigned heavy cleaning chores? If good mothers are supposed to stay at home with their children, then why are U.S. Black women on public assistance forced to find jobs and leave their children in day care? If women's highest calling is to become mothers, then why are Black teen mothers pressured to use Norplant and Depo Provera? In the absence of a viable Black feminism that investigates how intersecting oppressions of race, gender, and class foster these contradictions, the angle of vision created by being deemed devalued workers and failed mothers could easily be turned inward, leading to internalized oppression. But the legacy of struggle among U.S. Black women suggests that a collectively shared, Black women's oppositional knowledge has long existed. This collective wisdom in turn has spurred U.S. Black women to generate a more specialized knowledge, namely, Black feminist thought as critical social theory. Just as fighting injustice lay at the heart of U.S. Black women's experiences, so did analyzing and creating imaginative responses to injustice characterize the core of Black feminist thought.

Historically, while they often disagreed on its expression—some U.S. Black women were profoundly reformist while more radical thinkers bordered on the revolutionary—African-American women intellectuals who were nurtured in social conditions of racial segregation strove to develop Black feminist thought as critical social theory. Regardless of social class and other differences among U.S. Black women, all were in some way affected by intersecting oppressions of race, gender, and class. The economic, political, and ideological dimensions of U.S. Black women's oppression suppressed the intellectual production of individual Black feminist thinkers. At the same time, these same social conditions simultaneously stimulated distinctive patterns of U.S. Black women's activism that also influenced and was influenced by individual Black women thinkers. Thus, the dialectic of oppression and activism characterizing U.S. Black women's experiences with intersecting oppressions also influenced the ideas and actions of Black women intellectuals.

The exclusion of Black women's ideas from mainstream academic discourse and the curious placement of African-American women intellectuals in feminist thinking, Black social and political theories, and in other important thought such as U.S. labor studies has meant that U.S. Black women intellectuals have found themselves in outsider-within positions in many academic endeavors (Hull et al. 1982; Christian 1989). The assumptions on which full group membership are based—Whiteness for feminist thought, maleness for Black social and political thought, and the combination for mainstream scholarship—all negate Black women's realities. Prevented from becoming full insiders in any of these areas of inquiry, Black women remained in outsider-within locations, individuals whose marginality provided a distinctive angle of vision on these intellectual and political entities.

Alice Walker's work exemplifies these fundamental influences within Black women's intellectual traditions. Walker describes how her outsider-within location influenced her thinking: "I believe … that it was from this period—from my solitary, lonely position, the position of an outcast—that I began really to see people and things, really to notice relationships" (Walker 1983, 244). Walker realizes that "the gift of loneliness is sometimes a radical vision of society or one's people that has not previously been taken into account" (p. 264). And yet marginality is not the only influence on her work. By reclaiming the works of Zora Neale Hurston and in other ways placing Black women's experiences and culture at the center of her work, she draws on alternative Black feminist worldviews.

Developing Black Feminist Thought

Starting from the assumption that African-American women have created independent, oppositional yet subjugated knowledges concerning our own subordination, contemporary U.S. Black women intellectuals are engaged in the struggle to reconceptualize all dimensions of the dialectic of oppression and activism as it applies to African-American women. Central to this enterprise is reclaiming Black feminist intellectual traditions (see, e.g., Harley and Terborg-Penn 1978; Hull et al. 1982; James and Busia 1993; and Guy-Sheftall 1995a, 1995b).

For many U.S. Black women intellectuals, this task of reclaiming Black women's subjugated knowledge takes on special meaning. Knowing that the minds and talents of our grandmothers, mothers, and sisters have been suppressed stimulates many contributions to the growing field of Black women's studies (Hull et al. 1982). Alice Walker describes how this sense of purpose affects her work: "In my own work I write not only what I want to read—understanding fully and indelibly that if I don't do it no one else is so vitally interested, or capable of doing it to my satisfaction—I write all the things *I should have been able to read*" (Walker 1983, 13).

Reclaiming Black women's ideas involves discovering, reinterpreting, and, in many cases, analyzing for the first time the works of individual U.S. Black women thinkers who were so extraordinary that they did manage to have their ideas preserved. In some cases this process involves locating unrecognized and unheralded works, scattered and long out of print. Marilyn Richardson's (1987) painstaking editing of the writings and speeches of Maria Stewart, and Mary Helen Washington's (1975, 1980, 1987) collections of Black women's writings typify this process. Similarly, Alice Walker's (1979) efforts to have Zora Neale Hurston's unmarked grave recognized parallel her intellectual quest to honor Hurston's important contributions to Black feminist literary traditions.

Reclaiming Black women's ideas also involves discovering, reinterpreting, and analyzing the ideas of subgroups within the larger collectivity of U.S. Black women who have been silenced. For example, burgeoning scholarship by and about Black lesbians reveals a diverse and complex history. Gloria Hull's (1984) careful compilation of the journals of Black feminist intellectual Alice Dunbar-Nelson illustrates the difficulties of being closeted yet still making major contributions to African-American social and political thought. Audre Lorde's (1982) autobiography, *Zami*, provides a book-length treatment of Black lesbian communities in New York. Similarly, Kennedy, and Davis's (1994) history of the formation of lesbian communities in 1940s and 1950s Buffalo, New York, strives to understand how racial segregation influenced constructions of lesbian identities.

Reinterpreting existing works through new theoretical frameworks is another dimension of developing Black feminist thought. In Black feminist literary criticism, this process is exemplified by Barbara Christian's (1985) landmark volume on Black women writers, Mary Helen Washington's (1987) reassessment of anger and voice in *Maud Martha*, a much-neglected work by novelist and poet Gwendolyn Brooks, and Hazel Carby's (1987) use of the lens of race, class, and gender to reinterpret the works of nineteenth-century Black women novelists. Within Black feminist historiography the tremendous strides that have been made in U.S. Black women's history are evident in Evelyn Brooks Higginbotham's (1989) analysis of the emerging concepts and paradigms in Black women's history, her study of women in the Black Baptist Church (1993), Stephanie Shaw's (1996) study of Black professional women workers during the Jim Crow era, and the landmark volume *Black Women in America: An Historical Encyclopedia* (Hine et al. 1993).

Developing Black feminist thought also involves searching for its expression in alternative institutional locations and among women who are not commonly perceived as intellectuals. As defined in this volume, Black women intellectuals are neither all academics nor found primarily in the Black middle class. Instead, all U.S. Black women who somehow contribute to Black feminist thought as critical social theory are deemed to be "intellectuals." They may be highly educated. Many are not. For example, nineteenth-century Black feminist activist Sojourner Truth is not typically seen as an intellectual.[3] Because she could neither read nor write, much of what we know about her has been recorded by other people. One of her most famous speeches, that delivered at the 1851 women's rights convention in Akron, Ohio, comes to us in a report written by a feminist abolitionist some time after the event itself (Painter 1993). We do not know what Truth actually said, only what the recorder claims that she said. Despite this limitation, in that speech Truth reportedly provides an incisive analysis of the definition of the term *woman* forwarded in the mid-1800s:

> That man over there says women need to be helped into carriages, and lifted over ditches, and to have the best place everywhere. Nobody ever helps me into carriages, or over mud puddles, or gives me any best place! And ain't I a woman? Look at me! Look at my arm! I have ploughed, and planted, and gathered into barns, and no man could head me! And ain't I a woman? I could work as much and eat as much as a man—when I could get it—and bear the lash as well! And ain't I a woman? I have borne thirteen

children, and seen them most all sold off to slavery, and when I cried out with my mother's grief, none but Jesus heard me! And ain't I a woman? (Loewenberg and Bogin 1976, 235)

By using the contradictions between her life as an African-American woman and the qualities ascribed to women, Sojourner Truth exposes the concept of woman as being culturally constructed. Her life as a second-class citizen has been filled with hard physical labor, with no assistance from men. Her question, "and ain't I a woman?" points to the contradictions inherent in blanket use of the term *woman*. For those who question Truth's femininity, she invokes her status as a mother of thirteen children, all sold off into slavery, and asks again, "and ain't I a woman?" Rather than accepting the existing assumptions about what a woman is and then trying to prove that she fit the standards, Truth challenged the very standards themselves. Her actions demonstrate the process of deconstruction— namely, exposing a concept as ideological or culturally constructed rather than as natural or a simple reflection of reality (Collins 1998, 137–45). By deconstructing the concept *woman*, Truth proved herself to be a formidable intellectual. And yet Truth was a former slave who never learned to read or write.

Examining the contributions of women like Sojourner Truth suggests that the concept of *intellectual* must itself be deconstructed. Not all Black women intellectuals are educated. Not all Black women intellectuals work in academia. Furthermore, not all highly-educated Black women, especially those who are employed in U.S. colleges and universities, are *automatically* intellectuals. U.S. Black women intellectuals are not a female segment of William E. B. Du Bois's notion of the "talented tenth." One is neither born an intellectual nor does one become one by earning a degree. Rather, doing intellectual work of the sort envisioned within Black feminism requires a process of self-conscious struggle on behalf of Black women, regardless of the actual social location where that work occurs.

These are not idle concerns within new power relations that have greatly altered the fabric of U.S. and Black civil society. Race, class, and gender still constitute intersecting oppressions, but the ways in which they are now organized to produce social injustice differ from prior eras. Just as theories, epistemologies, and facts produced by any group of individuals represent the standpoints and interests of their creators, the very definition of who is legitimated to do intellectual work is not only politically contested, but is changing (Mannheim 1936; Gramsci 1971). Reclaiming Black feminist intellectual traditions involves much more than developing Black feminist analyses using standard epistemological criteria. It also involves challenging the very terms of intellectual discourse itself.

Assuming new angles of vision on which U.S. Black women are, in fact, intellectuals, and on their seeming dedication to contributing to Black feminist thought raises new questions about the production of this oppositional knowledge. Historically, much of the Black women's intellectual tradition occurred in institutional locations other than the academy. For example, the music of working-class

Black women blues singers of the 1920s and 1930s is often seen as one important site outside academia for this intellectual tradition (Davis 1998). Whereas Ann duCille (1993) quite rightly warns us about viewing Black women's blues through rose-colored glasses, the fact remains that far more Black women listened to Bessie Smith and Ma Rainey than were able to read Nella Larsen or Jessie Fauset. Despite impressive educational achievements that have allowed many U.S. Black women to procure jobs in higher education and the media, this may continue to be the case. For example, Imani Perry (1995) suggests that the music of Black women hip-hop artists serves as a new site of Black women intellectual production. Again, despite the fact that hip-hop contains diverse and contradictory components (Rose 1994) and that popularity alone is insufficient to confer the title "intellectual," many more Black women listen to Queen Latifah and Salt 'N' Pepa than read literature by Alice Walker and Toni Morrison.

Because clarifying Black women's experiences and ideas lies at the core of Black feminist thought, interpreting them requires collaborative leadership among those who participate in the diverse forms that Black women's communities now take. This requires acknowledging not only how African-American women outside of academia have long functioned as intellectuals by representing the interests of Black women as a group, but how this continues to be the case. For example, rap singer Sister Souljah's music as well as her autobiography *No Disrespect* (1994) certainly can be seen as contributing to Black feminist thought as critical social theory. Despite her uncritical acceptance of a masculinist Black nationalist ideology, Souljah is deeply concerned with issues of Black women's oppression, and offers an important perspective on contemporary urban culture. Yet while young Black women listened to Souljah's music and thought about her ideas, Souljah's work has been dismissed within feminist classrooms in academia as being "nonfeminist." Without tapping these nontraditional sources, much of the Black women's intellectual tradition would remain "not known and hence not believed in" (Williams 1987, 150).

At the same time, many Black women academics struggle to find ways to do intellectual work that challenges injustice. They know that being an academic and an intellectual are not necessarily the same thing. Since the 1960s, U.S. Black women have entered faculty positions in higher education in small but unprecedented numbers. These women confront a peculiar dilemma. On the one hand, acquiring the prestige enjoyed by their colleagues often required unquestioned acceptance of academic norms. On the other hand, many of these same norms remain wedded to notions of Black and female inferiority. Finding ways to temper critical responses to academia without unduly jeopardizing their careers constitutes a new challenge for Black women who aim to be intellectuals within academia, especially intellectuals engaged in developing Black feminist thought (Collins 1998, 95–123).

Surviving these challenges requires new ways of doing Black feminist intellectual work. Developing Black feminist thought as critical social theory involves including the ideas of Black women not previously considered intellectuals—many of whom may be working-class women with jobs outside academia—as well as those ideas emanating from more formal, legitimated scholarship. The ideas we share with one another as mothers in extended families, as othermothers in Black communities, as members of Black churches, and as teachers to the Black community's children have formed one pivotal area where African-American women have hammered out a multifaceted Black women's standpoint. Musicians, vocalists, poets, writers, and other artists constitute another group from which Black women intellectuals have emerged. Building on African-influenced oral traditions, musicians in particular have enjoyed close association with the larger community of African-American women constituting their audience. Through their words and actions, grassroots political activists also contribute to Black women's intellectual traditions. Producing intellectual work is generally not attributed to Black women artists and political activists. Especially in elite institutions of higher education, such women are typically viewed as objects of study, a classification that creates a false dichotomy between scholarship and activism between thinking and doing. In contrast, examining the ideas and actions of these excluded groups in a way that views them as subjects reveals a world in which behavior is a statement of philosophy and in which a vibrant, both/and, scholar/activist tradition remains intact.

Notes

1. Numerous Black women intellectuals have explored the core themes first articulated by Maria W. Stewart (see Hull et al. 1982). Sharon Harley and Rosalyn Terborg-Penn's (1978) ground-breaking collection of essays on Black women's history foreshadowed volumes on Black women's history such as those by Giddings (1984), and D. White (1985) and the important historical encyclopedia by Hine et al. (1993). A similar explosion in Black women's literary criticism has occurred, as evidenced by the publication of book-length studies of Black women writers such as those by Barbara Christian (1985), Hazel Carby (1987), and Ann duCille (1996).

2. My use of the term *subjugated knowledge* differs somewhat from Michel Foucault's (1980a) definition. According to Foucault, subjugated knowledges are "those blocs of historical knowledge which were present but disguised," namely, "a whole set of knowledges that have been disqualified as inadequate to their task or insufficiently elaborated: naive knowledges, located low down on the hierarchy, beneath the required level of cognition or scientificity" (p. 82). I suggest that Black feminist thought is not a "naive knowledge" but has been made to appear so by those controlling knowledge validation procedures. Moreover, Foucault argues that subjugated knowledge is "a particular, local, regional knowledge, a differential knowledge incapable of unanimity and which owes its force only to the harshness with which it is opposed by everything surrounding it" (p. 82). The component of Black feminist thought that analyzes Black women's oppression fits this definition, but the long-standing, independent, African-derived influences within Black women's thought are omitted from Foucault's analysis.

3. Sojourner Truth's actions exemplify Antonio Gramsci's (1971) contention that every social group creates one or more "strata of intellectuals which give it homogeneity and an awareness of its own function not only in the economic but also in the social and political fields" (p. 5). Academics are the intellectuals trained to represent the interests of groups in power. In contrast, "organic" intellectuals depend on common sense and represent the interests of their own group. Sojourner Truth typifies an "organic" or everyday intellectual, but she may not be certified as such by the dominant group because her intellectual activity threatens the prevailing social order. The outsider-within position of Black women academics encourages us to draw on the traditions of both our discipline of training and our experiences as Black women but to participate fully in neither (Collins 1986).

32.
SEPARATING LESBIAN THEORY
FROM FEMINIST THEORY
Cheshire Calhoun

Heidi Hartmann once said of the marriage of Marxism and feminism that it "has been like the marriage of husband and wife depicted in English common law: marxism and feminism are one, and that one is marxism."[1] Lesbian theory and feminism, I want to suggest, are at risk of falling into a similar unhappy marriage in which "the one" is feminism.

Although lesbian feminist theorizing has significantly contributed to feminist thought, it has also generally treated lesbianism as a kind of applied issue. Feminist theories developed outside of the context of lesbianism are brought to bear on lesbianism in order to illuminate the nature of lesbian oppression and women's relation to women within lesbianism. So, for example, early radical lesbians played off the feminist claim that all male-female relationships are dominance relationships. They argued either that the lesbian is *the* paradigm case of patriarchal resister because she refuses to be heterosexual or that she fits on a continuum of types of patriarchal resisters.[2] In taking this line, lesbian theorists made a space for lesbianism by focusing on what they took to be the inherently feminist and antipatriarchal nature of lesbian existence. Contemporary lesbian theorists are less inclined to read lesbianism as feminist resistance to male dominance.[3] Instead, following the trend that feminist theory has itself taken, the focus has largely shifted to women's relation to women: the presence of ageism, racism, and anti-Semitism among lesbians, the problem of avoiding a totalizing discourse that speaks for all lesbians without being sensitive to differences, the difficulty of creating community in the face of political differences (e.g., on the issue of sadomasochism [s/m]), and the need to construct new conceptions of female agency and female friendship.[4] All of these are issues that have their birthplace in feminist theory. They become lesbian issues only because the general concern with women's relation to women is narrowed to lesbians' relation to fellow lesbians. Once again, lesbian thought becomes applied feminist thought.

Now, there is nothing wrong with using feminist tools to analyze lesbianism. Indeed, something would be wrong with feminist theory if it could not be usefully applied to lesbianism in a way that both illuminates lesbianism and extends feminist theory itself. And there would surely be something lacking in lesbian thought if it did not make use of feminist insights. My worry is that if this is all that lesbian feminism amounts to then there is no lesbian *theory*. Lesbian theory and feminist theory are one, and that one is feminist theory. What more could one want?

When Hartmann complained that Marxism had swallowed feminism, her point was that because traditional Marxism lacks a notion of sex-class, and thus of patriarchy as a political system distinct from capitalism, it must treat women's oppression as a special case of class oppression. Marxism is of necessity blind to the irreducibly gendered nature of women's lives. A parallel complaint might be raised about feminist theory. To the extent that feminist theory lacks a concept of hetero-sexuals and nonheterosexuals as members of different sexuality classes and thus of heterosexuality as a political structure separable from patriarchy, feminist theory must treat lesbian oppression as a special case of patriarchal oppression and remain blind to the irreducibly lesbian nature of lesbian lives.

Lesbian feminism is for several reasons at high risk of doing just that. First, the most extensive analyses of heterosexuality available to feminists are those developed in the late 1970s and early 1980s by Charlotte Bunch, Gayle Rubin, Adrienne Rich, Monique Wittig, and Kate Millett.[5] Heterosexuality, on this account, is both product and essential support of patriarchy. Women's heterosexual orientation perpetuates their social, economic, emotional, and sexual dependence on and accessibility by men. Heterosexuality is thus a system of male ownership of women, participation in which is compulsory for men and especially for women. The lesbian's and heterosexual woman's relation to heterosexuality on this account is fundamentally the same. Both experience it as the demand that women be dependent on and accessible by men. Both are vulnerable to penalties if they resist that demand. Thus heterosexuality is equally compulsory for heterosexual women and lesbians; and compulsory heterosexuality means the same thing for both. There is no specifically lesbian relation to heterosexuality.

Second, lesbian feminists have had to assert their differences from gay men and thus their distance from both the political aims and the self-understanding of the gay movement. The gay rights movement has suffered from at least two defects. On the one hand, in focusing on lesbians' and gays' shared status as sexual deviants, the gay rights movement was unable to address the connection between lesbian oppression and women's oppression. On the other hand, it tended to equate gay with gay male and failed to address the patriarchal attitudes embedded in the gay movement itself.[6] Making clear the difference between lesbians and gay men meant that lesbian feminists' focus had to be on the experience of lesbians in a patriarchal culture, not on their experience as deviants in a heterosexist culture.

Third, the fact that to be lesbian is to live out of intimate relation with men and in intimate relation with women encourages the reduction of "lesbian" to "feminist."[7] Early radical feminists were quite explicit about this, claiming that lesbians are the truly woman-identified women. Contemporary lesbian feminists, recognizing that lesbians may share patriarchal attitudes toward women, resist such grand claims. But even if lesbian feminism is no longer at risk of equating being lesbian with being a "true" feminist, the danger remains that it may equate "lesbian issue" with "feminist" issue. If what count as lesbian issues are only those visible through a feminist lens, then lesbian issues will simply be a special class of feminist ones.

Finally, the historical circumstances that gave birth to lesbian feminism had a decided impact on the direction that lesbian feminism took. The first major lesbian feminist statement, "The Woman Identified Woman," was a direct response to Betty Friedan's charge that lesbians posed a "lavender menace" to the women's movement.[8] In Friedan's and many National Organization for Women (NOW) members' view, the association of feminism with lesbianism, and thus with deviancy, undermined the credibility of women's rights claims. Threatened with ostracism from the women's movement, the Radicalesbians argued in "The Woman Identified Woman" that lesbians, because they love women and refuse to live with or devote their energies to the oppressor, are the paradigm feminists.[9] The political climate of the 1970s women's movement thus required lesbian feminists to assert their allegiance to feminist aims and values rather than calling attention to lesbians' differences from their heterosexual sisters. It was neither the time nor the place for lesbians to entertain the possibility that heterosexuality might itself be a political system and that heterosexual women and men, as a consolidated and powerful class, might have strong interests in maintaining a system of heterosexual privileges. In affirming their commitment to opposing patriarchy, lesbian feminists instead committed themselves to a specifically feminist account of the interests motivating the maintenance of a heterosexual system: men have patriarchal interests in securing sexual/emotional access to women, and heterosexual women have complicitous interests in securing access to a system of male privileges. This move effectively barred lesbian feminists from asking whether heterosexual women and men have, as heterosexuals, a class interest in constructing heterosexual sex as the only real, nonimitative sex, in eliminating historical, literary, and media representations of lesbians and gay men, in reserving jobs, public accommodations, and private housing for heterosexuals only, in barring lesbians and gay men from access to children in the educational system, children's service organizations, and adoption and artificial insemination agencies, in reducing lesbianism and homosexuality to biologically or psychodevelopmentally rooted urges while propagating the myth of a magical heterosexual romantic love, and in securing for the married heterosexual couple exclusive pride of place in the social world. Nor could or did lesbian feminists ask whether these privileges taken as a set could provide a sufficient motivating interest for maintaining a heterosexual system even in the absence of patriarchy.

For all four reasons, treating sexual orientation on a par with gender, race, and economic class—that is, as a distinct and irreducible dimension of one's political identity—may not come naturally to lesbian feminist thinking. But separating sexuality politics from gender politics is exactly what must happen if there is to be a specifically *lesbian* feminist theory rather than simply feminist theory applied to lesbians. A lesbian feminist theory would need, among other things, to focus on what is distinctive about the lesbian's relation to heterosexuality, to the category "woman," and to other women. That is, it would need to put into clear view the difference between being a lesbian who resists heterosexuality, being a woman, and loving men rather than women and being a feminist who resists the same things.

In what follows, I will be arguing that, like patriarchy and capitalism, or white imperialism, patriarchy and heterosexual dominance are two, in principle, separable systems. Even where they work together, it is possible conceptually to pull the patriarchal aspect of male-female relationships apart from their heterosexual dimension....

The Lesbian Not-Woman

Monique Wittig ends "The Straight Mind" with this sentence: "Lesbians are not women."[10] Wittig denies that "man" and "woman" are natural categories, arguing instead that the two sex-classes—men, women—are the product of heterosexual social relations in which "men appropriate for themselves the reproduction and production of women and also their physical persons by means of a contract called the marriage contract."[11] Thus, "it is oppression that creates sex and not the contrary."[12] Lesbians, however, refuse to participate in heterosexual social relations. Like runaway slaves who refuse to have their labor appropriated by white masters, lesbians are runaways who refuse to allow men to control their productive and reproductive labor within a nuclear family. Thus Wittig observes, "Lesbianism is the only concept I know of which is beyond the categories of sex (woman and man), because the designated subject (lesbian) is not a woman, either economically, or politically, or ideologically. For what makes a woman is a specific social relation to a man, a relation that we have previously called servitude, a relation which implies personal and physical obligation as well as economic obligation ("forced residence," domestic corvée, conjugal duties, unlimited production of children, et cetera), a relation which lesbians escape by refusing to become or to stay heterosexual."[13] What I want to highlight in Wittig's explanation of what bars lesbians from the category "woman" is that it claims both too much and too little for lesbians as well as reads lesbianism from a peculiarly heterosexual viewpoint. To say that only lesbians exist beyond sex categories (in Wittig's particular sense of what this means) claims too much for lesbians. If to be a woman just means living in a relation of servitude to men, there will be other ways short of lesbianism of evading the category "woman." The heterosexual celibate, virgin, single-parent head of household, marriage resister, or the married woman who insists on an egalitarian marriage contract all apparently qualify as escapees from the category "woman."[14]

Although Wittig does remark that runaway wives are also escaping their sex class, she clearly thought that lesbians are in some special sense *not women*. But her own analysis does not capture lesbians' special deviancy from the category "woman." There is indeed no conceptual space in Wittig's framework for pursuing the question of how a heterosexual woman's refusal to be a woman differs from a lesbian's refusal to be a woman. It is in that failure that she claims too little for lesbians. Because lesbians and heterosexual resisters must have, on her account, the same relation to the category "woman," there can be no interesting differences between the two. This, I think, is a mistake, and I will argue in a moment that lesbians are in a quite special sense not-women.

Finally, to equate lesbians' escape from heterosexuality and the category 'woman' with escape from male control is to adopt a peculiarly heterosexual viewpoint on lesbianism. The fact that heterosexuality enables men to control women's domestic labor is something that would be salient only to a *heterosexual* woman. Only heterosexual women do housework for men, raise children for men, have their domiciles determined by men, and so on. Thus, from a heterosexual standpoint lesbianism may indeed appear to offer a liberating escape from male control. But from the standpoint of a woman unaccustomed to living with men, that is, from a lesbian standpoint, lesbianism is not about a refusal to labor for men. Nor is heterosexuality experienced primarily as a form of male dominance over women, but instead as heterosexual dominance over lesbians and gay men. Nor is the daily experience of lesbianism one of liberation but, instead, one of acute oppression.

Because Wittig looks at lesbianism from a (heterosexual) feminist perspective, asking how lesbians escape the kinds of male control to which paradigmatically heterosexual women are subject, she misses the penalties attached to lesbians' exit from heterosexuality. Indeed, contrary to Wittig's claim, the lesbian may as a rule have *less* control over her productive and reproductive labor than her married heterosexual sister. Although the lesbian escapes whatever control *individual* men may exercise over their wives within marriage, she does not thereby escape control of her productive and reproductive labor either in her personal life with another woman or in her public life. To refuse to be heterosexual is simply to leap out of the frying pan of individual patriarchal control into the fire of institutionalized heterosexual control. Wittig's claim that "lesbianism provides for the moment the only social form in which we can live freely" vastly underestimates the coercive forces brought to bear on the lesbian for her lesbianism.[15] She may be unable to adopt children or be denied custody of and visiting privileges to her children. In order to retain her job, she will most likely have to hide her lesbianism and pretend to be heterosexual. She will likely be punished for public displays of affection. She may be denied the housing of her choice or be forced to move from her home as a result of harassment by neighbors. If she is "out," she will find herself alternately abused and subjected to lascivious interest by heterosexual men. Even if she is no longer at risk of being burned at the stake or subjected to clitoridectomy or electroshock, she may still be subjected to "therapies" that insist that she cannot be both lesbian and a healthy, mature adult. She will be labeled a dyke and scrutinized for symptoms of mannishness in her anatomy, dress, behavior, and interests. She will not see her lesbian sexuality or romantic love for another woman reflected in the public media. And both because there are no publicly-accessible models of lesbian relationships and because such coercive pressure is brought to bear against lesbian relationships, sustaining a stable personal life will be very difficult. The lesbian may be free from an individual man in her personal life, but she is not free.

What these criticisms suggest is, first, that the political structure that oppresses heterosexual women is patriarchy; but the political structure that most acutely oppresses lesbians is more plausibly taken to be heterosexuality. Second, these criticisms suggest that heterosexual women's (especially heterosexual feminists') and lesbians' relation to the category "woman" are not the same.

From a feminist point of view, the problem with the category 'woman' is not so much that there is one. The problem lies in its specific construction within patriarchal society. "Woman" has been constructed as the Other and the deficient in relation to 'man'. To "woman" have been assigned all those traits that would both rationalize and perpetuate women's lack of power in relation to men. Women are weak, passive, dependent, emotional, irrational, nurturant, closer to nature, maternal, and so on. This is to say that, from a feminist point of view, the problem with the category "woman" is that "woman" has been equated with subordination to men. The feminist task, then, is to rupture that equation. With the exception of early liberal feminists' recommendation of androgyny and possibly contemporary French feminists' deconstruction of "woman," the feminist project has not been the elimination of the category "woman." Instead, the project has been one of reconstructing that category. That reconstructive project has had two phases within feminism. The first phase tried to reconstruct the category "woman" so that it could no longer be used to rationalize male dominance. So, for example, some feminine traits were rejected, others, such as nurturance, were revalued and/or redefined, and some masculine traits (e.g., strength) were appropriated with or without redefinition.[16] The more recent phase has been devoted to reconstructing the category "woman" employed within feminism itself so that it cannot be used to rationalize white, middle-class, college-educated, heterosexual, Christian women's dominance within feminism.[17] This latter reconstruction has required the postulate of multiple categories of "woman" to capture the intersection of gender with other political identities.[18]

The feminist experience of her relation to the category "woman," thus, has been the experience of *being* a woman in a male dominant, as well as racist and classist, society, which imposes on her a conception of what it means to be a woman that she rejects. Her refusal to be a woman has extended only to refusal to be the kind of woman that a patriarchal, racist, and classist society demands that she be. And that refusal has gone hand in hand with claiming the category "woman" (or categories of "women") for herself and insisting on a woman-identified construction of that category.

This is not the lesbian relation to the category "woman." Although partly mistaken, I think, in her reasons, Wittig was correct to say that to be lesbian is to exit the category "woman" altogether. It is to be ungendered, unsexed, neither woman nor man. This is because (here following Wittig) sex/gender is the result of institutionalized heterosexuality.[19] Heterosexual systems are ones that organize reproduction via hetero*sexual* practice. That practice requires the production of two sex/genders so that sexual desire can be heterosexualized. It also requires that sex/gender map onto reproductive differences. Thus, within heterosexual systems, "'intelligible' genders are those which in some sense institute and maintain relations of coherence and continuity among sex, gender, sexual practice, and desire."[20] Individuals who violate the unity of reproductive anatomy, heterosexual desire, and gender behavior fall out of the domain of intelligible gender identity. At best, lesbians are not-women. That is, for them the closest available category of sex/gender identity is one that does not fit. Neither anatomy nor desire nor gender can link her securely to the category "woman." Within heterosexist ideology her anatomy itself is suspect. Much was made, for example, in the sexologists' literature of physical masculinity in the lesbian, including reports of an enlarged clitoris. The postulate of a biological basis of homosexuality and lesbianism continues to guide research today. And many lesbians' insistence on having been born lesbian reinforces such suspicions about anatomical differences from heterosexual women. In addition, her anatomy cannot link her to "woman" because what lesbianism reveals is the fundamental lie that differences in male and female anatomy destine a difference in males' and females' sexual and social relation to females, that is, destine one to be functionally a man or a woman. The lesbian's female body in no way bars her from functioning as a man in relation to women. She shares with members of the category "man" a sexual desire for and love of women. Also, the very traits that Wittig took to be definitive of "man"—the enactment of masculine dominance over women, physically, psychologically, socially, and economically—are an option for her in a way that they are not an option for heterosexual women. The lesbian thus exits the category of "woman", though without thereby entering the category "man".

Gender-deviant heterosexual women (i.e., women who resist patriarchal understandings of what it means to be a woman) do not similarly exit the category "woman". Gender deviance would result in not-woman status only if the content of the category "woman" were fully exhausted by a description, such as Wittig's, of what it means to be a woman. I have been suggesting, on the contrary, that heterosexuality is a critical component of the category "woman." Heterosexuality secures one's status as a "natural" woman, which is to say, as having a body whose sex as female is above suspicion. Heterosexuality also guarantees a significant nonidentity between one's own and men's relation to women. The heterosexual woman will not have a sexual, romantic, marital, coparenting relation to other women; she will have instead a *woman's* relation to women. Thus even in her gender deviance, the heterosexual resister of patriarchally defined gender remains unambiguously a woman.

Because the lesbian stands outside the category "woman," her experience of womanliness and its oppressive nature is not identical to that of the heterosexual feminist, who stands within the category "woman," even if resistantly. Womanliness is not something the lesbian has the option of refusing or reconstructing for a better fit. It is a fundamental impossibility for her. To be a not-woman is to be incapable of *being* a woman within heterosexual society. The lesbian can thus be womanly only in the modes of being in drag and of passing. And if she experiences womanliness—the demand that she look like a woman, act like a woman—as oppressive, it is not because womanliness requires subordination to men (although this may also be her experience). It is instead because the demand that she be womanly is the demand that she pretend that the sex/gender "woman" is a natural possibility for her and that she pass as a woman. It is thus also a demand that she not reveal the nonexhaustiveness and, potentially, the nonnaturalness of the binary categories "woman" and "man."

The lesbian experience of her relation to the category "woman", thus, is the experience of being a not-woman in a heterosexual society that compels everyone to be either a woman or a man and requires that she be a woman.[21] It is also the experience of being oppressed by a womanliness that denies her desire for women, and of being deviantly outside of sex/gender categories. That deviancy is harshly punished. In an attempt to compel her back into the category "woman", her lesbian desire and unwomanly relation to women are punished or treated. At the same time, she is denied the heterosexual privileges to which "real" women have access.

From a lesbian perspective, the category "woman" is oppressive because, within heterosexual societies, that category is compulsory for all anatomically female individuals. Feminist reconstructions of "woman" do not typically challenge compulsory sex/gender. They implicitly assume that "woman" and "man" exhaust the field of possible sorts of persons to be (even if it takes multiple categories of each to exhaust the taxonomy). Furthermore, insofar as lesbians are automatically and uncritically subsumed under the feminist category "woman," feminist theorizing presumes that membership in that category is determined by anatomy and ignores the extent to which the femaleness of the lesbian body is suspect. The lesbian objection to being a woman is not met by admissions that the category "woman" as well as what it means to be anatomically female are open to social construction and reconstruction. Nor is it met by the suggestion that there is no single category "woman" but instead multiple categories of women. From a lesbian perspective what has to be challenged is heterosexual society's demand that females be women. For that demand denies the lesbian option. The lesbian option is to be a not-woman, where being a not-woman is played out by insisting on being neither identifiably woman nor man, or by enacting femininity as drag, or by insisting on switching gender categories and thus being a man, which within patriarchy means being dominant in relation to women and potentially also misogynistic.

Failure to see the difference between feminist and lesbian relations to the category "woman" may well result in mislocating lesbian politics and failing to see the potential friction between feminist and lesbian politics. I take the feminist critique of butch and femme lesbianism as a case in point. On that critique, both the lesbian appropriation of femininity by femmes (and more recently by lipstick lesbians) and the lesbian appropriation of masculinity through butch sexual-social dominance repeat between women the power politics and misogyny that typifies male-female relations in a patriarchal society. Julia Penelope, for instance, argues that "those aspects of behavior and appearance labeled "femininity" in HP [heteropatriarchy] are dangerous for us. We still live *in* a heteropatriarchy and Lesbians who incorporate male ideas of appropriate female behaviors into their lives signal their acceptance of the HP version of reality."[22] In particular, the feminine lesbian confirms heteropatriarchy's acceptance of the feminine woman and rejection of any trace of mannishness in women.

From a feminist point of view there is no way of rendering politically harmless the appropriation of a role that requires sexual-social passivity and subordination, even if the appropriation is by a not-woman and even if she is not passive or subordinate primarily in relation to men. Here the argument against femininity in lesbians directly parallels the argument against the masochist role in lesbian s/m. The femme's and masochist's appeal to the voluntariness of their choices, the privacy of their practices, and the pleasure they derive from femininity and masochism, respectively, do not go all the way toward making what they do purely personal. Both femininity and female masochism acquire their meaning from what Penelope calls "heteropatriarchal semantics" as well as from the historical and material conditions of women's oppression. Those meanings cannot be dissolved at will.[23] To adopt either femininity or female masochism for oneself is to make use of a set of meanings produced through and sustained by men's oppression of women. It is thus to reveal one's personal failure to come to critical grips with the politics of women's position within patriarchy. Even if the femme's or masochist's personal choices are not political in the sense that they also publicly endorse femininity or masochism in women, they are still political in the sense that they make use of public meanings which are tied to gender politics.

Nor, the feminist critic might add, can the appropriation of masculine dominance, aggression, and misogyny be rendered politically harmless. What the butch (as well as the sadist in lesbian s/m) confirms is the patriarchal equation of power with sexual dominance and superiority with masculinity. Janice Raymond's caustic remarks about lesbian s/m might equally express the feminist critique of butch-femme roles: "It is difficult to see what is so advanced or progressive about a position that locates 'desire,' and that imprisons female sexual dynamism, vitality, and vigor, in old forms of sexual objectification, subordination, and violence, this time initiated by women and done with women's consent. The libertarians offer a supposed sexuality stripped naked of feminine taboo, but only able to dress itself in masculine garb. It is a male-constructed sexuality in drag."[24]

I have no intention of disagreeing with the claim that butch-femme role-playing runs contrary to feminist politics. What I do intend to take issue with is the assumption that feminist politics are necessarily lesbian politics. Judith Butler gives a quite different reading of the multiple appropriations of femininity and masculinity within the lesbian/gay community by butches, femmes, queens, dykes, and gay male girls. It is a reading that I take to be closer to a lesbian perspective, even if farther from a feminist one.

What the feminist critique omits is the fact that "Within lesbian contexts, the 'identification' with masculinity that appears as butch identity is not a simple assimilation of lesbianism back into the terms of heterosexuality. As one lesbian femme explained, she likes her boys to be girls. . . . As a result, that masculinity, if that it can be called, is always brought into relief against a culturally intelligible "female body." It is precisely this dissonant juxtaposition and the sexual tension that its transgression generates that constitute the object of desire."[25] It is also precisely this dissonant juxtaposition of masculinity and female body that enables the butch to enact a comedic parody of masculinity that denaturalizes the category "man". Heterosexual society assumes that masculinity is naturally united to the male body and desire for women. Similarly, it assumes that femininity is naturally united to the female body and desire for men. Butler argues, however, that gender identity is not natural but the result of continuous gender performances. One can be a man, for example, only by continuously performing masculinity and desire for women through a male body. Heterosexual society sustains the illusion of natural gender identities—"heterosexual man," "heterosexual woman"—by outlawing alternative performances. The butch lesbian gives an outlawed performance. She performs masculinity and desire for women through a female body. The butch gay man similarly gives an outlawed performance by performing masculinity in tandem with desire for men through a male body. Such multiple locations of masculinity—on the heterosexual male body, the lesbian body, the gay man's body—help create a condition in which "after a while, everyone starts to look like a drag queen."[26] The categories of "woman" and "man" cease to appear natural. Without such clearly natural or original gender identities, lesbians' subordinate status cannot be rationalized on the grounds that lesbians are unnatural, imitative beings. And, one might add, the exclusively heterosexual organization of sexuality, romantic love, marriage, and the family begin to appear arbitrary.

Because challenging heterosexual dominance and compulsory compliance with heterosexual sex/gender categories depends on deviant performances that reconfigure the elements of "man" and "woman," Butler rejects feminist attempts to "outlaw" butch and femme lesbian identities.

> Lesbianism that defines itself in radical exclusion from heterosexuality deprives itself of the capacity to resignify the very heterosexual constructs by which it is partially and inevitably constituted. As a result, that lesbian strategy would consolidate compulsory heterosexuality in its oppressive forms.
>
> The more insidious and effective strategy it seems is a thoroughgoing appropriation and redeployment of the categories of identity themselves.[27]

...But [has] Butler...really responded to the *feminist* critique of butch-femme role-playing? I think not. A feminist might well raise the following objection: butch and femme lesbianism may indeed undermine heterosexual society. It does not follow, however, that butch-femme lesbianism undermines patriarchy. The original objection still stands: butch lesbianism leaves in place the patriarchal equation of masculinity with power and dominance, while femme lesbianism leaves in place the patriarchal equation of femininity with weakness and subordination. Butler's...political program would at best simply replace heterosexuality-based patriarchy (male power), with masculinity-based patriarchy (masculine power).

Under masculinity-based patriarchy, anatomical females and males would have an equal opportunity to appropriate masculine power over feminine individuals, who themselves could be either anatomically male or female.

What the disagreement between Butler and many feminists reveals is the fact that challenging heterosexual society and challenging patriarchy are not the same thing. The feminist political opposition to patriarchal power relations disables lesbians from effectively challenging heterosexual society. The lesbian political opposition to compulsory heterosexual gender performances disables feminists from effectively challenging patriarchal society. But neither Butler nor feminists who critique butch and femme lesbians see this. Both assume the *identity* of feminist politics and lesbian politics. This is simply a mistake. Heterosexuality and patriarchy are analytically distinct social systems, just as capitalism and patriarchy are distinct. Patriarchy can survive just as easily to a nonheterosexual society as it can in a noncapitalist society. Butch-femme culture is a case in point. On the flip side, heterosexuality can survive in a nonpatriarchal society. Heterosexual societies simply require that masculinity be united with a male body and desire for women and that femininity be united with a female body and desire for men. Heterosexual systems do *not* depend on femininity and masculinity being defined and valued the way they are in patriarchal societies. Matriarchies are heterosexual systems.[28]

Given this, one should expect that feminist politics and lesbian politics, though typically overlapping, may sometimes part company. Moreover, when those politics do conflict, there is no reason to expect that feminist lesbians will or should give priority to feminist politics. Being a woman (or better, being mistaken for a woman) and being oppressed as a woman are often not the most important facts in a lesbian's life. Being a lesbian and being oppressed as a lesbian often matter more.

Which Heterosexuality?

.... I intend to begin this section by expanding on the argument against reducing the institution of heterosexuality to (a part of) the institution of male dominance. I will then turn to Janice Raymond's and Sarah Hoagland's feminist attempts to avoid claiming too much for lesbians. Their strategy involves locating the political problem in a particular *style* of heterosexualist interaction rather than in heterosexuality itself. This strategy, I will argue, results in claiming too little for lesbians by denying that there is anything intrinsically political in lesbians' revolt against the rule of heterosexuality. I will conclude with a quite different reading of heterosexuality, one that I take to be closer to a lesbian view, if farther from a feminist one.

Heterosexuality as Male Dominance
Heterosexuality, in Wittig's view, is a political and economic system of male dominance. The heterosexual social contract (to which only men have consented) stipulates that women belong to men. In particular, women's reproductive labor, including both child rearing and domestic chores, belongs to men by "natural" right much as a slave's labor belongs to its master's by natural right. It is thus heterosex-

uality that enables men to appropriate women's labor and that supports a system of male dominance. In Wittig's view, lesbian refusal to be heterosexual challenges this system of male dominance because being lesbian fundamentally means refusing to accept the "economic, ideological and political power of men."[29] Wittig's equation of lesbian resistance with feminist resistance is both obvious and explicit. She claims that to be a feminist is to fight for the disappearance of the sex-class "woman" by refusing to participate in the heterosexual relations that created the sex-class "woman" in the first place.[30] To be a feminist just *is* to be a lesbian.

In "Lesbians in Revolt," Charlotte Bunch similarly equates heterosexuality with male control over women's labor; and like Wittig, she regards lesbianism as a political revolt against a system in which neither a woman nor her labor belong to herself. "The lesbian . . . refuses to be a man's property, to submit to the unpaid labor system of housework and childcare. She rejects the nuclear family as the basic unit of production and consumption in capitalist society."[31] In Bunch's view, commitment to heterosexuality is necessarily a commitment to supporting a male world, and thus a barrier to struggle against women's oppression. "Being a lesbian means ending identification with, allegiance to, dependence on, and support of heterosexuality. It means ending your personal stake in the male world so that you join women individually and collectively in the struggle to end oppression."[32]

At least two different objections might be raised to Wittig's and Bunch's implicit claim that one must be a lesbian to be a feminist. First, lesbianism only challenges male control of women in the family. But women's labor power is also extensively controlled in the public sphere through male bosses, absence of maternity leave, sexual harassment, the job requirement of an "appropriately" feminine appearance, insufficient availability of day care, sex segregation of women into lower paid jobs, and so on. As Ann Ferguson observes, enforced heterosexuality "may be one of the mechanisms [of male dominance], but it surely is not the single or sufficient one. Others, such as the control of female biological reproduction, male control of state and political power, and economic systems involving discrimination based on class and race, seem analytically distinct from coercive heterosexuality, yet are causes which support and, perpetuate male dominance."[33] Moreover, given both the decline of male power within the nuclear family and of the nuclear family itself, one might well claim that the public control of women's productive and reproductive labor is far more critical to the maintenance of patriarchy than the private control of women's labor within the nuclear family.

While the first objection focuses on the way that lesbianism may not be the only or even most fundamental means of resisting patriarchy, a second objection focuses on the fact that the kind of resistance being claimed for lesbians in fact belongs generally to feminists. As an empirical generalization about heterosexual relations, it is true that men continue to exercise control over women's private and public work lives. As Wittig might put it, it "goes without saying" in the heterosexual social contract that women will assume primary responsibility for child rearing and domestic labor, that they will adjust their public work lives to the exigencies of their male partner's, and that they will be at least partially economically dependent on their male partner's income. But there are any number of ways of evading the terms of this contract without ceasing to be heterosexual. Thus the claim that heterosexual relations are male dominant ones is insufficient to support the claim that only lesbians are genuine resisters. Indeed, the heterosexual feminist who insists on a more equal partnership may resist patriarchy more effectively than many lesbians. As both Janice Raymond and Sarah Hoagland have argued, the importation of hetero-relations into lesbian relationships enables patriarchal ways of thinking to be sustained within lesbian relationships themselves.[34]

Heterosexualism versus Heterosexuality

Both Raymond and Hoagland avoid equating "lesbian" with "feminist" by distinguishing heterosexuality from "hetero-relations" (Raymond) and "heterosexualism" (Hoagland). Within their writing, "heterosexuality" retains its customary referent to sexual object choice. "Heterorelations" and "heterosexualism" refer to the patriarchal nature of male-female relations in both the private and public spheres. According to Raymond, in a hetero-relational society, "most of women's personal, social, political, professional, and economic relations are defined by the ideology that woman is for man."[35] Hoagland similarly claims that heterosexualism "is a particular economic, political, and emotional relationship between men and women: men must dominate women and women must subordinate themselves to men in any number of ways. As a result, men presume access to women while women remain riveted on men and are unable to sustain a community of women."[36] It is, in their view, hetero-relationalism, not heterosexuality, per se, that subordinates women to men.

By distinguishing hetero-relations and heterosexualism from heterosexuality Raymond and Hoagland avoid exaggerating the feminist element in lesbianism. Both recognize the potential failure of lesbians to disengage from heterosexualism. Lesbians themselves may be misogynistic and may engage in the same dominance-subordinance relations that typify heterosexualism. Thus lesbian resistance to heterosexuality is not automatically a resistance to patriarchy. Because Raymond and Hoagland are sensitive to this fact, they are able to subject lesbian relations to feminist critique in a productive way. In addition, by recognizing that heterosexual women can redefine their relations to men in such a way that they both leave space for gyn-affectionate relations with women and refuse to participate in hetero-relations with men, Raymond avoids pitting lesbians against heterosexual women within the feminist community in a battle over who counts as a "true" feminist.

Their attempt, however, to avoid claiming too much for lesbianism comes at the cost of ultimately claiming too little for it. By putting the concept of hetero-relations or heterosexualism at the center of their lesbian feminism, both effectively eliminate space for a *lesbian* theory. Within their work, lesbian resistance to heterosexuality does not, in itself, have either political or conceptual significance. Whatever political significance lesbian personal lives may have is due entirely to the presence of or resistance to hetero-relations within those lives. The reduction of lesbian politics to feminist politics is quite obvious in Raymond's "Putting the

Politics Back into Lesbianism."[37] There, Raymond sharply criticizes lesbian lifestylers and sexual libertarians for failure to see that in advocating an anything-goes sexuality (including lesbian pornography and s/m) as the path to liberation, they are simply repeating the patriarchal image of woman as essentially sexual being. Moreover, as I mentioned earlier, insofar as lesbian lifestylers advocate aggressive and violent forms of sexuality, they are simply putting a "male-constructed sexuality in drag."[38] What I want to underscore in Raymond's critique is that putting politics into lesbianism means putting *feminist* politics into lesbianism. She does not demand that lesbians put resistance to heterosexuality and to lesbian oppression at the center of their lives. Thus she does not ask whether or not lesbian s/m promotes *lesbian* politics.

One important consequence of equating lesbian with feminist politics in this way is that lesbians who have suffered the worst oppression, for example, the 1950s butches and femmes who risked repeated arrest and police harassment, often turn out to be the least politically interesting from a feminist point of view. Shane Phelan's criticism of Adrienne Rich for marginalizing "real" lesbians who resisted heterosexuality and for giving nonlesbians who resisted dependency on men pride of place on her lesbian continuum applies generally to those who equate lesbian politics with feminist politics. . . .

From a feminist point of view whose political yardstick measures only distance from patriarchal practices and institutions, butches and femmes, lesbian sex radicals who promote pornography and s/m, lesbian mothers, and married lesbians all fail to measure up. All are vulnerable to the charge of appropriating for women and between women the very practices and institutions that have served so well to oppress women. Yet it is precisely these women, who insist on the reality and value of romance, sexuality, parenting, and marriage between women, who resist most strongly heterosexual society's reservation of the private sphere for male-female couples only. From a lesbian point of view whose political yardstick measures resistance to heterosexuality and heterosexual privilege, they are neither politically uninteresting nor assimilationist.

Not only does this focus on heterosexualism rather than heterosexuality leave no space for understanding the inherently political nature of lesbianism, it also leaves no space for understanding the significance of specifically lesbian love. For instance, like Rich's notion of a lesbian continuum that includes both lesbians and heterosexual women, Raymond's "use of the term *Gyn/affection* expresses a *continuum* of female friendship" that includes some (but not all) lesbian love as well as friendships between heterosexual women.[39] In her view, it is in gyn/affection that women seize power from men and engage in a woman-identified act. Thus it is gyn/affection that is politically significant. Specifically lesbian sexual and romantic attraction to women is left without any politically or conceptually interesting place to be. Raymond is by no means the first or only lesbian feminist to marginalize lesbian love in favor of a form of love between women that is more directly tied to feminist solidarity. Bunch, for example, claims that "the lesbian, woman-identified-woman commits herself to women not only as an alternative to oppressive male-female relationships but primarily because she *loves* women."[40] That this is not a particularized conception of love but rather feminist "love" of women as a class becomes clear in the way she connects lesbian love with class solidarity: "When women do give primary energies to other women, then it is possible to concentrate fully on building a movement for our liberation."[41] In a more recent piece, Nett Hart similarly equates lesbian love with love of women as a class: "We love women as a class and we love specific women. We embrace the concept that women can be loved, that women are inherently worthy of love."[42] In both Bunch and Hart, there is a conceptual slide from "love" in the sense of a sexual-romantic love of a particular woman to "love" in the sense of valuing and respecting members of the category "woman." Although Raymond differs in being much more careful to keep the two sorts of love conceptually separated, all three prioritize love of women as a class. From a feminist point of view it is indeed the capacity to value members of the category "woman" and to form strong primary bonds of friendship with many women that matters politically. But this is not lesbian love. Lesbians fall in love with, want to make love to, decide to set up a household with a particular other woman, not a class of women. It is for this particularized, sexualized love that lesbians are penalized in heterosexual society. Because of this, lesbian theory needs to move specifically lesbian love to the center of its political stage.

None of these remarks are intended either to undercut the value for feminists of work being done by lesbians or the need to subject lesbian practice to feminist critique. They are meant to suggest that a full-blown lesbian feminism cannot afford to reduce the political institution of heterosexuality to an institution of male dominance.

Heterosexuality as a Political System

I have been arguing so far that reading heterosexuality and lesbianism solely in relation to patriarchal gender politics fails to yield an adequate picture of lesbians' political position. I turn now to an exploration of the thesis that heterosexuality is itself a political system that shapes our social structure as systematically as do patriarchal, racial imperialist, and class systems.

I do not mean to deny that in patriarchal societies heterosexuality enables what Gayle Rubin called the "traffic in women." I *do* mean to deny that heterosexual systems' only function is to support a system of male privilege. I suggest instead that heterosexual systems, whether patriarchal or not, function to insure reproduction by making the male-female unit fundamental to social structure, particularly, though not exclusively, to the structure of what might broadly be called the private sphere. That is, heterosexual systems assign the heterosexual couple-based family a privileged social status as the only legitimate site of sexuality, child bearing, child rearing, the care of individuals' physical and emotional needs, the maintenance of a household, and the creation of kinship bonds. It is because the purpose of heterosexual systems is to sustain reproduction that threats to that system—for example, the education of women, or homosexuality—inevitably evoke in Anglo-American history some version of the race suicide argument.

Heterosexuality then is not just a matter of the orientation of individual sexual desire. It is a method of socially organizing a broad spectrum of reproductive activities. Accordingly, the taboo on homosexuality does not simply outlaw same-sex desire. More basically it outlaws the female-female or male-male couple as the site of any reproductive activities.[43] Thus, if one wants a complete set of the regulations that constitute the taboo on lesbianism and homosexuality, one needs to look at all of the practices that directly or indirectly insure that the family will be built around a male-female pair. The social and legal prohibition of same-sex sex is only the tip of the iceberg of the systematic heterosexualization of social life.

This socially foundational status of the male-female couple gets ideologically expressed and reinforced through the language of naturalness: the individuals who make up society are taken to be naturally gendered as men or women, naturally heterosexual, and naturally inclined to establish a family based around the male-female reproductive unit. The alleged natural inevitability of gender differences, heterosexual desire, and heterosexually reproductive families enables heterosexual societies to take it for granted that "of course" the social, economic, and legal structure of any society will, and ought to, reflect these basic facts.

Social practices, norms, and institutions are designed to meet heterosexual systems' need to produce sex/gender dimorphism—masculine males and feminine females—so that desire can then be heterosexualized. Gendered behavioral norms, gendered rites of passage, a sexual division of labor, and the like produce differently gendered persons out of differently sexed persons. Prohibitions against gender crossing (e.g., against cross-dressing, effeminacy in men, mannishness in women) also help sustain the dimorphism necessary to heterosexualize desire.

Children and especially adolescents are carefully prepared for heterosexual interaction. They are given heterosexual sex education, advice for attracting the opposite sex, norms for heterosexual behavior, and appropriate social occasions (such as dances or dating rituals) for enacting desire. Adult heterosexuality is further sustained through erotica and pornography, heterosexualized humor, heterosexualized dress, romance novels, and so on.

Heterosexual societies take it for granted that men and women will bond in an intimate relationship, ultimately founding a family. As a result, social conventions, economic arrangements, and the legal structure treat the heterosexual couple as a single, and singularly important, social unit. The couple is represented linguistically (boyfriend-girlfriend, husband-wife) and is treated socially as a single unit (e.g., in joint invitations or in receiving joint gifts). It is legally licensed and legally supported through such entitlements as communal property, joint custody or adoption of children, and the power to give proxy consent within the couple. The couple is also recognized in the occupational structure via such provisions as spousal health care benefits and restrictions on nepotism. Multiple practices and institutions help heterosexual individuals to couple and create families and support the continuation of those couples and couple-based families. These include dating services, matchmakers, introductions to eligible partners, premarital counseling, marriage counseling, marriage and divorce law, adoption services, reproductive technologies, family rates, family health care benefits, tax deductions for married couples, and so on.

The sum total of all the social, economic, and legal arrangements that support the sexual and relational coupling of men with women constitutes heterosexual privilege. And it is privilege of a peculiar sort. Heterosexuals do not simply claim *greater* socio-politico-legal standing than nonheterosexuals. They claim as natural and normal an arrangement where *only* heterosexuals have socio-politico-legal standing. Lesbians and gay men are not recognized as social beings because they cannot enter into the most basic social unit, the male-female couple. Within heterosexual systems the only social arrangements that apply to nonheterosexuals are eliminative in nature. The coercive force of the criminal law, institutionalized discrimination, "therapeutic" treatment, and individual prejudice and violence is marshaled against the existence of lesbians and gay men. At best, lesbians and gay men have negative social reality. Lesbians are not-women engaged in nonsex within nonrelationships that may constitute a nonfamily.

It would be a mistake to think that legal prohibition of discrimination on the basis of sexual orientation or legal recognition of domestic partnerships would give lesbians and gay men any genuine socio-politico-legal standing. The legal reduction of lesbianism to mere sexuality which is implicit in "sexual orientation" legislation only reconfirms the heterosexual assumption that lesbianism cannot itself provide the site for the broad spectrum of reproductive activities. Only heterosexuality, which "everyone knows" is more than mere sexual desire, can provide this site in the form of the heterosexual couple. Because lesbianism is supposedly mere sex and not a mode of sociality, no fundamental alteration needs to be made in the social practices and institutions that constitute the private sphere. Domestic partnership laws fall in the same boat. They set up what amount to separate but allegedly equal spheres for heterosexuals and nonheterosexuals. Heterosexuals retain coverage by marriage laws. All other possible private arrangements are covered under domestic partnerships. The point of excluding lesbian and gay marriages from marriage law itself is, of course, to reaffirm heterosexual society's most basic belief that only the male-female couple constitutes a natural, basic social unit.

In short, unlike the heterosexual woman, including the heterosexual feminist, the lesbian experience of the institution of heterosexuality is of a system that makes her sexual, affectional, domestic, and reproductive life unreal. Within heterosexual society, the experience between women of sexual fulfillment, of falling in love, of marrying, of creating a home, of starting a family have no social reality. Unlike the heterosexual feminist, the lesbian has no socially supported private sphere, not even an oppressive one.

Failure to see the difference between the heterosexual feminist's and the lesbian's relation to the institution of heterosexuality may well result in mislocating lesbian politics. From a feminist point of view, sexual interaction, romantic love, marriage, and the family are all danger zones because all have been distorted to serve male interests. It thus does not behoove feminist politics to begin by championing the importance of sexual interaction, romantic love, marriage, and the (couple-based) family. But it does behoove lesbian politics to start in precisely these places. Her recognition as a social being, and thus as an individual with socio-politico-legal standing, depends upon the female-female couple being recognized as a primary social unit. That in turn cannot be done without directly challenging the reservation of the primary structures of the private sphere for heterosexuals. Just as the heart of male privilege lies in the "right" of access to women, so the heart of heterosexual privilege lies in the "right" of access to sexual-romantic-marital-familial relationships.

Notes

1. Heidi Hartmann, "The Unhappy Marriage of Marxism and Feminism, " in *Feminist Frameworks,* ed. Alison M. Jaggar and Paula S. Rothenberg, 2d ed. (New York: McGraw-Hill, 1984), p. 172.

2. On the former, see, e.g., Charlotte Bunch, "Lesbians in Revolt," in her *Passionate Politics, Essays 1968–1986* (New York: St. Martin's, 1987); and Monique Wittig, *The Straight Mind and Other Essays* (Boston: Beacon, 1992). Regarding the latter see Adrienne Rich, "Compulsory Heterosexuality and the Lesbian Continuum," in *The Signs Reader: Women, Gender, and Scholarship,* ed. Elizabeth Abel and Emily K. Abel (Chicago: University of Chicago Press, 1983).

3. For instance, Jeffner Allen states in her introduction to the anthology *Lesbian Philosophies and Cultures,* ed. Jeffner Allen (Albany, N.Y.: SUNY Press, 1990), "The primary emphasis of this book is *lesbian* philosophies and cultures, rather than lesbianism considered in relation to or in contrast to, patriarchy, or heterosexuality" (p. 1).

4. See, e.g., the recent anthology, Allen, ed., *Lesbian Philosophies and Cultures;* as well as Sarah Lucia Hoagland's *Lesbian Ethics: Toward New Value* (Palo Alto, Calif.: Institute of Lesbian Studies, 1990); and Janice G. Raymond's *A Passion for Friends* (Boston: Beacon, 1986).

5. Charlotte Bunch, "Lesbians in Revolt," "Learning from Lesbian Separatism," and "Lesbian-Feminist Theory," all in her *Passionate Politics;* Gayle Rubin, "The Traffic in Women," in *Toward an Anthropology of Women,* ed. Rayna Reiter (New York: Monthly Review, 1975); Kate Millett, *Sexual Politics* (New York: Doubleday, 1969); Rich; Wittig, The Straight Mind.

6. See, e.g., Marilyn Frye's critical assessment of the gay rights movement in "Lesbian Feminism and the Gay Rights Movement: Another View of Male Supremacy, Another Separatism," in her *The Politics of Reality* (Freedom, Calif.: Crossing, 1983); as well as John Stoltenberg's "Sadomasochism: Eroticized Violence, Eroticized Powerlessness," in *Against Sadomasochism,* ed. Robin Ruth Linden et al. (San Francisco: Frog in the Well, 1982).

7. Charlotte Bunch, e.g., observes that "lesbianism and feminism are both about women loving and supporting women and women revolting against the so-called supremacy of men and the patriarchal institutions that control us" ("Lesbian-Feminist Theory," p. 196).

8. For brief historical discussions of this event, see Shane Phelan's "The Woman-identified Woman," in her *Identity Politics: Lesbian Feminism and the Limits of Community.* (Philadelphia: Temple University Press, 1989); and Terralee Bensinger's "Lesbian Pornography: The Re/Making of (a) Community," *Discourse* 15 (1992): 69–93.

9. Radicalesbians, "The Woman Identified Woman," in *Radical Feminism,* ed. Anne Koedt et al. (New York: Quandrangle, 1973).

10. Monique Wittig, "The Straight Mind," in *The Straight Mind and Other Essays,* p. 32.

11. Monique Wittig, "The Category of Sex," in *The Straight Mind and Other Essays,* p. 6.

12. Ibid., p. 2.

13. Monique Wittig, "One Is Not Born a Woman," in *The Straight Mind and Other Essays,* p 20.

14. This point has been made by a number of authors, including Marilyn Frye ("Some Reflections on Separatism and Power," in *The Politics of Reality*) and Kathryn Pyne Addelson ("Words and Lives," *Signs* 7 [1981]: 187–99).

15. Wittig, "One Is Not Born a Woman," p. 20.

16. Joyce Trebilcott neatly summarizes these reconstructive strategies in "Conceiving Women: Notes on the Logic of Feminism," *Sinister Wisdom*, vol. 11 (1979), reprinted in *Women and Values: Readings in Recent Feminist Philosophy*, ed. Marilyn Pearsall (Belmont, Calif.: Wadsworth, 1986).

17. See, e.g., Marilyn Frye's "A Response to *Lesbian Ethics*: Why Ethics?" in *Feminist Ethics*, ed. Claudia Card (Lawrence: University Press of Kansas, 1991); and Elizabeth V. Spelman's *Inessential Woman: Problems of Exclusion in Feminist Thought* (Boston: Beacon, 1988).

18. Spelman argues elegantly for the necessity of multiple categories in *Inessential Woman*.

19. I use "sex/gender" rather than "gender" throughout the argument that lesbians are not-women in order to avoid implying that what makes lesbians not-women is simply their gender deviance (e.g., their butchness or refusal to be subordinate to men). I want to stress instead that lesbians are not clearly female. It is sex deviance combined with gender deviance that I think results in lesbians' exit from the category "woman."

20. Judith Butler, *Gender Trouble: Feminism and the Subversion of Identity* (New York: Routledge, 1990), p. 17.

21. Frye quite vividly describes the phenomenon of compulsory sex/gender in "Sexism," in *The Politics of Reality*.

22. Julia Penelope, "Heteropatriarchal Semantics and Lesbian Identity: The Ways a Lesbian Can Be," in her *Call Me Lesbian: Lesbian Lives, Lesbian Theory* (Freedom, Calif: Crossing, 1992).

23. For critical discussions of the meanings employed within s/m, see esp. Susan Leigh Star, "Swastikas: The Street and the University," in Linden et al., eds.; and Stoltenberg.

24. Janice G. Raymond, "Putting the Politics Back into Lesbianism," *Women's Studies International Forum* 12 (1989): 149–56.

25. Butler, *Gender Trouble*, p. 123. For additional discussion of the creation of an apparently natural gender identity through repetitive gender performances, see Judith Butler, "Imitation and Gender Insubordination," in *Inside/Out: Lesbian Theories, Gay Theories*, ed. Diana Fuss (New York: Routledge, 1991).

26. Quote of the week from Allan Berubé in *City on a Hill* 26, no. 30 (1992): 10. In "Sexism," Frye similarly comments that "heterosexual critics of queers' 'role-playing' ought to look at themselves in the mirror on their way out for a night on the town to see who's in drag. The answer is, everybody is" (p. 29).

27. Butler, *Gender Trouble*, p. 128.

28. Wittig makes this point in "One Is Not Born a Woman," p. 10.

29. Wittig, "One Is Not Born a Woman," p. 13.

30. Ibid., p. 14.

31. Bunch, "Lesbians in Revolt," p. 165.

32. Ibid., p. 166.

33. Ann Ferguson, "Patriarchy, Sexual Identity, and the Sexual Revolution," in Ann Ferguson, Jacquelyn N. Zita, and Kathryn Pyne Addelson, "Viewpoint: On 'Compulsory Heterosexuality and Lesbian Existence': Defining the Issues," *Signs* 7 (1981): 147–88, p. 159.

34. Hoagland.

35. Raymond, *A Passion for Friends*, p. 11.

36. Hoagland, p. 29.

37. Raymond, "Putting the Politics Back into Lesbianism." See also her criticisms of lesbian s/m in the chapter "Obstacles to Female Friendship," in *A Passion for Friends*.

38. Raymond, "Putting the Politics Back into Lesbianism," p. 150.

39. Raymond, *A Passion for Friends*, p. 15

40. Bunch, "Lesbians in Revolt," p. 162.

41. Ibid.

42. Nett Hart, "Lesbian Desire as Social Action," in Allen, ed., p. 297.

43. This helps to explain why it is relatively easy to garner toleration of lesbianism and homosexuality as private bedroom practices, while attempts to sanction lesbian and gay parenting and marriages meet with intense resistance. I thank Mary Going for bringing me to see the critical importance of challenging the heterosexual couple-based family.

33.

THEORIZING DIFFERENCE
FROM MULTIRACIAL FEMINISM
Maxine Baca Zinn and Bonnie Thornton Dill

Women of color have long challenged the hegemony of feminisms constructed primarily around the lives of white middle-class women. Since the late 1960s, U.S. women of color have taken issue with unitary theories of gender. Our critiques grew out of the widespread concern about the exclusion of women of color from feminist scholarship and the misinterpretation of our experiences,[1] and ultimately "out of the very discourses, denying, permitting, and producing difference."[2] Speaking simultaneously from "within and against" *both* women's liberation *and* antiracist movements, we have insisted on the need to challenge systems of domination,[3] not merely as gendered subjects but as women whose lives are affected by our location in multiple hierarchies.

Recently, and largely in response to these challenges, work that links gender to other forms of domination is increasing. In this article, we examine this connection further as well as the ways in which difference and diversity infuse contemporary feminist studies. Our analysis draws on a conceptual framework that we refer to as "multiracial feminism."[4] This perspective is an attempt to go beyond a mere recognition of diversity and difference among women to examine structures of domination, specifically the importance of race in understanding the social construction of gender. Despite the varied concerns and multiple intellectual stances which characterize the feminisms of women of color, they share an emphasis on race as a primary force situating genders differently. It is the centrality of race, of institutionalized racism, and of struggles against racial oppression that link the various feminist perspectives within this framework. Together, they demonstrate that racial meanings offer new theoretical directions for feminist thought.

Tensions in Contemporary Difference Feminism

Objections to the false universalism embedded in the concept "woman" emerged within other discourses as well as those of women of color.[5] Lesbian feminists and postmodern feminists put forth their own versions of what Susan Bordo has called "gender skepticism."[6]

Many thinkers within mainstream feminism have responded to these critiques with efforts to contextualize gender. The search for women's "universal" or "essential" characteristics is being abandoned. By examining gender in the context of other social divisions and perspectives, difference has gradually become important—even problematizing the universal categories of "women" and "men." Sandra Harding expresses the shift best in her claim that "there are no gender relations *per se*, but only gender relations as constructed by and between classes, races, and cultures."[7]

Many feminists now contend that difference occupies center stage as *the* project of women studies today.[8] According to one scholar, "difference has replaced equality as the central concern of feminist theory."[9] Many have welcomed the change, hailing it as a major revitalizing force in U.S. feminist theory.[10] But if *some* priorities within mainstream feminist thought have been refocused by attention to difference, there remains an "uneasy alliance"[11] between women of color and other feminists.

If difference has helped revitalize academic feminisms, it has also "upset the apple cart" and introduced new conflicts into feminist studies.[12] For example, in a recent and widely discussed essay, Jane Rowland Martin argues that the current preoccupation with difference is leading feminism into dangerous traps. She fears that in giving privileged status to a predetermined set of analytic categories (race, ethnicity, and class), "we affirm the existence of nothing but difference." She asks, "How do we know that for us, difference does not turn on being fat, or religious, or in an abusive relationship?"[13]

We, too, see pitfalls in some strands of the difference project. However, our perspectives take their bearings from social relations. Race and class differences are crucial, we argue, not as individual characteristics (such as being fat) but insofar as they are primary organizing principles of a society which locates and positions groups within that society's opportunity structures.

Despite the much-heralded diversity trend within feminist studies, difference is often reduced to mere pluralism: a "live and let live" approach where principles of relativism generate a long list of diversities which begin with gender, class, and race, and continue through a range of social structural—as well as personal—characteristics.[14] Another disturbing pattern, which bell hooks refers to as "the commodification of difference," is the representation of diversity as a form of exotica, "a spice, seasoning that livens up the dull dish that is mainstream white culture."[15] The major limitation of these approaches is the failure to attend to the power relations that accompany difference. Moreover, these approaches ignore the inequalities that cause some characteristics to be seen as "normal" while others are seen as "different" and thus, deviant.

Maria C. Lugones expresses irritation at those feminists who see only the *problem* of difference without recognizing *difference*.[16] Increasingly, we find that difference is recognized. But this in no way means that difference occupies a "privileged" theoretical status. Instead of using difference to rethink the category of women, difference is often a euphemism for women who differ from the traditional norm. Even in purporting to accept difference, feminist pluralism often creates a social reality that reverts to universalizing women:

> So much feminist scholarship assumes that when we cut through all of the diversity among women created by differences of racial classification, ethnicity, social class, and

sexual orientation, a "universal truth" concerning women and gender lies buried underneath. But if we can face the scary possibility that no such certainty exists and that persisting in such a search will always distort or omit someone's experiences, with what do we replace this old way of thinking? Gender differences and gender politics begin to look very different if there is no essential woman at the core.[17]

What Is Multiracial Feminism?

A new set of feminist theories have emerged from the challenges put forth by women of color. Multiracial feminism is an evolving body of theory and practice informed by wide-ranging intellectual traditions. This framework does not offer a singular or unified feminism but a body of knowledge situating women and men in multiple systems of domination. U.S. multiracial feminism encompasses several emergent perspectives developed primarily by women of color: African Americans, Latinas, Asian Americans, and Native Americans, women whose analyses are shaped by their unique perspectives as "outsiders within"—marginal intellectuals whose social locations provide them with a particular perspective on self and society.[18] Although U.S. women of color represent many races and ethnic backgrounds—with different histories and cultures—our feminisms cohere in their treatment of race as a basic social division, a structure of power, a focus of political struggle, and hence a fundamental force in shaping women's and men's lives.

This evolving intellectual and political perspective uses several controversial terms. While we adopt the label "multiracial," other terms have been used to describe this broad framework. For example, Chela Sandoval refers to "U.S. Third World feminisms,"[19] while other scholars refer to "indigenous feminisms." In their theory text-reader, Alison M. Jagger and Paula M. Rothenberg adopt the label "multicultural feminism."[20]

We use "multiracial" rather than "multicultural" as a way of underscoring race as a power system that interacts with other structured inequalities to shape genders. Within the U. S. context, race, and the system of meanings and ideologies which accompany it, is a fundamental organizing principle of social relationships.[21] Race affects all women and men, although in different ways. Even cultural and group differences among women are produced through interaction within a racially stratified social order. Therefore, although we do not discount the importance of culture, we caution that cultural analytic frameworks that ignore race tend to view women's differences as the product of group-specific values and practices that often result in the marginalization of cultural groups which are then perceived as exotic expressions of a normative center. Our focus on race stresses the social construction of differently situated social groups and their varying degrees of advantage and power. Additionally, this emphasis on race takes on increasing political importance in an era where discourse about race is governed by color-evasive language[22] and a preference for individual rather than group remedies for social inequalities. Our analyses insist upon the primary and pervasive nature of race in contemporary U.S. society while at the same time acknowledging how race both shapes and is shaped by a variety of other social relations.

In the social sciences, multiracial feminism grew out of socialist feminist thinking. Theories about how political economic forces shape women's lives were influential as we began to uncover the social causes of racial ethnic women's subordination. But socialist feminism's concept of capitalist patriarchy, with its focus on women's unpaid (reproductive) labor in the home failed to address racial differences in the organization of reproductive labor. As feminists of color have argued, "reproductive labor has divided along racial as well as gender lines, and the specific characteristics have varied regionally and changed over time as capitalism has reorganized."[23] Despite the limitations of socialist feminism, this body of literature has been especially useful in pursuing questions about the interconnections among systems of domination.[24]

Race and ethnic studies was the other major social scientific source of multiracial feminism. It provided a basis for comparative analyses of groups that are socially and legally subordinated and remain culturally distinct within U.S. society. This includes the systematic discrimination of socially constructed racial groups and their distinctive cultural arrangements. Historically, the categories of African American, Latino, Asian American, and Native American were constructed as both racially and culturally distinct. Each group has a distinctive culture, shares a common heritage, and has developed a common identity within a larger society that subordinates them.[25]

We recognize, of course, certain problems inherent in an uncritical use of the multiracial label. First, the perspective can be hampered by a biracial model in which only African Americans and whites are seen as racial categories and all other groups are viewed through the prism of cultural differences. Latinos and Asians have always occupied distinctive places within the racial hierarchy, and current shifts in the composition of the U.S. population are racializing these groups anew.[26]

A second problem lies in treating multiracial feminism as a single analytical framework, and its principle architects, women of color, as an undifferentiated category. The concepts "multiracial feminism," "racial ethnic women," and "women of color" "homogenize quite different experiences and can falsely universalize experiences across race, ethnicity, sexual orientation, and age."[27] The feminisms created by women of color exhibit a plurality of intellectual and political positions. We speak in many voices, with inconsistencies that are born of our different social locations. Multiracial feminism embodies this plurality and richness. Our intent is not to falsely universalize women of color. Nor do we wish to promote a new racial essentialism in place of the old gender essentialism. Instead, we use these concepts to examine the structures and experiences produced by intersecting forms of race and gender.

It is also essential to acknowledge that race is a shifting and contested category whose meanings construct definitions of all aspects of social life.[28] In the United States it helped define citizenship by excluding everyone who was not a white, male property owner. It defined labor as slave or free, coolie or contract, and family as available only to those men whose marriages were recognized or whose wives could immigrate with them. Additionally, racial meanings are contested both within groups and between them.[29]

Although definitions of race are at once historically and geographically specific, they are also transnational, encompassing diasporic groups and crossing traditional geographic boundaries. Thus, while U.S. multiracial feminism calls attention to the fundamental importance of race, it must also locate the meaning of race within specific national traditions.

The Distinguishing Features of Multiracial Feminism

By attending to these problems, multiracial feminism offers a set of analytic premises for thinking about and theorizing gender. The following themes distinguish this branch of feminist inquiry.

First, multiracial feminism asserts that gender is constructed by a range of interlocking inequalities, what Patricia Hill Collins calls a "matrix of domination."[30] The idea of a matrix is that several fundamental systems work with and through each other. People experience race, class, gender, and sexuality differently depending upon their social location in the structures of race, class, gender, and sexuality. For example, people of the same race will experience race differently depending upon their location in the class structure as working class, professional managerial class, or unemployed; in the gender structure as female or male; and in structures of sexuality as heterosexual, homosexual, or bisexual.

Multiracial feminism also examines the simultaneity of systems in shaping women's experience an identity. Race, class, gender, and sexuality are not reducible to individual attributes to be measured and assessed for their separate contribution in explaining given social outcomes, an approach that Elizabeth Spelman calls "popbead metaphysics," where a woman's identity consists of the sum of parts neatly divisible from one another.[31] The matrix of domination seeks to account for the multiple ways that women experience themselves as gendered, raced, classed, and sexualized.

Second, multiracial feminism emphasizes the intersectional nature of hierarchies at all levels of social life. Class, race, gender, and sexuality are components of both social structure and social interaction. Women and men are differently embedded in locations created by these cross-cutting hierarchies. As a result, women and men throughout the social order experience different forms of privilege and subordination, depending on their race, class, gender, and sexuality. In other words, intersecting forms of domination produce *both* oppression *and* opportunity. At the same time that structures of race, class, and gender create disadvantages for women of color, they provide unacknowledged benefits for those who are at the top of these hierarchies—whites, members of the upper classes, and males. Therefore, multiracial feminism applies not only to racial ethnic women but also to women and men of all races, classes, and genders.

Third, multiracial feminism highlights the relational nature of dominance and subordination. Power is the cornerstone of women's differences.[32] This means that women's differences are *connected* in systematic ways.[33] Race is a vital element in the pattern of relations among minority and white women. As Linda Gordon argues, the very meanings of being a white woman in the United States have been affected by the existence of subordinated women of color: "They intersect in conflict and in occasional cooperation, but always in mutual influence."[34]

Fourth, multiracial feminism explores the interplay of social structure and women's agency. Within the constraints of race, class, and gender oppression, women create viable lives for themselves, their families, and their communities. Women of color have resisted and often undermined the forces of power that control them. From acts of quiet dignity and steadfast determination to involvement in revolt and rebellion, women struggle to shape their own lives. Racial oppression has been a common focus of the "dynamic oppositional agency" of women of color. As Chandra Talpade Mohanty points out, it is the nature and organization of women's opposition which mediates and differentiates the impact of structures of domination.[35]

Fifth, multiracial feminism encompasses wide-ranging methodological approaches, and like other branches of feminist thought, relies on varied theoretical tools as well. Ruth Frankenberg and Lata Mani identify three guiding principles of inclusive feminist inquiry: "building complex analyses, avoiding erasure, specifying location."[36] In the last decade, the opening up of academic feminism has focused attention on social location in the production of knowledge. Most basically, research by and about marginalized women has destabilized what used to be considered as universal categories of gender. Marginalized locations are well suited for grasping social relations that remained obscure from more privileged vantage points. Lived experience, in other words, creates alternative ways of understanding the social world and the experience of different groups of women within it. Racially informed standpoint epistemologies have provided new topics, fresh questions, and new understandings of women and men. Women of color have, as Norma Alarcón argues, asserted ourselves as subjects, using our voices to challenge dominant conceptions of truth.[37]

Sixth, multiracial feminism brings together understandings drawn from the lived experiences of diverse and continuously changing groups of women. Among Asian Americans, Native Americans, Latinas, and Blacks are many different national cultural and ethnic groups. Each one is engaged in the process of testing, refining, and reshaping these broader categories in its own image. Such internal differences heighten awareness of and sensitivity to both commonalities and differences, serving as a constant reminder of the importance of comparative study and maintaining a creative tension between diversity and universalization.

Difference and Transformation

Efforts to make women's studies less partial and less distorted have produced important changes in academic feminism. Inclusive thinking has provided a way to build multiplicity and difference into our analyses. This has led to the discovery that race matters for everyone. White women, too, must be reconceptualized as a category that is multiply defined by race, class, and other differences. As Ruth

Frankenberg demonstrates in a study of whiteness among contemporary women, all kinds of social relations, even those that appear neutral, are, in fact, racialized. Frankenberg further complicates the very notion of a unified white identity by introducing issues of Jewish identity.[38] Therefore, the lives of women of color cannot be seen as a *variation* on a more general model of white American womanhood. The model of womanhood that feminist social science once held as "universal" is also a product of race and class.

When we analyze the power relations constituting all social arrangements and shaping women's lives in distinctive ways, we can begin to grapple with core feminist issues about how genders are socially constructed and constructed differently. Women's difference is built into our study of gender. Yet this perspective is quite far removed from the atheoretical pluralism implied in much contemporary thinking about gender.

Multiracial feminism, in our view, focuses not just on differences but also on the way in which differences and domination intersect and are historically and socially constituted. It challenges feminist scholars to go beyond the mere recognition and inclusion of difference to reshape the basic concepts and theories of our disciplines. By attending to women's social location based on race, class, and gender, multiracial feminism seeks to clarify the structural sources of diversity. Ultimately, multiracial feminism forces us to see privilege and subordination as interrelated and to pose such questions as: How do the existences and experiences of all people—women and men, different racial-ethnic groups, and different classes—shape the experiences of each other? How are those relationships defined and enforced through social institutions that are the primary sites for negotiating power within society? How do these differences contribute to the construction of both individual and group identity? Once we acknowledge that all women are affected by the racial order of society, then it becomes clear that the insights of multiracial feminism provide an analytical framework, not solely for understanding the experiences of women of color but for understanding *all* women, and men, as well.

Notes

1. Maxine Baca Zinn, Lynn Weber Cannon, Elizabeth Higginbotham, and Bonnie Thornton Dill, "The Costs of Exclusionary Practices in Women's Studies," *Signs* 11 (winter 1986): 290–303.
2. Chela Sandoval, "U.S. Third World Feminism: The Theory and Method of Oppositional Consciousness in the Postmodern World," *Genders* (spring 1991): 1–24.
3. Ruth Frankenberg and Lata Mani, "Cross Currents, Crosstalk: Race, 'Postcoloniality,' and the Politics of Location," *Cultural Studies* 7 (May 1993): 292–310.
4. We use the term "multiracial feminism" to convey the multiplicity of racial groups and feminist perspectives.
5. A growing body of work on difference in feminist thought now exists. Although we cannot cite all the current work, the following are representative: Michèle Barrett, "The Concept of Difference," *Feminist Review* 26 (July 1987): 29–42; Christina Crosby, "Dealing with Difference," in *Feminists Theorize the Political*, ed. Judith Butler and Joan W. Scott (New York: Routledge, 1992), 130–43; Elizabeth Fox-Genovese, "Difference, Diversity, and Divisions in an Agenda for

the Women's Movement," in *Color, Class, and Country: Experiences of Gender*, ed: Gay Young and Bette J. Dickerson (London: Zed Books, 1994), 232–48; Nancy A. Hewitt, "Compounding Differences," *Feminist Studies* 18 (summer 1992): 313–26; Maria C. Lugones, "On the Logic of Feminist Pluralism," in *Feminist Ethics*, ed. Claudia Card (Lawrence: University of Kansas Press, 1991), 35–44; Rita S. Gallin and Anne Ferguson, "The Plurality of Feminism: Rethinking 'Difference,'" in *The Woman and International Development Annual* (Boulder: Westview Press, 1993), 3: 1–16; and Linda Gordon, "On Difference," *Genders* 10 (spring 1991): 91–111.

6. Susan Bordo, "*Feminism, Postmodernism,* and Gender Skepticism," in Feminism/ Postmodernism, ed. Linda J. Nicholson (London: Routledge, 1990), 133–56.

7. Sandra G. Harding, *Whose Science? Whose Knowledge? Thinking from Women's Lives* (Ithaca: Cornell University Press, 1991), 179.

8. Crosby, 131.

9. Fox-Genovese, 232.

10. Faye Ginsberg and Anna Lowenhaupt Tsing, Introduction to *Uncertain Terms, Negotiating Gender in American Culture*, ed. Faye Ginsberg and Anna Lowenhaupt Tsing (Boston: Beacon Press, 1990), 3.

11. Sandoval, 2.

12. Sandra Morgan, "Making Connections: Socialist-Feminist Challenges to Marxist Scholarship," in *Women and a New Academy: Gender and Cultural Contexts*, ed. Jean F. O'Barr (Madison: University of Wisconsin Press, 1989), 149.

13. Jane Rowland Martin, "Methodological Essentialism, False Difference, and Other Dangerous Traps," *Signs* 19 (spring 1994): 647.

14. Barrett, 32.

15. bell hooks, *Black Looks: Race and Representation* (Boston: South End Press, 1992), 21.

16. Lugones, 35–44.

17. Patricia Hill Collins, Foreword to *Women of Color in U.S. Society*, ed. Maxine Baca Zinn and Bonnie Thornton Dill (Philadelphia: Temple University Press, 1994), xv.

18. Patricia Hill Collins, "Learning from the Outsider Within: The Sociological Significance of Black Feminist Thought," *Social Problems* 33 (December1986): 514–32.

19. Sandoval, 1.

20. Alison M. Jagger and Paula S. Rothenberg, *Feminist Frameworks: Alternative Theoretical Accounts of the Relations between Women and Men*, 3d ed. (New York: McGraw-Hill, 1993).

21. Michael Omi and Howard Winant, *Racial Formation in the United States: From the 1960s to the 1980s*, 2d ed. (New York: Routledge, 1994).

22. Ruth Frankenberg, *White Women. Race Matters: The Social Construction of Whiteness* (Minneapolis: University of Minnesota Press, 1993).

23. Evelyn Nakano Glenn, "From Servitude to Service Work: Historical Continuities in the Racial Division of Paid Reproductive Labor," *Signs* 18 (autumn 1992): 3. See also Bonnie Thornton Dill, "Our Mothers' Grief: Racial-Ethnic Women and the Maintenance of Families," *Journal of Family History* 13, no. 4 (1988): 415–31.

24. Morgan, 146.

25. Maxine Baca Zinn and Bonnie Thornton Dill, "Difference and Domination," in *Women of Color in U.S. Society*, 11–12.

26. See Omi and Winant, 53–76, for a discussion of racial formation.

27. Margaret L. Andersen and Patricia Hill Collins, *Race, Class, and Gender: An Anthology* (Belmont, Calif.: Wadsworth, 1992), xvi.

28. Omi and Winant.

29. Nazli Kibria, "Migration and Vietnamese American Women: Remaking Ethnicity," in *Women of Color in U.S. Society*, 247–61.

30. Patricia Hill Collins, *Black Feminist Thought: Knowledge, Consciousness, and the Politics of Empowerment* (Boston: Unwin Hyman, 1990).

31. Elizabeth Spelman, *Inessential Women: Problems of Exclusion in Feminist Thought* (Boston: Beacon Press, 1988), 136.

32. Several discussions of difference make this point. See Baca Zinn and Dill, Gordon, 106; and Lynn Weber, in the "Symposium on West and Fenstermaker's 'Doing Difference,'" *Gender & Society* 9 (August 1995): 515–19.

33. Glenn, 10.

34. Gordon, 106.

35. Chandra Talpade Mohanty, "Cartographies of Struggle: Third World Women and the Politics of Feminism," in *Third World Women and the Politics of Feminism*, ed. Chandra Talpade Mohanty, Ann Russo, and Lourdes Torres (Bloomington: Indiana University Press, 1991), 13.

36. Frankenberg and Mani, 306.

37. Norma Alarçon, "The Theoretical Subject(s) of *This Bridge Called My Back* and Anglo-American Feminism," in *Making Face, Making Soul, Haciendo Caras: Creative and Critical Perspectives by Women of Color*, ed. Gloria Anzaldúa (San Francisco: Aunt Lute, 1990), 356.

38. Frankenberg. See also Evelyn Torton Beck, "The Politics of Jewish Invisibility." *NWSA Journal* (fall 1988): 93–102.

POSTSTRUCTURALIST
THEORIES

34.
MULTIPLE MEDIATIONS: FEMINIST SCHOLARSHIP IN THE AGE OF MULTINATIONAL RECEPTION
Lata Mani

"unusual knowing," a cognitive practice, a form of consciousness that is not primordial, universal, or coextensive with human thought. [. . .] but historically determined and yet subjectively and politically assumed. (de Lauretis, March 1990)

On the acupuncturist's table, Berkeley, California, July 1988.

> *I am lying in wait for the complex verbal negotiation that attends each visit to my acupuncturist. I want a diagnosis—a definable illness, a definite cure. He is disdainful of this desire for clarity and resolution and insists on treating my body as a zone in which energies rise and fall, sometimes rebelliously, at other times gracefully and once even, as he put it, "stroppily". As I ponder the frustrating untranslatability of his idiom, he asks the dreaded question: "Well, what is your Ph.D. thesis about?"*
>
> *I stare at the infra-red lamp and wonder which version to present. The various responses I have elicited over the years race through my mind like a film running at high speed. My usual strategy is to assess the cultural politics of those addressing me (such as I can discern them), the tenor of the question (is this a serious inquiry or merely a polite one?) and my frame of mind at the time (do I want to educate, be patronized, or try to avoid both by being vague, but thereby risking the impression that I know not what I am doing?). I did not, however, have time for such musings. I was trapped under the beady eye of my white American doctor of needles who, having taken my pulse, was awaiting a reply. So I blurted out what I consider my minimalist "no-nonsense" description: "I am working on the debate between colonial officials, missionaries, and the indigenous male elite on sati (widow burning) in colonial India."*
>
> *I felt weak, as though it had been a confession extorted from me after intense cross-examination. I sighed inwardly. Meanwhile, my declaration had provoked what turned out to be a half-hour lecture on the dilemmas of cross-cultural understanding. He said that such practices would always be difficult for Westerners to comprehend, hastily adding that it was important none the less not to impose alien values and that sati probably had a particular significance within Indian culture which it would be enlightening to know. At this point he turned away from my foot, into which he had just finished inserting needles, and asked, "So how do you understand widow burning?"*
>
> *I felt myself stiffen. He had thrown me a challenge that would require a command performance in colonial and post-colonial history and discourse, one that I did not feel equal to at the time. So I said evasively, "It's a long story and I'm trying to sort it out."*

"Good" said the genial man in the white coat tapping my arm. Not waiting for a response, he continued. "Of course, you are Westernized and your ideas have probably changed from living here. I wonder what women in India feel about it?' So saying, he left the room.

I was furious. I had not interrupted his liberal, relativist, patronizing discourse, and was as a result caught in its pincer movement: an apparent but ultimately repressive toler-ance, a desire for "true" knowledge, and a demand for authenticity that was impossible for me to meet, given that any agreement between us, however fragile and superficial, would immediately make me "Westernized": not like "them" but like "him." I wished for the mil-lionth time that I had been working on a less contentious topic, one that, unlike sati, *had not served as metonym for Indian society itself... or had had the panache to wag my fin-ger like him and say, "Read my book and you'll find out."*

The Emergence of a Politics of Location

This paper explores questions of positionality and location and their relation to the production of knowledge as well as its reception. These issues have animated feminism from its inception. Here they are approached through a set of intercon-nected reflections, on the processes that shaped my study of debates on *sati* under British colonialism, and on the different ways in which this analysis has been received in Britain and in India. Such alternative readings thematize the politics of intellectual work in neo/post-colonial contexts, and the difficulties of achieving an international feminism sensitive to the complex and diverse articulations of the local and the global.

Contemporary theory in feminism and in the humanities has brought a criti-cal self-consciousness to bear both on the place and mode of enunciation (who speaks and how) and that of its reception (how it is interpreted and why). As claims to universality and objectivity have been shown to be the alibis of a largely masculinist, heterosexist, and white Western subject, both readers and writers have had to confront their particularity and history. Gender, race, class, sexuality, and historical experience specify hitherto unmarked bodies, deeply compromising the fictions of unified subjects and disinterested knowledges.

Such developments, or should I say acknowledgements, require attentiveness to the theoretical and political impulses that shape our projects, and an openness to the inevitable fact that different agendas may govern their reception. Needless to say, there have always been multiple investments and diverse audiences. Our accounting of these phenomena today simply attests to the successful struggles for discursive spaces of those overlapping and hitherto marginalized groups, women, Third World people, gays and lesbians. Institutional concessions to the heterogene-ity of the social landscape has prompted the emergence of new fields of study within U.S. universities, for instance ethnic studies and women's studies. It has also given new momentum to interdisciplinary work. The current mobilization of tal-ents and energies around culture studies is a case in point.[1]

The revolt of the particular against that masquerading as the general, of what Donna Haraway has called "situated" as against "disembodied knowledges"

(Haraway, 1988), has brought to the fore theoretical and political questions regarding positionality and identity. This issue has probably been most fully developed within feminism, in part in debates about the relationship between experience and knowledge. One locus of such discussion in the Euro-American context has been the related struggles over racism and white centredness of dominant feminism (Moraga and Anzaldua, 1981; hooks, 1981, Amos et al., 1984; Bhavnani and Coulson, 1986, among others) and its replication of elements of colonial discourse (Spivak, 1981; Mohanty, 1984; Minh-Ha 1986, 1987; Lazreg, 1988). Feminists have called for a revised politics of location—"revised" because, unlike its initial articulation, the relation between experience and knowledge is now seen to be one not of correspondence, but fraught with history, contingency and struggle. (In addition to the authors already cited, see Bulkin et al., 1984; Segrest, 1985; Rich, 1986; de Lauretis, 1986; Kaplan, 1987.)[2] These terms powerfully suggest some of the problems of positionality as they confront me: a post-colonial Third World feminist working on India in the United States.

Chandra Talpade Mohanty argues that developing a politics of location requires exploration of "the historical, geographic, cultural, psychic and imaginative boundaries which provide the ground for political definition and self-definition" (Mohanty, 1987: 31). Location, in her terms, is not a fixed point but a "temporality of struggle" (p. 40), characterized by multiple locations and nonsynchronous processes of movement "between cultures, languages, and complex configurations of meaning and power" (p. 42). These processes, in Mohanty's view, enable "a paradoxical continuity of self, mapping and . . . political location. . . . [M]y location forces and enables specific modes of reading and knowing the dominant. The struggles I choose to engage in are then the intensification of these modes of knowing" (p. 42). This definition of the space of politics very nicely illuminates the dynamics of how my conception of a project on the debate on *sati* in colonial India bears the traces of movement between cultures and configurations of meaning, multiple locations, and specific modes of knowing.

My research examines colonial official, missionary, and indigenous elite discourses on *sati* in Britain and India in the late eighteenth- and early-nineteenth centuries. I investigate the conditions of production and the burden of each of these discourses, the intersections, differences, and tensions between them, and the competing and overlapping ways in which they were deployed. Among other things, I argue that a specifically colonial discourse on India framed the debate on *sati* producing troubling consequences for how "the woman's question" in India was to be posed thereafter, whether by Indian nationalists, or Western feminists (Mani, 1989).

One of the things that has prompted and sustained my energy through hours of plodding through archival documents and reels of dizzying microfilm has been a conviction of the importance of the contemporary ideological and political legacy of such debates about women and culture. I have always been aware that this legacy has had a differential trajectory in India and in, for example, the U.S. or Britain: that the relation of this earlier discourse to contemporary knowledges, popular and specialist, about India in the West, was different from its relation to the contemporary self-knowledge of Indians. It is the contours of this difference that this paper will now explore.

The following section reflects on the experience of presenting my work (Mani, 1987) to groups in the U.S., Britain, and India, and discovering that the audiences in these places seized on entirely different aspects of my work as politically significant. These responses in turn have caused me to reflect on how moving between different "configurations of meaning and power" can prompt different "modes of knowing." The experience has also required me squarely to confront a problem not adequately theorized in discussions of positionality or of the function of theory and criticism: the politics of simultaneously negotiating not multiple but discrepant audiences, different "temporalities of struggle."[3]

Back to the Future: The After-Lives of Colonial Discourses

"Colonial" or Eurocentric discourses on India, and on the Third World more generally, have an abiding presence in the U.S. and Britain, the two Western countries with which I am most familiar. Television documentaries, scholarly writing and popular wisdom circulate such notions as the centrality of religion—whether framed as the essential "spirituality" of the East or as the dominance of caste (Inden, 1986; Appadurai, 1988)—the antiquity of Indian "culture," and the victimization of women. These ideas "hail" those of us living here with a systematicity that, over time, makes them truly oppressive. As a Marxist-feminist who had come to feminism in India, I initially responded to the predominance of culturalist understandings of Indian society with surprise and bemusement at the ignorance they betrayed. I assumed that such ignorance must also account for my having so often to explain the supposed anomaly of being an Indian feminist.

The repetition of such incidents as my encounter with the acupuncturist, the dynamics of which I would barely have been able to fathom when I first arrived in the U.S., compelled me to think seriously about the prehistory of such knowledges about India and Indian women. I brought this new sensibility to bear on reading the debate on *sati*. It has been, I believe, by and large productive. For although I have read many of the same documents as other historians, Indian and non-Indian, an alertness to how British colonialism may have shaped knowledge about colonized society has turned up unexpected disjunctures, contests and determinations, for instance, over what constitutes "tradition." Given a context in which elements of this nineteenth-century discourse continue to circulate, on occasion virtually unreconstructed, in the service of British racism and U.S. cultural imperialism, I consider excavation of the colonial prehistory of such ideas to be a political gesture.

By and large, most discussions that followed presentations of my work in the U.S. or Britain tended to focus on the contemporary replications, resonances or rearticulations of what I had sketched. In Britain, for instance, we explored how the British state manipulates women's "oppression" in Indian and Pakistani "culture" to legitimate virginity tests, immigration controls, and policing of Asian marriages and family life. This "civilizing" racist British state has placed black feminists in Britain in a position analogous to that of nineteenth-century Indian male social reformers, who defended "culture" and "women" in a similarly overdetermined context (Parmar, 1982; Amos et al., 1984; Grewal et al., 1988). The significant difference between then and now is that black feminists (unlike many male nationalists) have insisted on keeping women at the centre of the struggle, refusing to let themselves become mere pawns in a contest between the state and community. They have charted a complex strategy. On the one hand, they have challenged the self-serving appropriation of "women's issues" by a racist British state. Simultaneously, they have resisted both the "protection" of men in the black community when it has come with a defence of practices oppressive to women, and white feminist attempts to rescue them from patriarchy. In short, black feminists in Britain have refused "salvation," whether by the state in the name of civilized modernity, by black men on behalf of tradition and community integrity, or by white feminists in the interest of ethnocentric versions of women's liberation. In this context, discussions after my presentations explored, among other things, questions of rhetoric and strategy: how to argue for women's rights in ways that were not complicit in any way with patriarchal, racist or ethnocentric formulations of the issues. Thus, given that the British state draws on key elements of nineteenth-century discourses on India to further its own current projects, my delineation of the colonial dimension of these discourses was seen to have an explicitly political character.

In India, however, this dimension of my project was interpreted quite differently, primarily as an academic and historical argument. To some extent this is not surprising. Notions of "timeless textual traditions" or the essential spirituality of Indian society have a different afterlife in the Indian public domain. Quite simply, they are not, as in Britain, critical to the elaboration of hegemony. Certainly, development policies explicitly embrace the logic of modernity, brahmanical texts have come to represent quintessential Hinduism, and the colonial legacy of making religious scriptures the basis of civil law has enormously complicated feminist projects of legal reform. However, notions like "timeless traditions" function most often to inspire literature from the Indian Tourist Development Corporation or to feed the fantasy life of petit-bourgeois middle- and high-caste Indians regarding the glory of ancient India (read: "of their own lineage"). Except in the case of Government of India documentaries on tribal peoples, or sometimes in relation to remote rural areas, there does not exist a serious convention of representing Indian citizens as lacking agency, inhabiting a timeless zone, and immobilized by "tradition." Indeed, this kind of analysis would be difficult to sustain, given that the authority of the Indian state has been continually challenged since independence, and is bolstered today not by a democratic consensus but through a brutal and increasingly unashamed use of violence.

The Indian context thus presents a sharp contrast to the West; naming something "colonial" in India has, accordingly, a different import. It becomes a question of periodization, rather than a crucial move in developing an oppositional, anti-imperialist critical practice. Such a reading is further comprehensible because, in a palpable, existential sense, when one is in India, colonialism does indeed seem like a thing long past. Despite India's economically dependent status in the world economy and its wilful exploitation by multinationals and agencies like the World Bank, "the West" as an ideological and political presence articulates with such a density of indigenous institutions, discourses, histories, and practices that its identity as "Western" is refracted and not always salient. This is not to say that Indians are naive about the impact of the West. (There was, for example, little confusion about the ultimate culpability of the U.S.-based corporation Union Carbide, in the Bhopal industrial disaster.) What I am suggesting is that, unlike, for example, many nations in the Caribbean or in Central America, in India it is not the boot of imperialism that is felt as an identifiable weight upon one's neck. The pressure one feels compelled to resist is rather that of the nation state, dominant social and political institutions, and religious "fundamentalisms" of various kinds. No doubt, the activities of the nation state are themselves related in complex ways to regional and global geopolitical trends, but it is the local face of this international phenomenon against which one is moved to struggle.

It comes as no surprise, then, that in India, the "political" dimension of my work is seen to be expressed primarily in my engagement with nationalism, the limited parameters within which nationalists posed the question of women's status, the marginality of women to nineteenth-century discussions supposedly about them, and the legacy of colonialism in contemporary discussion of women's issues. This last point was made in my presentation in relation to the recent controversy over reform of Islamic law provoked by the "Shahbano case." The case was one in which the Supreme Court had upheld the application of a Muslim woman, Shahbano, for life-long maintenance from her ex-husband. The Supreme Court's verdict became a rallying point for many Muslims who felt that the court had (contrary to its claims) violated Islamic law and thus undermined the only legal protection Indian Muslims enjoyed as a religious minority (Punwani, 1985; Kishwar, 1986; Engineer, 1987; Pathak and Sunder Rajan, 1989). In analyzing the case, it was possible to point out how, in this as in many instances in the nineteenth century, contests over women's rights were being debated as contests over scriptural interpretation, and as struggles over a community's autonomy and right to self-determination. While these terms do not exhaust the arguments made in relation to the case, they point to significant parallels between nineteenth- and twentieth-century debates on women (Mani, 1987: 153–6). My interest in such continuities was in the ways in which they constrained the form and content of contemporary discussions. I did not assume that the persistence of certain discursive elements implied unchanged significance, meanings or effects; ideas are potentially available for different kinds of appropriation by different social forces. Suffice it to say that the case, more than any theoretical argument about "colonial discourse", served to convey some of the political impulses of my project. Even here, however, the "colonial" dimension was of academic interest. The burden of the discussion, not inappropriately, fell to the practical problems of building coalitions between Hindu and Muslim women in the wake of the divisiveness produced by the Shahbano case and the growth of communalism in Indian politics.

Situating Our Interventions

These differing receptions of my work in Britain and India raise questions regarding the relationship between "experience" and "theory," one's geographical location and the formulation of one's projects. It seems to me that travelling to the U.S. and living under its regimes of truth regarding India and the Third World more generally have intensified for me certain "modes of knowing." The disjunctions between how I saw myself and the kinds of knowledge about me that I kept bumping into in the West, opened up new questions for social and political inquiry.

Reading Edward Said's *Orientalism* in this context was enormously productive and energizing (Said, 1979). It contextualized the phenomena, discourses and attitudes I was encountering and helped me in the task of situating personal experiences within a historical problematic. It quickened my impulse to take more seriously than I had previously been inclined to, colonial official and missionary discourses on India. My interest in these was not merely that of a historian of ideas, but of someone curious about the history of the present. I can only wonder at how my project might have been fashioned in the absence of this experience of travel to a different economy of power and knowledge. In this regard, I find it significant that an Indian friend of mine once remarked that the full force of Said's argument in *Orientalism* had come home to her only after spending time in Europe. Prior to this she had believed, and this is a fairly common perception in India, that Said was perhaps overstating his case, stretching a point.[4]

It seems to me that the politics and epistemology of differing readings such as these dramatizes the dilemma of post-colonial intellectuals working on the Third World in the West. One diagnosis of this situation accuses such intellectuals of inauthenticity or ideological contamination by the West. This charge may be levelled by First World intellectuals demanding a spurious authenticity of their Third World colleagues. It often works to challenge the latter groups' credibility, by implying that their politics are exceptional and ungeneralizable. This analysis may, however, also be shared by Third World intellectuals working in the Third World. The criticism in this instance may be rooted in the assumption, not always unwarranted, that intellectuals abroad are, so to speak, selling out. It is, however, ultimately simplistic because it overgeneralizes, and one does not, of course, have to leave home to sell out. Alternatively, assertions about ideological contamination are often shorthand allusions to genuine issues, such as asymmetries in the material conditions of scholarship in metropolitan and Third World contexts. Such problems are, however, not clarified by a moralistic formulation of the issue in terms of purity or pollution.

In the face of this discourse of authenticity, some Third World intellectuals working in the First World have reterritorialized themselves as hybrid. This strategy is compelling when such a demonstration of hybridity becomes, as in Gloria

Anzaldúa's *Borderlands* (1987) an enabling moment for the possibility of a collective politics attentive to difference and contradiction. When, however, the elaboration of hybridity becomes an end in itself, serving only to undo binary oppositions, it runs the risk of dodging entirely the question of location. To this one must say, "necessary but insufficient."

Finally, for those intellectuals from the geographical Third World who have an elsewhere to return to, there is the possibility of adopting a tactic which would separate projects into what is deemed appropriate or inappropriate to do "while one is in the West." Here again we have a prescription which may make sense in specific instances, for political and practical reasons. On the other hand this strategy also has the potential for side-stepping the issue. It implicitly conceives of the West and non-West as autonomous spaces and thereby evades the thorny issue of their intersections and mutual implications (Mohanty, 1989).

How, then, would I proceed to delineate, in my own case, the potential and limits of my location, working on the Third World in the belly of the First? For one thing, it seems to me that the mode of knowing enabled by the experience of existing between discursive systems makes it difficult for me to isolate colonialism as a distinct historical period with little claim on the present. Consequently, I have tried to train myself to look for discontinuities in apparently smooth surfaces, and continuities across the dominant and oppositional. Secondly, the deadening essentialism of much historical and contemporary Western representation of the Third World has confirmed for me, albeit in a different way, a lesson learnt earlier from Marxism: an abiding suspicion of primarily cultural explanations of social phenomena. At the same time, perhaps not paradoxically, experiences of such a persistent privileging of "culture" have in turn compelled me to take very seriously the domain designated by it. What counts as "culture"? How is it conceived and represented? With what consequences? In short, I have been persuaded of the need to open to critical reflection the vexed and complex issue of the relationship between colonialism and questions of culture.

This is a problem that is, to my mind, yet to be adequately thematized in the literature on colonialism in India. Historiography on nineteenth-century India, for instance, has produced sophisticated analysis of the impact of colonialism on India's economy and politics, but has paid comparatively little attention to its impact on culture or on conceptions of it. Perhaps the ways in which I may be tempted to frame the problem will be marked by the fact that it became an issue for me as a result of my experience of Britain and the U.S. It may be that I accent the colonial rather more heavily than my imagined counterpart, the feminist writing in India. But as I reflect on what moves me, I also need to be aware that I now inescapably participate in multiple conversations, not all of which overlap. As for the gains of being situated in the interstices, only time will tell. In the meantime, it seems to me that my attempt to specify location might also be fruitfully undertaken in dialogue with feminists in India. After all, the dangers of reading the local as global are potentially present both in India and in the West: in the former through minimizing colonialism, in the latter through aggrandizing it.

Priorities Redetermined: The Aftermath of Roop Kanwar's Burning

The difficulties of straddling different temporalities of struggle cannot, however, always be resolved through listening for and talking about our specificities. There are political moments which pose limits to the possibility of conceiving of international feminist exchanges (whether between First and Third World women in the West or between Third World women cross-nationally) as negotiated dialogues which, while they may alternately diverge and intersect, are ultimately benign and noncontradictory.

On 22 September 1987, Roop Kanwar died on the funeral pyre of her husband in Deorala, Rajasthan. The incident has sparked off a nationwide controversy on *sati* in India, unearthed the information that there have been at least thirty-eight widow immolations in Rajasthan since independence, and dragged out of the closet vociferous supporters of the practice. In this recent case, the government of India vacillated in taking action against family members found to have coerced Roop. State officials were present along with an estimated 300,000 others at an event "honouring" the episode thirteen days after the burning, and when the state finally banned glorification of *sati*, the response was too little, too late.

Meanwhile, a massive debate on *sati* had been set in motion, with opponents and defenders staking out their claims in terms that were in many ways remarkably reminiscent of the nineteenth-century controversy which is the subject of my own research. As in the colonial period, issues of scriptural interpretation, the so-called traditional nature of *sati*, its barbarity, the role of the state, women's social conditioning and the question of the widow's consent, all emerged as key items in the debate.

Four positions were discernible in the discussions that followed upon Roop Kanwar's death. Each of these is more elaborate than my characterization of it suggests, but my purpose here is merely to sketch in broad strokes the discursive space that was constituted, referring readers to others who have analyzed them more thoroughly (Patel and Kumar, 1988; Sangari, 1988, among others). There was firstly, a "liberal" position, critical of *sati* as "traditional," "religious," and barbaric and arguing that the incident represented the failure of the project of modernization. Secondly, and opposed to this, was the conservative, pro-*sati* lobby. This valorized *sati's* "traditional" and "religious" status and argued that the rationality of the practice was necessarily inaccessible to westernized, urban Indians.

Ostensibly critical of both these positions, although reserving the burden of its critique for the former and ultimately aligning itself with the latter, was a third stance (Nandy, 1987, 1988a, 1988b). Ashis Nandy, a trenchant critic of the philosophies of modernization and development, castigated liberal condemnation of *sati* as the response of a rootless, decultured urban bourgeoisie, unable, if not unwilling, to comprehend the masses. We may agree with Nandy that the incomprehension of *sati* expressed by the liberal media required examination and critique: after all, *sati* is only one among many practices exploitative of women. In a sense, contemporary liberal incomprehension parallels nineteenth-century colonial horror. Both cast *sati* simultaneously as an exceptional practice *and* one that is emblematic of society as a whole. The sense of its exceptionalism emerges in analyses of *sati* which treat it in isolation from women's subordination in general, while its emblematic status is dramatized in the way in which the incident has provoked anxiety about the nature and extent of India's social progress.

This, however, is not the direction in which Nandy develops his argument. Nandy's ire is directed mainly at what he perceives as the "Western" modes of denouncing *sati* reproduced by "modernists". Nandy's stand on *sati* has drawn sharp criticism from feminists (Qadeer and Hasan, 1987; Patel and Kumar, 1988, Sangari, 1988; Philipose and Setalvad, 1988) whom he scorns as modernist, overlooking thereby important distinctions between feminist and liberal critiques of the practice (Nandy, 1988b). What is even more curious, however, is that Nandy's critique of the colonial mentality of these modernists itself reproduces three key moves of colonial discourse. He reaffirms the "tradition"/"modernity" dichotomy in analyzing the practice, and replicates the colonial oppositions, "glorious past/degraded present" and "authentic/inauthentic *sati*." The latter two are brought together in his positive evaluation of the original, mythological *sati*, said to express women's sacred and magical powers, as against his negative description of contemporary widow burning which, he claims, is merely the product of a dehumanized market morality.

The fourth, and to my mind, genuinely anti-imperialist position (even though, unlike Nandy's it was not articulated as such) was that taken by feminists. Not surprisingly, concern for women's lives was very much at the centre of feminist discourse. Feminists insisted that Roop Kanwar's death should be understood in the context of the general subordination of women in Indian society, challenged attempts to frame the issue as one of tradition or religion and located the Deorala incident within post-independent political and economic developments in Rajasthan (Kishwar and Vanita, 1987; Bhasin and Menon, 1988; Vaid, 1988; among others). Feminists also pointed to the modernity of the incident and to the character of the pro-*sati* lobby, whose members were urban, educated men in their twenties and thirties. For example, Madhu Kishwar and Ruth Vanita argued that Deorala was not a rural backwater, but rather a prosperous town with electricity, tap water and a 70 percent literacy rate (Kishwar and Vanita, 1987). Further, they pointed out that Roop Kanwar was a city-educated woman while her husband had a degree in science and her father-in-law, one of the abettors, was employed as a school teacher. In addition to the insufficiency of derisively analyzing *sati* as "traditional," feminists argued that such a ploy would play into the hands of pro-*sati* "traditionalists". Religious arguments were similarly exposed as serving to legitimate the oppression of women. Again, Kishwar and Vanita described how the daily rituals around the spot where the burning had taken place resembled victory celebrations, not religious devotion. In arguing that cries of "religion" could not absolve anyone of murder, Indira Jaising put it thus: "just as the personal is political, the religious is secular where women are concerned," (Jaising, 1987).

Finally, feminists warned against the danger of demanding more stringent laws and greater state intervention, the recurring pleas of liberal opponents of *sati*. They highlighted the appalling lack of will demonstrated by the state in prosecuting

Roop's in-laws, and the possibility that the state would merely abuse the greater powers that would accrue to it. These fears have largely been realized. Local police have used their powers to harass journalists and others investigating the case and, despite the law against abetting and glorifying *sati*, an estimated 8,000 people gathered at Deorala in September 1988 to "celebrate" the one year anniversary of the burning of Roop Kanwar (Pachauri, 1988). And perhaps worst of all, one of the provisions of the legislative act on *sati* makes its victims liable to punishment: women who attempt *sati* are hereafter to be subject to fine or imprisonment!

The events that have followed Roop Kanwar's burning have radically changed the Indian context for my work. Widow burning is no longer, as it had been when I began, a "historical" problem, but very much a charged and explosive contemporary issue. Although my own discussion here has focused most on feminist arguments, they are, alas, marginal to the current debate. The discursive space is principally being defined by conservatives and liberals. The former are more active in mobilizing a constituency and have had the support of political parties more wedded to securing votes than to fundamental rights of any kind. This context has made it imperative to contextualize and frame in particular ways some of the arguments I develop in my thesis.

How, for instance, might my critique of the civilizing mission be appropriated in the current situation? Part of my argument has been to show, in some detail, what is occluded in the following statement which represents a dominant story about colonialism and the question of woman: "we came, we saw, we were horrified, we intervened." Taking the instance of *sati*, whose abolition by the British in 1829 supposedly illuminates, *par excellence*, the legitimacy of this account, I have tried to suggest that the story is much more complicated. Among other things, I point out that legislative prohibition of *sati* was preceded by its legalization, a procedure that involved British officials in determining and enforcing a colonial version of the practice deemed traditional and authentic; that intervention in *sati* provided grounds for intervention in civil society; and that a fundamental ambivalence to *sati* structured colonial attitudes to the practice (Mani, 1987). I argue that missionary involvement in *sati* was similarly complex and ambivalent, with horror being reserved primarily for fundraising material produced for a British public. My point is that ultimately, for both officials and missionaries, women were not really at issue. Women rather provided ground for the development of other agendas.

I make a related argument about nineteenth-century indigenous discourses on *sati*. I argue that these developed within the constraints of a discourse on Indian society privileged by the British, that ambivalence to the practice is discernible even among those passionately opposed to *sati*, and that here too, concern for women seems secondary to concern for "tradition" or for the general good of society. Women thus appear as obstacles to societal reform, and as individuals who must be trained to take up the duties of modern life with its own requirements of good wife and mother. My argument, then, has called into question the overly positive evaluation of the civilizing impulses of colonialism and the modernizing desires of proto-nationalism and nationalism: not because women did not gain from them, but because neither seemed to me to be selfless and benign in their espousal of women's rights, nor even centrally concerned with them.

How will such a critique of colonialist and nationalist arguments against *sati* resonate in India today? Is there any danger that my critique of the *terms* of these arguments will be read reductively as support for *sati*? Authorial intention, it is generally conceded, guarantees nothing. Considerable care will be necessary in framing my discussion in such a way that only a deliberate misreading can appropriate my arguments to reactionary ends. In addition, perhaps in my discussion of the nineteenth-century debate on *sati* I should also explicitly engage the contemporary moment so as to clarify how once again, with the signal exception of feminists and some progressives, arguments about women's rights have provided the basis for a further entrenchment of patriarchy in the name of "tradition" (a point made by many Indian feminists) and for the arrogation of greater powers to the state in the name of "modernity".

I was lucky to be in India in the aftermath of Deorala. Lucky, because, in and of themselves, newspaper clippings and magazine articles could not have conveyed to me the political temperature there. Grasping the situation required the cumulative experience of countless conversations with friends, family members- and neighbours, chance encounters on buses and trains, reports from feminists and civil libertarians who had travelled to Deorala, public meetings, and accounts of group discussions held in schools, colleges, political and community organizations. Much of this would obviously have been unavailable in print. My combined impressions strongly suggest that great care will have to be exercised in making arguments such as a critique of the Western civilizing mission.

The possible implications of other issues, such as exploration of the question of women's agency, appear to be even more treacherous. The problem of women's agency occupies a paradoxical position in feminist thinking in that, despite being a central concern, it remains poorly theorized. This is equally true of post-structuralist theory which, while being critical of the bourgeois conception of agency as the free will of an autonomous self, has yet to produce an adequate alternative formulation.

The widow's will has been a recurring theme in both the nineteenth- and twentieth-century debates on *sati*. Here, discussion of agency is framed around the limited and analytically unhelpful binary terms, coercion and consent. Those defending *sati* have, then as now, made claims about the "voluntary" nature of the act. Against this, opponents of *sati* have emphasized coercion, and questioned the meaning of consent. In the earlier debate, consent was sometimes conceived as impossible by definition: women were simply deemed incapable of it. At other times, the issue was formulated more broadly in terms of women's social position and of the meagre alternatives available to them. For instance, it was pointed out that one could hardly speak of consent when widowhood imposed its own regimes of misery. By and large, those against *sati* today have developed this latter argument, feminists far more consistently than liberals. In the colonial situation, this dualistic conception of agency led to legislation requiring women to be cross-examined at the pyre and being permitted to burn if their action was declared to be voluntary. A static conception of agency intersected with the assumption of religious hegemony to marginalize the ways in which women actively negotiated and struggled against the social and familial constraints upon them. Nowhere is this more evident than in colonial eyewitness accounts of *sati*, which consistently effaced signs of women's agency in struggle, resistance, and coercion (Mani, 1989).

I have long felt anxious about how a broader consideration of women's agency is foreclosed by its reductive translation into an issue of whether or not the widow went willingly. Limiting discussion of women's agency in this way makes it difficult to engage simultaneously women's systematic subordination *and* the ways in which they negotiate oppressive, even determining, social conditions (Ong, 1987 and Gordon, 1989 develop such complex analyses of women's agency). I know that part of my own concern with these questions comes from a sense of the extent to which Third World peoples are consistently represented in Eurocentric discourses as lacking agency. I also know that it comes from a conviction that structures of domination are best understood if we can grasp how we remain agents even in the moments in which we are being intimately, viciously oppressed.

The discourse of woman as victim has been invaluable to feminism in pointing to the systematic character of gender domination. But if it is not employed with care, or in conjunction with a dynamic conception of agency, it leaves us with reductive representations of women as primarily beings who are passive and acted upon. In other words we are left with that common figure of Eurocentric feminist discourse: the Third World woman as "always, already victim," (Mohanty, 1984). What is forsaken here is the notion of women's oppression as a multifaceted and contradictory social process. It is crucial to stress in this regard, however, that when Indian feminists speak of woman as victim it is in a complex material sense. It is also important to note than in emphasizing women's systematic subordination rather than debating questions of agency, Indian feminists are specifically attempting to counter right-wing discourse that falsely proposes women's total freedom.[5]

Questions of agency provoke issues at the heart of feminism. But in raising them in the current Indian context, one walks a tightrope. First, given the dominant discourse on *sati*, to claim that women are agents even in their coercion is to court the possibility of misappropriation by the right wing. Second, current legislation on *sati*, by making women attempting *sati* liable to punishment, implicitly conceives of them as "free agents". The law states that any such punishment must take account of the circumstances in which the woman's decision was taken. But given that legal and political institutions routinely punish victims instead of perpetrators, why should we trust that this proviso will not work against women? In the short term, then, it seems safest to counter the notion of woman as free agent by emphasizing her victimization. However, unless we include in this a complex sense of agency, we run the risk of producing a discourse which sets women up to be saved. This would situate women within feminist analysis in ways that are similar to their positioning within colonialist or nationalist discourse.

The example of women's agency is a particularly good instance of the dilemmas confronted in simultaneously attempting to speak within different historical moments and to discrepant audiences. What might be a valuable pushing of the limits of current rethinking of agency in Anglo-American feminism, may, if not done with extreme care, be an unhelpful, if not disastrous move in the Indian context. If criticism is to be "worldly" (Said, 1983: 1–30) or "situated" (Haraway, 1988), or engaged, it must take account of the worlds in which it speaks. Perhaps to Bruce Robbins' suggestion that theory is a "when" not a "what" (Robbins, 1987/1988: 5), we should also add the notion of a "where."

Notes

Lata Mani received her Ph.D. from the University of California, Santa Cruz in 1989. She has been active in feminist struggles in India and in feminist and antiracist work in the U.S.

Kum-Kum Bhavnani, Vivek Dhareshwar, Ruth Frankenberg, Mary John, and Kamala Visweswaran have left the imprint of their critical readings on the final version of this paper. I am also indebted to Indian feminists and progressives whose political insight and imaginative interventions in the contemporary debate on widow burning have been inspiring and instructive. An earlier version of this paper appeared in *Inscriptions*, no. 5, University of California, Santa Cruz, 1989.

1. The relative rapidity with which the concept of "culture studies" has found institutional support in the U.S. academy compared to ethnic or women's studies should give us pause. bell hooks (Gloria Watkins) and Gayatri C. Spivak have recently mapped out what is at stake intellectually and politically in the kinds of theoretical and curricular agendas being privileged and excluded in the institutionalization of "Third World" or "culture studies." bell hooks, "Critical integration: talking race, resisting racism," Conference on Feminisms and Cultural Imperialism: The Politics of Difference, Cornell University, 1989 April 22–3; Gayatri C. Spivak, "Post-coloniality and the field of value," Conference on Feminisms and Cultural Imperialism: The Politics of Difference, Cornell University, 1989, April 22–3.
2. As a whole, however, as Norma Alarcon (1990), Aida Hurtado (1989), and Chela Sandoval (1991) have recently argued, the critique of U.S. white feminism has been taken up very unevenly and has failed fundamentally to transform dominant feminist thinking.
3. Edward Said (1986) raises the problem of discrepant experiences and constituencies but develops instead a case for foregrounding the *shared* intellectual and political terrain produced by colonialism. See also, Said, 1983: 226–47.
4. There may be many reasons for a critique of Said's *Orientalism*, some more persuasive than others (Mani and Frankenberg, 1985). There is first the theoretical resistance of those working within an objectivist paradigm to his social constructionist approach. Then there is the question of the scope of his argument. Many Indian readers, for example, felt that the book's value for them was seriously limited by its primary focus on the West and its lack of analysis of internal class and power relations in colonized territories. My point here, then, is not that there are no grounds to criticize *Orientalism*: rather that, in India, the political and ideological impetus of Said's project has generally not been apprehended as compelling, a response tied to both geographical location and historical experience.
5. Rajeswari Sunder Rajan is approaching the problem of the widow's subjectivity in *sati* from a different perspective. She argues that the "methodological impasse" generated by the "coercion-consent" framework can be avoided if the question of the widow's subjectivity is engaged via an exploration of "both the phenomenology of pain and a politics that recognizes pain as constitutive of the subject." (forthcoming).

35.
DECONSTRUCTING EQUALITY-VERSUS-DIFFERENCE: OR, THE USES OF POSTSTRUCTURALIST THEORY FOR FEMINISM
Joan W. Scott

That feminism needs theory goes without saying (perhaps because it has been said so often). What is not always clear is what that theory will do, although there are certain common assumptions I think we can find in a wide range of feminist writings. We need theory that can analyze the workings of patriarchy in all its manifestations—ideological, institutional, organizational, subjective—accounting not only for continuities but also for change over time. We need theory that will let us think in terms of pluralities and diversities rather than of unities and universals. We need theory that will break the conceptual hold, at least, of those long traditions of (Western) philosophy that have systematically and repeatedly construed the world hierarchically in terms of masculine universals and feminine specificities. We need theory that will enable us to articulate alternative ways of thinking about (and thus acting upon) gender without either simply reversing the old hierarchies or confirming them. And we need theory that will be useful and relevant for political practice.

It seems to me that the body of theory referred to as poststructuralism best meets all these requirements. It is not by any means the only theory nor are its positions and formulations unique. In my own case, however, it was reading poststructuralist theory and arguing with literary scholars that provided the elements of clarification for which I was looking. I found a new way of analyzing constructions of meaning and relationships of power that called unitary, universal categories into question and historicized concepts otherwise treated as natural (such as man/woman) or absolute (such as equality or justice). In addition, what attracted me was the historical connection between the two movements. Poststructuralism and contemporary feminism are late-twentieth-century movements that share a certain self-conscious critical relationship to established philosophical and political traditions. It thus seemed worthwhile for feminist scholars to exploit that relationship for their own ends.[1]...

...What seems most useful here is to give a short list of some major theoretical points and then devote most of my effort to a specific illustration. The first part of this article is a brief discussion of concepts used by poststructuralists that are also useful for feminists. The second part applies some of these concepts to one of the hotly contested issues among contemporary (U.S.) feminists—the "equality-versus-difference" debate.

Among the useful terms feminists have appropriated from poststructuralism are language, discourse, difference, and deconstruction.

Language. Following the work of structuralist linguistics and anthropology, the term is used to mean not simply words or even a vocabulary and set of grammatical rules but, rather, a meaning-constituting system: that is, any system—strictly verbal or other—through which meaning is constructed and cultural practices organized and by which, accordingly, people represent and understand their world, including who they are and how they relate to others. "Language," so conceived, is a central focus of poststructuralist analysis.

Language is not assumed to be a representation of ideas that either cause material relations or from which such relations follow; indeed, the idealist/materialist opposition is a false one to impose on this approach. Rather, the analysis of language provides a crucial point of entry, a starting point for understanding how social relations are conceived, and therefore—because understanding how they are conceived means understanding how they work—how institutions are organized, how relations of production are experienced, and how collective identity is established. Without attention to language and the processes by which meanings and categories are constituted, one only imposes oversimplified models on the world, models that perpetuate conventional understandings rather than open up new interpretive possibilities.

The point is to find ways to analyze specific "texts"—not only books and documents but also utterances of any kind and in any medium, including cultural practices—in terms of specific historical and contextual meanings. Poststructuralists insist that words and texts have no fixed or intrinsic meanings, that there is no transparent or self-evident relationship between them and either ideas or things, no basic or ultimate correspondence between language and the world. The questions that must be answered in such an analysis, then, are how, in what specific contexts, among which specific communities of people, and by what textual and social processes has meaning been acquired? More generally, the questions are: How do meanings change? How have some meanings emerged as normative and others have been eclipsed or disappeared? What do these processes reveal about how power is constituted and operates?

Discourse. Some of the answers to these questions are offered in the concept of discourse, especially as it has been developed in the work of Michel Foucault. A discourse is not a language or a text but a historically, socially, and institutionally specific structure of statements, terms, categories, and beliefs. Foucault suggests that the elaboration of meaning involves conflict and power, that meanings are locally contested within discursive "fields of force," that (at least since the Enlightenment) the power to control a particular field resides in claims to (scientific) knowledge embodied not only in writing but also in disciplinary and professional organizations, in institutions (hospitals, prisons, schools, factories), and in social relationships (doctor/patient, teacher/student, employer/worker, parent/ child, husband/wife). Discourse is thus contained or expressed in organizations and institutions as well as in words; all of these constitute texts or documents to be read.[2]

Discursive fields overlap, influence, and compete with one another; they appeal to one another's "truths" for authority and legitimation. These truths are assumed to be outside human invention, either already known and self-evident or discoverable through scientific inquiry. Precisely because they are assigned the status of objective knowledge, they seem to be beyond dispute and thus serve a powerful legitimating function. Darwinian theories of natural selection are one example of such legitimating truths; biological theories about sexual difference are another. The power of these "truths" comes from the way they function as givens or first premises for both sides in an argument, so that conflicts within discursive fields are framed to follow from rather than question them. The brilliance of so much of Foucault's work has been to illuminate the shared assumptions of what seemed to be sharply different arguments, thus exposing the limits of radical criticism and the extent of the power of dominant ideologies or epistemologies.

In addition, Foucault has shown how badly even challenges to fundamental assumptions often fared. They have been marginalized or silenced, forced to underplay their most radical claims in order to win a short-term goal, or completely absorbed into an existing framework. Yet the fact of change is crucial to Foucault's notion of "archaeology," to the way in which he uses contrasts from different historical periods to present his arguments. . . . Although some have read Foucault as an argument about the futility of human agency in the struggle for social change, I think that he is more appropriately taken as warning against simple solutions to difficult problems, as advising human actors to think strategically and more self-consciously about the philosophical and political implications and meanings of the programs they endorse. From this perspective, Foucault's work provides an important way of thinking differently (and perhaps more creatively) about the politics of the contextual construction of social meanings, about such organizing principles for political action as "equality" and "difference."

Difference. An important dimension of poststructuralist analyses of language has to do with the concept of difference, the notion (following Ferdinand de Saussure's structuralist linguistics) that meaning is made through implicit or explicit contrast, that a positive definition rests on the negation or repression of something represented as antithetical to it. Thus, any unitary concept in fact contains repressed or negated material; it is established in explicit opposition to another term. Any analysis of meaning involves teasing out these negations and oppositions, figuring out how (and whether) they are operating in specific contexts. Oppositions rest on metaphors and cross-references, and often in patriarchal discourse, sexual difference (the contrast masculine/feminine) serves to encode or establish meanings that are literally unrelated to gender or the body. In that way, the meanings of gender become tied to many kinds of cultural representations, and these in turn establish terms by which relations between women and men are organized and understood. The possibilities of this kind of analysis have, for obvious reasons, drawn the interest and attention of feminist scholars.

Fixed oppositions conceal the extent to which things presented as oppositional are, in fact, interdependent—that is, they derive their meaning from a particularly established contrast rather than from some inherent or pure antithesis. Furthermore, according to Jacques Derrida, the interdependence is hierarchical with one term dominant or prior, the opposite term subordinate and secondary. The Western philosophical tradition, he argues, rests on binary oppositions: unity/diversity, identity/difference, presence/absence, and universality/specificity. The leading terms are accorded primacy; their partners are represented as weaker or derivative. Yet the first terms depend on and derive their meaning from the second to such an extent that the secondary terms can be seen as generative of the definition of the first terms.[3] If binary oppositions provide insight into the way meaning is constructed, and if they operate as Derrida suggests, then analyses of meaning cannot take binary oppositions at face value but rather must "deconstruct" them for the processes they embody.

Deconstruction. Although this term is used loosely among scholars—often to refer to a dismantling or destructive enterprise—it also has a precise definition in the work of Derrida and his followers. Deconstruction involves analyzing the operations of difference in texts, the ways in which meanings are made to work. The method consists of two related steps: the reversal and displacement of binary oppositions. This double process reveals the interdependence of seemingly dichotomous terms and their meaning relative to a particular history. It shows them to be not natural but constructed oppositions, constructed for particular purposes in particular contexts.[4]...

Deconstruction is, then, an important exercise, for it allows us to be critical of the way in which ideas we want to use are ordinarily expressed, exhibited in patterns of meaning that may undercut the ends we seek to attain. A case in point—of meaning expressed in a politically self-defeating way—is the "equality-versus-difference" debate among feminists. Here a binary opposition has been created to offer a choice to feminists, of either endorsing "equality" or its presumed antithesis "difference." In fact, the antithesis itself hides the interdependence of the two terms, for equality is not the elimination of difference, and difference does not preclude equality.

In the past few years, "equality-versus-difference" has been used as a shorthand to characterize conflicting feminist positions and political strategies.[5] Those who argue that sexual difference ought to be an irrelevant consideration in schools, employment, the courts, and the legislature are put in the equality category. Those who insist that appeals on behalf of women ought to be made in terms of the needs, interests, and characteristics common to women as a group are placed in the difference category. In the clashes over the superiority of one or another of these strategies, feminists have invoked history, philosophy, and morality and have devised new classificatory labels: cultural feminism, liberal feminism, feminist separatism, and so on.[6] Most recently, the debate about equality and difference has been used to analyze the Sears case, the sex discrimination suit brought against the retailing giant by the Equal Employment Opportunities Commission (EEOC) in 1979, in which historians Alice Kessler-Harris and Rosalind Rosenberg testified on opposite sides.

There have been many articles written on the Sears case, among them a recent one by Ruth Milkman. Milkman insists that we attend to the political context of seemingly timeless principles: "We ignore the political dimensions of the equality-versus-difference debate at our peril, especially in a period of conservative resurgence like the present." She concludes:

> As long as this is the political context in which we find ourselves, feminist scholars must be aware of the real danger that arguments about "difference" or "women's culture" will be put to uses other than those for which they were originally developed. That does not mean we must abandon these arguments or the intellectual terrain they have opened up; it does mean that we must be self-conscious in our formulations, keeping firmly in view the ways in which our work can be exploited politically.[7]

Milkman's carefully nuanced formulation implies that equality is our safest course, but she is also reluctant to reject difference entirely. She feels a need to choose a side, but which side is the problem. Milkman's ambivalence is an example of what the legal theorist Martha Minow has labeled in another context "the difference dilemma." Ignoring difference in the case of subordinated groups, Minow points out, "leaves in place a faulty neutrality," but focusing on difference can underscore the stigma of deviance. "Both focusing on and ignoring difference risk recreating it. This is the dilemma of difference."[8] What is required, Minow suggests, is a new way of thinking about difference, and this involves rejecting the idea that equality-versus-difference constitutes an opposition. Instead of framing analyses and strategies as if such binary pairs were timeless and true, we need to ask how the dichotomous pairing of equality and difference itself works. Instead of remaining within the terms of existing political discourse, we need to subject those terms to critical examination. Until we understand how the concepts work to constrain and construct specific meanings, we cannot make them work for us.

A close look at the evidence in the Sears case suggests that equality-versus-difference may not accurately depict the opposing sides in the Sears case. During testimony, most of the arguments against equality and for difference were, in fact, made by the Sears lawyers or by Rosalind Rosenberg. They constructed an opponent against whom they asserted that women and men differed, that "fundamental differences"—the result of culture or long-standing patterns of socialization—led to women's presumed lack of interest in commission sales jobs. In order to make their own claim that sexual difference and not discrimination could explain the hiring patterns of Sears, the Sears defense attributed to EEOC an assumption that no one had made in those terms—that women and men had identical interests.[9] Alice Kessler-Harris did not argue that women were the same as men; instead, she used a variety of strategies to challenge Rosenberg's assertions. First, she argued that historical evidence suggested far more variety in the jobs women actually took than Rosenberg assumed. Second, she maintained that economic considerations usually offset the effects of socialization in women's attitudes to employment. And, third, she pointed out that, historically, job segregation by sex was the consequence of employer preferences, not employee choices. The question of women's choices could not be resolved, Kessler-Harris maintained, when the hiring process itself predetermined the outcome, imposing generalized gendered criteria that were not necessarily relevant to the work at hand. The debate joined then not around equality-versus-difference but around the relevance of general ideas of sexual difference in a specific context.[10]

To make the case for employer discrimination, EEOC lawyers cited obviously biased job applicant questionnaires and statements by personnel officers, but they had no individuals to testify that they had experienced discrimination. Kessler-Harris referred to past patterns of sexual segregation in the job market as the product of employer choices, but mostly she invoked history to break down Rosenberg's contention that women as a group differed consistently in the details of their behavior from men, instead insisting that variety characterized female job choices (as it did male job choices), that it made no sense in this case to talk about women as a uniform group. She defined equality to mean a presumption that women and men might have an equal interest in sales commission jobs. She did not claim that women and men, by definition, had such an equal interest. Rather, Kessler-Harris and the EEOC called into question the relevance for hiring decisions of generalizations about the necessarily antithetical behaviors of women and men. EEOC argued that Sears's hiring practices reflected inaccurate and inapplicable notions of sexual difference; Sears argued that "fundamental" differences between the sexes (and not its own actions) explained the gender imbalances in its labor force.

The Sears case was complicated by the fact that almost all the evidence offered was statistical. The testimony of the historians, therefore, could only be inferential at best. Each of them sought to explain small statistical disparities by reference to gross generalizations about the entire history of working women; furthermore, neither historian had much information about what had actually happened at Sears. They were forced, instead, to swear to the truth or falsehood of interpretive generalizations developed for purposes other than legal contestation, and they were forced to treat their interpretive premises as matters of fact. Reading the cross-examination of Kessler-Harris is revealing in this respect. Each of her carefully nuanced explanations of women's work history was forced into a reductive assertion by the Sears lawyers' insistence that she answer questions only by saying yes or no. Similarly, Rosalind Rosenberg's rebuttal to Alice Kessler-Harris eschewed the historian's subtle contextual reading of evidence and sought instead to impose a test of absolute consistency. She juxtaposed Kessler-Harris's testimony in the trial to her earlier published work (in which Kessler-Harris stressed differences between female and male workers in their approaches to work, arguing that women were more domestically oriented and less individualistic than men) in an effort to show that Kessler-Harris had misled the court.[11] Outside the courtroom, however, the disparities of the Kessler-Harris argument could also be explained in other ways. In relationship to a labor history that had typically excluded women, it might make sense to overgeneralize about women's experience, emphasizing difference in order to demonstrate that the universal term "worker" was really a male reference that could not account for all aspects of women's job experiences. In relationship to an employer who sought to justify discrimination by reference to sexual difference, it made more sense to deny the totalizing effects of difference by stressing instead the diversity and complexity of women's behavior and motivation. In the first case, difference served a positive function, unveiling the inequity hidden in a presumably neutral term; in the second case, difference served a negative purpose, justifying what Kessler-Harris believed to be unequal treatment. Although the inconsistency might have been avoided with a more self-conscious analysis of the "difference dilemma," Kessler-Harris's different positions were quite legitimately different emphases for different contexts; only in a courtroom could they be taken as proof of bad faith.[12]

The exacting demands of the courtroom for consistency and "truth" also point out the profound difficulties of arguing about difference. Although the testimony of the historians had to explain only a relatively small statistical disparity in the numbers of women and men hired for full-time commission sales jobs, the explanations that were preferred were totalizing and categorical.[13] In cross-examination, Kessler-Harris's multiple interpretations were found to be contradictory and confusing, although the judge praised Rosenberg for her coherence and lucidity.[14] In part, that was because Rosenberg held to a tight model that unproblematically linked socialization to individual choice; in part it was because her descriptions of gender differences accorded with prevailing normative views. In contrast Kessler-Harris had trouble finding a simple model that would at once acknowledge difference *and* refuse it as an acceptable explanation for the employment pattern of Sears. So she fell into great difficulty maintaining her case in the face of hostile questioning. On the one hand, she was accused of assuming that economic opportunism equally affected women and men (and thus of believing that women and men were the same). How, then, could she explain the differences her own work had identified? On the other hand, she was tarred (by Rosenberg) with the brush of subversion, for implying that all employers might have some interest in sex typing the labor force, for deducing from her own (presumably Marxist) theory, a "conspiratorial" conclusion about the behavior of Sears.[15] If the patterns of discrimination that Kessler-Harris alluded to were real, after all, one of their effects might well be the kind of difference Rosenberg pointed out. Caught within the framework of Rosenberg's use of historical evidence, Kessler-Harris and her lawyers relied on an essentially negative strategy, offering details designed to complicate and undercut Rosenberg's assertions. Kessler-Harris did not directly challenge the theoretical shortcomings of Rosenberg's socialization model, nor did she offer an alternative model of her own. That would have required, I think, either fully developing the case for employer discrimination or insisting more completely on the "differences" line of argument by exposing the "equality-versus-difference" formulation as an illusion.

In the end, the most nuanced arguments of Kessler-Harris were rejected as contradictory or inapplicable, and the judge decided in Sears's favor, repeating the defense argument that an assumption of equal interest was "unfounded" because of the differences between women and men.[16] Not only was EEOC's position rejected, but the hiring policies of Sears were implicitly endorsed. According to the judge, because difference was real and fundamental, it could explain statistical variations in Sears's hiring. Discrimination was redefined as simply the recognition of "natural" difference (however culturally or historically produced), fitting in nicely with the logic of Reagan conservatism. Difference was substituted for inequality, the appropriate antithesis of equality, becoming inequality's explanation and legitimation. The judge's decision illustrates a process literary scholar Naomi Schor has described in another context: it "essentializes difference and naturalizes social inequity."[17]

The Sears case offers a sobering lesson in the operation of a discursive, that is a political field. Analysis of language here provides insight not only into the manipulation of concepts and definitions but also into the implementation and justification of institutional and political power. References to categorical differences between women and men set the terms within which Sears defended its policies *and* EEOC challenged them. Equality-versus-difference was the intellectual trap within which historians argued not about tiny disparities in Sears's employment practices, but about the normative behaviors of women and men. Although we might conclude that the balance of power was against EEOC by the time the case was heard and that, therefore, its outcome was inevitable (part of the Reagan plan to reverse affirmative action programs of the 1970s), we still need to articulate a critique of what happened that can inform the next round of political encounter. How should that position be conceptualized?

When equality and difference are paired dichotomously, they structure an impossible choice. If one opts for equality, one is forced to accept the notion that difference is antithetical to it. If one opts for difference, one admits that equality is unattainable. That, in a sense, is the dilemma apparent in Milkman's conclusion cited above. Feminists cannot give up "difference"; it has been our most creative analytic tool. We cannot give up equality, at least as long as we want to speak to the principles and values of our political system. But it makes no sense for the feminist movement to let its arguments be forced into preexisting categories and its political disputes to be characterized by a dichotomy we did not invent. How then do we recognize and use notions of sexual difference and yet make arguments for equality? The only response is a double one: the unmasking of the power relationship constructed by posing equality as the antithesis of difference and the refusal of its consequent dichotomous construction of political choices.

Equality-versus-difference cannot structure choices for feminist politics; the oppositional pairing misrepresents the relationship of both terms. Equality, in the political theory of rights that lies behind the claims of excluded groups for justice, means the ignoring of differences between individuals for a particular purpose or in a particular context. Michael Walzer puts it this way: "The root meaning of equality is negative; egalitarianism in its origins is an abolitionist politics. It aims at eliminating not all differences, but a particular set of differences, and a different set in different times and places."[18] This presumes a social agreement to consider obviously different people as equivalent (not identical) for a stated purpose. In this usage, the opposite of equality is inequality or inequivalence, the noncommensurability of individuals or groups in certain circumstances, for certain purposes. Thus, for purposes of democratic citizenship, the measure of equivalence has been, at different times, independence or ownership of property or race or sex. The political notion of equality thus includes, indeed depends on, an acknowledgment of the existence of difference. Demands for equality have rested on implicit and usually unrecognized arguments from difference; if individuals or groups were identical or the same there would be no need to ask for equality. Equality might well be defined as deliberate indifference to specified differences.

The antithesis of difference in most usages is sameness or identity. But even here the contrast and the context must be specified. There is nothing self-evident or transcendent about difference, even if the fact of difference—sexual difference, for example—seems apparent to the naked eye. The questions always ought to be, What qualities or aspects are being compared? What is the nature of the comparison? How is the meaning of difference being constructed? Yet in the Sears testimony and in some debates among feminists (sexual) difference is assumed to be an immutable fact, its meaning inherent in the categories female and male. The lawyers for Sears put it this way: "The reasonableness of the EEOC's a priori assumptions of male/female sameness with respect to preferences, interests, and qualifications is... the crux of the issue."[19] The point of the EEOC challenge, however, was never sameness but the irrelevance of categorical differences.

The opposition men/women, as Rosenberg employed it, asserted the incomparability of the sexes, and although history and socialization were the explanatory factors, these resonated with categorical distinctions inferred from the facts of bodily difference. When the opposition men/women is invoked, as it was in the Sears case, it refers a specific issue (the small statistical discrepancy between women and men hired for commission sales jobs) back to a general principle (the "fundamental" differences between women and men). The differences within each group that might apply to this particular situation—the fact, for example, that some women might choose "aggressive" or "risk-taking" jobs or that some women might prefer high- to low-paying positions—were excluded by definition in the antithesis between the groups. The irony is, of course, that the statistical case required only a small percentage of women's behaviors to be explained. Yet the historical testimony argued categorically about "women." It thus became impossible to argue (as EEOC and Kessler-Harris tried to) that within the female category, women typically exhibit and participate in all sorts of "male" behaviors, that socialization is a complex process that does not yield uniform choices. To make the argument would have required a direct attack on categorical thinking about gender. For the generalized opposition male/female serves to obscure the differences among women in behavior, character, desire, subjectivity, sexuality, gender identification, and historical experience. In the light of Rosenberg's insistence on the primacy of sexual difference, Kessler-Harris's insistence on the specificity (and historically variable aspect) of women's actions could be dismissed as an unreasonable and trivial claim.

The alternative to the binary construction of sexual difference is not sameness, identity, or androgyny. By subsuming women into a general "human" identity, we lose the specificity of female diversity and women's experiences; we are back, in other words, to the days when "Man's" story was supposed to be everyone's story, when women were "hidden from history," when the feminine served as the negative counterpoint, the "Other," for the construction of positive masculine identity. It is not sameness *or* identity between women and men that we want to claim but a more complicated historically variable diversity than is permitted by the opposition male/female, a diversity that is also differently expressed for different purposes in different contexts. In effect, the duality this opposition creates draws one line of difference, invests it with biological explanations, and then treats each side of the opposition as a unitary phenomenon. Everything in each category (male/female) is assumed to be the same; hence, differences within either category are suppressed. In contrast, our goal is to see not only differences between the sexes but also the way these work to repress differences within gender groups. The sameness constructed on each side of the binary opposition hides the multiple play of differences and maintains their irrelevance and invisibility.

Placing equality and difference in an antithetical relationship has, then, a double effect. It denies the way in which difference has long figured in political notions of equality and it suggests that sameness is the only ground on which equality can be claimed. It thus puts feminists in an impossible position, for as long as we argue within the terms of a discourse set up by this opposition we grant the current conservative premise that because women cannot be identical to men in all respects, we cannot expect to be equal to them. The only alternative, it seems to me, is to refuse to oppose equality to difference and insist continually on differences—differences as the condition of individual and collective identities, differences as the constant challenge to the fixing of those identities, history as the repeated illustration of the play of differences, differences as the very meaning of equality itself.

Alice Kessler-Harris's experience in the Sears case shows, however, that the assertion of differences in the face of gender categories is not a sufficient strategy. What is required in addition is an analysis of fixed gender categories as normative statements that organize cultural understandings of sexual difference. This means that we must open to scrutiny the terms *women* and *men* as they are used to define one another in particular contexts—workplaces, for example. The history of women's work needs to be retold from this perspective as part of the story of the creation of a gendered workforce. In the nineteenth century, for example, certain concepts of male skill rested on a contrast with female labor (by definition unskilled). The organization and reorganization of work processes was accomplished by reference to the gender attributes of workers, rather than to issues of training, education, or social class. And wage differentials between the sexes were attributed to fundamentally different family roles that preceded (rather than followed from) employment arrangements. In all these processes the meaning of "worker" was established through a contrast between the presumably natural qualities of women and men. If we write the history of women's work by gathering data that describes the activities, needs, interests, and culture of "women workers," we leave in place the naturalized contrast and reify a fixed categorical difference between women and men. We start the story, in other words, too late, by uncritically accepting a gendered category (the "woman worker") that itself needs investigation because its meaning is relative to its history.

If in our histories we relativize the categories woman and man, it means, of course, that we must also recognize the contingent and specific nature of our political claims. Political strategies then will rest on analyses of the utility of certain arguments in certain discursive contexts, without, however, invoking absolute qualities for women or men. There are moments when it makes sense for mothers to demand consideration for their social role, and contexts within which motherhood is irrelevant to women's behavior; but to maintain that womanhood is motherhood is to obscure the differences that make choice possible. There are moments when it makes sense to demand a reevaluation of the status of what has been socially constructed as women's work ("comparable worth" strategies are the current example) and contexts within which it makes much more sense to prepare women for entry into "nontraditional" jobs. But to maintain that femininity predisposes women to certain (nurturing) jobs or (collaborative) styles of work is to naturalize complex economic and social processes and, once again, to obscure the differences that have characterized women's occupational histories. An insistence on differences undercuts the tendency to absolutist, and in the case of sexual difference, essentialist categories. It does not deny the existence of gender difference, but it does suggest that its meanings are always relative to particular constructions in specified contexts. In contrast, absolutist categorizations of difference end up always enforcing normative rules.

It is surely not easy to formulate a "deconstructive" political strategy in the face of powerful tendencies that construct the world in binary terms. Yet there seems to me no other choice. Perhaps as we learn to think this way, solutions will become more readily apparent. Perhaps the theoretical and historical work we do can prepare the ground. Certainly we can take heart from the history of feminism, which is full of illustrations of refusals of simple dichotomies and attempts instead to demonstrate that equality requires the recognition and inclusion of differences. Indeed, one way historians could contribute to a genuine rethinking of these concepts, is to stop writing the history of feminisms as a story of oscillations between demands for equality and affirmations of difference. This approach inadvertently strengthens the hold of the binary construction, establishing it as inevitable by giving it a long history. When looked at closely, in fact, the historical arguments of feminists do not usually fall into these neat compartments; they are instead attempts to reconcile theories of equal rights with cultural concepts of sexual difference, to question the validity of normative constructions of gender in the light of the existence of behaviors and qualities that contradict the rules, to point up rather than resolve conditions of contradiction, to articulate a political identity for women without conforming to existing stereotypes about them.

In histories of feminism and in feminist political strategies there needs to be at once attention to the operations of difference and all insistence on differences, but not a simple substitution of multiple for binary difference for it is not a happy pluralism we ought to invoke. The resolution of the "difference dilemma" comes neither from ignoring nor embracing difference as it is normatively constituted. Instead, it seems to me that the critical feminist position must always involve *two* moves. The first is the systematic criticism of the operations of categorical difference, the exposure of the kinds of exclusions and inclusions—the hierarchies—it constructs, and a refusal of their ultimate "truth." A refusal, however, not in the name of an equality that implies sameness or identity, but rather (and this is the second move) in the name of an equality that rests on differences—differences that confound, disrupt, and render ambiguous the meaning of any fixed binary opposition. To do anything else is to buy into the political argument that sameness is a requirement for equality, an untenable position for feminists (and historians) who know that power is constructed on and so must be challenged from the ground of difference.

Notes

1. On the problem of appropriating poststructuralism for feminism, see Biddy Martin, "Feminism, Criticism, Foucault," *New German Critique* 27 (Fall 1982): 3–30.
2. Examples of Michel Foucault's work include *The Archaeology of Knowledge* (New York: Harper & Row, 1976), *The History of Sexuality*, vol. 1, An Introduction (New York: Vintage, 1980), and *Power/Knowledge: Selected Interviews and Other Writings, 1972–1977* (New York: Pantheon, 1980). See also Hubert L. Dreyfus and Paul Rabinow, *Michel Foucault: Beyond Structuralism and Hermeneutics* (Chicago: University of Chicago Press, 1983).
3. The Australian philosopher Elizabeth Gross puts it this way: "What Derrida attempts to show is that within these binary couples, the primary or dominant term derives its privilege from a curtailment or suppression of its opposite. Sameness or identity, presence, speech, the origin, mind, et cetera are all privileged in relation to their opposites, which are regarded as debased, impure variants of the primary term. Difference, for example, is the lack of identity or sameness; absence is the lack of presence; writing is the supplement of speech, and so on." See her "Derrida, Irigaray, and Deconstruction," *Left-wright, Intervention*: 20 (1986): 73. See also Jacques Derrida, *Of Grammatology* (Baltimore: Johns Hopkins University Press, 1976); and Jonathan Culler, *On Deconstruction: Theory and Criticism after Structuralism* (Ithaca: Cornell University Press, 1982).
4. Again, to cite Elizabeth Gross's formulation: "Taken together, reversal and its useful displacement show the necessary but unfounded function of these terms in Western thought. One must both reverse the dichotomy and the values attached to the two terms, as well as displace the excluded term, placing it beyond its oppositional role, as the internal condition of the dominant term. This move makes clear the violence of the hierarchy and the debt the dominant term owes to the subordinate one. It also demonstrates that there are other ways of conceiving these terms than dichotomously. If these terms were only or necessarily dichotomies, the process of displacement would not be possible. Although historically necessary, the terms are not logically necessary." See Gross, 74.
5. Most recently, attention has been focused on the issue of pregnancy benefits. See, for example, Lucinda M. Finley, "Transcending Equality Theory: A Way Out of the Maternity and the

Workplace Debate," *Columbia Law Review* 86 (October 1986): 1118–83. See Sylvia A. Law, "Rethinking Sex and the Constitution," *University of Pennsylvania Law Review* 132 (June 1984): 955–1040.

6. Recently, historians have begun to cast feminist history in terms of the equality-versus-difference debate. Rather than accept it as an accurate characterization of antithetical positions, however, I think we need to look more closely at how feminists used these arguments. A close reading of nineteenth-century French feminist texts, for example, leads me to conclude that they are far less easily categorized into difference or equality positions than one would have supposed. I think it is a mistake for feminist historians to write this debate uncritically into history for it reifies an "antithesis" that may not actually have existed. We need instead to "deconstruct" feminist arguments and read them in their discursive contexts, all as explorations of "the difference dilemma."

7. Ruth Milkman, "Women's History and the Sears Case," *Feminist Studies* 12 (Summer 1986): 394–95. In my discussion of the Sears case, I have drawn heavily on this careful and intelligent article, the best so far of the many that have been written on the subject.

8. Martha Minow, "Learning to Live with the Dilemma of Difference: Bilingual and Special Education," *Law and Contemporary Problems* 48, 2 (1984): 157–211; quotation is from p. 160; see also pp. 202–6.

9. There is a difference, it seems to me, between arguing that women and men have identical interests and arguing that one should presume such identity in all aspects of the hiring process. The second position is the only strategic way of not building into the hiring process prejudice or the wrong presumptions about differences of interest.

10. Rosenberg's "Offer of Proof" and Kessler-Harris's "Written Testimony" appeared in *Signs* 11 (Summer 1986): 757–79. The "Written Rebuttal Testimony of Dr. Rosalind Rosenberg" is part of the official transcript of the case, U.S. District Court for the Northern District of Illinois, Eastern Division, *EEOC vs Sears*, Civil Action No. 79-C-4373. (I am grateful to Sanford Levinson for sharing the trial documents with me and for our many conversations about them.)

11. Appendix to the "Written Rebuttal Testimony of Dr. Rosalind Rosenberg," 1–12.

12. On the limits imposed by courtrooms and the pitfalls expert witnesses may encounter, see Nadine Taub, "Thinking about Testifying," *Perspectives* (American Historical Association Newsletter) 24 (November 1986): 10–11.

13. On this point, Taub asks a useful question: "Is there a danger in discrimination cases that historical or other expert testimony not grounded in the particular facts of the case will reinforce the idea that it is acceptable to make generalizations about particular groups?" (p. 11).

14. See the cross-examination of Kessler-Harris, *EEOC vs Sears*, 16376–619.

15. The Rosenberg "Rebuttal" is particularly vehement on this question: "This assumption that all employers discriminate is prominent in her (Kessler-Harris's) work.... In a 1979 article, she wrote hopefully that women harbor values, attitudes, and behavior patterns potentially subversive to capitalism" (p. 11). "There are, of course, documented instances of employers limiting the opportunities of women. But the fact that some employers have discriminated does not prove that all do" (p. 19). The rebuttal raises another issue about the political and ideological limits of a courtroom or, perhaps it is better to say, about the way the courtroom reproduces dominant ideologies. The general notion that employers discriminate was unacceptable (but the general notion that women prefer certain jobs was not). This unacceptability was underscored by linking it to subversion and Marxism, positions intolerable in U.S. political discourse. Rosenberg's innuendos attempted to discredit Kessler-Harris on two counts—first, by suggesting she was making a ridiculous generalization and, second, by suggesting that only people outside acceptable politics could even entertain that generalization.

16. Milkman, 391.

17. Naomi Schor, "Reading Double: Sand's Difference," in *The Poetics of Gender*, ed. Nancy K. Miller (New York: Columbia University Press, 1986), 256.

18. Michael Walzer, *Spheres of Justice: A Defense of Pluralism and Equality* (New York: Basic Books, 1983), xii. See also Minow, 202–3.

19. Milkman, 384.

36.
SITUATED KNOWLEDGES: THE SCIENCE QUESTION IN FEMINISM AND THE PRIVILEGE OF PARTIAL PERSPECTIVE
Donna Haraway

Academic and activist feminist inquiry has repeatedly tried to come to terms with the question of what *we* might mean by the curious and inescapable term "objectivity." We have used a lot of toxic ink and trees processed into paper decrying what *they* have meant and how it hurts *us*. The imagined "they" constitute a kind of invisible conspiracy of masculinist scientists and philosophers replete with grants and laboratories. The imagined "we" are the embodied others, who are *not* allowed not to have a body, a finite point of view, and so an inevitably disqualifying and polluting bias in any discussion of consequence....

It has seemed to me that feminists have both selectively and flexibly used and been trapped by two poles of a tempting dichotomy on the question of objectivity. Certainly I speak for myself here, and I offer the speculation that there is a collective discourse on these matters. Recent social studies of science and technology, for example, have made available a very strong social constructionist argument for *all* forms of knowledge claims, most certainly and especially scientific ones.[1] According to these tempting views, no insider's perspective is privileged, because all drawings of inside-outside boundaries in knowledge are theorized as power moves not moves toward truth.... Social constructionists make clear that official ideologies about objectivity and scientific method are particularly bad guides to how scientific knowledge is actually *made*. Just as for the rest of us, what scientists believe or say they do and what they really do have a very loose fit....

In any case, social constructionists might maintain that the ideological doctrine of scientific method and all the philosophical verbiage about epistemology were cooked up to distract our attention from getting to know the world *effectively* by practicing the sciences. From this point of view, science—the real game in town—is rhetoric, a series of efforts to persuade relevant social actors that one's manufactured knowledge is a route to a desired form of very objective power. Such persuasions must take account of the structure of facts and artifacts, as well as of language-mediated actors in the knowledge game. Here, artifacts and facts are parts of the powerful art of rhetoric. Practice is persuasion, and the focus is very much on practice. All knowledge is a condensed node in an agonistic power field.

The strong program in the sociology of knowledge joins with the lovely and nasty tools of semiology and deconstruction to insist on the rhetorical nature of truth, including scientific truth. History is a story Western culture buffs tell each other; science is a contestable text and a power field; the content is the form.[2] Period.

So much for those of us who would still like to talk about *reality* with more confidence than we allow to the Christian Right when they discuss the Second Coming and their being raptured out of the final destruction of the world. We would like to think our appeals to real worlds are more than a desperate lurch away from cynicism and an act of faith like any other cult's, no matter how much space we generously give to all the rich and always historically specific mediations through which we and everybody else must know the world. But the further I get in describing the radical social constructionist program and a particular version of postmodernism, coupled with the acid tools of critical discourse in the human sciences, the more nervous I get. The imagery of force fields, of moves in a fully textualized and coded world, which is the working metaphor in many arguments about socially negotiated reality for the postmodern subject, is, just for starters, an imagery of high-tech military fields, of automated academic battlefields, where blips of light called players disintegrate (what a metaphor!) each other in order to stay in the knowledge and power game. Technoscience and science fiction collapse into the sun of their radiant (ir)reality-war.[3] It shouldn't take decades of feminist theory to sense the enemy here. Nancy Hartsock got all this crystal clear in her concept of abstract masculinity.[4]

I, and others, started out wanting a strong tool for deconstructing the truth claims of hostile science by showing the radical historical specificity, and so contestability, of *every* layer of the onion of scientific and technological constructions, and we end up with a kind of epistemological electroshock therapy, which far from ushering us into the high stakes tables of the game of contesting public truths, lays us out on the table with self-induced multiple personality disorder. We wanted a way to go beyond showing bias in science (that proved too easy anyhow) and beyond separating the good scientific sheep from the bad goats of bias and misuse. It seemed promising to do this by the strongest possible constructionist argument that left no cracks for reducing the issues to bias versus objectivity, use versus misuse, science versus pseudoscience. We unmasked the doctrines of objectivity because they threatened our budding sense of collective historical subjectivity and agency and our "embodied" accounts of the truth, and we ended up with one more excuse for not learning any post-Newtonian physics and one more reason to drop the old feminist self-help practices of repairing our own cars. They're just texts anyway, so let the boys have them back.

Some of us tried to stay sane in these disassembled and dissembling tunes by holding out for a feminist version of objectivity. Here, motivated by many of the same political desires, is the other seductive end of the objectivity problem. Humanistic Marxism was polluted at the source by its structuring theory about the domination of nature in the self-construction of man and by its closely related impotence in relation to historicizing anything women did that didn't qualify for a wage. But Marxism was still a promising resource as a kind of epistemological feminist mental hygiene that sought our own doctrines of objective vision. Marxist starting points offered a way to get to our own versions of standpoint theories, insistent embodiment, a rich tradition of critiquing hegemony without disempowering positivisms and relativisms and a way to get to nuanced theories of mediation. Some versions of psychoanalysis were of aid in this approach especially anglophone object relations theory....

Another approach, "feminist empiricism," also converges with feminist uses of Marxian resources to get a theory of science which continues to insist on legitimate meanings of objectivity and which remains leery of a radical constructivism conjugated with semiology and narratology.[5] Feminists have to insist on a better account of the world; it is not enough to show radical historical contingency and modes of construction for everything. Here, we, as feminists, find ourselves perversely conjoined with the discourse of many practicing scientists, who, when all is said and done, mostly believe they are describing and discovering things *by means of* all their constructing and arguing. Evelyn Fox Keller has been particularly insistent on this fundamental matter, and Sandra Harding calls the goal of these approaches a "successor science." Feminists have stakes in a successor science project that offers a more adequate, richer, better account of a world, in order to live in it well and in critical, reflexive relation to our own as well as others' practices of domination and the unequal parts of privilege and oppression that make up all positions. In traditional philosophical categories, the issue is ethics and politics perhaps more than epistemology.

So, I think my problem, and "our" problem, is how to have *simultaneously* an account of radical historical contingency for all knowledge claims and knowing subjects, a critical practice for recognizing our own "semiotic technologies" for making meanings, *and* a no-nonsense commitment to faithful accounts of a "real" world, one that can be partially shared and that is friendly to earthwide projects of finite freedom, adequate material abundance, modest meaning in suffering, and limited happiness....

The Persistence of Vision

I would like to proceed by placing metaphorical reliance on a much maligned sensor system in feminist discourse: vision.[6] Vision can be good for avoiding binary oppositions. I would like to insist on the embodied nature of all vision and so reclaim the sensory system that has been used to signify a leap out of the marked body and into a conquering gaze from nowhere.... I would like a doctrine of embodied objectivity that accommodates paradoxical and critical feminist science projects: Feminist objectivity means quite simply *situated knowledges*.

The eyes have been used to signify a perverse capacity—honed to perfection in the history of science tied to militarism, capitalism, colonialism, and male supremacy—to distance the knowing subject from everybody and everything in the interests of unfettered power. The instruments of visualization in multinationalist, postmodernist culture have compounded these meanings of disembodiment. The visualizing technologies are without apparent limit.…

But, of course, that view of infinite vision is an illusion, a god trick. I would like to suggest how our insisting metaphorically on the particularity and embodiment of all visions (although not necessarily organic embodiment and including technological mediation), and not giving in to the tempting myths of vision as a route to disembodiment and second-birthing allows us to construct a usable, but not an innocent, doctrine of objectivity. I want a feminist writing of the body that metaphorically emphasizes vision again, because we need to reclaim that sense to find our way through all the visualizing tricks and powers of modern sciences and technologies that have transformed the objectivity debates. We need to learn in our bodies, endowed with primate color and stereoscopic vision, how to attach the objective to our theoretical and political scanners in order to name where we are and are not, in dimensions of mental and physical space we hardly know how to name. So, not so perversely, objectivity turns out to be about particular and specific embodiment and definitely not about the false vision promising transcendence of all limits and responsibility. The moral is simple: only partial perspectives promise objective vision. All Western cultural narratives about objectivity are allegories of the ideologies governing the relations of what we call mind and body, distance and responsibility. Feminist objectivity is about limited location and situated knowledge, not about transcendence and splitting of subject and object. It allows us to become answerable for what we learn how to see.

These are lessons that I learned in part walking with my dogs and wondering how the world looks without a fovea and very few retinal cells for color vision but with a huge neural processing and sensory area for smells. It is a lesson available from photographs of how the world looks to the compound eyes of a insect or even from the camera eye of a spy satellite or the digitally transmitted signals of space probe-perceived differences "near" Jupiter that have been transformed into coffee table color photographs. The "eyes" made available in modern technological sciences shatter any idea of passive vision; these prosthetic devices show us that all eyes, including our organic ones, are active perceptual systems, building on translations and specific *ways* of seeing, that is, ways of life. There is no unmediated photograph or passive camera obscura in scientific accounts of bodies and machines; there are only highly specific visual possibilities, each with a wonderfully detailed, active, partial way of organizing worlds. All these pictures of the world should not be allegories of infinite mobility and interchangeability but of elaborate specificity and difference and the loving care people might take to learn how to see faithfully from another's point of view, even when the other is our own machine. That's not alienating distance; that's a *possible* allegory for feminist versions of objectivity. Understanding how these visual systems work, technically, socially, and psychically, ought to be a way of embodying feminist objectivity.

Many currents in feminism attempt to theorize grounds for trusting especially the vantage points of the subjugated; there is good reason to believe vision is better from below the brilliant space platforms of the powerful.[7] Building on that suspicion, this essay is an argument for situated and embodied knowledges and an argument against various forms of unlocatable, and so irresponsible, knowledge claims. Irresponsible means unable to called into account. There is a premium on establishing the capacity to see from the peripheries and the depths. But here there also lies serious danger of romanticizing and/or appropriating the vision of the less powerful while claiming to see from their positions. To see from below is neither easily learned nor unproblematic, even if "we" "naturally" inhabit the great underground terrain of subjugated knowledges. The positionings of the subjugated are not exempt from critical reexamination, decoding, deconstruction, and interpretation; that is, from both semiological and hermeneutic modes of critical inquiry. The standpoints of the subjugated are not "innocent" positions. On the contrary, they are preferred because in principle they are least likely to allow denial of the critical and interpretive core of all knowledge. They are knowledgeable of modes of denial through repression, forgetting, and disappearing acts—ways of being nowhere while claiming to see comprehensively. The subjugated have a decent chance to be on to the god trick and all its dazzling—and, therefore, blinding—illuminations. "Subjugated" standpoints are preferred because they seem to promise more adequate, sustained, objective, transforming accounts of the world. But *how* to see from below is a problem requiring at least as much skill with bodies and language, with the mediations of vision, as the "highest" technoscientific visualizations.

Such preferred positionings is as hostile to various forms of relativism as to the most explicitly totalizing versions of claims to scientific authority. But the alternative to relativism is not totalization and single vision, which is always finally the unmarked category whose power depends on systematic narrowing and obscuring. The alternative to relativism is partial, locatable, critical knowledges sustaining the possibility of webs of connections called solidarity in politics and shared conversations in epistemology. Relativism is a way of being nowhere while claiming to be everywhere equally. The "equality" of positioning is a denial of responsibility and critical inquiry. Relativism is the perfect mirror twin of totalization in the ideologies of objectivity; both deny the stakes in location, embodiment, and partial perspective; both make it impossible to see well. Relativism and totalization are both "god tricks" promising vision from everywhere and nowhere equally and fully, common myths in rhetorics surrounding Science. But it is precisely in the politics and epistemology of partial perspectives that the possibility of sustained, rational, objective inquiry rests.

So, with many other feminists, I want to argue for a doctrine and practice of objectivity that privileges contestations, deconstruction, passionate construction, webbed connections, and hope for transformation of systems of knowledge and ways of seeing. But not just any partial perspective will do; we must be hostile to easy relativisms and holisms built out of summing and subsuming parts. "Passionate detachment"[8] requires more than acknowledged and self-critical partiality. We are also bound to seek perspective from those points of view, which can never be known in advance, that promise something quite extraordinary, that is, knowledge potent for constructing worlds less organized by axes of domination....

A commitment to mobile positioning and to passionate detachment is dependent on the impossibility of entertaining innocent "identity" politics and epistemologies as strategies for seeing from the standpoints of the subjugated in order to see well. One cannot "be" either a cell or molecule—or a woman, colonized person, laborer, and so on—if one intends to see and see from these positions critically. "Being" is much more problematic and contingent. Also, one cannot relocate in any possible vantage point without being accountable for that movement. Vision is *always* a question of the power to see—and perhaps of the violence implicit in our visualizing practices. With whose blood were my eyes crafted? These points also apply to testimony from the position of "oneself." We are not immediately present to ourselves. Self-knowledge requires a semiotic-material technology to link meaning and bodies. Self-identity is a bad visual system. Fusion is a bad strategy of positioning. The boys in the human sciences have called this doubt about self-presence the "death of the subject" defined as a single ordering point of will and consciousness. That judgment seems bizarre to me. I prefer to call this doubt the opening of nonisomorphic subjects, agents, and territories of stories unimaginable from the vantage point of the cyclopean, self-satiated eye of the master subject. The Western eye has fundamentally been a wandering eye, a traveling lens. These peregrinations have often been violent and insistent on having mirrors for a conquering self—but not always. Western feminists also *inherit* some skill in learning to participate in revisualizing worlds turned upside down in earth-transforming challenges to the views of the masters. All is not to be done from scratch.

The split and contradictory self is the one who can interrogate positionings and be accountable, the one who can construct and join rational conversations and fantastic imaginings that change history.[9] Splitting, not being, is the privileged image for feminist epistemologies of scientific knowledge. "Splitting" in this context should be about heterogeneous multiplicities that are simultaneously salient and incapable of being squashed into isomorphic slots or cumulative lists. This geometry pertains within and among subjects. Subjectivity is multidimensional; so, therefore, is vision. The knowing self is partial in all its guises, never finished, whole, simply there and original; it is always constructed and stitched together imperfectly, and *therefore* able to join with another, to see together without claiming to be another. Here is the promise of objectivity: a scientific knower seeks the subject position, not of identity, but of objectivity, that is, partial connection. There is no way to "be" simultaneously in all, or wholly in any, of the privileged (i.e., subjugated) positions structured by gender, race, nation, and class. And that is a short list of critical positions. The search for such a "full" and total position is the search for the fetishized perfect subject of oppositional history, sometimes appearing in feminist theory as the essentialized Third Word Woman.[10] Subjugation is not ground for an ontology; it might be a visual clue. Vision requires instruments of vision; an optics is a politics of positioning. Instruments of vision mediate standpoints; there is no immediate vision from the standpoints of the subjugated. Identity, including self-identity, does not produce science; critical positioning does, that is, objectivity. Only those occupying the positions of the dominators are self-identical, unmarked, disembodied, unmediated, transcendent, born again. It is unfortunately possible for the subjugated to lust for and even scramble into that subject position—and then disappear from view. Knowledge from the point of view of the unmarked is truly fantastic, distorted, and irrational. The only position from which objectivity could not possibly be practiced and honored is the stand-point of the master, the Man, the One God, whose Eye produces, appropriates, and orders all difference. No one ever accused the God of monotheism of objectivity, only of indifference. The god trick is self-identical, and we have mistaken that for creativity and knowledge, omniscience even.

Positioning is, therefore, the key practice in grounding knowledge organized around the imagery of vision, and much Western scientific and philosophic discourse is organized in this way. Positioning implies responsibility for our enabling practices. It follows that politics and ethics ground struggles for and contests over what may count as rational knowledge. That is, admitted or not, politics and ethics ground struggles over knowledge projects in the exact, natural, social, and human sciences. Otherwise, rationality is simply impossible, an optical illusion projected from nowhere comprehensively. Histories of science may be powerfully told as histories of the technologies. These technologies are skilled practices. How to see? Where to see from? What limits to vision? What to see for? Whom to see with? Who gets to have more than one point of view? Who gets blinded? Who wears blinders? Who interprets the visual field? What other sensory powers do we wish to cultivate besides vision? Moral and political discourse should be the paradigm for rational discourse about the imagery and technologies of vision. . . . Struggles over what will count as rational accounts of the world are struggles over *how* to see. The terms of vision: the science question in colonialism, the science question in exterminism,[11] the science question in feminism.

The issue in politically engaged attacks on various empiricisms, reductionisms, or other versions of scientific authority should not be relativism—but location. A dichotomous chart expressing this point might look like this:

universal rationality	ethnophilosophies
common language	heteroglossia
new organon	deconstruction
unified field theory	oppositional positioning
world system	local knowledges
master theory	webbed accounts

But a dichotomous chart misrepresents in a critical way the positions of embodied objectivity that I am trying to sketch. The primary distortion is the illusion of symmetry in the chart's dichotomy, making any position appear, first, simply alternative and, second, mutually exclusive. A map of tensions and resonances between the fixed ends of a charged dichotomy better represents the potent politics and epistemologies of embodied, therefore accountable objectivity. For example, local knowledges have to be in tension with the productive structurings that force unequal translations and exchanges—material and semiotic—within the webs of knowledge and power. Webs *can* have the property of being systematic, even of being centrally structured global systems with deep filaments and tenacious tendrils into time, space, and consciousness, which are the dimensions of world history. Feminist accountability requires a knowledge tuned to resonance, not to dichotomy. Gender is a field of structured and structuring difference, in which the tones of extreme localization, of the intimately personal and individualized body, vibrate in the same field with global high-tension emissions. Feminist embodiment, then, is not about fixed location in a reified body, female or otherwise, but about nodes in fields, inflections in orientations, and responsibility for difference in material-semiotic fields of meaning. Embodiment is significant prosthesis; objectivity cannot be about fixed vision when what counts as an object is precisely what world history turns out to be about.

How should one be positioned in order to see, in this situation of tensions, resonances, transformations, resistances, and complicities? Here, primate vision is not immediately a very powerful metaphor or technology for feminist political-epistemological clarification, because it seems to present to consciousness already processed and objectified fields; things seem already fixed and distanced. But the visual metaphor allows one to go beyond the fixed appearances, which are only the end products. The metaphor invites us to investigate the varied apparatuses of visual production, including the prosthetic technologies interfaced with our biological eyes and brains. And here we find highly particular machineries for processing regions of the electromagnetic spectrum into our pictures of the world. It is in the intricacies of these visualization technologies in which we are embedded that we will find metaphors and means for understanding and intervening in the patterns of objectification in the world—that is, the patterns of reality for which we must be accountable. In these metaphors, we find means for appreciating simultaneously *both* the concrete, "real" aspect and the aspect of semiosis and production in what we call scientific knowledge.

I am arguing for politics and epistemologies of location, positioning, and situating, where partiality and not universality is the condition of being heard to make rational knowledge claims. These are claims on people's lives. I am arguing for the view from a body, always a complex, contradictory, structuring, and structured body, versus the view from above, from nowhere, from simplicity. Only the god trick is forbidden....

Feminism loves another science: the sciences and politics of interpretation, translation, stuttering, and the partly understood. Feminism is about the sciences of the multiple subject with (at least) double vision. Feminism is about a critical vision consequent upon a critical positioning in unhomogeneous gendered social space.[12] Translation is always interpretive, critical, and partial. Here is a ground for conversation, rationality, and objectivity—which is power-sensitive, not pluralist, "conversation.".... There is no single feminist standpoint because our maps require too many dimensions for that metaphor to ground our visions. But the feminist standpoint theorists' goal of an epistemology and politics of engaged, accountable positioning remains eminently potent. The goal is better accounts of the world, that is, "science."

Above all, rational knowledge does not pretend to disengagement: to be from everywhere and so nowhere, to be free from interpretation, from being represented, to be fully self-contained or fully formalizable. Rational knowledge is a process of ongoing critical interpretation among "fields" of interpreters and decoders. Rational knowledge is power-sensitive conversation.[13] Decoding and transcoding plus translation and criticism; all are necessary. So science becomes the paradigmatic model, not of closure, but of that which is contestable and contested. Science becomes the myth, not of what escapes human agency and responsibility in a realm above the fray, but rather, of accountability and responsibility for translations and solidarities linking the cacopohonous visions and visionary voices that characterize the knowledges of the subjugated. A splitting of senses, a confusion of voice and sight, rather than clear and distinct ideas, becomes the metaphor for the ground of the rational. We seek not the knowledges ruled by phallogocentrism (nostalgia for the presence of the one true Word) and disembodied vision. We seek those ruled by partial sight and limited voice—not partiality for its own sake but, rather, for the sake of the connections and unexpected openings situated knowledges make possible. Situated knowledges are about communities, not about isolated individuals. The only way to find a larger vision is to be somewhere in particular. The science question in feminism is about objectivity as positioned rationality. Its images are not the products of escape and transcendence of limits (the view from above) but the joining of partial views and halting voices into a collective subject position that promises a vision of the means of ongoing finite embodiment, of living within limits and contradictions—of views from somewhere.

Objects as Actors: The Apparatus of Bodily Production

Throughout this reflection on "objectivity," I have refused to resolve the ambiguities built into referring to science without differentiating its extraordinary range of contexts. Through the insistent ambiguity, I have foregrounded a field of commonalities binding exact, physical, natural, social, political, biological, and human sciences; and I have tied this whole heterogeneous field academically (and industrially, e.g., in publishing, the weapons trade, and pharmaceuticals) institutionalized knowledge production to a meaning, a science that insists on its potency in ideological struggles. But, partly in order to give play to both the specificities and the highly permeable boundaries of meanings in discourse on science, I would like to suggest a resolution to one ambiguity. Throughout the field of meanings constituting science, one of the commonalities concerns the status of any object of knowledge and of related claims about the faithfulness of our accounts to a "real world," no matter how mediated for us and no matter how complex and contradictory these worlds may be. Feminists, and others who have been most active as critics of the sciences and their claims or associated ideologies, have shied away from doctrines of scientific objectivity in part because of the suspicion that an "object" of knowledge is a passive and inert thing. Accounts of such objects can seem to be either appropriations of a fixed and determined world reduced to resource for instrumentalist projects of destructive Western societies, or they can be seen as masks for interests, usually dominating interests.

For example, "sex" as an object of biological knowledge appears regularly in the guise of biological determinism, threatening the fragile space for social constructionism and critical theory, with their attendant possibilities for active and transformative intervention, which were called into being by feminist concepts of gender as socially, historically, and semiotically positioned difference. And yet, to lose authoritative biological accounts of sex, which set up productive tensions with gender seems to be to lose too much; it seems to be to lose not just analytic power within a particular Western tradition but also the body itself as anything but a blank page for social inscription, including those of biological discourse. The same problem of loss attends the radical "reduction" of the objects of physics or of any science to the ephemera of discursive production and social construction.[14]

But the difficulty and loss are not necessary. They derive partly from the analytic tradition, deeply indebted to Aristotle and to the transformative history of "White Capitalist Patriarchy" (how may we name this scandalous Thing?) that turns everything into a resource for appropriation, in which an object of knowledge is finally itself only matter for the seminal power, the act, of the knower. Here, the object both guarantees and refreshes the power of the knower, but any status as *agent* in the productions of knowledge must be denied the object. It—the world—must, in short, be objectified as a thing, not as an agent; it must be matter for the self-formation of the only social being in the productions of knowledge, the human knower.... Nature is only the raw material of culture, appropriated, preserved, enslaved, exalted, or otherwise made flexible for disposal by culture in the logic of capitalist colonialism. Similarly, sex is only matter to the act of gender; the productionist logic seems inescapable in traditions of Western binary oppositions. This analytical and historical narrative logic accounts for my nervousness about the sex/gender distinction in the recent history of feminist theory. Sex is "resourced" for its representation as gender, which "we" can control. It has seemed all but impossible to avoid the trap of an appropriationist logic of domination built into the nature/culture opposition and its generative lineage, including the sex/gender distinction.

It seems clear that feminist accounts of objectivity and embodiment—that is, of a world—of the kind sketched in this essay require a deceptively simply maneuver within inherited Western analytical traditions, a maneuver begun in dialectics but stopping short of the needed revisions. Situated knowledges require that the object of knowledge be pictured as an actor and agent, not as a screen or a ground or a resource, never finally as slave to the master that closes off the dialectic in his unique agency and his authorship of "objective" knowledge.... Accounts of a "real" world do not, then, depend on a logic of "discovery" but on a power-charged social relation of "conversation." The world neither speaks itself nor disappears in favor of a master decoder. The codes of the world are not still, waiting only to be read....

My simple, perhaps simple-minded, maneuver is obviously not new in Western philosophy, but it has a special feminist edge to it in relation to the science question in feminist and to the linked question of gender as situated difference and the question of female embodiment. Ecofeminists have perhaps been most insistent on some version of the world as active subject, not as resource to be mapped and appropriated in bourgeois, Marxist, or masculinist projects. Acknowledging the agency of the world in knowledge makes room for some unsettling possibilities, including a sense of the world's independent sense of humor. Such a sense of humor is not comfortable for humanists and others committed to the world as resource. There are, however, richly evocative figures to promote feminist visualization of the world as witty agent. We need not lapse into appeals to a primal mother resisting her translation into resource. The Coyote or Trickster, as embodied in Southwest native American accounts, suggests the situation we are in when we give up mastery but keep searching for fidelity, knowing all the while that we will be hoodwinked. I think these are useful myths for scientists who might be our allies. Feminist objectivity makes room for surprises and ironies at the heart of all knowledge production; we are not in charge of the world. We just live here and try to strike up noninnocent conversations by means of our prosthetic devices, including our visualization technologies. No wonder science fiction has been such a rich writing practice in recent feminist theory. I like to see feminist theory as a reinvented coyote discourse obligated to its sources in many heterogeneous accounts of the world.

Another rich feminist practice in science in the last couple of decades illustrates particularly well the "activation" of the previously passive categories of objects of knowledge. This activation permanently problematizes binary distinctions like sex and gender, without eliminating their strategic utility. I refer to the reconstructions in primatology (especially, but not only, in women's practice as primatologists, evolutionary biologists, and behavioral ecologists) of what may count as sex, especially as female sex, in scientific accounts.[15] The *body*, the object of biological discourse, becomes a most engaging being. Claims of biological determinism can never be the same again. When female "sex" has been so thoroughly retheorized and revisualized that it emerges as practically indistinguishable from "mind," something basic has happened to the categories of biology. The biological female peopling current biological behavioral accounts has almost no passive properties left. She is structuring and active in every respect; the "body" is an agent, not a resource. Difference is theorized *biologically* as situational, not intrinsic, at every level from gene to foraging pattern, thereby fundamentally changing the biological politics of the body. The relations between sex and gender need to be categorically reworked within these frames of knowledge. I would like to suggest that this trend in explanatory strategies in biology is an allegory for interventions faithful to projects of feminist objectivity. The point is not that these new pictures of the biological female are simply true or not open to contestation and conversation—quite the opposite. But these pictures foreground knowledge as situated conversation at every level of its articulation. The boundary between animal and human is one of the stakes in this allegory, as is the boundary between machine and organism....

Objectivity is not about disengagement but about mutual *and* usually unequal structuring, about taking risks in a world where "we" are permanently mortal, that is, not in "final" control.... Feminist embodiment, feminist hopes for partiality, objectivity, and situated knowledges, turn on conversations and codes at this potent node in fields of possible bodies and meanings. Here is where science, science fantasy, and science fiction converge in the objectivity question in feminism. Perhaps our hopes for accountability, for politics, for ecofeminism, turn on revisioning the world as coding trickster with whom we must learn to converse.

Notes

1. For example, see Karin Knorr-Cetina and Michael Mulkay, eds., *Science Observed: Perspectives on the Social Study of Science* (London: Sage, 1983); Wiebe E. Bijker, Thomas P. Hughes, and Trevor Pinch, eds., *The Social Construction of Technological Systems* (Cambridge: MIT Press, 1987); and esp. Bruno Latour's *Les microbes, guerre et paix, suivi de irréductions* (Paris: Métailié, 1984); and *The Pasteurization of France, Followed by Irreductions: A Politico-Scientific Essay* (Cambridge: Harvard University Press, 1988).

2. For an elegant and very helpful elucidation of a noncartoon version of this argument, see Hayden White, *The Content of the Form: Narrative Discourse and Historical Representation* (Baltimore: Johns Hopkins University Press, 1987). I still want more; and unfulfilled desire can be a powerful seed for changing the stories.

3. In "Through the Lumen: Frankenstein and the Optics of Re-Origination" (Ph.D. diss. University of California at Santa Cruz, 1988), Zoe Sofoulis has produced a dazzling (she will forgive me the metaphor) theoretical treatment of technoscience, the psychoanalysis of science fiction culture, and the metaphorics of extraterrestrialism, including a wonderful focus on the ideologies and philosophies of light, illumination, and discovery in Western mythics of science and technology. My essay was revised in dialogue with Sofoulis's arguments and metaphors in her dissertation.

4. Nancy Hartsock, *Money, Sex, and Power: An Essay on Domination and Community* (Boston: Northeastern University Press, 1984).

5. Harding, 24–26, 161–162.

6. John Varley's science fiction short story, "The Persistence of Vision," in *The Persistence of Vision* (New York: Dell, 1978), 263–316, is part of the inspiration for this section. In the story, Varley constructs a utopian community designed and built by the deaf-blind. He then explores these people's technologies and other mediations of communication and their relations to sighted children and visitors....

7. See Hartsock, "The Feminist Standpoint: Developing the Ground for a Specifically Feminist Historical Materialism"; and Chela Sandoval, *Yours in Struggle: Women Respond to Racism* (Oakland: Center for Third World Organizing, n.d.); Harding; and Gloria Anzaldua, *Borderlands/La Frontera* (San Francisco: Spinsters/Aunt Lute, 1987).

8. Annette Kuhn, *Women's Pictures: Feminism and Cinema* (London: Routledge & Kegan Paul, 1982), 3–18.

9. Joan Scott reminded me that Teresa de Lauretis put it like this: "Differences among women may be better understood as differences within women.... But once understood in their constitutive power—once it is understood, that is, that these differences not only constitute each woman's consciousness and subjective limits but all together define the *female subject of feminism* in its very specificity, is inherent and at least for now irreconcilable contradiction—these differences, then cannot be again collapsed into a fixed identity, a sameness of all women as Woman, or a representation of Feminism as a coherent and available image." See Theresa de Lauretis,

"Feminist Studies/Critical Studies: Issues, Terms, and Contexts," in her *Feminist Studies/Critical Studies* (Bloomington: Indiana University Press, 1986), 14–15.

10. Chandra Mohanty, "Under Western Eyes," *Boundary* 2/3 (1984): 333–58.

11. See Sofoulis, unpublished manuscript.

12. In *The Science Question in Feminism* (p. 181), Harding suggests that gender has three dimensions, each historically specific: gender symbolism, the social-sexual division of labor, and processes of constructing individual gendered identity....

13. Katie King, "Canons without Innocence" (Ph.D. diss., University of California at Santa Cruz, 1987).

14. Evelyn Fox Keller, in "The Gender/Science System: Or, Is Sex to Gender As Nature Is to Science?" (*Hypatia* 2 [Fall 1987]: 37–49), has insisted on the important possibilities opened up by the construction of the intersection of the distinction between sex and gender, on the one hand, and nature and science, on the other. She also insists on the need to hold to some nondiscursive grounding in "sex" and "nature," perhaps what I am calling the "body" and "world."

15. Donna Haraway, *Primate Visions: Gender, Race, and Nature in the World of Modern Science* (New York: Routledge & Kegan Paul 1989).

37.
THE THEORETICAL SUBJECT(S) OF
THIS BRIDGE CALLED MY BACK AND ANGLO-
AMERICAN FEMINISM
Norma Alarcón

This Bridge Called My Back: Writings by Radical Women of Color, edited by Chicana writers Cherríe Moraga and Gloria Anzaldúa,[1] was intended as a collection of essays, poems, tales, and testimonials that would give voice to the contradictory experiences of "women of color." In fact, the editors state:

> We are the colored in a white feminist movement.
> We are the feminists among the people of our culture.
> We are often the lesbians among the straight.[2]

By giving voice to such experiences, each according to her style, the editors and contributors believed they were developing a theory of subjectivity and culture that would demonstrate the considerable differences between them and Anglo-American women, as well as between them and Anglo-European men and men of their own culture. As speaking subjects of a new discursive formation, many of *Bridge*'s writers were aware of the displacement of their subjectivity across a multiplicity of discourses: feminist/lesbian, nationalist, racial, socioeconomic, historical, et cetera. The peculiarity of their displacement implies a multiplicity of positions from which they are driven to grasp or understand themselves and their relations with the real, in the Althusserian sense of the word.[3] *Bridge* writers, in part, were aware that these positions are often incompatible or contradictory, and others did not have access to the maze of discourses competing for their body and voice. The self-conscious effort to reflect on their "flesh and blood experiences to concretize a vision that can begin to heal our "wounded knee"[4] led many *Bridge* speakers to take a position in conflict with multiple intercultural and intracultural discursive interpretations in an effort to come to grips with "the many-headed demon of oppression."[5]

Since its publication in 1981, *Bridge* has had a diverse impact on Anglo-American feminist writings in the United States. Teresa de Lauretis, for example, claims that *Bridge* has contributed to a "shift in feminist consciousness,"[6] yet her explanation fails to clarify what the shift consists of and for whom. There is little doubt, however, that *Bridge*, along with the 1980s writings by many women of color in the United States, has problematized many a version of Anglo-American feminism, and has helped open the way for alternative feminist discourses and theories. Presently, however the impact among most Anglo-American theorists appears to be more cosmetic than not because, as Jane Flax has recently noted, "The modal 'person' in feminist theory still appears to be a self-sufficient individual adult."[7] This particular "modal person" corresponds to the female subject most admired in literature which Gayatri Chakravorty Spivak had characterized as one who "articulates herself in shifting relationship to . . . the constitution and 'interpellation' of the subject not only as individual but as 'individualist'."[8] Consequently, the "native female" or "woman of color" can be excluded from the discourse of feminist theory. The "native female"—object of colonialism and racism—is excluded because, in Flax's terms, white feminists have not "explored how our understanding of gender relations, self, and theory are partially constituted in and through experiences of living in a culture in which asymmetric race relations are a central organizing principle of society."[9] Thus, the most popular subject of Anglo-American feminism is an autonomous, self-making, self determining subject who first proceeds according to the *logic of identification* with regard to the subject of consciousness, a notion usually viewed as the purview of man, but now claimed for women.[10] Believing that in this respect she is the same as man, she now claims the right to pursue her own identity, to name herself, to pursue self-knowledge, and, in the words of Adrienne Rich, to effect "a change in the concept of sexual identity."[11]

Though feminism has problematized gender relations, indeed, as Flax observes, gender is "the single most important advance in feminist theory,"[12] it has not problematized the subject of knowledge and her complicity with the notion of consciousness as "synthetic unificatory power, the centre and active point of organization of representations determining their concatenation."[13] The subject (and object) of knowledge is now a woman, but the inherited view of consciousness has not been questioned at all. As a result, some Anglo-American feminist subjects of consciousness have tended to become a parody of the masculine subject of consciousness, thus revealing their ethnocentric liberal underpinnings. In 1982, Jean Bethke Elshtain had noted the "masculine cast" of radical feminist language, for example, noting the terms of "raw power, brute force, martial discipline, law and order with a feminist face—and voice."[14] Also in critiquing liberal feminism and its language, she notes that "no vision of the political community that might serve as the ground work of a life in common is possible within a political life dominated by a self-interested, predatory individualism."[15] Althusser argues that this tradition "has privileged the category of the 'subject' as Origin, Essence and Cause, responsible in its internality for all determinations of the external object. In other words, this tradition has promoted Man, in his ideas and experience, as the source of knowledge, morals and history."[16] By identifying in this way with this tradition, standpoint epistemologists have substituted, ironically, woman for man. This "logic of identification" as a first step in constructing the theoretical subject of feminism is often veiled from standpoint epistemologists because greater attention is given to naming female identity, and describing women's ways of knowing as being considerably different than men's.[17] By emphasizing "sexual difference," the second step takes place, often called oppositional thinking (counteridentifying).

However, this gendered standpoint epistemology leads to feminism's bizarre position with regard to other liberation movements, working inherently against the interests of non-white women and no one else. For example, Sandra Harding argues that oppositional thinking (counteridentification) with white men should be retained even though "[t]here are suggestions in the literature of Native Americans, Africans, and Asians that what feminists call feminine versus masculine personalities, ontologies, ethics, epistemologies, and world views may be what these other liberation movements call Non-Western versus Western personalities and world views.... I set aside the crucial and fatal complication for this way of thinking—the fact that one half of these people are women and that most women are not Western."[18] She further suggests that feminists respond by relinquishing the totalizing "master theory" character of our theory-making: "This response to the issue [will manage] to retain the categories of feminist theory... and simply set them alongside the categories of the theory making of other subjugated groups.... Of course, it leaves bifurcated (and perhaps even more finely divided) the identities of all except ruling-class white Western women...."[19] The apperception of this situation is precisely what led to the choice of title for the book *All the Women Are White, All the Blacks Are Men, But Some of Us Are Brave*, edited by Gloria T. Hull, Patricia Bell Scott, and Barbara Smith.[20]

Notwithstanding the power of *Bridge* to affect the personal lives of its readers, *Bridge*'s challenge to the Anglo-American subject of feminism has yet to effect a newer discourse. Women of color often recognize themselves in the pages of *Bridge*, and write to say, "The women writers seemed to be speaking to me, and they actually understood what I was going through. Many of you put into words feelings I have had that I had no way of expressing.... The writings justified some of my thoughts telling me I had a right to feel as I did."[21] On the other hand, Anglo feminist readers of *Bridge* tend to appropriate it, cite it as an instance of difference between women, and proceed to negate that difference by subsuming women of color into the unitary category of woman/women. The latter is often viewed as the "common denominator" in an oppositional (counteridentifying) discourse with some white men, that leaves us unable to explore relationships among women.

Bridge's writers did not see the so-called "common denominator" as the solution for the construction of the theoretical feminist subject. In the call for submissions the editors clearly stated: "We want to express to all women—especially to white middle class women—the experiences which divide us as feminists; we want to explore the causes, and sources of, and solutions to these divisions. We want to create a definition that expands what 'feminist' means to US."[22] Thus, the female subject of *Bridge* is highly complex. She is and has been constructed in a crisis of meaning situation which includes racial and cultural divisions and conflicts. The psychic and material violence that gives shape to that subjectivity cannot be underestimated nor passed over lightly. The fact that not all of this violence comes from men in general but also from women renders the notion of "common denominator" problematic.

It is clear, however, that even as *Bridge* becomes a resource for the Anglo-American feminist theory classroom and syllabus, there's a tendency to deny differences if those differences pose a threat to the "common denominator" category. That is, unity would be purchased with silence, putting aside the conflictive history of groups' interrelations and interdependence. In the words of Paula Treichler, "[h]ow do we address the issues and concerns raised by women of color, who may themselves be even more excluded from theoretical feminist discourse than from the women's studies curriculum?. . . Can we explore our 'common differences' without overemphasizing the division that currently seems to characterize the feminism of the United States and the world?"[23] Clearly, this exploration appears impossible without a reconfiguration of the subject of feminist theory, and her relational position to a multiplicity of others, not just white men.

Some recent critics of the "exclusionary practices in Women's Studies" have noted that its gender standpoint epistemology leads to a 'tacking on' of "material about minority women" without any note of its "significance for feminist knowledge."[24] The common approaches noted were the tendency to 1) treat race and class as secondary features in social organization (as well as representation) with primacy given to female subordination; 2) acknowledge that inequalities of race, class and gender generate different experiences and then set race and class inequalities aside on the grounds that information was lacking to allow incorporation into an analysis; 3) focus on descriptive aspects of the ways of life, values, customs, and problems of women in subordinate race and class categories with little attempt to explain their source or their broader meaning. In fact, it may be impossible for gender standpoint epistemology to ever do more than a "pretheoretical presentation of concrete problems."[25] Since the subject of feminist theory and its single theme—gender—go largely unquestioned, its point of view tends to suppress and repress voices that question its authority, and as Jane Flax remarks, "The suppression of these voices seems to be a necessary condition for the (apparent) authority, coherence, and universality of our own."[26] This may account for the inability to include the voices of "women of color" into feminist discourse, though they are not necessarily under-represented in the reading list.

For the standpoint epistemologists, the desire to construct a feminist theory based solely on gender, on the one hand, and the knowledge or implicit recognition that such an account might distort the representation of many women and/or correspond to that of some men, on the other, gives rise to anxiety and ambivalence with respect to the future of that feminism, especially in Anglo-America. At the core of that attitude is the often unstated recognition that if the pervasiveness of women's oppression is virtually "universal" on some level, it is also highly diverse from group to group and that women themselves may become complicitous with that oppression. "Complicity arises," says Macdonell, "where through lack of a positive starting point either a practice is driven to make use of prevailing values or a critique becomes the basis for a new theory."[27] Standpoint epistemologists have made use of the now gendered and feminist notion of consciousness, without too much question. (This notion, of course, represents the highest value of European culture since the Enlightenment.) The inclusion of other analytical categories such as race and class becomes impossible for a subject whose consciousness refuses to acknowledge that "one becomes a woman" in ways that are much more complex than in a simple opposition to men. In cultures in which "asymmetric race and class relations are a central organizing principle of society," one may also "become a woman" in opposition to other women. In other words, the whole category of woman may also need to be problematized, a point that I shall take up later. In any case, one should not step into that category nor that of man that easily or simply.

Simone de Beauvoir and her key work *The Second Sex* have been most influential in the development of feminist standpoint epistemology. She may even be responsible for the creation of Anglo-American feminist theory's "episteme": a highly self–conscious ruling class white Western female subject locked in a struggle to the death with "Man." De Beauvoir has shaken the world of women, most especially with the ramification of her phrase, "One is not born, but rather becomes, a woman."[28] For over 400 pages of text after that statement, de Beauvoir demonstrates how a female is constituted as a "woman" by society as her freedom is curtailed from childhood. The curtailment of freedom incapacitates her from affirming "herself as a subject."[29] Very few women, indeed, can escape the cycle of indoctrination except perhaps the writer/intellectual because "[s]he knows that she is a conscious being, a subject."[30] This particular kind of woman can perhaps make of her gender a project and transform her sexual identity.[31] But what of those women who are not so privileged, who neither have the political freedom nor the education? Do they now, then, occupy the place of the Other (the "Brave") while some women become subjects? Or do we have to make a subject of the whole world?

Regardless of our point of view in this matter, the way to becoming a female subject has been effected through consciousness-raising. In 1982, in a major theoretical essay, "Feminism, Method and the State: An Agenda for Theory," Catharine A. MacKinnon cited *Bridge* as a book that explored the relationship between sex and race and argued that "consciousness-raising" was *the* feminist method.[32] The reference to *Bridge* was brief. It served as an example, along with other texts, of the challenge that race and nationalism have posed for Marxism. According to her, Marxism has been unable to account for the appearance of these emancipatory discourses nor has it been able to assimilate them. Nevertheless, MacKinnon's major point was to demonstrate the epistemological challenge that feminism and its primary method, "consciousness-raising," posed for Marxism. Within Marxism, class as method of analysis has failed to reckon with the historical force of sexism. Through "consciousness-raising" (from women's point of view), women are led to know the world in a different way. Women's experience of politics, of life as sex objects, gives rise to its own method of appropriating that reality: feminist method. It challenges the objectivity of the "empirical gaze" and "rejects the distinction between knowing subject and known object."[33] By having women be the subject of knowledge, the so-called objectivity of men is brought into question. Often, this leads to privileging women's way of knowing in opposition to men's way of knowing, thus sustaining the very binary opposition that feminism would like to change or transform. Admittedly, this is only one of the many paradoxical procedures in feminist think-ing, as Nancy Cott confirms: "It acknowledges diversity among women while posit-ing that women recognize their unity. It requires gender consciousness for its basis, yet calls for the elimination of prescribed gender roles."[34]

However, I suspect that these contradictions or paradoxes have more profound implications than is readily apparent. Part of the problem may be that as feminist practice and theory recuperate their sexual differential, through "consciousness-raising," women reinscribe such a differential as feminist epistemology or theory. With gender as the central concept in feminist thinking, epistemology is flattened out in such a way that we lose sight of the complex and multiple ways in which the subject and object of possible experience are constituted. The flattening effect is multiplied when one considers that gender is often solely related to white men. There's no inquiry into the knowing subject beyond the fact of being a "woman." But what is a "woman," or a "man" for that matter? If we refuse to define either term according to some "essence," then we are left with having to specify their conven-tional significance in time and space, which is liable to change as knowledge increases or interests change. The fact that Anglo-American feminism has appropri-ated the generic term for itself leaves many a woman in this country having to call herself otherwise, i.e., "woman of color," which is equally "meaningless" without further specification. It also gives rise to the tautology "Chicana women." Needless to say, the requirement of gender consciousness only in relationship to man leaves us in the dark about a good many things, including interracial and intercultural relations. It may be that the only purpose this type of differential has is as a political strategy. It does not help us envision a world beyond binary restrictions, nor does it help us to reconfigure feminist theory to include the "native female." It does, how-ever, help us grasp the paradox that within this cultural context one cannot be a feminist without becoming a gendered subject of knowledge, which makes it very difficult to transcend gender at all and to imagine relations between women.

In *Feminist Politics and Human Nature*, Alison M. Jaggar, speaking as a socialist feminist, refers repeatedly to *Bridge* and other works by women of color. In that work, Jaggar states that subordinated women are unrepresented in feminist theory. Jaggar claims that socialist feminism is inspired by Marxist and radical feminist politics though the latter has failed to be scientific about its insights. *Bridge* is cited various times to counter the racist and classist position of radical feminists.[35] Jaggar charges that "[r]adical feminism has encouraged women to name their own expe-rience but it has not recognized explicitly that this experience must be analyzed, explained and theoretically transcended."[36] In a sense, Jaggar's charge amounts to the notion that radical feminists were flattening out their knowledge by an inade-quate methodology, i.e., gender consciousness raising. Many of Jaggar's observa-tions are a restatement of *Bridge's* challenge to Anglo-American feminists of all persuasions, be it Liberal, Radical, Marxist, and Socialist, the types sketched out by Jaggar. For example, "[a] representation of reality from the standpoint of women must draw on the variety of all women's experience"[37] may be compared to Barbara

Smith's view in *Bridge* that "Feminism is the political theory and practice to free *all* women: women of color, working-class women, poor women, physically challenged women, lesbians, old women, as well as white economically privileged heterosexual women."[38] Jaggar continues, "Since historically diverse groups of women, such as working class women, women of color, and others have been excluded from intellectual work, they somehow must be enabled to participate as subjects as well as objects of feminist theorizing."[39] Writers in *Bridge* did appear to think that "consciousness-raising" and the naming of one's experience would deliver some theory and yield a notion of "what 'feminist' means to us."[40] Except for Smith's statement, there is no overarching view that would guide us as to "what 'feminist' means to us." Though there is a tacit political identity—gender/class/race-encapsulated in the phrase "women of color" that connects the pieces—they tend to split apart into "vertical relations" between the culture of resistance and the culture resisted or from which excluded. Thus, the binary restrictions become as prevalent between race/ethnicity of oppressed versus oppressor as between the sexes. The problems inherent in Anglo-American feminism and race relations are so locked into the "Self/Other" theme that it is no surprise that *Bridge's* co-editor Moraga would remark, "In the last three years I have learned that Third World feminism does not provide the kind of easy political framework that women of color are running to in droves. The *idea* of Third World feminism has proved to be much easier between the covers of a book than between real live women."[41] She refers to the United States, of course, because feminism is alive and well throughout the Third World largely within the purview of women's rights, or as a class struggle.[42]

The appropriation of *Bridge's* observations in Jaggar's work differs slightly from the others in its view of linguistic use, implying to a limited extent that language is also reflective of material existence. The crucial question is how, indeed, can women of color be subjects as well as objects of feminist theorizing? Jaggar cites María Lugones' doubts: "We cannot talk to you in our language because you do not understand it.... The power of white Anglo women vis-à-vis Hispanas and Black women is in inverse proportion to their working knowledge of each other.... Because of their ignorance, white Anglo women who try to do theory with women of color inevitably disrupt the dialogue. Before they can contribute to collective dialogue, they need to 'know the text,' to have become familiar with an alternative way of viewing the world.... You need to learn to become unintrusive, unimportant, patient to the point of tears, while at the same time open to learning any possible lessons. You will have to come to terms with the sense of alienation, of not belonging, of having your world thoroughly disrupted, having it criticized and scrutinized from the point of view of those who have been harmed by it, having important concepts central to it dismissed, being viewed with mistrust."[43] One of *Bridge's* breaks with prevailing conventions is linguistic. Lugones' advice to Anglo women to listen was post *Bridge*. If prevailing conventions of speaking/writing had been observed, many a contributor would have been censored or silenced. So would have many a major document or writing of minorities. *Bridge* leads us to understand that the silence and silencing of people begins with the dominating enforcement of linguistic conventions, the resistance to relational dialogues, as well as the disenablement of peoples by outlawing their forms of speech. Anglo-American feminist theory assumes a speaking subject who is an autonomous, self-conscious individual woman. Such theory does not discuss the linguistic status of the person. It takes for granted the linguistic status which founds subjectivity. In this way it appropriates woman/women for itself, and turns its work into a theoretical project within which the rest of us are compelled to "fit." By "forgetting" or refusing to take into account that we are culturally constituted in and through language in complex ways and not just engendered in a homogeneous situation, the Anglo-American subject of consciousness cannot come to terms with her (his) own class-biased ethnocentrism. She is blinded to her own construction not just as a woman but as an Anglo-American one. Such a subject creates a theoretical subject that could not possibly include all women just because we are women. It is against this feminist backdrop that many "women of color" have struggled to give voice to their subjectivity and which effected the publication of the writings collected in *Bridge*. However, the freedom of women of color to posit themselves as multiple-voiced subjects is constantly in peril of repression precisely at that point where our constituted contradictions put us at odds with women different from ourselves.

The pursuit of a "politics of unity" solely based on gender forecloses the "pursuit of solidarity" through different political formations and the exploration of alternative theories of the subject of consciousness. There is a tendency in more sophisticated and elaborate gender standpoint epistemologists to affirm "an identity made up of heterogeneous and heteronomous representations of gender, race, and class, and often indeed across languages and cultures"[44] with one breath, and with the next to refuse to explore how that identity may be theorized or analyzed, by reconfirming a unified subjectivity or "shared consciousness" through gender. The difference is handed over with one hand and taken away with the other. If it be true, as Teresa de Lauretis has observed, that "[s]elf and identity...are always grasped and understood within particular discursive configurations,"[45] it does not necessarily follow that one can easily and self-consciously decide "to reclaim [an identity] from a history of multiple assimilations,"[46] and still retain a "shared consciousness." Such a practice goes counter to the homogenizing tendency of the subject of consciousness in the United States. To be oppressed means to be disenabled not only from grasping an "identity," but also from reclaiming it. In this culture, to grasp or reclaim an identity means always already to have become a subject of consciousness. The theory of the subject of consciousness as a unitary and synthesizing agent of knowledge is always already a posture of domination. One only has to think of Gloria Anzaldúa's essay in Bridge, "Speaking in Tongues: A Letter to Third World Women Writers."[47] Though de Lauretis concedes that a racial "shared consciousness" may have prior claims than gender, she still insists on unity through gender: "the female subject is always constructed and defined in gender, starting from gender."[48] One is interested in having more than an account of gender, there are other relations to be accounted for. De Lauretis insists, in most of her work, that "the differences among women may be better understood as differences within women."[49] This position returns us all to our solitary, though different, consciousness, without noting that some differences are (have been) a result of relations of domination of women by women; that differences may be purposefully constituted for the purpose of domination or exclusion, especially in oppositional thinking. Difference, whether it be sexual, racial, social, has to be conceptualized within a political and ideological domain.[50] In *Bridge*, for example, Mirtha Quintanales points out that "in this country, in this world, racism is used *both* to create false differences among us and to mask very significant ones—cultural, economic, political."[51]

One of the most remarkable tendencies in the work reviewed is the implicit or explicit acknowledgement that women of color are excluded from feminist theory, on the one hand, and on the other the reminder that though excluded from theory, their books are read in the classroom and/or duly footnoted. It is clear that some of the writers in *Bridge* thought at some point in the seventies that feminism could be the ideal answer to their hope for liberation. Chrystos, for example, states her disillusionment as follows: "I no longer believe that feminism is a tool which can eliminate racism or even promote better understanding between different races and kinds of women."[52] The disillusionment is eloquently reformulated in the theme poem by Donna Kate Rushin, "The Bridge Poem."[53] The dream of helping the people who surround her to reach an interconnectedness that would change society is given up in favor of self-translation into a "true self." In my view, the speaker's refusal to play "bridge," an enablement to others as well as self, is the acceptance of defeat at the hands of political groups whose self-definition follows the view of self as unitary, capable of being defined by a single "theme." The speaker's perception that the "self" is multiple ("I'm sick of mediating with your worst self/on behalf of your better selves,"[54]) and its reduction harmful, gives emphasis to the relationality between one's selves and those of others as an ongoing process of struggle, effort and tension. Indeed, in this poem the better "bridging self" of the speaker is defeated by the overriding notion of the unitary subject of knowledge and consciousness so prevalent in Anglo-American culture. Consciousness as a site of multiple voicings is the theoretical subject, par excellence, of *Bridge*. Concomitantly, these voicings (or thematic threads) are not viewed as necessarily originating with the subject, but as discourses that transverse consciousness and which the subject must struggle with constantly. Rosario Morales, for example, says "I want to be whole. I want to claim myself to be puertorican, and U. S. American, working class and middle class, housewife and intellectual, feminist, marxist and anti-imperialist."[55] Gloria Anzaldúa observes, "What am I? *A third world lesbian feminist with marxist and mystic leanings.* They would chop me up into little fragments and tag each piece with a label."[56] The need to assign multiple registers of existence is an effect of the belief that knowledge of one's subjectivity cannot be arrived at through a single discursive "theme." Indeed, the multiple-voiced subjectivity is lived in resistance to competing notions for one's allegiance or self-identification. It is a process of disidentification[57] with prevalent formulations of the most forcefully theoretical subject of feminism. The choice of one or many themes is both theoretical and a political decision. Like gender epistemologists and other emancipatory movements, the theoretical subject of *Bridge* gives credit to the subject of consciousness as the site of knowledge but problematizes it by representing it as a weave. In Anzaldúa's terms, the woman of color has a "plural personality." Speaking of the new mestiza in *Borderlands/La Frontera*, she says, "[s]he learns to juggle cultures.... [the] juncture where the mestiza stands is where phenomena tend to collide."[58] As an object of multiple indoctrinations that heretofore have collided upon her, their new recognition as products of the oppositional thinking of others can help her come to terms with the politics of varied discourses and their antagonistic relations.

Thus, current political practices in the United States make it almost impossible to go beyond an oppositional theory of the subject, which is the prevailing feminist strategy and that of others; however, it is not the theory that will help us grasp the subjectivity of women of color. Socially and historically, women of color have been now central, now outside antagonistic relations between races, classes, and gender(s); this struggle of multiple antagonisms, almost always in relation to culturally different groups and not just genders, gives configuration to the theoretical subject of *Bridge*. It must be noted, however, that each woman of color cited here, even in her positing of a "plurality of self," is already privileged enough to reach the moment of cognition of a situation for herself. This should suggest that to privilege the subject, even if multiple-voiced, is not enough.

Notes

1. Hereafter cited as *Bridge*, the book has two editions. I use the second edition published by Kitchen Table Press, 1983. The first edition was published by Persephone Press, 1981.
2. Moraga and Anzaldúa, 2–3.
3. Louis Althusser, *Lenin and Philosophy and Other Essays*, Ben Brewster, tr. (London: New Left Books, 1971).
4. Moraga and Anzaldúa, 23.
5. Moraga and Anzaldúa, 195.
6. Teresa de Lauretis, *Technologies of Gender* (Bloomington: Indiana University Press, 1987), 10.
7. Jane Flax, "Postmodernism and Gender Relations in Feminist Theory," *Signs* 12:4 (Summer 1987), 640.
8. Gayatri Chakravorty Spivak, "Three Women's Texts and a Critique of Imperialism," *Critical Inquiry* 12:1 (Autumn 1985), 243–44.
9. Flax, 640.
10. Julia Kristeva. "Women's Time," *Signs* 7:1 (Autumn 1981), 19.
11. Adrienne Rich, *On Lies, Secrets and Silence* (New York: W. W. Norton, 1979), 35.
12. Flax, 627.
13. Michel Pecheux, *Language, Semantics and Ideology* (New York: St. Martin's Press, 1982), 122.
14. Jean Bethke Elshtain, "Feminist Discourse and Its Discontents: Language, Power, and Meaning," *Signs* 7:3 (Spring 1981), 611.
15. Elshtain, 617.
16. Diane Macdonell, *Theories of Discourses: An Introduction* (New York: Basil Blackwell, 1986), 76.
17. For an intriguing demonstration of these operations, see Seyla Benhabib, "The Generalized and the Concrete Other: The Kohlberg-Gilligan Controversy and Feminist Theory" in Seyla

Benhabib and Drucilla Cornell, *Feminism as Critique* (Minneapolis: University of Minnesota Press, 1987), 77–95.

18. Sandra Harding, "The Instability of the Analytical Categories of Feminist Theory," *Signs* 11:4 (Summer 1986), 659.

19. Harding, 660.

20. Gloria T. Hull, Patricia B. Scott, and Barbara Smith, eds., *All the Women Are White, All the Blacks Are Men, But Some of Us Are Brave* (Westbury, NY: Feminist Press, 1982).

21. Moraga and Anzaldúa, Introduction to the Second Edition, n.p.

22. Moraga and Anzaldúa, Introduction to the First Edition, xxiii.

23. Paula Treichler, "Teaching Feminist Theory," *Theory in the Classroom*, Cary Nelsen, ed. (Urbana: University of Illinois Press, 1986), 79.

24. Maxine Baca Zinn, Lynn Weber Cannon, Elizabeth Higginbotham, and Bonnie Thornton Dill, "The Cost of Exclusionary Practices in Women's Studies," *Signs* 11:1 (Summer 1986), 296.

25. Baca Zinn et al., 296–97.

26. Flax, 633.

27. Macdonell, 62.

28. Simone de Beauvoir, *The Second Sex* (New York: Vintage Books, 1974), 301.

29. de Beauvoir, 316.

30. de Beauvoir, 761.

31. For a detailed discussion of this theme, see Judith Butler, "Variations on Sex and Gender: Beauvoir, Wittig, and Foucault" in Benhabib and Cornell, 128–42.

32. Catharine MacKinnon, "Feminism, Marxism, Method and the State: An Agenda for Theory," *Signs* 7:3 (Spring 1982), 536–38.

33. MacKinnon, 536.

34. Nancy F. Cott, "Feminist Theory and Feminist Movements: The Past Before Us," *What Is Feminism: A ReExamination*, Juliet Mitchell and Ann Oakley, eds. (New York: Pantheon Books, 1986), 49.

35. Alison M. Jaggar, *Feminist Politics and Human Nature* (Totowa, NJ: Rowman & Allanheld, 1983), 249–50; 295–96.

36. Jaggar, 381.

37. Jaggar, 386.

38. Moraga and Anzaldúa, 61.

39. Jaggar, 386.

40. Moraga and Anzaldúa, Introduction, xxiii.

41. Moraga and Anzaldúa, Foreword to the Second Edition, n.p.

42. Miranda Davies, *Third World: Second Sex* (London: Zed Books, 1987).

43. Jaggar, 386.

44. Teresa de Lauretis, "Feminist Studies/Critical Studies: Issues, Terms, and Contexts," *Feminist Studies/Critical Studies*, Teresa de Lauretis, ed. (Bloomington: Indiana University Press 1986), 9.

45. de Lauretis, *Feminist Studies*, 8.

46. de Lauretis, *Feminist Studies*, 9.

47. Moraga and Anzaldúa, 165–74.

48. de Lauretis, *Feminist Studies*, 14.

49. de Lauretis, *Feminist Studies*, 14.

50. Monique Wittig, cited in Elizabeth Meese. *Crossing the Double-Cross: The Practice of Feminist Criticism* (Chapel Hill: University of North Carolina Press, 1986), 74.

51. Moraga and Anzaldúa, 153.

52. Moraga and Anzaldúa, 69.

53. Moraga and Anzaldúa, xxi–xxii.

54. Moraga and Anzaldúa, xxii.

55. Moraga and Anzaldúa, 91.

56. Moraga and Anzaldúa, 205.

57. Pecheux, 158–59.

58. Gloria Anzaldúa, *Borderlands/La Frontera: The New Mestiza* (San Francisco: Spinsters/Aunt Lute, 1987), 79.

38.
PERFORMATIVE ACTS AND GENDER CONSTITUTION: AN ESSAY IN PHENOMENOLOGY AND FEMINIST THEORY
Judith Butler

Philosophers rarely think about acting in the theatrical sense, but they do have a discourse of "acts" that maintains associative semantic meanings with theories of performance and acting. For example...the phenomenological theory of "acts," espoused by Edmund Husserl, Maurice Merleau-Ponty, and George Herbert Mead, among others, seeks to explain the mundane way in which social agents *constitute* social reality through language, gesture, and all manner of symbolic social sign. Though phenomenology sometimes appears to assume the existence of a choosing and constituting agent prior to language (who poses as the sole source of its constituting acts), there is also a more radical use of the doctrine of constitution that takes the social agent as an *object* rather than the subject of constitutive acts.

When Simone de Beauvoir claims, "one is not born, but, rather, *becomes* a woman," she is appropriating and reinterpreting this doctrine of constituting acts from the phenomenological tradition.[1] In this sense, gender is in no way a stable identity of locus of agency from which various acts proceed; rather, it is an identity tenuously constituted in time—an identity instituted through a stylized repetition of acts. Further, gender is instituted through the stylization of the body and, hence, must be understood as the mundane way in which bodily gestures, movements, and enactments of various kinds constitute the illusion of an abiding gendered self. This formulation moves the conception of gender off the ground of a substantial model of identity to one that requires a conception of a constituted *social temporality*. Significantly, if gender is instituted through acts which are internally discontinuous, then the *appearance of substance* is precisely that, a constructed identity, a performative accomplishment which the mundane social audience, including the actors themselves, come to believe and to perform in the mode of belief. If the ground of gender identity is the stylized repetition of acts through time, and not a seemingly seamless identity, then the possibilities of gender transformation are to be found in the arbitrary relation, between such acts, in the possibility of a different sort of repeating, in the breaking or subversive repetition of that style.

Through the conception of gender acts sketched above, I will try to show some ways in which reified and naturalized conceptions of gender might be understood as constituted and, hence, capable of being constituted differently. In opposition to theatrical or phenomenological models which take the gendered self to be prior to

its acts, I will understand constituting acts not only as constituting the identity of
the actor, but constituting that identity as a compelling illusion, an object of *belief*.
In the course of making my argument, I will draw from theatrical, anthropological,
and philosophical discourses, but mainly phenomenology, to show that what is
called gender identity is a performative accomplishment compelled by social sanction and taboo. In its very character as performative resides the possibility of contesting its reified status.

I. Sex/Gender: Feminist and Phenomenological Views

Feminist theory has often been critical of naturalistic explanations of sex and sexuality that assume that the meaning of women's social existence can be derived
from some fact of their physiology. In distinguishing sex from gender, feminist theorists have disputed causal explanations that assume that sex dictates or necessitates certain social meanings for women's experience. Phenomenological theories
of human embodiment have also been concerned to distinguish between the various physiological and biological causalities that structure bodily existence and the
meanings that embodied existence assumes in the context of lived experience. In
Merleau-Ponty's reflections in *The Phenomenology of Perception* on "the body in its
sexual being," he takes issue with such accounts of bodily experience and claims
that the body is "an historical idea" rather than "a natural species."[2] Significantly, it
is this claim that Simone de Beauvoir cites in *The Second Sex* when she sets the
stage for her claim that "woman," and by extension, any gender, is an historical situation rather than a natural fact.[3]

In both contexts, the existence and facticity of the material or natural dimensions of the body are not denied, but reconceived as distinct from the process by
which the body comes to bear cultural meanings. For both Beauvoir and Merleau-
Ponty, the body is understood to be an active process of embodying certain cultural and historical possibilities, a complicated process of appropriation which any
phenomenological theory of constitution needs to describe. In order to describe
the gendered body, a phenomenological theory of constitution requires an expansion of the conventional view of acts to mean both that which constitutes meaning
and that through which meaning is performed or enacted. In other words, the acts
by which gender is constituted bear similarities to performative acts within theatrical contexts. My task, then, is to examine in what ways gender is constructed
through specific corporeal acts, and what possibilities exist for the cultural transformation of gender through such acts.

Merleau-Ponty maintains not only that the body is an historical idea but a set
of possibilities to be continually realized. In claiming that the body is an historical
idea, Merleau-Ponty means that it gains its meaning through a concrete and historically mediated expression in the world. That the body is a set of possibilities
signifies (a) that its appearance in the world, for perception, is not predetermined
by some manner of interior essence, and (b) that its concrete expression in the
world must be understood as the taking up and rendering specific of a set of his-

torical possibilities. Hence, there is an agency which is understood as the process of rendering such possibilities determinate. These possibilities are necessarily constrained by available historical conventions. The body is not a self-identical or merely factic materiality; it is a materiality that bears meaning, if nothing else, and the manner of this bearing is fundamentally dramatic. By dramatic I mean only that the body is not merely matter but a continual and incessant *materialization* of possibilities. One is not simply a body, but, in some very key sense, one does one's body and, indeed, one does one's body differently from one's contemporaries and from one's embodied predecessors and successors as well.

It is, however, clearly unfortunate grammar to claim that there is a "we" or an "I" that does its body, as if a disembodied agency preceded and directed an embodied exterior. More appropriate, I suggest, would be a vocabulary that resists the substance metaphysics of subject-verb formations and relies instead on an ontology of present participles. The "I" that is its body is, of necessity, a mode of embodying, and the "what" that it embodies is possibilities. But here again the grammar of the formulation misleads, for the possibilities that are embodied are not fundamentally exterior or antecedent to the process of embodying itself. As an intentionally organized materiality, the body is always an embodying *of* possibilities both conditioned and circumscribed by historical convention. In other words, the body *is* a historical situation, as Beauvoir has claimed, and is a manner of doing, dramatizing, and *reproducing* a historical situation.

To do, to dramatize, to reproduce, these seem to be some of the elementary structures of embodiment. This doing of gender is not merely a way in which embodied agents are exterior, surfaced, open to the perception of others. Embodiment clearly manifests a set of strategies or what Sartre would perhaps have called a style of being or Foucault, "a stylistics of existence." This style is never fully self-styled, for living styles have a history, and that history conditions and limits possibilities. Consider gender, for instance, as *a corporeal style*, an "act," as it were, which is both intentional and performative, where "performative" itself carries the double-meaning of "dramatic" and "non-referential."

When Beauvoir claims that "woman" is a historical idea and not a natural fact, she clearly underscores the distinction between sex, as biological facticity, and gender, as the cultural interpretation or signification of that facticity. To be female is, according to that distinction, a facticity which has no meaning, but to be a woman is to have *become* a woman, to compel the body to conform to an historical idea of "woman," to induce the body to become a cultural sign, to materialize oneself in obedience to an historically delimited possibility, and to do this as a sustained and repeated corporeal project. The notion of a "project," however, suggests the originating force of a radical will, and because gender is a project which has cultural survival as its end, the term *"strategy"* better suggests the situation of duress under which gender performance always and variously occurs. Hence, as a strategy of survival, gender is a performance with clearly punitive consequences. Discrete genders are part of what "humanizes" individuals within contemporary culture; indeed, those who fail to do their gender right are regularly punished. Because there is neither an "essence" that gender expresses or externalizes nor an objective ideal to which gender aspires; because gender is not a fact, the various acts of gender, and without those acts would be no gender at all. Gender is, thus, a construction that regularly conceals its genesis. The tacit collective agreement to perform, produce, and sustain discrete and polar genders as cultural fictions is obscured by the credibility of its own production. The authors of gender become entranced by their own fictions whereby the construction compels one's belief in its necessity and naturalness. The historical possibilities materialized through various corporeal styles are nothing other than those punitively regulated cultural fictions that are alternately embodied and disguised under duress.

How useful is a phenomenological point of departure for a feminist description of gender? On the surface it appears that phenomenology shares with feminist analysis a commitment to grounding theory in lived experience, and in revealing the way in which the world is produced through the constituting acts of subjective experience. Clearly, not all feminist theory would privilege the point of view of the subject (Kristeva once objected to feminist theory as "too existentialist"),[4] and yet, the feminist claim that the personal is political suggests, in part, that subjective experience is not only structured by existing political arrangements, but effects and structures those arrangements in turn. Feminist theory has sought to understand the way in which systemic or pervasive political and cultural structures are enacted and reproduced through individual acts and practices, and how the analysis of ostensibly personal situations is clarified through situating the issues in a broader and shared cultural context. Indeed, the feminist impulse, and I am sure there is more than one, has often emerged in the recognition that my pain or my silence or my anger or my perception is finally not mine alone, and that it delimits me in a shared cultural situation which in turn enables and empowers me in certain unanticipated ways. The personal is thus implicitly political inasmuch as it is conditioned by shared social structures, but the personal has also been immunized against political challenge to the extent that public/private distinctions endure. For feminist theory, then, the personal becomes an expansive category, one which accommodates, if only implicitly, political structures usually viewed as public. Indeed, the very meaning of the political expands as well. At its best, feminist theory involves a dialectical expansion of both of these categories. My situation does not cease to be mine just because it is the situation of someone else, and my acts, individual as they are, nevertheless reproduce the situation of my gender, and do that in various ways. In other words, there is, latent in the personal is political formulation of feminist theory, a supposition that the life-world of gender relations is constituted, at least partially, through the concrete and historically mediated *acts* of individuals. Considering that "the" body is invariably transformed into his body or her body, the body is only known through its gendered appearance. It would seem imperative to consider the way in which this gendering of the body occurs. My suggestion is that the body becomes its gender through a series of acts which are renewed, revised, and consolidated through time. From a feminist point of view, one might try to reconceive the gendered body as the legacy of sedimented acts rather than a predetermined or foreclosed structure, essence or fact, whether natural, cultural, or linguistic.

The feminist appropriation of the phenomenological theory of constitution might employ the notion of an *act* in a richly ambiguous sense. If the personal is a category which expands to include the wider political and social structures, then the *acts* of the gendered subject would be similarly expansive. Clearly, there are political acts which are deliberate and instrumental actions of political organizing, resistance, and collective intervention with the broad aim of instating a more just set of social and political relations. There are thus acts which are done in the name of women, and then there are acts in and of themselves, apart from any instrumental consequence, that challenge the category of women itself. Indeed, one ought to consider the futility of a political program which seeks radically to transform the social situation of women without first determining whether the category of woman is socially constructed in such a way that to be a woman is, by definition, to be in an oppressed situation. In an understandable desire to forge bonds of solidarity, feminist discourse has often relied upon the category of woman as a universal presupposition of cultural experience which, in its universal status, provides a false ontological promise of eventual political solidarity. In a culture in which the false universal of "man" has for the most part been presupposed as coextensive with humanness itself, feminist theory has sought with success to bring female specificity into visibility and to rewrite the history of culture in terms which acknowledge the presence, the influence, and the oppression of women. Yet, in this effort to combat the invisibility of women as a category, feminists run the risk of rendering visible a category which may or may not be representative of the concrete lives of women. As feminists, we have been less eager, I think, to consider the status of the category itself and, indeed, to discern the conditions of oppression which issue from an unexamined reproduction of gender identities which sustain discrete and binary categories of man and woman.

When Beauvoir claims that woman is an "historical situation," she emphasizes that the body suffers a certain cultural construction, not only through conventions that sanction and proscribe how one acts one's body, the "act" or performance that one's body is, but also in the tacit conventions that structure the way the body is culturally perceived. Indeed, if gender is the cultural significance that the sexed body assumes, and if that significance is codetermined through various acts and their cultural perception, then it would appear that from within the terms of culture it is not possible to know sex as distinct from gender. The reproduction of the category of gender is enacted on a large political scale, as when women first enter a profession or gain certain rights, or are reconceived in legal or political discourse in significantly new ways. But the more mundane reproduction of gendered identity takes place through the various ways in which bodies are acted in relationship to the deeply entrenched or sedimented expectations of gendered existence. Consider that there is a sedimentation of gender norms that produces the peculiar phenomenon of a natural sex, or a real woman, or any number of prevalent and compelling social fictions, and that this is a sedimentation that over time has produced a set of corporeal styles which, in reified form, appear as the natural configuration of bodies into sexes which exist in a binary relation to one another.

II. Binary Genders and the Heterosexual Contract

To guarantee the reproduction of a given culture, various requirements, well-established in the anthropological literature of kinship, have instated sexual reproduction within the confines of a heterosexually-based system of marriage which requires the reproduction of human beings in certain gendered modes which, in effect, guarantee the eventual reproduction of that kinship system. As Foucault and others have pointed out, the association of a natural sex with a discrete gender and with an ostensibly natural "attraction" to the opposing sex/gender is an unnatural conjunction of cultural constructs in the service of reproductive interests.[5] Feminist cultural anthropology and kinship studies have shown how cultures are governed by conventions that not only regulate and guarantee the production, exchange, and consumption of material goods, but also reproduce the bonds of kinship itself, which require taboos and a punitive regulation or reproduction to effect that end. Levi-Strauss has shown how the incest taboo works to guarantee the channeling of sexuality into various modes of heterosexual marriage.[6] Gayle Rubin has argued convincingly that the incest taboo produces certain kinds of discrete gendered identities and sexualities.[7] My point is simply that one way in which this system of compulsory heterosexuality is reproduced and concealed is through the cultivation of bodies into discrete sexes with "natural" appearances and "natural" heterosexual dispositions. Although the enthnocentric conceit suggests a progression beyond the mandatory structures of kinship relations as described by Levi-Strauss, I would suggest, along with Rubin, that contemporary gender identities are so many marks or "traces" of residual kinship. The contention that sex, gender, and heterosexuality are historical products which have become conjoined and reified as natural over time has received a good deal of critical attention not only from Michel Foucault, but Monique Wittig, gay historians, and various cultural anthropologists and social psychologists in recent years.[8] These theories, however, still lack the critical resources for thinking radically about the historical sedimentation of sexuality and sex-related constructs if they do not delimit and describe the mundane manner in which these constructs are produced, reproduced, and maintained within the field of bodies.

Can phenomenology assist a feminist reconstruction of the sedimented character of sex, gender, and sexuality at the level of the body? In the first place, the phenomenological focus on the various acts by which cultural identity is constituted and assumed provides a felicitous starting point for the feminist effort to understand the mundane manner in which bodies get crafted into genders. The formulation of the body as a mode of dramatizing or enacting possibilities offers a way to understand how a cultural convention is embodied and enacted. But it seems difficult, if not impossible, to imagine a way to conceptualize the scale and systemic character of women's oppression from a theoretical position which takes constituting acts to be its point of departure. Although individual acts do work to maintain and reproduce systems of oppression, and, indeed, any theory of personal political responsibility presupposes such a view, it doesn't follow that oppression is a sole consequence of such acts. One might argue that without human beings whose various acts, largely construed, produce and maintain oppressive conditions, those conditions would fall away, but note that the relation between acts and conditions is neither unilateral nor unmediated. There are social contexts and conventions within which certain acts not only become possible but become conceivable as acts at all. The transformation of social relations becomes a matter, then, of transforming hegemonic social conditions rather than the individual acts that are spawned by those conditions. Indeed, one runs the risk of addressing the merely indirect, if not epiphenomenal, reflection of those conditions if one remains restricted to a politics of acts.

But the theatrical sense of an "act" forces a revision of the individualist assumptions underlying the more restricted view of constituting acts within phenomenological discourse. As a given temporal duration within the entire performance, "acts" are a shared experience and "collective action." Just as within feminist theory the very category of the personal is expanded to include political structures, so is there a theatrically-based and, indeed, less individually-oriented view of acts that goes some of the way in defusing the criticism of act theory as "too existentialist." The act that gender is, the act that embodied agents *are* inasmuch as they dramatically and actively embody and, indeed, *wear* certain cultural significations, is clearly not one's act alone. Surely, there are nuanced and individual ways of *doing* one's gender, but *that* one does it, and that one does it in *accord with* certain sanctions and proscriptions, is clearly not a fully individual matter. Here again, I don't mean to minimize the effect of certain gender norms which originate within the family and are enforced through certain familial modes of punishment and reward and which, as a consequence, might be construed as highly individual, for even there family relations recapitulate, individualize, and specify preexisting cultural relations; they are rarely, if ever, radically original. The act that one does, the act that one performs, is, in a sense, an act that has been going on before one arrived on the scene. Hence, gender is an act which has been rehearsed, much as a script survives the particular actors who make use of it, but which requires individual actors in order to be actualized and reproduced as reality once again. The complex components that go into an act must be distinguished in order to understand the kind of acting in concert and acting in accord which acting one's gender invariably is.

In what senses, then, is gender an act? As anthropologist Victor Turner suggests in his studies of ritual social drama, social action requires a performance which is *repeated*. This repetition is at once a reenactment and reexperiencing of a set of meanings already socially established; it is the mundane and ritualized form of their legitimation.[9] When this conception of social performance is applied to gender, it is clear that although there are individual bodies that enact these significations by becoming stylized into gendered modes, this "action" is immediately public as well. There are temporal and collective dimensions to these actions, and their public nature is not inconsequential; indeed, the performance is effected with the strategic aim of maintaining gender within its binary frame. Understood in pedagogical terms, the performance renders social laws explicit.

As a public action and performative act, gender is not a radical choice or project that reflects a merely individual choice, but neither is it imposed or inscribed upon the individual, as some post-structuralist displacements of the subject would contend. The body is not passively scripted with cultural codes, as if it were a lifeless recipient of wholly pregiven cultural relations. But neither do embodied selves preexist the cultural conventions which essentially signify bodies. Actors are always already on the stage, within the terms of the performance. Just as a script may be enacted in various ways, and just as the play requires both text and interpretation, so the gendered body acts its part in a culturally restricted corporeal space and enacts interpretations within the confines of already existing directives.

Although the links between a theatrical and a social role are complex and the distinctions not easily drawn (Bruce Wilshire points out the limits of the comparison in *Role-Playing and Identity: The Limits of Theatre as Metaphor*),[10] it seems clear that, although theatrical performances can meet with political censorship and scathing criticism, gender performances in nontheatrical contexts are governed by more clearly punitive and regulatory social conventions. Indeed, the sight of a transvestite onstage can compel pleasure and applause while the sight of the same transvestite on the seat next to us on the bus can compel fear, rage, even violence. The conventions which mediate proximity and identification in these two instances are clearly quite different. I want to make two different kinds of claims regarding this tentative distinction. In the theatre, one can say, "this is just an act," and de-realize the act, make acting into something quite distinct from what is real. Because of this distinction, one can maintain one's sense of reality in the face of this temporary challenge to our existing ontological assumptions about gender arrangements; the various conventions which announce that "this is only a play" allows strict lines to be drawn between the performance and life. On the street or in the bus, the act becomes dangerous, if it does, precisely because there are no theatrical conventions to delimit the purely imaginary character of the act, indeed, on the street or in the bus, there is no presumption that the act is distinct from a reality; the disquieting effect of the act is that there are no conventions that facilitate making this separation. Clearly, there is theatre which attempts to contest or, indeed, break down those conventions that demarcate the imaginary from the real (Richard Schechner brings this out quite clearly in *Between Theatre and Anthropology*).[11] Yet in those cases one confronts the same phenomenon, namely, that the act is not contrasted with the real, but *constitutes* a reality that is in some sense new, a modality of gender that cannot readily be assimilated into the preexisting categories that regulate gender reality. From the point of view of those established categories, one may want to claim, but oh, this is *really* a girl or a woman, or this is *really* a boy or a man, and further that the *appearance* contradicts the *reality* of the gender, that the discrete and familiar reality must be there, nascent, temporarily unrealized, perhaps realized at other times or other places. The transvestite, however, can do more than simply express the distinction between sex and gender, but challenges, at least implicitly, the distinction between appearance and reality that structures a good deal of popular thinking about gender identity. If the "reality" of gender is constituted by the performance itself, then there is no recourse to an essential and unrealized "sex" or "gender" which gender performances ostensibly express. Indeed, the transvestite's gender is as fully real as anyone whose performance complies with social expectations.

Gender reality is performative which means, quite simply, that it is real only to the extent that it is performed. It seems fair to say that certain kinds of acts are usually interpreted as expressive of a gender core or identity, and that these acts either conform to an expected gender identity or contest that expectation in some way. That expectation, in turn, is based upon the perception of sex, where sex is understood to be the discrete and *factic datum* of primary sexual characteristics. This implicit and popular theory of acts and gestures as *expressive* of gender suggests that gender itself is something prior to the various acts, postures, and gestures by which it is dramatized and known; indeed, gender appears to the popular imagination as a substantial core which might well be understood as the spiritual or psychological correlate of biological sex.[12] If gender attributes, however, are not expressive but performative, then these attributes effectively constitute the identity they are said to express or reveal. The distinction between expression and performativeness is quite crucial, for if gender attributes and acts, the various ways in which a body shows or produces its cultural signification, are performative, then there is no preexisting identity by which an act or attribute might be measured; there would be no true or false, real or distorted acts of gender, and the postulation of a true gender identity would be revealed as a regulatory fiction. That gender reality is created through sustained social performances means that the very notions of an essential sex, a true or abiding masculinity or femininity, are also constituted as part of the strategy by which the performative aspect of gender is concealed.

As a consequence, gender cannot be understood as a *role* which either expresses or disguises an interior "self," whether that "self" is conceived as sexed or not. As performance which is performative, gender is an "act," broadly construed, which constructs the social fiction of its own psychological interiority. As opposed to a view such as Erving Goffman's which posits a self which assumes and exchanges various "roles" within the complex social expectations of the "game" of modern life,[13] I am suggesting that this self is not only irretrievably "outside," constituted in social discourse, but that the ascription of interiority is itself a publicly regulated and sanctioned form of essence fabrication. Genders, then, can be neither true nor false, neither real nor apparent. And yet, one is compelled to live in a world in which genders constitute univocal signifiers, in which gender is stabilized, polarized, rendered discrete and intractable. In effect, gender is made to comply with a model of truth and falsity which not only contradicts its own performative fluidity, but serves a social policy of gender regulation and control. Performing one's gender wrong initiates a set of punishments both obvious and indirect, and performing it well provides the reassurance that there is an essentialism of gender identity after all. That this reassurance is so easily displaced by anxiety, that culture so readily punishes or marginalizes those who fail to perform the illusion of gender essentialism should be sign enough that on some level there is social knowledge that the truth or falsity of gender is only socially compelled and in no sense ontologically necessitated.[14]

III. Feminst Theory: Beyond an Expressive Model of Gender

This view of gender does not pose as a comprehensive theory about what gender is or the manner of its construction, and neither does it prescribe an explicit feminist political program. Indeed, I can imagine this view of gender being used for a number of discrepant political strategies. Some of my friends may fault me for this and insist that any theory of gender constitution has political presuppositions and implications, and that it is impossible to separate a theory of gender from a political philosophy of feminism. In fact, I would agree, and argue that it is primarily political interests which create the social phenomena of gender itself, and that without a radical critique of gender constitution, feminist theory fails to take stock of the way in which oppression structures the ontological categories through which gender is conceived. Gayatri Spivak has argued that feminists need to rely on an operational essentialism, a false ontology of women as a universal in order to advance a feminist political program.[15] She knows that the category of "women" is not fully expressive, that the multiplicity and discontinuity of the referent mocks and rebels against the univocity of the sign, but suggests it could be used for strategic purposes. Kristeva suggests something similar, I think, when she prescribes that feminists use the category of women as a political tool without attributing ontological integrity to the term, and adds that, strictly speaking, women cannot be said to exist.[16] Feminists might well worry about the political implications of claiming that women do not exist, especially in light of the persuasive arguments advanced by Mary Anne Warren in her book, *Gendercide.*[17] She argues that social policies regarding population control and reproductive technology are designed to limit and, at times, eradicate the existence of women altogether. In light of such a claim, what good does it do to quarrel about the metaphysical status of the term, and perhaps, for clearly political reasons, feminists ought to silence the quarrel altogether.

But it is one thing to use the term and know its ontological insufficiency and quite another to articulate a normative vision for feminist theory which celebrates or emancipates an essence, a nature, or a shared reality which cannot be found. The option I am defending is not to redescribe the world from the point of view of women. I don't know what that point of view is, but whatever it is, it is not singular, and not mine to espouse. It would only be half-right to claim that I am interested in how the phenomenon of a men's or women's point of view gets constituted, for while I do think that those points of views are, indeed, socially constituted, and that a reflexive genealogy of those points of view is important to do, it is not primarily the gender episteme that I am interested in exposing, deconstructing, or reconstructing. Indeed, it is the presupposition of the category of "woman" itself that requires a critical genealogy of the complex institutional and discursive means by which it is constituted. Although some feminist literary critics suggest that the presupposition of sexual difference is necessary for all discourse, that position reifies sexual difference as the founding moment of culture and precludes an analysis not only of how sexual difference is constituted to begin with but how it is continuously constituted, both by the masculine tradition that preempts the universal point of view, and by those feminist positions that construct the univocal category of "women" in the name of expressing or, indeed, liberating a subjected class. As Foucault claimed about those humanist efforts to liberate the criminalized subject, the subject that is freed is even more deeply shackled than originally thought.[18]

Clearly, though, I envision the critical genealogy of gender to rely on a phenomenological set of presuppositions, most important among them the expanded conception of an "act" which is both socially shared and historically constituted, and which is performative in the sense I previously described. But a critical genealogy needs to be supplemented by a politics of performative gender acts, one which both redescribes existing gender identities and offers a prescriptive view about the kind of gender reality there ought to be. The redescription needs to expose the reifications that tacitly serve as substantial gender cores or identities, and to elucidate both the act and the strategy of disavowal which at once constitute and conceal gender as we live it. The prescription is invariably more difficult, if only because we need to think a world in which acts, gestures, the visual body, the clothed body, the various physical attributes usually associated with gender, *express nothing*. In a sense, the prescription is not utopian, but consists in an imperative to acknowledge the existing complexity of gender which our vocabulary invariably disguises and to bring that complexity into a dramatic cultural interplay without punitive consequences.

Certainly, it remains politically important to represent women, but to do that in a way that does not distort and reify the very collectivity the theory is supposed to emancipate. Feminist theory which presupposes sexual difference as the necessary and invariant theoretical point of departure clearly improves upon those humanist discourses which conflate the universal with the masculine and appropriate all of culture as masculine property. Clearly, it is necessary to reread the texts of western philosophy from the various points of view that have been excluded, not only to reveal the particular perspective and set of interests informing those ostensibly transparent descriptions of the real, but to offer alternative descriptions and prescriptions; indeed, to establish philosophy as a cultural practice, and to criticize its tenets from marginalized cultural locations. I have no quarrel with this procedure, and have clearly benefited from those analyses. My only concern is that sexual difference not become a reification which unwittingly preserves a binary restriction on gender identity and an implicitly heterosexual framework for the description of gender, gender identity, and sexuality. There is, in my view, nothing about femaleness that is waiting to be expressed; there is, on the other hand, a good deal about the diverse experiences of women that is being expressed and still needs to be expressed, but caution is needed with respect to that theoretical language, for it does not simply report a prelinguistic experience, but constructs that experience as well as the limits of its analysis. Regardless of the pervasive character of patriarchy and the prevalence of sexual difference as an operative cultural distinction, there is nothing about a binary gender system that is given. As a corporeal field of cultural play, gender is a basically innovative affair, although it is quite clear that there are strict punishments for contesting the script by performing out of turn or through unwarranted improvisation. Gender is not passively scripted on the body, and neither is it determined by nature, language, the symbolic, or the overwhelming history of patriarchy. Gender is what is put on, invariably, under constraint, daily and incessantly, with anxiety and pleasure, but if this continuous act is mistaken for a natural or linguistic given, power is relinquished to expand the cultural field bodily through subversive performances of various kinds.

Notes

1. For a further discussion of Beauvoir's feminist contribution to phenomenological theory, see my "Variations on Sex and Gender: *Beauvoir's The Second Sex*," *Yale French Studies* 172 (1986) .
2. Maurice Merleau-Ponty, "The Body in its Sexual Being," in *The Phenomenology of Perception*, trans. Colin Smith (Boston: Routledge and Kegan Paul, 1962).
3. Simone de Beauvoir, *The Second Sex*, trans. H. M. Parshley (New York: Vintage, 1974), p. 38.
4. Julia Kristeva, *Histoire d'amour* (Paris: Editions Denoel, 1983), p. 242.
5. See Michel Foucault, *The History of Sexuality: An Introduction*, trans. Robert Hurley (New York: Random House, 1980), p. 154: "the notion of 'sex' made it possible to group together, in an artificial unity, anatomical elements, biological functions, conducts, sensations, and pleasures, and it enabled one to make use of this fictitious unity as a causal principle."
6. See Claude Levi-Strauss, *The Elementary Structures of Kinship* (Boston: Beacon, 1965).
7. Gayle Rubin, "The Traffic in Women: Notes on the 'Political Economy' of Sex," in *Toward an Anthropology of Women*, ed. Rayna R. Reiter (New York: Monthly Review Press, 1975), pp. 178–85.
8. See my "Variations on Sex and Gender: Beauvoir, Wittig, and Foucault," in *Feminism as Critique*, ed. Seyla Benhabib and Drucila Cornell (London: Basil Blackwell, 1987 [distributed by the University of Minnesota Press]).
9. See Victor Turner, *Dramas, Fields, and Metaphors* (Ithaca: Cornell University Press, 1974). Clifford Geertz suggests in "Blurred Genres: The Refiguration of Thought," in *Local Knowledge: Further Essays in Interpretive Anthropology* (New York: Basic, 1983), that the theatrical metaphor is used by recent social theory in two, often opposing, ways. Ritual theorists like Victor Turner focus on a notion of social drama of various kinds as a means for settling internal conflicts within a culture and regenerating social cohesion. On the other hand, symbolic action approaches, influenced by figures as diverse as Emile Durkheim, Kenneth Burke, and Michel Foucault, focus on the way in which political authority and questions of legitimation are thematized and settled within the terms of performed meaning. Geertz himself suggests that the tension might be viewed dialectically; his study of political organization in Bali as a "theatre-state" is a case in point. In terms of an explicitly feminist account of gender as performative, it seems clear to me that an account of gender as ritualized, public performance must be combined with an analysis of the political sanctions and taboos under which that performance may and may not occur within the public sphere free of punitive consequence.

10. Bruce Wilshire, *Role-Playing and Identity: The Limits of Theatre as Metaphor* (Boston: Routledge and Kegan Paul, 1981).

11. Richard Schechner, *Between Theatre and Anthropology* (Philadelphia: University of Pennsylvania Press, 1985). See especially, "News, Sex, and Performance," pp. 295–324.

12. In *Mother Camp: Female Impersonators in America* (Englewood Cliffs, NJ: Prentice-Hall, 1972), Anthropologist Esther Newton gives an urban ethnography of drag queens in which she suggests that all gender might be understood on the model of drag. In *Gender: An Ethnomethodological Approach* (Chicago: University of Chicago Press, 1978), Suzanne J. Kessler and Wendy McKenna argue that gender is an "accomplishment" which requires the skills of constructing the body into a socially legitimate artifice.

13. See Erving Goffmann, *The Presentation of Self in Everyday Life* (Garden City, NY: Doubleday, 1959).

14. See Michel Foucault's edition of *Herculine Barbin: The Journals of a Nineteenth Century French Hermaphrodite*, trans. Richard McDougall (New York: Pantheon, 1984), for an interesting display of the horror evoked by intersexed bodies. Foucault's introduction makes clear that the medical delimitation of univocal sex is yet another wayward application of the discourse on truth-as-identity. See also the work of Robert Edgerton in *American Anthropologist* on the cross-cultural variations of response to hermaphroditic bodies.

15. Remarks at the Center for Humanities, Wesleyan University, Spring, 1985.

16. Julia Kristeva, "Woman Can Never Be Defined," trans. Marilyn A. August, in *New French Feminisms*, ed. Elaine Marks and Isabelle de Courtivron (New York: Schocken, 1981).

17. Mary Anne Warren, *Gendercide: The Implications of Sex Selection* (New Jersey: Rowman and Allanheld, 1985).

18. Ibid.; Michel Foucault, *Discipline and Punish: The Birth of the Prison*, trans. Alan Sheridan (New York: Vintage, 1978).

39.
A TALE OF TWO FEMINISMS: POWER AND VICTIMIZATION IN CONTEMPORARY FEMINIST DEBATE
Carolyn Sorisio

We have heard the old tale—how Betty Friedan's *The Feminine Mystique* brushed against a generation of women's lips with a hard kiss, waking Adrienne Rich's dead. The feminist movement of the 1960s and 1970s brought tangible change. In my field of feminist literary criticism, the newly resurrected struggled for representation of women writers in the curriculum and a better understanding of women in history. Thinkers as diverse as Héléne Cixous and the team of Sandra M. Gilbert and Susan Gubar held one common assumption—"woman" was a category that merited serious scrutiny; it was a word with weight. Yet now we hear another tale. We are postfeminist. Women don't want to call themselves the "f" word. Heavily influenced by the Reagan-Bush years, young Americans "completely recoil at anything too militant, too angry, too extremist."[1] Worse yet, feminism is cast as a tragic hero crafting its own demise. A monolithic "we" considers women passive victims of male sexual and economic violence. "We" have deployed a "fem police" that regulates the thoughts, sexuality, and choices of women in the name of equality.[2] Our dogma is stale, our ideology rigid, our fashion tastes hopelessly passé.

Although by no means uniform, much of the criticism aimed at feminism in the media for the past several years focuses on a few points of contention. First, feminists are charged with prescribing "correct" forms of feminine behavior, especially in relation to sexuality. Sally Quinn, in the *Washington Post*, contends that feminist leaders are not able "to separate the work place from the bedroom" and want "to regulate people's behavior in their personal lives."[3] Second, white, middle-class feminists allegedly revel in their self-imposed status of victims. For example, Wendy Kaminer pauses before reviewing Katie Roiphe's *The Morning After: Rape, Fear, and Feminism on Campus* to explain that the "expression of oppression" is a general rule in feminism. "Protesting their sexual victimization enables privileged, heterosexual white women to claim a share of the moral high ground ceded to the victims of racism, classism, and homophobia," she maintains.[4]

Even more severe sins are laid at academic feminists' feet. We are denounced as rigidly dogmatic and irreparably esoteric. Writers refer to a sinister "sisterhood" that controls dissent and, ever conspiratorial, wields unprecedented power. Daphne Patai claimed in 1992 that women of color controlled the women's studies department at the University of Massachusetts at Amherst, despite the fact that she was then its acting director. She writes in the *Chronicle of Higher Education* that "as if in compensation for past oppression, no one can challenge or gainsay their version of reality."[5] Christina Hoff Sommers, author of *Who Stole Feminism: How Women Have Betrayed Women*, caricatures women's studies as impossibly trite. Nonetheless, she accuses an allegedly potent feminist clique of manipulating information about rape, sexual harassment, gender bias, and other women's issues. "The steady stream of errors, myths and screw-ups are not accidental" she told a crowd of undergraduates.[6] Denying any common ground, she informed the *Washington Post* that "The thing is, we're not a tribe. We're not a class. We do not have a shared vision."[7]

If not downright conspiratorial, academic feminists are nonetheless characterized as out of touch, confining ourselves to a realm of theory with no tangible significance in either the political or the personal sphere. A columnist in the *New York Times* chides, "try telling a welfare mother or a harried secretary that they should worry about being a victim of the unconscious process of phallocentric language."[8] Naomi Wolf thinks American female feminists seize on poststructural French feminist thought, as if to prove that we are as complex as many male intellectuals. "Here's something of our own that's just as hard," she imagines academics reasoning. "We'll teach it to our own kids, and no one will know what *we're* talking about either."[9]

In the 1980s and 1990s, feminism has become a paradox. On the one hand, it is perceived as so powerful that it has initiated a backlash, as is evidenced by the now truly banal "political correctness" wars. In this framework, women and people of color are awarded far more power than they actually exert. On the other hand, Susan Faludi's *Backlash: The Undeclared War against American Women* (1991) reveals the somber truth that, contrary to perception, women in the 1980s suffered major economic, legal, and cultural setbacks.[10] In my field on a national level, women writers and writers of color are not being included, beyond a few tokens, in the majority of classes.[11] Is it possible that feminism has become Virginia Woolf's Mrs. Ramsay? Is it so ubiquitous as to be diffused?

This is a depressing conclusion. Unlike so many women of my generation who the media tells me have disowned feminism, I have always considered myself a feminist. And unlike the women who unwittingly depict themselves as victims of an allegedly victim-producing movement, I consider feminism a quest that we continually redefine, rather than a doctrine that seeks to confine me. The question translates, for me, into what feminist scholarship is doing for women in general. I take the charges against academic feminists earnestly. However, it is too facile to dismiss theoretical sophistication as irrelevant to women's progress and to imply that feminism should somehow be anti-intellectual. . . . Movements can take many forms, and although theory may not translate directly or perceivably into material gains, it has a role to play. Nonetheless, I am concerned that academics all too often talk only within our own circle, and need to make a more concerted effort to participate as clearly as possible in cultural debate.

The charges against both academic and mainstream feminism deserve serious consideration. Three recently published books raise concerns that also surface in the media: Katie Roiphe's *The Morning After: Sex, Fear, and Feminism on Campus* (1993), Naomi Wolf's *Fire with Fire: The New Female Power and How It Will Change the Twenty-First Century* (1993), and Camille Paglia's *Sex, Art, and American Culture* (1992).[12] These three women obtained considerable attention in the 1990s, and all contribute to the debate about victimization, dogmatic rigidity, and theoretical obscurity. By examining the relationship between popular feminist critique and issues within contemporary feminist scholarship, I hope to help bridge the gap between the two and to suggest ways in which academic feminists can best serve contemporary causes.[13]

Katie Roiphe's 1991 *New York Times* column "Date Rape Hysteria"[14] set off a wave of media attention and spawned *The Morning After*. Roiphe argues that white middle- and upper-class feminists have exaggerated incidents of date rape and sexual harassment to secure precocious power through victim identity. Although she spends some space challenging statistics about the number of sex crimes on campuses, Roiphe is more concerned with evaluating rhetoric. Describing a "Take Back the Night" rally at Princeton, Roiphe concludes that "there is strength in numbers, and unfortunately right now there is strength in being the most oppressed," (44). She interprets educational materials as regressing to Victorian ideas of the passionless woman. "Again and again," she charges, "the rape-crisis movement peddles images of gender relations that deny female desires and infantilize women," (65). By overstating the prevalence of sex offenses, feminists debilitate women by fostering an environment of fear. It is not rape or harassment, but rather the feminist response to these practices, that frightens this young champion of individual agency. Likewise, it is not sexual harassment that creates a "chilly" atmosphere for women on campus, but rather feminist surveillance of professors' actions. She charges feminists with generating "an atmosphere of suspicion and distrust" that "can lead professors to keep female students at a distance," (92–93).

Like her younger counterpart, the self-proclaimed heir of the 1960s, Camille Paglia, also accuses mainstream feminism of wallowing in victimization:

> Never in history have women been freer than they are here. And this idea, this bitching, bitching, kvetching about capitalism and America and men, this whining—it's infantile, it's an adolescent condition, it's *bad* for women. It's very, very bad to convince young women that they have been victims and that their heritage is nothing but victimization. (274)

Also similar to Roiphe, Paglia expends her greatest energy on her analysis of feminism and sexuality, calling for a new kind of feminism "that stresses personal responsibility and is open to art and sex in all their dark, unconsoling mysteries," (vii). Paglia gained national media attention for her outlandish claims, such as suggesting that date rape was really the result of "white middle-class girls coming out of pampered homes, expecting to do whatever they want," and then crying victim when they are attacked (268). She also smacks of primitivism, portraying working-class and ethnic women as celebrating the rawness of their culture. "Everyone knows throughout the world," Paglia asserts in her characteristically sweeping way, "that many of these working-class relationships where women get beat up have hot sex. . . . Maybe she won't leave him because the sex is very hot," (65).

Paglia's attack on the academy contains similar generalizations. Repeatedly, she portrays women's studies as slapped together haphazardly, as a "disaster" that should be eliminated (281–82). Yet she fires her heaviest artillery at the French, particularly at Jacques Lacan and his "overpraised feminist propagandists Hélène Cixous and Luce Irigaray." In a front-page 1991 *New York Times Book Review* essay, Paglia rebukes American academics for being "down on their knees kissing French egos." Not one for wasting time on theoretical specification, Paglia assesses French theory: "Of course the French felt decentered: they had just been crushed by Germany." Ever the tourist in "exotic" cultures, Paglia juxtaposes the intellectually deadened French to African American culture, which, presumably in a sort of preintellectual libidinal state, is "alive and ecstatic."[15]

Although both Roiphe and Paglia critique victimization, they have opposite beliefs about the origin of gendered behavior. Roiphe does not want to reduce identity to biology. Therefore, her sharpest assault is on Catharine MacKinnon, whom she accuses of presenting essentialist notions of identity. In MacKinnon's worldview, Roiphe charges, "men and women are inexorably locked into their roles," (158). Paglia's work is informed by the antithetical belief; she contends that men are physiologically more aggressive than women. "Hunt, pursuit, and capture are biologically programmed into male sexuality," she argues (51). Complaining that no one wants to talk about nature, Paglia laments the "contempt for science" that is going on in the humanities and charges feminists with ignoring biological difference (258).

Wolf's *Fire with Fire*, which is better researched and better argued than Roiphe's and Paglia's work, also advocates "power feminism" rather than "victim feminism." Wolf concedes that the image of feminism generated by the male-run media estranges many women but she concentrates on what she sees as alienating aspects within feminism itself (60). The secret to women's success—one she believes many feminists have ignored—lies in women knowing how to end their own victimization and claim power. "Women are suffering from much subordination for no more pressing reason than that we have stopped short of compelling it to end," she suggests in an optimistically willful way (50–51). The answer? Wolf urges women to do three things: "to fantasize political retribution for an insult to sex, to claim and use money, and to imagine and enjoy winning" (36).

Like Roiphe and Paglia, Wolf also maintains that feminism restricts sexuality, creating "an elaborate vocabulary with which to describe sexual harm done by men, but almost no vocabulary in which a woman can celebrate sex with men," (184). Wolf proceeds to "come clean" with her "subjective truth": "I am sick of the opposition trying to make me choose between being sexual and serious; and I am sick of being split the same way by victim feminism. I want to be a serious thinker and not have to hide the fact that I have breasts; I want female sexuality to accompany, rather than undermine, female political power" (185). Except for her references to Andrea Dworkin, who hardly speaks for all feminists, Wolf is never clear as to how her socially sanctioned heterosexuality has been silenced. Yet her "subjective truth" is still a serious accusation; the movement that embraced sexual liberation is now being accused of silencing, even policing, sexuality.

More important to Wolf's argument than her heterosexual confessions is her critique of Marxist feminism, which she depicts as pathetically 1960s. Although Marxism once usefully linked issues of gender, money, and power, its hangover now results in "victim feminism." "These attitudes, which are passé now almost everywhere else in the world, are foolish burdens to carry," Wolf explains (68). "Power feminism," as defined by Wolf, makes capital the primary means of solidarity among women: "It calls for alliances based on economic self-interest and economic giving back rather than on a sentimental and workable fantasy of cosmic sisterhood" (53). Claiming "there is no more 'radical' system imaginable than the one we have inherited," Wolf encourages women to expand American liberal democratic ideology (115). Capitalism and individualism can be radical, and women must learn "to ask for more, always more" (243). By rejecting what she calls the "sentimental" and endorsing capitalistic individualism, Wolf effectively dismisses any feminist critique of American national identity. This stance is particularly troublesome, as it ignores the negative impact on women in other nations when American women seek "more, always more" of the world's resources....

By refusing to name the feminist theorists she implicates or to analyze their ideas seriously, Roiphe creates an inaccurately monolithic portrayal of what is a very complex, dynamic, and contentious field. She repeats the common pattern of replacing specific people and arguments with the all-encompassing category "feminists." Wolf, a Yale graduate, is also suspect for her "subjective truths." Reading both books, I get the unsettling feeling that, much like the 1970s feminist work they implicitly rebel against, both Roiphe and Wolf extrapolate too readily from their personal experiences to comment on feminism in general. Contrary to what they imply, all of America does not follow the Ivy League.

Nonetheless, the challenges they pose must be addressed. The charge of "victim feminism" seems to have generated the most attention. To attribute this recognition solely to an antifeminist backlash ignores other aspects crucial to the debate. Let's be clear here. The language of "victimization," much like "political correctness" several years ago, has been co-opted for a political agenda that goes far beyond gender. Critiques of "victim feminism" appeal to the myth of rugged individualism, the belief that anyone can overcome obstacles and succeed in American society. Pouring historically exploited groups into one victimization mold enables some Americans to disclaim any debt we may have as citizens who greatly benefit from gender, class, and race inequity. It obscures the true dynamics of power and absolves responsibility....

Perceiving gender as the primary identity marker led many scholars to ignore race, class, and cultural differences that are not incidental but absolutely essential to feminism. In a sense, Roiphe, Paglia, and Wolf correctly call "victim feminism" harmful. However, it is not for the reasons they explore. Rather, it is injurious because it allows white bourgeois women to inaccurately absorb others' experiences into their own, to force them into a rhetoric of "sisterhood" or a category of "woman" that may not adequately describe different women's experiences. bell hooks makes this argument in her *Feminist Theory: From Margin to Center* (1984). She contends that bonding as victims allows white women to avoid confronting their responsibility for sexism, racism, and classism.[16] She maintains:

> A central tenet of modern feminist thought has been the assertion that "all women are oppressed."... Sexism as a system of domination is institutionalized but it has never determined in an absolute way the fate of all women in this society.... Many women in this society do have choices (as inadequate as they are)[;] therefore exploitation and discrimination are words that more accurately describe the lot of women collectively in the United States.[17]

hooks suggests that one of the reasons many black women do not identify themselves as feminists is the tendency of white middle-class women to cling to a theory of common oppression. She argues that women who are exploited or oppressed daily cannot afford to relinquish the belief that they exercise some measure of control, however relative, over their lives. It would be psychologically demoralizing for these women to bond with other women on the basis of shared victimization.[18]

hooks's critique of feminism is powerful, on the mark, and clearly stated. Yet you won't find it—or any sustained, substantial analysis of feminists of color—in Roiphe, Paglia, or Wolf.[19] These three foes of "victim feminism" could remind feminists who might begin work with an a priori assumption of oppression that not all women share the same experiences. This, in turn, could lead us to intensify our interrogation of the relationship among gender, race, class, and nationality. However, I am not hopeful that this will happen. Quite simply, these books leave their implied white middle- and upper-class readers feeling just too good about their own power as Americans. For them, victimization gets in the way of the relatively privileged. It somehow messes up their access to the boys' world of sex and capital. This is not the direction that feminism should take....

Although aspects of "victim feminism" are important, another implication of the debate also needs to be addressed. Lurking behind all of these arguments is anxiety about the cause of gendered behavior. For Roiphe, this concern surfaces in her apprehension regarding prescribed sexuality. Her most sophisticated argument comes when she interprets the language of date-rape pamphlets: "The movement against rape, then, not only dictates the way sex *shouldn't be* but also the way it *should be*. Sex should be gentle, it should not be aggressive; it should be absolutely equal, it should not involve domination and submission," (60). Similarly, Wolf's "victim feminism" is really another way of discussing essentialism. What she objects to most forcefully is feminism that claims a universally passive, nurturing female nature. She describes this mode:

> Women are not hierarchical but egalitarian.... Men want to dominate and separate; women want to communicate and connect. Men—especially Western men—are individualistic autocrats; women are communitarian healers. Men objectify women while women want commitment. Men kill; women give life. (144)

Unlike Roiphe and Wolf, Paglia, as I have mentioned, insists that gender difference is physiological and natural.

Historically, it makes sense that all of these books focus on essentialism. Essentialism first took root in America early in the nineteenth century and remains a powerful force today. As women of all races and African American and Native American men and women fought for democratic rights in the relatively new Republic, scientists and social conservatives began to argue that non-Caucasians and women were innately different and inferior.[20] In the complex and turbulent years that have followed, an essential feminine nature has been asserted by both advocates and opponents of women's rights. What is disturbing about Roiphe, Paglia, and Wolf is not that they once again highlight essentialism, but rather that they seem to derive no benefit from the excellent historical and theoretical work that has been published on the issue. They indicate that academic feminists must intensify efforts to speak to the overall feminist community. Otherwise, we will constantly remain in the same place, reinvent the same wheel, and learn nothing from the past....

If we view essentialism as a tool employed by women for specific reasons in both the 1870s and the 1970s, we can begin to ask questions about both its effectiveness and its liabilities. Similarly, we can analyze poststructuralism as a methodology that comes from a distinctive historical moment and is exploited by feminists for definable gains. Unlike essentialism, poststructuralism offers an alluring theoretical escape from the bodies that are said to relegate us to a subordinate societal role. It is quite possible that poststructuralism lures some feminists into thinking of gender only as a construct, not as a tangible presence that must be dealt with politically. Perhaps, we muse in an imaginary liberatory space, our bodies are not ourselves. Tania Modleski aptly summarizes the attraction:

> Since feminism has a great stake in the belief, first articulated by Simone de Beauvoir, that one is not *born* a woman, one *becomes* a woman (for if this were *not* the case it would be difficult to imagine social change), thinkers like Lacan and Foucault have provided the analytical tools by which we may begin the arduous task of unbecoming women.[21]

Besides allowing us to comprehend femininity as constructed, poststructuralism also equipped us with another valuable device. Through theory, we were able to grasp the binary nature of identity. We learned that to have "woman," one must have "man." To have "black," one must have "white." Poststructuralism, either directly or indirectly, allowed many scholars to begin to question male and white identity. It took the white Western male out of the center, out of a seemingly natural state, placing him instead under the category of construct. He became a set of expectations, rather than a universal and foreordained tyrant.

Yet when taken to extremes, some theory can hinder claims made on the basis of group identity. Modleski cautions that the "once exhilarating proposition that there is no 'essential' female nature has been elaborated to the point where it is now often used to scare 'women' away from making any generalizations about or political claims on behalf of a group called 'women.'"[22] Likewise, Barbara Christian questions the timing of the so-called death of the subject:

> I see the language it creates as one which mystifies rather than clarifies our condition, making it possible for a few people who know that particular language to control the critical scene—the language surfaced, interestingly enough, just when the literature of peoples of color, of black women, of Latin Americans, of Africans began to move to the "center."[23]

As Christian points out, although identity is not necessarily essential, we do not want to theorize ourselves out of a position from which to act. Because of this paradox, feminist scholars must work with multiple consciousness. We must attempt to understand how theories, even our own, have been used against us in the past, and we must learn from both material and theoretical history to avoid uncomfortable appropriation. We must repeatedly move beyond the harmful paradigms placed upon feminism that give us just "two tales," and into a more nuanced understanding of history, power, and struggle....

Notes

1. Paula Kamen came to this conclusion after conducting 236 interviews for her book *Feminist Fatale: Voices from the "Twentysomething" Generation Explore the Future of the Women's Movement* (New York: Fine, 1991). See Suzanne Gordon, "Don't Call Them Feminists," *Philadelphia Inquirer*, 19 February 1992.

2. Naomi Wolf describes how her friends joke, "Don't tell the Sisterhood," or, "Promise you won't turn me in to the fem police?" when they want to confide "unsanctioned sexual longings or 'frivolous' concern about clothes or vulnerability or men." Naomi Wolf, *Fire with Fire: The New Female Power and How It Will Change the Twenty-First Century* (New York: Random House, 1993), 62.

3. Sally Quinn, "Who Killed Feminism? Hypocritical Movement Leaders Betrayed Their Own Cause," *Washington Post*, 19 January 1992.

4. Wendy Kaminer, review of *The Morning After: Sex, Fear, and Feminism on Campus*, by Katie Roiphe, *New York Times* Book Review, 19 September 1993, 1.

5. Daphne Patai, "The Struggle for Feminist Purity Threatens the Goals of Feminism," *Chronicle of Higher Education*, 5 February 1992.

6. Christina Hoff Sommers, quoted in Marie McCullough, "Feminist Debate Comes to Swarthmore," *Philadelphia Inquirer*, 29 April 1994.

7. Christina Hoff Sommers, quoted in Megan Rosenfeld, "The Feminist Mistake? Christina Hoff Sommers Sees a Tyranny of the Sisterhood," *Washington Post*, 7 July 1994. Teachers for a Democratic Culture devoted the majority of its fall 1994 newsletter to critiques of Sommers. *Teachers for a Democratic Culture* 3 (1994).

8. Susan Jane Gilman, "Why the Fear of Feminism?" *New York Times*, 1 September 1991.

9. Wolf, *Fire with Fire*, 125.

10. Susan Faludi, *Backlash: The Undeclared War against American Women* (New York: Crown, 1991).

11. See Paul Lauter, *Canons and Contexts* (New York: Oxford University Press, 1991), 97–101.

12. Katie Roiphe, *The Morning After: Sex, Fear, and Feminism on Campus* (New York: Little, Brown, 1993); Wolf, *Fire with Fire*; and Camille Paglia, *Sex, Art, and American Culture: Essays* (New York: Random House, 1992). Subsequent references to these works appear parenthetically in the text.

13. bell hooks also links these three authors, criticizing them for advancing their careers through a combative, argumentative style and for erasing class and race difference. She comments that "without Paglia as trailblazer and symbolic mentor, there would be no cultural limelight for white girls such as Katie Roiphe and Naomi Wolf." bell hooks, *Outlaw Culture: Resisting Representations* (New York: Routledge, 1994), 86.

14. Katie Roiphe, "Date Rape Hysteria," *New York Times*, 20 November 1991.

15. Camille Paglia, "Ninnies, Pedants, Tyrants, and Other Academics," *New York Times Book Review*, 5 May 1991, 29.

16. See bell hooks, *Feminist Theory: From Margin to Center* (Boston: South End, 1984), 46.

17. Ibid., 5.

18. Ibid., 45.

19. hooks also comments in *Outlaw Culture* on this lack of representation, arguing that "Paglia never mentions the critical writing of any African American," (85); that Wolf's writing reflects a new kind of work by feminists that "completely ignores issues of race and class," (93); and that she (hooks) is disturbed by the "overall erasure of the voices and thoughts of women of color" in Roiphe's work (103).

20. For analysis of essentialism in relation to race, see George Fredrickson, *The Black Image in the White Mind: The Debate on Afro-American Character and Destiny, 1817–1914* (New York: Harper & Row, 1971). See also Reginald Horsman, *Race and Manifest Destiny: The Origins of Americas: Racial Anglo-Saxonism* (Cambridge: Harvard University Press, 1981); and Robert E. Bieder, *Science Encounters the Indian, 1820–1880* (Norman: University of Oklahoma Press, 1986). Cynthia Eagle Russett, in *Sexual Science: The Victorian Construction of Womanhood* (Cambridge: Harvard University Press, 1989), offers an excellent summary of the rise of gendered essentialism in the nineteenth century.

21. Tania Modleski, *Feminism without Women: Culture and Criticism in a "Postfeminist" Age* (New York: Routledge, 1991), 15.

22. Ibid.

23. Barbara Christian, "The Race for Theory," *Feminist Studies* 14, no. 1 (1988): 51–63.

LOCATIONS
AND COALITIONS

40.
REPORT FROM THE BAHAMAS
June Jordan

I am staying in a hotel that calls itself The Sheraton British Colonial. One of the photographs advertising the place displays a middle-aged Black man in a waiter's tuxedo, smiling. What intrigues me most about the picture is just this: while the Black man bears a tray full of "colorful" drinks above his left shoulder, both of his feet, shoes and trouserlegs, up to ten inches above his ankles, stand in the also "colorful" Caribbean salt water. He is so delighted to serve you he will wade into the water to bring you Banana Daquiris while you float! More precisely, he will wade into the water, fully clothed, oblivious to the ruin of his shoes, his trousers, his health, and he will do it with a smile.

I am in the Bahamas. On the phone in my room, a spinning complement of plastic pages offers handy index clues such as CAR RENTAL and CASINOS. A message from the Ministry of Tourism appears among these travellers tips. Opening with a paragraph of "WELCOME," the message then proceeds to "A PAGE OF HISTORY," which reads as follows:

> New World History begins on the same day that modern Bahamian history begins—October 12, 1492. That's when Columbus stepped ashore—British influence came first with the Eleutherian Adventurers of 1647—After the Revolutions. American Loyalists fled from the newly independent states and settled in the Bahamas. Confederate blockade-runners used the island as a haven during the War between the States, and after the War, a number of Southerners moved to the Bahamas.

There it is again. Something proclaims itself a legitimate history and all it does is track white Mr. Columbus to the British Eleutherians through the Confederate Southerners as they barge into New World surf, land on New World turf, and nobody saving one word about the Bahamian people, the Black peoples, to whom the only thing new in their island world was this weird succession of crude intruders and its colonial consequences.

This is my consciousness of race as I unpack my bathing suit in the Sheraton British Colonial. Neither this hotel nor the British nor the long ago Italians nor the white Delta airline pilots belong here, of course. And every time I look at the photograph of that fool standing in the water with his shoes on I'm about to have a West Indian fit, even though I know he's no fool; he's a middle-aged Black man who needs a job and this is his job—pretending himself a servile ancillary to the pleasures of the rich. (Compared to his options in life, I am a rich woman.

Compared to most of the Black Americans arriving for this Easter weekend on a three nights four days' deal of bargain rates, the middle-aged waiter is a poor Black man.)

We will jostle along with the other (white) visitors and join them in the tee shirt shops or, laughing together, learn ruthless rules of negotiation as we, Black Americans as well as white, argue down the price of handwoven goods at the nearby straw market while the merchants, frequently toothless Black women seated on the concrete in their only presentable dress, humble themselves to our careless games:

"Yes? You like it? Eight dollar."

"Five."

"I give it to you. Seven."

And so it continues, this weird succession of crude intruders that, now, includes me and my brothers and my sisters from the North.

This is my consciousness of class as I try to decide how much money I can spend on Bahamian gifts for my family back in Brooklyn. No matter that these other Black women incessantly weave words and flowers into the straw hats and bags piled beside them on the burning dusty street. No matter that these other Black women must work their sense of beauty into these things that we will take away as cheaply as we dare, or they will do without food.

We are not white, after all. The budget is limited. And we are harmlessly killing time between the poolside rum punch and "The Native Show on the Patio" that will play tonight outside the hotel restaurant.

This is my consciousness of race and class and gender identity as I notice the fixed relations between these other Black women and myself. They sell and I buy or I don't. They risk not eating. I risk going broke on my first vacation afternoon.

We are not particularly women anymore; we are parties to a transaction designed to set us against each other.

"Olive" is the name of the Black woman who cleans my hotel room. On my way to the beach I am wondering what "Olive" would say if I told her why I chose The Sheraton British Colonial; if I told her I wanted to swim. I wanted to sleep. I did not want to be harassed by the middle-aged waiter, or his nephew. I did not want to be raped by anybody (white or Black) at all and I calculated that my safety as a Black woman alone would best be assured by a multinational hotel corporation. In my experience, the big guys take customer complaints more seriously than the little ones. I would suppose that's one reason why they're big; they don't like to lose money anymore than I like to be bothered when I'm trying to read a goddamned book underneath a palm tree I paid $264 to get next to. A Black woman seeking refuge in a multinational corporation may seem like a contradiction to some, but there you are. In this case it's a coincidence of entirely different self-interests: Sheraton/cash = June Jordan's short run safety.

Anyway, I'm pretty sure "Olive" would look at me as though I came from someplace as far away as Brooklyn. Then she'd probably allow herself one indignant query before righteously removing her vacuum cleaner from my room; "and why in the first place you come down you without your husband?"

I cannot imagine how I would begin to answer her.

My "rights" and my "freedom" and my "desire" and a slew of other New World values; what would they sound like to this Black woman described on the card atop my hotel bureau as "Olive the Maid"? "Olive" is older than I am and I may smoke a cigarette while she changes the sheets on my bed. Whose rights? Whose freedom? Whose desire?

And why should she give a shit about mine unless I do something, for real, about hers?

It happens that the book that I finished reading under a palm tree earlier today was the novel, *The Bread Givers*, by Anzia Yezierska. Definitely autobiographical. Yezierska lays out the difficulties of being both female and "a person" inside a traditional Jewish family at the start of the twentieth century. That any Jewish woman became anything more than the abused servant of her father or her husband is really an improbable piece of news. Yet Yezierska managed such an unlikely outcome for her own life. In *The Bread Givers*, the heroine also manages an important, although partial, escape from traditional Jewish female destiny. And in the unpardonable, despotic father, the Talmudic scholar of that Jewish family, did I not see my own and hate him twice, again? When the heroine, the young Jewish child, wanders the streets with a filthy pail she borrows to sell herring in order to raise the ghetto rent and when she cries, "Nothing was before me but the hunger in our house, and no bread for the next meal if I didn't sell the herring. No longer like a fire engine, but like a houseful of hungry mouths my heart cried, 'herring—herring! Two cents apiece!' who would doubt the ease, the sisterhood of conversation possible between that white girl and the Black women selling straw bags on the streets of paradise because they do not want to die? And is it not obvious that the wife of that Talmudic scholar and "Olive," who cleans my room here at the hotel, have more in common than I can claim with either one of them?

This is my consciousness of race and class and gender identity as I collect wet towels, sunglasses, wristwatch, and head towards a shower.

I am thinking about the boy who loaned this novel to me. He's white and he's Jewish and he's pursuing an independent study project with me, at the State University where I teach whether or not I feel like it, where I teach without stint because, like the waiter, I am no fool. It's my job and either I work or I do without everything you need money to buy. The boy loaned me the novel because he thought I'd be interested to know how a Jewish-American writer used English so that the syntax, and therefore the cultural habits of mind expressed by the Yiddish language, could survive translation. He did this because he wanted to create another connection between us on the basis of language, between his knowledge/his love of Yiddish and my knowledge/my love of Black English.

He has been right about the forceful survival of the Yiddish. And I had become excited by this further evidence of the written voice of spoken language protected from the monodrone of "standard" English, and so we had grown closer on this account. But then our talk shifted to student affairs more generally, and I had learned that this student does not care one way or the other about currently jeopardized Federal Student Loan Programs because, as he explained it to me, they do not affect him. He does not need financial help outside his family. My own son, however, is Black. And I am the only family help available to him and that means, if Reagan succeeds in eliminating Federal programs to aid minority students, he will have to forget about furthering his studies, or he or I or both of us will have to hit the numbers pretty big. For these reasons of difference, the student and I had moved away from each other, even while we continued to talk.

My consciousness turned to race, again, and class.

Sitting in the same chair as the boy, several weeks ago, a graduate student came to discuss her grade. I praised the excellence of her final paper; indeed it had seemed to me an extraordinary pulling together of recent left brain/right brain research with the themes of transcendental poetry.

She told me that, for her part, she'd completed her reading of my political essays. "You are so lucky!" she exclaimed.

"What do you mean by that?"

"You have a cause. You have a purpose to your life."

I looked carefully at this white woman; what was she really

saying to me? "What do you mean?" I repeated.

"Poverty. Police violence. Discrimination in general."

(Jesus Christ, I thought: Is that her idea of lucky?)

"And how about you?" I asked.

"Me?"

"Yeah, you. Don't you have a cause?"

"Me? I'm just a middle-aged woman: a housewife and a mother. I'm a nobody." For a while, I made no response.

First of all, speaking of race and class and gender in one breath, what she said meant that those lucky preoccupations of mine, from police violence to nuclear wipe-out, were not shared. They were mine and not hers. But here she sat, friendly as an old stuffed animal, beaming good will or more "luck" in my direction.

In the second place, what this white woman said to me meant that she did not believe she was "a person" precisely because she had fulfilled the traditional female functions revered by the father of that Jewish immigrant, Anzia Yezierska. And the woman in front of me was not a Jew. That was not the connection. The link was strictly female. Nevertheless, how should that woman and I, another female connect, beyond this bizarre exchange?

If she believed me lucky to have regular hurdles of discrimination then why shouldn't I insist that she's lucky to be a middle class white Wasp female who lives in such well-sanctioned and normative comfort that she even has the luxury to deny the power of the privileges that paralyze her life?

If she deserts me and "my cause" where we differ, if, for example, she abandons me to "my" problems of race, then why should I support her in "her" problems of housewifely oblivion?

Recollection of this peculiar moment brings me to the shower in the bathroom cleaned by "Olive." She reminds me of the usual Women's Studies curriculum

because it has nothing to do with her or her job: you won't find "Olive" listed anywhere on the reading list. You will likewise seldom hear of Anzia Yezierska. But yes,
you will find, from Florence Nightingale to Adrienne Rich, a white procession of
independently well-to-do women writers. (Gertrude Stein/Virginia Woolf/Hilda
Doolittle are standard names among the "essential" women writers.)

In other words, most of the women of the world—Black and First World and
white who work because we must—most of the women of the world persist far
from the heart of the usual Women's Studies syllabus.

Similarly, the typical Black History course will slide by the majority experience
it pretends to represent. For example, Mary McLeod Bethune will scarcely receive
as much attention as Nat Turner, even though Black women who bravely and efficiently provided for the education of Black people hugely outnumber those few
Black men who led successful or doomed rebellions against slavery. In fact, Mary
McLeod Bethune may not receive even honorable mention because Black History
too often apes those ridiculous white history courses which produce such dangerous gibberish as The Sheraton British Colonial "history" of the Bahamas. Both
Black and white history courses exclude from their central consideration those
people who neither killed nor conquered anyone as the means to new identity,
those people who took care of every one of the people who wanted to become "a
person," those people who still take care of the life at issue: the ones who wash and
who feed and who teach and who diligently decorate straw hats and bags with all of
their historically unrequired gentle love: the women.

> *Oh the old rugged cross*
> *on a hill far away*
> *Well I cherish the old rugged cross*

It's Good Friday in the Bahamas. Seventy-eight degrees in the shade. Except for
Sheraton territory, everything's closed.

It so happens that for truly secular reasons I've been fasting for three days. My
hunger has now reached nearly violent proportions. In the hotel sandwich shop,
the Black woman handling the counter complains about the tourists; why isn't the
shop closed and why don't the tourists stop eating for once in their lives. I'm fam-
ished and I order chicken salad and cottage cheese and lettuce and tomato and a
hard-boiled egg and a hot cross bun and apple juice.

She eyes me with disgust.

To be sure, the timing of my stomach offends her serious religious practices.
Neither one of us apologizes to the other. She seasons the chicken salad to the pep-
pery max while I listen to the loud radio gospel she plays to console herself. It's a
country Black version of "The Old Rugged Cross."

As I heave much chicken into my mouth tears start. It's not the pepper. I am,
after all, a West Indian daughter. It's the Good Friday music that dominates the
humid atmosphere.

Well I cherish the old rugged cross

And I am back, faster than a 747, in Brooklyn, in the home of my parents where we are wondering, as we do every year, if the sky will darken until Christ has been buried in the tomb. The sky should darken if God is in His heavens. And then, around 3 p.m., at the conclusion of our mournful church service at the neighborhood St. Phillips, and even while we dumbly stare at the black cloth covering the gold altar and the slender unlit candles, the sun should return through the high gothic windows and vindicate our waiting faith that the Lord will rise again, on Easter.

How I used to bow my head at the very name of Jesus: ecstatic to abase myself in deference to His majesty.

My mouth is full of salad. I can't seem to eat quickly enough. I can't think how I should lessen the offence of my appetite. The other Black woman on the premises, the one who disapprovingly prepared this very tasty break from my fast, makes no remark. She is no fool. This is a job that she needs. I suppose she notices that at least I included a hot cross bun among my edibles. That's something in my favor. I decide that's enough.

I am suddenly eager to walk off the food. Up a fairly steep hill I walk without hurrying. Through the pastel desolation of the little town, the road brings me to a confectionary pink and white plantation house. At the gates, an unnecessarily large statue of Christopher Columbus faces me down, or tries to. His hand is fisted to one hip. I look back at him, laugh without deference, and turn left.

It's time to pack it up. Catch my plane. I scan the hotel room for things not to forget. There's that white report card on the bureau.

"Dear Guests:" it says, under the name "Olive." "I am your maid for the day. Please rate me: Excellent. Good. Average. Poor. Thank you."

I tuck this momento from the Sheraton British Colonial into my notebook. How would "Olive" rate *me*? What would it mean for us to seem "good" to each other? What would that rating require?

But I am hastening to leave. Neither turtle soup nor kidney pie nor any conch shell delight shall delay my departure. I have rested, here, in the Bahamas, and I'm ready to return to my usual job, my usual work. But the skin on my body has changed and so has my mind. On the Delta flight home I realize I am burning up, indeed.

So far as I can see, the usual race and class concepts of connection, or gender assumptions of unity, do not apply very well. I doubt that they ever did. Otherwise why would Black folks forever bemoan our lack of solidarity when the deal turns real. And if unity on the basis of sexual oppression is something natural, then why do we women, the majority people on the planet, still have a problem?

The plane's ready for takeoff. I fasten my seatbelt and let the tumult inside my head run free. Yes: race and class and gender remain as real as the weather. But what they must mean about the contact between two individuals is less obvious and, like the weather, not predictable.

And when these factors of race and class and gender absolutely collapse is whenever you try to use them as automatic concepts of connection. They may serve well as indicators of commonly felt conflict, but as elements of connection they seem about as reliable as precipitation probability for the day after the night before the day.

It occurs to me that much organizational grief could be avoided if people understood that partnership in misery does not necessarily provide for partnership for change: *When we get the monsters off our backs all of us may want to run in very different directions.*

And not only that: even though both "Olive" and "I" live inside a conflict neither one of us created, and even though both of us therefore hurt inside that conflict, I may be one of the monsters she needs to eliminate from her universe and, in a sense, she may be one of the monsters in mine.

I am reaching for the words to describe the difference between a common identity that has been imposed and the individual identity any one of us will choose, once she gains that chance.

That difference is the one that keeps us stupid in the face of new, specific information about somebody else with whom we are supposed to have a connection because a third party, hostile to both of us, has worked it so that the two of us, like it or not, share a common enemy. *What happens beyond the idea of that enemy and beyond the consequences of that enemy?*

I am saying that the ultimate connection cannot be the enemy. The ultimate connection must be the need that we find between us. It is not only who you are, in other words, but what we can do for each other that will determine the connection.

I am flying back to my job. I have been teaching contemporary women's poetry this semester. One quandary I have set myself to explore with my students is the one of taking responsibility without power. We had been wrestling ideas to the floor for several sessions when a young Black woman, a South African, asked me for help, after class.

Sokutu told me she was "in a trance" and that she'd been unable to eat for two weeks.

"What's going on?" I asked her, even as my eyes startled at her trembling and emaciated appearance.

"My husband. He drinks all the time. He beats me up. I go to the hospital. I can't eat. I don't know what/anything."

In my office, she described her situation. I did not dare to let her sense my fear and horror. She was dragging about, hour by hour, in dread. Her husband, a young Black South African, was drinking himself into more and more deadly violence against her.

Sokutu told me how she could keep nothing down. She weighed 90 lbs. at the outside, as she spoke to me. She'd already been hospitalized as a result of her husband's battering rage.

I knew both of them because I had organized a campus group to aid the liberation struggles of Southern Africa.

Nausea rose in my throat. What about this presumable connection: this husband and this wife fled from that homeland of hatred against them, and now what? He was destroying himself. If not stopped, he would certainly murder his wife.

She needed a doctor, right away. It was a medical emergency. She needed protection. It was a security crisis. She needed refuge for battered wives and personal therapy and legal counsel. She needed a friend.

I got on the phone and called every number in the campus directory that I could imagine might prove helpful. Nothing worked. There were no institutional resources designed to meet her enormous, multifaceted, and ordinary woman's need.

I called various students. I asked the Chairperson of the English Department for advice. I asked everyone for help.

Finally, another one of my students, Cathy, a young Irish woman active in campus IRA activities, responded. She asked for further details. I gave them to her.

"Her husband," Cathy told me, "is an alcoholic. You have to understand about alcoholics. It's not the same as anything else. And it's a disease you can't treat any old way."

I listened, fearfully. Did this mean there was nothing we could do?

"That's not what I'm saying," she said. "But you have to keep the alcoholic part of the thing central in everybody's mind, otherwise her husband will kill her. Or he'll kill himself."

She spoke calmly. I felt there was nothing to do but to assume she knew what she was talking about.

"Will you come with me?" I asked her, after a silence. "Will you come with me and help us figure out what to do next?"

Cathy said she would but that she felt shy: Sokutu comes from South Africa. What would she think about Cathy?

"I don't know," I said. "But let's go."

We left to find a dormitory room for the young battered wife.

It was late, now, and dark outside.

On Cathy's VW that I followed behind with my own car, was the sticker that reads BOBBY SANDS FREE AT LAST. My eyes blurred as I read and reread the words. This was another connection: Bobby Sands and Martin Luther King Jr. and who would believe it? I would not have believed it; I grew up terrorized by Irish kids who introduced me to the word "nigga."

And here I was following an Irish woman to the room of a Black South African. We were going to that room to try to save a life together.

When we reached the little room, we found ourselves awkward and large. Sokutu attempted to treat us with utmost courtesy, as though we were honored guests. She seemed surprised by Cathy, but mostly Sokutu was flushed with relief and joy because we were there, with her.

I did not know how we should ever terminate her heartfelt courtesies and address, directly, the reason for our visit: her starvation and her extreme physical danger.

Finally, Cathy sat on the floor and reached out her hands to Sokutu. "I'm here," she said quietly, "Because June has told me what has happened to you. And I know what it is. Your husband is an alcoholic. He has a disease. I know what it is. My father was an alcoholic. He killed himself. He almost killed my mother. I want to be your friend."

"Oh," was the only small sound that escaped from Sokutu's mouth. And then she embraced the other student. And then everything changed and I watched all of this happen so I know that this happened: this connection.

And after we called the police and exchanged phone numbers and plans were made for the night and for the next morning, the young South African woman walked down the dormitory hallway, saying goodbye and saying thank you to us.

I walked behind them, the young Irish woman and the young South African, and I saw them walking as sisters walk, hugging each other, and whispering and sure of each other and I felt how it was not who they were but what they both know and what they were both preparing to do about what they know that was going to make them both free at last.

And I look out the windows of the plane and I see clouds that will not kill me and I know that someday soon other clouds may erupt to kill us all.

And I tell the stewardess No thanks to the cocktails she offers me. But I look about the cabin at the hundred strangers drinking as they fly and I think even here and even now I must make the connection real between me and these strangers everywhere before those other clouds unify this ragged bunch of us, too late.

41.
NOTES TOWARD A POLITICS OF LOCATION[1]
Adrienne Rich

I am to speak these words in Europe, but I have been searching for them in the United States of America. A few years ago I would have spoken of the common oppression of women, the gathering movement of women around the globe, the hidden history of women's resistance and bonding, the failure of all previous politics to recognize the universal shadow of patriarchy, the belief that women now, in a time of rising consciousness and global emergency, may join across all national and cultural boundaries to create a society free of domination, in which "sexuality, politics, . . . work, . . . intimacy . . . thinking itself will be transformed."[2]

I would have spoken these words as a feminist who "happened" to be a white United States citizen, conscious of my government's proven capacity for violence and arrogance of power, but as self-separated from that government, quoting without second thought Virginia Woolf's statement in *Three Guineas* that "as a woman I have no country. As a woman I want no country. As a woman my country is the whole world."

This is not what I come here to say in 1984. I come here with notes but without absolute conclusions. This is not a sign of loss of faith or hope. These notes are the marks of a struggle to keep moving, a struggle for accountability.

Beginning to write, then getting up. Stopped by the movements of a huge early bumblebee which has somehow gotten inside this house and is reeling, bumping, stunning itself against windowpanes and sills. I open the front door and speak to it, trying to attract it outside. It is looking for what it needs, just as I am, and, like me, it has gotten trapped in a place where it cannot fulfill its own life. I could open the jar of honey on the kitchen counter, and perhaps it would take honey from that jar; but its life process, its work, its mode of being cannot be fulfilled inside this house.

And I, too, have been bumping my way against glassy panes, falling half-stunned, gathering myself up and crawling, then again taking off, searching.

I don't hear the bumblebee any more, and I leave the front door. I sit down and pick up a secondhand, faintly annotated student copy of Marx's *The German Ideology*, which "happens" to be lying on the table.

I will speak these words in Europe, but I am having to search for them in the United States of North America. When I was ten or eleven, early in World War II, a girlfriend and I used to write each other letters which we addressed like this:

Adrienne Rich
14 Edgevale Road

Baltimore, Maryland
The United States of America
The Continent of North America
The Western Hemisphere
The Earth
The Solar System
The Universe

You could see your own house as a tiny fleck on an ever widening landscape, or as the center of it all from which the circles expanded into the infinite unknown.

It is that question of feeling at the center that gnaws at me now. At the center of what?

As a woman I have a country; as a woman I cannot divest myself of that country merely by condemning its government or by saying three times "As a woman my country is the whole world." Tribal loyalties aside, and even if nation-states are now just pretexts used by multinational conglomerates to serve their interests, I need to understand how a place on the map is also a place in history within which as a woman, a Jew, a lesbian, a feminist I am created and trying to create.

Begin, though, not with a continent or a country or a house, but with the geography closest in—the body. Here at least I know I exist, that living human individual whom the young Marx called "the first premise of all human history."[3] But it was not as a Marxist that I turned to this place, back from philosophy and literature and science and theology in which I had looked for myself in vain. It was as a radical feminist.

The politics of pregnability and motherhood. The politics of orgasm. The politics of rape and incest, of abortion, birth control, forcible sterilization. Of prostitution and marital sex. Of what had been named sexual liberation. Of prescriptive heterosexuality. Of lesbian existence.

And Marxist feminists were often pioneers in this work. But for many women I knew, the need to begin with the female body—our own—was understood not as applying a Marxist principle *to* women, but as locating the grounds from which to speak with authority *as* women. Not to transcend this body, but to reclaim it. To reconnect our thinking and speaking with the body of this particular living human individual, a woman. Begin, we said, with the material, with matter, mma, madre, mutter, moeder, modder, etc., etc.

Begin with the material. Pick up again the long struggle against lofty and privileged abstraction. Perhaps this is the core of revolutionary process, whether it calls itself Marxist or Third World or feminist or all three. Long before the nineteenth century, the empirical witch of the European Middle Ages, trusting her senses, practicing her tried remedies against the anti-material, anti-sensuous, anti-empirical dogmas of the Church. Dying for that, by the millions. "A female-led peasant rebellion"?—in any event, a rebellion against the idolatry of pure ideas, the belief that ideas have a life of their own and float along above the heads of ordinary people— women, the poor, the uninitiated.[4]

Abstractions severed from the doings of living people, fed back to people as slogans.

Theory—the seeing of patterns, showing the forest as well as the trees—theory can be a dew that rises from the earth and collects in the rain cloud and returns to earth over and over. But if it doesn't smell of the earth, it isn't good for the earth.

I wrote a sentence just now and x'd it out. In it I said that women have always understood the struggle against free-floating abstraction even when they were intimidated by abstract ideas. I don't want to write that kind of sentence now, the sentence that begins "Women have always...." We started by rejecting the sentences that began "Women have always had an instinct for mothering" or "Women have always and everywhere been in subjugation to men." If we have learned anything in these years of late twentieth-century feminism, it's that that "always" blots out what we really need to know: When, where, and under what conditions has the statement been true?

The absolute necessity to raise these questions in the world: where, when, and under what conditions have women acted and been acted on, as women? Wherever people are struggling against subjection, the specific subjection of women, through our location in a female body, from now on has to be addressed. The necessity to go on speaking of it, refusing to let the discussion go on as before, speaking where silence has been advised and enforced, not just about our subjection, but about our active presence and practice as women. We believed (I go on believing) that the liberation of women is a wedge driven into all other radical thought, can open out the structures of resistance, unbind the imagination, connect what's been dangerously disconnected. Let us pay attention now, we said, to women: let men and women make a conscious act of attention when women speak; let us insist on kinds of process which allow more women to speak; let us get back to earth—not as paradigm for "women," but as place of location.

Perhaps we need a moratorium on saying "the body." For it's also possible to abstract "the" body. When I write "the body," I see nothing in particular. To write "my body" plunges me into lived experience, particularity: I see scars, disfigurements, discolorations, damages, losses, as well as what pleases me. Bones well nourished from the placenta; the teeth of a middle-class person seen by the dentist twice a year from childhood. White skin, marked and scarred by three pregnancies, an elected sterilization, progressive arthritis, four joint operations, calcium deposits, no rapes, no abortions, long hours at a typewriter—my own, not in a typing pool—and so forth. To say "the body" lifts me away from what has given me a primary perspective. To say "my body" reduces the temptation to grandiose assertions. This body. White, female; or female, white. The first obvious, lifelong facts. But I was born in the white section of a hospital which separated Black and white women in labor and Black and white babies in the nursery, just as it separated Black and white bodies in its morgue. I was defined as white before I was defined as female.

The politics of location. Even to begin with my body. I have to say that from the outset that body had more than one identity. When I was carried out of the hospital into the world, I was viewed and treated as female, but also viewed and treated as white—by both Black and white people. I was located by color and sex as surely as a Black child was located by color and sex—though the implications of white identity were mystified by the presumption that white people are the center of the universe.

To locate myself in my body means more than understanding what it has meant to me to have a vulva and clitoris and uterus and breasts. It means recognizing this white skin, the places it has taken me, the places it has not let me go.

The body I was born into was not only female and white, but Jewish—enough for geographic location to have played, in those years, a determining part. I was a *Mischling*, four years old when the Third Reich began. Had it been not Baltimore, but Prague or Lódz or Amsterdam, the ten-year-old letter writer might have had no address. Had I survived Prague, Amsterdam, or Lódz and the railway stations for which they were deportation points, I would be some body else. My center, perhaps, the Middle East or Latin America, my language itself another language. Or I might be in no body at all.

But I am a North American Jew, born and raised three thousand miles from the war in Europe.

Trying as women to see from the center. "A politics," I wrote once, "of asking women's questions."[5] We are not "the woman question" asked by somebody else; we are the women who ask the questions.

Trying to see so much, aware of so much to be seen, brought into the light, changed. Breaking down again and again the false male universal. Piling piece by piece of concrete experience side by side, comparing, beginning to discern patterns. Anger, frustration with Marxist or Leftist dismissals of these questions, this struggle. Easy now to call this disillusionment facile, but the anger was deep, the frustration real, both in personal relationships and political organizations. I wrote in 1975: *Much of what is narrowly termed "politics" seems to rest on a longing for certainty even at the cost of honesty, for an analysis which, once given, need not be reexamined. Such is the deadendedness—for women—of Marxism in our time.*[6]

And it has felt like a dead end wherever politics has been externalized, cut off from the ongoing lives of women or of men, rarefied into an elite jargon, an enclave, defined by little sects who feed off each others' errors.

But even as we shrugged away Marx along with the academic Marxists and the sectarian Left, some of us, calling ourselves radical feminists, never meant anything less by women's liberation than the creation of a society without domination; we never meant less than the making new of all relationships. The problem was that we did not know whom we meant when we said "we."

The power men everywhere wield over women, power which has become a model for every other form of exploitation and illegitimate control.[7] I wrote these words in 1978 at the end of an essay called "Compulsory Heterosexuality and Lesbian Existence," patriarchy as the "model" for other forms of domination—this idea was not original with me. It has been put forward insistently by white Western feminists, and in 1972 I had quoted from Leví-Strauss: *I would go so far as to say that even before slavery or class domination existed, men built an approach to women that would serve one day to introduce differences among us all.*[8]

Living for fifty-some years, having watched even minor bits of history unfold, I am less quick than I once was to search for single "causes" or origins in dealings among human beings. But suppose that we could trace back and establish that patriarchy has been everywhere the model. To what choices of action does that lead us in the present? Patriarchy exists nowhere in a pure state; we are the latest to set foot in a tangle of oppressions grown up and around each other for centuries. This isn't the old children's game where you choose one strand of color in the web and follow it back to find your prize, ignoring the others as mere distractions. The prize is life itself, and most women in the world must fight for their lives on many fronts at once.

We . . . often find it difficult to separate race from class from sex oppression because in our lives they are most often experienced simultaneously. We know that there is such a thing as racial-sexual oppression which is neither solely racial nor solely sexual. . . . We need to articulate the real class situation of persons who are not merely raceless, sexless workers but for whom racial and sexual oppression are significant determinants in their working/economic lives.

This is from the 1977 Combahee River Collective statement, a major document of the U.S. women's movement, which gives a clear and uncompromising Black-feminist naming to the experience of simultaneity of oppressions.[9]

Even in the struggle against free-floating abstraction, we have abstracted. Marxists and radical feminists have both done this. Why not admit it, get it said, so we can get on to the work to be done, back down to earth again? The faceless, sexless, raceless proletariat. The faceless, raceless, classless category of "all women." Both creations of white Western self-centeredness.

To come to terms with the circumscribing nature of (our) whiteness.[10] Marginalized though we have been as women, as white and Western makers of theory, we also marginalize others because our lived experience is thoughtlessly white, because even our "women's cultures" are rooted in some Western tradition. Recognizing our location, having to name the ground we're coming from, the conditions we have taken for granted—there is a confusion between our claims to the white and

Western eye and the woman—seeing eye,[11] fear of losing the centrality of the one even as we claim the other.

How does the white Western feminist define theory? Is it something made only by white women and only by women acknowledged as writers? How does the white Western feminist define "an idea"? How do we actively work to build a white Western feminist consciousness that is not simply centered on itself, that resists white circumscribing?

It was in the writings but also the actions and speeches and sermons of Black United States citizens that I began to experience the meaning of my whiteness as a point of location for which I needed to take responsibility. It was in reading poems by contemporary Cuban women that I began to experience the meaning of North America as a location which had also shaped my ways of seeing and my ideas of who and what was important, a location for which I was also responsible. I traveled then to Nicaragua, where, in a tiny impoverished country, in a four-year-old society dedicated to eradicating poverty, under the hills of the Nicaragua-Honduras border, I could physically feel the weight of the United States of North America, its military forces, its vast appropriations of money, its mass media, at my back; I could feel what it means, dissident or not, to be part of that raised boot of power, the cold shadow we cast everywhere to the south.

I come from a country stuck fast for forty years in the deepfreeze of history. Any United States citizen alive today has been saturated with Cold War rhetoric, the horrors of communism, the betrayals of socialism, the warning that any collective restructuring of society spells the end of personal freedom. And, yes, there have been horrors and betrayals deserving open opposition. But we are not invited to consider the butcheries of Stalinism, the terrors of the Russian counterrevolution alongside the butcheries of white supremacism and Manifest Destiny. We are not urged to help create a more human society here in response to the ones we are taught to hate and dread. Discourse itself is frozen at this level. Tonight as I turned a switch searching for "the news," that shinily animated silicone mask was on television again, telling the citizens of my country we are menaced by communism from El Salvador, that communism—Soviet variety, obviously—is on the move in Central America, that freedom is imperiled, that the suffering peasants of Latin America must be stopped, just as Hitler had to be stopped.

The discourse has never really changed; it is wearingly abstract. (Lillian Smith, white anti-racist writer and activist, spoke of the "deadly sameness" of abstraction.)[12] It allows no differences among places, times, cultures, conditions, movements. Words that should possess a depth and breadth of allusions—words like *socialism, communism, democracy, collectivism*—are stripped of their historical roots, the many faces of the struggles for social justice and independence reduced to an ambition to dominate the world.

Is there a connection between this state of mind—the Cold War mentality, the attribution of all our problems to an external enemy—and a form of feminism so focused on male evil and female victimization that it, too, allows for no differences among women, men, places, times, cultures, conditions, classes, movements? Living in the climate of an enormous either/or, we absorb some of it unless we actively take heed.

In the United States large numbers of people have been cut off from their own process and movement. We have been hearing for forty years that we are the guardians of freedom, while "behind the Iron Curtain" all is duplicity and manipulation, if not sheer terror. Yet the legacy of fear lingering after the witch hunts of the fifties hangs on like the aftersmell of a burning. The sense of obliquity, mystery, paranoia surrounding the American Communist party after the Khrushchev Report of 1956: the party lost 30,000 members within weeks, and few who remained were talking about it. To be a Jew, a homosexual, any kind of marginal person was to be liable for suspicion of being "Communist." A blanketing snow had begun to drift over the radical history of the United States.

And, though parts of the North American feminist movement actually sprang from the Black movements of the sixties and the student left, feminists have suffered not only from the burying and distortion of women's experience, but from the overall burying and distortion of the great movements for social change.[13]

The first American woman astronaut is interviewed by the liberal-feminist editor of a mass-circulation women's magazine. She is a splendid creature, healthy, young, thick dark head of hair, scientific degrees from an elite university, an athletic self-confidence. She is also white. She speaks of the future of space, the potential uses of space colonies by private industry, especially for producing materials which can be advantageously processed under conditions of weightlessness. Pharmaceuticals for example. By extension one thinks of chemicals. Neither of these two spirited women speak of the alliances between the military and the "private" sector of the North American economy. Nor do they speak of Depo-Provera, Valium, Librium, napalm, dioxin. *When big companies decide that it's now to their advantage to put a lot of their money into production of materials in space . . . we'll really get the funding that we need,* says the astronaut. No mention of who "we" are and what "we" need funding for; no questions about the poisoning and impoverishment of women here on earth or of the earth itself. Women, too, may leave the earth behind.[14]

The astronaut is young, feels her own power, works hard for her exhilaration. She has swung out over the earth and come back, one more time passed all the tests. It's not that I expect her to come back to earth as Cassandra. But this experience of hers has nothing as yet to do with the liberation of women. A female proletariat—uneducated, ill nourished, unorganized, and largely from the Third World—will create the profits which will stimulate the "big companies" to invest in space.

On a split screen in my brain I see two versions of her story: the backward gaze through streaming weightlessness to the familiar globe, pale blue and green and white, the strict and sober presence of it, the true intuition of relativity battering the heart; and the swiftly calculated move to a farther suburb, the male technocrats and the women they have picked and tested, leaving the familiar globe behind: the toxic rivers, the cancerous wells, the strangled valleys, the closed-down urban hospitals, the shattered schools, the atomic desert blooming, the lilac suckers run wild, the blue grape hyacinths spreading, the ailanthus and kudzu doing their final desperate part—the beauty that won't travel, that can't be stolen away.

A movement for change lives in feelings, actions, and words. Whatever circumscribes or mutilates our feelings makes it more difficult to act, keeps our actions reactive, repetitive: abstract thinking, narrow tribal loyalties, every kind of self-righteousness, the arrogance of believing ourselves at the center. It's hard to look back on the limits of my understanding a year, five years ago—how did I look without seeing, hear without listening? It can be difficult to be generous to earlier selves, and keeping faith with the continuity of our journeys is especially hard in the United States, where identities and loyalties have been shed and replaced without a tremor, all in the name of becoming "American." Yet how, except through ourselves, do we discover what moves other people to change? Our old fears and denials—what helps us let go of them? What makes us decide we have to re-educate ourselves, even those of us with "good" educations? A politicized life ought to sharpen both the senses and the memory.

The difficulty of saying I—a phrase from the East German novelist Christa Wolf.[15] But once having said it, as we realize the necessity to go further, isn't there a difficulty of saying "we"? *You cannot speak for me. I cannot speak for us.* Two thoughts: there is no liberation that only knows how to say "I"; there is no collective movement that speaks for each of us all the way through.

And so even ordinary pronouns become a political problem.[16]

- 64 cruise missiles in Greenham Common and Molesworth.
- 112 at Comiso.
- 96 Pershing II missiles in West Germany.
- 96 for Belgium and the Netherlands.

That is the projection for the next few years.[17]

- Thousands of women, in Europe and the United States, saying *no* to this and to the militarization of the world.

An approach which traces militarism back to patriarchy and patriarchy back to the fundamental quality of maleness can be demoralizing and even paralyzing.... Perhaps it is possible to be less fixed on the discovery of "original causes." It might be more useful to ask, How do these values and behaviors get repeated generation after generation?[18]

The valorization of manliness and masculinity. The armed forces as the extreme embodiment of the patriarchal family. The archaic idea of women as a "home front" even as the missiles are deployed in the backyards of Wyoming and

Mutlangen. The growing urgency that an anti-nuclear, anti-militarist movement must be a feminist movement, must be a socialist movement, must be an anti-racist, anti-imperialist movement. That it's not enough to fear for the people we know, our own kind, ourselves. Nor is it empowering to give ourselves up to abstract terrors of pure annihilation. The anti-nuclear, anti-military movement cannot sweep away the missiles as a movement to save white civilization in the West.

The movement for change is a changing movement, changing itself, demasculinizing itself, de-Westernizing itself, becoming a critical mass that is saying in so many different voices, languages, gestures, actions: *It must change; we ourselves can change it.*

We who are not the same. We who are many and do not want to be the same.

Trying to watch myself in the process of writing this, I keep coming back to something Sheila Rowbotham, the British socialist feminist, wrote in *Beyond the Fragments*:

> *A movement helps you to overcome some of the oppressive distancing of theory and this has been a . . . continuing creative endeavour of women's liberation. But some paths are not mapped and our footholds vanish. . . . I see what I'm writing as part of a wider claiming which is beginning. I am part of the difficulty myself. The difficulty is not out there.*[19]

My difficulties, too, are not out there—except in the social conditions that make all this necessary. I do not any longer *believe*—my feelings do not allow me to believe—that the white eye sees from the center. Yet I often find myself thinking as if I still believed that were true. Or, rather, my thinking stands still. I feel in a state of arrest, as if my brain and heart were refusing to speak to each other. My brain, a woman's brain, has exulted in breaking the taboo against women thinking, has taken off on the wind, saying, *I am the woman who asks the questions.* My heart has been learning in a much more humble and laborious way, learning that feelings are useless without facts, that all privilege is ignorant at the core.

The United States has never been a white country, though it has long served what white men defined as their interests. The Mediterranean was never white. England, northern Europe, if ever absolutely white, are so no longer. In a Leftist bookstore in Manchester, England, a Third World poster: *WE ARE HERE BECAUSE YOU WERE THERE.* In Europe there have always been the Jews, the original ghetto dwellers, identified as a racial type, suffering under pass laws and special entry taxes, enforced relocations, massacres: the scapegoats, the aliens, never seen as truly European but as part of that darker world that must be controlled, eventually exterminated. Today the cities of Europe have new scapegoats as well: the diaspora from the old colonial empires. Is anti-Semitism the model for racism, or racism for anti-Semitism? Once more, where does the question lead us? Don't we have to start here, where we are, forty years after the Holocaust, in the churn of Middle Eastern violence, in the midst of decisive ferment in South Africa—not in some debate over origins and precedents, but in the recognition of simultaneous oppressions?

I've been thinking a lot about the obsession with origins. It seems a way of stopping time in its tracks. The sacred Neolithic triangles, the Minoan vases with staring eyes and breasts, the female figurines of Anatolia—weren't they concrete evidence of a kind, like Sappho's fragments, for earlier woman-affirming cultures, cultures that enjoyed centuries of peace? But haven't they also served as arresting images, which kept us attached and immobilized? Human activity didn't stop in Crete or Catal Huyuk. We can't build a society free from domination by fixing our sights backward on some long-ago tribe or city.

    The continuing spiritual power of an image lives in the interplay between what it reminds us of—what it *brings to mind*—and our own continuing actions in the present. When the labrys becomes a badge for a cult of Minoan goddesses, when the wearer of the labrys has ceased to ask herself what she is doing on this earth, where her love of women is taking her, the labrys, too, becomes abstraction—lifted away from the heat and friction of human activity. The Jewish star on my neck must serve me both for reminder and as a goad to continuing and changing responsibility.

When I learn that in 1913, mass women's marches were held in South Africa which caused the rescinding of entry permit laws; that in 1956, 20,000 women assembled in Pretoria to protest pass laws for women, that resistance to these laws was carried out in remote country villages and punished by shootings, beatings, and burnings; that in 1959, 2,000 women demonstrated in Durban against laws which provided beerhalls for African men and criminalized women's traditional home brewing; that at one and the same time, African women have played a major role alongside men in resisting apartheid, I have to ask myself why it took me so long to learn these chapters of women's history, why the leadership and strategies of African women have been so unrecognized as theory in action by white Western feminist thought. (And in a book by two men, entitled *South African Politics* and published in 1982, there is one entry under "Women" [franchise] and no reference anywhere to women's political leadership and mass actions.)[20]

    When I read that a major strand in the conflicts of the past decade in Lebanon has been political organizing by women of women, across class and tribal and religious lines, women working and teaching together within refugee camps and armed communities, and of the violent undermining of their efforts through the civil war and the Israeli invasion, I am forced to think.[21] Iman Khalife, the young teacher who tried to organize a silent peace march on the Christian-Moslem border of Beirut—a protest which was quelled by the threat of a massacre of the participants—Iman Khalife and women like her do not come out of nowhere. But we Western feminists, living under other kinds of conditions, are not encouraged to know this background.

And I turn to Etel Adnan's brief, extraordinary novel *Sitt Marie Rose*, about a middle-class Christian Lebanese woman tortured for joining the Palestinian Resistance, and read:

> She was also subject to another great delusion believing that women are protected from repression, and that the leaders considered political fights to be strictly between males. In fact, with women's greater access to certain powers, they began to watch them more closely, and perhaps with even greater hostility. Every feminine act, even charitable and seemingly unpolitical ones, were regarded as a rebellion in this world where women had always played servile roles. Marie Rose inspired scorn and hate long before the fateful day of her arrest.[22]

Across the curve of the earth, there are women getting up before dawn, in the blackness before the point of light, in the twilight before sunrise; there are women rising earlier than men and children to break the ice, to start the stove, to put up the pap, the coffee, the rice, to iron the pants, to braid the hair, to pull the day's water up from the well, to boil water for tea, to wash the children for school, to pull the vegetables and start the walk to market, to run to catch the bus for the work that is paid. I don't know when most women sleep. In big cities at dawn women are traveling home after cleaning offices all night, or waxing the halls of hospitals, or sitting up with the old and sick and frightened at the hour when death is supposed to do its work.

In Peru: "Women invest hours in cleaning tiny stones and chaff out of beans, wheat and rice; they shell peas and clean fish and grind spices in small mortars. They buy bones or tripe at the market and cook cheap, nutritious soups. They repair clothes until they will not sustain another patch. They search...out the cheapest school uniforms, payable in the greatest number of installments. They trade old magazines for plastic washbasins and buy second-hand toys and shoes. They walk long distances to find a spool of thread at a slightly lower price."[23]

This is the working day that has never changed, the unpaid female labor which means the survival of the poor.

In minimal light I see her, over and over, her inner clock pushing her out of bed with her heavy and maybe painful limbs, her breath breathing life into her stove, her house, her family, taking the last cold swatch of night on her body, meeting the sudden leap of the rising sun.

In my white North American world they have tried to tell me that this woman—politicized by intersecting forces—doesn't think and reflect on her life. That her ideas are not real ideas like those of Karl Marx and Simone de Beauvoir. That her calculations, her spiritual philosophy, her gifts for law and ethics, her daily emergency political decisions are merely instinctual or conditioned reactions. That only certain kinds of people can make theory; that the white-educated mind is capable of formulating everything; that white middle-class feminism can know for "all women"; that only when a white mind formulates is the formulation to be taken seriously.

In the United States, white-centered theory has not yet adequately engaged with the texts—written, printed, and widely available—which have been for a decade or more formulating the political theory of Black American feminism: the Combahee River Collective statement, the essays and speeches of Gloria I. Joseph, Audre Lorde, Bernice Reagon, Michele Russell, Barbara Smith, June Jordan, to name a few of the most obvious. White feminists have read and taught from the anthology *This Bridge Called My Back: Writings by Radical Women of Color*, yet often have stopped at perceiving it simply as an angry attack on the white women's movement. So white feelings remain at the center. And, yes, I need to move outward from the base and center of my feelings, but with a corrective sense that my feelings are not *the* center of feminism.[24]

And if we read Audre Lorde or Gloria Joseph or Barbara Smith, do we understand that the intellectual roots of this feminist theory are not white liberalism or white Euro-American feminism, but the analyses of Afro-American experience articulated by Sojourner Truth, W. E. B. Du Bois, Ida B. Wells-Barnett, C. L. R. James, Malcolm X, Lorraine Hansberry, Fannie Lou Hamer, among others? That Black feminism cannot be marginalized and circumscribed as simply a response to white feminist racism or an augmentation of white feminism; that it is an organic development of the Black movements and philosophies of the past, their practice and their printed writings? (And that, increasingly, Black American feminism is actively in dialogue with other movements of women of color within and beyond the United States?)

To shrink from or dismiss that challenge can only isolate white feminism from the other great movements for self-determination and justice within and against which women define ourselves.

Once again: Who is *we*?

This is the end of these notes, but it is not an ending.

Notes

1. Talk given at the First Summer School of Critical Semiotics, Conference on Women, Feminist Identity and Society in the 1980s, Utrecht, Holland, June 1, 1984. Different versions of this talk were given at Cornell University for the Women's Studies Research Seminar, and as the Burgess Lecture, Pacific Oaks College, Pasadena, California.
2. Adrienne Rich, *Of Woman Born: Motherhood as Experience and Institution* (New York: W. W. Norton, 1976), p. 286.
3. Karl Marx and Frederick Engels, *The German Ideology*, ed. C. J. Arthur (New York: International Publishers, 1970), p. 42.
4. Barbara Ehrenreich and Deirdre English, *Witches, Midwives, and Nurses: A History of Women Healers* (Old Westbury, N.Y.: Feminist Press, 1973).
5. Adrienne Rich, *On Lies, Secrets, and Silence: Selected Prose 1966–1978* (New York: W. W. Norton, 1979), p. 17.
6. *Ibid.*, p. 193. [A.R., 1986: For a vigorous indictment of dead-ended Marxism and a call to "revolution in permanence," see Raya Dunayevskaya, *Women's Liberation and the Dialectics of Revolution* (Atlantic Highlands, N.J.: Humanities Press, 1985).]
7. Adrienne Rich, "Compulsory Heterosexuality and Lesbian Existence," in Rich 1986, p. 68.

8. Rich, *On Lies, Secrets, and Silence*, p. 84.

9. Barbara Smith, ed., *Home Girls: A Black Feminist Anthology* (New York: Kitchen Table/Women of Color Press, 1983), pp. 171–183. See also Audre Lorde, *Sister Outsider: Essays and Speeches* (Trumansburg, N.Y.: Crossing Press, 1984). See Hilda Bernstein, *For Their Triumphs and for Their Tears: Women in Apartheid South Africa* (London: International Defence and Aid Fund, 1978), for a description of simultaneity of African women's oppressions under apartheid. For a biographical and personal account, see Ellen Kuzwayo, *Call Me Woman* (San Francisco: Spinsters/Aunt Lute, 1985).

10. Gloria I. Joseph, "The Incompatible Menage à Trois: Marxism, Feminism and Racism," in *Women and Revolution*, ed. Lydia Sargent (Boston: South End Press, 1981).

11. See Marilyn Frye, *The Politics of Reality* (Trumansburg, N.Y.: Crossing Press, 1983), p. 171.

12. Lillian Smith, "Autobiography as a Dialogue between King and Corpse," in *The Winner Names the Age*, ed. Michelle Cliff (New York: W. W. Norton, 1978), p. 189.

13. See Elly Bulkin, "Hard Ground: Jewish Identity, Racism, and Anti-Semitism," in E. Bulkin, M. B. Pratt, and B. Smith, *Yours in Struggle: Three Feminist Perspectives on Anti-Semitism and Racism* (Brooklyn, N.Y.: Long Haul, 1984.)

14. *Ms.* (January 1984): 86.

15. Christa Wolf, *The Quest for Christa T*, trans. Christopher Middleton (New York: Farrar, Straus & Giroux, 1970), p, 174.

16. See Bernice Reagon, "Turning the Century," in Smith, pp. 356–368; Bulkin, pp. 103, 190–193.

17. Information as of May 1984, thanks to the War Resisters League.

18. Cynthia Enloe, *Does Khaki Become You? The Militarisation of Women's Lives* (London: Pluto Press, 1983), ch. 8.

19. Sheila Rowbotham, Lynne Segal, and Hilary Wainwright, *Beyond the Fragments: Feminism and the Making of Socialism* (Boston: Alyson, 1981), pp. 55–56.

20. *Women under Apartheid* (London: International Defence and Aid Fund for Southern Africa in cooperation with the United Nations Centre Against Apartheid, 1981), pp. 87–99; Leonard Thompson and Andrew Prior, *South African Politics* (New Haven, Conn.: Yale University Press, 1981). An article in *Sechaba* (published by the African National Congress) refers to "the rich tradition of organization and mobilization by women" in the Black South African struggle ([October 1984]: p. 9).

21. Helen Wheatley, "Palestinian Women in Lebanon: Targets of Repression," *TWANAS, Third World Student Newspaper*, University of California, Santa Cruz (March 1984).

22. Etel Adnan, *Sitt Marie Rose*, trans. Georgina Kleege (Sausalito, Calif.: Post Apollo Press, 1982), p. 101.

23. Blanca Figueroa and Jeanine Anderson, "Women in Peru," *International Reports: Women and Society* (1981). See also Ximena Bunster and Elsa M. Chaney, *Sellers and Servants: Working Women in Lima Peru* (New York: Praeger, 1985), and Madhu Kishwar and Ruth Vanita, In *Search of Answers: Indian Women's Voices from "Manushi"* (London: Zed, 1984), pp. 56–57.

24. Gloria Anzaldúa and Cherrìe Moraga, eds., *This Bridge Called My Back: Writings by Radical Women of Color* (Watertown, Mass.: Persephone, 1981; distributed by Kitchen Table/Women of Color Press, Albany, New York).

42.
FEMINIST ENCOUNTERS:
LOCATING THE POLITICS OF EXPERIENCE
Chandra Talpade Mohanty

Feminist and anti-racist struggles in the 1990s face some of the same urgent questions encountered in the 1970s. After two decades of engagement in feminist political activism and scholarship in a variety of sociopolitical and geographical locations, questions of difference (sex, race, class, nation), experience and history remain at the centre of feminist analysis. Only, at least in the U.S. academy, feminists no longer have to contend as they did in the 1970s with phallocentric denials of the legitimacy of gender as a category of analysis. Instead, the crucial questions in the 1990s concern the construction, examination and, most significantly, the institutionalization of difference *within* feminist discourses. It is this institutionalization of difference that concerns me here. Specifically, I ask the following question: how does the politics of location in the contemporary U.S.A. determine and produce experience and difference as analytical and political categories in feminist "cross-cultural" work? By the term "politics of location" I refer to the historical, geographical, cultural, psychic, and imaginative boundaries which provide the ground for political definition and self-definition for contemporary U.S. feminists.[1]

Since the 1970s, there have been key paradigm shifts in western feminist theory. These shifts can be traced to political, historical, methodological, and philosophical developments in our understanding of questions of power, struggle, and social transformation. Feminists have drawn on decolonization movements around the world, on movements for racial equality, on peasant struggles and gay and lesbian movements, as well as on the methodologies of Marxism, psychoanalysis, deconstruction, and post-structuralism to situate our thinking in the 1990s. While these developments have often led to progressive, indeed radical analyses of sexual difference, the focus on questions of subjectivity and identity which is a hallmark of contemporary feminist theory has also had some problematic effects in the area of race and Third World/postcolonial studies. One problematic effect of the post-modern critique of essentialist notions of identity has been the dissolution of the category of race—however, this is often accomplished at the expense of a recognition of racism. Another effect has been the generation of discourses of diversity and pluralism which are grounded in an apolitical, often individualized identity politics.[2] Here, questions of *historical interconnection* are transformed into questions of discrete and separate histories (or even herstories) and into questions of identity politics.[3] While I cannot deal with such effects in detail here, I work through them in a limited way by suggesting the importance of analysing and theorizing difference in the context of feminist cross-cultural work. Through this theorization of experience, I suggest that historicizing and locating political agency is a necessary alternative to formulations of the "universality" of gendered oppression and struggles. This universality of gender oppression is problematic, based as it is on the assumption that the categories of race and class have to be invisible for gender to be visible. In the 1990s, the challenges posed by black and Third World feminists can point the way towards a more precise, transformative feminist politics. Thus, the juncture of feminist and anti-racist/Third World/post-colonial studies is of great significance, materially as well as methodologically.[4]

Feminist analyses which attempt to cross national, racial, and ethnic boundaries produce and reproduce difference in particular ways. This codification of difference occurs through the naturalization of analytic categories which are supposed to have cross-cultural validity. I attempt an analysis of two recent feminist texts which address the turn of the century directly. Both texts also foreground analytic categories which address questions of cross-cultural, cross-national differences among women. Robin Morgan's "Planetary Feminism: The Politics of the 21st Century" and Bernice Johnson Reagon's "Coalition Politics: Turning the Century" are both *movement* texts and are written for diverse mass audiences. Morgan's essay forms the introduction to her 1984 book, *Sisterhood Is Global: The International Women's Movement Anthology*, while Reagon's piece was first given as a talk at the West Coast Women's Music Festival in 1981, and has since been published in Barbara Smith's 1983 anthology, *Home Girls: A Black Feminist Anthology.*[5] Both essays construct contesting notions of experience, difference, and struggle within and across cultural boundaries. I stage an encounter between these texts because they represent for me, despite their differences from each other, an alternative presence—a thought, an idea, a record of activism and struggle—which can help me both locate and position myself in relation to "history." Through this presence, and with these texts, I can hope to approach the end of the century and not be overwhelmed. . . .

"A Place on the Map is Also a Place in History"[6]

The last decade has witnessed the publication of numerous feminist writings on what is generally referred to as an international women's movement, and we have its concrete embodiment in *Sisterhood Is Global,* a text which in fact describes itself as "The International Women's Movement Anthology." There is considerable difference between international feminist networks organized around specific issues like sex-tourism and multinational exploitation of women's work, and the notion of *an* international women's movement which, as I attempt to demonstrate, implicitly *assumes* global or universal sisterhood. But it is best to begin by recognizing the significance and value of the publication of an anthology such as this. The value of documenting the indigenous histories of women's struggles is unquestionable.

Morgan states that the book took twelve years in conception and development, five years in actual work, and innumerable hours in networking and fundraising. It is obvious that without Morgan's vision and perseverance this anthology would not have been published. The range of writing represented is truly impressive. At a time when most of the globe seems to be taken over by religious fundamentalism and big business, and the colonization of space takes precedence over survival concerns, an anthology that documents women's organized resistance has significant value in helping us envision a better future. In fact, it is because I recognize the value and importance of this anthology that I am concerned about the political implications of Morgan's framework for cross-cultural comparison. Thus my comments and criticisms are intended to encourage a greater internal self-consciousness within feminist politics and writing, not to lay blame or induce guilt.

Universal sisterhood is produced in Morgan's text through specific assumptions about women as a cross-culturally singular, homogeneous group with the same interests, perspectives and goals and similar experiences. Morgan's definitions of "women's experience" and history lead to a particular self-presentation of western women, a specific codification of differences among women, and eventually to what I consider to be problematic suggestions for political strategy.[7] Since feminist discourse is productive of analytic categories and strategic decisions which have material effects, the construction of the category of universal sisterhood in a text which is widely read deserves attention. In addition, *Sisterhood Is Global* is still the only text which proclaims itself as the anthology of *the* international women's movement. It has had worldwide distribution, and Robin Morgan herself has earned the respect of feminists everywhere. And since authority is always charged with responsibility, the discursive production and dissemination of notions of universal sisterhood is a significant political event which perhaps solicits its own analysis.

Morgan's explicit intent is "to further the dialogue between and solidarity of women everywhere" (p. 8). This is a valid and admirable project to the extent that one is willing to assume, if not the reality, then at least the possibility, of universal sisterhood on the basis of shared good will. But the moment we attempt to articulate the operation of contemporary imperialism with the notion of an international women's movement based on global sisterhood, the awkward political implications of Morgan's task become clear. Her particular notion of universal sisterhood seems predicated on the erasure of the history and effects of contemporary imperialism. Robin Morgan seems to situate *all* women (including herself) outside contemporary world history, leading to what I see as her ultimate suggestion that transcendence rather than engagement is the model for future social change. And this, I think, is a model which can have dangerous implications for women who do not and cannot speak from a location of white, western, middle-class privilege. A place on the map (New York City) is, after all, also a locatable place in history.

What is the relation between experience and politics in Robin Morgan's text? In "Planetary Feminism" the category of "women's experience" is constructed within two parameters: woman as victim, and, woman as truth-teller. Morgan suggests that it is not mystical or biological commonalities which characterize women across cultures and histories, but rather a common condition and world view.... This may be convincing up to a point, but the political analysis that underlies this characterization of the commonality among women is shaky at best. At various points in the essay, this "common condition" that women share is referred to as the suffering inflicted by a universal "patriarchal mentality" (p. 1), women's opposition to male power and androcentrism, and the experience of rape, battery, labour and childbirth. For Morgan, the magnitude of suffering experienced by most of the women in the world leads to their potential power as a world political force, a force constituted in opposition to Big Brother in the U.S., Western and Eastern Europe, Moscow, China, Africa, the Middle East and Latin America. The assertion that women constitute a potential world political force is suggestive; however, Big Brother is *not exactly the same* even in, say, the U.S. and Latin America. Despite the similarity of power interests and location, the two contexts present significant differences in the manifestations of power and hence of the possibility of struggles against it. I part company with Morgan when she seems to believe that Big Brother is the same the world over because "he" simply represents male interests, notwithstanding particular imperial histories or the role of monopoly capital in different countries.

In Morgan's analysis, women are unified by their shared perspective (for example, opposition to war), shared goals (betterment of human beings) and shared experience of oppression. Here the homogeneity of women as a group is produced not on the basis of biological essentials (Morgan offers a rich, layered critique of biological materialism), but rather through the psychologization of complex and contradictory historical and cultural realities. This leads in turn to the assumption of women as a unified group on the basis of secondary sociological universals. What binds women together is an ahistorical notion of the sameness of their oppression and, consequently, the sameness of their struggles. Therefore in Morgan's text cross-cultural comparisons are based on the assumption of the singularity and homogeneity of women as a *group*. This homogeneity of women as a group, is, in turn, predicated on a definition of the *experience of oppression* where difference can only be understood as male/female....

Assumptions pertaining to the relation of experience to history are evident in Morgan's discussion of another aspect of women's experience: woman as truth-teller. According to her, women speak of the "real" unsullied by "rhetoric" or "diplomatic abstractions." They, as opposed to men (also a coherent singular group in this analytic economy), are authentic human beings whose "freedom of choice" has been taken away from them: "Our emphasis is on the individual voice of a woman speaking not as an official representative of her country, but rather as a truth- teller, with an emphasis on reality as opposed to rhetoric" (p. xvi). In addition, Morgan asserts that women social scientists are "freer of androcentric bias"and "more likely to elicit more trust and...more honest responses from female respondents of their studies" (p. xvii). There is an argument to be made for

women interviewing women, but I do not think this is it. The assumptions underlying these statements indicate to me that Morgan thinks women have some kind
of privileged access to the "real," the "truth," and can elicit "trust" from other
women purely on the basis of their being not-male. There is a problematic conflation here of the biological and the psychological with the discursive and the ideological. "Women" are collapsed into the "suppressed feminine" and men into the
dominant ideology....

What, then, does this analysis suggest about the status of experience in this
text? In Morgan's account, women have a sort of cross-cultural coherence as distinct from men. The status or position of women is assumed to be self-evident.
However, this focus on the position of women whereby women are seen as a coherent group in *all* contexts, regardless of class or ethnicity, structures the world in
ultimately Manichaean terms, where women are always seen in opposition to men,
patriarchy is always essentially the invariable phenomenon of male domination,
and the religious, legal, economic, and familial systems are implicitly assumed to
be constructed by men. Here, men and women are seen as whole groups with
already constituted experiences as groups, and questions of history, conflict, and
difference are formulated from what can only be this privileged location of knowledge.

I am bothered, then, by the fact that Morgan can see contemporary imperialism only in terms of a "patriarchal mentality" which is enforced by men as a *group*.
Women across class, race, and national boundaries are participants to the extent
that we are "caught up in political webs not of our making which we are powerless
to unravel" (p. 25). Since women as a unified group are seen as unimplicated in the
process of history and contemporary imperialism, the logical strategic response for
Morgan appears to be political transcendence: "To fight back in solidarity, however, as a real political force requires that women transcend the patriarchal barriers
of class and race, and furthermore, transcend even the solutions the Big Brothers
propose to the problems they themselves created" (p. 18). Morgan's emphasis on
women's transcendence is evident in her discussions of 1) women's deep opposition to nationalism as practised in patriarchal society, and 2) women's involvement
in peace and disarmament movements across the world, because, in her opinion,
they desire peace (as opposed to men who cause war). Thus, the concrete reality of
women's involvement in peace movements is substituted by an abstract "desire" for
peace which is supposed to transcend race, class, and national conflicts among
women. Tangible responsibility and credit for organizing peace movements is
replaced by an essentialist and psychological unifying desire. The problem is that in
this case women are not seen as political agents; they are merely allowed to be well
intentioned. Although Morgan does offer some specific suggestions for political
strategy which require resisting "the system," her fundamental suggestion is that
women transcend the left, the right, and the centre, the law of the father, God, and
the system. Since women have been analytically constituted outside real politics or
history, progress for them can only be seen in terms of transcendence.

The *experience* of struggle is thus defined as both personal and ahistorical. In other words, the political is *limited to* the personal and all conflicts among and within women are flattened. If sisterhood itself is defined on the basis of personal intentions, attitudes, or desires, conflict is also automatically constructed on only the psychological level. Experience is thus written in as simultaneously individual (that is, located in the individual body/psyche of woman) and general (located in women as a preconstituted collective). There seem to be two problems with this definition. First, experience is seen as being immediately accessible, understood and named. The complex relationships between behaviour and its representation are either ignored or made irrelevant; experience is collapsed into discourse and vice-versa. Second, since experience has a fundamentally psychological status, questions of history and collectivity are formulated on the level of attitude and intention. In effect, the sociality of collective struggles is understood in terms of something like individual-group relations, relations which are common-sensically seen as detached from history. If the assumption of the *sameness* of experience is what ties woman (individual) to women (group), regardless of class, race, nation, and sexualities, the notion of experience is anchored firmly in the notion of the individual self, a determined and specifiable constituent of European modernity. However, this notion of the individual needs to be self-consciously historicized if as feminists we wish to go beyond the limited bourgeois ideology of individualism, especially as we attempt to understand what cross-cultural sisterhood might be made to mean....

Universal sisterhood, defined as the transcendence of the "male" world, thus ends up being a middle-class, psychologized notion which effectively erases material and ideological power differences within and among groups of women, especially between First and Third World women (and, paradoxically, removes us all as actors from history and politics). It is in this erasure of difference as inequality and dependence that the privilege of Morgan's political "location" might be visible. Ultimately in this reductive utopian vision, men *participate* in politics while women can only hope to *transcend* them. Morgan's notion of universal sisterhood *does* construct a unity. However, for me, the real challenge arises in being able to craft a notion of political unity without relying on the logic of appropriation and incorporation and, just as significantly, a denial of *agency*. For me the unity of women is best understood not as *given*, on the basis of a natural/psychological commonality; it is something that has to be worked for, struggled towards—*in history*. What we need to do is articulate ways in which the historical forms of oppression relate to the category "women," and not to try to deduce one from the other. In other words, it is Morgan's formulation of the relation of synchronous, alternative histories (herstories) to a diachronic, dominant historical narrative (History) that is problematic. One of the tasks of feminist analysis is uncovering alternative, non-identical histories which challenge and disrupt the spatial and temporal location of a hegemonic history. However, sometimes attempts to uncover and locate alternative histories code these very histories as either totally dependent on and determined by a dominant narrative, or as isolated and autonomous narratives, untouched in their essence by the dominant figurations. In these rewritings, what is lost is the recognition that it is the very co-implication of histories with History which helps us situate and understand oppositional agency. In Morgan's text, it is the move to characterize alternative herstories as separate and different from history that results in a denial of feminist agency. And it is this potential repositioning of the relation of oppositional histories/spaces to a dominant historical narrative that I find valuable in Bernice Reagon's discussion of coalition politics.

"It Ain't Home No More": Rethinking Unity

While Morgan uses the notion of sisterhood to construct a cross-cultural unity of women and speaks of "planetary feminism as the politics of the 21st century," Bernice Johnson Reagon uses *coalition* as the basis to talk about the cross-cultural commonality of struggles, identifying *survival*, rather than *shared oppression*, as the ground for coalition. She begins with this valuable political reminder: "You don't go into coalition because you *like* it. The only reason you would consider trying to team up with somebody who could possibly kill you, is because that's the only way you can figure you can stay alive" (p. 357).

The governing metaphor Reagon uses to speak of coalition, difference and struggle is that of a "barred room." However, whereas Morgan's barred room might be owned and controlled by the Big Brothers in different countries, Reagon's internal critique of the contemporary left focuses on the barred rooms constructed by oppositional political movements such as feminist, civil rights, gay and lesbian, and chicano political organizations. She maintains that these barred rooms may provide a "nurturing space" for a little while, but they ultimately provide an illusion of community based on isolation and the freezing of difference. Thus, while sameness of experience, oppression, culture, et cetera. may be adequate to construct this space, the moment we "get ready to clean house" this very sameness in community is exposed as having been built on a debilitating ossification of difference.

Reagon is concerned with differences *within* political struggles, and the negative effects, in the long run, of a nurturing, "nationalist" perspective: "At a certain stage nationalism is crucial to a people if you are going to ever impact as a group in your own interest. Nationalism at another point becomes reactionary because it is totally inadequate for surviving in the world with many peoples" (p. 358). This is similar to Gramsci's analysis of oppositional political strategy in terms of the difference between wars of manoeuvre (separation and consolidation) and wars of position (re-entry into the mainstream in order to challenge it on its own terms). Reagon's insistence on breaking out of barred rooms and struggling for coalition is a recognition of the importance—indeed the inevitable necessity—of wars of position. It is based, I think, on a recognition of the need to resist the imperatives of an expansionist U.S. state, and of imperial History. It is also, however, a recognition of the limits of identity politics. For once you open the door and let others in, "the room don't feel like the room no more. And it ain't home no more" (p. 359).

The relation of coalition to home is a central metaphor for Reagon. She speaks of coalition as opposed, by definition, to home.[8] In fact, the confusion of home with coalition is what concerns her as an urgent problem, and it is here that the status of experience in her text becomes clear. She criticizes the idea of enforcing "women-only" or "woman-identified" space by using an "in-house" definition of woman. What concerns her is not a sameness which allows us to identify with each other as women, but the exclusions particular normative definitions of "woman" enforce. It is the exercise of violence in creating a legitimate *inside* and an illegitimate *outside* in the name of identity that is significant to her—or, in other words, the exercise of violence when unity or coalition is confused with home and used to enforce a premature sisterhood or solidarity. According to her this "comes from taking a word like 'women' and using it as a code" (p. 360). The experience of being woman can create an illusory unity, for it is not the experience of being woman, but the meanings attached to gender, race, class, and age at various historical moments that is of strategic significance.

Thus, by calling into question the term "woman" as the automatic basis of unity, Bernice Reagon would want to splinter the notion of experience suggested by Robin Morgan. Her critique of nationalist and culturalist positions, which after an initial necessary period of consolidation work in harmful and exclusionary ways, provides us with a fundamentally political analytic space for an understanding of experience. By always insisting on an analysis of the operations and effects of power in our attempts to create alternative communities, Reagon foregrounds our *strategic* locations and positionings. Instead of separating experience and politics and basing the latter on the former, she emphasizes the politics that always define and inform experience (in particular, in left, anti-racist and feminist communities). By examining the differences and potential divisions *within* political subjects as well as collectives, Reagon offers an implicit critique of totalizing theories of history and social change. She underscores the significance of the traditions of political struggle, what she calls an "old-age perspective"—and this is, I would add, a global perspective. What is significant, however, is that the global is forged on the basis of memories and counter-narratives, not on an ahistorical universalism. For Reagon, global, old-age perspectives are founded on humility, the gradual chipping away of our assumed, often ethnocentric centres of self/other definitions.

Thus, her particular location and political priorities lead her to emphasize a politics of engagement (a war of position), and to interrogate totalizing notions of difference and the identification of exclusive spaces as "homes." Perhaps it is partly also her insistence on the urgency and difficult nature of political struggle that leads Reagon to talk about difference in terms of racism, while Morgan often formulates difference in terms of cultural pluralism. This is Bernice Reagon's way of "throwing yourself into the next century":

> Most of us think that the space we live in is the most important space there is, and that the condition we find ourselves in is the condition that must be changed or else. That is only partially the case. If you analyse the situation properly, you will know that there

might be a few things you can do in your personal, individual interest so that you can experience and enjoy change. But most of the things that you do, if you do them right, are for people who live long after you are forgotten. That will happen if you give it away.... The only way you can take yourself seriously is if you can throw yourself into the next period beyond your little meager human-body-mouth talking all the time. (p. 365)

...I have looked at two recent feminist texts and argued that feminist discourse must be self-conscious in its production of notions of experience and difference. The rationale for staging an encounter between the two texts, written by a white and black activist respectively, was not to identify "good" and "bad" feminist texts. Instead, I was interested in foregrounding questions of cross-cultural analysis which permeate "movement" or popular (not just academic) feminist texts, and in indicating the significance of a politics of location in the U.S. of the 1980s and the 1990s. Instead of privileging a certain limited version of identity politics, it is the current *intersection* of anti-racist, anti-imperialist, and gay and lesbian struggles which we need to understand to map the ground for feminist political strategy and critical analysis.[9] A reading of these texts also opens up for me a temporality of *struggle*, which disrupts and challenges the logic of linearity, development, and progress which are the hallmarks of European modernity.

But why focus on a temporality of struggle? And how do I define *my* place on the map? For me, the notion of a temporality of struggle defies and subverts the logic of European modernity and the "law of identical temporality." It suggests an insistent, simultaneous, non-synchronous process characterized by multiple locations, rather than a search for origins and endings which, as Adrienne Rich says, 'seems a way of stopping time in its tracks."[10] The year 2000 is the end of the Christian millennium, and Christianity is certainly an indelible part of post-colonial history. But we cannot afford to forget those alternative, resistant spaces occupied by oppositional histories and memories. By not insisting on *a* history or *a* geography but focusing on a temporality of struggle, I create the historical ground from which I can define myself in the U.S.A. of the 1990s, a place from which I can speak to the future—not the end of an era but the promise of many.

The U.S.A. of the 1990s: a geopolitical power seemingly unbounded in its effects, peopled with "natives" struggling for land and legal rights, and "immigrants" with their own histories and memories. Alicia Dujovne Ortiz writes about Buenos Aires as "the very image of expansiveness."[11] This is also how I visualize the U.S.A. of the 1990s. Ortiz writes of Buenos Aires:

A city without doors. Or rather, a port city, a gateway which never closes. I have always been astonished by those great cities of the world which have such precise boundaries that one can say exactly where they end. Buenos Aires has no end. One wants to ring it with a beltway, as if to point an index finger, trembling with uncertainty, and say: "You end there. Up to this point you are you. Beyond that, God alone knows!"... a city that is impossible to limit with the eye or the mind. So, what does it mean to say that one is a native of Buenos Aires? To belong to Buenos Aires, to be *Porteno*—to come from this

Port? What does this mean? What or who can we hang onto? Usually we cling to history or geography. In this case, what are we to do? Here geography is merely an abstract line that marks the separation of the earth and sky.[12]

If the logic of imperialism and the logic of modernity share a notion of time, they also share a notion of space as territory. In the North America of the 1990s geography seems more and more like "an abstract line that marks the separation of the earth and sky." Witness the contemporary struggle for control over oil in the name of "democracy and freedom" in Saudi Arabia. Even the boundaries between space and outer space are not binding any more. In this expansive and expanding continent, how does one locate oneself? And what does location as I have inherited it have to do with self-conscious, strategic location as I choose it now?

A National Public Radio news broadcast announces that all immigrants to the United States now have to undergo mandatory AIDS testing. I am reminded very sharply of my immigrant status in this country, of my plastic identification card which is proof of my legitimate location in the U.S. But location, for feminists, necessarily implies self- as well as collective definition, since meanings of the self are inextricably bound up with our understanding of collectives as social agents. For me, a comparative reading of Morgan's and Reagon's documents of activism precipitates the recognition that experience of the self, which is often discontinuous and fragmented, must be historicized before it can be generalized into a collective vision. In other words, experience must be historically interpreted and theorized if it is to become the basis of feminist solidarity and struggle, and it is at this moment that an understanding of the politics of location proves crucial.

In this country I am, for instance, subject to a number of legal/political definitions: "post-colonial," "immigrant," "Third World." These definitions, while in no way comprehensive, do trace an analytic and political space from which I can insist on a temporality of struggle. Movement *between* cultures, languages, and complex configurations of meaning and power have always been the territory of the colonized. It is this *process*, what Caren Kaplan in her discussion of the reading and writing of home/exile has called "a continual reterritorialization, with the proviso that one moves on,"[13] that I am calling a temporality of struggle. It is this process, this reterritorialization through struggle, that allows me a paradoxical continuity of self, mapping and transforming my political location. It suggests a particular notion of political agency, since my location forces and enables specific modes of reading and knowing the dominant. The struggles I choose to engage in are then an intensification of these modes of knowing—an engagement on a different level of knowledge. There is, quite simply, no transcendental location possible in the U.S.A. of the 1990s.

I have argued for a politics of engagement rather than a politics of transcendence, for the present and the future. I *know*—in my own non-synchronous temporality—that by the year 2000 apartheid will be discussed as a nightmarish chapter in black South Africa's history, the resistance to and victory over the efforts of the U.S. government and multinational mining conglomerates to relocate the Navajo and

Hopi reservations from Big Mountain, Arizona, will be written into elementary-school textbooks, and the Palestinian homeland will no longer be referred to as the "Middle East question"—it will be a reality. But that is my preferred history: what I hope and struggle for, I garner as *my* knowledge, create it as the place from where I seek to know. After all, it is the way in which I understand, define and engage in feminist, anti-imperialist and anti-racist collectives and movements that anchors my belief in the future and in the efficacy of struggles for social change.

Notes

1. I am indebted to Adrienne Rich's essay, "Notes Toward a Politics of Location" (1984), for the notion of the "politics of location" (in her *Blood, Bread, and Poetry: Selected Prose 1979–1985* [W.W. Norton & Company, New York, 1986], pp. 210–31). In a number of essays in this collection, Rich writes eloquently and provocatively about the politics of her own location as a white, Jewish, lesbian feminist in North America. See especially "North American Tunnel Vision" (1983) and "Blood, Bread and Poetry: The Location of the Poet" (1984). While I attempt to modify and extend Rich's notion, I share her sense of urgency as she asks feminists to re-examine the politics of our location in North America:

   > A natural extension of all this seemed to me the need to examine not only racial and ethnic identity, but location in the United States of North America. As a feminist in the United States it seemed necessary to examine how we participate in mainstream North American cultural chauvinism, the sometimes unconscious belief that white North Americans possess a superior right to judge, select, and ransack other cultures, that we are more "advanced" than other peoples of this hemisphere... It was not enough to say "As a woman I have no country; as a woman my country is the whole world." Magnificent as that vision may be, we can't explode into breadth without a conscious grasp on the particular and concrete meaning of our location here and now, in the United States of America. ("North American Tunnel Vision," p. 162)

2. I address one version of this, the management of race and cultural pluralism in the U.S. academy, in some depth in my essay "On Race and Voice: Challenges for Liberal Education in the 1990s," *Cultural Critique*, 14 (1989–90), pp. 179–208.

3. Two recent essays develop the point I am trying to suggest here. Jenny Bourne identifies the problems with most forms of contemporary identity politics which equalize notions of oppression, thereby writing out of the picture any analysis of structural exploitation or domination. See her "Jewish Feminism and Identity Politics," *Race and Class*, XXIX (1987), pp. 1–24.

   In a similar vein, S.P. Mohanty uses the opposition between "History" and "histories" to criticize an implicit assumption in contemporary cultural theory that pluralism is an adequate substitute for political analyses of dependent relationships and larger historical configurations. For Mohanty, the ultimate target is the cultural and historical *relativism* which he identifies as the unexamined philosophical "dogma" underlying political celebrations of pure difference. This is how he characterizes the initial issues involved:

   > Plurality [is] thus a political ideal as much as it [is] a methodological slogan. But... a nagging question [remains]: How do we negotiate between my history and yours? How would it be possible for us to recover our commonality, not the humanist myth of our shared human attributes which are meant to distinguish us all from animals, but, more significantly, the imbrication of our various pasts and presents, the ineluctable relationships of shared and contested meanings, values, material resources? It is necessary to assert our dense particularities, our lived and imagined differences. But could we afford to leave unexamined the question of how our differences are intertwined and indeed hierarchically organized? Could we, in other words, really afford to have entirely different histories, to see ourselves as living—and having lived—in entirely heterogeneous and discrete spaces?

See his "Us and Them: On the Philosophical Bases of Political Criticism," *The Yale Journal of Criticism*, 2 (1989), pp. 1–31; p. 13.

4. For instance, some of the questions which arise in feminist analyses and politics which are situated at the juncture of studies of race, colonialism, and Third World political economy pertain to the systemic production, constitution, operation and reproduction of the institutional manifestations of power. How does power operate in the constitution of gendered and racial subjects? How do we talk about contemporary political praxis, collective consciousness and collective struggle in the context of an analysis of power? Other questions concern the discursive codification of sexual politics and the corresponding feminist political strategies these codifications engender. Why is sexual politics defined around particular issues? One might examine the cultural and historical processes and conditions under which sexuality is constructed during conditions of war. One might also ask under what historical conditions sexuality is defined as sexual violence, and investigate the emergence of gay and lesbian sexual identities. The discursive organization of these questions is significant because they help to chart and shape collective resistance. Some of these questions are addressed by contributors in a collection of essays I have co-edited with Ann Russo and Lourdes Torres, entitled *Third World Women and the Politics of Feminism* (Indiana University Press, Bloomington, Ind., and Indianapolis, 1991).

5. Robin Morgan, "Planetary Feminism: The Politics of the 21st Century," in her *Sisterhood Is Global: The International Women's Movement Anthology* (Anchor Press/Doubleday, New York, 1984), pp. 1–37; I also refer to the "Prefatory Note and Methodology" section (pp. xiii–xxiii) of *Sisterhood Is Global* in this essay. Bernice Johnson Reagon, "Coalition Politics: Turning the Century," in Barbara Smith (ed.), *Home Girls: A Black Feminist Anthology* (Kitchen Table, Women of Color Press, New York, 1983), pp. 356–68.

6. Rich, "Notes Toward a Politics of Location," p. 212.

7. Elsewhere I have attempted a detailed analysis of some recent western feminist social science texts about the Third World. Focusing on works which have appeared in an influential series published by Zed Press of London, I examine this discursive construction of women in the Third World and the resultant western feminist self-representations. See "Under Western Eyes: Feminist Scholarship and Colonial Discourses," *Feminist Review*, 30 (1988), pp. 61–88.

8. For an extensive discussion of the appeal and contradictions of notions of home and identity in contemporary feminist politics, see Biddy Martin and Chandra Talpade Mohanty, "Feminist Politics: What's Home Got to Do With It?" in de Lauretis, *Feminist Studies/Critical Studies*, pp. 191–212.

9. For a rich and informative account of contemporary racial politics in the U.S., see Michael Omi and Howard Winant, *Racial Formation in the United States: From the 1960s to the 1980s* (Routledge and Kegan Paul, New York and London, 1986). Surprisingly, this text erases gender and gay politics altogether, leading me to wonder how we can talk about the "racial state" without addressing questions of gender and sexual politics. A good companion text which in fact emphasizes such questions is G. Anzaldúa and Moraga (eds.), *This Bridge Called My Back: Writings By Radical Women of Color* (Kitchen Table, Women of Color Press, New York, 1983). Another, more contemporary text which continues some of the discussions in *This Bridge*, also edited by Gloria Anzaldúa, is entitled *Making Face, Making Soul, Haciendo Caras, Creative and Critical Perspectives by Women Color* (Aunt Lute, San Francisco, 1990).

10. Rich, "Notes Toward a Politics of Location," p. 227.

11. Alicia Dujovne Ortiz, "*Buenos Aires* (an excerpt)," *Discourse*, 8 (1986–7), pp. 73–83; p. 76.

12. Ibid., p. 76.

13. Caren Kaplan, "The Poetics of Displacement in Buenos Aires," *Discourse*, 8 (1986–87), pp. 94–102; p. 98.

43.
BEYOND BEAN COUNTING
JeeYeun Lee

I came out as a woman, an Asian American and a bisexual within a relatively short span of time, and ever since then I have been guilty of the crime of bean counting, as Bill Clinton oh-so-eloquently phrased it. Every time I am in a room of people gathered for any reason, I automatically count those whom I can identify as women, men, people of color, Asian Americans, mixed-race people, whites, gays and lesbians, bisexuals, heterosexuals, people with disabilities. So when I received the call for submissions for this anthology, I imagined opening up the finished book to the table of contents and counting beans; I then sent the call for submissions to as many queer Asian/Pacific American women writers as I knew.

Such is the nature of feminism in the 1990s: an uneasy balancing act between the imperatives of outreach and inclusion on the one hand, and the risk of tokenism and further marginalization on the other. This dynamic has indelibly shaped my personal experiences with feminism, starting from my very first encounter with organized feminism. This encounter happened to be, literally, Feminist Studies 101 at the university I attended. The content of the class was divided into topics such as family, work, sexuality and so forth, and for each topic we studied what various feminist paradigms said about it: "liberal feminism," "socialist feminism," "radical feminism" and "feminism and women of color."

Taking this class was an exhilarating, empowering and very uneasy experience. For the first time I found people who articulated those murky half-formed feelings that I could previously only express incoherently as "But that's not fair!" People who agreed, sympathized, related their own experiences, theorized, helped me form what I had always known. In seventh grade, a teacher made us do a mock debate, and I ended up arguing with Neil Coleman about whether women or men were better cooks. He said more men were professional chefs, therefore men were better. I responded that more women cooked in daily life, therefore women were better. He said it was quality that mattered, not quantity, and left me standing there with nothing to say. I knew there was something wrong with his argument, something wrong with the whole issue as it was framed, and felt extremely annoyed at being made to consent to the inferiority of my gender, losing in front of the whole class. I could never defend myself when arguments like this came up, invariably with boys who were good at debates and used to winning. They left me seething with resentment at their manipulations and frustrated at my speechlessness. So to come to a class that addressed these issues directly and gave me the words for all those pent-up feelings and frustrations was a tremendously affirming and empowering experience.

At the same time, it was an intensely uncomfortable experience. I knew "women of color" was supposed to include Asian American women, but I could not find any in the class readings. Were there no Asian American feminists? Were there none who could write in English? Did there even exist older Asian American women who were second or third generation? Were we Asian American students in the class the first to think about feminism? A class about women, I thought, was a class about me, so I looked for myself everywhere and found nothing. Nothing about Asian American families, immigrant women's work patterns, issues of sexuality and body image for Asian women, violence against Asian American women, Asian American women in the seventies feminist movement, nothing anywhere. I wasn't fully conscious then that I was searching for this, but this absence came out in certain feelings. First of all, I felt jealous of African American and Chicana feminists. Their work was present at least to some degree in the readings: They had research and theories, they were eloquent and they *existed*. Black and Chicana women in the class could claim them as role models, voices, communities—I had no one to claim as my own. My emerging identification as a woman of color was displaced through the writings of black and Chicana women, and I had to read myself, create my politics, through theirs; even now, to a certain extent, I feel more familiar with their issues than those of Asian American women. Second, I felt guilty. Although it was never expressed outright, I felt that there was some pressure on me to represent Asian American issues, and I could not. I felt estranged from the Asian American groups on campus and Asian American politics and activism in general, and guilty about this ignorance and alienation.

Now mind you, I'm still grateful for this class. Feminism was my avenue to politics: It politicized me; it raised my consciousness about issues of oppression, power and resistance in general. I learned a language with which I could start to explain my experiences and link them to larger societal structures of oppression and complicity. It also gave me ways that I could resist and actively fight back. I became interested in Asian American politics, people of color politics, gay/lesbian/bisexual politics and other struggles because of this exposure to feminism. But there is no excuse for this nearly complete exclusion of Asian/Pacific American women from the class. Marginalization is not simply a politically correct buzzword, it is a material reality that affects people's lives—in this case, my own. I would have been turned off from feminism altogether had it not been for later classes that dealt specifically with women of color. And I would like to name names here: I went to Stanford University, a bastion of privilege that pretends to be on the cutting edge of "multiculturalism." Just under twenty-five percent of the undergraduate population is Asian/Pacific American, but there was no mention of Asian/Pacific American women in Feminist Studies 101. All the classes I took on women of color were taught by graduate students and visiting professors. There was, at that time, only one woman of color on the feminist studies faculty. I regret that I realized the political importance of these facts only after I left Stanford.

I understand that feminists in academia are caught between a rock and a hard place—not too many of us hold positions of decision-making power in universities. And I must acknowledge my gratitude for their struggles in helping to establish feminist studies programs and produce theories and research about women, all of which create vital opportunities and affirmation. But other women's organizations that are not constrained by such explicit forces are also lily-white. This obviously differs from group to group, and I think many of them are very conscientious about outreach to historically marginalized women. But, for instance, in 1992 and 1993, at the meetings I attended of the Women's Action Coalition (WAC) in New York City, out of approximately two hundred women usually fewer than twenty women of color were present.

But this is not a diatribe against feminism in general. I want to emphasize that the feminism that I and other young women come to today is one that is at least sensitive to issues of exclusion. If perhaps twenty years ago charges of racism, classism, and homophobia were not taken seriously, today they are cause of extreme anguish and soul-searching. I am profoundly grateful to older feminists of color and their white allies who struggled to bring U.S. feminist movements to this point. At the same time, I think that this current sensitivity often breeds tokenism, guilt, suspicion, and self-rightousness that have very material repercussions on women's groups. I have found these uneasy dynamics in all the women's groups I've come across, addressed to varying degrees. At one extreme, I have seen groups that deny the marginalizing affects of their practices, believing that issues of inclusion really have nothing to do with their specific agendas. At the other extreme, I have seen groups ripped apart by accusations of political correctness, immobilized by guilt, knowing they should address a certain issue but not knowing how to begin, and still wondering why "women of color just don't come to our meetings." And tokenism is alive and well in the nineties. Those of us who have been aware of our tokenization often become suspicious and tired of educating others, wondering if we are invested enough to continue to do so, wondering if the overall goal is worth it.

In this age when "political correctness" has been appropriated by conservative forces as a derogatory term, it is extremely difficult to honestly discuss and confront any ideas and practices that perpetuate dominant norms—and none of us is innocent of such collusion. Many times, our response is to become defensive, shutting down to constructive critiques and actions, or to individualize our collusion as solely a personal fault, as if working on our individual racist or classist attitudes would somehow make things better. It appears that we all have a lot of work to do still.

And I mean *all.* Issues of exclusion are not the sole province of white feminists. I learned this very vividly at a 1993 retreat organized by the Asian Pacifica Lesbian Network. It has become somewhat common lately to speak of "Asian and Pacific Islanders" or "Asian/Pacific Americans" or, as in this case, "Asian Pacifica." This is meant to be inclusive, to recognize some issues held in common by people from Asia and people from the Pacific Islands. Two women of Native Hawaiian descent and some Asian American allies confronted the group at this retreat to ask for more than lip service in the organization's name: If the group was seriously committed to being an inclusive coalition, we needed to educate ourselves about and actively advocate Pacific Islander issues. And because I don't want to relegate them to a footnote, I will mention here a few of these issues: the demand for sovereignty for Native Hawaiians, whose government was illegally overthrown by the U.S. in 1893; fighting stereotypes of women and men that are different from those of Asian people; decrying U.S. imperialist possession and occupation of the islands of Guam, the Virgin Islands, American Samoa, the Marshall Islands, Micronesia, the Northern Mariana Islands and several others.

This was a retreat where one would suppose everyone had so much in common—after all, we were all queer API women, right? Any such myth was effectively destroyed by the realities of our experiences and issues: We were women of different ethnic backgrounds, with very different issues among East Asians, South Asians, Southeast Asians, and Pacific Islanders; women of mixed race and heritage; women who identified as lesbians and those who identified as bisexuals; women who were immigrants, refugees, illegal aliens, or second generation or more; older women, physically challenged women, women adopted by white families, women from the Midwest. Such tangible differences brought home the fact that no simplistic identity politics is *ever* possible, that we had to conceive of ourselves as a coalition first and foremost; as one woman on a panel said, our identity as queer API women must be a *coalitional* identity. Initially, I thought that I had finally found a home where I could relax and let down my guard. This was true to a certain degree, but I discovered that this was the home where I would have to work the hardest because I cared the most. I would have to be committed to push myself and push others to deal with all of our differences, so that we *could* be safe for each other. And in this difficult work of coalition, one positive action was taken at the retreat: We changed the name of the organization to include "bisexual," thus becoming the Asian Pacifica Lesbian and Bisexual Network, a name that people started using immediately.

All this is to say that I and other young women have found most feminist movements today to be at this point, where there is at least a stated emphasis on inclusion and outreach with the accompanying risk of tokenism. I firmly believe that it is always the margins that push us further in our politics. Women of color do not struggle in feminist movements simply to add cultural diversity, to add the viewpoints of different kinds of women. Women of color feminist theories challenge the fundamental premises of feminism, such as the very definition of "women," and call for recognition of the constructed racial nature of *all* experiences of gender. In the same way, heterosexist norms do not oppress solely lesbians, bisexuals and gay men, but affect all of our choices and non-choices; issues posed by differently abled women question our basic assumptions about body image, health care, sexuality and work; ecofeminists challenge our fundamental ideas about living on and with the earth, about our interactions with animals, plants, food, agriculture and industry. Many feminists seem to find the issues of class the most difficult to address; we are always faced with the fundamental inequalities inherent to late-twentieth-century multinational capitalism and our unavoidable implication in its structures. Such an overwhelming array of problems can numb and immobilize us, or make us concentrate our energies too narrowly. I don't think that we have to address everything fully at the same time, but we *must* be fully aware of the limitations of our specific agendas. Progressive activists cannot afford to do the masters' work for them by continuing to carry out oppressive assumptions and exclusions.

These days, whenever someone says the word "women" to me, my mind goes blank. What "women"? What is this "women" thing you're talking about? Does that mean me? Does that mean my mother, my roommates, the white woman next door, the checkout clerk at the supermarket, my aunts in Korea, half of the world's population? I ask people to specify and specify, until I can figure out exactly what they're talking about, and I try to remember to apply the same standards to myself, to deny myself the slightest possibility of romanticization. Sisterhood may be global, but who is in that sisterhood? None of us can afford to assume anything about anybody else. This thing called "feminism" takes a great deal of hard work, and I think this is one of the primary hallmarks of young feminists' activism today: We realize that coming together and working together are by no means natural or easy.

WORKS CITED

The sources cited in parenthetical citations throughout all introductions and essays are listed below. Otherwise, footnoted materials are included at the end of each essay.

Adam, Gyorgy. 1975. Multinational Corporations and Worldwide Sourcing. In *International Firms and Modern Imperialism*, ed. Hugo Radice. New York: Penguin.

Adams, Alayne, and Sarah Castle. 1994. Gender Relations and Household Dynamics. In *Population Policies Reconsidered*, ed. Gita Sen, Adrienne Germain, and Lincoln C. Chen, pp. 161–73. Cambridge: Harvard University Press.

Agarwal, Bina. 1992. The Gender and Environment Debate: Lessons from India. *Feminist Studies* 18 (1): 119–58.

Aguilar–San Juan, Karin. 1996. Review of *The Very Inside. Amerasia Journal* 22: 161–64.

Ahmed, L. 1992. *Women and Gender in Islam.* New Haven: Yale University Press.

Alarcon, Norma. 1990. The Theoretical Subject(s) of *This Bridge Called My Back* and Anglo-American Feminism. In *Making Face, Making Soul*, ed. Gloria Anzaldúa, pp. 356-69. San Francisco: Aunt Lute Books.

Alcoff, Linda. 1988. Cultural Feminism vs. Poststructuralism. *Signs* 13: 405–35.

Alexander, M. Jacqui, and Chandra Talpade Mohanty, eds. 1997. *Feminist Genealogies, Colonial Legacies, Democratic Futures.* New York: Routledge.

Alvarez, Sonia E. 1997. Even Fidel Can't Change That: Trans/national Feminist Advocacy Strategies and Cultural Politics in Latin America. Unpublished paper presented at the Department of Cultural Anthropology, Duke University.

———. 1998. Latin American Feminisms "Go Global": Trends of the 1990's and Challenges for the New Millennium. In *Cultures of Politics/Politics of Cultures*, ed. Sonia E. Alvarez, Evelina Dagnino, and Arturo Escobar. Boulder: Westview Press.

American Association of University Women and the Wellesley College Center for Research on Women. 1992. *How Schools Shortchange Girls.* New York: Marlowe and Company.

Amos, Valerie, and Pratibha Parmar. 1984. Challenging Imperial Feminism. *Feminist Review* 17: 3–19.

Amos, V., G. Lewis, A. Mama, and P. Parmar, eds. 1984. Many Voices, One Chant: Black-Feminist Perspectives. *Feminist Review* 17.

Amott, Teresa, and Julie Matthaei. 1991. *Race, Gender, and Work.* Boston: South End Press.

Anderson, Benedict. 1983. *Imagined Communities.* London: Verso.

Anderson, Margaret. 1991. Feminism and the American Family Ideal. *Journal of Comparative Family Studies* 22 (2): 235–46.

Appadurai, A. 1988. Putting Hierarchy in Its Place. *Cultural Anthropology* 3 (1).

Archer, John, and Barbara Lloyd. 1985. *Sex and Gender*, rev. ed. Cambridge: Cambridge University Press.

Ashcroft, Bill, Gareth Griffiths, and Helen Tiffin. 1998. *Keywords in Post-Colonial Studies.* London: Routledge.

Asian and Pacific Women's Resource Collection Network. 1990. *Asia and Pacific Women's Resource and Action Series: Health.* Kuala Lumpur: Asia and Pacific Development Centre.

Awkward, Michael. 1996. A Black Man's Place(s) in Black Feminist Criticism. In *Representing Black Men*, ed. Marcellus Blount and George P. Cunningham, pp. 3–26. New York: Routledge.

Baloyi, Danisa E. 1995. Apartheid and Identity: Black Women in South Africa. In *Connecting Across Cultures and Continents: Black Women Speak Out on Identity, Race and Development*, ed. Achola Pala. New York: United Nations Development Fund for Women.

(Bambara), Toni Cade, ed. 1970. *The Black Woman: An Anthology*. New York: Signet.

Bang, R. 1989. High Prevalence of Gynecological Diseases in Rural Indian Women. *Lancet* 337: 85–88.

Barriosde Chungara, Domatila. 1977. *Let Me Speak: Testimony of Domatila, a Woman of the Bolivian Mines*, trans. by Victoria Ortiz. London: Monthly Review Press.

Basu, A. M. 1990. Cultural Influences on Health Care Use: Two Regional Groups in India. *Studies in Family Planning* 21: 275–86.

Beal, Frances. 1970. Double Jeopardy: To Be Black and Female. In *Liberation Now*, ed. Deborah Babcox and Madeline Belkin. New York: Dell.

Becker, Gary Stanley. 1957. *The Economics of Discrimination*. Chicago: University of Chicago Press.

Belenky, Mary, et al. 1986. *Women's Ways of Knowing*. New York: Basic Books.

Benmayor, R., R. M. Torruellas, and A. L. Juarbe. 1992. *Responses to Poverty Among Puerto Rican Women*. New York: Centro de Estudios Puertorriqueños, Hunter College.

Berer, M. 1990. What Would a Feminist Population Policy Be Like? *Women's Health Journal* 18: 4–7.

———. 1993. Population and Family Planning Policies: Women-Centered Perspectives. *Reproductive Health Matters* 1: 4–12.

Berry, Mary Frances. 1994. *Black Resistance, White Law*. New York: Penguin.

Bhabha, Homi. 1990. *Nation and Narration*. New York: Routledge.

———. 1994. *The Location of Culture*. New York: Routledge.

Bhasin, K., and N. Khan. 1986. *Some Questions on Feminism for Women in South Asia*. New Delhi: Kali.

Bhasin, K., and R. Menon. 1988. The Problem. *Seminar* 342, special issue on sati.

Bhatt, Radha. 1989. Laksmi Ashram: A Gandhian Perspective in the Himalayan Foothills. In *Healing the Wounds*, ed. Judith Plant, pp. 167–73. Boston: South End Press.

Bhavnani, Kum Kum. 2001. *Feminism and Race*. New York: Oxford University Press.

Bhavnani, K. K., and M. Coulson. 1986. Transforming Socialist-Feminism: The Challenge of Racism. *Feminist Review* 23.

Biehl, Janet. 1989. *Rethinking Ecofeminist Politics*. Boston: South End Press.

Blachman, M. 1973. *Eve in an Adamocracy*, Occasional Papers No. 5, New York University.

Blaxall, Martha, and Barbara Reagan, eds. 1976. *Women and the Workplace*. Chicago: University of Chicago Press.

Blunt, Alison, and Gilliam Rose, eds. 1994. *Writing, Women, and Space: Colonial and Postcolonial Geographies*. New York: Guilford Press.

Boland, Reed, Sudhakar Rao, and George Zeidenstein. 1994. Honoring Human Rights in Population Policies: From Declaration to Action. In *Population Policies Reconsidered*, ed. Gita Sen, Adrienne Germain, and Lincoln C. Chen, pp. 89–105. Cambridge: Harvard University Press.

Bonaparte, Marie. 1953. *Female Sexuality*. New York: Grove Press.

Bordo, Susan. 1986. The Cartesian Masculinization of Thought. *Signs* 11: 439–56.

Boserup, Ester. 1970. *Woman's Role in Economic Development*. London: Allen and Unwin.

Braidotti, Rosi et al. 1994. *Women, the Environment, and Sustainable Development*. London: Zed Books.

Brewer, Rose. 1993. Theorizing Race, Class and Gender: The New Scholarship of Black Feminist Intellectuals and Black Women's Labor. In *Theorizing Black Feminism*, ed. Stanlie M. James and Abena P. A. Busia, pp. 13–30. New York: Routledge.

Brosius, Peter. 1994. "Mere Observers: Writing in the Ethnographic Present in Sarawak, East Malaysia." Paper presented at the American Anthropological Association meeting, November, Washington, D.C.

Brown, Cynthia Strokes, ed. 1986. *Ready from Within: Septima Clark and the Civil Rights Movement*. Navarro, CA: Wild Trees Press.

Brown, Elaine. 1992. *A Taste of Power: A Black Woman's Story.* New York: Pantheon.

Brown, Elsa Barkley. 1994. Negotiating and Transforming the Public Sphere: African American Political Life in the Transition from Slavery to Freedom. *Public Culture* 7 (1): 107–46.

Brown, Wendy. 1995. *States of Injury: Power and Freedom in Late Modernity.* Princeton: Princeton University Press.

Bruce, J. 1990. Fundamental Elements of the Quality of Care. *Studies in Family Planning* 21: 61–91.

Brydon, L., and S. Chant. 1989. *Women in the Third World.* Aldershot: Edward Elgar.

Buck, Elizabeth. 1993. *Paradise Remade: The Politics of Culture and History in Hawai'i.* Philadelphia: Temple University Press.

Bulkin, E., M. B. Pratt, and B. Smith. 1984. *Yours in Struggle: Feminist Perspectives on Racism and Anti-Semitism.* New York: Long Haul Press.

Bunch, Charlotte. 1979. Feminism and Education: Not By Degrees. *Quest* 1: 1–7.

———. 1990. Women's Rights as Human Rights. *Human Rights Quarterly* 12: 486–98.

Bunch, Charlotte, and Susana Fried. 1996. Bejing' 95: Moving Women's Human Rights From Margin to Center. *Signs* 22: 203.

Burnham, Margaret A. An Impossible Marriage: Slave Law and Family Law. *Law and Inequality* 5: 187–225.

Burris, Barbara. 1973. The Fourth World Manifesto. In *Radical Feminism*, ed. Anne Koedt, Ellen Levine, and Anita Rapone, pp. 322–57. New York: Quadrangle.

Butler, Judith. 1990. Gender Trouble, Feminist Theory, and Psychoanalytic Discourse. In Linda Nicholson, *Feminism/Postmodernism*, pp. 324–340. New York: Routledge.

Calderon, Hector, and Jose D. Saldivar, eds. 1991. *Chicano Criticism in a Social Context*, Durham: Duke University Press.

Cantarow, Ellen. 1980. *Moving the Mountain.* New York: Feminist Press.

Caprio, Frank S. 1953 and 1966. *The Sexually Adequate Female.* New York: Fawcett Books.

Caraway, Nancie. 1991. *Segregated Sisterhood: Racism and the Politics of American Feminism.* Knoxville: University of Tennessee Press.

Carby, Hazel. 1987. *Reconstructing Womanhood: The Emergence of the Afro-American Woman Novelist.* New York: Oxford University Press.

———. 1992. The Multicultural Wars. In *Black Popular Culture*, ed. Michele Wallace and Gina Dent. Seattle: Bay Press.

Cardoso, R. C. L. 1984. Movimentos Sociais Urbanos: Balanço Critico. In *Sociedade e Politica no Brasil Pos-1964*, ed. B. Sorj and M. H. de Almeida. São Paulo: Editora Brasiliense: 226–39.

Centre for Contemporary Cultural Studies. 1982. *The Empire Strikes Back: Race and Racism in 70s Britain.* London: Hutchinson.

Chan, Sucheng. 1991. *Asian Americans: An Interpretive History.* Boston: Twayne, 1991.

Chaney, E. 1979. *Supermadre: Women in Politics in Latin America.* Austin: University of Texas Press.

Chesler, E. 1992. *Woman of Valor.* New York: Simon & Schuster.

Childress, Alice. [1956] 1986. *Like One of the Family.* Boston: Beacon.

Chincilla, Norma. 1997. Marxism, Feminism and the Struggle for Democracy in Latin America. In *Materialist Feminism*, ed. Rosemary Hennessy and Chrys Ingraham, pp. 214–26. New York: Routledge.

Chodorow, Nancy. 1978. *The Reproduction of Mothering.* Berkeley: University of California Press.

Chow, Esther Ngan-Ling. 1996. Making Waves, Moving Mountains: Reflections on Bejing' 95 and Beyond. *Signs* 22: 187, 189.

Christian, Barbara. 1985. *Black Feminist Criticism, Perspectives on Black Women Writers.* New York: Pergmon.

Christian, Barbara. 1989. But Who Do You Really Belong to—Black Studies or Women's Studies? *Women's Studies* 17 (1–2): 17–23.

———. 1994. Diminishing Returns: Can Black Feminism(s) Survive the Academy? In *Multiculturalism: A Critical Reader*, ed. David Theo Goldberg. Cambridge: Basil Blackwell.

Chuchryk, P. 1989. Subversive Mothers: The Opposition to the Military Regime in Chile. In *Women, the State and Development*, ed. S. M. Charlton, J. Everett, and K. Staudt. Albany: SUNY Press.

Cockburn, Cynthia. 1998. *The Space Between Us: Negotiating Gender and National Identities in Conflict.* London: Zed Books.

Collins, Patricia Hill. 1986. Learning from the Outsider Within: The Sociological Significance of Black Feminist Thought. *Social Problems* 33 (6): 14–32.

———. 1998. *Fighting Words: Black Women and the Search for Justice.* Minneapolis: University of Minnesota Press.

"Consciousness Raising." 1973. In *Radical Feminism,* ed. Anne Koedt, Ellen Levine, and Anita Rapone, pp. 280–81. New York: Quadrangle.

Cook, R. J. 1993a. International Human Rights and Women's Reproductive Health. *Studies in Family Planning* 24: 73–86.

———. 1993b. Women's International Human Rights Law. *Human Rights Quarterly* 15: 230–61.

Copelon, Rhonda. 1994. Intimate Terror: Understanding Domestic Violence as Torture. In *International Women's Human Rights,* ed. R. J. Cook. Philadelphia: University of Pennsylvania.

Corcoran-Nantes, V. 1988. "Women in Grassroots Protest Politics in São Paulo, Brazil," Ph.D. Thesis, University of Liverpool.

———. 1990. Women and Popular Urban Social Movements in São Paulo, Brazil. *Bulletin of Latin American Research* 9 (2): 249–64.

Correa, Sonia. 1993. "Sterilization in Brazil: Reviewing the Analysis." Unpublished.

Cott, Nancy. 1986a. Feminist Theory and Feminist Movements. In *What is Feminism,* ed. Juliet Mitchell and Ann Oakley, pp. 49–62. New York: Pantheon.

———. 1986b. *The Grounding of Modern Feminism.* New Haven: Yale University Press.

Crenshaw, K. 1991. Demarginalizing the Intersection of Race and Sex: Black Feminist Critique of Anti-Discrimination Doctrine, Feminist Theory, and Anti-Racist Politics. In *Feminist Legal Theory,* ed. K. T. Bartlett and R. Kennedy. Boulder: Westview Press.

Cruse, Harold. 1967. *The Crisis of the Negro Intellectual.* New York: William Morrow.

Cutrufelli, M. R. 1983. *Women of Africa: Roots of Oppression.* London: Zed Books.

Daly, Mary. 1978. *Gyn/Ecology.* New York: Beacon Press.

Dankelman, Irene, and Joan Davidson, eds. 1988. *Women and Environment in the Third World.* London: Earthscan Publications.

Darcy de Oliveira and Thais Corral, eds. 1990. Terra Femina. Germany and Brazil: Frauen Anstiftung. The Institute of Cultural Action (IDAG), and the Network in Defense of Human Species (REDEH).

Davis, Angela Y. 1981. *Women, Race and Class.* New York: Random House.

———. 1989. *Women, Culture, and Politics.* New York: Random House.

———. 1998. *Blues Legacies and Black Feminism.* New York: Vintage.

De Lauretis, T., ed. 1986. *Feminist Studies/Critical Studies.* Bloomington: Indiana University Press.

De Lauretis, T. 1990. Eccentric Subjects: Feminist Theory and Historical Consciousness. *Feminist Studies.* 16 (1): 115–50.

Delmar, Rosalind. 1986. What Is Feminism? In *What Is Feminism,* ed. Juliet Mitchell and Ann Oakley, pp. 8–33. New York: Pantheon.

Delphy, Christine. 1980. A Materialist Feminism Is Possible. *Feminist Review* 4.

Derrida, Jacques. 1976. *Of Grammatology.* Baltimore: John Hopkins University Press.

Desai, Sonalde. 1994. Women's Burdens: Easing the Structural Constraints. In *Population Policies Reconsidered,* ed. Gita Sen, Adrienne Germain, and Lincoln C. Chen, pp. 139–50. Cambridge: Harvard University Press.

Diamond, Irene. 1994. *Fertile Ground: Women, Earth, and the Limits of Control.* Boston: Beacon Press.

Diamond, Irene, and Gloria Feman Orenstein, eds. 1990. *Reweaving the World.* San Francisco: Sierra Club Books.

Dill, Bonnie Thornton. 1979. The Dialectics of Black Womanhood. *Signs* 4 (3): 543–55.

———. 1983. Race, Class, and Gender: Prospects for an All-Inclusive Sisterhood. *Feminist Studies* 9 (1): 131–50.

Diop, Cheikh. 1974. *The African Origin of Civilization: Myth or Reality?* New York: L. Hill.

Dixon-Mueller R. 1993. *Population Policy and Women's Rights.* Westport, CT: Praeger.

D'Souza, Corrine Kumar. 1988. New Healing Movement, A New Hope: West Wind, and the Wind from the South. In *Healing the Wounds,* ed. Judith Plant, pp. 67–76. Boston: South End Press.

Du Bois, W. E. B. 1969. *The Souls of Black Folks*. New York: New American Library.

DuCille, Ann. 1993. Blues Notes on Black Sexuality. In *American Sexual Politics*, ed. John C. Fout and Maura Shaw Tantillo, pp. 193–219. Chicago: University of Chicago Press.

———. 1996. *Skin Trade*. Cambridge: Harvard University Press.

Dyson, Michael Eric. 1996. *Race Rules: Navigating the Color Line*. New York: Vintage.

Eisenstein, Hester, and Alice Jardine, ed. 1980. *The Future of Difference*. Boston: G. K. Hall.

Eisenstein, Zillah, ed. 1978. *Capitalist Patriarchy and the Case for Socialist Feminism*. New York: Monthly Review Press.

———. 1983. *The Radical Future of Liberal Feminism*. Boston: Northeastern University Press.

———. 1994. *The Color of Gender*. Berkeley: University of California Press.

Ejlersen, Mette. 1968. *I Accuse (Jeg Anklager)*. Chr. Erichsens Forlag.

Elias, C. 1991. *Sexually Transmitted Diseases and the Reproductive Health of Women in Developing Countries*. New York: Population Council.

Ellman, Mary. 1968. *Thinking About Women*. New York: Harcourt, Brace & World.

Elshtain, J. B. 1981. *Public Man, Private Woman*. Princeton: Princeton University Press.

Engels, Frederick. 1972. *The Origin of Family, Private Property, and the State*, ed. Eleanor Burke Leacock. New York: International Publishers.

Engineer, A. A. 1987. *The Shahbano Controversy*. Bombay: Orient Longman.

Escoffier, Jeffrey. 1995. Community and Academic Intellectuals: The Contest for Cultural Authority in Identity Politics. In *Cultural Politics and Social Movements*, ed. Marcy Darnovsky, Barbara Epstein, and Richard Flacks, pp. 20–34. Philadelphia: Temple University Press.

Evans, Sara. 1979. *Personal Politics*. New York: Vintage.

Evers, T., C. Muller-Plantenberg, and S. Spessart. 1982. Movimentos de Bairro e Estado: Lutas na Esfera de Reprodução na America Latina. In *Cidade, Povo e Poder*, ed. J. A. Moises, pp. 110–60. Rio de Janeiro: Paz e Terra.

Expert Group Meeting on Population and Women. 1992 (October). *Substantive Preparations for the Conference—Recommendations*. New York: United Nations Economic and Social Council.

Ezeh, A. C. 1993. The Influence of Spouses over Each Other's Contraceptive Attitudes in Ghana. *Studies in Family Planning* 24: 163–74.

Faber, Daniel, ed. 1998. *The Struggle for Ecological Democracy*. New York: Guilford Press.

Fabros, M. L. 1991. The WRRC's Institutional Framework and Strategies on Reproductive Rights. *Flights* 4. Official Publication of the Women's Resource and Research Center, Quezon City, Philippines.

Fausto-Sterling, Anne. 1995. Gender, Race and Nation: The Comparative Anatomy of 'Hottentot' Women in Europe, 1815–1817. In *Deviant Bodies*, ed. Jennifer Terry and Jacqueline Urla. Bloomington: Indiana University Press.

———. 2000. *Sexing the Body*. New York: Basic Books.

Fernández-Kelly, Maria Patricia. 1982. Mexican Border Industrialization, Female Labour Force Participation and Migration. Working Paper. Center for the Study, Education and Advancement of Women. University of California, Berkeley.

Filet Abreu de Souza, J. 1980. Paid Domestic Service in Brazil. *Latin American Perspectives* 24 (7).

Fischer, L. 1962. *The Essential Gandhi*. New York: Vintage.

Foucault, Michel. 1980. *Power/Knowledge: Selected Interviews and Other Writings*, 1972–1977. ed. Colin Gordon. New York: Pantheon.

Fraser, Nancy. 1992. Rethinking the Public Sphere: A Contribution to the Critique of Actually Existing Democracy." In *Habermas and the Public Sphere*, ed. Craig Calhoun. Cambridge: MIT Press.

Freedman, L. P., and S. L. Isaacs. 1993. Human Rights and Reproductive Choice. *Studies in Family Planning* 24: 18–30.

Freire, Paulo. 1970. *The Pedagogy of the Oppressed*. New York: Herder & Herder.

Friedman, M. 1992. Feminism and Modern Friendship. In *Communitarianism and Individualism*, ed. S. Avineri and A. de-Shalit. New York: Oxford University Press.

Fröbel, Folker, Jürgen Heinrichs, and Otto Kreye. 1978. Export-Oriented Industrialization of Underdeveloped Countries. *Monthly Review* 30, (6): 22–27.

Fröbel, Folker. 1980. *The New International Division of Labour*. Cambridge: Cambridge University Press.

Frye, Marilyn. 1983. *The Politics of Reality*. Trumansburg, NY: Crossing Press.

Gaard, Greta, ed. 1991. *Ecofeminism: Women, Animals, Nature*. Philadelphia: Temple University Press.

Garcia-Moreno, Claudia, and Amparo Claro. 1994. Challenges from the Women's Health Movement: Women's Rights versus Population Control. In *Population Policies Reconsidered*, ed. Gita Sen, Adrienne Germain, and Lincoln C. Chen, pp. 47–61. Cambridge: Harvard University Press.

Gaucher, David, ed. 1993. *Heroes: Twelve Tales of Environmental Victory*. San Francisco: Mercury House.

Giddings, Paula. 1984. *When and Where I Enter*. New York: William Morrow.

Gilkes, Cheryl Townsend. 1985. "Together and in Harness": Women's Traditions in the Sanctified Church. *Signs* 10 (4): 678–99.

Gilligan, Carol. 1982. *In a Different Voice*. Cambridge: Harvard University Press.

Gordon, Linda. 1976. *Woman's Body, Woman's Right*. New York: Penguin.

Gordon, L. 1989. *Heroes of their Own Lives, The Politics and History of Family Violence*. New York: Penguin.

Gramsci, Antonio. 1971. *Selections from the Prison Notebooks*. London: Lawrence and Wishart.

Grant, Judith. 1993. *Fundamental Feminism*. New York: Routledge.

Grewal, S., J. Kay, L. Landor, G. Lewis, P. Parmar, eds. 1988. *Charting the Journey: Writings by Black and Third World Women*. London: Sheba.

Gross, Jeanne. 1977. Feminist Ethics from a Marxist Perspective. *Radical Religion* 3 (2): 52–56.

Grossman, Rachel. 1979. Women's Place in the Integrated Circuit. *Southeast Asia Chronicle, Pacific Research*, 9 (5–6).

Guillaumin, Colette. 1982. The Question of Difference. *Feminist Issues* 2 (2).

———. 1985. The Masculine: Denotations/Connotations. *Feminist Issues* 5 (1).

Gutman, Herbert. 1976. *The Black Family in Slavery and Freedom, 1750–1975*. New York: Random House.

Guy–Sheftall, Beverly. 1986. Remembering Sojourner Truth: On Black Feminism. *Catalyst* (Fall): 54–57.

———. 1995a. The Evolution of Feminist Consciousness among African American Women. In *Words of Fire*, ed. Beverly Guy-Sheftall, pp. 1–22. New York: New Press.

———, ed. 1995b. *Words of Fire*. New York: New Press.

Gwaltney, John Langston. 1980. *Drylongso, A Self-Portrait of Black America*. New York: Vintage.

Hamilton, Dale Colleen. 1989. The Give and Take. In *Healing the Wounds*, ed. Judith Plant, pp. 134–44. Boston: South End Press.

Haraway, Donna. 1988 Situated Knowledges: The Science Question in Feminism and the Privilege of Partial Perspective. *Feminist Studies* 14 (3): 575–599.

———. 1989. *Primate Visions*. New York and London: Routledge.

Harding, S., and M. Hintikka. 1983. *Discovering Reality*. Dordrecht: Reidel.

Harding, S. 1986. *The Science Question in Feminism*. Ithaca: Cornell University Press.

Harding, S., and J. O'Barr, eds. 1987. *Sex and Scientific Inquiry*. Chicago: University of Chicago Press.

Harding, Sandra. 1998. *Is Science Multicultural?* Bloomington: Indiana University Press.

Harley, Sharon, and Rosalyn Terborg-Penn, eds. 1978. *The Afro-American Woman*. Port Washington, NY: Kennikat Press.

Hartsock, Nancy. 1990. Foucault on Power: A Theory for Women? In *Feminism/Postmodernism*, ed. Linda Nicholson, pp. 157–75. New York: Routledge.

Heise, L. 1992. Violence against Women: The Missing Agenda. In *Women's Health: A Global Perspective*, ed. M. A. Koblinsky, J. Timyan, and J. Gay. Boulder: Westview Press.

Heller, A. 1992. Rights, Modernity, Democracy. In *Deconstruction and the Possibility of Justice*, ed. D. Cornell, M. Rosenfeld, and D. G. Carlson. New York: Routledge.

Hernton, Calvin. 1985. The Sexual Mountain and Black Women Writers. *Black Scholar* 16 (4): 2–11.

Hesford, Wendy S., and Wendy Kozol. 2001. *Haunting Violations: Feminist Criticism and the Crisis of the "Real."* Urbana: University of Illinois Press.

Higginbotham, Evelyn Brooks. 1989. Beyond the Sound of Silence: Afro-American Women in History. *Gender and History* 1 (1): 50–67.

———. 1993. *Righteous Discontent: The Women's Movement in the Black Baptist Church, 1880–1920*. Cambridge: Harvard University Press.

Hine, Darlene Clark, Elsa Barkley Brown, and Rosalyn Terborg-Penn, eds. 1993. *Black Women in America: An Historical Encyclopedia.* New York: Carlson.

Hing, Bill Ong. 1993. *Making and Remaking Asian America Through Immigration Policy 1850–1990.* Palo Alto: Stanford University Press.

Hodgson, Dorothy. 1995a. The Politics of Gender, Ethnicity, and "Development": Images, Interventions, and the Reconfiguration of Maasai Identities, 1916–1993. Ph.D. Dissertation, University of Michigan.

———. 1995b. Critical Interventions: The Politics of Studying Indigenous Development. Paper presented at the American Anthropological Association meeting, November, Washington, D.C.

hooks, bell. 1981. *Ain't I A Woman: Black Women and Feminism.* Boston: South End Press.

Hull, Gloria T., Patricia Bell Scott, and Barbara Smith, eds. 1982. *Black But Some of Us Are Brave.* New York: Feminist Press.

Hull, Gloria T., ed. 1984. *Give Us Each Day: The Diary of Alice Dunbar-Nelson.* New York: Norton.

Humphries, Jane. 1977. Class Struggle and the Persistence of the Working-Class Family. *Cambridge Journal of Economics* 1, 241–58.

Hurtado, A. 1989. Relating to Privilege: Seduction and Rejection in the Subordination of White Women and Women of Color. *Signs* 14 (4).

Hurtig, Marie-Claude, and Marie-France Pichevin. 1985. La Variable Sexe en Psychologie: Donne ou Construct? *Cahiers de Psychologie Cognitive* 5 (2): 187–228.

———. 1986. *La Différence des Sexes.* Paris: Tierce.

Huston, P. 1992. *Motherhood by Choice.* New York: Feminist Press.

Inden, R. 1986. Orientalist Constructions of India. *Modern Asian Studies* 20 (3).

Jackson, Cecile. 1993. Women/Nature or Gender/History? A Critique of Ecofeminist Development. *Journal of Peasant Studies* 20 (3): 389–419.

Jacobs, Jane. 1993. Earth Honoring: Western Desires and Indigenous Knowledges. In *Writing Women and Space: Colonial and Postcolonial Geographies,* ed. Alison Blunt and Gilliam Rose, pp. 169–96. New York: Guilford Press.

Jaggar, Alison M. 1990. Love and Knowledge: Emotion in Feminist Epistemology. In *Gender/Body/Knowledge: Feminist Reconstructions of Being and Knowing,* ed. Alison M. Jaggar and Susan R. Bordo, pp. 145–171. New Brunswick, NJ: Rutgers University Press.

Jain, Anrudh, Judith Bruce, and B. Mensch. 1992. Setting Standards of Quality in Family Planning Programs. *Studies in Family Planning* 23: 392–95.

Jain, Anrudh, and Judith Bruce. A Reproductive Health Approach to the Objectives and Assessment of Family Planning Programs. In *Population Policies Reconsidered,* ed. Gita Sen, Adrienne Germain, and Lincoln C. Chen, pp. 193–209. Cambridge: Harvard University Press.

Jaising, I. 1987. Women, Religion and the Law. *The Lawyers Collective* 2 (11).

James, Adeola. 1990. *In Their Own Voices: African Women Writers Talk.* Portsmouth, NH: Heinemann.

James, Stanlie, and Abena Busia, eds. 1993. *Theorizing Black Feminisms.* New York: Routledge.

Jaquette, J. 1980. Female Political Participation in Latin America. In *Sex and Class in Latin America,* ed. J. Nash. and H. Safa. New York: Bergin Publishers.

———. ed., 1989. *The Women's Movement in Latin America: Feminism and the Transition to Democracy.* London: Unwin Hyman.

Jayawardena, K. 1993. *With a Different Voice: White Women and Colonialism in South Asia.* London: Zed Books.

Jeffery, P., R. Jeffery, and A. Lyon. 1989. *Labour Pains and Labour Power: Women and Childbearing in India.* London: Zed Books.

Jewell, K. Sue. 1993. *From Mammy to Miss America and Beyond.* New York: Routledge.

Johnson-Reagon, Bernice. 1983. Coalition Politics: Turning the Century. In *Homegirls: A Black Feminist Anthology,* ed. Barbara Smith, pp. 356–68. New York: Kitchen Table Press.

Jones, Jacqueline. 1985. *Labor of Love, Labor of Sorrow.* New York: Basic Books.

Jordan, June. 1981. *Civil Wars.* Boston: Beacon.

Joseph, Gloria. 1981. The Incompatible Menage-à-Trois: Marxism, Feminism, and Racism. In *Women and Revolution,* ed. Lydia Sargent, pp. 91–107. Boston: South End Press.

Kaplan, C. 1987. Deterritorializations: The Rewriting of Home and Exile in Western Feminist Discourse. *Cultural Critique* 6.

Kaplan, Caren, Norma Alarcon, and Minoo Moallem, eds. 1999. *Between Woman and Nation.* Durham: Duke University Press.

Kaplan, Robert D. 1994. The Coming Anarchy. *Atlantic Monthly* 273 (February): 44–76.

Keck, Margaret, and Kathryn Sikkink. 1998. *Activists beyond Borders.* Ithaca: Cornell University Press.

Keller, E. F. 1985. *Reflections on Gender and Science.* New Haven: Yale University Press.

Kelly, G. Lombard. 1951 and 1965. *Sexual Feelings in Married Men and Women.* New York: Pocketbooks.

Kelly, J. 1984. *Women, History, and Theory.* Chicago: University of Chicago Press.

Kelly, Petra. 1989. "Preface," in *Healing the Wounds,* ed. Judith Plant, pp. ix–xi. Boston: South End Press.

Kennedy, Elizabeth Lapovsky, and Madeline Davis. 1994. *Boots of Leather, Slippers of Gold.* New York: Penguin.

Kessler, Suzanne. 2000. *Lessons from the Intersexed.* New Brunswick: Rutgers University Press.

Khattab, H. 1992. *The Silent Endurance.* Amman: UNICEF; Cairo: Population Council.

Kim, Seung-kyung, and Carole McCann. 1998. Internationalizing Theories of Feminism. *Women's Studies Quarterly* 26 (Fall/Winter): 115–32.

King, Deborah. 1988. Multiple Jeopardy, Multiple Consciousness: The Context of a Black Feminist Ideology. *Signs* 14 (1): 42–72.

King, Katie. 1994. *Theory in Its Feminist Travels.* Bloomington: Indiana University Press.

King, Mae. 1973. The Politics of Sexual Stereotypes. *Black Scholar* 4 (6–7): 12–23.

King, Ynestra. 1989. "Healing the Wounds: Feminism, Ecology, and the Nature/Culture Dualism." In *Reweaving the World,* ed. Irene Diamond and Gloria Feman Orenstein, pp. 106–21. San Francisco: Sierra Club Books.

Kinsey, Alfred C. 1953. *Sexual Behavior in the Human Female.* New York: Pocketbooks.

Kishwar, M. 1986. Pro-Woman or Anti-Muslim? The Shahbano Controversy. *Manushi* 32.

Kishwar, M., and Vanita R. 1987. The Burning of Roop Kanwar. *Manushi* 42–3.

Komarovsky, Mirra. 1950. Functional Analysis of Sex Roles. *American Sociological Review* 15 (4).

Kucinski, B. 1982. *Abertura Uma Historia de Uma Crise.* São Paula: Brasil Debates.

Kumar, Radha. 1995. From Chipko to Sati: The Contemporary Indian Women's Movement. In *Challenge of Local Feminisms,* ed. Amrita Basu. Boulder: Westview Press.

LaChapelle, Dolores. 1989. Sacred Land, Sacred Sex. In *Healing the Wounds,* ed. Judith Plant, pp. 155–67. Boston: South End Press.

Landsberg, Martin. 1979. Export-led Industrialization in the Third World: Manufacturing Imperialism. *Review of Radical Political Economics* 11 (4): 50–63.

The Latina Feminist Group. 2001. *Telling to Live: Latina Feminist Testimonios.* Durham: Duke University Press.

Lazreg, M. 1988. Feminism and Difference: The Perils of Writing as a Woman on Women in Algeria. *Feminist Studies,* 14 (1).

Leach, Melissa. 1993. *Rainforest Relations: Gender and Resource Use Among the Mende of Gola, Sierra Leone.* Washington, D.C.: Smithsonian Institution Press.

Leontiades, James. 1971. International Sourcing in the Less-developed Countries. *Columbia Journal of World Business* 6 (6): 19–26.

Leví-Strauss Claude. 1969. *The Elementary Structures of Kinship.* London: Eyre and Spottiswoode.

Li, Huey-li. 1993. A Cross-Cultural Critique of Ecofeminism. In *Ecofeminism: Women, Animals, Nature,* ed. Greta Gaard, pp. 272–94. Philadelphia: Temple University Press.

Lim, Linda Y. C. 1978a. Multinational Firms and Manufacturing for Export in Less-developed Countries: The Case of the Electronics Industry in Malaysia and Singapore. Ph.D. Dissertation, University of Michigan.

———. 1978b. *Women Workers in Multinational Corporations: The Case of the Electronics Industry in Malaysia and Singapore.* Michigan Occasional Papers, no. 9. Ann Arbor, Michigan: University of Michigan, Women Studies Program.

Lim-Hing, Sharon, ed. 1994. *The Very Inside: An Anthology of Writing by Asian and Pacific Islander Lesbian and Bisexual Women.* Toronto: Sister Vision.

Lipschutz, Ronnie. 1992. Reconstructing World Politics: The Emergence of Global Society. *Millennium* 21 (3): 389–420.

Lloyd, G. 1984. *The Man of Reason.* Minneapolis: University of Minnesota Press.

Loewenberg, Bert J., and Ruth Bogin, eds. 1976. *Black Women in Nineteenth-Century American Life.* University Park: Pennsylvania State University Press.

Lopez, I. 1993. Constrained Choices: An Ethnography of Sterilization and Puerto Rican Women in New York City. Unpublished manuscript.

Lorber, Judith. 1994. *Paradoxes of Gender.* New Haven: Yale University Press.

Lorde, Audre. 1981. An Open Letter to Mary Daly. In *This Bridge Called My Back,* ed. Cherrie Moraga and Gloria Anzaldúa, pp. 94–97. New York: Kitchen Table Press.

Lorde, Audre. 1982. *Zami, A New Spelling of My Name.* Trumansberg, NY: Crossing Press.

———. 1984. Age, Race, Class, and Sex. In *Sister Outsider,* pp. 114–23. Freedom, CA: Crossing Press.

———. 1984. *Sister Outsider.* Trumansberg, NY: Crossing Press.

Lubiano, Wahneema. 1992. Black Ladies, Welfare Queens, and State Minstrels: Ideological War by Narrative Means. *Race-ing Justice, En-Gendering Power,* ed. Toni Morrison, pp. 323–63. New York: Pantheon.

Lynch, Cecilia. 1998. Social Movements and the Problem of Globalization. *Alternatives* 23: 149–73.

Machado, L. 1988. The Participation of Women in the Health Movement of Jardim Nordeste, in the Eastern Zone of San Paulo, Brazil: 1976–1985. *Bulletin of Latin American Research* 7 (1): 47–43.

MacKinnon, Catharine. 1987. *Feminism Unmodified.* Cambridge: Harvard University Press.

Macy, Joanna. 1989. Awakening to the Ecological Self. In *Healing the Wounds,* ed. Judith Plant, pp. 201–11. Boston: South End Press.

Madhubuti, Haki R., ed. 1990. *Confusion by Any Other Name: Essays Exploring the Negative Impact of the Blackman's Guide to Understanding the Black Woman.* Chicago: Third World Press.

Mani, L., and R. Frankenberg. 1985. The Challenge of Orientalism. *Economy and Society* 14 (2).

Mani, L. 1987. Contentious Traditions: The Debate on *Sati* in Colonial India. *Cultural Critique* no. 7; also published in Sangari and Vaid 1989.

———. 1989. Contentious Traditions: The Debate on *Sati* in Colonial India, 1780–1833. Ph.D. Diss. University of California, Santa Cruz.

Mannheim, Karl. 1936. *Ideology and Utopia.* New York: Harcourt, Brace & World.

Marable, Manning. 1983. Grounding with My Sisters: Patriarchy and the Exploitation of Black Women. In *How Capitalism Underdeveloped Black America,* pp. 69–104. Boston: South End Press.

Marx, Karl. 1977. The German Ideology. In *Karl Marx: Selected Writings,* ed. David McLellan, pp. 159–91. New York: Oxford University Press.

Masters, William H. and Virginia E. Johnson. 1966. *Human Sexual Response.* New York: Little Brown.

Mathieu, Nicole-Claude. 1980. Masculinity/Femininity. *Feminist Issues* 1 (1).

———. 1991. *L'Anatomie Politique. Categorisations et Ideologies du Sexe.* Paris: Côté-femmes.

Mattelart, M. 1980. The Feminine Version of the Coup d'Etat. In *Sex and Class in Latin America,* ed. J. Nash and H. I. Safa. New York: Bergin Publishers.

McCarthy, J., and D. Maine. 1992. A Framework for Analyzing the Determinants of Maternal Mortality. *Studies in Family Planning* 23: 23–33.

McDermott, Patrice. 1994. *Politics and Scholarship: Feminist Academic Journals and the Production of Knowledge.* Urbana: University of Illinois Press.

———. 1998. Internationalizing the Core Curriculum. *Women's Studies Quarterly* 26 (Fall/Winter): 88–98.

McIntosh, Peggy. White Privilege and Male Privilege: A Personal Account of Coming to See Correspondences through Work in Women's Studies. Working Paper No. 189. Wellesley, MA: Center for Research on Women, Wellesley College.

Mead, Margaret. 1935. *Sex and Temperament in Three Primitive Societies.* New York: William Morrow.

Merchant, Carolyn. 1989. Ecofeminism and Feminist Theory. In *Reweaving the World,* ed. Irene Diamond and Gloria Feman Orenstein, pp. 100–105. San Francisco: Sierra Club Books.

Michel, Andrée. 1959. *Famille, Industrialisation, Logement.* Paris: Centre National de Recherche Scientifique.

———. 1960. La Femme Dans la Famille Française. *Cahiers Internationaux de Sociologie* 111.

Mies, Maria. 1986. *Patriarchy and Accumulation on a World Scale.* London: Zed Books.

———. 1988. *Women: The Last Colony.* London: Zed Books.

Mill, John Stuart. 1883. *The Subjection of Women*. New York: Henry Holt and Co.

Millet, Kate. 1970. *Sexual Politics*. New York: Avon.

Minh-Ha, Trihn T., ed. 1986/1987. She the Inappropriate/d Other. *Discourse* 8.

Mintzes, B., ed. 1992. *A Question of Control: Women's Perspectives on the Development and Use of Contraceptives*. Amsterdam: WEMOS, Women & Pharmaceuticals Project.

Mirza, Heidi Safia, ed. 1997. *Black British Feminism*. New York: Routledge.

Mitchell, Juliet, and Ann Oakley. 1986. Introduction. *What Is Feminism?* pp. 1–7. New York: Pantheon.

Moghadam, Valentine M. 1996a. Feminists Networks North and South: DAWN, WIDE and WLUML. *Journal of International Communication* 3 (1): 111–25.

———. 1996b. The Fourth World Conference on Women: Dissension and Consensus. *Bulletin of Concerned Asian Scholars* (January–March): 28.

Mohanty, Chandra Talpade. 1991a. Cartographies of Struggle: Third World Women and the Politics of Feminism. In *Third World Women and the Politics of Feminism*, ed. Chandra Talpade Mohanty, Ann Russo, and Lourdes Torres, pp. 1–47. Bloomington: University of Indiana Press.

———. 1991b. Under Western Eyes: Feminist Scholarship and Colonial Discourses. In *Third World Women and the Politics of Feminism*, eds. Chandra Talpade Mohanty, Ann Russo, and Lourdes Torres, pp. 51–80. Bloomington: University of Indiana Press.

Mohanty, S. P. 1989. Us and Them: On the Philosophical Bases of Political Criticism. *Yale Journal of Criticism* 2 (2).

Moia, Martha. 1981. *La Saumone*. Paris: Mercure de France.

Molyneux, Maxine. 2000. Analysing Women's Movements. In *Women's Movements in International Perspective: Latin America and Beyond*. New York: Palgrave.

Money, John, and Anke Ehrhardt. 1972. *Man and Woman, Boy and Girl*. Baltimore: Johns Hopkins University Press.

Moraga, Cherrie, and Gloria Anzaldúa, eds. 1981, 1986. *This Bridge Called My Back: Writings by Radical Women of Color*. New York: Kitchen Table Press.

Morgan, Robin, ed. 1984. *Sisterhood Is Global*. New York: Anchor Press/Doubleday.

Morsy, S. 1994. Maternal Mortality in Egypt: Selective Health Strategy and the Medicalization of Population Control. In *Conceiving the New World Order*, ed. Faye Ginsburg and Rayna Rapp. Berkeley: University of California Press.

Morton, Patricia. 1991. *Disfigured Images*. New York: Praeger.

Moser, C. O. N. 1987. Mobilisation Is Women's Work: The Struggle for Infrastructure in Guayaquil, Ecuador. In *Women, Human Settlements and Housing*, ed. C. O. N. Moser and L. Peaks, pp. 166–94. London: Tavistock Publications.

Moses, Claire. 1998a. What's in a Name? On Writing the History of Feminism, an unpublished paper presented to the International Academic Conference on Women' Studies and Development in the Twenty-First Century, Peking University, June.

———. 1998b. Made in America: French Feminism in Academia. *Feminist Studies* 24 (Summer): 241–73.

Moxon, Richard W. 1974. Offshore Production in Less-developed Countries—A Case Study of Multinationality in the Electronics Industry. *Bulletin* 8–99 (July). New York University: Graduate School of Business Administration, Institute of Finance.

Mullings, Leith. 1997. *On Our Own Terms*. New York: Routledge.

Murdock, George. 1949. *Social Structure*. New York: Macmillan.

Murray, Pauli. 1970. The Liberation of Black Women. In *Voices of the New Feminism*, ed. Mary Lou Thompson, pp. 87–102. Boston: Beacon.

Musallam, B. F. 1983. *Sex and Society in Islam*. Cambridge: Cambridge University Press.

Myrdal, Alva, and Viola Klein. 1956. *Women's Two Roles—Home and Work*. London: Routledge and Kegan Paul.

Nandy, A. 1987. The Sociology of *Sati*. *Indian Express* (October 5).

———. 1988a. The Human Factor. *The Illustrated Weekly of India* (January 17).

———. 1988b. *Sati* in Kaliyuga. *Economic and Political Weekly* (September 17).

Narayan, Uma. 1997. *Dislocating Cultures: Identities, Traditions, and Third World Feminisms*. New York: Routledge.

National Research Council. 1989. *Contraception and Reproduction: Health Consequences for Women and Children in the Developing World.* Washington, D.C.: National Academy Press.

Nayyar, Deepak. 1978. Transnational Corporations and Manufactured Exports from Poor Countries. *Economic Journal* 88: 58–84.

Nedelsky, J. 1989. Reconceiving Autonomy. *Yale Journal of Law and Feminism* 1: 7–36.

Oakley, Ann. 1972. *Sex, Gender and Society.* New York: Harper & Row.

Offe, K. 1985. New Social Movements: Challenging the Boundaries of Institutional Politics. *Social Research* 52: 817–68.

O'Flaherty, W. D. 1980. *Women, Androgynes, and Other Mythical Beasts.* Chicago: University of Chicago Press.

Okin, Susan. 1979. *Women in Western Political Thought.* Princeton: Princeton University Press.

Olsen, F. 1984. Statutory Rape: A Feminist Critique of Rights Analysis. *Texas Law Review* 63: 387–432.

Omi, Michael, and Howard Winant. 1994. *Racial Formation in the United States.* New York: Routledge.

Omolade, Barbara. 1994. *The Rising Song of African American Women.* New York: Routledge.

Ong, A. 1987. *Spirits of Resistance and Capitalist Resistance: Factory Women in Malaysia.* Albany: SUNY Press.

Pachauri, P. 1988. Turning a Blind Eye: Glorification of *Sati* Continues Despite the Law. *India Today* (October 15).

Paglaban, E. 1978. Philippines: Workers in the Export Industry. *Pacific Research* 9 (3–4).

Painter, Nell. 1993. Sojourner Truth. In *Black Women in the United States: An Historical Encyclopedia,* ed. Darlene Clark Hine, Elsa Barkley Brown, and Rosalyn Terborg-Penn, Vol. II 72–76. New York: Carlson.

Pang Eng Fong, and Linda Y. C. Lim. 1977. *The Electronics Industry in Singapore.* Economic Research Centre, University of Singapore, Research Monograph Series, 7.

Paris, Peter J. 1995. *The Spirituality of African Peoples.* Minneapolis: Fortress.

Parmar, P. 1982. Gender, Race and Class: Asian Women in Resistance. In Centre for Contemporary Cultural Studies, ed., *The Empire Strikes Back: Race and Racism in 70's Britain.* London: Hutchinson.

Parsons, Talcott. 1954. *Essays in Sociological Theory.* Glencoe, Illinois: Free Press.

Patel, S. and K. Kumar. 1988. Defenders of *Sati. Economic and Political Weekly* (January 23).

Pathak, Z. and R. Sunder Rajan. 1989. Shahbano. *Signs* 14 (3).

Pearce, T. O. 1994. Women's Reproductive Practices and Biomedicine. In *Conceiving the New World Order,* ed. Faye Ginsburg and Rayna Rapp. Berkeley: University of California Press.

Perry, Imani. 1995. It's My Thang and I'll Swing It the Way That I Feel! In *Gender, Race and Class in Media,* ed. Gail Dines and Jean Humez, pp. 524–30. Thousand Oaks, CA: Sage.

Petchesky, Rosalind. 1979. Reproductive Choice in the Contemporary United States: A Social Analysis of Female Sterilization. In *And The Poor Get Children,* ed. K. Michaelson. New York: Monthly Review Press.

———. 1990. *Abortion and Woman's Choice: The State, Sexuality and Reproductive Freedom,* rev. ed. Boston: Northeastern University Press.

———. 1994. The Body as Property: A Feminist Revision. In *Conceiving the New World,* ed. Faye Ginsburg and Rayna Rapp. Berkeley: University of California Press.

Petchesky, R. P., and J. Weiner. 1990. *Global Feminist Perspectives on Reproductive Rights and Reproductive Health.* New York: Reproductive Rights Education Project, Hunter College.

Philipose, P., and T. Setalvad. 1988. Demystifying *Sati. The Illustrated Weekly of India* (March 13).

Philipose, Pamela. 1989. Women Act: Women and Environmental Protection in India. In *Healing the Wounds,* ed. Judith Plant, pp. 67–76. Boston: South End Press.

Pies, C. n.d. *Creating Ethical Reproductive Health Care Policy.* San Francisco: Education Programs Associates, Inc.

Powers, Samantha. 2002. *A Problem from Hell: America and the Age of Genocide.* New York: Basic Books.

Protacio, N. 1990. "From Womb to Tomb: The Filipino Women's Struggle for Good Health and Justice." Paper presented at the Fourth International Interdisciplinary Congress on Women, June 12, Hunter College, New York.

Pulido, Laura. 1998. Ecological Legitimacy and Cultural Essentialism: Hispano Grazing in the Southwest. In *The Struggle for Ecological Democracy*, ed. Daniel Faber, pp. 293–311. New York: Guilford Press.

Punwani, J. 1985. The Strange Case of Shahbano. *The Sunday Observer* (November 24).

Qadeer, I., and Z. Hasan. 1987. Deadly Politics of the State and Its Apologists. *Economic and Political Weekly* (November 14).

Radicalesbians. 1973. Woman Identified Woman. In *Radical Feminism*, ed. Anne Koedt, Ellen Levine, and Anita Rapone, pp. 240–45. New York: Quadrangle.

Ramasubban, R. 1990. "Sexual Behaviour and Conditions of Health Care: Potential Risks for HIV Transmission in India." Paper prepared for the International Union for the Scientific Study of Population Seminar on Anthropological Studies Relevant to the Sexual Transmission of HIV, Sonderborg, Denmark.

Ramusack, B. N. 1989. Embattled Advocates: The Debate over Birth Control in India, 1920–40. *Journal of Women's History* 1: 34–64.

Rao, Aruna. 1991. *Women's Studies International: Nairobi and Beyond.* New York: Feminist Press.

Rao, Brinda. 1991. Dominant Constructions of Women and Nature in Social Science Literature Capitalism, Nature, Socialism, pamphlet 2. New York: Guilford Press.

Ravindran, T. K. S. 1993. Women and the Politics of Population and Development in India. *Reproductive Health Matters* 1: 26–38.

Reiter, Rayna, ed. 1975. *Toward an Anthropology of Women.* New York: Monthly Review Press.

Reynis, Lee Ann. 1976. The Proliferation of U.S. Firm Third World Sourcing in the Mid-to-Late 1960's: An Historical and Empirical Study of the Factors which Occasioned the Location of Production for the U.S. Market Abroad. Ph.D. diss., University of Michigan.

Rich, Adrienne. 1979. Disloyal to Civilization: Feminism, Racism, Gynephobia. In *On Lies, Secrets, and Silences*, pp. 275–310. New York: Norton.

———. 1986. Compulsory Heterosexuality. In *Blood Bread and Poetry: Selected Essays, 1979–1985.* W. W. Norton.

Richardson, Marilyn, ed. 1987. *Maria W. Stewart, America's First Black Woman Political Writer.* Bloomington: Indiana University Press.

Robbins, B. 1987/1988. The Politics of Theory. *Social Text* 18.

Rosaldo, Michelle, and Louise Lamphere, eds. 1974. *Woman, Culture, and Society.* Palo Alto: Stanford University Press.

Rose, Tricia. 1994. *Black Noise: Rap Music and Black Culture in Contemporary America.* Hanover, NH: Wesleyan University Press.

Rosenfeld, M. 1992. Deconstruction and Legal Interpretation. In *Deconstruction and the Possibility of Justice*, ed. D. Cornel, J. M. Rosenfeld, and D. G. Carlson. New York: Routledge.

Rosenfelt, Deborah. 1998. Crossing Boundaries: Thinking Globally and Teaching Locally about Women's Lives. *Women's Studies Quarterly* 26 (Fall/Winter): 4–16.

Rubin, Gayle. 1975. The Traffic in Women: Notes on the "Political Economy" of Sex. In *Toward an Anthropology of Women*, ed. Rayna Reiter, pp. 157–210. New York: Monthly Review Press.

Ruddick, Sara. 1989. *Maternal Thinking: Toward a Politics of Peace.* Boston: Beacon Press.

Ruthven, M. 1984. *Islam in the World.* New York: Oxford University Press.

Safa, H. I. 1990. Women's Social Movements in Latin America. *Gender and Society* 4 (3).

Said, Edward. 1978. *Orientalism.* New York: Pantheon Books.

———. 1983. *The World, The Text and the Critic.* Cambridge: Harvard University Press.

———. 1986. Intellectuals in the Post-Colonial World. *Salmagundi*, 70–71.

———. 1990. Feminism and Race: A Report on the 1981 National Women's Studies Association Conference. In *Making Face, Making Soul*, ed. Gloria Anzaldúa, pp. 55–71. San Francisco: Aunt Lute Books.

Sandoval, Chela. 1991. U.S. Third World Feminism: The Theory and Method of Oppositional Consciousness in the Postmodern World. *Genders* 10 (Spring): 1–23.

Sangari, K. K. 1988. Perpetuating the Myth. *Seminar*, no. 342, special issue on *sati*.

Sangari, K. K., and S. Vaid, eds. 1989. *Recasting Women: Essays on Colonial History.* New Delhi: Kali.

Sanger, M. 1920. *Woman and the New Race.* New York: Brentano's.

Saussure, Ferdinand de. 1959. *Course in General Linguistics*, trans, W. Baskin. London: The Philosophical Library.

Scales-Trent, Judy. 1989. Black Women and the Constitution: Finding Our Place, Asserting Our Rights, *Harvard Civil Rights–Civil Liberties Law Review* 24 (Winter): 9–43.

Schmitz, Betty, Deborah Rosenfelt, Johnella Butler, and Beverly Guy-Sheftall. 1995. Women's Studies and Curriculum Transformation. In *Handbook of Research on Multicultural Education,* ed. James A. Banks, pp. 708–28. New York: Macmillan Publishing.

Schneider, E. M. 1991. The Dialectic of Rights and Politics: Perspectives from the Women's Movement. In *Feminist Legal Theory,* ed. K. T. Bartlett and R. Kennedy. Boulder: Westview Press.

Schroeder, Richard. 1993. Shady Practice: Gender and the Political Ecology of Resource Stabilization in Gambian Garden/Orchards. *Economic Geography* 69 (4): 349–65.

———. 1995. "Co-opted Critiques: Gender, Environment and Development Discourse." Paper presented at the American Anthropological Association meeting, November, Washington, D.C.

Scott, James. 1985. *Weapons of the Weak: Everyday Forms of Peasant Resistance.* New Haven: Yale University Press.

Scott, Joan. 1992. Experience. In *Feminists Theorize the Political,* ed. Judith Butler and Joan Scott, pp. 22–40. New York: Routledge.

———. 1993. The Evidence of Experience. *The Lesbian and Gay Studies Reader,* ed. Henry Abelove, Michèle Aina Barale, and David V. Halperin, pp. 397–415. New York: Routledge.

Scott, Joan, Cora Kaplan, and Debra Keates, eds. 1997. *Transitions, Translations, Environments.* New York: Routledge.

Segrest, Mab. 1985. *My Mama's Dead Squirrel: Lesbian Essays on Southern Culture.* Ithaca, NY: Firebrand Books.

———. 1994. *Memoir of a Race Traitor.* Boston: South End Press.

Sen, Gita. 1980. The Sexual Division of Labor and the Working-Class Family. *The Review of Radical Political Economics* 12 2: 76–85.

———. 1992. *Women, Poverty and Population.* Cambridge: Center for Population and Development Studies, Harvard University.

Shange, Ntozake. 1975. *For Colored Girls Who Have Considered Suicide/When the Rainbow Is Enuf.* New York: Macmillan.

Shaw, Stephanie J. 1996. *What a Woman Ought to Be and to Do: Black Professional Women Workers During the Jim Crow Era.* Chicago: University of Chicago Press.

Shiva, Vandana. 1998. *Staying Alive: Women, Ecology, and Development.* New Delhi: Kali.

———. 1994. *Close to Home: Women Reconnect Ecology, Health and Development Worldwide.* Philadelphia: New Society Publishers.

———. 1998. Development, Ecology and Women. In *Healing the Wounds,* ed. Judith Plant, pp. 80–90. Boston: South End Press.

———. 1990. Development as a New Project of Western Patriarchy. In *Reweaving the World,* ed. Irene Diamond and Gloria Feman Orenstein, pp. 189–200. San Francisco: Sierra Club Books.

Sivanandan, A. 1980. Imperialism in the Silicon Age. *Monthly Review* 32 (3): 24–42.

Slater, D., ed. 1985. *New Social Movements and the State in Latin America.* Amsterdam: CEDLA, Latin American Studies 29.

Smith, Barbara, and Beverly Smith. 1981. Across the Kitchen Table: A Sister to Sister Dialogue. In *This Bridge Called My Back,* ed. Cherrie Moraga and Gloria Anzaldúa, pp. 113–27. New York: Kitchen Table Press.

Smith, Barbara. 1982. Racism and Women's Studies. In *But Some of Us Are Brave,* ed. Gloria T. Hull, Patricia Bell Scott, and Barbara Smith, pp. 48–51. New York: Feminist Press.

———, ed. 1983. *Home Girls: Black Feminist Anthology.* New York: Kitchen Table Press.

Smith, Dorothy. 1987. *The Everyday World as Problematic.* Boston: Northeastern University Press.

Smith, Michael Peter. 1994. Can You Imagine? Transnational Migration and the Globalization of Grassroots Politics. *Social Text* 39: 15–33.

Smitherman, Geneva. 1977. *Talkin and Testifyin: The Language of Black America.* Boston: Houghton Mifflin.

Snow, Robert. 1977. Dependent Development and the New Industrial Worker: The Export Processing Zone in the Philippines. Ph.D. diss., Harvard University.

Sobel, Mechal. 1979. *Tabelin' On: The Slave Journey to an Afro-Baptist Faith.* Princeton: Princeton University Press.

Souljah, Sister. 1994. *No Disrespect.* New York: Random House.

Special Section on French Feminism. 1981. *Signs* 7 (Autumn): 5–86.

Spelman, Elizabeth. 1988. *Inessential Woman.* New York: Beacon Press.

Spivak, Gayatri. 1981. French Feminism in an International Frame. *Yale French Studies* 62.

———. 1988. Can the Subaltern Speak? In *Marxism and Interpretation,* ed. Cary Nelson and Lawrence Grossberg, pp. 271–313. Chicago: University of Illinois.

———. 1990. *The Post-Colonial Critic,* ed. Sarah Harasym. New York: Routledge.

Squires, Gregory D. 1994. *Capital and Communities in Black and White.* Albany: SUNY Press.

Staples, Robert. 1979. The Myth of Black Macho: A Response to Angry Black Feminists. *Black Scholar* 10 (6): 24–33.

Stevens, E. 1973. Machismo and Marianismo. *Society* 10 (6).

Stone-Mediatore, Shari. 2000. Chandra Mohanty and the Revaluing of Experience. In *Decentering the Center,* ed. Uma Narayan and Sandra Harding, pp. 110–27. Bloomington: Indiana University Press.

Sturgeon, Noël. 1997. *Ecofeminist Natures.* New York: Routledge.

Sudarkasa, Niara. 1981. Interpreting the African Heritage in Afro-American Family Organization. In *Black Families,* ed. Harriette Pipes McAdoo, pp. 37–53. Beverly Hills, CA: Sage.

Sunder Rajan, R. (forthcoming) The Subject of *Sati:* Pain and Death in the Contemporary Discourse on Sati. *Yale Journal of Criticism.*

Tabak, F. 1983. *Autoritarismo e Participação da Mulher.* Rio de Janeiro: Edições Graal Ltda.

Tabet, Paula. 1982. Hands, Tools, Weapons. *Feminist Issues* 2 (2).

Takeo, Tsuchiya. 1978. Free Trade Zones in Southeast Asia. *Monthly Review* 29 (9): 29–39.

Taylor, Carole Anne. 1993. Positioning Subjects and Objects: Agency, Narration, Relationality. *Hypatia* 8 (Winter): 55–80.

Taylor, Harriet. 1983. *Enfranchisement of Women.* London: Virago.

Taylor, Peter, and Frederick Buttel. 1992. How Do We Know We Have Global Environmental Problems? Science and the Globalization of Environmental Discourse. *Geoform* 23 (3): 405–416.

Trinh, T. Minh-Ha. 1989. *Woman, Native, Other.* Bloomington: Indiana University Press.

Tronto, Joan C. 1990. Women and Caring: What Can Feminists Learn about Morality from Caring? In *Gender/Body/Knowledge: Feminist Reconstructions of Being and Knowing,* ed. Alison M. Jaggar and Susan R. Bordo, pp. 172–187. New Brunswick, NJ: Rutgers University Press.

Tsing, Anna. 1994. From the Margins. *Cultural Anthropology* 9 (3): 279–97.

———. 1997. Environmentalisms: Transitions as Translations. In *Transitions, Translations, Environments,* ed. Joan Scott, Cora Kaplan, and Debra Keates. New York: Routledge.

Tushnet, M. 1984. An Essay on Rights. *Texas Law Review* 62: 1363–1403.

Unger, R. 1983. The Critical Legal Studies Movement. *Harvard Law Review* 96 (3): 561–675.

United Nations Industrial Development Organization (UNIDO). 1979. Redeployment of Industries from Developed to Developing Countries. Industrial Development Conference 419 (October 3).

———. 1980. Women in the Redeployment of Manufacturing Industry to Developing Countries. UNIDO Working Papers on Structural Change, no. 18, UNIDO/ICIS (July 8).

Vaid, S. 1988. Politics of Widow Immolation. *Seminar,* no. 342, special issue on *sati.*

Van den Hombergh, Heleen. 1993. *Gender, Environment and Development.* Utrecht: International Books.

Varikas, Eleni. 1987. Droit Naturel, Nature Féminine et Egalité de Sexes, *L'Homme et la Société* 3–4.

Vasquez, Carmen. Towards a Revolutionary Ethics. *Coming Up* (January 1983): 11.

Walker, Alice, ed. 1979. *I Love Myself When I Am Laughing, And Then Again When I Am Looking Mean and Impressive.* New York: Feminist Press.

Walker, Alice. 1983. *In Search of Our Mother's Gardens.* New York: Harcourt Brace Jovanovich.

Wallace, Audrey. 1993. Sowing Seeds of Hope. In *Eco-Heroes: Twelve Tales of Environmental Victory,* ed. David Gancher, pp. 1–22. San Francisco: Mercury House.

Wallace, Michele. 1978. *Black Macho and the Myth of the Superwoman.* New York: Dial Press.

———. 1990. *Invisibility Blues.* New York: Verso.

Wanderley, L. E. 1980. Movimientos Sociales Populares: Aspectos Económicos e Políticos. *Encontros com a Civilização Brasileira* 25: 107–31.

Wapner, Paul. 1995. Politics Beyond the State: Environmental Activism and World Civic Politics. *World Politics* 47: 311–40.

Ware, Cellestine. 1970. *Woman Power: The Movement for Women's Liberation.* New York: Tower Publications.

Washington, Mary Helen, ed. 1975. *Black-Eyed Susans: Classic Stories by and about Black Women.* Garden City, NY: Anchor.

———. 1980. *Midnight Birds.* Garden City, NY: Anchor.

———, ed. 1987. *Invented Lives: Narratives of Black Women 1860–1960.* Garden City, NY: Anchor.

Wasserheit, J. 1993. The Costs of Reproductive Tract Infections in Women. In *Women and HIV/AIDS: An International Resource Book,* ed. M. Berer and S. Ray. London: Pandora.

Webber, Thomas L. 1978. *Deep Like the Rivers.* New York: Norton.

Weeks, J. 1981. *Sex, Politics and Society.* New York: Longman.

West, Cornell. 1977–1978. Philosophy and the Afro-American Experience. *Philosophical Forum* 2–3: 117–48.

———. 1993. *Race Matters.* Boston: Beacon.

White, Deborah Gray. 1985. *Ar'n't I a Woman?: Female Slaves in the Plantation South.* New York: Norton.

Williams, Fannie Barrier. 1987. The Colored Girl. In *Invented Lives: Narratives of Black Women 1860–1960,* ed. Mary Helen Washington, pp. 150–59. Garden City, NY: Anchor.

Williams, P. J. 1991. *The Alchemy of Race and Rights.* Cambridge: Harvard University.

Wilshire, Donna. 1990. The Uses of Myth, Image, and the Female Body in Re-visioning Knowledge. In *Gender/Body/Knowledge/: Feminist Reconstructions of Being and Knowing,* ed. Alison M. Jaggar and Susan R. Bordo, pp. 92–114. New Brunswick, NJ: Rutgers University Press.

Wittig, Monique. 1992. *The Straight Mind and Other Essays.* Boston: Beacon Press.

Wollstonecraft, Mary. 1975. *A Vindication of the Rights of Woman.* New York: Penguin.

Women's Global Network for Reproductive Rights. 1991. *Statement of Purpose.*

Young, Iris. 1980. Socialist Feminism and the Limits of Dual Systems Theory. *Socialist Review* 50/51: 169–88.

———. 1981. Beyond the Unhappy Marriage: A Critique of Dual Systems Theory. In *Women and Revolution,* ed. Lydia Sargent, pp. 43–69. Boston: South End Press.

Young, Iris Marion. 1990. *Justice and the Politics of Difference.* Princeton: Princeton University Press.

Yuval-Davis, Nira. 1997. *Gender and Nation.* Thousand Oaks, CA: Sage.

Zimmerman, M. et al. 1990. Assessing the Acceptability of Norplant® Implants in Four Countries. *Studies in Family Planning* 21: 92–103.

Zinn, Maxine Baca, et al. 1986. The Costs of Exclusionary Practices in Women's Studies. *Signs* 11 (2): 290–303.

PERMISSIONS

INDEX